WESTERN CIVILIZATION
Recent Interpretations

Volume I
FROM EARLIEST TIMES TO 1715

Volume I
FROM
EARLIEST TIMES TO 1715

Edited by
Charles D. Hamilton

UNIVERSITY OF CHICAGO

WESTERN CIVILIZATION
Recent Interpretations

THOMAS Y. CROWELL COMPANY
NEW YORK   ESTABLISHED 1834

Library of Congress Cataloging in Publication Data

HAMILTON, CHARLES DANIEL   comp.
  Western civilization: recent interpretations.

  Includes bibliographical references.
  CONTENTS: v. 1.   From earliest times to 1715.
Edited by Charles D. Hamilton.—v. 2.   From 1715 to the
present.   Edited by C. Stewart Doty.
    1.   Civilization—History.   2.   Civilization,
Occidental.   I.   Doty, Charles Stewart.   II.   Title.
CB59.H34   1973   910'.03'1821   72-13456
ISBN 0-690-87469-3 (v. 1)

For
Jeremiah F. O'Sullivan
and
Donald Kagan
Who Taught Me to Love History

Manufactured in the United States of America

1   2   3   4   5   6   7   8   9   10

Preface

The purpose of this volume is to bring together a variety of short supplementary readings in western civilization that are not always accessible in order to introduce students to the nature and importance of historical investigation and to stimulate further thought and discussion about history. Three general groups of materials have been chosen for these readings: those containing new interpretations or research on fundamental themes in western civilization not yet incorporated into the textbooks; those setting forth the basic positions on current controversies in historical interpretation of major events; and those provocatively or evocatively probing those historical events, people, or developments which students find difficult to understand and which, as a result, are often too briefly treated by teachers with too little time and textbooks with too few pages. Rather than being an anthology of snippets, this volume is composed of complete, readable essays which originally appeared as articles, scholarly papers, lectures, or self-contained chapters in larger works. Moreover, the selections are up-to-date, a majority of them having been published in the last decade.

Each selection is introduced by a headnote pointing out the importance of the subject and the significance of the selection to understanding the issue under discussion. Each headnote raises questions for individual study and class discussion. The author's footnotes are eliminated except where they are necessary to the understanding of his message, and the editor has added some explanatory footnotes to aid students. Each selection contains a full bibliographic citation so that the student can consult the original.

We hope that this book will correct the impression too often conveyed by textbooks that history is a narrative, to be unfolded once and for all. No matter how learned any man is, no matter how skillfully, objectively and comprehensively he can write, a single man's view of any historical period will always remain personal, and will reflect his personal interests, concerns and abilities, as well as his limitations. The same may be said of a collaborative effort to write on something as diverse as "Western Civilization." "Everyman his own historian," or "each generation must write its own history"—however one states it, the proposition remains valid that history is in some sense a personal thing. What is important or significant to one person or one age may be meaningless to another. Hence this collection is meant to introduce the student to a broad range of historians and historical writing. In this way the student's appreciation of western history may be enriched, and he may be exposed to a variety of viewpoints and interpretations. At the same time, it must not be thought that historical investigation, that is, the formulation of questions, the research and weighing of evidence, and the drawing of conclusions, is done without method. As any practicing historian knows, there are certain canons of historical scholarship, and definite methods of approaching and interpreting evidence. Another objective of the present collection, therefore, is to make the student aware of some of the difficulties the historian faces in the pursuit of his craft and to illustrate how some of the best contemporary historians have pursued their investigations. Methodology, evaluation of evidence, historical inference and generalization—these and other aspects of historical writing are touched on in these selections.

In short, the idea of this anthology is to stimulate and stretch the minds of this generation of students with provocative, recent interpretations of basic historical problems in western civilization that will be meaningful to them and to their teachers.

I should like to express my gratitude to those students whom I have taught at Cornell, the University of Wisconsin, and the University of Chicago, and who have done much to stimulate my own thinking about Western Civilization and about history in general. I would also like to thank my colleagues on the Western Civilization staff in the College of the University of Chicago whose conversation, comradeship and example in teaching have helped to deepen and broaden my knowledge of history; in particular, Keith Baker, Sumner Benson, Hanna Gray, Emile Karafiol, William Sewell and Karl Weintraub. Finally, my deepest debt is to my wife, Mary Ellen, whose encouragement and understanding have meant the most.

Contents

THE ANCIENT WORLD

PART I

IT has been customary for several centuries now to divide Western history into three general periods, ancient, medieval, and modern. A majority of modern scholars are dissatisfied with this schematic division because in many ways it represents little more than an attempt to organize and compartmentalize human experience in order to make it more intelligible. The so-called ancient world manifests more diversity and variation than either of the other two major periods, but it has become convenient to treat all the developments that occurred in the Near East and the Mediterranean world before the dissolution of Roman political power in the fifth century as belonging to "antiquity." The various different civilizations thus embraced in the somewhat artificial construct of the "ancient world" differ radically one from another in certain respects: the basic world view of ancient Egypt is not that of Mesopotamia (as John Wilson's selection demonstrates); the Greeks' reliance on reason rather than tradition and mythology to understand the world marks them off from the ancient oriental civilizations; and the creative, theoretical Greek character finds its virtual antithesis in the pragmatic, tradition-oriented Roman mind. Fundamental differences in outlook among the numerous civilizations whose histories comprise the ancient world would seem, therefore, to negate their treatment as a unitary period.

Another set of considerations, however, make it legitimate for us to speak of the ancient world. For one thing, many of the basic discoveries, inventions, and advances in social organization, government, economics, cultural and intellectual activity, and religion which have had a lasting impact on subsequent Western civilization were made in this period and brought together and transmitted by the Roman Empire. A second basic similarity among the various ancient civilizations is the relative scarcity of surviving documentary evidence and the peculiar problems of interpretation that this presents to the modern scholar. Finally, the achievements and contributions of most of the ancient civilizations were either forgotten or at best imperfectly understood until a process of rediscovery and reinterpretation, which began in the fourteenth century, brought them to light again.

The following selections have been chosen to illustrate and elucidate some of the most significant contributions to subsequent Western civilization that were made in antiquity, as well as to show how historians cope with the problem of sources in an attempt to understand the past. The selections by Kathleen Kenyon, John Wilson, and Samuel Kramer on the ancient Orient are concerned with basic advances in agriculture and settled life, in the establishment of governmental sanctions to provide order and security, and in the fundamental mastery of writing. At the same time, each selection suggests some of the difficulties and methods of the ancient historian, and especially of the archaeologist. The articles by Sterling Dow, C. M. Bowra, and Donald Kagan focus on the Greeks and likewise discuss substantive questions of importance: who were the Greeks, and where did they come from? What is the relationship between their own traditions and such facts as archaeology can establish? How did they come to recognize the function of reason in human understanding, which has been a characteristic of Western thought ever since? What was the nature of this accomplishment of theirs? How did they come to wage a great war that dealt a heavy blow to their marvelously energetic and creative civilization? Here again, the selections provide new information and interpretations of crucial developments, and demonstrate the progress of scholarship. The articles by Henry Boren and F. H. Lawson deal with the origin of Rome's struggle to integrate the fruits of conquest into her national life, which ultimately led to civil war and the establishment of power in the hands of one man, the emperor; and the nature and significance of one of her most important contributions to civilization, Roman Law. Finally, the last two selections are concerned with Christianity, which grew up in the Roman Empire and succeeded in dominating virtually all of European society for a thousand years. Joachim Jeremias discusses the problems that scholars face in trying to approach the "Jesus of history" and his relationship to early Christianity; Robert Grant deals with the acceptance of Christianity by Constantine, an event with fateful consequences both for the Roman state and for Christianity.

These readings will provide a reasonable topical coverage both of significant subjects and of historical method and interpretation. They will also serve as a foundation for many of the readings that follow in the next two parts of this book.

1. The
First
Jericho

KATHLEEN M. KENYON

The long process whereby man developed, biologically and culturally, beyond the level of other intelligent life can be recovered by modern investigators only in its main outlines. The anthropologist, biologist, botanist, geologist, and other specialists have aided the archaeologist in his attempts to recover man's prehistory, so called because prehistoric man could leave no record of his thoughts or ideas until he had discovered the art of writing. For many important discoveries and inventions in mankind's development, such as the discovery of language as a means of communication, or the use and control of fire, or the invention of the wheel, the historian can discover no trace of when or how the achievement was made. Such is not the case, however, with one of the most crucial stages in this process. Archaeology affords sufficient evidence to permit discussion of what the eminent prehistorian V. Gordon Childe, in Man Makes Himself, *has termed "the Neolithic Revolution," that is, the mastery of agriculture and the beginnings of permanent settlement. Men had moved beyond the nomadic stage of food-gathering and hunting, and they could assure themselves of an adequate, sometimes abundant supply of food. With the basic problem of survival met, population could expand, specialization of labor could be introduced, social and political organization could advance, and perhaps most significant of all for the history of civiliza-*

Source: Kathleen M. Kenyon, *Digging Up Jericho* (London: Ernest Benn, Ltd., 1957), pp. 51–52, 56–60, 65–76. Copyright © 1957 by Kathleen M. Kenyon. Reprinted by permission of Ernest Benn Ltd., London, and Praeger Publishers, Inc., New York.

tion, some men could be freed from the necessity of food production to turn their minds to other things.

How did this "revolution" take place? Where, and when? In the absence of written records, how does the modern scholar go about attempting to answer these questions? What problems does he face, both in obtaining information to elucidate these questions and in interpreting such information? What are the limitations of his knowledge, and what caveats should we bear in mind in reading the archaeologist's reconstruction of the culture he studies? These and other questions are touched on in Kenyon's description of one of the earliest known sites of settled, perhaps even "urban" life.

Kathleen Kenyon is a specialist in Palestinian archaeology and prehistory, and her publications include, in addition to numerous specialized publications of the excavations at Jericho and Jerusalem, Beginning in Archaeology *(1961),* Archaeology in the Holy Land *(1965), and* Digging Up Jericho *(1957) from which the following selection is taken.*

Her book affords a glimpse of the archaeologist at work and provides a gradually unfolding picture of the ancient town, season by season, as the excavations proceed. She describes with flair and skill the principal finds at Jericho and indicates their significance in our understanding of prehistory.

From this selection, the student can learn much about the problems and techniques of archaeology, as well as about several important early accomplishments in man's struggle to assure his need for food and shelter.

The title of this chapter may in due course have to be altered, for we are not yet at the beginning of its history. In the course of five seasons' work, we have excavated a considerable number of successive levels of a very remarkable early phase, and we have obtained glimpses of a still earlier stage to which I shall return. But first I must describe the buildings and culture of the phase which has made Jericho famous.

This phase is that of a Neolithic community which has not yet begun to manufacture pottery. For long it has been accepted that one of the earliest crafts developed when man ceased to be a wanderer and adopted a settled way of life, was the manufacture of pottery. As a nomadic hunter he had not the leisure to undertake such a manufacturing process, nor, as a wanderer would he be expected to be able to encumber himself with an extensive household equipment, especially such a fragile one as the earliest pots would have constituted. Therefore it can be accepted that the absence of pottery is a primitive trait. It could however be argued that the Jordan Valley was something of a backwater, out of touch with the main centres of progress. From this it might follow that it was not necessary to ascribe any great antiquity to the pre-pottery Neolithic occupation of Jericho. But it will be shown that there is reason to believe that this is not so. There are there just enough links between later material and that from other sites to suggest that it is in fact the third stage at Jericho which corresponds with the earliest occupation yet discovered at most other Neolithic sites in the Near East. Since these sites appear to date to the fifth millennium B.C., we can on this evidence alone fairly confidently place the end of the pre-pottery stage at Jericho round about 5000 B.C. It will be seen that the stage lasted a very long time, and I shall return to the question of how early we are to place its beginnings in due course.

One site in the Near East appears to have a comparable history. At Jarmo, situated on the foothills of north-eastern Iraq, there is also a pre-pottery phase in a site producing evidence of a fairly prolonged settled occupation, evidently succeeded by a phase with pottery. A Carbon-14 analysis, by which the age of organic material can be estimated from its surviving radio-activity, has given a date of approximately 4750 B.C. for early Jarmo. It may be, therefore, that there was a parallel development there, though on a considerably lesser scale than at Jericho. The finds at the two sites are however quite different, and there is nothing to suggest any direct connection.

There is also a site in Cyprus, Khirokitia, in which pottery was not used, though the architectural development shows that it was a firmly established settlement. There again, the architecture and equipment is completely different from that at Jericho. The date suggested for this culture is 3700–3400 B.C.

It would thus appear that there were a number of primitive communities in different parts of the Near East, with no direct connection between them, and possibly of very varying dates. The great interest of Jericho lies in the fact that it must be very early in date, and at this very early date it reached such a high degree of development.

. . . . .

The whole impression of the houses is that of good, solid, well-planned lay-out. There is even evidence of a considerable degree of comfort, for we have found that the floors of several of the rooms were covered by rush mats. These survive only as a thin white film, but the texture of the rushes which made them, and the weave of the mats is perfectly clear. One was apparently rectangular, and there are four examples of round mats of varying sizes. One of these even shows the track of a white ant which ate its way across it.

As I have already said, the occupants of these houses had no pottery vessels or containers. Their dishes and bowls were made of stone, mostly of a soft local limestone which can be polished to a high and beautiful finish. No doubt other containers were of wood or skin, which have not survived.

Their tools and weapons were mainly made of flint, but occasionally of obsidian. There are many varieties and sizes of blades, which served as knives. There are borers and scrapers which would serve for manufacturing garments and containers of skin. Arrowheads showed that hunting still supplemented food production, though the numbers are not very great in proportion to the other implements. Some of the most attractive flints are the sickle blades, which are very numerous. The edges are very finely serrated, and the making of these teeth shows high technical skill. The use of these toothed blades for cutting grain is shown by the high gloss which is produced by the silica in the stalks they have cut, and the number of the sickle blades shows the extent to which grain was a staple diet. Some of the blades were in the form of short sections and must have been set in bone or wooden mounts. Others were longer and had a double cutting edge; these must have been hafted like knives.

Further evidence of the use of grain comes from the frequent find of querns. These are of a type which so far is unique to Jericho. They consist of a roughly oblong block of conglomerate stone, with a grinding hollow which always runs out to one edge of the block, while at the other end is a flat ledge on which perhaps the operator sat, and there is a narrower flat ledge along the two sides. The grinding stones are also characteristic, and are finely worked ovals of hard stone. There is also a very varied collection of other stone vessels and implements; hammer-stones, grinders, pestles and polishers. The most attractive of these are the polishing stones. The finest ones are shaped like cakes of soap, with two convex surfaces polished to an almost mirror-like finish. Others are of all sizes down to quite small pebbles showing highly polished patches. The larger stones were presumably used for burnishing the plastered floors, which are such a characteristic feature of the culture, while the smaller ones must have served for purposes such as polishing the stone bowls, bone tools and so on.

A curious feature is the almost complete lack of heavier tools, such as axes or adzes for heavy woodworking, and picks or hoes for working the soil. We know from the presence of sockets in the walls that the inhabitants were able to fell and dress substantial timbers, but there is no evidence of what tools were used. It is possible that the answer to what implements were used for digging is provided by a number of pierced stones which may have served as weights for digging sticks, such as are used by some primitive tribes today.

As to how these people were clothed, we have not much evidence. Some small stone disks might be spindle-whorls, and as such be evidence of spinning, and some smooth bone tools might be for use in weaving, and heavy stones with holes through them might have served as loomweights. Bone pins made out of the metapodial bones of animals, with one articular end making the head, could have been used as dress-fasteners. As evidence of ornaments, we have a considerable number of beads fashioned from malachite. It is probable, too, that the pierced shells found in considerable numbers were used as ornaments. The piercing is natural, but the shells must have been brought from the seashore, and were presumably collected because they could so easily be strung into necklaces.

One class of small stone objects may have been used as ornaments, or may have had some religious significance. We call them miniature axe amulets. They are of green stone, and are shaped just like miniature polished stone axes, though whether they do actually imitate axes may be doubted, as one of the notable things about the flint industry is the almost complete lack of real polished stone axes. These small green stone objects are not pierced for suspension, which one would have expected whether they were intended for amulets or as ornaments. It is difficult to believe they were functional in any way. So their purpose must remain enigmatic, and archaeologists are always apt to ascribe a cult use to anything for which they can suggest no other use, so we call them amulets.

Similarly archaeologists tend to call buildings, which do not conform to the usual plan of domestic houses, shrines or temples. It is naturally of great interest to trace what we can of the religion of these people who lie so near the beginning of civilisation, and there are a certain number of definite indications. One little room can hardly be anything but a shrine. It was formed by dividing off a section in a house which originally had had the normal plan. In one of the end-walls so formed, a small niche was constructed, and set in the base of this was found a rough stone to serve as a pedestal. In the debris of the collapse of the building, not far away, was found a remarkable stone. The material was volcanic rock, probably brought from the Nebi Musa district about eight miles away. It was .46 m. high, .18 m. wide, and elaborately chipped to a pointed oval in section. This little column exactly fitted the pedestal and the niche. There can be little doubt that we have here a cult object, a recognition that there was a supernatural force which could be anonymously represented in this way, and an ancestor in conception if not in lineal ascent of the Semitic ritual stone, the *mazzebah*.

This small room should perhaps be likened to a family chapel. Another building can be described as a temple, though its attribution to religious uses is not so certain. Its central feature is a large rectangular room, the largest room found, about six metres in one direction and more than four metres (the north wall lay beyond the excavated area) in the other. In its centre, neatly aligned on the walls, was a little basin. The floor, walls and basin were all covered with the usual fine, highly burnished plaster, which in the neighborhood of the basin was strongly scorched by fire. At each end of the rectangular central room were annexes of a curious rounded plan, with walls curving inwards in elevation, as if to form domes. This building is so unusual in plan, and with this suggestion of ceremonial in the central basin, that we are inclined to suggest that it was a temple. Even if its use was not religious, it was almost certainly a public building, which is also of interest.

Some of the small objects found also suggest a religious significance. This is reasonably certain in the case of two little female figurines. The better of these is perfectly preserved except for her head, which is missing. The attitude is typical of the conventional Mother Goddess figurines found in connection with so many Near Eastern cultures of later dates. She has a long flowing robe, gathered at the waist. The arms are akimbo, and her hands are placed beneath her breasts. The second figurine is similar, though less well-preserved, and they are strongly suggestive of a Mother Goddess or fertility cult, very natural for a community closely dependent on the productivity of the soil for their existence. A number of little animal figurines might also be interpreted as being associated with fertility rites, and this is the interpretation often put on such objects, but unless they are found in, unequivocal positions, it is difficult to be sure that they are not in fact children's toys.

An interesting little object is a small bone bead carved in the form of a human face. The features are neatly incised by boring. The back of the object is flat, and it seems probable that it was not intended as a pendant but to be sewn on, the attachment hole being vertically and not horizontally bored, and near the centre of the oval and not at the top.

The most remarkable manifestation of customs which can best be explained in terms of cult practices might be called a Cult of Skulls. An interest in the human head is shown by the little bead described in the last paragraph. But the full practice involved the careful preservation of actual human skulls. Our first evidence of this was the find of the skull of an elderly man, without any of the other bones of the body, carefully set in the angle of a room, beneath the floor. It looked as if the inhabitants wished to preserve his wisdom for subsequent generations. . . .

Our finds have thus shown that the people of Jericho were both culturally and technically highly developed. We have also established the fact that the settlement of the period was of considerable size. The first houses of the type I have described were found by Professor Garstang towards the north-east end of the *tell*. Early in the excavations of 1952, we were surprised to find similar houses within six feet of the surface in the centre of the west side . . . This showed that the settlement covered at least half the area of the later town. It was obviously desirable to establish its full size, so Trench II at the north end and Trench III at the south end were begun through the slopes of the *tell*. These showed that the pre-pottery Neolithic settlement extended at least as far as the Bronze Age town. It was in fact probably larger, for on the three sides examined, the levels of this period are cut by the outermost Middle Bronze Age wall; how much farther they extended cannot be established, for when this wall was built, the rock at its foot was cleared of all accumulations and the soil from them piled up as a bank inside, in order to make the defences more impregnable. On the east side, the modern road has cut into the *tell,* so the position here cannot be investigated. The exact size of the settlement cannot therefore be established, but from the points which have been fixed we know it covered at least eight acres. A modern oriental town of this size might house about three thousand people. There are too many uncertain factors for one to be able to say with assurance that Neolithic Jericho housed a similar number, but one can guess that it may have been in that region.

The settlement is quite clearly on the scale, not of a village, but of a town. Its claim to a true civic status is established by the discovery, the first of the exciting finds to be produced by the present excavations, that it possessed a massive defensive wall. This was first found in 1952. . . . It was built of large, undressed stones, and survived to the height of 2.50 m. It looked most impressive as one peered down at it, with its base at what then seemed to us the great depth of 7 m. . . . We cannot as yet say whether it enclosed the whole settlement, as it is of course not impossible that it enclosed only a citadel area. But whether or not it enclosed the whole town, it is clear evidence of community organisation. No one small group or family could have carried out an undertaking of this sort, and someone or some corporate body must have provided the organisation to bring the great boulders from the stream beds at the foot of the mountains, half a mile or so away, someone must have ordained its line and someone have supervised its construction.

The wall was free-standing only on its outer side. On the inner side, the contemporary level was 2.80 m. higher than the external one. This terrace was constructed by cutting away the earlier levels on the outer side, and piling them up on the inside, the wall being built against this pile. The wall must originally have stood at least two metres higher than the surviving top, giving a total minimum height of about five metres, for on the inside it served also as a house wall, and the additional two metres is necessary to give headroom within the house.

It was in this house that the plastered skulls must have been preserved, for they were found discarded in its debris, beneath the floor of the next succeeding building. In the fill beneath the floor of the house, put in when the wall was built, was found the surprising number of burials, from which the skulls must have been derived. It is the association of the great defensive wall with the mass burial that makes it tempting to interpret as a massacre the disaster which the number of burials suggests. If a violent attack on a town at that time undefended had resulted in the death of a large number of the citizens, it would be reasonable that when it was rebuilt, a defensive wall should be added. But this can only be a hypothesis, for the surviving portions of the skeletons do not show any identifiable signs of injuries.

After a period, this wall apparently collapsed. After the first collapse, it was rebuilt on the same line. But after a second collapse, a new wall was built 6.50 m. in advance, against the debris which buried the face of the original one. The new one was on the same principle as the old one, with a free-standing outer face and a higher terrace inside, and the internal house was extended over the new fill, probably up to the new wall, but erosion has destroyed the actual junction. This same erosion makes it impossible to say whether the eight succeeding house levels belonging to the pre-pottery Neolithic period, all with the same type of plan, structure and plastered floors, also run up to the new wall, or to some successor.

As I have just said, the town in the stages preceding the first of these two walls was undefended. But in 1954 we found that they were not the earliest on the site. Beneath the first of them was a deep tipped fill, partly bricky and partly ashy. This dipped down steeply to the west, over the face of a yet earlier wall. As this gradually emerged, it became clear that it was much more impressive than the later one which overlay it. It was not built of such large stones, but it had a considerably more regular face, though the stones were likewise undressed. Moreover, it survived to a height of six metres, with its foundations resting on bedrock at a depth of fifteen metres (nearly fifty feet) from the surface of the mound. Like the later one, it was free-standing only on the outer face, and was built on a slight batter against an interior fill.

In the following two seasons, further details of the system of fortification to which this wall belongs have emerged. On the outer side was a great rock-cut ditch, nine metres wide and three metres deep. The labour involved in excavating this ditch out of the solid rock must have been tremendous. As we have discovered nothing in the way of heavy flint picks, one can only suppose that it was carried out with stone mauls, perhaps helped by splitting by fire and water.

Still more remarkable is the adjunct to the wall on the inner side. This is a massive tower, nine metres in diameter, and solidly built of stone. In conception and construction, this tower would not disgrace one of the more grandiose medieval castles. In its centre is a stone-built staircase with twenty steps, leading down to a horizontal passage. The treads of the stairs are formed by great stone slabs more than .75 m. across, hammer-dressed to a smooth finish, and the roofs of the staircase and the passage are formed of still larger slabs, .95 m. across and up to a metre long, similarly dressed. The whole thing is excellent in both architecture and masonry, and everyone who sees it finds it impossible to believe that it was built eight thousand years or more ago.

We have not yet solved the problem of the purpose of the staircase. The passage at its base most unfortunately leads to just that point in the circumference of the tower which lies beyond the edge of our excavations, and to clear down to its entrance on the outside will mean shifting some fifty feet of filling, as well as twenty feet of our own dump on top. As found, the passage was full of skeletons, twelve in all, jammed in extremely tightly. But this was certainly not the primary purpose, since when they were put in, the fill in the passage had risen to within two feet of the roof. For this same reason, one cannot give the dramatic interpretation that they were the last heroic defenders of the tower. Clearly the passage had ceased to be functional at that stage, and the bodies were put in, after it had gone out of use, simply because it was a convenient hole.

Even the stage of this great wall, ditch and tower is not the beginning of the story of the defences of Jericho. The tower has two outer skins surrounding a stone core. The outermost is not continuous, but is associated with some curiously shaped rooms on the north-west side. These skins proved to represent successive building phases, and it is only to the last of these that the town wall just described belongs, for it is built against the outermost skin, with which it was structurally contemporary. To the north of the tower, the town wall was built against a filling of stone chips, clearly derived from the cutting of the ditch, which is therefore contemporary with it. These chips were piled up against a yet earlier massive stone wall, which survives, free-standing on both faces, to a height of four metres. This wall was cut through by the inner skin surrounding the tower. It is therefore earlier than it, and it almost certainly is the town wall going with the core of the tower, which must represent its earliest phase. The wall contemporary with the intermediate phase, in which the inner skin was added to the core, may be represented by the lower part of the later wall, which is in a different and rather rougher style of building.

We have, therefore, indications that the elaborate system of defences has a very long history. The earlier stages have not yet been fully traced, and it will indeed be difficult to do so without disturbing more than is desirable of the stage at present exposed, which must represent the climax of this remarkable achievement. But the earliest so far traced, with the nucleus of the tower, and a free-standing stone wall must in itself have been sufficiently magnificent, and again and again one returns to the feeling of amazement at the very great antiquity of the remains, and at the evidence they provide for the high degree of organisation and technical ability of their builders.

One question which for long puzzled us was why such fine structures as the town wall and the tower should have been allowed to go out of use. To this question the 1956 season of excavations provided the answer. In the deep excavations towards the north-east end of the *tell* . . . a whole series of superimposed houses with the typical burnished plastered floors, walls built of thumb-impressed bricks, . . . had been excavated. In 1956 it became clear that we were penetrating down into a different phase. The most noticeable change was that the floors were of mud and not plaster. Moreover, the walls were curved and the plan of the houses seemed to be round, and when the walls were dissected, the bricks were found to be of a new type. The shape of the bricks was an elongated oval, the base flat and the upper surface curved or hog-backed. As the area was further cleared, another fact emerged. Along the north side of the site the walls and floors were missing, and in their places were deposits of water-laid silt and gravel. This in due course defined itself as a silted-up stream bed. At some stage, therefore, a stream had partially destroyed the houses, cutting into the accumulated walls and floors to a depth of at least 1.50 m. The lines of fill showed that the stream bed had silted up twice and the water had then cut down again, so the stream had three successive periods of activity. Immediately overlying the final silting-up was the floor of the first house with the typical plastered floors. The cutting of the stream therefore neatly divides the phase with the houses built of hog-back bricks from the succeeding phase of the houses with plastered floors. It shows that there was an actual time-gap between them as well as a break in building style. The length of that gap is conjectural. Presumably each fresh cutting down represents a winter's rains, for the stream was almost certainly cut by storm water and not by that of a spring. But rainfall, at any rate locally, in this area is not sufficiently consistent for there to be a strong enough flood to cut the channel out each year to the full depth. The gap may therefore be anything from three years to, say, ten or much more.

It was thus in Site E that the break between two pre-pottery Neolithic phases was sharply defined. But buildings of the earlier phase were reached, in 1956, in two other sites, M and D, and the characteristics of this phase are now becoming familiar. It seems probable that the rooms were of a beehive shape, with the walls circular in plan, and inclining slightly inward in elevation. The floors were sunk below the external level, and in two cases the steps down into the entrance passage are well preserved. In one instance it is clear that the treads of the steps were of wooden planks. Timber was extensively used, for remains of burnt beams are found in all the areas. A curious feature is that in several instances there is a basis of heavy cobbling below the floors, with a deep trough of cobbles along the line of the walls. Not only is the architecture different from that of the later phase, but also most of the articles of equipment are new, the flints of a hitherto unknown type, a remarkably fine and rich bone industry, and greenstone amulets of a different shape. The familiar querns are no longer found, the earlier type having a much less elaborately shaped grinding hollow, and the stone bowls being more roughly shaped.

Though there is so much that is different, the earlier people had one thing in common with the later one. They also had a cult of skulls, and already a considerable number of skulls separated from the bodies have been found. But even here there is a difference, for the skulls are found arranged in groups, in one case closely packed in a circle, all looking inwards, in another arranged in three sets of three, all looking in the same direction. In the third instance there is an unpleasant suggestion of infant sacrifice, for beneath a curious bath-like structure of mud-plaster there is, besides one complete infant burial, a collection of infant skulls with the neck vertebrae attached, showing that the heads were cut off and not merely collected from burials. The ordinary method of disposing of the dead was, as in the later phase, burial beneath the house floors but in deep pits.

It is the break between the hog-back-brick phase and the plaster-floor phase which is responsible for the great town wall and the tower going out of use. The buildings contemporary with the various phases of the tower are in the earlier technique, and those which succeed the layers of debris which cover the face of the wall and tail up over the top of the tower are in the plastered-floor technique. The layers of debris are therefore the equivalent of the stream bed in Site E.

The massive system of defences therefore acquires a new interest, for it belongs to the earliest phase in the history of the town. It might be safer to qualify this statement by adding the phrase 'so far discovered', but we have now reached bedrock in several places without finding any suggestion of a yet earlier phase, though it might be claimed that all our sites are towards the periphery of the mound, and earlier remains might lie beneath the centre.

There is thus abundant evidence that the pre-pottery Neolithic phases at Jericho cover a long period of time. The ruins of the successive buildings raised a mound some forty-five feet in height before the first pottery appeared on the site, a type of pottery which precedes the later type which can . . . be linked with the early village settlements elsewhere in the Near East belonging to the fifth millennium B.C. In the excavation area in the centre of the west side of the *tell* . . . nineteen successive building stages belonging to the plastered-floor phase can be identified. In Site E, where the remains of at least two building stages had been removed in the 1955–6 excavations, we have excavated fourteen main stages. Earlier than this whole phase, and separated from it by a gap of unknown duration, is the hog-back-brick phase with all its ramifications, as yet only glimpsed. We are thus carried back a very long way.

To establish any sort of absolute dating, archaeologists have today available what is known as the Carbon-14 method of dating. This is based on the fact that all organic material while living absorbs radio-activity. When it dies, for instance when a tree is felled, it starts to give it up. The rate at which the radio-active matter is lost has been calculated, and measurements can be made of the amount present in suitable specimens. This gives, within a standard deviation, the number of years ago the organism ceased to live. The standard deviation may give a margin of three hundred years or so either way, but when one is dealing with objects several thousand years old, this does not affect the general picture very much.

The material found on ancient sites which is most useful for this purpose is charcoal, and as much charcoal as possible has therefore been collected from all our levels. The process of examination, and the elimination of all possible sources of error, is a complicated one, and so far only preliminary results have been obtained. They concern, moreover, only the plaster-floor stage. From the debris overlying the fourteenth building of this stage from the top in Site F, charcoal fragments have given a date of *c.* 5850 B.C. Below it are five more stages before the debris overlying the hog-back-brick phase is reached. In Site E, a date of *c.* 6250 B.C. has been given for the sixth from the top of the fourteen stages excavated by us. It is thus apparent that a period when the people of the plaster-floor phase had long been established on the site must be dated as long ago as the seventh millennium B.C. Behind it lies all the hog-back-brick phase and the beginning of the plaster-floor phase.*

The finds at Jericho are completely revolutionary for the established ideas of the beginnings of settled life and civilisation. Hitherto, our evidence of the earliest settlements has been of villages of the fifth millennium, primitive, small and unpretentious. Not till towards 3000 B.C. did these develop into anything like towns. Both stratification and the Carbon-14 dating place Neolithic Jericho long before this. We have abundant evidence that, from size, fortifications and general community undertakings, Jericho of the plaster-floor phase must be considered as a town. We do not yet know the full size of the settlement of the hog-back-brick phase, but in all other respects it also must be considered as a town.

Such a community must have been supported by an efficient agriculture, for the number of persons congregated together which is suggested

---

* Since this was written a Carbon-14 dating of *c.* 6800 B.C. has been obtained for a level comparatively late in the hog-back-brick phase.

by the size of the settlement could not have been dependent on the wild produce, animal or vegetable, obtainable within convenient reach. In this, the natural resources of the site certainly play a part. The alluvial soil of the Jordan Valley is very fertile, but the very great heat of the district parches vegetation unless there is abundant water. In Jericho this is provided by the spring which emerges at the foot of the ancient site, and this must have been as important in antiquity as it is today. Today, the fertility of the oasis is dependent on an elaborate irrigation system. It is reasonable to assume that fields or gardens, extensive enough to support the considerable population of Neolithic Jericho, could also only have been made available by a system of irrigation, for otherwise the water would not have reached a sufficient area. Our knowledge of the growth of the later towns in Mesopotamia and Egypt has shown what an important part irrigation plays in the development of a community. Community organisation is required for the control of the irrigation channels, and this control provides sanctions which can become the basis of community laws. Thus an agglomeration of families is welded into a unit. Once such community organisation comes into being, other community undertakings can follow. At Jericho we have the evidence of these in the town walls and in the buildings which would appear to be public. The whole process is an interlocking one of cause and effect.

But our most recent evidence shows that Jericho cannot have been unique, though so far it is the only site known. We have suspected this for some time, since for a community to have found it necessary to defend itself by such massive town walls, there must have been some enemies that were feared. The discovery of the two distinct cultures, implying two distinct sets of people, provides part of the answer. The defences of the hog-back-brick people were against the plaster-floor people, who eventually overcame them. But it was not a case of townsfolk defending themselves against envious nomads. The plaster-floor people arrived with a fully developed civilisation and a fully developed and even stereotyped architecture, for the houses which immediately succeed the break have all the characteristics which last throughout the long occupation which follows. They therefore come from other towns, and from towns sufficiently near to be an obvious menace to the earlier occupants of Jericho. Somewhere, and moreover somewhere probably in the Jordan Valley, other equally early towns are to be found.

We can therefore deduce that in the sixth and probably seventh millennium B.C. there was a growth of civilisation hitherto completely unsuspected. Any general deductions must await the discovery of other sites, so any further theories must be hypothetical. But since our evidence carries us so very far back, we know that we are getting near to the Pleistocene, the period of the Ice Ages of Europe, which ended about 10,000 B.C. In the Mediterranean and Near East, the counterpart of the Ice Ages was the Pluvials, in which areas now desert must have been fertile. As a hypothesis, it may be suggested that favourable climatic and vegetational conditions may at this time have stimulated a growth of agriculture and therefore of settlement, of which Jericho provides the only evidence so far found. After a long period of flourishing town life, increasing desiccation as conditions approached those of today may have stifled this premature development. The villages of the fifth millennium, which undoubtedly at Jericho represent a period of retrogression, may mark a fresh beginning and a gradual adaptation of settlement to new and less favourable conditions.

We may therefore envisage pre-pottery Neolithic Jericho as a culture with all the attributes of civilisation, except that of a written language. The town must have been almost modern, or at least medieval in appearance, and it must have been surrounded by fertile fields. In the neighbourhood we can assume that there were other similar towns, and since materials such as obsidian, turquoise matrix and cowrie shells must have been obtained from a considerable distance away, we can assume trade with and relations between neighbouring districts. This is the revolutionary picture that Jericho has given us of a period nine or ten thousand years ago.

15

Kenyon

THE FIRST
JERICHO

2. The Search for Security and Order

JOHN A. WILSON

History, it has been asserted, is the study of change over time. Yet of the two earliest centers of civilization, the river valleys of the Nile and of the Tigris and Euphrates, the civilization of Egypt presents an essentially unchanging aspect for many centuries. Is this appearance the result of limited evidence at the disposal of the Egyptologist, or is it an integral part of the world view of the ancient Egyptian? John A. Wilson, one of the most eminent American Egyptologists, argues that the Egyptian was inordinately complacent and self-satisfied with his civilization and extremely optimistic about life, at least in comparison with contemporary civilizations in Mesopotamia. In an essay on ancient Egypt in Before Philosophy *(1949), edited by Henri Frankfort, he argues that this attitude was due in large part to the peculiarly favorable and benign geographical and climatic conditions that Egypt enjoyed, as compared to the harsher and less predictable situation of Mesopotamia. The questions of how and why the Egyptians developed their particular outlook on life, and why these remained constant for the better part of two millennia, deserve discussion.*

In The Burden of Egypt *Wilson sets out to explore these and other intriguing questions about the civilization of ancient Egypt. He is not writing a "his-*

Source: John A. Wilson, *The Culture of Ancient Egypt* (Chicago: University of Chicago Press, 1951), pp. 43–52, 61–67. Copyright © 1951 by the University of Chicago Press. Reprinted by permission of the author and publisher. [Footnotes omitted.]

tory," that is, a connected account of political, social, or intellectual development, but rather an interpretive study of important aspects of Egyptian thought and achievement. This interpretation is based on a long career of teaching, writing, and fieldwork in Egypt, during much of which Wilson was associated with the Oriental Institute of the University of Chicago.

In the selections presented here, Wilson stresses particularly the differences between Egypt and Mesopotamia in two areas: the idea of the ruler, and the concept of justice or order. In Mesopotamia the ruler was usually considered the representative of the patron-god, whereas in Egypt Pharaoh was a god. Likewise, in the preface to the law-code of Hammurabi, the king receives the code from a god and is held responsible for maintaining it, while in Egypt ma'at, meaning right, order, justice, and so forth is identified with Pharaoh's personal will. These points are merely two of several on which Egyptian and Mesopotamian attitudes differ in fundamental ways. Wilson's study points up many more great differences in moral and social values between these ancient civilizations and our contemporary culture.

As Wilson says, the problem of discovering the origins of outlook, especially in antiquity, is often really insoluble. But even if the scholar must often speculate without the possibility of attaining certainty, the exercise frequently produces greater insight and appreciation of the problems under consideration.

The Early Dynastic Period was obviously of critical importance in setting modes of thought for all of Egyptian civilization, and Wilson's discussion of the age will remain valuable and provocative. Further study could focus on A. Gardiner's Egypt of the Pharaohs (1961) and the recently written chapters of W. S. Smith in volume I of the Cambridge Ancient History (1970).

Dynasties 1–3 (about 3100–2700 B.C.)

What happened at the beginning of the First Dynasty? At a certain date we change from predynastic to dynastic, from prehistory to history, from the unrecorded prologue to a stage with the curtain up but the lights dimmed down to a minimum. Why did Egyptian historical tradition claim that a certain Menes united the Two Lands into a single nation and began the first of a series of dynasties? We can give certain answers based on our limited range of observations, but the essentials of the process must evade us. We can see much of what happened, but we cannot establish the driving forces which produced the nation.

To be sure, a single date for the beginning of a nation is always an arbitrary figure, selected from a number of different dates: that is, at this point we consider that the nation really become effective. There must have been a long process of preparation before that time, and there was probably a long process of consolidation and justification after that time. If we could establish our early Egyptian chronology with certainty and state that Menes held a ceremonial of "the Uniting of the Two Lands" on certain days in some specific year in the range of 3100 B.C., we should still have to face the problems of what went before and what came after that date.

What we do know is fragmentary and has little true significance. A ruling family of Upper Egypt came north, by conquest united the two parts of the land, set up a capital at Memphis near the junction of the Two Lands, and thus started the long series of dynasties, a series which lasted for about three thousand years. However, we do not know the antecedents of these conquerors from the south; we do not know whether Menes was an actual historical figure or only a later composition of legend; we do not know precisely what the word "conquest" means; we do not know whether the conquest was effected in a generation or two or lasted some centuries; and we do not know whether the role of Memphis was suddenly and immediately effective or whether it had long antecedents and later development. Above all, we lack the psychology of the process: was this a painful imposition of rule by force against long-drawn-out opposition or was Egypt ready and ripe for nationhood, with the only question one of internal competition for the rule?

We can only bring certain observations to play upon these questions. It seems that the first two dynasties were times of consolidation; for perhaps four hundred years after the founding of the First Dynasty, the culture of final predynastic times continued; then, in the Third and Fourth Dynasties, the new state was stable and secure enough to express itself in a distinctively new and "Egyptian" way. This change to new cultural expression appears to have come about with relative abruptness. The inference is that the new state could not at first address itself to matters of culture, such as architecture, art, and literature, while it was preoccupied with matters of government, such as the setting-up of force and bureaus and the securing of the acceptance of rule. This is a negative argument, but it can be bolstered with the positive observation that there are scattered records of fighting and an apparent rebellion within the First and Second Dynasties. It would seem that the new state had to have plenty of time to discover and extend its powers.

Another problem, very difficult to state, is the role of the newly established king within this newly established state. In later times he was stated by the official dogma to be of other nature, a god reigning over humans. Was he so accepted from the beginnings? Probably not, for the conquest should have been more rapid if the conqueror had been widely accepted as a god. Did dogma from the beginning claim that he was a god, but did this claim gain slow acceptance because of competing claims? Or was the dogma of the divinity of the pharaoh a concept which the new state worked out over the early dynasties, in order to establish securely the new rule? In other words, did this new ruler find it necessary to promote himself from the role of the paramount mortal, whose authority might be challenged by other strong mortals, to the role of the god who could not be challenged?

This question is important because it deals with the central doctrine of the Egyptian state in all its aspects, the doctrine of the god-king. To understand that concept, we should like to know how, when, and why it came into being. It is false to assume that the divinity of the ruler belongs to a certain developmental stage of any culture. When we look at the comparable and contemporary cultures of Mesopotamia and Israel, we see that they looked upon their kings quite differently from the way the Egyptians did. In those other cultures the king ruled *for* the gods but not *as* a god. In Egypt the pharaoh ruled as the god who was upon earth and among mortals. Can we understand why the Egyptians fixed upon this dogma? Can we discover when the dogma came into being?

We can give no firm and final answers to these questions. We can only pose certain hypotheses, which may or may not fit the case. The chief of these hypotheses goes back to the geographic nature of Egypt, at once isolated and divided. Egypt was the land which was cut off from major contacts and thus enjoyed a happy sense of security and special election. Her destiny was exceptional because divine providence had set her apart—distinctly apart—from her neighbors. The gods of the larger cosmos did not need to hover over her, cautiously deputizing a mortal to rule on their behalf but retaining to themselves the functional elements of power and control. No; they could go confidently about their cosmic business because one of their number, the pharaoh who was himself a god, carried the functions of power and control and resided in Egypt. The geographic security of the land, so different from Israel or Mesopotamia, gave the gods a sense of confidence about the land, so that rule could safely come down to earth *de jure* and need not be extended through a deputy on earth.

However, the geographic nature of Egypt provides a paradox, which may seem to vitiate both ends of our argument. Viewed in her external isolation, Egypt was a unity, a land apart. Viewed in her internal dualism, Egypt was a disunity, a land split apart. To the Egyptian, Egypt was at the same time "the land" and "the Two Lands." Upper Egypt and Lower Egypt were always distinctly conscious that they were different, one from the other. In any time of weakened rule they broke apart. What held them together was their common dependence upon the Nile and the accepted dogma that Egypt was ruled not by an Upper Egyptian nor by a Lower Egyptian but by a god, in whom could reside the essential forces of each part of the Two Lands. If Lower Egypt accepted this dogma, it could not object to being ruled by a being whose family seemed to have been resident in Upper Egypt but who was, by definition, not of a geographic region in this world but of the realm of the gods.

If this be true, it is probable that it took some time to secure nationwide acceptance of the dogma that this apparent human was not a mortal but was of other being. He proclaimed himself to be a Horus, a god of the distant spaces, of the sky, like a falcon. He proclaimed himself to be "the Two Ladies"; that is, his being incorporated the beings of the two goddesses who stood, respectively, for Upper and Lower Egypt. These two claims took him away from any part of the soil of Egypt and yet rooted him in both parts of Egypt. Ultimately, by the Fifth Dynasty, he would claim to be the divine son of the sun-god Re, the supreme god. How did such a dogma secure acceptance?

To answer that question, we must make a distinction between the acceptance of the dogma as a theory of rule and the acceptance of the dogma as applying specifically to one conquering dynasty. We have argued above that the geography of Egypt supplied a propensity toward acceptance of divine kingship. An added argument would flow out of the psychology of the ancient Egyptian mind. Those people were neither mystics nor modern scientific rationalists. They were basically practical, eager to accept what worked in practice and to try several different approaches to attain an end. What was useful, effective, or advantageous was good. This does not mean that they were hardheaded, efficient, and categorical in a modern sense. Their reasoning never sought to penetrate to the essence of phenomena, and their easy-going pragmatism did not attempt to find the one single way; rather, different and disparate ways were acceptable if they gave some indication of practical effectiveness. Unlike their Asiatic neighbors, Babylonians and Hebrews, the Egyptians made little attempt to systematize a coherent scheme, with separate categories for distinct phenomena. Under a warmer sun the Egyptians blandly blended phenomena which might have been kept resolutely apart. They were lazily tolerant and catholic-minded. Ancient psychology gave animation to everything in the universe—sun, wind, water, tree, rock—and made no sharp boundaries among states of being—human and animal, living and dead, human and divine. Therefore, the Egyptian's all-embracing catholicity saw no essential difference in substance in the several components of the universe. To him the various visible and tangible phenomena of his existence were only superficially or temporarily different, but essentially of one substance, blended into a great spectrum of overlapping colors without sharp margins. Since he felt no necessity for making clear-cut categories, it was easy for him to move comfortably from the human to the divine and to accept the dogma that this pharaoh, who lived among men as if of mortal flesh and blood, was actually a god, graciously residing upon earth in order to rule the land of Egypt. One may believe that the dogma of divine kingship was easy and natural for the Egyptian and thus may have had its roots deep in his prehistoric past.

However, it is a different question when we come to the application of the dogma to a new and conquering dynasty. When the First Dynasty came out of Upper Egypt and set up its claim to divine rule over all of Egypt, did that easygoing tolerance of the conquered territories promote immediate acceptance? Did they say to themselves: "This works; we're a practical people; we accept these rulers as our divine kings"? We do not know the answer to this question. Was there any precedent for uniting the two parts of Egypt into a single nation? It has been claimed that there had been a predynastic union of the land, probably several centuries before the First Dynasty and followed by some centuries of disunion. Unfortunately, it is impossible to say whether that predynastic union was historical fact or later historical fiction. If it was fact, then there was a precedent for the union of Egypt by the rule of a god on earth, but the precedent had been broken by a long period of disunion. If the predynastic union was not fact, then the fiction of such a union must have been built up under the earliest dynasties to justify the dynastic union by a mythical prototype.

It has already been noted in this chapter that the first two dynasties appear to have been concerned with conquest and consolidation. We should therefore propose the working theory that the idea of divine kingship was native to Egypt and had long been present as a loosely formulated concept, that the first dynasties seized upon that concept to give sanction to their new rule, and that the dogma of the divine pharaoh as we know it was therefore worked out in detailed application and achieved formal acceptance under the earliest dynasties. It must be admitted that this cannot be proved, but it can stand as a theory until additional evidence may be adduced to prove or disprove it.

Before picking up the loose thread of historical narrative, we must wrestle with another concept which, like the divine kingship, gave stability and authority to the new state. That concept lies in the Egyptian word *ma'at,* variously translated as "truth," "justice," "righteousness," "order," and so on. Each of those translations may be apt in a certain context, but no one English word is always applicable. *Ma'at* was a quality which belonged to good rule or administration, but it cannot be translated as "rule," "government," "administration," or "law." *Ma'at* was the proper quality of such applied functions. Basically, *ma'at* had some of the same flexibility as our English terms "right," "just," "true," and "in order." It was the cosmic force of harmony, order, stability, and security, coming down from the first creation as the organizing quality of created phenomena and reaffirmed at the accession of each god-king of Egypt. In the temple scenes the pharaoh exhibited *ma'at* to the other gods every day, as the visible evidence that he was carrying out his divine function of rule on their behalf. Thus there was something of the unchanging, eternal, and cosmic about *ma'at.* If we render it "order," it was the order of created things, physical and spiritual, established at the beginning and valid for all time. If we render it "justice," it was not simply justice in terms of legal administration; it was the just and proper relationship of cosmic phenomena, including the relationship of the rulers and the ruled. If we render it "truth," we must remember that, to the ancient, things were true not because they were susceptible of testing and verification but because they were recognized as being in their true and proper places in the order created and maintained by the gods. *Ma'at,* then, was a created and inherited rightness, which tradition built up into a concept of orderly stability, in order to confirm and consolidate the *status quo.* Particularly the continuing rule of the pharaoh. The opposites of *ma'at* were words which we translate as "lying," "falsehood," and "deceit." That which was not consonant with the established and accepted order could be denied as being false. *Ma'at* comes closest to the moral connotation of our word "good."

To the human mind the future has fearful uncertainty, and passing time brings change, even decay. If man could arrest the flight of time, he would discharge some of his feeling of uncertainty and insecurity. It is possible to cut down on the ravages of time and the peril of the future by asserting the eternal and unchanging. If temporary and transitory phenomena can be related to the timeless and stable, doubts and fears can be reduced. The ancient did this by the process of mythmaking, whereby the phenomena and activities of his little world were asserted to be momentary flashes of the everlasting, rocklike order of the gods. So this little pharaoh who sat upon the throne of Egypt was no transitory human but was the same "good god" that he had been from the Beginning and would be for all time. So the relationship of being was not something which had to be worked out painfully in an evolution toward even better conditions but was magnificently free from change, experiment, or evolution, since it had been fully good from the Beginning and needed only to be reaffirmed in its unchanging rightness. Aspects of the divine kingship and of *ma'at* might be subject to temporary misfortune or challenge, but the generalities of these two concepts came to be fundamental in acceptance because they gave timid man freedom from doubt through the operation of the immutable.

It is our theory that these two concepts had already been present in Egyptian consciousness before the dynasties, because they seem natural to Egypt and not artificial constructions, but that the early dynasties had the problem of articulating the concepts to that new nation which they were constructing. Until that specific application had been worked out in its many relationships and interpretations, the new nation was tentative and formative. When, finally, the application had become accepted as the eternal tradition of Egypt, the state was truly in being, and ancient Egypt ended her adolescence and entered upon her characteristic career of essential sameness for fifteen hundred years. We believe that the adolescence took up much of the energies of the new state for the first two dynasties, perhaps four centuries, and that it was not until the Third Dynasty that Egypt really became Egypt.

Thus we assume the process of the first two or three dynasties to have been highly centripetal, with the setting-up of a state with the pharaoh as its essential nucleus. He, as a god, *was* the state. To be sure, it was necessary for him to have officials of a government which had spread and which would become increasingly elaborated, but our evidence indicates that they were his officers, appointed by him, responsible to him alone, and holding office subject to his divine pleasure. To be sure, it was necessary for a new state to have rules and regulations for administrative procedure and precedent, but our negative evidence suggests that there was no codification of law, impersonally conceived and referable by magistrates without consideration of the crown. Rather, the customary law of the land was conceived to be the word of the pharaoh, articulated by him in conformance with the concept of *ma'at* and ever subject to his divine pleasure, within his interpretation of *ma'at* and of his function as a god. These suggestions derive from observations of later times and from our theory that the construction of the state was achieved in these earliest dynasties, to be valid for all later times. In later times there was visible no impersonal and continuing body of law, like one of the Mesopotamian codes, until we come down into Persian and Greek days; the centralization of the state in the person of the king apparently forbade such impersonal law. The authority of codified law would have competed with the personal authority of the pharaoh. We theorize that magistrates operated under customs and practices as locally known to them, all conceived to be the expression of royal will and immediately changeable by royal whim. The only qualification to such rigidly personalized and centralized government was the concept of *ma'at,* that which was right and true and in conformance with divine order; but, since the king was himself a god, he was the earthly interpreter of *ma'at* and—in theory, at least—was subject to the control of *ma'at* only within the limits of his conscience, if a god needs to have a conscience.

These forms and this philosophy of rule are invisible to us in the earliest dynasties. It is the analogy of visible forms which leads us to suggest that the invisible forms were being worked out at this time. Physically, the culture of the first three dynasties is shown in architecture, sculpture, minor arts, and a small amount of writing. Such forms show the first two dynasties to have been a continuation of the physical culture of the final predynastic period, particularly as affected by the stimulation from Mesopotamia. Those borrowings of monumental architecture with recessed brick paneling, of cylinder seals, and of certain motifs in relief sculpture continued through the first two dynasties and only began to receive alteration or substitution in the Third and Fourth Dynasties. Our argument is, thus, that the first three dynasties were too busy setting up the state and the tradition of the state to undertake any modification of the forms of culture. When that state was finally and firmly set upon its base of the divine kingship, then Egypt was ready to express her own characteristic forms, worked out independently upon native soil.

The royal and noble tombs of the final predynastic and earliest dynastic times are the largest visible sign of the physical culture. These were low, flat-topped structures of thick brick walls and sloping sides, called *mastabas* in Egyptian archeology. The sides were relieved by decorative paneling, with bricks set into recessed niches. All this was Mesopotamian in origin. Mesopotamia had only brick. Egypt, of course, had brick, but stone was abundant and easy to work. It is significant that stone came in only slowly, first as a mere adjunct of a brick structure. Under the First Dynasty one pharaoh tried the experiment of flooring his burial pit with slabs of cut and fitted granite. Thus the central chamber in his eternal home had a pavement of more enduring material than the rest of the brick tomb. Under the Second Dynasty a pharaoh had a complete chamber of his brick tomb constructed of hewn and fitted limestone, and for the same period there is literary evidence of a temple or shrine built in stone. Such construction was unusual enough to warrant significant mention in the royal annals. It was in the Third Dynasty that stone really came into its own, in the great complex around the Step Pyramid of King

Djoser at Sakkarah. Perhaps it is wrong to say that stone "came into its own," because the stone of this structure was cut into small bricks, laid as if the stone blocks were mud bricks, and paneled in the same way as the previous brick tombs were. However, the great complex was built entirely in stone, even though experience and tradition dictated that stone should be treated as though it were brick. As yet, the architects and masons had not dared to realize the qualities of stone for massiveness, strength, and durability. There were also decorative elements in the brick construction which told of the weight of conservatism in an architecture which had dared to be revolutionary in the medium used. The columns supporting the roof blocks were pieced together out of limestone bricks and carved with flutings, to represent a bundle column of reeds smeared with mud, an earlier architectural form from a much simpler structure. The stone roof blocks were carved and painted on their undersides to represent palm logs, the earlier roofing material. This great complex of buildings was a magnificent achievement, and the architect who conceived it and laid it out was an inventive and bold genius. However, even an adventurer may explore new territory in ways that are familiar to him, with due regard for precedent, particularly if the sacred sanctions are involved.

As a generalization, the ancient Egyptian was neither adventurous nor experimental; he preferred to continue the pattern which had been handed down through long ages. However, that pattern must have been developed through experimentation at some time, and the earliest dynasties were a period of trial and discovery. Then the Egyptian worked out the forms of expression which were so thoroughly to his liking that he attempted to hold them unchanging for the rest of his cultural existence. It is a great pity that we know so little about this earliest historical period and that most of our knowledge is derived by inference or reference from later periods. Over the many centuries of ancient Egyptian history the charge that this people was not adventurous or creative is true. They preferred to cling firmly to the status which they had inherited—from the gods, in their dogma. The great majority of those new elements which came into the physical culture of later pharaonic Egypt consisted of borrowings and adaptations from abroad, not local inventions. But, of course, the status to which they clung so fervidly had been worked out at some time. For the most part, that time was the first five dynasties. If that is true, we do face the question of whether this status which made up the characteristic Egyptian culture was also a borrowing from abroad. We have seen the effect of the fructification from Mesopotamia at the end of the predynastic period. Was the "Egyptian cultural expression" which was devised in the earliest dynasties also a borrowing or adaptation from abroad?

The answer to that question is in part an argument from silence. It is difficult to see anything in that Egyptian cultural expression which can be referred to any foreign neighbor, and it is possible to ascribe every new development to domestic activity only. Thus far we have mentioned only monumental architecture in stone, taking the place of construction in brick. It was pointed out that Mesopotamia had been forced to build in brick, because of the absence of stone, whereas Egypt had an abundance of building stone in great variety. It might further be pointed out that the architectural types worked out in stone were Egyptian in spirit. The columns imitating reed bundles, the roof slabs imitating palm trunks, the cornice roll, and the torus molding—all went back to Nilotic models and not to any known antecedents elsewhere. Further, the characteristic batter of the walls of tombs and temples has its direct analogy in the sloping cliff walls which border the Nile, so that these structures were artistically fitted to their setting against or upon those cliffs. Ultimately, that battered wall found its logical expression in the sloping sides of the pyramid, a structure which is characteristically Egyptian and has no sensible analogies elsewhere. . . .

If it be true that the earliest dynasties were a period in which the characteristic structure of the Egyptian culture was worked out in its historical form, what do we know about the beginnings of institutions in that period? What do we know about the setting-up of a national government, of the articulation of the former local states into the nation, of the building-up of an officialdom, of the legal sanctions whereby the state controlled the people? What do we know about the social and economic status of the people? Did a new government bring into being new ruling classes, and therefore new social classes? Did a single government, controlling the land from the First Cataract to the Mediterranean, so improve the economic standing of the nation that there was a newly rich class and a notable increase in population? These are highly important questions, but we cannot answer any of them. Documentary evidence in the form of records is virtually lacking for the first three dynasties and is very scarce in the fourth. Evidence from art or from physical remains is too scanty to bear much weight. It is again necessary to ignore such questions in the lack of evidence or to resort to pure speculation; and it must be stressed that speculation is highly subjective.

The wall reliefs of the Old Kingdom, in the Fifth and Sixth Dynasties, showed scenes of hunting in jungle marshes, suggesting that the task of draining such jungles and then irrigating the resultant land was still incomplete. It seems possible that the arable land of Egypt was relatively slight before there was a unified state. With national order established for the length of Egypt, there would be domestic peace and an opportunity to concentrate on agricultural advance, and there would be one single government regulating the use of water and land, forbidding malpractice, and encouraging wider irrigation and planting, in the interests of higher taxes. There would be a freer flow of commerce, more urban centers for the distribution of goods, and thus a greater market for increasing products. We have already discussed the concept of an "urban revolution" and have seen that it was probably a slow process of evolution rather than of revolution. When we consider the factor of one strong, central, and regulating government, it seems likely that a great stimulation to the process of the urban revolution lay in the union of Egypt under the dynasties. If that be true, a major part of the draining of the swamps, the irrigating of new land, the increase in crops and in population, the stimulation of commerce, the specialization of working function, and the appearance of a wealthy and leisured class may have been a result of national government rather than a process leading to national government. In any case, the beginnings of this urban revolution lay in prehistory, even though we may assume that the setting-up of a state was an essential to the progress of the revolution.

In the process of winning new agricultural land, the pharaoh was a leader. Credit went to him, as the embodiment of the state, for the presence and control of the life-giving waters. An early relief shows him active in the ceremonial of opening a new canal. His government had a definite interest in the annual height of the Nile and the consequent prosperity of the land. The early royal annals give a measurement for each year, which can only be the height of the River above or below some fixed datum. Prosperity belonged to the pharaoh and had to be credited to his divine activity on behalf of his land; adversity was probably ascribed to the hostile activity of other gods, whom the pharaoh would have to propitiate in order to rescue his land.

Mention has been made of royal annals, and we do possess a fragmentary and cryptic series of notations for the reigns of a few kings from the First to the Fifth Dynasty, in the Palermo Stone and related fragments. Each year was memorialized because of some significant happening and was marked with a record of the height of the Nile. At any rate, the happening was significant at the time when the record was made, although many of the notations have little meaning to us. Most of them seem to belong to religious ceremonials related to the kingship. Perhaps it is significant that there is very little of political history, in the sense of wars and conquests. For the recording of the years, the peaceful activity of royal ritual, journeys, and buildings was of major importance.

For the first three dynasties we know little about the kings, less about the nobility, and practically nothing about the people. We must stifle our curiosity about social conditions in a changing age. One small series of observations must bear an inordinate amount of weight, because it is all that we have to go on. That deals with the relation of pharaoh to his people at the point of death.

The Egyptian belief in a life after death, an immortality which repeated the best features of the life in this world, was one of the extraordinary factors in the culture. In its developed form it promised every good man a happy eternity. There may be some question as to the definition of that term "good man," particularly as it related to the common masses, but the evidence which comes down to us from the articulate populace indicates that any man might win for himself immortality. When and how did that belief originate? Are its origins lost in the predynastic past, or can we see some development of the idea in historic times?

Like so many of the questions in this book, these can receive only tentative answers. The first observation is that there was a belief in some kind of survival in the earliest predynastic period, as evidenced by the equipment which accompanied the dead in burial and the fact that the burial position was commonly in relation to the rising sun. Whether that survival was thought to be limited in time or in scope we do not know. At any rate, in the predynastic period burial was localized in the several provinces in an apparent independence of rulers. The final predynastic and the first dynasties show a contrast, in that the burial of important personages was commonly in close juxtaposition to the royal tomb. It would seem that the development of the idea of the state and of the divinity of the pharaoh was reflected in a burial custom in which the noble clearly expressed his dependence upon his god-king. What does this mean?

We may accompany this observation with the recent discovery of the burial of a First Dynasty princess together with her personal and domestic servants, each having the tools and materials of his or her trade and apparently all put to death at the time of the princess' interment. In other words, the princess, as the daughter or wife or mother of the god-king, was assured of a continuing existence after death in essentially the same terms as in this life. For that afterlife she needed her own physical equipment, which was placed in her tomb, and she needed her own servants, who were slaughtered to accompany her. We cannot know their state of mind at this mass execution on behalf of their lady. Presumably, there was a doctrine that their afterlife was nonexistent or very limited unless they were needed by someone who was certain of immortality. Therefore, their chance of immortality rested solely on their physical and temporal juxtaposition to her in death. This discovery is the clearest indication of a primitive custom which had been suspected from other evidence. However, the practice of mass sacrifice seems not to have survived into later times in Egypt. The accompaniment of the lord by the servant thereafter became ritual, magical, and symbolic.

Thus the close juxtaposition of the tomb of the noble to the tomb of the pharaoh, particularly in early times down into the Fifth Dynasty, has its meaning. There was no mass sacrifice at the time of the king's death or burial; the accompaniment was spatial rather than temporal. The pharaoh, as a god, was assured of eternal and blessed existence. At the beginning of Egyptian history the noble was not so assured; his best chance of happy immortality lay in his close relation to and service of his god-king. If he could be buried close to the royal *mastaba* or pyramid, if his titles as carved on his tomb clearly stated his service to the pharaoh, and if the inscriptions of his tomb expressed his dependence upon royal pleasure, he might then be needed as an agent in that continued rule which the deceased pharaoh would enjoy in other realm. We shall note the Pyramid Texts, which served to beatify the pharaoh after death, and the absence of similar texts in the tombs of nobles; and we shall there note the beginnings of a process of decentralization and independence of the king. Here we claim that, in the earliest dynasties, only those were sure of eternal life after death who carried within them the germ of divinity—king and queen, prince and princess—and that the noble class apparently depended upon royal need of their services in order to gain such eternal life. This was the doctrine of divine kingship carried out in grim earnest.

As to the lower grades of society—merchants, artisans, peasants, serfs, and slaves—we have no real evidence on their hopes of immortality at this early period. Probably, they, like the nobles, depended upon their immediate overlords. If a Queen Meres-enekh was graciously pleased to record the name, title, and figure of her mortuary priest Khemetnu in her tomb, she had some need of him and he had some chance of survival in her service. Carrying out the same principle, when a noble had the figures of domestic servants placed in his tomb or carved on the walls of the tomb, his servants in this world might have hope of continued existence in accompanying and waiting upon him, just as he himself lived on because he accompanied and waited upon the pharaoh. This, however, is an argument based on rather slim evidence. It assumes that the next world was essentially the same as this world in its happiest and most successful aspects. Since the central factor in this world was the divine nature of the king, who owned and controlled everything within Egypt, the next world would be based on the same absolute authority. Life after death, independent of the pharaoh, would thus be out of the question for this early period.

Many of our arguments in this chapter have been derived from fragmentary and slim evidence. We might similarly speculate on the political tensions and struggles of the first three or four dynasties, as indicated in the apparent popularity of certain gods, some of whom had geographic or functional location. For example, the pharaoh was the god Horus, embodiment of far-reaching rule. What does it mean that briefly in the Second Dynasty the pharaoh was also the god Seth, a factor opposite to Horus? Was this a rebellion by a part of Egypt devoted to Seth or a rebellion within the doctrine of divine kingship? Here we simply note the fact as indicating the struggle of the state to work out national acceptance.

A different problem, which may be of far greater importance, lay in the struggle between two religious systems, the solar and the Osirian. That some such struggle went on, down into historic times, seems highly probable. To be sure, the struggle is visible chiefly as a conflict between two different mortuary religions, the relation of the dead to the sun, which sinks to rest but rises again in glory every day, and the relation of the dead to Osiris, a mortuary god of obscure origins. Whether Osiris was originally an earthly king, who died and thus became the king of the dead; was a god of the earth, in which the dead were buried; or was the god of the Nile, which also died and came to life again is uncertain. By the beginning of the dynasties he had come to be the god who was dead but still lived and therefore to be the dead ruler and ruler of the dead. Thus the deceased pharaoh came to be Osiris, and his son who followed him on the throne came to be the dutiful son Horus, who took action to keep his deceased father alive in another world. Increasingly this concept of death overshadowed the concept in which the deceased went into the company of the sun. It is clear that the two doctrines were, to our modern minds, competing and therefore irreconcilable. However, it is not necessary that the tolerant and catholic Egyptian found them irreconcilable. To him it may simply have been an enlargement of the idea of life in death that there were alternatives, that the deceased had wide scope and different phases of being. Perhaps this conflict between two different mortuary systems was no bitter struggle at all.

Certainly, the conflict between the solar god Re and the mortuary god Osiris was no social and economic class struggle between the haves and the have-nots, between the king and the state religion, on the one side, and the people and the religion of the masses, on the other. That is clear from the fact that the earliest mortuary religion that we can read in the texts limits both the solar and the Osirian phases of future life to the pharaoh alone. He was the only one who, as a god, went to join the sun-god in his journeys; he was the only one who, as a dead king, became Osiris, the king of the dead. At the beginning and for most of the course of the Old Kingdom, these were royal religions, denied to the masses. That "democratization" which was to come at the end of the Old Kingdom and in the First Intermediate Period was quite a different process. It may have seized upon the Osirian faith for its extension of future happiness to wider numbers of the populace, but the Osirian faith was not in itself "democratic." On the contrary, it began in the highest degree as a limitation to the god-king alone.

It is a great tragedy that we know so little about these first dynasties because there are clear indications that this formative period of ancient Egyptian history was of critical importance and that, for once, the Egyptian spirit was one of eager adventure and advance. Now that the prologue has been read, the stage lights become brighter, and we see a culture which had already been formed in its essentials, which was satisfied with those essentials, and which embarked upon a long career of attempting to maintain those essentials unchanged against the wear of time and changing circumstance. Of course, that attempt could not be absolutely successful, for the centuries did bring constant change and reinterpretation of the essentials of the culture; but Egypt was basically the same in her outlook on life from about 2700 to about 1200 B.C., and that is an extraordinarily long time to maintain a status. The social-political essential was the assertion that Egypt was owned and ruled by a god, who assured the land of divine blessings and whose knowledge, power, and oversight were complete and absolute. The spiritual essential was that Egypt was the most blessed of lands, so that setbacks could be only temporary and one might be free to relish life in its simple and homely terms. That basic optimism about life in this world was soon to be extended to an optimism about the life to come as eternally blessed for all good Egyptians.

3. The Sumerian School

SAMUEL NOAH KRAMER

Although people had been aware of the existence and of the achievements of Egyptian civilization from antiquity through the modern period, Sumerian civilization had been lost for thousands of years, and it was only in the last century or so that scholars have recognized not only that an advanced level of human society was reached in the southern region of Mesopotamia by about 3000 B.C., but also that it may well have been the mysterious Sumerians rather than the Egyptians who "invented" many seminal techniques and practices. Samuel Noah Kramer, whose entire career has been devoted to Sumerian studies, expounds in a series of studies on multiple aspects of life, History Begins at Sumer *(1961), the view that many human "firsts" should be attributed to the Sumerians.*

Kramer's work raises several problems of methodology: What does the scholar do when his tablet, baked of clay and inscribed with the wedge-shaped (cuneiform) characters that the Sumerians devised, has broken off? How does he interpret words of uncertain meaning? What inferences about life in general can he safely make from the evidence, often of a particular and limited kind, at his disposal?

Clearly one of the most important inventions for the subsequent history of civilized society was that of writing. The Sumerians appear to have been the

Source: Samuel Noah Kramer, *The Sumerians* (Chicago: University of Chicago Press, 1963), pp. 229–248. Copyright © 1963 by the University of Chicago Press. Reprinted by permission of the author and the publisher.

*first to devise an effective system of communication by symbols intelligible
to anyone trained in their interpretation. But the need for training in reading
and writing, self-evident perhaps to the twentieth-century mind, meant a specialized class in antiquity. In his chapter on "The Sumerian School" Kramer
explores such questions as how the school operated; what requirements and
subjects formed the curriculum; who sought an "education" in ancient Sumer;
and what purposes the educational system served in society.*

*Kramer writes with wit and sympathy about this long-dead civilization, and
he brings to his writing a vivid sense of the continuity of human experience.
In several of the selections of texts dealing with Sumerian education that he
discusses, it is evident that he feels the Sumerians were much like contemporary man in motivation and daily activity. Their society was a vigorous and
dynamic one, and their contributions to the development of the human community are amazing to recognize. Kramer's writings provide a solid introduction for the layman to this gifted and intelligent people to whom we are indebted, directly or indirectly, for many aspects of civilization. The transmission of Sumerian culture in antiquity through successive periods is well treated
in L. Oppenheim's* Ancient Mesopotamia *(1964).*

From the point of view of the history of civilization, Sumer's supreme
achievements were the development of the cuneiform system of writing
and the formal system of education which was its direct outgrowth. It is
no exaggeration to say that had it not been for the inventiveness and per-
severance of the anonymous, practically oriented Sumerian pundits and
teachers who lived in the early third millennium B.C., it is hardly likely
that the intellectual and scientific achievements of modern days would
have been possible; it was from Sumer that writing and learning spread
the world over. To be sure, the inventors of the earliest Sumerian signs,
the pictographs, could hardly have anticipated the system of schooling as
it developed in later days. But even among the oldest known written
documents—those found in Erech—consisting of more than a thousand small pictographic clay tablets inscribed primarily with bits of economic and administrative memoranda, there are several which contain
word lists intended for study and practice; that is, as early as 3000 B.C.,
some scribes were already thinking in terms of teaching and learning.
Progress was slow in centuries that followed; but by the middle of the
third millennium B.C., there must have been a number of schools throughout Sumer where writing was taught formally. In ancient Shuruppak, the
home city of the Sumerian Noah, quite a number of school "textbooks"
dating from about 2500 B.C. were excavated some fifty years ago, consisting of lists of gods, animals, artifacts, and a varied assortment of words
and phrases.

However, it was in the course of the last half of the third millennium
that the Sumerian school system matured and flourished. From this period
tens of thousands of clay tablets have already been excavated, and there is
little doubt that hundreds of thousands more lie buried in the ground
awaiting the future excavator. The vast majority are administrative in

character and cover every phase of Sumerian economic life. From these we learn that the number of scribes who practiced their craft throughout those years ran into the thousands; there were junior scribes and "high" scribes, royal and temple scribes, scribes who were highly specialized for particular categories of administrative activities, and scribes who became leading officials in state and government. There is every reason to assume, therefore, that numerous scribal schools of considerable size and importance flourished throughout the land.

But none of these early tablets deals directly with the Sumerian school system, its organization and method of operation. For this type of information, we must go to the first half of the second millennium B.C. From this later period excavators have discovered hundreds of practice-tablets filled with all sorts of exercises prepared by the pupils themselves as part of their daily schoolwork; their script ranges from the sorry scratches of the "first-grader" to the elegantly made signs of the far-advanced student about to become a "graduate." By way of inference, these ancient copybooks tell us not a little about the method of teaching current in the Sumerian school and about the nature of the curriculum. Better yet, the ancient professors and teachers themselves liked to write about school life, and several of their essays on this subject have been recovered at least in part. From all these sources we get a picture of the Sumerian school, its aims and goals, its students and faculty, its curriculum and teaching techniques, which is quite unique for so early a period in the history of man.

The Sumerian school was known as *edubba*, "tablet house." Its original goal was what we would term "professional," that is, it was first established for the purpose of training the scribes necessary to satisfy the economic and administrative needs of the land, primarily, of course, those of the temple and palace. This continued to be the major aim of the Sumerian school throughout its existence. However, in the course of its growth and development, and particularly as a result of the ever widening curriculum, it came to be the center of culture and learning in Sumer. Within its walls flourished the scholar-scientist, the man who studied whatever theological, botanical, zoölogical, geographical, mathematical, grammatical, and linguistic knowledge was current in his day and who in some cases added to this knowledge.

Moreover, rather unlike present-day institutions of learning, the Sumerian school was also the center of what might be termed creative writing. It was here that the literary creations of the past were studied and copied; it was here, too, that new ones were composed. While it is true, therefore, that the large majority of graduates from the Sumerian schools became scribes in the service of the temple and palace and among the rich and powerful of the land, there were some who devoted their lives to teaching and learning. Like the university professor of today, many of these ancient scholars depended for their livelihood on their teaching salaries and devoted themselves to research and writing in their spare time. The Sumerian school, which probably began as a temple appendage, became in time a secular institution; the teachers were paid, as far as we can see, out of the tuition fees collected from the students. The curriculum, too, was largely secular in character.

Education was, of course, neither universal nor compulsory. The greater part of the students came from the more wealthy families; the poor could hardly afford the cost and the time which a prolonged education demanded. Until recently this was assumed a priori to be the case. But about a decade ago, a Luxembourg cuneiformist by the name of Nikolaus Schneider ingeniously proved it from contemporary sources. In the thousands of published economic and administrative documents from about 2000 B.C., some five hundred individuals list themselves as scribes, and for further identification many of them add the names of their fathers and their occupations. Schneider compiled a list of these data and found that the fathers of the scribes, that is, of the school graduates, were governors, "city fathers," ambassadors, temple administrators, military officers, sea captains, high tax officials, priests of various sorts, managers, supervisors, foremen, scribes, archivists, and accountants—in short, all the wealthier citizens of an urban community. Only one single woman is listed as a scribe in these documents, and the likelihood is, therefore, that the student body of the Sumerian school consisted of males only.

The head of the Sumerian school was the *ummia*, "expert," "professor," who was also called "school-father," while the pupil was called "school-son" and the alumnus "the school-son of days past." The assistant professor was known as "big brother," and some of his duties were to write the new tablets for the pupils to copy, examine the students' copies, and hear them recite their studies from memory. Other members of the faculty were, for example, "the man in charge of drawing" and "the man in charge of Sumerian." There were also monitors in charge of attendance and special proctors responsible for discipline. We know nothing of the relative rank of the school personnel, except, of course, that the headmaster was the "school-father."

If we now turn to the curriculum of the Sumerian school, we have at our disposal a wealth of data from the schools themselves, which is indeed unique in the history of early man. For in this case there is no need to depend on the statements made by the ancients or on inference from scattered bits of information; we have the actual written products of the schoolboys themselves, from the beginner's first attempts to the copies of the advanced student, which were so well prepared that they were hardly to be distinguished from those of the professor. It is from these school products that we realize that the Sumerian school's curriculum consisted of two primary groups; the first may be described as semiscientific and scholarly and the second as literary and creative.

In considering the first, or semiscientific, group of subjects, it is important to stress that it did not stem from what we may call the scientific urge, the search for truth for truth's sake; rather, it grew and developed out of the main school aim, which was to teach the scribe how to write the Sumerian language. For in order to satisfy this pedagogical need, the Sumerian scribal teachers devised a system of instruction which consisted primarily of linguistic classification; that is, they classified the Sumerian language into groups of related words and phrases and had the students memorize and copy them until they could reproduce them with ease. In the course of the third millennium B.C., these textbooks became ever more complete and gradually grew to be more or less stereotyped and standard for all the schools of Sumer. Among them we find long lists of names of trees and reeds, of all sorts of animals (including birds), of countries, cities, and villages, and of all sorts of stones and minerals. All in all, these compilations show a considerable acquaintance with what might be termed botanical, zoölogical, geographical, and mineralogical lore, a fact that is only now beginning to be realized by historians of science.

Our schoolmen also prepared all sorts of mathematical tables and many detailed mathematical problems together with their solutions. And in the field of linguistics, we find the study of Sumerian grammar well represented; a number of the school tablets are inscribed with long lists of substantive complexes and verbal forms which indicate a highly sophisticated grammatical approach. Moreover, as a result of the gradual conquest of the Sumerians by the Semitic Akkadians in the last quarter of the third millennium B.C., our ancient professors prepared what are by all odds the oldest dictionaries known to man. For the Semitic conquerors not only borrowed the Sumerian script; they also treasured highly the Sumerian literary works and studied and imitated them long after Sumerian had become extinct as a spoken language—hence, the pedagogical need for dictionaries in which the Sumerian words and phrases were translated into the Akkadian language.

As for the literary and creative aspects of the Sumerian curriculum, they consisted primarily of studying, copying, and imitating the large and diversified group of literary compositions that must have originated and developed primarily in the latter half of the third millennium B.C. The number of these ancient works ran into the hundreds; they were almost all poetic in form and ranged in length from close to a thousand to less than fifty lines. As recovered to date, they are seen to consist in the main of the following genres: myths and epic tales in the form of narrative poems celebrating the deeds and exploits of the Sumerian gods and heroes; hymns to gods and kings; lamentations, that is, poems bewailing the not infrequent destruction of the Sumerian cities; wisdom compositions, including proverbs, fables, and essays. Of the approximately five thousand literary tablets and fragments recovered from the ruins of Sumer, not a few are in the immature hand of the ancient pupils themselves.

Little is known as yet of the teaching methods and techniques practiced in the Sumerian school. In the morning, upon his arrival in school, the pupil studied the tablet that he had prepared the day before. After this, the "big brother," that is, the assistant professor, prepared a new tablet, which the student then proceeded to copy and study. Both the "big brother" and "school-father" would examine his copies to see if they were correct. Memorizing, no doubt, played a very large role in the student's work. Then, too, the teacher and the assistants must have supplemented the bare lists, tables, and literary texts that the student was copying and studying with considerable oral and explanatory material. But these "lectures," which would no doubt prove invaluable for our understanding of Sumerian scientific, religious, and literary thought, were in all probability never written down and hence are lost to us forever.

While the Sumerian school was in no way "tainted" by what we could call progressive education, the curriculum was pedagogically oriented at least to some extent. Thus the neophyte began his studies with quite elementary syllabic exercises such as tu-ta-ti, nu-na-ni, bu-ba-bi, zu-za-zi, etc. This was followed by the study and practice of a sign list of some nine hundred entries which gave single signs along with their pronunciation. Then came lists containing hundreds of words that had come to be written, for one reason or another, not by one sign but by a group of two or more signs. These were followed by collections containing literally thousands of words and phrases arranged according to meaning. Thus in the field of the "natural sciences," there were lists of the parts of the animal and human body, of wild and domestic animals, of birds and fishes, of trees and plants, of stones and stars. The lists of artifacts included wooden objects—more than fifteen hundred items ranging from pieces of raw wood to boats and chariots; objects made of reed, skin, leather, and metal; assorted types of pottery, garments, foods, and beverages. A special group of these lists dealt with place names—lands, cities, and hamlets as well as rivers, canals, and fields. A collection of the most common expressions used in administrative and legal documents was also included as well as a list of some eight hundred words denoting professions, kinship relations, deformities of the human body, etc.

It was only when the student had become well acquainted with the writing of the complex Sumerian vocabulary that he began to copy and memorize short sentences, proverbs, and fables, and also collections of "model" contracts, this last being essential for the redaction of legal documents, which played a large role in the economic life of Sumer. Along with this linguistic training, the student was also given instruction in mathematics, which took the form of studying and copying metrological tables, with the equivalence of measures of capacity, length, and weight, as well as multiplication and reciprocal tables for computation purposes. Later, the student was put to solving practical problems dealing with wages, canal-digging, and construction work.

In the matter of discipline—and as will be seen below, discipline seems to have been a major problem in the Sumerian school—there was no sparing of the rod. While the teachers no doubt encouraged their students to do good work by means of praise and commendation, they depended primarily on the cane for correcting the student's faults and inadequacies. The student did not have an easy time of it. He attended school daily from sunrise to sunset; he must have had some vacation throughout the year, but we have no information on the point. He devoted many years to his school studies; he stayed in school from his early youth to the day when he became a young man. It would be most interesting to know if—and when and to what extent—the students were expected to specialize in one study or another. But on this point, as indeed on many other matters concerned with school activities, our sources fail us.

In conclusion, we may say just a word about the school building. In the course of several Mesopotamian excavations, buildings have been uncovered which for one reason or another were identified as possible schoolhouses; one in Nippur, another in Sippar, and a third in Ur. But except for the fact that a large number of tablets were found in the rooms, there seems little to distinguish them from ordinary house rooms, and the identification may be mistaken. However, some fifteen years ago, the French who excavated ancient Mari far to the west of Nippur uncovered two rooms which definitely seem to show physical features that might be characteristic of a schoolroom; in particular, they contain several rows of benches made of baked brick, capable of seating one, two, and four people.

There may be a reference to the shape and form of the school building in an enigmatic riddle that an ancient Sumerian professor contrived, which reads as follows:

(What is it:)
A house which like heaven has a plow,
Which like a copper kettle is cloth-covered,
Which like a goose stands on a base,
He whose eyes are not open enters it,
He whose eyes are (wide) open comes out of it?

Its solution is: It's the school.

While the first part of this riddle, which is found on a still unpublished tablet excavated at Ur and copied by Cyril J. Gadd of the British Museum, is altogether obscure, the last two lines sum up succinctly the purpose of the school; to turn the ignorant and illiterate into a man of wisdom and learning.

As already noted, we have at our disposal quite a number of essays relating to education which the ancient schoolmen themselves prepared for the edification of their students, and these give a graphic and vivid picture of various aspects of school life, including the interrelationships between faculty, students, parents, and graduates. Following are four of the better preserved essays, which, to judge from the contents, may be entitled (1) "Schooldays," (2) "School Rowdies (The Disputation between Enkimansi and Girnishag)," (3) "A Scribe and His Perverse Son," and (4) "Colloquy between an *ugula* and a Scribe."

The essay "Schooldays," which deals with the day-to-day activities of the schoolboy as recounted by an "old grad" with some of the nostalgic details that the modern alumnus recounts at his class reunion, is one of the most human documents excavated in the ancient Near East. Originally composed by an anonymous schoolteacher who lived about 2000 B.C., its simple, straightforward words reveal how little human nature has really changed throughout the millenniums. We find our ancient schoolboy, not unlike his modern counterpart, terribly afraid of coming late to school "lest his teacher cane him." When he awakes he hurries his mother to prepare his lunch. In school he misbehaves and is caned more than once by the teacher and his assistants; we are quite sure of the rendering "caning" since the Sumerian sign consists of "stick" and "flesh." As for the teacher, his pay seems to have been as meager then as it is now; at least, he is only too happy to make a "little extra" from the parents to eke out his earnings.

The composition, which was no doubt the creation of one of the *ummia*'s in the *edubba,* begins with a direct question to an old alumnus which reads: "Old Grad, where did you go (when you were young)?" The latter answers: "I went to school." The professor-author then asks: "What did you do in school?" This is the cue for the old grad to reminisce about his school activities thus:

> I recited my tablet, ate my lunch, prepared my (new) tablet, wrote it, finished it; then my model tablets were brought to me; and in the afternoon my exercise tablets were brought to me. When school was dismissed, I went home, entered the house, and found my father sitting there. I explained (?) my exercise-tablets to my father, (?) recited my tablet to him, and he was delighted, (so much so) that I attended him (with joy).

The author now has the schoolboy turn to the house servants (it was evidently quite a well-to-do home) with these words:

> I am thirsty, give me water to drink; I am hungry, give me bread to eat; wash my feet, set up (my) bed, I want to go to sleep. Wake me early in the morning, I must not be late lest my teacher cane me.

Presumably all this was done, for we next find our schoolboy saying:

> When I arose early in the morning, I faced my mother and said to her: "Give me my lunch, I want to go to school!" My mother gave me two rolls, and I set out; my mother gave me two rolls, and I went to school. In school the fellow in charge of punctuality said: "Why are you late?" Afraid and with pounding heart, I entered before my teacher and made a respectful curtsy.

But curtsy or not, it was a bad day for our ancient pupil—at least as the old grad remembered it rather nostalgically—he had to take canings from various members of the school staff. Or, in the words which the author puts in the mouth of the alumnus:

> My headmaster read my tablet, said:
> "There is something missing," caned me.
> (There follow two unintelligible lines)
> The fellow in charge of neatness (?) said:

"You loitered in the street and did not straighten up (?) your clothes (?)," caned me.

(There follow five unintelligible lines)

The fellow in charge of silence said:

"Why did you talk without permission," caned me.

The fellow in charge of the assembly (?) said:

"Why did you 'stand at ease (?)' without permission," caned me.

The fellow in charge of good behavior said:

"Why did you rise without permission," caned me.

The fellow in charge of the gate said:

"Why did you go out from (the gate) without permission," caned me.

The fellow in charge of the whip said:

"Why did you take . . without permission," caned me.

The fellow in charge of Sumerian said:

"Why didn't you speak Sumerian," caned me.

My teacher (*ummia*) said:

"Your hand is unsatisfactory," caned me.

(And so) I (began to) hate the scribal art, (began to) neglect the scribal art.

My teacher took no delight in me; (even) [stopped teaching (?)] me his skill in the scribal art; in no way prepared me in the matters (essential) to the art (of being) a "young scribe," (or) the art (of being) a "big brother."

In despair, according to our old grad, he turned to his father, saying:

Give him a bit extra salary, (and) let him become more kindly (?); let him be free (for a time) from arithmetic; (when) he counts up all the school affairs of the students, let him count me (too among them; that is, perhaps, let him not neglect me any longer).

From here on, the author himself takes over, describing the events as if he had been there and had·witnessed them, thus:

To that which the schoolboy said, his father gave heed. The teacher was brought from school, and after entering in the house, he was seated on the "big chair." The schoolboy attended and served him, and whatever he learned of the scribal art, he unfolded to his father. Then did the father in the joy of his heart say joyfully to the headmaster of the school: "My little fellow has opened (wide) his hand, (and) you made wisdom enter there; you showed him all the fine points of the scribal art; you made him see the solutions of the mathematical and arithmetical (problems), you (taught him how) to make deep (?) the cuneiform script (?).

The author now has the father turn to his household servants, saying:

Pour for him *irda*-oil, bring it to the table for him. Make fragrant oil flow like water on his stomach (and) back; I want to dress him in a garment, give him some extra salary, put a ring on his hand.

The servants do as they are bidden, and then the teacher speaks to the schoolboy:

Young fellow, (because) you hated not my words, neglected them not, (may you) complete the scribal art from beginning to end. Because you gave me everything without stint, paid me a salary larger than my efforts (deserve), (and) have honored me, may Nidaba, the queen of guardian angels, be your guardian angel; may your pointed stylus write well for you; may your exercises contain no faults. Of your brothers, may you be their leader; of your friends may you be their chief; may you rank the highest among the schoolboys, satisfy (?) all who walk (?) to and from in (?) the palaces. Little fellow, you "know" (your) father, I am second to him; that homage be paid to you, that you be blessed—may the god of your father bring this about with firm hand; he will bring prayer and supplication to Nidaba, your queen, as if it were a matter for your god. Thus, when you put a kindly hand on the . . . of the teacher, (and) on the forehead of the "big brother," then (?) your young comrades will show you favor. You have carried out well the school's activities, you are a man of learning. You have exalted Nidaba, the queen of learning; O Nidaba, praise!

From the preceding essay it is not easy to decide whether the faculty of the Sumerian school consisted largely of sadists or whether its student body consisted of rowdies and roughnecks. That the latter may have been true at least in part seems to be corroborated by the second of our essays, "The Disputation between Enkimansi and Girnishag." According to this document, the ancient pedagogues seem to have had their hands full trying to control pupils who took pleasure in pushing, shouting, quarreling, and cursing.

This one hundred and sixty line Sumerian essay has only recently been pieced together from seven tablets and fragments by Cyril J. Gadd, professor emeritus of the School of Oriental and African Studies of the University of London, and the author of this book [*The Sumerians*]. Two of these were excavated at Ur by Sir Leonard Woolley about twenty-five years ago; they were published in part by Professor Gadd in 1956, under the title "Teachers and Students in the Oldest Schools," as an inaugural lecture at the School of Oriental and African Studies. But these two tablets contained only the beginning and end of the essay. A fuller text is now available as a result of the identification of five pieces excavated at Nippur, one of which, a large eight-column tablet containing a whole collection of Sumerian essays, proved to be of particular importance for the restoration of the text of our essay. Excavated some sixty years ago, it is now in the Hilprecht Collection of the Friedrich-Schiller University of Jena in East Germany, and its contents were only recently made available. It must be stressed, however, that in spite of the more complete text now available, much of the meaning of the essay and not a few of its implications are still quite uncertain, since many of the passages are only partially preserved. The sketch here presented must therefore be taken as preliminary and tentative, and future discoveries may modify the interpretation considerably.

One rather unexpected and not uninteresting bit of comparative cultural information provided by our essay concerns the literal meaning and derogatory implications of the word "sophomore," which is first known to have been used as an English word in Cambridge in 1688. There is reason to believe that this word, "sophomore," is the English form of a Greek compound word "sophos-moros," which means literally "clever-fool." Now, as Professor Gadd was first to point out, our Sumerian essay contains the exact equivalent of the Greek "sophos-moros." In the course of the bitter and abusive arguments between the two school rivals which constitute the main part of the essay, one of them taunts the other with being a *"galam-huru,"* a Sumerian compound word meaning literally "clever-fool," that is, "sophomore." The composition consists primarily of a bitter verbal contest between two schoolmates named Enkimansi and Girnishag, both of whom are far advanced in their studies; in fact, Girnishag may have reached the height of being "big brother," that is, an assistant instructor in the school. In the course of the disputation each talks up his own virtues and talents in glowing terms and talks down his opponent with withering sneers and vituperative insults. Thus near the very beginning of the document, one of these worthies addresses the other as follows:

> You dolt, numskull, school pest, you illiterate, you Sumerian ignoramus, your hand is terrible; it cannot even hold the stylus properly; it is unfit for writing and cannot take dictation. (And yet you say) you are a scribe like me.

To this the other worthy answers:

> What do you mean I am not a scribe like you? When you write a document it makes no sense. When you write a letter it is illegible (?). You go to divide up an estate, but are unable to divide up the estate. For when you go to survey the field, you can't hold the measuring line. You can't hold a nail in your hand; you have no sense. You don't know how to arbitrate between the contesting parties; you aggravate the struggle between the brothers. You are one of the most incompetent of tablet writers. What are you fit for, can any one say (?)?

To which his rival retorts:

> Why, I am competent all around. When I go to divide an estate, I divide the estate. When I go to survey the field, I know how to hold the measuring line. I know how to arbitrate between the contesting parties. I know how to pacify the struggle between the brothers and soothe their feelings. But you are the laziest (?) of scribes, the most careless (?) of men. When you do multiplication, it is full of mistakes (?) . . . In (computing) areas you confuse (?)

length with width. Squares, triangles, circles (?), and sectors—you treat them all without understanding as if. . . . You chatterbox, scoundrel, sneerer, and bully, you (dare say) that you are the "heart" of the student body!

Taking this sentence as a cue, his opponent begins with the query: "What do you mean I am not the 'heart' of the student body?" He then continues with a description of his talents as a keeper of accounts and ends with these lines:

Me, I was raised on Sumerian, I am the son of a scribe. But you are a bungler, a windbag. When you try to shape a tablet, you can't even smooth (?) the clay (?). When you try to write a line, your hand can't manage (?) the tablet. . . . You "sophomore," cover your ears! cover your ears! (Yet) you (claim to know) Sumerian like me!

At this point a long passage follows which is so poorly preserved that it is difficult to follow even the shift of speakers. Finally, someone (probably the *ugula,* that is, a monitor of some sort) became so incensed at one student—Enkimansi—that he was ready to lock him up and put him in chains, to judge from the following passage toward the very end of the composition, which in the following tentative translation reads:

Why do you behave like this! Why do you push, curse, and hurl insults at each other! Why do you raise a commotion in the school!
. . . (There follow four unintelligible lines.) The commotion has reached him! Why were you insolent (?), inattentive (?), (why do you) curse, and hurl insults against him who is your "big brother" and has taught you the scribal art to your own advantage (?)! Even the *ummia* who knows everything shook his head violently (?) (saying): "Do to him what you please." If I (really) did to you what I pleased—to a fellow who behaved like you (and) was inattentive (?) to his "big brother"—I would (first) beat you with a mace—what's a wooden board (when it comes to beating!)—(and) having put copper chains on your feet, would lock you up in the house (and) for two months would not let you out of the school (building).

Following four unintelligible lines, the composition closes with the words: "In the dispute between Girnishag and Enkimansi the *ummia* gave the verdict."

As can be surmised from the two preceding essays, the Sumerian school was rather formidable and uninviting; the curriculum was "stiff," the teaching methods drab, the discipline harsh. No wonder, then, that at least some of the pupils played truant when possible and became "problem children" to their teacher and parents. Which supposition brings us to the third of our school essays, "A Scribe and His Perverse Son," a text pieced together from more than a score of tablets and fragments. This essay is noteworthy as one of the first documents in the history of man in which the word "humanity" (Sumerian, *namlulu*) is used not only to designate mankind but in the sense of conduct and behavior befitting human beings.

The composition, which is about one hundred eighty lines in length, begins with an introduction consisting of a more or less friendly dialogue between father and son in which the latter is admonished to go to school, work diligently, and report back without loitering in the streets. To make sure the lad has paid close attention, the father has him repeat his words verbatim.

From this point on, the essay is a monologue on the part of the father. It starts with a series of practical instructions to help make a man of his son: not to gad about in the streets and boulevards; to be humble before his monitor; to go to school and learn from the experience of man's early past. There follows a bitter rebuke to the wayward son, who, his father claims, has made him sick unto death with his perennial fears and inhuman behavior. He, the father, is deeply disappointed at the son's ingratitude; he never made him work behind plow or ox, nor did he ever ask him to bring firewood or to support him as other fathers make their sons do. And yet his son has turned out to be less of a man than the others.

Like many a disappointed parent of today, the father seems to be especially hurt that his son refuses to follow his professional footsteps and become a scribe. He admonishes him to emulate his companions, brothers, and friends and to follow his own profession, the scribal art, in spite of the fact that it is the most difficult of all professions that the god of arts and crafts thought up and brought into being. It is most useful, the father argues, for the poetic transmission of man's experiences. But in any case, he continues, it is decreed by Enlil, the king of all the gods, that a son should follow his father's profession.

After a final upbraiding for the son's pursuit of materialistic success rather than humanistic endeavor, the text becomes rather obscure; it seems to consist of brief, pithy sayings intended, perhaps, to guide the son in true wisdom. In any case, the essay closes on a happy note, with the father blessing his son and praying that he find favor in the eyes of his personal god, the moon-god, Nanna, and his wife, the goddess Ningal.

Here now is a quite literal, if tentative, translation of the more intelligible portions of the essay, omitting only here and there an obscure phrase or a broken line. The father begins by asking his son:

> "Where did you go?"
> "I did not go anywhere."
> "If you did not go anywhere, why do you idle about? Go to school, stand before your 'school-father' (professor), recite your assignment, open your schoolbag, write your tablet, let your 'big brother' write your new tablet for you. After you have finished your assignment and reported to your monitor, come to me, and do not wander about in the street. Come now, do you know what I said?"
> "I know, I'll tell it to you."

"Come, now, repeat it to me."

"I'll repeat it to you."

"Tell it to me."

"I'll tell it to you."

"Come on, tell it to me."

"You told me to go to school, recite my assignment, open my schoolbag, write my tablet, while my 'big brother' is to write my new tablet. After finishing my assignment, I am to proceed to my work and to come to you after I have reported to my monitor. That's what you told me."

"Come now, be a man. Don't stand about in the public square or wander about the boulevard. When walking in the street, don't look all around. Be humble and show fear before your monitor. When you show terror, the monitor will like you.

(About fifteen lines destroyed)

"You who wander about in the public square, would you achieve success? Then seek out the first generations. Go to school, it will be of benefit to you. My son, seek out the first generations, inquire of them.

"Perverse one over whom I stand watch—I would not be a man did I not stand watch over my son—I spoke to my kin, compared its men, but found none like you among them.

"What I am about to relate to you turns the fool into a wise man, holds the snake as if by charms, and will not let you accept false phrases.

"Because my heart had been sated with weariness of you, I kept away from you and heeded not your fears and grumblings—no, I heeded not your fears and grumblings. Because of your clamorings, yes, because of your clamorings, I was angry with you—yes, I was angry with you. Because you do not look to your humanity, my heart was carried off as if by an evil wind. Your grumblings have put an end to me, you have brought me to the point of death.

"I, never in all my life, did I make you carry reeds to the cane-brake. The reed rushes which the young and the little carry, you, never in your life did you carry them. I never said to you 'Follow my caravans.' I never sent you to work, to plow my field. I never sent you to work, to dig up my field. I never sent you to work as a laborer. 'Go, work and support me,' I never in my life said to you.

"Others like you support their parents by working. If you spoke to your kin and appreciated them, you would emulate them. They provide 10 *gur* of barley each—even the young ones provided their fathers with 10 *gur* each. They multiplied barley for their father, maintained him in barley, oil, and wool. But you, you're a man when it comes to perverseness, but compared to them you're not a man at all. You certainly don't labor like them—they are the sons of fathers who make their sons labor, but me—I didn't make you work like them.

"I, night and day am I tortured because of you. Night and day you waste in pleasures. You have accumulated much wealth, have expanded far and wide, have become fat, big, broad, powerful, and puffed. But your kin waits expectantly for your misfortune and will rejoice at it because you looked not to your humanity."

(Here follows an obscure passage of forty-one lines which seems to consist of proverbs and old saws; the essay then concludes with the father's poetic blessing:)

From him who quarrels with you may Nanna, your god, save you,
From him who attacks you may Nanna, your god, save you,
May you find favor before your god,
May your humanity exalt you, neck and breast,
May you be the head of your city's sages,
May your city utter your name in favored places,
May your god call you by a good name,
May you find favor before your god Nanna,
May you be regarded with favor by the goddess Ningal.

If in spite of the heavy and far from exciting curriculum, the harsh punishments by his teachers, and the bitter rivalry of his more aggressive fellow classmates the ambitious and persevering student succeeded in graduating from school, there were several job possibilities open to him; he could, for example, enter the services of the palace or temple, or he could become the managing scribe and accountant of one of the larger estates which dotted the land. In the fourth of the school essays, "Colloquy between an *ugula* and a Scribe," we find the *edubba* graduate, now a full-fledged scribe on one such estate, having an argument with the *ugula* (probably its superintendent), who himself was an alumnus of the *edubba*. The composition, which consists of seventy-eight lines reconstructed from a dozen tablets and fragments, begins with an address by the *ugula* which reads:

Old Grad, come here to me (and) let me tell you what my *ummia* (the professor in charge of the *edubba*) told me.

I, too, like you was (once) a little fellow and had a "big brother."

The *ummia* would assign me work (that was even too much) for a (grown) man.

(But) I darted about like a darting reed, became absorbed in the work, neglected not my *ummia*'s words, did not act according to my own self(ish spirit), (and as a result) the "big brother" was pleased with my accomplishment.

He rejoiced because I humbled myself before him and spoke (?) in my favor (?).

Whatever he sketched for me I made, I put everything in its place—(even a fool could easily (?) follow (?) his instructions.

He guided my hand on the clay, showed me how to behave

properly, "opened" my mouth with words, uttered good counsel, fo-cused (?) (my) eyes on the rules which guide the man of achieve-ment: diligence is the very essence (literally "lot") of achievement, time-wasting is taboo, the fellow who gads about (and) wastes time at his assignment has failed his assignment.

He (the "big brother") vaunted not his knowledge, his words are restrained—had he vaunted his knowledge, eyes would "pop."

Attend him (therefore) before the sun rises (and) before the night cools; do not turn back the pleasure of being by the side of the "big brother"; having come close to the "big foreheads" your words will become honored.

He (the "big brother" (?)) did not turn back a second time the fastened eyes . . . , he bound about your neck a garland (?) of man's courtesy and respect (?).

The heart of the afflicted (?) having been soothed, he is freed of guilt.

The man (who brings) milk (?) sacrifices (?), made adequate (?) his gift; the man of wealth has pressed his knee-bent kid to his breast—so (?) must you be courteous to man, supervisor, and owner, must make their heart content.

So much for the *ugula's* rather diffuse and long-winded speech. Following an introductory line which reads; "The learned scribe humbly answers his *ugula,*" the text continues with what seems to be a far from humble re-sponse:

You recounted to me . . like a . . , (but) now I will let you have the answer to it; as for your ox-like bellow, you will not turn me into an ignoramus with its lack of understanding—I will answer it fully (?) (literally, perhaps, "sixty times").

Like a puppy (your) eyes are wide part (?) (even if) you act (like) a human being.

Why do you lay down rules for me as if I am an idler?

Anyone who heard you would drop (?) his hands in despair (?).

Let me explain to you carefully (literally, "let me put into your hand") the art of being a scribe since (?) you have mentioned it.

You have put me in charge over your house (and) never have I let you find me idling about.

I held the slave girls, slaves, and (the rest of) your household to their task; saw to it that they enjoyed their bread, clothing, and fat (and) that they work properly (literally, "as is their way").

You did not (have to) follow your slave in the house of your master; I did the unpleasant (?) task (?) (and) followed him like a sheep.

I have said daily the protecting (?) prayers which you have or-dered; your sheep (and) your oxen are pleasing (and) bring joy to your god; on the day when your god's boat is moored they (the priests (?)) lay hands on you (in blessing). You assigned me the breast (that is, perhaps, the high, unirrigated part) of the field (and) I made the men work there—a challenging task which permits no sleep either by night or in the heat of day.

(Yet) all the . . . . (and (?)) the sons of the farmers nod (?) approval (?).

I applied the kindly hand in your field (and) folks spoke well of me; I made the ox bring in whatever filled (?) your path (?), made him carry (?) his load for you.

From my youth you raised me, watched over my behavior, treated me kindly like goodly silver, (and) did not . . . . I (therefore) kept away (?) from you that which "walks not in greatness," like something which is taboo for you; I kept away from you the "small winds (?)" (and) did not let them exist for you.

Raise now your head high, you who were formerly a little fellow, you can (now) turn your hand against (?) (any) man, (so) act (?) as is befitting.

Here probably ends the scribe's answer, although there is no introductory line to indicate a change of speaker. The rather unexpectedly amiable response of the *ugula*, which concludes the composition, reads as follows:

You who paid homage (?) to me, who blessed (?) me, who brought instruction into my body like edible milk (and) fat—because (?) you stood not about in idleness I have obtained the earth's favors, have not suffered its misfortunes. The *ummia*, the "word-knowers" nod (?) approval (?), tell (?) all about you in their houses (?), wherever they are (?). Your name is uttered (only) for good, your commands are well received (?). The ox-drivers (?) [halt (?)] their strife at your sweet songs; at your sweet songs the contenders (?) will drop (?) [(their) contention (?)]. The *ummia* pays you (?) homage with joyful heart (saying): "You who (as a) little fellow sat at my words, pleased my heart—Nidaba (the patron goddess of the *edubba*) has given in your hand the honor of (being an) *ummia*; you are the consecrated of Nidaba, may you rise heaven high. May you be blessed with joyous heart, [suffer] no heartache; may you [excel (?)] in whatever is in the *edubba*, the house of learning; [may] the loftiness of Nidaba [bring (?) you un]rivaled (?) rejoicing. At your kindly wisdom strife [will halt (?)]; the little fellows will drop (?) [their contention (?) in] . . . . The craftsmen will utter [your name for good]; the . . . will recount [your]. . . . In the song-echoing (?) street, the street where . . . , you have brought the unrivaled *me;* you have mastered (?) the direction of harmonious (?) conduct."

There follows the typical closing phrase: "O Nidaba, praise!" To all of which the modern professor and teacher might well respond with a wistful and envious "Amen!"

4. The Greeks in the Bronze Age

STERLING DOW

*About their origins as a people, and especially about the legendary characters
who had dominated the early, heroic days of Greek civilization, the Greeks
preserved many detailed if not always harmonious traditions from at least
the eighth century* B.C. *onward. The most spectacular and influential of these
found expression in the two great epics ascribed to the blind poet Homer—
the* Iliad *and the* Odyssey. *For many centuries after the political decline of
Greece and its absorption into the Roman Empire, many people believed
more or less implicitly in the stories of Greek tradition. In the late eighteenth
century, however, a German philologist, Friedrich Wolf, published a striking
work entitled* Prolegomena ad Homerum, *in which he challenged the unity
and authorship of both poems and opened the modern discussion of many
interrelated problems having to do with Greek prehistory, which are called
collectively "the Homeric question."*

*Not long after Wolf wrote, Greece was liberated from Ottoman rule, and for-
eigners found it easier to visit and travel in Greece. Exploration and rediscovery of many ancient Greek monuments and antiquities began, but proceeded in a more or less haphazard manner until the startling discovery in
the 1870's of the remains of a great city on the site of Troy by a retired German*

Source: Sterling Dow, "The Greeks in the Bronze Age," in *Rapports du XIe
Congrès International des Sciences Historiques* (Stockholm, 1960), pp. 2–26. Reprinted by permission of Almqvist & Wiksells, Uppsala, Sweden. [Footnotes omitted.]

*businessman, Heinrich Schliemann. He followed up this discovery with equal-
ly striking finds in southern Greece, at Mycenae, the legendary capital of Agamemnon. Positive proof seemed at hand that the Homeric poems, and Greek
historical tradition generally, contained a good deal of truth and accuracy. But
problems remained. In many cases the descriptions of Homer did not agree
with the evidence of the archaeologist's spade. The great question then became,
What precisely was the relationship between Homer and history? Some
scholars saw in the poems a close connection with the Greeks at least of the late
Bronze Age; others claimed only a superficial similarity, the result of distortion in oral tradition over long centuries before the Homeric poems were
finally put into written form. Furthermore, with the rediscovery of a great
civilization on Crete, called "Minoan" after the Cretan king of Greek tradition, there arose the question of the relationship between Crete and Mycenae
in the Bronze Age. A major breakthrough came in 1954 with the decipherment
of a hitherto unreadable script, Linear B, which was found both at Knossos on
Crete and at Mycenaean sites on the mainland, and which was proved to be
Greek. Now contemporary written evidence in Greek dating from the Bronze
Age had come to light and forced a re-evaluation of much of the other evidence
and many older hypotheses about the Greeks in this period.*

*Sterling Dow, the author of this selection, is Professor Emeritus of
Classics and History at Harvard University. He has published numerous
articles and papers in Greek history and is a specialist in Greek epigraphy,
the study of inscriptions. He discusses here some of the leading questions of
Greek prehistory. Who were the Greeks, and where did they come from? What
was their relationship with Minoan civilization on Crete? How did their civilization develop? How reliable are the legends and stories that are found in
Homer? Although not every scholar accepts all of Dow's arguments or conclusions, his article is a remarkable synthesis of most of the information and
of the modern literature that was available a decade ago. It makes clear the
particular difficulties faced by the historian in trying to understand Greece in
the Bronze Age. For further reading on some of the topics treated, see J. Chad-
wick's exciting book on* The Decipherment of Linear B *(1958), G. S. Kirk's*
The Songs of Homer *(1962), or E. Vermeule's* Greece in the Bronze Age
(1964).

I. The Settlement of Greece

Before the end of the Dark Age, the population of Greece had been made
up for the rest of Antiquity. As finally constituted, the population consisted of four groups of peoples, viz. two groups of non-Greeks and two
groups of Greeks. The order of arrival of these four groups is the first
problem.

About one of them, viz. the Dorians, there is no question: they were
the fourth and last to arrive. Their impact spread itself over many years,
both before and after 1100 B.C., the approximate date usually given for
convenience. With them came the Dark Age, and iron began to be used.

The major uncertainties are back in the Stone and Bronze Ages, long
anterior to 1100 B.C. The three groups of peoples which have to be settled

in Greece before (4) the Dorians are: (1) Neolithic peoples, (2) Anatolian peoples, (3) non-Dorian Greeks. No reliable explicit statement from Antiquity tells us when any of these peoples arrived, and it is still true that after the (metal-less) Neolithic period, no particular kind of archaeological remains—buildings, weapons, pottery, burials, or the like—comes to us positively associated with any of them. Indeed argument is needed to show that there *were* three groups of peoples, and that no one group is identical with one of the others.

Archaeology does reveal, on many sites, though by no means on all sites, three distinct strata of general destruction; each destruction was followed, soon or late, by new kinds of pottery and other remains. Such interruptions of cultural continuity are usually and rightly taken to signalize the arrival of a new people. The Interruptions (if we may use the word as a specific term) are as follows: (A) end of Neolithic to beginning of Early Helladic; (B) end of Early Helladic to beginning of Middle Helladic; and (C) end of Late Helladic, i.e. end of the Bronze Age to beginning of Sub-Minoan, and then of Protogeometric, i.e. beginning of the Iron Age. This last Interruption (C) undoubtedly marks the arrival of (4) the Dorians. The two earlier Interruptions, (A) and (B), must mark the arrival of two out of the three earlier peoples.

The (2) Anatolians are known to have been in Greece from the fact that many place-names in Greece have certain specific suffixes, which have been virtually proved not to be Greek. These place-name suffixes are abundant, however, in Asia Minor. They are found also in Crete and in the Islands. The natural presumption is that people from Asia Minor spread over the Aegean, moving at about the same time into both Crete and Greece. The immigration introduced a degree of cultural unity sufficient to spread similar place names over Crete, over the Mainland, the Islands, and North into Macedonia. The question was put: When did such unity prevail over the whole area? The answer was: Clearly *not* in the Neolithic period; *nor* in Middle Helladic; *nor* in Late Helladic, because in Late Helladic a common culture developed only in the last phase, and a simultaneous Anatolian (or any other) invasion of Crete, the Islands, and the Mainland in that period is out of the question. Archaeology does, however, prove a common and unified culture in the Early Helladic period. This being so, the (2) Anatolians are conjectured to have arrived at the Interruption (A) between Neolithic and Early Helladic.

It has long been assumed that Mykenai in its great days was under Greek domination—back into the Middle Helladic period, sometime not long before ca. 1600 B.C. and down to Agamemnon, whose name is Greek. The development reflected in the graves at Mykenai appeared to be continuous, but there was a gap between the graves (ending at ca. 1300 B.C.) and Agamemnon (then dated ca. 1200).

Although it was all but certain that Greece was in Greek hands, still nothing clinched the argument. The evidence was primarily archaeological, but it amounted only to features of Mainland culture which were Northern, and which persisted in the face of strong Minoanization (the Minoans who inhabited Crete and spread their Minoan culture to the

Mainland were certainly not Greeks). There was also linguistic evidence, but it was merely the interpretation, still disputed, of some names in Hittite documents to give recognizable Greek names. Add tradition, mostly Homeric—which after all is only myth for this period, including names such as Agamemnon—and the evidence available was exhausted.

Now there is much more. The decipherment of the Linear B script as Greek proves absolutely that there were Greeks in Pylos by ca. 1200 B.C., where they were well established, with a complicated bureaucracy certainly not created overnight. It proves also that Greeks were in control of Knossos (and Crete) by 1400 B.C., whereas earlier this had merely seemed to some scholars highly probable on archaeological grounds. If Greeks controlled Crete in 1400, they must have been based on the Mainland, i.e. presumably on Mykenai. In Mykenai (or wherever) they could not have just arrived, but the whole long development, uninterrupted and organic, back through the great Tholos Tomb Dynasty, and beyond that through the Shaft Grave Dynasty, must be Greek. And so the decipherment of Linear B has shown, what no one is likely ever to doubt again, that Greeks were firmly in control of the country during all the five Late Helladic centuries, ca. 1600 to ca. 1100 B.C. Since, moreover, there is no sharp archaeological break (i.e. no level of destruction) between Middle and Late Helladic, it is proper to assume that the Greeks were in Greece during the Middle Helladic period also, and hence that the first (i.e. non-Dorian) Greeks came to Greece at the beginning of the Middle Helladic period, ca. 2000 B.C. The signal of their arrival is the stratum of destruction, Interruption (B) at the end of Early Helladic III. To non-Dorian Greeks, therefore, belong the Middle and Late Helladic periods.

These findings are helpful. As we have seen, the arrival of the (4) Dorian Greeks at the end of Late Helladic, ca. 1100 B.C., i.e. at Interruption (C), is undisputed. The decipherment of Linear B as Greek provides assurance that the (3) non-Dorian Greeks came to Greece at the end of Early Helladic, ca. 2000 B.C., i.e. at Interruption (B). By elimination, Interruption (A), at the end of Neolithic, is confirmed as the time of arrival of the (2) Anatolians. This reinforces the conclusion already reached by Blegen in 1928 on the basis of archaeological evidence, as we have seen.

The resulting scheme is more solid than ever before:

Number	Interruption	People	Time of arrival
(1)		Neolithic	Some remote date, unknown.
(2)	(A)	Anatolians	Beginning of early Helladic, ca. 3000 B.C. (Also to Crete.)
(3)	(B)	Non-Dorian Greeks	Beginning of Middle Helladic, ca. 2000 B.C. (None to Crete.)
(4)	(C)	Dorian Greeks	Beginning of Dark (Iron) Age, usual date ca. 1100 B.C. (Also to Crete.)

Greeks came to Greece by the start of MH I: that may be regarded now as certain.

II. *Background: Early Periods and Sites*

1. NEOLITHIC

The Neolithic peoples of the Mainland were quite different in culture from those of Crete; they did not settle even the Kyklades. Probably therefore they came by land. Culturally, they are said to have remained provincial throughout a period of tremendous duration, viz. "the Neolithic and to a large extent the Early Bronze Age." No one contribution of theirs to the later Greece of the Hellenes has been definitely specified, but something historical can perhaps be learned from the principal site of the second of the two main Neolithic periods.

Dimini. Whatever its absolute dates, Dimini in Thessaly is a fortified Neolithic town, of which there are few. Its neighbor and precedecessor, Sesklo, preserves only one apparent stretch of city wall, but Dimini boasted a sextuple circumvallation, a thing unique in Greece at any period. The walls were curved to follow the contours of the hill, so that at times the walls are close together. There were no towers. The height of the walls is stated, on no obvious basis, to have been probably not over ca. 2.90 m; there was a low parapet behind. The design makes the purpose clear: the walls were breast-works. The purpose was not to put six successive obstacles in front of the enemy, but rather to give body protection to many rows of archers and slingers. Taken by itself, as a type, this is doubtless an early fortification, but in relative chronology its phase of Thessalian Neolithic (the second of two phases) may be so late in absolute time as to come after e.g. the fortification of Lerna (*infra*). This impairs the value of Dimini as a monument of the military art. Be this as it may, the innermost-topmost wall is the thickest, approaches most to a rectangular shape, and encloses a court on the long axis of which is a "megaron." No scheme could more strongly suggest monarchy, control literally central. Such as it is, this is the first major fact—or better, not "fact" but "observation" —in the political history of Europe.

2. EARLY HELLADIC

Since their place-names are found in the Islands, the Anatolian peoples probably came by sea. Many more long centuries were drawn out before Greeks arrived, but in the Early Helladic periods as in the Neolithic, there were spectacular events and achievements of which some memory may have been transmitted until finally the Greeks heard it. On the whole, to be sure, the Anatolian peoples on the Greek Mainland, as in Crete, seem to have lived quietly, in towns numerous, small, unwalled, and self-contained. Commerce was minimal, war apparently unusual. But to all this there is one known startling exception.

Lerna. At Lerna there was that long continuity of occupation which is favorable to a high culture. There had been two Neolithic phases. In the second phase, levels could be counted, and the deposit from the first phase, where no such definite count could be made, but which is approximately as deep, suggests somewhat the same order of duration. At the beginning of Early Helladic occupation, a distinct break occurred. Early Helladic also is divided into two phases, the first of which had at least six architectural stages.

In this first EH phase, two different fortification walls were built at Lerna, an earlier wall and a later; the later, so far as it has been recovered, replaced the earlier. The earlier appears, though we cannot judge, to have been simple. Over it was built a massive new fortification, consisting of two thick walls joined at intervals by heavy cross-walls which strengthened the whole and formed chambers. Towers projected from the angles. Again, as at Dimini (but quite different in form), we encountered a developed design without known antecedents on the site (the earlier wall being so fragmentary that its form cannot be fully made out, but apparently it was a single wall without towers). A house ('BG') of equally massive construction—we may as well call it the then palace—and showing two or three building periods, stood within this impressive and (for EH times) uncommon fort.

A sensational sequence of events followed. Palace BG and the fortification walls were razed to the ground in order to build a new and perhaps even grander palace, 'The House of the Tiles.' Defences were evidently considered superfluous, but the sequel suggests that this was an error. Not at once but after some little time the House of the Tiles was destroyed in a great conflagration. Whether the House was first pillaged is not clear, but the catastrophe was evidently no mere accident, since the building was never replaced. Instead, the debris was reverently gathered into a low tumulus, perfectly circular in plan, ringed with stones, and evidently forbidden to be built upon. During the long remainder of EH, a series of three or four lesser building periods produced only small houses, and no fortification. The tumulus was not violated.

The House of the Tiles is the greatest known monument of the Anatolians in Greece. After its destruction, the culminating peak of the culture was past, so that when the Greeks arrived, they could learn only the humbler crafts, not strong monarchy symbolized by grand palaces. A few other Early Bronze sites had walls, and enough of them may have survived (not at Lerna but Aigina) to teach the Greeks their first lessons in military architecture, and perhaps to endow them with a small but pernicious heritage of inter-polis warfare.

3. MIDDLE HELLADIC

Like their predecessors the Anatolians, the Greeks came to most areas as violent conquerors, but to some areas peacefully enough so that their arrival was not disruptive nor marked by conflagrations. With this evidence of archaeology, the one known cultural borrowing agrees. Enough Anatolians survived throughout most of Greece, and their intercourse with the new settlers was peaceful and prolonged enough, to communicate the names of natural features, town-sites, and a few other words; the latter two items suggest some continuity of occupation.

Beyond this all is guess-work. The Greeks may well have learned much in a minor way from the inhabitants—crafts and skills, local lore, legends of men and walled cities, tales of gods and heroes, and most important, sea-faring. It *might* even be true that just as the Greeks later (from 1600 B.C. on) received their higher education from the Minoans (who were kin to the Anatolian inhabitants of Greece), so earlier the Greeks received elementary education from the Neolithic peoples (if anything survived from them) and more importantly from the Anatolian inhabitants of Greece. Analogies could be given, however, to show how easily false inferences can be made about cultural borrowings by conquerors from the conquered: a new, superior people may adopt place-names and vegetables but little else. In the present instance, moreover, there is the fact of pottery: the invaders used, or came to use, pottery wares ('Minyan') superior to anything known earlier in Greece, and moreover the frequent imitation of metal shapes indicates that the newcomers disposed of enough metal so that not infrequently they could afford to make a vessel of it.

For history the most significant general fact is that some of the Middle Helladic sites were fortified: Aigina, Malthi, Mykenai, Tiryns are the ones known to have been. The fortifications are not impressive compared either to those of Dimini and of Lerna, or to later walls, and in some instances the MH walls may have been constructed primarily not against massive attacks—none of the MM cities is known to have been violently destroyed within the period—but merely against stray marauders.

Dorion-Malthi, however, in the middle of the Middle Helladic period, was made into a real fort. In the Neolithic and Early Helladic periods it had been an unfortified country town and it never became a city and a power of consequence, even comparable for instance to Gla; but from its hilltop north-west of Mt. Ithome it dominated the route from the north into the plain of Messenia. The first distinction of Malthi is a rare one: it was possible to excavate the whole.

After residing there awhile, the Middle Helladic occupants, who had conquered and burned the old EH country town, decided to make the site a strong-point. Excavation showed that the plans went well beyond mere fortifications, to include other features of some interest. Among these, the palace itself is the least impressive, being not conspicuously larger than the other buildings, nor isolated, nor planted on a central axis. Nevertheless it is recognizable. Sharing with it the central, topmost terrace were a series of artisans' shops—smiths, millers, potters. This central, topmost area was surrounded by a wall of its own, which in places served also as a retaining wall. Less than a half of the heavy construction is preserved, but there were evidently five gates, some of them flanked by towers.

A fairly large area surrounded this central fort all the way round: there was space for some 320 houses in all, plus certain areas evidently left empty for markets, herds, or whatnot. But not all the buildings were houses. Along part of the west side, and using the city-wall itself for a back-wall, 15 commodious magazines were constructed. They were obviously built as part of the whole plan. The dominating feature is the city wall, which can be traced throughout most of its length. The gates are narrow. Outworks of some sort were noted at three points: they may have been towers. The wall follows the contours of the hill.

Whoever the people were who built this city ("Dorion IV"), and whatever the source of their inspiration, plainly the whole reflects strong central authority. But powerful monarchy was not evident at first. The first city built on the site by the Middle Helladic occupiers, "Dorion III," was apparently not thus planned, unified, and fortified. The conquest itself may have been led by an autocrat; if so, it took his successors some time to learn the architectural possibilities. But they were bold and imaginative. No classical polis is quite so literally centralized and so schematically neat as Malthi.

A still more remarkable feature, but never commented upon, is the presence of artisans' shops near the palace, and the great row of capacious magazines along the outer wall. In a sense the city appears to be actually in large part if not wholly an extension of the palace. As elsewhere, far the larger number of the community would live outside. And so here at Malthi, as early as at distant Knossos, and far earlier than at nearby Pylos, we may recognize the characteristic Mykenaian combination of manufacturing, storage, and military facilities which supported, and were directed by, a palace bureaucracy.

III. The Minoan Thalassocracy

Knossos and Crete in Late Minoan I. For more than a millennium, Cretan culture had developed undisturbed, indeed essentially uninfluenced, from outside, passing through many phases. If the history of the palace is any indication, the power of the leading city, Knossos, at first had grown only slowly. But the consolidation of the Palace, in Middle Minoan II, i.e. in the first half of the Second Millennium B.C., may well have been preceded and supported by an extension of territory, income, and, in a mild form, of military strength. In Late Minoan I, the Palace attained its maximum size. Concomitantly, the power of its kings reached out landwards.

There is some evidence that not only the Palace itself at Knossos, but also some of the other sites in Crete, had had walls of a sort in the Middle Minoan period. In no case, apparently, were the fortifications powerful; when expansion started, Knossos was not impeded by them. Mallia, almost a neighbor, was her greatest rival, and there is some reason to think that Knossos destroyed Mallia at this very time.

The only other large power, Phaistos, was reduced to accepting peaceful co-existence. Knossos took as much of Crete as she wanted, which was doubtless as much as she thought she could control. An extensive road system was developed, with numerous stations which may have been military guard-posts. In Late Minoan I Crete, Knossos occupied a commanding position.

There need be no doubt also that Cretan foreign relations were Knossian foreign relations. It was Knossos which brought the advanced arts to the Mainland of Europe and civilized the Greeks. With regard, moreover, to economic and political power, quite apart from the civilizing arts, it was natural that the city which had gained the hegemony of Crete should not stop at the water's edge, but should seek markets and spheres of influence overseas.

The Minoanization of the Mainland. The story told by the six famous Shaft Graves of Mykenai is familiar and undisputed. The 19 burials, unviolated, of royal persons can plausibly be assigned to one dynasty. In the span of their rule, which reached from sometime in Middle Helladic III down into Late Minoan I, roundly from ca. 1600 B.C. to ca. 1500, Minoan cultural influence on Mainland Greece can be followed from an early stage to a mounting ascendancy. In content and in manner the culture of the Mainland became Minoan. Major arts and minor crafts were equally and completely affected; so much so that it is often impossible to say whether a given object, such as a dagger with multiple metal inlays, was made in Crete and exported, or was made on the Mainland by a Cretan craftsman who had gone abroad to make his fortune, or was made on the Mainland by a Mainland craftsman trained in Crete. The first really powerful Greeks failed to develop plastic arts of their own, but they learned with utter thoroughness from others.

The fact of Cretan influence on the Mainland ("Minoanization") has been familiar long enough so that we fail to consider that it was not inevitable that the civilizing arts should have been imported from Crete and from Crete alone. Asia Minor and Egypt had much to offer. Hence, behind the tremendous Minoan cultural impetus, one expects to find extensive commerce, and behind the commerce very likely some political and military power.

The Empire: Founder, Date, Character. The first individual man named by Thucydides in his History (1.4) is put down as Minos, and the first specific organized power is stated to be Minos' Sea Empire. Of the person still nothing positive is known. "Minos" may have been merely a title. It may also have been a title which came from the proper name of an actual famous emperor; we shall see that the circumstances surrounding the myth are such as virtually to make him real.

The date of the Empire is not difficult to determine. In Middle Minoan III, Knossian power at home is still not consolidated, and Minoan cultural influence abroad has to establish itself. But if we come down as far as Late Minoan II, on the other hand, i.e. to the period from ca. 1450 to ca. 1400, Minoan Knossos was in no position to control anybody, as we shall see *infra;* and this condition may have begun as early as say 1480, though 1460 or even 1450 might be the correct date for the beginning of Knossian helplessness. In any case at least 100 years (1580–1480) are available, and they are *the* 100 years when Knossos has been seen to be at her peak, viz. in Late Minoan I. The Minoan Thalassocracy probably occupied most of this century.

The Minoans plainly loved sport more than war, but very dangerous sport. They had a military organization, with officers distinguished from privates—it was no mere rabble, but *may* have been a professional army—and they hired mercenaries from distant parts, doubtless because the manpower on which they could draw was limited. None of their cities being walled, they knew nothing of siege warfare.

Whether their navy included any ships specially constructed for combat may be doubted. Ships interested their artists, but the representations are all small, so that the comparatively large ships, which doubtless existed, could not be adequately depicted. Certainly they used sails as well as oars, but one fact alone proves that the ships were larger than mere sailing rowboats: they could (then or a very little later, *infra*) transport horses, which requires a larger ship. Timbers of any desired size were doubtless available, and carpentry was well advanced. Adhering, however, to minimum probabilities for this, the first thalassocracy, it is proper to imagine small fleets of one-masted merchant vessels which, aided by a store of arms, turned pirate when the occasion seemed favorable, and likewise descended upon seacoast towns.

But it would not take long to discover that devastating raids might well cut down future booty. The next step would be the exaction of tribute, presently fixed in amounts and payable on the occasion of regular visits. Unless the seacoast towns were large and armed, this was not difficult. If a town was too large to control, or was too well fortified, or was inaccessible, the fleets of Minos simply got what they could by trade.

The most promising area for exploitation was not Egypt or the strong states of Asia, but the Aegean—the islands and the coasts of the Mainland. Mykenai was altogether too strong, hence trade was indicated. But precisely as in the case of the Athenian Empire later (Thucydides was right in seeing a general resemblance), the islands and many coastal hamlets were helpless, and trade was replaced by seizure. So long as Knossos, like Athens later, had strong naval superiority, it was not difficult. The peculiarity of a sea empire is precisely that imperial command of the sea prevents subjects from uniting, and without being garrisoned they can be bilked separately for tribute.

Outposts and Organization. In time, no doubt, the advantages became apparent of permanent stations of some sort (trading posts, factories) with perhaps enough troops in each for protection and to make easier the collection of regular tribute. The name Minoa was given, or became attached, to several of these trading posts. All the known Minoas are on the coast; the trading-revenue fleet would put in for supplies and to help in collecting tribute. It may well be significant that none of them became a large or powerful city: they occupied fringe positions: they were only supply depots for the fleets, plus a modicum of trade. The (general) location and the name are all that is positively known.

But again, in time, the further advantages became apparent of actual Minoan cities, permanently rooted, perhaps inland, and supported not merely by trade and tribute but by agriculture and industry. And so Crete sent out the first European colonies. There may not have been many: only two have as yet been discovered, Phylakopi in Melos, and Ialysos in Rhodes; Miletos in Asia Minor is doubtful. In contrast with all the Minoas, these known colonies became important towns.

The Minoan Thalassocracy was far-flung but not grandiose. On a map it would be patches of tribute-paying areas—necessarily the coastal areas of Greece too weak to maintain independence—plus a few colonies; the rest would be trade. Knossos flooded the Mainland with works of the arts and the crafts; her fresco painters and other technicians travelled from city to city. Coinage being virtually non-existent, the form of payment can only be conjectured; one natural conjecture is precious metals.

The organization of this first European Empire need not be imagined as impressive. In other Cretan palaces, and doubtless also at Knossos, bureaucratic records were kept on clay tablets, but the tablets (Linear A) have a slovenly appearance. The Minoans never became great organizers; were never rigorous enough to develop fierce bureaucratic precision or to burn cities (unless Mallia?). The reason for their easy-going ways was not so much that they were at an early stage of imperialism, as that the gay Minoan temperament, developed in many centuries of insular security, would never have found the exacting tasks of governing a big empire congenial at any stage. Their enthusiasm for records and writings was indeed so weak that although they transmitted, and secured the full acceptance of graphic images in abundance, hardly anyone outside Crete learned Linear A writing.

The Myth of the Minotaur. Minoan culture was loved, as it deserved to be, but Minoan tribute was hated. No doubt they were harsh masters. In revenge the Athenians concocted the myth of the Minotaur. Several of its features are palpably inventions. Theseus was inevitably made the hero, and the revenge motif required that he, like Aeneas, jilt the loving enemy princess after heroic conduct and a safe escape. The tribute too is personalized: for seven youths and seven maidens read X measures of wheat or barley, *vel sim.* Myth loves "human" touches. The Athenians did not love paying tribute, yet their myth presupposes tribute. Myth often puts a good face on things, sometimes concealing the truth almost completely, as the Romans for instance concealed in myth the fact of a century of hated Etruscan domination. The Athenians could not do likewise. It is notable, for instance, the Minos himself is left alive: Theseus is not made to kill the hated oppressor. That claim would have been absurd, so the myth adhered to fact. Again, if the Athenians were to conceal the tribute, the story would have no point. But they would never in the world invent so disgraceful a circumstance. The myth embodies a fact, the fact of tribute.

If this were all, it would still be telling evidence for the existence of a

Minoan Thalassocracy. But besides the "human elements" which were certainly invented, and the bitter facts which had to be kept, the myth has certain other elements, occurring uniquely in this one myth, chiefly the *Minotaur,* and the maze-like *labyrinth* in which he was kept. Recalling the place-name suffix -inth-, we see that *labyrinthos* should mean "place of the labrys"; and "labrys" means double-axe. The Palace at Knossos is eminently the place of double-axes; they are incised in its very piers. "Minotaur" is Greek for "minos-bull," and is patently a monstrous duplication of Minos himself. The Minoans were devoted to a peculiar and very hazardous bull-sport, in which girls as well as youths participated. Most recently there is evidence that the performances took place, not outside, but in the central courtyards of the palaces themselves. There is no need to add that the very plan of the Palace at Knossos is labyrinthine in its maze-like elaboration.

No myth whatever from all Antiquity preserves more truthfully such a constellation of facts otherwise unknowable later; the 27,000 + lines of Homer have nothing to compare with this. The Cretan local details of the myth can reasonably be held to be corroboration of the truth of the underlying facts. Minos was known far and wide; more place-names echoed his name than any other mortal's till Alexander the Great; and an immortal myth, telling of Athenian dislike, tells also perforce of Minos' Empire. Later, Herodotus, who had heard too many good stories to be easily convinced by any, passed it by without a thought; but Thucydides, intent on piercing through to the realities, saw reality in Minos' Thalassocracy. True, Thucydides could only fill out the picture by sketching in general details of the Athenian Empire of his own time; the area was the same, and the fundamental conditions were similar enough to make his account plausible.

Centralized freebooting rather than an empire, Minos nevertheless inspired respect and hate. It was doubtless just what might be expected of Cretans: wild, irregular, venturesome, colorful. It succeeded because there was no organized opposition. The Greeks had come as conquerors, but after two or three placid centuries not all were able to face Minos. Such was the first supra-national entity of European history.

IV. The Greeks in Crete

The Conquest. Beginning in the period Middle Minoan III, Cretan merchants and craftsmen had come to the Mainland. Presently, in return, Greeks from Mykenai and other cities, travelling as merchants, sailors, envoys, or mere tourists, doubtless visited the great metropolis of culture. But they did not all go to genuflect. Athens and the other places in the Empire hated the levies of tribute and resented subjugation. Mykenai herself doubtless became tired of learning, paying, admiring, and envying. It may not have taken the visitors long to observe that Knossos, unwalled, was defended by troops without body armor; and to observe that the Mainland, perhaps Mykenai alone with her immediate allies, was stronger than Knossos.

Two facts about the conquest are known. One is that command of the sea was a pre-requisite. Under the eyes of the Cretans, Mykenai created a navy: it was probably easy, since already Mykenai had extensive commerce, and so far as is known, merchantmen were the only warships, i.e. there were no ships specialized solely for combat. Allied fleets were doubtless enlisted: if so, the coalition against Troy was not the first foreign expedition Mykenai had commanded.

On the whole peaceful, the Cretans were mainly a dagger people, or a dagger-and-rapier people, in contrast to the Mykenaian kings, who were buried with a small arsenal of slashing swords. The Cretans were only good enough at military affairs to maintain for a few generations their ramshackle, piratical "empire." There was of course no siege, no long exacerbating campaign such as would lead to furious carnage and destruction: archaeology records no destruction.

Like the Macedonians later, the Mykenaians struck against their civilizers (and it may well be that one battle, like Khaironeia, sufficed). What Athens earlier, under "Theseus," would have liked to do but could not, Mykenai did. Knossos, unconquered since the Bronze Age began, was defeated, and Greeks occupied the Labyrinth.

Permanent occupation with full control of a foreign city was perhaps itself a new thing in the Aegean world. Like Minos before, the new Thalassocracy could ill afford the men. But Mykenai now held Knossos itself, an incomparable treasure: the schoolmaster of Greece more fundamentally than Athens ever was to be, Knossos had also been, again as Athens was to be, a tyrannical denier of liberties. The Greeks stayed in Knossos, mainly no doubt for profit, secondarily to prevent revival of tyranny; but also, as it turned out, to go on learning.

To account for far-flung Knossian overseas power, it was necessary to assume that Knossos controlled other cities. The Linear B tablets now appear to tell us that Greek Knossos was master of many cities in Crete, perhaps of the whole island. The cities were defenseless, i.e. unwalled, and had had no experience in forming a union of their own, i.e. not under Knossos. Some few may have got themselves destroyed by rebelling later, when the Greeks were well established, but none is alleged to have been destroyed at the time of the conquest.

Date of the Greek Conquest. The kind of changes shown by archaeology in Late Minoan II at Knossos would have taken some time to develop. The script also, as we see it in the tablets, which were inscribed presumably in the last year or two before the destruction, is well standardized, fixed for 200 years. The Greeks would have taken years to settle in (it was a foreign country they were trying to rule), to conquer as much as they wanted, to observe Linear A, to get the elaborate new Linear B signary developed, to teach it and to use it. Late Minoan II is usually dated from ca. 1450, i.e. the changes, except the script, become clearly marked about then. The conquest itself, for a guess, may have been as early as 1480 or as late as 1460. If the impression gained from Linear B is correct, by ca. 1410 an elaborate bureaucratic system has been built up. The earlier date, ca. 1480, seems preferable for the conquest itself.

Knossos under Greeks. The capture of Knossos was followed by military occupation. In addition to being, as before, a royal residence, a cult center, a place of (bull) sports, an administrative capital with archives, and a battery of magazines (for the storage of payment in kind), the Palace now became an arsenal. A conspicuous new feature was the numerous chariots; large numbers of horses must have been stabled near the palace. For the first time troops were seen drilling in body armor. The number of arrows in the arsenal was high in the thousands, though not more than should be expected. But the Palace remained unprotected by any fortification: like their predecessors, the Mykenaians doubtless asked, Whom have we to fear?

In the building itself the Greeks made few changes. Most conspicuous was the creation of a Throne Room. It was not a very large chamber, and we do not know what went on in it: but definitely it is similar to the design of Mainland throne rooms. At the humble other extreme, Mainland pottery, the so-called Palace Style, was introduced; it was of course ultimately Minoan-derived, but certain shapes of vase and of decoration distinguished it.

The Creation of Linear B. In a sense, literacy had existed in Crete for some three centuries; but the Minoans had made little use of it. The surviving Linear A tablets, as we have seen, are so poor clerically as to suggest negligence if not actual incompetence. It is not strange that very little writing had crossed to the Mainland, which may be regarded as virtually illiterate until Knossos was captured. At Knossos, including the neighboring sites, only 16 Linear A inscriptions have survived; but on the analogy of Hagia Triada, we may imagine that the Greeks found accounts being kept there in Linear A. Such accounts were the more necessary because Knossos controlled a large part of Crete.

Upon capturing Knossos and its Cretan holdings, the Greeks were faced with administrative tasks never faced by them before. They pressed into their own service some at least of the Knossian administrative staff, and in no time at all (we may imagine) the Greeks learned from the scribes the advantages for administration of the ability to write and read. The language had to be Greek, but trial showed that Linear A, doubtless none too good for the Minoan language, was impossible for Greek. Accordingly orders were given to the (Minoan) scribes, and largely by them Linear B was created. The basis was of course Linear A; but the process of creation, so far as it is now understood, was by no means completely systematic. The result was what might be expected. A syllabary need not be, for Greek, grossly defective, and Linear B conceivably could be worse. On the other hand, and without being able to judge, except from external appearances, about Linear A, one can only say that an instrument was created barely adequate to the administrative records for which the Greeks wanted it.

The Wanax at Knossos. The Linear B tablets have revealed a fact of prime historical importance. The head of state at Knossos bore the title *Wanax* (ἄναξ), the Linear B word for King (actually attested only at

Pylos on the Mainland). With him too there was a *Lawagetas,* a high official whose duties and relationship to the Wanax are unknown. Knossos, in short, was under rulers whose titles suggest an independent kingdom. For instance, in Mykenai Agamemnon was doubtless called Wanax, and Nestor in Pylos. It might well seem therefore that Knossos was not part of an empire, but rather was as completely independent of Mykenai as was, e.g., Pylos. The objections to this view are strong but not conclusive. They are two. In the first place, some Mainland power had to organize and pay for a large-scale expedition: it is unlikely that that power would voluntarily forego the profits. On the contrary, wealth derived from Crete would be one likely source of funds to pay for the walls, the palace, and the tholoi (with their lost furnishings) at Mykenai. In the second place, Linear B was transmitted to the Mainland with such utter faithfulness as to suggest that close touch with Knossos was maintained. Possibly the Wanax of Knossos belonged, like Menelaos, to a cadet branch of the house of Mykenai, or may otherwise have been under Mykenaian control.

The Destruction in ca. 1400 B.C. One April day when there was a brisk wind blowing, the Palace at Knossos was burned throughout. The almost complete lack of valuable objects found by the excavators makes it appear that the Palace was looted first, and consequently that the fire was intentional. Stone vases were left where they were being made, and the Throne Room was in confusion.

At or about the same time, other places were destroyed or were abandoned without destruction: Tylissos, Nirou Khani, perhaps Plate. A couple of decades earlier, apparently, the same thing had happened to Phaistos itself (and Hagia Triada), to several places in the East, to Gournia and other small towns. It has sometimes been suggested, strangely, that these were acts of natives directed against their Greek masters. To burn a dozen cities of your own is no sure way to rid yourself of tyranny, but only to invite, as in World War II, savage reprisals at once and worse tyranny to follow. The way to get rid of an occupying force is to kill its troops, and there is every reason to believe that the Cretans were powerless against the arms stacked at Knossos and their users. Neither is there any evidence or probability that any foreign, i.e. non-Greek, power invaded Crete and destroyed cities. No foreign power at this time is known to have launched great overseas expeditions. The perpetrators must be identified by more positive reasoning.

The first clue is that certain of the towns now deserted were not reoccupied for over a thousand years: Mokhlos, Pseira, Nirou Khani. The Palace itself at Knossos was apparently deserted for a time, then cleared and partly repaired.

The evidence can be extended. In J. D. S. Pendlebury, *Archaeology of Crete* (London, 1939), all the known sites of Crete were mapped and also tabulated. For all three Late Minoan sub-periods together (LM I, LM II, LM III, plus sites assignable only to LM as a whole), the total is 192. The figure is large enough to encourage further exploration. LM II, being a local (Knossian) period, may be omitted, and of course the sites assignable only to LM as a whole. For LM I alone, 69 sites are known; for LM III, a longer period, 88.

This is not the place to discuss the various refinements and qualifications which caution may suggest: when they are taken into account and the necessary allowances are made the conclusions will not be impaired. The striking fact is that of the 69 LM I sites, only 22 sites, which constitute only 11 per cent of the total of 192 different sites for LM as a whole, are known to have been occupied in both LM I and LM III.

Evidently there was a major disruption before the beginning of LM III. The disruption extended beyond the 12 cities where there is definite evidence of destruction or sudden abandonment. The sites themselves, physically, were as good as before. One suspects that the explanation may be grim, viz. enslavement or the massacre of all who did not escape to the hills. Even little Trianda in Rhodes was abandoned suddenly; the people left cheap things (pots etc.) on the floor just where they happened to be. It is ominous that there was a Mykenaian town nearby.

In all this there is nothing to suggest a foreign invasion, nor is it the kind of disruption which a civil disturbance would suggest. The destruction was rather an act of hate. Further light on who did it is shed by the subsequent fate of Crete. During the entire next period, Late Minoan III, or more generally Late Bronze III (formerly called "Mycenaean" but that is no longer possible), Crete was reduced to being isolated and quiet. That is the evidence of archaeology. Except for what the Homeric epics, and most specifically the Catalogue of Ships, allege about participation in the Trojan Expedition, Crete has no part in the events of LB III. It seems that Mykenai, after the destruction, left Crete to itself for some time. The outside power had been there in full control: the Linear B tablets make that plain. It is natural, and I think correct, to assume that the power which had the control was the power which abandoned the island. Mykenai was supreme. It was Mykenai which committed the enslavements, massacres, and burnings. On some of the sites, where these awful events had taken place, including Knossos itself for a time, the Cretans no longer wished to live.

Why did Mykenai kill a goose that was laying golden eggs? An explanation is not hard to imagine. The Cretans have never been comfortable to govern. A dagger people from way back, gay and irresponsible ("all Cretans are liars," said a Cretan), they doubtless took their first conquest hard. The pride of an island free of invasion longer than even England has been, aware that recently they had ruled the seas and educated their future conquerors, was a pride which could turn to any and all forms of desperation. There may have been a long series of incidents, culminating in some such act as the assassination of a *wanax*.

It is a construction, but I think it fits. Mykenai presently had had enough. To hold the island in chains was out of the question. They lacked the manpower. They could find (and did find) more tranquil fields to dominate. And so, in utter exasperation, Mykenai pillaged, massacred, burned, and withdrew.

Later, in the long Late Bronze age, a Greek dynasty returned, somehow managed better, and sent the mighty King Idomeneus, with Meriones and 80 ships, a large contingent, to Troy.

Tradition. The decipherment of the Linear B tablets has had yet one further result, hitherto unnoticed. We know now that at some time there was massive Greek conquest not only of Knossos but also of the erstwhile dependencies of Knossos. Such an achievement makes the capture of poor little Troy VIIa seem petty. We know also that Knossos and many other places in Crete, and even Minoan colonies outside Crete, at some later time were pillaged and destroyed. Here were awful and mighty acts: why is there no epic about them? Theseus earlier was remembered in a story that proved to be unforgettable. Troy later was remembered in two epics that are immortal. Yet neither myth nor tradition in any other form remembered the events of ca. 1480 or of ca. 1400 B.C. The fact calls for understanding.

An explanation can, I think, be given, and it is fundamental to the nature of mythical tradition. The *Chanson de Roland,* by whomever composed (evidently the process of its development was not precisely the same as that of the *Iliad*), selected a petty rearguard action, that at Roncesvalles, and proceeded to make a hero and a villain and a moving story out of unlikely material. Plainly in the formation of epic there can operate what may be called a principle of whimsicality. In the second place, study of modern living epics in Jugoslavia has shown that a large number of epics normally co-exist. Each singer has several. The epics compete for favor, and those that achieve popularity persist because of the story, and because of the talent some unusual singers expend upon it. Quite likely there *were* epics about Knossos. They lacked intrinsic interest, and no singer, adopting their themes, made them live. We have the *Iliad,* the *Odyssey,* and parts of many other epics clustered about them: the inferiority of these others is evident even in the fragments, and they illustrate the process, essentially whimsical and in a sense accidental, which normally operates. History is the loser on a vast scale; but the singers are concerned, not with history in our sense, but with history as material which they can use to please and enthrall their hearers.

V. The Mykenaian Hegemony

Mykenai in Greece. Apart from the usual farms, pastures, and groves, the resources of Mykenai are altogether unknown to us: how was procured the gold of the Shaft Graves and the wherewithal to build a fleet. Mykenai itself was well situated, but so were many other towns. With silver, marble, and clay, Classical Athens had at least modest non-agricultural resources for Empire; but for Mykenai no special local sources of wealth whatever can be specified.

It was the start which was difficult. In time, perhaps early in the 300–400 years of Greek occupation before Grave Circle A, territory was surely added. The minimum which ought to be imagined is shown best by Pylos in the Linear B tablets: however their detail is to be interpreted, unquestionably they show extensive territorial control. Something like this, as much or more, should be imagined for Mykenai.

A second stage, whenever attained, would be the close alliance, based on marriage perhaps rather than on conquest, with Lakedaimon, thus giving control all the way south to the Lakonian Gulf, also the Taygetan promontory, and in Messenia as far as, and including, Pedasos-Methone.

Earlier perhaps than this Mainland expansion was a third phase, the conquest of Crete. In any case the problem of resources, difficult (for us) in the Sixteenth Century—so that the obtaining of the gold etc. for the 19 burials in Grave Circle A remains a problem—in the later Fifteenth and in the Fourteenth Century is no problem at all. Revenues sufficed for the walls, the palace, the tholoi; for all the furnishings, of which just enough remains to give a hint, of the palace; and of the tholoi, where virtually nothing remains.

The Form of the Hegemony. If we try to formulate some notion of the organization of the Aegean under Mykenai, we find a number of indications as guides:

1. In the Ancient tradition as a whole, Mykenai is not given a thalassocracy. Thucydides makes Minos, but not Agamemnon, anticipate the features of the Athenian Empire. Agamemnon has naval power and islands, but their character would seem to be that of an extension of the kingdom.

2. The Catalogue of Ships, however doubtful its division of the Argolid into two, may well echo historical truth in not making the *relation* (not, of course, the absolute figures) of Agamemnon's naval power to the rest of Greece resemble that of Athens later. Agamemnon has available 160 ships, of which he loans the Arkadioi 60: the implicit suggestion that he could man only 100 is in the direction of realism. The next largest power, Pylos, has 90; then comes Tiryns and Crete each with 80.

3. The Linear B tablets from Knossos, as we have seen, reveal there a chief of state (*Wanax*) with a high official at his side, just as in an independent kingdom. Mykenai may well have controlled the place and received much of the income, but in form Knossos was apparently independent.

4. In the *Iliad,* Agamemnon does not by any means occupy the position of Emperor in relation to the other Kings. He is a *primus inter pares,* though with the emphasis on the *primus.* The weaker he appears personally, the more he must be conceded to owe to his acknowledged headship of Greece; close reading will show, I think, that this position is really conceded very fully by the poet, however much his plot forced him to make Agamemnon appear weak personally.

5. These considerations, varied in source and doubtless in value, accord best with the Hittite evidence as most recently interpreted.

This interpretation leads not for the first time, but more imperatively than before, to the identification of Rhodes as the great Greek power with which the Hittites dealt. Hittite documents of the Fourteenth and Thirteenth centuries refer some 20 times to Akhkhijawa, more easily transliterated Ahhijawa, which was evidently their (inaccurate) rendition of 'Αχαιία, that is, Achaea. If Ahhijawa cannot be Mykenai itself—the evidence is awkward both ways—then what we have is an independent state of considerable power in the eastern Aegean. Here again Mykenai appears as having no empire, or rather, Greek power is fragmented.

If the foregoing does not mislead, we can contrast the Minoan Thalassocracy with the Mykenaian Hegemony. Like Classical Corinth, perhaps, Mykenai was content with the profits of trade, and sought no empire. Colonies were sent out, but for the revenue of trade if for any; not for other power, and not for the extortion of tribute. As against the many Minoas, spread abroad, there is only the one Mykenai.

Tiryns, and a Theory of Walls. The Bronze Age is crowded with problems, of which one of the most intractable has been the walls of Tiryns. Tiryns is not much over six miles, or ten kilometres, from Mykenai, yet Tiryns managed to build walls (and subsequently enlarged them to double the free area protected) under the very eyes of Mykenai. Why did Mykenai permit it? So long as the question remains unanswered—a question inherent, not in fallible texts, but in solid visible facts—our knowledge of the very elements of the Bronze Age is incomplete. Yet no satisfactory answer has been given.

If a theory may be ventured, it will start from the size of the citadels in question. All are small. In two or three minutes a man could walk from one end to the other of the Athenian Akropolis. Mykenai was not larger, Tiryns was smaller. Dimini, Lerna (only a fraction is excavated, but there is no reason to believe that it had any unusual size), Malthi—the known forts of the past were no larger. Gla alone had any size, but that was because of terrain. This feature, smallness, has itself always been a difficulty, though usually not discussed. How could Troy stand a ten-year siege if it were so small that a swift runner, as D. L. Page points out, could cross it lengthwise in some 25 seconds?

The essential consideration is that fortifications can be defensive or offensive. Messene and the other Fourth-Century B.C. forts were offensive, i.e. built to encircle and contain Sparta. The classic walls of Messene enclosed a whole city, i.e. they sheltered an army which could sally forth to threaten any army passing by, or to ruin its communications. For this purpose size, speaking generally, is essential. Such walls are built to provide ample safe space.

Prehistoric walls were built around the palace. Their purpose was to protect the king's house and as much as was feasible of the cluster of offices, storerooms, workrooms, archives, etc., which excavation has discovered within them and which the Linear B tablets associate with the palace bureaucracy. Most of all, they were built to shelter the royal treasure. They were defensive. They would hold enough men to man the walls and, under the then conditions of siege warfare, to stand a siege. A small force could do it.

This being so, it seems likely enough that the Kings of Mykenai saw no reason to object to the building of walls at Tiryns. If the King of Tiryns wished to be safe, i.e. to build a fence around his valuables, that was unobjectionable. Even when enlarged, the fort would not hold enough men to block the access of Mykenai to the sea. Tiryns might harass Mykenaian traders going to and fro, but only at the price of a war which the two neighbors did not wish to contemplate; their lands were vulnerable even if their stored-up treasures were not. The walls were built as defences against more remote enemies.

Troy. If this view of Bronze Age fortifications is acceptable, the expedition against Troy can be explained in simple terms. The old notion that Troy obnoxiously controlled the Dardanelles, and thus Black Sea commerce, by levying toll on shipping, or on goods trans-shipped, is happily defunct. There was no such commerce, and the destruction of Troy VIIa did not open it up. Another explanation of the war is needed.

Like all such forts, Troy VIIa held royal treasure. It was not the rich place that Troy VI had been, but the prospective plunder was worth the effort. Epic poetry later altered the purpose to a romantic one, and glamorized the whole expedition, just as epic poetry would be expected to do.

A few facts appear to survive criticism. There *was* a Greek expedition against Troy VIIa; Mykenai under Agamemnon commanded it; numerous allies took part. The fort was packed with people, and proved hard to capture. The Greeks succeeded, after which they pillaged, burned, and departed. Epic exaggerated all the details, especially the size of the Greek force, and the time it took. Gross inaccuracies about the site crept in: they would not worry epic poets. So much seems clear. The real problems are in another sphere, viz. chronology.

The Relative Order of Events. Until closer absolute dates can be fixed from the pottery, the historian can only attempt a rational relative arrangement.

In Greece itself, all the great forts had already been built, probably in the Fourteenth Century. The danger envisaged at that time is totally unknown, but the fact that the walls were often repaired, improved, and sometimes extended shows that they were not built for mere display of strength; and they are much too strong to have been built against mere marauders. Danger did not materialize effectively until the end of the pottery period Myk III B. Close to the walls of Mykenai itself three fine houses, more likely to have been appurtenances of the Palace than mere private dwellings, were destroyed by fire at that time. The Kings of Pylos had presumably felt that their remote location and their wide domains were protection enough, and so they had built no walls. Also at the end of Myk III B, the attack on Pylos came by sea; moderate forces were dispatched to a series of possible landing-places, but it was a mistake (one can guess) thus to divide up the army—it is as if only raids were feared, whereas the actual attack was massive. The Palace was easily entered, savagely despoiled, and burned.

History records many acts of colossal folly, but it stretches credulity to put the Trojan expedition *after* such events—not to mention the violence such a dating would do to the tradition of a large fleet from Pylos, under the venerable and prominent Nestor. Moreover the likely dating of the pottery found in Troy VIIa is earlier. The traditional dating of the expedition to some year soon after 1200 B.C. is therefore coming to be generally regarded as improbable.

The great movement of peoples that attacked Egypt by land and sea ca. 1223 B.C. is the next earlier event. The age of unrest had already begun. There was another attack on Egypt, this time by a great fleet of sea raiders, in ca. 1190 B.C. The connection of these events somehow with the destructions at Mykenai and Pylos is surely mandatory. A Trojan expedition in the midst of all this may not be inconceivable, but would have been folly. Moreover the heroes on their returns would have encountered somewhere, sometime, the masses of migrants and raiders, but the tradition preserves no memory of it.

One further indication is the ending of the commerce of Mykenai. It had been extensive and voluminous, but at some date in the second half of the Thirteenth Century it is reduced to almost nothing. The cause, again, would be the movements of uprooted peoples, who must have been on the move for a score of years before they reached Egypt. The Trojan expedition *ought* not to have been launched when revenues from commerce were decimated, the world was unsettled abroad, and there was a threat to the home cities.

And yet it is impossible to recede very far in fixing a date for the Trojan expedition, because unlike its predecessor, Troy VIIa contains very little Mykenaian pottery: 80 sherds of Myk III B, none whatever of Myk III C. There are two choices. One is to suppose that the expedition was launched when conditions were already so upset that Mykenaian exports had dwindled. In that case it would have been a comparatively small but thoroughly desperate raid, wildly distorted by the poets later. And again there is the fact that forces were abroad sufficient to ruin very extensive commerce, yet of such forces the tradition preserves no memory. The alternative is to conceive that Troy itself, before world conditions were upset and commerce ruined, became too poor to import luxury wares from Greece, so that Myk III B wares, still being exported elsewhere in quantity, could rarely be afforded at Troy. This latter alternative would permit a date conformable to the conditions represented in the *Iliad* and *Odyssey,* i.e. a world not yet thrown into turmoil. The epics are surprisingly scrupulous, as if well informed generally, about, e.g., the Dorians; some knowledge of the peoples known to the Egyptians by name as their attackers might be expected if such peoples were then at large.

Of these two alternatives, neither of which is comfortable, the latter seems preferable. Troy fell, in that case, ca. 1240, but before Myk III B ceased to be exported.

The Destruction of the Palace Bureaucracies. Certain phenomena, when seen in relation, give an insight into the "mind" of Bronze Age Greece. (1) With their interest in astonishingly petty details, the tablets show a bookkeeping—shopkeeping mentality. (2) The economy in some sense is planned. The object of the plan, or at least *one* object, is to fill the palace magazines with agricultural produce (Knossos) and the shelves with thousands of vases (Pylos), the sale of which would increase the royal treasures (Mykenai, Grave Circle A). (3) In other royal economies, i.e. in states where the king's income is very large (taxes, tribute, booty), and his expenses (army/bodyguard, court, royal burials) are less, treasure can accumulate to enormous totals (cf. the Achaemenids and the Ptolemies). (4) The safety of the treasure naturally becomes a grave concern: hence walls are built if a menace exists. (5) The treasures cannot be kept secret, but become known, however inaccurately; hence wars such as the expedition against Troy, since people who are obsessed with their own treasures naturally want to add to them the treasures of others.

(6) Within each such state, and considering them from the point of view of the subjects, it seems clear that the authority of the monarch and his bureaucracy over a great many subjects was tremendous. People appear to have lived within an elaborate framework or *system,* features of which were specialization under central control, with writing used to communicate and preserve orders and records. To some extent intricate and complex, the different functions—commerce and agriculture and manufacture—depended on each other. If treasure and the safe-guarding of it were dominant concerns in the king's mind, subservience and care in fulfilling his duties in the system dominated the subject. The subject knew no other way of life.

All of this was highly "civilized" and one may conjecture that it was fragile. Destroy the palace, and the whole community was wrecked. This happened. Pylos, the last palace to be built, was perhaps the first to go, ca. 1200 B.C., the rest very soon, in the next decades, at latest not after 1150. The Dorian destroyers were savage enough to have ended less fragile organizations than the palace bureaucracies. As it was, the disruption of commerce brought down the whole of society. This fragility explains why, even without Dorians on the Akropolis, Attika also went under. The economy was geared to certain exports and imports; they ended, and the invaders were soon ravaging the Attic countryside. The Akropolis they could not take, but destruction was complete without that.

Linear B can teach us two large facts, still not wholly assimilated, about the destruction. One is about illiteracy. Hitherto it has been fairly clear that illiteracy was due to the failure of interest on the part of older people in teaching the younger to read and write; and in an equally complete failure of interest on the part of the younger to want to learn. Now we can understand much better the failure of interest. It was caused by the utter collapse of a system which had engrossed the lives of those who wrote and who read. When the system collapsed overnight, the incentive to literacy was not all that went with it, but people's very lives. There were no more careers for the palace bureaucrats, the craftsmen, the officers, even for the more highly trained slaves. Probably most of them had to go dig in the fields. There was a reversion to primitive economy.

The other large historical fact taught by Linear B is the abruptness of the governmental change. The Classical Greeks were inherently, persistently conservative, in that the greatest changes were regularly accompanied by retention of something old. As in Rome and in other states also, the King might be largely or almost completely supplanted; but there was still at Athens, throughout its history down to Constantine or beyond, an officer entitled *Basileus,* not to mention, for centuries at least, four *Phylobasileis.* But when the destruction of the Twelfth Century took place, the chief of state, the *Wanax,* was evidently completely abolished. He was part of the bureaucracy, the supreme part, so integral that his title did not survive, even in some conservative nominal manner, any more than did the bureaucracy. The epic tradition too lost any accurate and conscious memory of the office.

The effect of the Dorian invasions was not just the destruction of property. It was profoundly a mental event. The state was almost literally decapitated. The whole organization and the whole mentality at the top —that of the palace bureaucracy—went. Small local officials, numerous in each state, whose title had been *Basileus* and was signficantly kept, replaced the one Wanax. The state was broken up into smaller local units. Attika, for instance, had to be united all over again.

The Dorians and the three centuries *plus* of Dark Age which they initiated were the most fearful and (for civilization at the time) costly disaster in European history. But they were not an unmixed evil. Linear B literacy, had it lasted any length of time, would have been an incubus upon the Greek mind. That has been clear for some time. Can we not add to it a similar statement about the palace bureaucracies? They had created Mykenai, Tiryns, Pylos, much else; but their work was done, they had no future, at least none easily imagined. Even in cities where there may have been opportunities, as in Athens, no one tried to recreate palace bureaucracies. They too would have become an incubus, a faulty syllabary of thought where a flexible alphabet was needed. Even though fine things were rubbed out by the Dorians, too many and unnecessarily, on the whole it was well for Europe that the slate was wiped clean. Hesiod knew enough to deplore the Iron Age, yet without it there would have been no Hesiod, and all that came down to his greater compeer Homer would never have had the qualities which oral testing produces.

5. The Place of Reason

C. M. BOWRA

More than any other ancient people, the Greeks made fundamental contributions to the formation of Western thought; more than in any other area, the Greek emphasis on the human mind and the importance of reason in inquiry into the world around them gave a crucial cast to subsequent thought. Where Egyptian and Mesopotamian thought had been content with mythological explanations of the world and natural phenomena, the Greek mind moved beyond this stage and opened new horizons of knowledge. Although the Greeks might not have recognized the following as separate and distinct areas of inquiry, modern scholars credit them with delineating the fields of mathematics, philosophy, and natural science; for the Greeks, philosophia, love of wisdom, was a single all-embracing term.

In this selection from his acclaimed The Greek Experience, *C. M. Bowra, who has written numerous books on Greek literature and thought, discusses the importance of reason in Greek intellectual achievement. He surveys lucidly the most significant areas of accomplishment between the first critical investigations of natural phenomena in Ionia in the sixth century* B.C. *and the age of Plato. Bowra makes clear some rather complex material and clarifies the nature and significance of the Greek achievement. His essay indicates the stages through which Greek thought passed—the stimuli for various specific*

Source: C. M. Bowra, *The Greek Experience* (Cleveland, Ohio: World Publishing Co., 1957), pp. 165–185. Copyright © 1957 by C. M. Bowra. Reprinted by permission of The World Publishing Company and Weidenfeld (Publishers) Ltd. [Footnotes omitted.]

achievements; the differences between the Greeks and others of the ancients; and the peculiar characteristics of Greek rational thought. The student should gain a deeper appreciation of the role of the Greeks in formulating one of the most fundamental and characteristic aspects of Western civilization from this selection.

A more detailed treatment of some of the areas discussed here by Bowra may be found in W. K. C. Guthrie's volumes on Greek philosophy (in progress; two volumes have appeared), in Benjamin Farrington's Greek Science *(1953), and especially in the provocative work of Bruno Snell,* The Discovery of the Mind *(1953). As a useful contrast to the view that all was rationality among the Greeks, see E. R. Dodd's* The Greeks and the Irrational *(1951).*

In their archaic period the Greeks expressed their most significant speculations in poetry, and even when this was reinforced by sculpture and painting, their outlook was still largely shaped by their poetical education and the principles which it implied. Even if the traditional myths left much unexplained, and even contradicted each other on important matters, they provided an approach to experience, a way of thinking in concrete images, which satisfied a people who had no reason to doubt that the gods were at work everywhere and that a knowledge of them explained most phenomena, both physical and mental. But by the beginning of the sixth century a new spirit had been born, which grew and matured until it touched many branches of inquiry. This was a desire to understand things more exactly, to penetrate the mystery which enveloped them, to explain them in rational language, and to find principles and rules in nature rather than the inexplicable whims which myth ascribed to the gods. Such a movement was perhaps inevitable in a people so intelligent as the Greeks, but it was stimulated by social and political changes. It began in Ionia, and its first exponent was Thales of Miletus. The disappearance of the hereditary monarchies and their replacement by a new ruling class, which soon turned its attention to foreign trade, meant that the intellectual horizon was enlarged with the physical, and the establishment of trading-stations, like Naucratis in Egypt, brought Greeks into contact with an unfamiliar, if narrow, range of applied knowledge. At home building, sculpture, and metal-work posed technical problems which called for solution; the increased activity of sailors, who penetrated to the far western end of the Mediterranean, demanded a more than mythological acquaintance with geography and astronomy; the popularity of athletics encouraged a proper knowledge of the human body, if only to mend broken limbs and heal sprains. Events fostered a new spirit of inquiry into the visible world, and this inquiry took three main forms. Though there was some overlap between them each maintained its special character and obeyed its own laws of growth.

The first was mathematics. This was not a Greek invention, but had already been practised with some skill in Babylonia and Egypt, and it is from Egypt that Thales was said to have brought it. That perhaps is why he was able to determine the height of a pyramid by measuring its shadow. Egyptian mathematics seem to have been more practical than theoretical, and Thales marked the special character of Greek studies when he proved that a circle is bisected by its diameter and forecast the direction in which mathematical proof was thenceforth to move. The Greeks raised mathematics beyond the practical application which the Egyptians had given to it for such matters as building and emphasized its theoretical character. Just as in their arts they sought some reality behind appearances, so in mathematics they sought permanent principles which could be applied wherever conditions were the same. The possibilities of such an inquiry caught the imagination of Pythagoras and his disciples, who saw in numbers the key to most problems and asserted, 'Things are numbers'. If we do not take this too literally, it marks an important stage in intellectual development, since it establishes the principle that a large mass of phenomena can be understood if we can discover mathematically the laws which govern them. It is one of the surprises of history that Pythagoras was impelled towards mathematics by the study of music. He was concerned with establishing fixed relations between the several notes on a musical scale, and he saw that this could be solved as a matter of arithmetical proportion. From it he seems to have moved to the theorem, which still bears his name, that the square on the hypotenuse of a right-angled triangle is equal to the sum of the squares on the other two sides. This was known in a limited and practical form in Egypt and is said to have been discovered independently in India, but the Greek demonstration was a triumph of pure mathematical thinking without reference to practical considerations. Greek mathematics began with geometry and remained faithful to it through its long career.

The second form taken by the new movement was philosophy. This too was an attempt to find the reality behind phenomena, but its instrument was not numbers, but words. At its start it seems to have posed the question: 'What is the primary substance of things?' and Thales answered that it was water, Anaximenes that it was air. Such an inquiry was cosmological in that it sought to find a more satisfying theory than myths which told that Chaos gave birth to Light and Darkness and that each had its own appropriate progeny. In fact this question really contained two questions, 'what is the *origin* of things?' and 'what is the *nature* of things?' The philosophers faced both, and came to their several answers. But they agreed that these questions were indeed fundamental and could be answered by hard thought. In this way they laid the foundations of logic, of correct thinking, in which any contradiction between one proposition and another means that one at least of them is false. Though the philosophers might appeal to phenomena for the illustration and confirmation of their theories, the theories themselves were built on a coherent system of argument from assumed or accepted beginnings. In this respect they resembled the mathematicians, and though in its early stages philosophy was less abstract than mathematics, it certainly believed that no theory of being was adequate unless it was throughout coherent and consistent.

The third form was natural science. If this had something in common with philosophy in its desire to discover and explain the nature of phenomena, it differed in its methods. It believed not so much in the establishment of a consistent theory as in observation and experiment, and though in astronomy it relied largely upon mathematics, it controlled this by careful attention to established facts. Its most practical, most successful, and most strictly scientific inquiry was medicine. From the start medicine seems to have broken free from the presuppositions which underlay other branches of science and to have kept itself in well-defined limits. In replacing the traditional apparatus of magic by controlled diet and nursing, the doctors began a far-reaching revolution. Their task was to study the causes of disorder in the human body, when, on the analogy of music, its *harmoniâ,* or attunement, was broken, and to try to restore it to its normal state. In the fifth century Greek medicine, under the leadership of Hippocrates of Cos (479–399 BC), broke with the past and its belief in supernatural cures and developed a whole system based on scientific method. The writings of Hippocrates and his followers show a minute care in the examination of pathological symptoms. Every part of the body has to be examined, every unusual colour or movement or temperature noted. The doctor must find out about the patient's sense of taste and smell, his sleep and his dreams, his appetite or lack of it, his pains and his itches, his stools and his urine. Once the evidence had been collected and the symptoms compared with other recorded cases, the physician felt that he could proceed to diagnosis and treatment, confident that he knew all that he could about the case and that he could within limits prognosticate what was going to happen:

> It is necessary to learn accurately each constitution of the seasons as well as the disease; what common element in the constitution or the disease is good, and what common element in the constitution or the disease is bad; what malady is long and fatal, what is long and likely to end in recovery; what acute illness is fatal, what acute illness is likely to end in recovery. With this knowledge it is easy to examine the order of the critical days and to prognosticate from it. He who knows these matters can know what he ought to treat as well as the time and the method of treatment.

Here the spirit of scientific inquiry relies on careful observation and is able to give some forecast of what is likely to happen. The author does not claim that, even when he knows what the disease is, he can cure it; he is content to diagnose it and avoid errors in its treatment. The principles of Greek medicine were those of natural science today, and it is appropriate that the Greeks made this momentous revolution through their care for the human body.

Though mathematics, philosophy, and natural science had their separate assumptions and principles and methods of work, they had also a good deal in common and shared certain basic characteristics which belonged to the age of Greek enlightenment. First, they were not in their early days in conflict with religion. Since, like religion, they dealt with questions of the nature and origins of things, it is not surprising that Thales should say, 'All things are full of gods', or Anaximander call the air a god. Such language was suitable in a society which saw gods everywhere and was not too troubled to define their exact spheres of activity. Just because the Greeks believed that the world of gods and of men is one, they had no difficulty in believing that what they saw around them had a divine as well as a physical side and that ultimately the two are not distinct. In their desire to find some universal principle, they assumed, as religious thinkers did, the existence of a cosmic order, and in elaborating their ideas of this they used the old language which ascribed divine control to various spheres of reality. Even if they could not finally unravel what laws governed phenomena, they could at least claim that such laws existed, and use mythical language to show what they meant. The first glimmerings of laws of nature were themselves derived from divine laws, and we can well understand how, when Anaximander wishes to display the balance of opposite forces as central to reality, he says: 'Things give satisfaction and reparation to one another for their injustice, as is appointed by the ordering of time', or when Heraclitus speaks for the regularity of the sun's movements, he says: 'The Sun will not overstep his measures; if he does, the Erinyes, handmaids of Justice, will find him out.' So long as the gods were taken for granted, it was not difficult for philosophers to fit their ideas into a system which was tolerably elastic and quite happy to welcome new functions for its gods.

These branches of inquiry all presuppose that it is both possible and proper for man to discover the truth about the nature of things and would in principle accept the saying of Heraclitus: 'Wisdom is one thing. It is to know the thought by which all things are steered through all things.' But at the start this was contrary to much common belief that, since the gods treat men as they please, it is impossible to be certain of anything. Pindar and Sophocles alike make men's ignorance of their own destiny a cardinal point of difference between them and the gods. But as science and philosophy developed, this idea was modified and fitted into the new ideal of knowledge. In the sixth century, Solon, who was well versed in traditional wisdom, follows a kind of ascending scale from utter ignorance to reasonable expectation. If the merchant and the farmer are at the mercy of the weather, which they cannot forecast or control, the craftsman, poet, seer, and physician have at least a divine patron who instructs and protects them and fortifies them in their knowledge of their own business. They may of course make mistakes and can never be quite sure what will happen, but they do not work in utter ignorance. Indeed, the possession of such knowledge was one of the means by which men could, no matter at what distance, become more like the gods and more able to control their own destinies. The practical answer was that, though men cannot hope for certainty, they can make good surmises, as the doctor, Alcmaeon of Croton (fl. 500 BC) says: 'About what is invisible, about what is mortal, the gods have clear knowledge, but to us as men, only inference on what is coming is possible.' This takes the old idea and gives it a practical application. Inference is after all something and may well be useful. Within limits a man may seek to resemble the gods, and if he remembers the vast difference between their powers and his, there is no reason why he should not regard knowledge as an attainable end, provided that he confines it to certain spheres and does not claim too much for it, especially in trying to forecast the future or to know what is reserved for the gods alone. This was a delicate position, and not always easy to hold, but if it was kept within certain limits, it avoided any overt breach with religious faith.

Philosophy and science had to come to terms with religion, if only because they themselves made similar assumptions. It was of course possible to adopt a purely negative position and dismiss science as futile, as Pindar did when he said that natural philosophers 'pick a useless fruit of knowledge'. This was natural enough for him, since the knowledge which he valued was much less of the physical world than of the gods. But few men seem to have gone so far as this, and even the devout Sophocles was at times touched by scientific notions, though they did no more than confirm his already strong religious faith. In fact the early philosophers treated their task in almost a religious spirit and aimed at presenting it as in some sense a revelation, not similar indeed in content to the old beliefs, but like them in its spirit and its methods. Though Heraclitus rejected with angry contempt the stories told by Homer and Hesiod, he proclaimed his own insight into the *Logos,* or Word, which directs all things. Parmenides not only asserts that his knowledge was given to him by a goddess but speaks of himself as one initiated into special mysteries and of his system as a Way. Pythagoras sought to find in numbers an instrument of salvation as well as of geometry. Greek philosophers were not in the beginning irreligious. Rather they proposed reformed versions of traditional assumptions and offered these in a language which ordinary men could understand. In this they were quite sincere. They believed that they had something to say which was divinely inspired and that their task was to present it in all its seriousness and urgency.

A special claim and characteristic of this task was the pursuit of truth through inquiry. The old view that truth was given in revelation by the gods was not actually denied, but quietly replaced by the conviction that men can find it out for themselves. It did not take a scientist to recognize that revealed truth is not always satisfactory. The Muses, who were credited with telling men about the gods and the past, were notoriously untrustworthy, and even Pindar admits that poetry creates illusions:

Beauty, who creates
All sweet delights for men,
Brings honour at will, and makes the false seem true
Time and again.

The traditional position was that men should be content with what truth they have and hope that time will reveal more to them. The scientists and philosophers emended this by insisting that truth is a first duty and that no effort must be spared to discover it. Xenophanes denies the old notion when he claims that in fact men find out things for themselves: 'The gods have not revealed everything to men from the beginning, but men by searching find out better in time.' Truth has its own appeal and makes its own claims on its servants, as Democritus saw when he said that he would rather find out the cause of a thing than have the kingdom of the Persians. It was indeed recognized that the pursuit of truth might be a high, even the highest, form of conduct, and Heraclitus implicitly rejects old views of *aretê* for his own conception of it: 'To think is the greatest virtue (*aretê*) and wisdom consists of speaking what is true and acting in obedience to nature.' The climax was reached when Socrates propounded his paradox that virtue is wisdom, and inspired far-reaching theories by it. The seriousness with which philosophers sought truth had indeed a religious earnestness and, when Anaxagoras built an altar to Truth, he showed what it meant to him. Such a spirit was not at war with established religion, which gave a welcome to new divinities even of this abstract nature, and anyhow it could hardly complain that men should wish to understand the nature of things and be humble in the presence of its mysteries.

Mathematics, philosophy, and natural science also shared a belief in the value of observation and experiment. They might differ greatly in the degree in which they used them, but none of them felt that they could entirely dispense with them. Because their sharp eyes were trained on the visual arts and took pleasure in noticing details, the Greeks were naturally keen observers and regarded observation as a human activity which called for no apology. Without it no important questions could be either posed or answered, and because it was natural to them, it stirred their intelligence and their speculations. In the sixth century Anaximenes noticed that clouds are formed from air and in turn by condensation become water. He concluded that the primal substance is air, and that everything is ultimately made from it. The theory was too simple to be true, but it was at least an attempt to answer a question forced on him by his own observation of facts. So too when Anaximander noticed that the structure of fishes is like that of human beings, he propounded, in advance of Darwin, the theory that life began in the sea and that men are descended from animals of another species. It was a bold idea, and he could not have foreseen its future justification, but at least he knew what his problem was and propounded his solution with a proper regard for what he had himself discovered. If theories of this kind seem to us to be insufficiently based and to be no more than inspired or ingenious guesses, we must remember that we know of them almost by accident and have almost no information on what evidence was put forward in their support. But there are indications that the first Greek scientists took trouble to collect facts which seemed relevant to their questions, and saw that proof is more than a stroke of happy insight. When Xenophanes tried to elucidate the relation of land to sea, he noted the presence of shells in inland districts and on hills, the imprint of a fish and of seaweed in the quarries of Syracuse, the form of an anchovy in the depth of the stone on Paros, and flat impressions of marine creatures on Malta. This shows a man who knew what to look for and took pains to find it, who was at once observant and systematic, a collector and a thinker. He came rightly to the conclusion that earth and water are not ultimately separate, and that they somehow invade one another. The conclusion is less interesting than the method, which shows that Xenophanes was a true inquirer in his assumption that the observation of hitherto unnoticed facts may be used to advance theories of far-ranging import.

These early investigators also did something to control observation by experiment. In this their efforts may look rather primitive, but they were at least a beginning and showed the right approach to their subject. This happened even in mathematics, when to demonstrate that the pitch of a musical note produced by a taut string depends on the length of the vibrating medium, the Pythagoreans used a movable bridge to vary the length of the string, and not only proved their point but found a means for measuring precisely a physical phenomenon. In philosophy Anaxagoras wished to show that the accuracy of the senses cannot be trusted beyond a certain point; he took two vessels, filled one with a white liquid and the other with a black, and mixed them drop by drop, until the eye could no longer distinguish between them. The same spirit prevailed both in the physical and the biological sciences. Empedocles demonstrated the corporeal nature of air by thrusting a funnel, with the upper end closed, into water and showing that the water could not get into it until the obstruction was removed and the air set free. In his inquiries into sense-perception Alcmaeon of Croton practised vivisection and dissection and came to the conclusion that the brain is the central organ of perception. If we make allowances for the almost complete lack of apparatus and for the absence of many materials which we have at our disposal, we need not be surprised that experiments were not conducted on a more elaborate scale. Their importance is their revelation of minds so vigorously at work and so certain what their problems are that they were able to add to observed facts by supplementing them with new facts of their own creation.

Greek thinkers had their own notion of the social implications of their task. They were not only convinced that their own form of activity was the best in itself but they maintained that it made men better morally and intellectually and that the pursuit of knowledge imposed social responsibilities and lessened the differences between man and man. The Hippocratic Oath, still used by doctors, shows how seriously the pioneers of medicine regarded their own task and how well they understood both its dangers and its duties, and it is no accident that a Hippocratic writer says, 'Where the love of mankind is, there also is the love of science', as if the knowledge of nature and the love of humanity could not ultimately be kept apart. No less striking are the words of Euripides on the happiness which comes from the study of nature:

Happy is he who has knowledge
That comes from enquiry. No evil he stirs
For his townsmen, nor gives himself
To unjust doings,
But surveys the unageing order
Of deathless nature, of what it is made,
And whence, and how.
In men of this kind the study
Of base acts never finds a home.

In the troubled conflicts of his time, when the old certainties were being shaken and the old balances broken, Euripides turned to the philosophic and scientific calm promised by inquiry into nature. In its detachment and its peace he saw a new hope for mankind and a cure for the ugly passions which were bred by political and social disorder.

Greek mathematics, philosophy, and science all survived the collapse of Athens in 404 BC, and all made some of their most notable contributions after it. Though mathematics never lost its connexion with astronomy, yet it remained largely 'pure' and *a priori*. This indeed was its glory. For the Greeks worked out a system by which mathematical proof can be conducted, and it has never been bettered. It begins with definition, and the definitions, as they survive in Euclid, are still models of conciseness and clarity. Next, it established analysis, in which, after making an assumption, we ask what the results will be, and so make the problem clear. Thirdly, it fashioned the form of exposition which still prevails in geometry, because it is ruled by strict logic. On these foundations the Greeks achieved their magnificent performance in mathematics, by which geometry not only was used for all that we now associate with it, but came near to performing operations like the integral calculus and founded statics and hydrostatics. The great genius of Archimedes (*c.* 287–213 BC) covered an almost unbelievable range of achievement, and long after him Greek mathematicians pursued his methods in the discovery of trigonometry, the theory of numbers, and the beginnings of algebra. When Plato had inscribed over the door of his Academy the words, 'Let no man enter who knows no geometry', he was not being eccentric, but paying his tribute to the Greek conviction that through geometry the world could be known as a rational whole. Because they were trained in it, the Greeks were able to make fundamental discoveries in astronomy, which culminated in the anticipation of Copernicus by Aristarchus of Samos (*c.* 310–230 BC) when he argued that 'the fixed stars and the sun remain unmoved, and the earth revolves about the sun in the circumference of a circle, the sun lying in the middle of the orbit'.

Like mathematics, Greek philosophy tried to grasp the world as a whole, and though its conclusions are not so final as those of geometry, it imposed on posterity its notion of what philosophy is and what problems should concern it. To it we owe such fundamental distinctions as those between the one and the many, reality and appearance, knowledge and opinion, being and not-being, form and matter, universals and particulars. In making such distinctions the Greeks tried to solve the discord between the infinite multiplicity and variety of phenomena and the need for some permanent reality behind or in them. They realized that for so precise and delicate a task words are by no means an ideal instrument, and they did their best to establish a vocabulary which should be both clear and consistent, and to see that the functions of words were understood as well as their meanings. With such an instrument they hoped to show what the sum of things is and how it works, and though their speculations might indeed carry them into bold constructions, they argued each step with a mathematical precision and tested their hypotheses with examples and instances which anyone could understand. In such a task they were inexorably forced beyond the visible world to a world of abstractions, which was for some more real than the common reality. Though the basis of their system was logic, they were not afraid of applying it to ethics, politics, and religion, or of summoning faith to their aid when argument had reached its limits and could do no more. Yet the strength of Greek philosophy lies not so much in its range as in its assumption that there is no problem which cannot be solved by hard and careful thought. It assumes that words are the instruments of thought and that thought is about things, no matter how remote or impalpable or complex.

Natural science did not in Greece have anything comparable to its present range, but in two main directions it laid the foundations of what we now think. The first is the atomic theory as it was propounded by Leucippus (*fl.* 440 BC) and Democritus (*c.* 460–370 BC). It has little in common with atomic physics as we know them, but is none the less their remote ancestor. It began as an attempt to solve the ultimate nature of things. The early answers that everything is derived from a single substance, such as water, air, or fire, were not satisfactory, nor was Empedocles' doctrine of the four elements, water, earth, air, and fire, since it left too much unexplained. The strength of the atomists was that they took note alike of the infinite variety of nature and of its ordered regularity. They put forward a theory of atoms, which are so small as to be invisible, and though all are made of the same stuff, they have an incalculable variety of shapes and sizes, and their relations with one another produce the variety of phenomena. The strength of the theory is that in it the physical universe is really physical, operated by natural laws, or, as Democritus said, 'necessity', and to this there are no exceptions. Even the gods belong to the phenomenal world and are explicable on the same principles as other phenomena. In effect the theory conforms to certain principles which lie at the heart of most scientific thinking. First, it assumes that all knowledge begins with the senses, and that without them no knowledge is possible. It is therefore not *a priori* and insists that theories must be verified by observed facts. Secondly, it dismisses the idea of any external power for that of inherent laws which operate absolutely everywhere and can for this reason be discovered. Thirdly, it treats even the human mind as a natural phenomenon, which can also be examined and discussed and explained. Fourthly, though it assumes the existence of a void in which the atoms move, a concept not easy to hold and liable to cause trouble, this notion is really no more than that of space as a field in which movement is possible and events take place. The atomic theory answered questions which had long troubled the Greeks and provided a working hypothesis for more discovery and more capacious theories of the nature of reality.

The second great achievement of Greek science was through medicine to biology. Early in the fifth century Alcmaeon of Croton saw that if a doctor is to understand the human body, he must study the bodies of animals and know how they work from the inside, and how enterprising this early biology was can be seen from the story that when a one-horned ram was brought, as an ominous portent, to Pericles, Anaxagoras had the skull cut in two and showed that the brain had not filled its proper position but had been shrunk to a point at the place in the cavity where the horn began. It was from experiments like this that in the next century Aristotle advanced to his prodigious studies in biology and his own enormous number of dissections. From the desire to cure sickness by finding out its causes Greek scientists advanced to the study of the physical frame of men, and therefore of animals, insects, and fishes. What began as a purely useful technique broadened into a true science, and continued to be relatively lively and creative until the second century AD. If the atomic theory illustrates the Greek gift for arguing from an abstract theory to a whole view of the universe, medicine shows the opposite process by which the accumulated knowledge of the surgery and the sick-room becomes a whole body of coherent information on the workings of something visible and tangible. If the one grew from the desire to find principles behind phenomena, the other grew from a vivid sense of the living scene and a lively curiosity about everything in it.

The spirit of inquiry which found its culmination in these great achievements was also applied to the study of man as a social being with a generous sense of what this means. It is not perhaps wrong to maintain that this was in the first place a result of medicine. When the Greeks saw that health was largely dependent on physical conditions, they attempted other researches which are the beginnings of anthropology, sociology, geography, and history. They knew that human physique is relatively stable, and tried to account for national variations by attributing them to climate or diet, as when a Hippocratic author explains the greater mildness and gentleness of Asiatics by the tamer conditions in which they live, and the endurance, industry, and high spirits of Europeans by their hard struggle for existence. Such questions belonged to *historiê* or inquiry, and the word, which was commonly associated with the study of man, is the ancestor of our own 'history'. From the start Greek historians followed certain fundamental principles. The first was that legends cannot be trusted, and Hecataeus of Miletus (*c.* 550–489 BC) may indeed be regarded as the founder of historical studies when he states his purpose: 'What I write here is the account of what I considered to be true. For the stories of the Greeks are numerous, and, in my opinion, ridiculous.' Legends of course had neither the authority nor the impregnability of Holy Writ, and a man was perfectly free to criticize them, but to criticize them on this scale was indeed revolutionary. Hecataeus perhaps went too far, for there is, as we now know, a kernel of truth in some ancient Greek legends, but he was justified by at least one aspect of antiquarian knowledge in his day. The Greeks liked to establish connexions with the past and did so by genealogies, but such genealogies were often created for political or personal reasons and their variety alone invited suspicion. Hecataeus wished to reform them and make them more sane and credible. This led to a second principle of Greek history. It saw man in his physical environment and attached great importance to geography. Hecataeus was at least as much a geographer as he was a historian, and though the information at his disposal was limited and often incorrect, he made a full use of it and did his best to construct a picture of the inhabited world as best he could. Anaximander had already constructed a map of it, and Hecataeus improved on this, not merely from information received from others but from his own travels. No doubt such a map was sketchy, inaccurate, and full of improbabilities, but it was in itself a remarkable step forward. Thirdly, Hecataeus, like his successors, chose prose and not verse for his work. This may seem an obvious and natural decision, but in fact it marked a great break in tradition. Hitherto poetry had been the normal method of remembering the past, and had been used not only by Homer for the heroic age but by later poets for stories of the Ionian migration, the wars against Lydia, and other relatively recent subjects. In choosing prose as his medium Hecataeus emphasized his break with the old view of the past as something inspired by the Muse and varied to taste by each poet, and substituted for it his own scientific ideal of something that could be found only by inquiry and called for qualities of detachment, hard work, and ability to sift evidence.

Though Herodotus does not agree with all that Hecataeus says, and may at times seem ungrateful to him, he continued his work on a grand scale in the true spirit of scientific investigation. It is true that Herodotus was also deeply touched by epic and tragedy and applied some of their methods to his telling of stories, but that was because he believed that this is how things happen, and there is no good reason to think that he was seriously wrong. Like Hecataeus, he learned much from his own extensive travels, and his observation of Egyptian customs and legends gave him a remarkable independence and breadth of outlook. Almost anything that concerned men interested him, and his history is a rich treasure of information on all manner of details relevant to the way in which men live. If on the one hand it made him sceptical of certain Greek claims, it also enabled him to understand his own people as only a man can who has external standards of comparison by which to judge them. For him 'barbarians' presented many points of interest, and he was not content to accept them as aberrations or monstrosities, but maintained that it is the heat of the sun which blackens faces and hardens skulls. He even made his own efforts to establish rules by which physical types and divisions can be classified, as when in discussing the Argippaei he distinguishes them from their neighbours the Scythians, by pointing out that though they wear Scythian dress, they are bald, snub-nosed, and bearded, speak a distinct language, and, unlike the Scythians, live off tree fruit. He established his observations on a system of *physis,* nature, and *nomos,* custom. The first means that each region has its own kind of physical growth, the second that modes of behaviour differ according to the demands of their surroundings. By this he explained the differences which the Greeks noticed, not without contempt, between themselves and the Egyptians, and even thought it 'natural' for certain Indians to eat dead parents; for, as Pindar said, 'Custom is king of all'. Yet he knew that even customs are not immutable, and that change of physical conditions may change them also.

His experience confirmed Herodotus in a natural openness of mind. Though he rejects some stories because they offend his sense of probability, and is often cautious about accepting others, it is characteristic of him that he gives in detail some stories about which he is himself sceptical. A signal example of this is the circumnavigation of Africa by Phoenicians sent by the Pharaoh Necho. The details which he gives, notably that at a certain point the sun 'rose on their right hand', confirm the truth of the story. Once he felt that he knew his way with a topic, he was not afraid to indulge in speculations which would have been thought intolerable in almost any century of the Christian era before the nineteenth. Of these the most remarkable is his sense of the length of historic and prehistoric time. He was bound by no dogma about the date of creation, and when he saw the alluvial deposits of the Nile in the Egyptian Delta, he compared them with five similar cases in the Aegean and ended by suggesting that, if the Nile were to reverse its course and flow into the Red Sea, it would take ten or twenty thousand years to fill it with soil. He believed indeed that 'everything could happen in the length of time', and it was this ability and willingness to welcome new facts and to see their importance that made him a true scientist.

In the next generation Thucydides (*c.* 460–*c.* 400 BC) wrote his history of the Peloponnesian War. In many ways the antithesis of Herodotus, he is also his heir and successor. In him the new science of history has matured by becoming more specialized, and he concentrates on what we call political history. If this means that he lacks the wide curiosity and the generous information of Herodotus, it also means that he works in a more critical temper and pays more attention to establishing the truth of even the smallest details. He examined eye-witnesses about recent events and applied to earlier periods a sharp, critical mind. Of the first he said:

> I have made it a principle not to write down the first story that came my way, and not even to be guided by my own general impressions; either I was present myself at the events which I have described or else I heard of them from eye-witnesses whose reports I

have checked with as much thoroughness as possible. Not that the truth was easy to discover: different eye-witnesses give different accounts of the same events, speaking out of partiality for one side or the other or else from imperfect memories.

and of the second:

We may claim instead to have used only the plainest evidence and to have reached conclusions which are reasonably accurate, considering that we have been dealing with ancient history.

Thucydides regarded as his first duty the careful assessment of evidence and the establishment of facts. When he had done that, he was prepared to advance, in his own austere and detached way, to suggest theories.

Like Herodotus, but in a different way, Thucydides owes something to medical science. He sets about the history of the Peloponnesian War in an almost clinical spirit, which first analyses Athens in its health and then the different flaws which corrupted its character and led to its downfall. He does this largely by indirect means, by showing the ideas which dominated the minds of the chief statesmen and politicians of the time and telling to what results these led in action. But though it is indirect, his method is that of science, at least of political science in a strict sense. He does not claim that his work will enable men to forecast the future, but he knows that a study of it will help them to understand events better, and at times he advances an abstract analysis, like that of class-war, which he certainly claims to be true of most conditions in which it arises. His concern is strictly with human actions, and he allows no part for supernatural forces, whether gods or cycles of fortune or destiny or other influences. Though he does not commit himself much about religion, he can hardly have believed in it, and he was certainly contemptuous of its more superstitious forms. He shows his scientific training in the paramount importance which he gives to intelligence. For him this is the first quality needed in a statesman, and he judges the different leaders of Athens by the degree in which they possess it. For him the barbarities demanded by Cleon or practised by the Athenians on Melos are errors of judgment, and all the more dangerous for that reason. He had indeed his own personal preferences, and he was well aware that religion and morality may be necessary to the well-being of a state, but he saw that in themselves they were not enough. Indeed, it is hard not to suspect a grave irony when he passes judgment on Nicias, who threw away the only hope of escape for the Athenian army from Syracuse by delaying in order to avert the menace of an eclipse: 'A man who, of all the Hellenes in my time, least deserved to come to so miserable an end, since the whole of his life had been devoted to the study and the practice of virtue.' Yet this outlook is itself inspired by deep convictions. The moral integrity of Thucydides is as great as his intellectual, and his love of the best things in Athens gives a special depth to his dispassionate curiosity. His respect for truth was equalled by his respect for certain moral qualities, especially those which take a civic or social form, and he is a supreme example of the ability of the Greeks to maintain high standards of conduct without demanding any supernatural sanction for them. In him, as in the pioneers of medicine, the visible world has pride of place and calls for its appropriate methods of study, but this attachment to it in no way detracts from his sense of the importance of what he studied or of the grave issues which he analyses with so unflinching an impartiality.

Though Greek science and philosophy began as the allies of religion, there came a point at which the alliance was not easy to maintain. It began to be clear that scientific explanations of phenomena might conflict with religious, and some skill was needed to avoid a crisis. The early physicians faced the issue in a calm enough spirit, as when a Hippocratic author discusses the nature of epilepsy, known as 'the sacred disease':

> This disease called sacred comes from the same causes as others, from the things that come to and go from the body, from cold, sun, and the variable restlessness of the winds. Such things are divine. So that there is no need to put the disease in a special class and to consider it more divine than others; they are all divine and all human. Each has a nature and a power of its own; none is hopeless or incapable of treatment.

Though we may legitimately suspect a nice irony, there is no reason to think that such words would not command acceptance. The gods were indeed thought to be everywhere, and their work manifest in everything; so a disease might well be both divine and human. Somewhat more complicated is the case of Herodotus, who undeniably saw the gods actively at work in the minds and passions of men, but had also a keen interest in scientific inquiry and accepted scientific explanations for inanimate nature. If religion and science were at variance, he too was capable of dodging the issue. When he mentions a Thessalian legend that the ravine through which the river Peneus flows to the sea was made by Posidon, he says: 'Their tale is plausible; and anyone who thinks that Posidon shakes the earth and that clefts produced by earthquakes are the works of that god would on seeing this mountain-ravine ascribe it to Posidon. For it appeared to me to be the result of an earthquake.' By this neat manoeuvre neither religion nor science is offended. It was possible to accept both, with certain unexpressed reservations but with no overt declaration of hostilities.

This became more difficult when science and philosophy turned their attention to the gods and gave their different explanations of them. The more thorough a theory was, the more difficult it might be to fit the gods into it. Democritus, who in fact eliminated them from the government of the universe, compromised by making them a kind of psychic phenomena, who can somehow bring good or bad fortune. Prodicus went further, and suggested that those things in nature which sustain life are looked upon as gods and honoured accordingly. This too undermines faith, since it reduces the gods to no more than physical forces and greatly restricts their activity. A third view, even more destructive, was that of Critias (*c.* 460–403), who made a character in a play say that the gods are an invention of some great teacher who wished to frighten men into keeping the laws and did so by saying that thunder and lightning are the work of gods:

With such dread terrors he encompassed them;
And neatly with a word he gave the gods
A habitation which well fitted them,
And so extinguished lawlessness with laws.

When such views were held, it is not surprising that Protagoras should sum up his own position: 'When it comes to the gods, I am unable to discover whether they exist or not, or even what they are like in form. For there are many things that stand in the way of this knowledge—the obscurity of the problem and the brevity of man's life.' Though philosophy began in a religious and even devout spirit, its very consistency and truth to its assumptions often forced it into either agnosticism or scepticism, and ordinary people began to feel that it was a danger to society.

Yet though many Greeks may have regarded these new developments with alarm, it is to the credit of their political tolerance that they took no strong measures against them. Indeed, the attack on the irreligious implications of natural science did not begin until the Peloponnesian War had begun to undermine self-confidence and to give a new boost to superstition. Even so we may suspect that political motives lay behind it. When his enemies wished to attack Pericles, one of their moves was to attack Anaxagoras, who not only declared that the moon was made of earth and the sun an incandescent rock bigger than the Peloponnese but discovered the true causes of solar and lunar eclipses. A dubious seer, called Diopithes, carried a decree authorizing the indictment of 'those who disbelieve in divine things or teach theories about what goes on in the sky'. Anaxagoras was tried and convicted, but fortunately escaped to Lampsacus, where he lived in peace and honour. Nor was this the only case of such persecution. Diagoras, Protagoras, and possibly Euripides were tried on similar charges, but the most notorious trial came after the end of the war, when in 399 BC Socrates was tried and executed. The accusation was skilfully framed and claimed that he 'does not recognize the gods recognized by the state but introduces new divinities'. Behind this lay political passion, since Socrates had been a friend of Critias, who as one of the Thirty had governed Athens with merciless brutality after its defeat in 404 BC. But the actual accusation appealed to a common prejudice that 'there is a certain Socrates, a wise man, who has studied what goes on in the sky and investigated everything under the earth'. Unfortunately there was, or had been, an element of truth in this. In his early life Socrates had been interested in natural phenomena, and as such had been pilloried in 423 BC by Aristophanes in the *Clouds,* in which the pupils of Socrates are taught that Zeus does not exist and his rule has passed to Dinos, or Vortex, and that rain, thunder, and lightning are not sent by the sky-god but come from unseemly disturbances in the clouds. The first half of the accusation against Socrates would certainly find support in a popular travesty of his views. The second half was no less important, and referred to the 'divine sign', which Socrates claimed as an important influence in his life and which was attached to no special god. The skillful combination of two charges, neither absolutely unfounded, was, in the angry atmosphere of the time, enough to get Socrates condemned to death. No doubt he did not make things easier for himself by his defence against accusations which he could not take seriously, but it is a strange irony that he, a sincerely religious man, should be martyred for a science which he had ceased to value.

The conflict between science and religion was matched by another conflict, no less serious, between science and philosophy. The old combination, which had in the past done so much for both, broke down on the fundamental question of the nature and possibility of knowledge. While science based its system on the senses and was content with what they had to give, philosophy felt that they could not be trusted and provided no sure basis for knowledge. On the one hand a medical author denies the validity of abstract argument:

> Conclusions which are merely verbal cannot bear fruit; only those do which are based on demonstrated fact. For affirmation and talk are deceptive and treacherous. Wherefore one must hold fast to fact in generalisations also, and occupy oneself with facts persistently if one is to acquire that ready and infallible habit which we call the art of medicine.

On the other hand, philosophy had always maintained that the reality, which is the object of thought, can be discovered only by the mind. Many views were held on the nature of this reality, but philosophy could hardly exist if its possibility were denied, and it was clear that gifts of the senses or 'facts' are not enough. The issue so presented was seen by Gorgias (*c.* 483–376 BC), who argued that the objects of sensation and the objects of knowledge are alike unreal, because both are concerned with not-being as well as with being, and it is impossible to distinguish between them. He concludes that there is nothing; that, even if there is anything, we cannot know it; and that, even if we could know it, we could not communicate it to anyone else. There is some paradox in this, and the notion of not-being is open to obvious objections, but it called for an answer, since it suggested that if the methods of philosophy were pushed to their limit, they made philosophy itself impossible. Protagoras tried to put forward a cure, when he taught that 'Man is the measure of all things' and that things *are* what they *seem*. Logically such a theory could lead only to solipsism and an infinite series of isolated, private universes, whose inmates are incommunicably severed from one another. By the end of the fifth century, the happy relations between philosophy and science had reached a crisis, and it looked as if they could not be restored.

It fell to Plato in the fourth century to make a heroic attempt to heal these wounds. The majestic fabric of his philosophy, constructed stage by stage through a long life, aimed at proving the possibility of knowledge and at finding a place for the observations of the senses. He saw that, just as in mathematics certain conclusions follow from certain premises, so in philosophy an argument may be developed with equal cogency from certain accepted assumptions. He distinguished, as others had before him, between Being and Becoming, but against the scientists he assumed that the first is real and the only proper object of knowledge, while the second, which depends on it, is mere appearance and the object of uncertain opinion. Reality for him consists of ideal Forms, which are at once logical universals, capable of being understood, and ideal particulars, capable of inspiring an almost mystical devotion. To establish his Forms he appealed, indirectly perhaps but no less certainly, to religion, and argued that we know them through recollection from a former existence. This might in fact mean no more than that our knowledge of them is innate, but in any case it is not derived from the senses. Though this impressive system removed doubts about the possibility of knowledge, it dealt a cruel blow to science. For it meant that observation and experiment gave place to *a priori* reasoning. Plato himself was so possessed by the notion that the universe is rational that he thought it possible to dictate its structure from his own conception of the way in which the Creator ought to have made it. In his search for certainty he failed to allow that on many matters we can hope for no more than a reasonable opinion and that this may be more valuable than any dogmatic assertion.

Yet Greek mathematics, philosophy, and science survived both the agony of the Peloponnesian War and Plato's counter-reformation, and continued to thrive for some four or five centuries. It is indeed a tribute to the firmness with which their foundations were laid and to the appeal which their questions still had for men. Yet in this there was an uneasy struggle between the old experimental methods and the *a priori* methods canonized by Plato, and in this struggle the honours went on the whole to the *a priori* school. Though the claims of experiment were upheld by biology and its sturdy ally, medicine, until at least the time of Galen (AD 129–199), in other fields of inquiry abstract thinking came to be thought more honourable than empirical science. Though Archimedes built engines for the defence of Syracuse and made astonishing discoveries in applied mathematics, he thought nothing of this part of his work and refused to commit it to writing. Greek mathematics, which had begun with practical learnings, became more and more abstract as it perfected its skill and its beauty. Philosophy indeed kept up its connexion with the world of action, and in Epicurus made the atomic theory a basis for conduct, but it gave little encouragement to scientific investigation, and in the end materialism made place for a world of transcendental abstractions. At the last even medicine gave way and preferred *a priori* speculation to examination of the human body. This indeed lies outside our scope, but it provides a comment on the history of mathematics, philosophy, and science in the classical age. Their strength was in their concern with the visible world, in which they sought to find permanent principles, and they can hardly be blamed if they asked questions so important and so difficult that in the end their successors paid more attention to these principles than to the phenomena which they were invoked to explain.

6. The Causes of the War

DONALD KAGAN

In 431 B.C. a great conflict broke out between Athens and Sparta which involved the majority of Greek states and, in the opinion of many classical scholars, altered the character and weakened the vitality of Greek civilization. This war had for its historian the Athenian Thucydides, a man with a sense of history and historical investigation scarcely equaled until the nineteenth century. At the outset of his history, Thucydides professed impartiality in the collection of evidence and promised to describe the origins of the war "so that no one should ever have to ask how it had come about," He also claimed to write for future generations, since "according to human nature, things will occur in the future in the same or a similar manner to the way they have in the past." By this Thucydides did not mean that history is cyclical, that things happen again and again according to a fixed pattern. Rather he seems to have been suggesting that in political contexts *similar problems have to be met and similar reactions can be expected from people in similar situations. Thus he hopes that his study of the war, and of the political events and decisions leading up to it, may prove useful to statesmen and politicians of future ages.*

Despite Thucydides' avowed attempt to explain the cause of the war, histo-

Source: Donald Kagan, *The Outbreak of the Peloponnesian War* (Ithaca, N.Y.: Cornell University Press, 1969), pp. 345–357, 372–374. Copyright © 1969 by Cornell University. Used by permission of Cornell University Press. [Footnotes omitted.]

rians have not been satisfied with his assertion that "the truest cause was the one most kept out of sight, namely the growth of Athenian power and the fear which this caused in Sparta." One school has attempted to prove that the war was occasioned by economic motivations; another that it was deliberately provoked by the Athenian leader Pericles for personal reasons; yet a third that Sparta was maneuvered into war by her ally Corinth, who was threatened politically and economically by Athens's power. However much historians may disagree with Thucydides' treatment of the specific causes of the war, almost everyone has accepted the view, implicit in Thucydides, that the war was inevitable.

Donald Kagan, Professor of History at Yale University, has examined the entire course of Greek diplomacy and political history, focusing on Athens and Sparta, from 478 to 431 B.C. in The Outbreak of the Peloponnesian War. *His principal and rather unorthodox conclusion is that the war was not inevitable; rather it came about through "bad decisions made by men in difficult situations." Kagan is a well-known student of ancient Greek politics and is the author of* A History of Greek Political Thought *(1965) in addition to numerous articles on Greek history. The following selections describe his view of the reasons for the coming of the war and his attempt to reconcile the discrepancy between Thucydides' view concerning the inevitability of the war and Kagan's own. His conclusions, provocative as they may be, deserve to be closely studied by historians of classical Greece. Indeed, his work promises to stimulate discussion not only of the origins of the war, but also about the nature of Greek politics, the historiographical methods of Thucydides, and the question of the inevitability of war in general. This last question especially should be of crucial significance to us as we attempt to move out of the Cold War and away from confrontation with the Soviet Union or China.*

It was Thucydides who invented the distinction between the underlying, remote causes of war and the immediate causes. In his history of the Peloponnesian War he considered the immediate causes, which in fact went back almost five years before the actual commencement of hostilities, to be far less important than the more remote cause that arose from the growth of the Athenian Empire almost fifty years before the start of the war. Thucydides' view that the war was the inevitable consequence of the growth of that empire, its insatiable demand for expansion, and the fear it must inspire in the Spartans has won widespread acceptance. Our investigation has led us to conclude that his judgment is mistaken. We have argued that Athenian power did not grow between 445 and 435, that the imperial appetite of Athens was not insatiable and gave good evidence of being satisfied, that the Spartans as a state seem not to have been unduly afraid of the Athenians, at least until the crisis had developed very far, that there was good reason to think that the two great powers and their allies could live side by side in peace indefinitely and thus that it was not the underlying causes but the immediate crisis that produced the war.

It is true, of course, that the war could not have taken place in the absence of certain pre-existing conditions. If there had been no history of

Athenian expansion and no sentiment in Sparta hostile to Athens, Corinth could never have driven the two powers into conflict. But tensions and suspicions exist in most diplomatic relationships; it remains to be proven that there is something in a particular historical situation which must permit those tensions and suspicions to bring on a war. It is far from clear, for instance, that the First World War was inevitable, but it can at least be argued with more than a little plausibility that some major change in the European situation must result from the disintegration of the power of Austria-Hungary, and that disintegration was not only inevitable, but already under way. The instability caused by that change in the European balance of power was unavoidable, and given the mutual suspicion and distrust of the major powers, there was a very good chance that war would result. The situation in Greece between the two Peloponnesian wars, however, was in no way parallel. There was no inherent instability; on the contrary, the settlement of 446/5, which was carefully adhered to by both sides, promised a greater stability than had been possible before. One may believe that the growing power of Athens and Sparta's fear of it made the First Peloponnesian War inevitable, but hardly the second.

Some scholars who have not been convinced by the Thycydidean formulation of the causes of the war have nonetheless been dissatisfied with an explanation arising from the events immediately preceding the war. They have discovered its origins not in the decisions and actions taken by statesmen in the period 435–431 but in forces, sometimes impersonal, that are greater than the men who are their instruments. Some have imagined that the cause of the war was naked Athenian aggression, which deliberately brought on the war to achieve greater conquests. In their view, Pericles carried out this policy, but it was the policy of the Athenians as a people. That judgment is contradicted by all the evidence we have and supported by none.

Others have rested their thesis of the inevitability of the war on such shadowy concepts as the conflict between Dorian and Ionian and between democracy and oligarchy. Although it is true that there were Dorians and Ionians, democrats and oligarchs, on either side, it is fair to say that the Athenian side was made up chiefly of Ionians and democrats, while the better part of the Spartan force was composed of Dorians and oligarchs. Yet there is not one whit of evidence for the view that these divisions contributed to the outbreak of war. Dorian, oligarchic Corinth had not hesitated to support Ionian, democratic Athens against Sparta in 506 and against Aegina in the 490's. Democratic, Ionian Athens had been willing to help Dorian, oligarchic Sparta in her war against the Messenians. Once decisions had been made on other grounds, similarities and differences of race and constitution could make relations between states easier or more difficult, but they were never an important factor in determining policy.

Economic causes in several forms, as we have seen, have been proposed as the real source of the conflict. Cornford's notion that there was a party of merchants from the Peiraeus who hoped to make great economic gains by seizing control of the route to the west via Megara, Acarnania, and

Corcyra and forced Pericles to drive Athens to war is altogether fanciful. In the first place, it is plain that the Athenians had no intention of seizing Megara at the beginning of the war. It is further clear that Athens' interest in Corcyra was strategic and not economic. Finally, although there were aggressively imperialistic Athenians who hoped to gain economically from the extension of empire, not all of them merchants from the Peiraeus, the simple fact is that they did not make Athenian policy. That policy was made by Pericles, who had fought them successfully in the past and was not swayed by them in the years of the final crisis.

Grundy's version of the economic causes of the war is no more acceptable. His conviction that the states of the Peloponnese were dependent on imported grain and went to war because Athenian domination of Corcyra threatened to cut them off from the granary of Italy and Sicily is wholly without support. The best refutation of his theory is that the Peloponnesians went through the long war, blockaded much of the time by the Athenian fleet, without starving. None of our sources mention widespread hunger in the Peloponnese, and they could not fail to do so if it had been there. Even poor Megara, whose starving farmers Aristophanes put on the stage with such comic effect, survived and even resisted an Athenian invasion and an internal revolution rather than yield. Grundy's view that the Athenians became involved at Corcyra likewise because of the search for western grain we have already dismissed. Nor is his suggestion that the Athenians must continue to expand in order to prevent unemployment at home at all persuasive. We have reason to think that at the time of the crisis Athens had disposed of its excess population and was even hard-pressed to fill up the quota of settlers for her colonies.

None of these economic explanations have won much support, but another one continues to have champions. It is that the rivalry between Corinth and Athens for the western trade was, if not the only cause of the war, at least a major factor in bringing it on. We have already seen that Corinth's involvement in the affairs of Epidamnus and her subsequent conflict with Corcyra were not caused by economic considerations. Her involvement with Athens arose out of the Corcyrean affair; there is no reason to believe it would have happened otherwise. The Corinthians at first did not try to bring on a war but merely attempted to persuade Athens to allow the humiliation of the Corcyreans. Pride and considerations of power, not economics, brought on the conflict between Athens and Corinth. It is perfectly true that Athenian trade in the western areas formerly dominated by Corinth had grown enormously. But the better part of that growth had taken place by the end of the sixth century and had not prevented Corinth from being very friendly to Athens. Thucydides tells us clearly just when and why the Corinthians first became hostile. It was in 459 when the Athenians helped the Megarians in their war against Corinth. The hatred Corinth thereafter felt toward Athens had little if anything to do with economics. If economic rivalry, moreover, is to explain the Corinthian hatred of Athens, we are at a loss to understand Corinth's decision to restrain the Spartan alliance from aiding the Samians in their rebellion from Athens. Surely the commercial rivalry with Athens, if there was one, did not significantly increase in intensity between 440 and 432, yet on the former occasion Corinth was outstandingly pacific and on the latter she was altogether bellicose. We are finally forced to conclude that economic rivalries did not make the Peloponnesian War inevitable and that economic considerations played no significant role in bringing on the war. Thucydides was altogether correct in fixing his attention on politics and power.

We have been presented lately with an up-dated version of the Thucydidean thesis that the war was the inevitable outcome of the division of the Greek world into two power blocs. In its new guise, the Thucydidean view is fortified with the weapons of modern social science. The condition that troubled the Greek world and brought on the war is discovered to be "bipolarity." Typically, such words are borrowed from the physical sciences to lend an air of novelty, clarity, and authority to a shopworn, vague, or erroneous idea. In our context, bipolarity is used to describe a condition in which "exclusive control of international politics was concentrated in two powers solely responsible for preserving the peace or making war." (The word bipolarity, incidentally, does not seem to have any advantage over the word polarity, another word borrowed from the physical sciences for use in other contexts.) That seems to be a fair statement of the way in which Thucydides saw the Greek world on the eve of the war, although it is hardly correct to assert that a consciousness of the "limitations which that power constellation has steadily imposed on the freedom of action of states" has been neglected. It has in fact been understood and given great weight by most scholars who have accepted the interpretation of Thucydides. It is true, of course, that they did not realize they were talking about bipolarity.

In any case, the argument runs something like this: The creation of the Athenian Empire after the Persian War and Sparta's refusal to "contain" its expansion produced a bipolar world. As the years passed, "the bipolar mold hardened." Thus, when the Corcyrean crisis came along, "there seemed to be no formula available that could lead out of the bipolar impasse." Political forces became too strong for the political leaders, and the war became a necessity. To be sure, this was not a metaphysical necessity, and in many situations the possibility of choice exists, but "events must be judged differently in a bipolar context." In such a context each side is in terror that the other will gain a monopoly of power and use it to enslave its rival. At some time in the growth of Athens, Sparta might have taken steps to check its rise, "but once the threshold of bipolarity was reached, events had passed the point at which peace could have been preserved indefinitely through settlements."

It is true that this particular formulation is not worth dissecting in detail, for it is the consequence of scattered piratical raids on the scholarly literature, ignores the evidence of the inscriptions, fails to consider the influence of internal politics, and makes only a cursory analysis of the final crisis. Yet it is valuable in putting into sharp relief the assumptions that underlie the view of Thucydides and dominate many modern interpretations of the causes of the war. The major assumptions are that the causes of the war must be sought chiefly, if not only, in Athens and Sparta, and that there was no way to avoid a final reckoning between these two great powers. But the Greek world of the years between the Persian War and the Peloponnesian War was not bipolar. By 435, Athens had come to dominate her allies to the degree that they were eliminated as independent factors in foreign affairs, but Sparta had not. Thebes and especially Corinth were free agents. To combat Athens with any hope of success, it is true, they must bring Sparta over to their cause. On the other hand—and this is decisive—Sparta could not prevent them from engaging in their own policies. This independent exercise of foreign policy was sometimes conducive to peace and sometimes to war; it was not, in any case, predictable. Its possibility is a serious argument against the inevitability of the war.

The unpersuasiveness of all theories of inevitability is best demonstrated by a resumé of the events that led to the war. At each step it is clear that the decisions were not preordained, although, of course, the options narrowed as time went on. Our analysis of the years between the wars shows that the theory that peace between Athens and Sparta could not last must be imposed on the facts from the outside; it does not arise from the evidence. The internal quarrel at Epidamnus had no relation to the outside world and need not have affected the international situation in any way. Corinth's decision to intervene was in no way the necessary consequence of previous conditions. Corinthian control of Epidamnus was not necessary for Corinth's economic well-being, her security, even her prestige. Corinth decided that the affair at Epidamnus would provide a splendid opportunity for revenge on its traditional enemies, the Corcyreans. The Corinthians could have chosen to refuse the Epidamnian appeal; had they done so there would have been no crisis and no war. To be sure, they knew in advance that intervention would probably mean war with Corcyra, and they did not flinch from the prospect, for they were confident that they could defeat Corcyra with the help of their Peloponnesian allies.

When some of their friends tried to dissuade them from their course out of fear that Corcyra would obtain the help of Athens and so bring on a larger war, the Corinthians ignored their counsel. They did not do so because they wanted a war with Athens, but because they expected that Athens would not fight. They were led to this belief by their interpretation of the informal détente between the Peloponnesians and the Athenians. Their interpretation was not correct, because Corcyra and its navy presented special problems not easily and obviously dealt with by the unspoken understanding that each side would be permitted freedom of action in its own sphere of influence. Sparta and Sicyon, at least, understood the danger, and the Corinthians should have too. They proceeded with their dangerous policy because they miscalculated the Athenian response. Their miscalculation arose not from a traditional hatred of Athens caused by a commercial rivalry, but rather from a combination of irrational hatred for the Corcyreans and wishful thinking, which led them to expect from Athens the response that they wanted. Had reason prevailed, the Corinthians would have accepted the Corcyrean offer of arbitration, which would have left them in a better position than when they first became involved at Epidamnus. The crisis would have ended before it ever involved either Athens or Sparta, and the war would have been averted.

By the time Athens became involved in 433, her freedom of action was somewhat limited. Corcyra was at war with Corinth. If Athens remained aloof, the Corinthians might win and attach the Corcyrean fleet to the Spartan alliance and challenge the unquestioned naval supremacy that was the basis of Athenian security. Once it became clear that Corinth would not retreat, the Athenians had no choice but to meet the challenge. It is clear, however, that the Athenians did not seek a confrontation with Corinth for commercial, imperial, or any other reasons; the conflict was forced on them. They first tried to limit their commitment in the hope that Corcyra would win with its own forces.

When the Battle of Sybota blocked this resolution, they did what they could to localize the conflict and avoid involving Sparta. The preparations they made for a likely conflict with Corinth were calculated to avoid giving the Corinthians a valid pretext for demanding Spartan assistance. Two of these measures, the ultimatum of Potidaea and the Megarian Decree, were errors in judgment by Pericles. In the case of Potidaea, he reacted too vigorously to the threat that Corinthian machinations might produce rebellion in the empire and gave the impression of Athenian tyranny and aggressiveness. In the case of Megara, again his reaction was greater than the situation required. He intended to punish Megara for helping the Corinthians in the Battle of Sybota and to issue a warning to them and to any other friends of Corinth to stay out of the affair and prevent its spread. The action was probably unnecessary, for Sparta seemed to be exercising a restraining hand on most of her allies; yet the decree had a very serious effect on the internal politics of Sparta. It appeared to be an attack on an ally of Sparta launched without sufficient provocation, and it reinforced the impression of Athens as a tyrant and an aggressor. Pericles misjudged the stability of the political situation at Sparta and unintentionally gave the war party a goad with which it could drive Sparta and its allies to war. If his judgment had been better and, perhaps, if the Athenian irritation with the Megarians had been less, he might have taken a gentler tone, avoided provocative actions, and allowed the friends of Athens and peace to keep their control of Spartan policy. If he had, there might not have been a majority of warlike ephors to promise help to Potidaea and to cooperate with the Corinthians in stirring up the war. Had the Athenians shown more restraint, there is a possibility that even after the Battle of Sybota a general war could have been prevented.

All this is not to say that there were no existing forces or conditions that helped bring on the war. The perfectly ordinary civil war in a remote and unimportant town on the fringes of the civilized world could hardly have led to a great war *ex nihilo*. Certainly there needed to be a solid core of suspicion and mutual distrust in Athens and Sparta. Another crucial factor originating long before the outbreak of the crisis was the deep and emotional hatred between Corinth and Corcyra. Still another was the organizational weakness of the Spartan alliance, which permitted a power of the second magnitude to drag the hegemonal power into a dangerous war for its own interests. Connected with that was the constitutional weakness of the Spartan executive, which divided the real responsibility for the formulation and conduct of foreign policy and permitted unpredictable shifts back and forth between policies in a rather short space of time. Such weaknesses made it difficult to restrain outbursts of passion and to follow a sober, cautious policy in times of crisis. After the death of Pericles, the Athenian constitution would show a similar weakness, but so long as he was alive Athens was free of this problem.

It is also true that the machinery of diplomacy was too rudimentary to preserve peace in time of crisis. The Thirty Years' Peace was open to varying interpretations, as are all diplomatic agreements, but it provided only one, rather clumsy, means for settling disagreements. It authorized the submission of all disputes to arbitration, but it made no provision for consultation before minor differences reached the level of disputes needing arbitration. By the time arbitration is required, disputants are often so hostile that they refuse to use it. When disputes reach the level of arbitration, they have become public issues and aroused powerful emotions not easily controlled.

All these may be considered as remote or underlying causes of the war. They may be seen as contributing to the situation that made war possible, but all of them together did not make war necessary. For that, a complicated chain of circumstances and decisions was needed. If any of its links had not been present, the war would not have come.

It is customary to apply the metaphor of the powder keg or tinderbox to international situations that are deemed the inevitable forerunners of war. The usual way of putting it is that the conflicting interests and passions of the contending parties provided the inflammatory material, and the final crisis was only a spark that had sooner or later to fall and cause the inevitable conflagration or explosion. If we were to apply this metaphor to the outbreak of the Second Peloponnesian War, we should put it this way: The growth of the Athenian Empire and Sparta's jealousy and fear of it provided the inflammable material that ignited into the First Peloponnesian War. The Thirty Years' Peace poured water on that flame and extinguished it. What was left of the flammable material was continually cooled and dampened by the mutual restraint of Athens and Sparta in the decade 445–435. To start the war, the spark of the Epidamnian trouble needed to land on one of the rare bits of flammable stuff that had not been thoroughly drenched. Thereafter it needed to be continually and vigorously fanned by the Corinthians, soon assisted by the Megarians, Potidaeans, Aeginetans, and the Spartan war party. Even then the spark might have been extinguished had not the Athenians provided some additional fuel at the crucial moment.

No one planned the Peloponnesian War, and no state wanted it, yet each of the three great states bears part of the blame for bringing it on. The Corinthians did not want war with Athens but a free hand against Corcyra. They were willing to risk such a war, however, because they hoped Athens would not really bring it on, because they counted on their proven ability to gain the help of Sparta in case of war, and because they were determined to have their way. Theirs is the greatest guilt, for they had the freest choice and sufficient warning of the consequences of their actions, yet they would not be deterred from their purpose.

The Spartans too deserve a share of the blame. They allowed their war party to frighten them with unfounded alarms of Athenian aggression and the Corinthians to blackmail them with empty threats of secession. They ignored the advice of Archidamus, which would have allowed them to avoid the war without any loss of power, honor, or influence. They rejected the opportunity to arbitrate specific disputes as specified in the treaty and were captured by the romantic vision of destroying the Athenian Empire, liberating Greece, and restoring Sparta to unchallenged primacy. They were quite right to go into the war burdened by a guilty conscience.

The Athenians, however, were not without guilt. To be sure, their security required that they accept the Corcyrean alliance and prepare for further conflict with Corinth. They need not, however, have behaved with such arrogance and harshness toward Potidaea and Megara. This frightened their rivals and lent plausibility to the charges of the Corinthians. In one sense, although probably not in the way they intended, the enemies of Pericles were right in fixing on the Megarian Decree as the cause of the war and on Pericles as its instigator. If he had not issued it, the Corinthians might not have been able to persuade the Spartans of the evil intentions of Athens and so to drive them to war. There is even some possibility that if he had been willing to rescind it at the request of the second Spartan embassy, the peace party might have returned to power and the war have been avoided. By that time, however, Pericles' war strategy dominated his thinking. It demanded a policy of firmness, and the Spartan offer was rejected. The political situation at Sparta made arbitration impossible; the intransigence of Pericles prevented any other solution.

All the statesmen involved suffered from what might be called "a failure of imagination." Each allowed war to come and even helped bring it on because he thought he could gain something at a reasonable cost. Each evolved a strategy largely based on past wars and expected the next war to follow his own plan. None seems to have considered the consequences of miscalculation. None had prepared a reserve plan to fall back on in case his original estimation should prove wrong. All expected a short war; none was ready even for the ten years of the Archidamian War, much less the full twenty-seven years that it took to bring the conflict to a conclusion. They all failed to foresee the evil consequences that such a war would have for everyone, victors and vanquished alike, that it would bring economic ruin, class warfare, brutality, erosion of moral standards, and a permanent instability that left Greece vulnerable to foreign conquest. Had they done so they would scarcely have risked a war for the relatively minor disputes that brought it on. Had they done so, we should admit at once, they would have been far better men than most statesmen who have faced similar decisions in the millennia since then. The Peloponnesian War was not caused by impersonal forces, unless anger, fear, undue optimism, stubbornness, jealousy, bad judgment, and lack of foresight are impersonal forces. It was caused by men who made bad decisions in difficult circumstances. Neither the circumstances nor the decisions were inevitable.

. . . . .

Our investigations have led us to conclusions that differ from those of Thucydides and the majority of modern scholars. That is a sobering thought, for perhaps it is only arrogance and a peculiar perversity that have led to such conclusions. A glance at the history of the question, however, may acquit us of these charges, for over the years Thucydides' account of the causes of the war has been found unsatisfactory even by those who accept his explanation. . . .

Finally we come to the question of why Thucydides chose the interpretation that he presents to us. Why does he offer an explanation for the coming of the war which is not clearly supported by the evidence he supplies? Part of the answer must lie in his polemical intentions. Popular opinion believed that the war was caused by Pericles and the Megarian Decree. That opinion was altogether simple-minded and wrong. Although the decree and Pericles were more important than Thucydides indicates, he was surely right to seek a more satisfactory explanation. It would be a mistake to believe, however, that Thucydides offers his interpretation merely to defend Pericles against the popular charges. Thucydides was an ardent admirer of Pericles and regarded him as the greatest statesman of his time. At the end of the war that had brought Athens so much grief and a crushing defeat, we may be sure that the reputation of Pericles had suffered great damage. Thucydides could not have been unmoved by the desire to restore that reputation, and his history must have contributed much to that end. Instead of believing that Pericles had driven his country into an unnecessary and disastrous war over a trifle, the reader of Thucydides is persuaded that Pericles was a wise and far-seeing statesman who knew that war was inevitable, evolved a sound strategy for winning it, and was thwarted only by such unforeseeable events as the plague and his own death, and by the foolishness of his successors, who would not carry out his strategy. Both versions are exaggerated, although we may be sure that Thucydides is far closer to the truth than Aristophanes and Ephorus. Thucydides would have been very pleased that his defense of Pericles has totally driven the opposition from the field.

Yet the desire to defend Pericles is not enough to explain the Thucydidean interpretation. The play of great impersonal forces is not confined merely to the coming of the war, but plays a leading part in the entire history. The purpose of the work is made very clear quite early. It is intended for those "who wish to see clearly the things that have happened and those things that, in accordance with human nature, will happen in the same or a similar way again in the future." His work is not intended only for the present, but as a "possession forever." Assuming the essential stability of human nature in the political realm, he tried to establish what amount almost to laws of political behavior. Mme. de Romilly's study of the place of imperialism in the work of Thucydides has shown that it is possible to derive from the history such fundamental laws. Nevertheless, he recognized the role of outstanding individuals who possessed wisdom and could affect the course of events. No doubt his book was intended for their use, and its purpose was to provide them with the principles of human political behavior that would enable them to make good judgments in the future. Thucydides wanted to describe and analyze the impersonal forces that operate in human society. A future Themistocles or a Pericles would have the wisdom to use the laws or principles that emerge from that analysis to guide his political actions.

If we keep this purpose in mind, we may arrive at a better understanding of why Thucydides interpreted the coming of the war as he did. Thucydides stood on the edge of philosophy. He was sufficiently a historian to feel compelled to establish the particulars, to present the data as accurately as he could, but he was no less, and perhaps more, concerned to convey the general truths that he had discovered. His passion for truth, his careful distinction between remote and immediate causes, his refusal to explain human events by celestial intervention have all led modern scholars to see him as very much like a modern historian. The fact is that in many ways he is far less modern than Herodotus. The canons of modern historical scholarship demand the presentation of a fair sample of the evidence. Evidence must be presented on both sides of an argument, and the interpretation must emerge from a demonstration that one thesis is better founded than another. Where there is conflicting evidence, the sources must be cited and reasons given for preferring one over the other. Relevant material known to the historian must be reported even though it contributes to a thesis that he believes mistaken. It should be perfectly plain that Herodotus complies with these demands far more than does Thucydides, who, in fact, violates every one of them at some time or another. Herodotus loves the phenomena in themselves; he is chiefly concerned with composing an interesting and honest narrative. He also wants to suggest some general truths, but that purpose is secondary. Thucydides has a different purpose. The phenomena and the narrative are not ends in themselves, but means whereby the historian can illustrate general truths.

This is not to say that Thucydides means to deceive. Quite the opposite is true. He is determined that the reader will not be deceived, so he selects his material in such a way as to emphasize and clarify the truth.

We must remember that his immediate audience knew much more than we do about the events that led to the Peloponnesian War. When Thucydides treated the Megarian Decree with such contempt, they were fully aware of all the evidence on the other side, and Thucydides knew it. His peculiar emphasis was not an attempt at deception but at interpretation. We should also remember that the great majority of the evidence that permits us to reject the Thucydidean interpretation is provided by Thucydides. The purpose of Thucydides was to set before us the truth as he saw it, but his truth need not be ours. If we are to use his history with profit, as we can and must, we must distinguish between the evidence he presents and the interpretation he puts on it. Only then can we use it as a "possession forever."

7. The Urban Side of the Gracchan Economic Crisis

HENRY C. BOREN

One of the most amazing phenomena in Western history is the rise of Rome from a provincial town at a river crossing to mistress of the world. Rome encountered many obstacles during her imperial expansion, but by the middle of the second century she had dealt with several external challenges to her position by conquering and incorporating willy-nilly virtually the entire Mediterranean world into an empire which she headed. Internally her constitution had grown by the adoption of compromises and the creation of new procedures and offices to meet changing conditions. Certainly one of the most remarkable aspects of Rome's internal development is the absence of violent conflict among her citizens during long periods of great stress. But all was far from well at Rome around 150 B.C.

The conquest of the Mediterranean had brought Rome wealth on an unprecedented scale, so that direct taxes were eliminated for citizens in 167 B.C. The warfare of the preceeding century, almost constant for over one hundred years, had caused a crisis in Italian economic life. Many citizens, formerly small farmers, found it impossible to return to their lands after long absences with the armies and drifted to the cities of Italy, especially Rome. Lands were bought up by the rich, both Roman citizens and Italian allies, and often converted into latifundia, *large estates worked by the cheap slave labor that*

Source: Henry C. Boren, "The Urban Side of the Gracchan Economic Crisis," *American Historical Review*, Vol. 63 (1958), pp. 890–902. Reprinted by permission of the author. [Footnotes omitted.]

resulted from the conquest of the East. Many conservatives, like Cato, also detected a corrupting influence on Roman morals and character from the importation of Greek and other Eastern tastes and values. In many areas of life then, the Romans were finding it necessary to make changes and were discovering that not all the results of world domination were positive.

A young Roman of noble family, Tiberius Sempronius Gracchus, was deeply disturbed by what appeared to him to be the disappearance of the Roman citizen-soldier, the backbone of Rome's might, and he proposed a plan to cure the ills of Rome. Gracchus's plan may have been impractical; it may have failed to assess and meet the real problems; that, however, is not so important as the fact that his persistence in pushing for agrarian reform in the teeth of opposition from many prominent members of Rome's ruling body, the Senate, plunged Rome into a century of internal strife that finally ended in Caesar's veiled monarchy. Why did the crisis become acute in the decade 133–123 B.C.? Why did some of the most prominent and respected senators resort to physical violence to curb Tiberius and his brother Gaius? What special circumstances can we cite to explain a shift away from the tradition of peaceful and reasoned response to crises in Rome's past?

Henry C. Boren, Professor of History at the University of North Carolina and a specialist in Roman Republican history, has done extensive research in the Gracchan period and has investigated these problems from a fresh vantage point. By studying numismatic evidence, archaeological remains, and literary texts, Boren has drawn some interesting conclusions about the city of Rome in and just prior to the Gracchan period. His most important thesis, presented in the following article, is that the city was in the midst of a severe crisis, characterized by a falling off of employment, and perhaps a shortage of grain with consequent price increases. Boren's work is significant historiographically, for he has studied an old problem by using new forms of evidence. He has thus produced not only new conclusions but also in effect a new body of evidence. It may be useful to compare Boren's article with the preceding study by Kagan to appreciate how the treatment of different historical questions changes, for while Boren has stressed the economic side of a problem generally considered from a political viewpoint, Kagan has a political explanation for a development that many historians have seen in essentially economic terms.

The critical period for the Roman Republic, it is often recognized, began in 133 B.C., the year of the tribuneship of Tiberius Gracchus. The measures which he and after him his brother Gaius (tribune in 123 and 122 B.C.) forced, over the opposition of most of the reluctant senatorial aristocracy, exposed the weaknesses of the Roman constitution with its dual development and divided responsibility and created new, irreconcilable factions whose strife eventually overthrew the Republic. The modern, who is likely to think of the English example of progress toward democracy through a series of concessions by the ruling classes, will perhaps conclude that the Gracchi only checked what might have been a similar evolution in Roman government. On the other hand, it is quite possible that Gaius

Gracchus intended to foster development toward democracy, but along Greek lines, that is, by setting himself up as a tyrant, a popular champion, who would ally himself with the merchant class to destroy the power of the aristocratic families. Uncompromising nobles like Scipio Nasica and Lucius Opimius, who did not hesitate to use violence against the Gracchi and their followers, must certainly be held chiefly accountable for the vicious nature of the subsequent factional strife which racked the state until Augustus. In any case, the Gracchan period was the beginning of the end for the Republic and is consequently worth careful study.

It is the thesis of this paper that the most pressing problems, those which precipitated the disastrous political tug of war, were economic and that they were of a peculiarly urban nature not before fully recognized by historians of Rome. These conclusions are based partly on new evidence but depend primarily upon heretofore overlooked negative evidence and a fresh look at the traditional sources.

In their discussions of the economic crisis of this period, the historians, following Appian, Plutarch, and Tiberius Gracchus himself, have emphasized the rise of the slave-operated *latifundia,* the decline of the small farmer, and the failure to enforce the centuries-old Licinian-Sextian laws limiting individual holdings of public land. This is quite proper, up to a point, for there is no doubt that there was a serious agrarian social and economic crisis from which stemmed many serious problems. But it will be seen that for Rome the most troublesome problems were urban, though these were related, certainly, to agrarian conditions; further, the urban economic situation was the most important factor in the immediate crisis.

103

Boren

THE URBAN SIDE
OF THE
GRACCHAN
ECONOMIC CRISIS

Evidence is presented in this paper to show that the city of Rome was generally prosperous during the middle of the second century, that spending on construction and luxuries was especially heavy in the years before the Gracchi, that there was a sharp decline in building and government spending generally just before 133, and that this decline, along with other economic factors, precipitated an especially acute crisis affecting particularly the city itself in 135–134, just as Tiberius Gracchus stood for office. It is inferred that the economy of the city had become geared closely to state expenditure, though, of course, it was also dependent upon heavy private spending in the area. The tremendous income and expenditure in the 140's and the sharp curtailment in succeeding years therefore reacted directly in every phase of the city's economy.

A survey of some widely used general works will show the extent to which this study modifies the customary views of the period. A. H. J. Greenidge, after giving some attention to the economic life of the city of Rome, says: "Italian agriculture was still the basis of the brilliant life of Rome. Had it not been so, the epoch of revolution could not have been ushered in by an agrarian law." But the agrarian law did not "usher in" the epoch; Tiberius' measures were not seriously opposed as revolutionary until constitutional issues were injected into the struggle, when he challenged senatorial control of the provinces and of the public purse and threatened to make the tribuneship completely independent of senatorial authority by "recall" of unpopular tribunes and successive reelection of popular ones.

Hugh Last writes of a general economic crisis in this period but refers primarily to the agricultural situation. He mentions the influx of large quantities of booty but notes the results only as they affected the rapid growth of the *latifundia*. He says: "Since there was no longer a livelihood to be got in the countryside, there was a movement to the towns. . . . An export trade was the only hope of employment for the fresh arrivals." Though undeniable in part, each of these views requires reexamination. Last recognizes that Tiberius' main problem was to reduce the number of "paupers" in Rome.

William E. Heitland discusses the subject in a conventional manner, remarking that "Gracchus . . . was right in recognizing the land-question as the fundamental problem of the state." Tenney Frank also treats the period in the usual fashion, and so, too, does H. H. Scullard, in his recent revision of Frank B. Marsh's survey of the later republic. A few writers recognize to some degree that the city of Rome had its own problems, that the influx of booty in the middle of the century had its effect on the economy, and even that the wars of the 130's seriously drained the treasury. The present writer, however, knows of no one who has sufficiently emphasized the impact of the influx of wealth on the economy of the city of Rome nor anyone who has closely considered the specifically urban side of the crisis with which Tiberius Gracchus tried to deal. Tiberius, of course, did make an agrarian law the core of his program, but the immediate crisis was less agrarian than urban, less concerned with land than with people. The land distribution law was merely his answer to the really pressing problem of what to do with the growing masses of the underprivileged in Rome.

Why had so many Latin and Italian small-holders streamed into the capital? It is not necessary to accept wholly the reasoning of Tiberius, who regarded the slave-operated *latifundia* as the chief factor in the migration. It would be equally logical to insist that the chief reason for the growing urban population in the United States today is the extensive adoption of modern farm machinery. The new and more profitable and efficient capitalistic farm operation in each instance certainly accounts for the dispossession of some farmers, but there are many reasons for such a migration. Early in the second century large numbers of men from the cities of the Italian allies already were flocking to Rome, and there is no real evidence that the movement was not for the most part voluntary. The average Roman or Italian peasant living on his tiny hereditary acreage scrabbled desperately for a bare existence. Surely he longed for something better. The ex-centurion who about 171 B.C. helped put down opposition to the military levy for the war against Perseus illustrates the bleak prospect the veterans faced. This man, after twenty-two years of service in the army, had been willing to return to his inheritance—a single *iugerum* of land (about three fifths of an acre) and a small hut—but how many such veterans could endure the old family farm after service in Greece or Asia? Soldiers who became acquainted with city life often preferred its numerous opportunities and varied activities to the farm. Moreover, those who held no land were exempt from military service.

During most of the first two thirds of the second century Rome was a busy place, requiring large numbers of laborers and artisans. There was much construction, financed by indemnities, booty, tribute, and the income from mines. The armies were supplied, and ships were built; numerous shops supplied the needs of the city's growing population. The extensive colonization programs of the 180's and 170's may indicate that during this period not all emigrating peasants could be assimilated into the urban population. Conversely, the cessation of colonization at mid-century (no Latin colonies were established after 181 and no Roman colonies between 157 and 122) indicates that for many years before the Gracchi the migrating Romans and Italians were readily absorbed into the swelling, bustling metropolis.

A survey of economic activity affecting Rome in the first half of the second century and a more detailed study of the decade prior to 133 B.C. will both suggest what opportunities were available to immigrants in this period and help to show, as the result of an obvious interconnection between income and spending and economic well-being, what were the fluctuations in the city's economy in these years.

The first third of the century saw an influx of money to the city from indemnities (chiefly from Carthage, Macedonia, and Syria) and bullion from the Spanish mines that amounted to an estimated 300,000,000 *denarii*. Much of the metal was quickly coined. It has been estimated that during a forty-three-year period 250,000,000 silver *denarii* were struck. There was even an issue of gold coinage in 167 due to the "enormous quantities of gold staters . . . imported to Rome, partly as spoils of war and partly as payments of tribute." Sale of slaves was a source of additional income. Individual soldiers brought back booty. Macedonian mines were reopened in 158 and yielded some precious metals. By 157, a considerable surplus was reported in the treasury. Despite a possible short deflationary period in the late 180's and 170's, the period generally was one of inflation—"inflation of a better kind, the issue of every-increasing amounts of good money." This new wealth of silver brought a change in the proportionate value of silver and copper, resulting in a gradual reduction of the weight of the bronze *as* from one ounce in 200 B.C. to half that amount at the end of the century (this may show merely that the *as* had become fiduciary coinage).

Money flowed rather freely in Rome in the decade of the 140's. Although the treasury was reported "in straits" from about 150 to about 146, booty from Carthage, Corinth, and Macedonia soon bolstered public and private purses. Unfortunately, the available information is not very exact. According to Pliny, Carthage yielded 4,370 pounds of silver and "much" gold. Frank estimates that Rome gained at least 45,000,000 *de-*

105

Boren

THE URBAN SIDE
OF THE
GRACCHAN
ECONOMIC CRISIS

narii from both Carthage and Corinth. Officers and soldiers brought back large amounts of private loot, especially from Corinth, and there were large numbers of slaves whose sale brought considerable sums. Rome, of course, had other sources of income. The productive mines in Spain, for example, increased in yield in this period. Newly acquired gold mines in the Piedmont operated by Roman companies about this time produced so much metal that there was a considerable although short-lived drop in the value of gold.

The extraordinary quantity of money moving into public and private coffers was not permitted to gather dust in the vaults. The years following 146 B.C. saw unusual spending in the city. Several important public buildings were put up in these years. Q. Caecilius Metellus, the conqueror of Macedonia, after his triumph built temples to Jupiter Stator and to Juno Regina, apparently within a magnificent portico erected shortly before. Greek architects and sculptors were called in to design these buildings, which were reported to be the first temples in Rome of all-marble construction. "Liberated" Greek art works graced their interiors; in the central area before the temples were set Lysippus' famous statues of Alexander's generals. L. Mummius, the spoiler of Corinth, vowed a temple to Hercules Victor, which seems to have been dedicated by himself as censor in 142. Pliny says Mummius filled Rome with statuary. He furnished works of art, including statues by Praxiteles, for the embellishment of a temple dedicated to Felicitas, which was erected soon after 146 by L. Licinius Lucullus from booty taken in a Spanish campaign of 150–151.

A major expenditure during the 140's was the construction of the Marcian aqueduct by Q. Marcius Rex at a cost of 180,000,000 *sesterces*. At the same time (144–140 B.C.) Marcius repaired the Aqua Appia and the Aqua Anio Vetus. These additions to the water supply system testify to the almost explosive population growth of the city. Other major construction projects of the 140's included the rebuilding of the Pons Aemilius and the fortification of the Janiculum in 142. Typical of the lavish expenditure of the times was the decision to gild the ceiling of the Capitoline temple, the first such ceiling in Rome. Another large temple was undertaken in 138 B.C. by D. Junius Brutus Callaicus. Placed in the Circus Flaminius and dedicated to Mars, it contained statuary by Scopas.

Significantly corroborative of heavy government spending in this period is the present author's statistical study of coin hoards of the time, which shows a relatively heavy volume of coinage for the 140's. Since the Roman *tresviri monetales* ordinarily struck coins only as they were needed to meet expenses of state, coinage volume is a reliable reflection of public expenditure. Issues of *denarii* (to which the study was confined) during these years were consistently large—as one would expect on the basis of evidence presented in the paragraphs above.

It can be surmised that the years which saw such an extensive public building program also witnessed heavy spending by private persons. Much booty from the profitable wars of the 140's fell into private purses. Pliny associates the fall and looting of Corinth and Carthage with the introduction of new standards of luxury into the state. In addition, contractors, artisans, and merchants would have prospered as a result of the heavy disbursements in and near Rome by the government. It must again be emphasized, however, that despite large private outlays which affected the prosperity level, it was inevitable that the general economy of the city should become intricately linked with the level of state expenditure and that any curtailment of that spending should immediately and disastrously react upon the economic fortunes of the masses of laborers and artisans at Rome.

In contrast with the prosperous 140's, the evidence—mostly negative—indicates a sharp reduction of public spending in the years after 138 B.C. Following construction of the temple to Mars in that year, there is no trace of further important public construction for thirteen years, until 125 B.C., when there was built the Tepulan aqueduct, less than a fifth as long as the Marcian, delivering less than a tenth the volume of water. This sudden drop in the scale of public spending is corroborated by the statistical coin study mentioned above. Although the issues of coins cannot be dated with sufficient accuracy to permit a year-by-year analysis, the statistics show with high probability that the pattern of consistently large issues of *denarii* in the 140's was not repeated in the 130's. The total volume of coins struck in these years was decidedly lower.

Additional evidence for the changed economic pattern of the 130's may be deduced from the nature of the wars Rome waged in this decade. These military operations, relatively minor, included wars against the Numantines in Spain, against the Scordisci in Macedonia, and against a slave revolt in Sicily. None of these conflicts could have produced much booty and no doubt, in fact, represented a net loss—which means that there was proportionally less available money to use for outlays in Rome. In the later stages of the Numantine War, Scipio Aemilianus used about sixty thousand troops; the city provided little spoil, and in his triumph Scipio distributed only seven *denarii* each to his soldiers—hardly enough for an extended spending spree in the big city! Probably the normal tribute from Spain was reduced by the disturbed conditions, and the flow of bullion from the mines may also have been lowered, although the most productive mines, near New Carthage, probably were not affected. The repulsion of the Scordisci in Macedonia in 135 was no doubt a small task, but for a time the tribute may have been lessened and income from the mines reduced. The most significant of these three military operations was the Sicilian Slave War, which worsened about 135 when Eunus organized the revolt into a war of serious proportions. Wide areas were devastated. The grain tithe, on which Rome had come to depend not only for income but also for food, was in large part uncollectible. This cut in grain imports did much to precipitate the immediate crisis in Rome—which must now be scrutinized more closely.

The multitude of immigrants into Rome during the years before the Gracchi could not have relished their existence in the city, even though

107

Boren

THE URBAN SIDE
OF THE
GRACCHAN
ECONOMIC CRISIS

they came, for the most part, with a wave of prosperity. Housing was inadequate, and the newcomers were crowded into large, many-storied apartment houses called *insulae*. The long, gradual inflation which characterized most decades of the century brought with it gradually rising prices and no doubt tended to benefit the commercial classes. But in an age when there were no labor unions or cost-of-living wage increases to compensate, the economic condition of the lowest classes could not have been satisfactory even during the prosperity of the 140's. "The rise in prices was more automatic and inevitable than the rise in pay." Moreover, the wars which brought huge booty to Rome had brought also large numbers of slaves. While many of these were used in farm operations, no doubt there was also a tendency in the city to replace free labor with slave labor, which during the 140's and for some years following was in such excellent supply. M. I. Rostovtzeff, noting that in Gracchan times there was unrest generally throughout the Mediterranean (and suggesting that this unrest was more important than the meager evidence indicates), attributes it in part to the abundance of cheap slave labor, which displaced free workers. Fritz M. Heichelheim attributes these uprisings to a general drastic rise in grain prices, which reduced many of the proletarians to starvation levels. The reported remarks to the Roman mob of Scipio Aemilianus, who called its members "step-children" of Italy and declared that he had brought most of them to Rome in chains, indicate that there were numerous freedmen or others of foreign birth in the jeering crowd. If the lower-class wage earner lagged behind financially in times of relative prosperity, the years of depression in the 130's must have brought widespread unemployment and unrelieved misery.

The factor in the situation which was most critical, which aroused the leaderless mob, which cried out for action, which led to the election of Tiberius Gracchus, and which influenced the direction his reform program would take was a shortage of grain and the consequent high price for bread, both chiefly the result of the Sicilian Slave War. This seems certain, even in the absence of literary evidence. Grain prices were already extremely high. The city of Rome had long depended on Sicily for grain. Cicero quotes old Cato as saying that Sicily was "the nation's storehouse, the nurse at whose breast the Roman people is fed." Rome was accustomed not only to receive the grain tithe in tribute from Sicily but also to purchase additional quantities of Sicilian grain on the open market. Perhaps as much as 25 or 30 per cent of the Sicilian crop thus furnished bread for Rome's thousands. Frank says that Rome, even before this period, was dependent for about half of all her grain on overseas imports, most, no doubt, from Sicily. The substantial diminution of the Sicilian tenth and of regular, addition imports from Sicily therefore meant a shortage of tremendous proportions in Rome. Speculation surely followed, as was usual at Rome. It appears also that grain prices in the Mediterranean area, already abnormally high, were further inflated by unusual pirate activity in this period. The result was that at a time of economic distress for many wage earners, the price of bread, the staple of their diet, shot up to prohibitive levels. In Rome there must have been danger of actual starvation. Perhaps it was at this time that Lucilius wrote

Deficit alma ceres,
Nec plebes pane potitur.

To Tiberius Gracchus, it seemed that in one stroke all the social and economic changes of recent decades showed their direful consequences: the new *latifundia,* using slave labor, had drastically lowered the numbers of the old peasant stock; the immigration to Rome had given the city a numerous, noisy, and economically stricken human substratum; the new agriculture had concentrated on crops such as the olive and the grape, so that the agricultural area no longer could supply the city with grain and Rome was forced to depend on importation. Whatever proportion of this latter development was caused by the inability of Roman grain to compete with state and other imports was probably overlooked by Tiberius. Faced with the starveling proletariat and convinced that the problems were all of a piece, Tiberius saw an easy solution. He would relieve the overcrowded city and the unemployed by putting the latter on small farms. This would partially eliminate the extreme dependence on imports of overseas grain and at the same time inhibit the further development of the *latifundia,* or even reduce their numbers.

From a broader view, with longer perspective, it can now be seen that Tiberius oversimplified the problem, that the agricultural approach could not possibly have been extensive enough or popular enough with the lower-class Romans to solve the crisis, even if enough land had been available for distribution. Tiberius was not, in short, attempting to solve the most immediate, emphatically urban, problem. He was trying to turn back the clock. It must be admitted that Tiberius was actuated by other motives, of course. Appian reports, for example, his concern for the declining numbers of citizens eligible for army duty.

The economic program begun by Gaius Gracchus ten years after the death of his brother is itself eloquent testimony that the problems with which he tried to deal were essentially urban. This has been rather generally recognized, though there has been a tendency to believe that these urban problems existed primarily as the result of the failure to solve the agrarian crisis. The material already presented will sufficiently modify this view. A reinterpretation of the literary evidence, with consideration of the negative evidence and with assistance from some new numismatic information, will serve to bring into clearer focus the conditions which the younger Gracchus faced.

The end of the Numantine War (133 B.C.) and the Sicilian Slave War (shortly after) ended the drain on the treasury from these unprofitable conflicts, and it may be assumed that normal income was restored from mines and tribute. The rich kingdom of Pergamum came to Rome by the will of Attalus III in 133 B.C., and although some years of military operations were required to establish firm Roman control, the full treasury appears immediately to have come to Rome; when in 132 the royal personal

109
Boren
THE URBAN SIDE
OF THE
GRACCHAN
ECONOMIC CRISIS

property was sold at public auction there, frenzied bidding was reported. Regardless of the depressed situation of the wage earners, there were those whose purses permitted them to buy these evidences of having arrived in society. If the Attalid treasury was actually used, as Tiberius Gracchus proposed, to stock the new small farms, this outlay may have had some effect on the city's economy. The numismatic study indicates at least some rise in public spending, but there is exceptional difficulty in establishing chronology of coin issues in these years.

The continued absence of public construction, which was not resumed until Gaius Gracchus' program demanded it, does not indicate a very complete recovery of an economy so dependent on state spending in the area. It has already been pointed out that the only major item of public building in the 120's before the tribunate of Gaius Gracchus was a relatively small aqueduct built in 125. The need for another aqueduct so soon after the construction of the huge Aqua Marcia in the 140's implies that neither Tiberius Gracchus' land distribution scheme nor the depression did much to reduce the population of the city.

A reform of the coinage, which probably took place in the late 120's, appears to have been a deliberately inflationary measure and was perhaps designed to relieve the load of the debtor class. Outstanding numismatists of this period have assigned this reform—revaluation of the *denarius* from ten to sixteen *asses*—to the interval between 133 and 122 and have usually connected it with the programs of one of the Gracchi. The present writer has shown conclusively that the early issues of the revalued *denarii* were quite small and consequently not connected with any large spending program. Since the *as* was the money of account or of reckoning, the measure was certainly inflationary. Later issues of the revalued *denarius* were much larger and are perhaps those which reflect the heavy spending of Gaius Gracchus. The implication, then, is that sometime during the 120's, most likely just before the election of Gaius, this revaluation was carried through because of the deflated state of the monetary system, with the intention of giving relief to debtor groups. This move may have aided the poorer citizens somewhat, but it would have helped most the aristocrats who had been trying to keep up with the "Joneses"—the moneyed equestrians—and had run their estates into debt. This was probably the answer of the senatorial aristocrats to the continued economic difficulties of the 120's. But it was not enough.

Perhaps, as in the year when Tiberius Gracchus was elected to office, there was a particularly acute crisis in 123, again involving the grain supply and hence the price of bread, still abnormally high. If Orosius may be trusted, a locust plague devoured the grain crops of Africa in 125 B.C. This would naturally have affected grain prices all over the Mediterranean. A little later, a Roman commander, Fabius, confiscated grain in Spain and sent it to Rome. Since it was normally unprofitable as well as unnecessary to ship grain that distance to Rome, there must have been great need for it. On the motion of Gaius Gracchus, Fabius was censured by the Senate—presumably for mistreating allies—and payment was ordered. Certain of Gaius' own measures to ensure a stable grain supply through the building of granaries and to supply grain to the Roman poor at reduced prices certainly reflect ruinous fluctuations both in supplies and prices of grain and may also bear testimony to a particularly acute crisis, which brought about his election to office.

The heavy government outlays of 123 and 122 B.C. may have "pump primed" the economy of the city of Rome back to a semblance of prosperity. Besides the building of granaries and the subsidization of a grain supply for the poor, Gracchus also furnished clothing free to citizens in the army, constructed many miles of graded, expensive roads, and established colonies. Plutarch describes him as continually surrounded by numerous contractors and builders. Gracchus' opponent in the tribunate in 122 B.C., Livius Drusus, with the backing of the Senate, also carried out a program to establish colonies, and some money would have been required for those which were actually established. Ordinary public construction resumed in Rome in 121 B.C. when the consul, Opimius, build a basilica and refurbished the temple of Concord, and Q. Fabius Allobrogicus constructed the first of the great arches so typical of the Roman *fora* in later times.

This enormous increase in spending in and about the city of Rome after 122 B.C.—corroborated in the author's numismatic statistical study—no doubt put an end, at least temporarily, to the long-drawn economic depression. The supply of grain may, for a time, have been sufficient to prevent a continuation of the especially onerous hardship of high-priced bread in a time of deflation and unemployment. Prices seem to have declined, but not to the level of mid-century. The problem of an adequate grain supply was not permanently solved and continued to plague the Roman authorities for centuries. Shortages of grain seem always to have given rise to an outcry of indignation demanding immediate action, as in the days of the Gracchi.

111

Boren

THE URBAN SIDE
OF THE
GRACCHAN
ECONOMIC CRISIS

The conclusions reached in this paper can be summarized as follows. It appears that both of the Gracchi were faced with approximately the same problems: an overcrowded city, unemployment, unrest, and economic depression, plus an acute crisis due to grain shortage and consequent high prices of bread. Tiberius tried to solve the dilemma by reestablishing a class of "sturdy yeomen" (to use a term Englishmen have applied to about the same sort of program); Gaius, recognizing the failure of his brother's agrarian law, adopted other methods. The depression, which was tied in closely with the reduced level of state spending in the immediate vicinity of Rome, seems to have endured almost continuously for about fifteen years. The measures of the younger Gracchus, plus other stabilizing factors, appear to have ended the worst of the depression by 122 B.C.

8. Roman Law

F. H. LAWSON

*The three areas in which the Romans made their most significant and endur-
ing contributions to Western civilization are language, architecture and engineering, and law. Although the Latin language is no longer a vital, living
tongue, having been supplanted in the last two centuries by the use of various
modern languages among scientists and scholars, and having been replaced
in the Roman Catholic liturgy by modern vernaculars in the last decade, it
survives indirectly as the basis for French, Italian, Spanish, Portuguese,
Roumanian and a few other Romance languages, and has contributed a large
portion of the vocabulary of English. Roman building techniques have also
left a lasting memorial in countless towns, bridges, and road systems of the
Mediterranean countries. Roman law, however, is much less visible and much
more difficult to evaluate in its effects on Western history, despite the role
that its existence and development played in the success of the Romans in
maintaining their political independence for almost a thousand years, and political dominance of the Mediterranean world for five hundred.*

*Professor Lawson recognizes the difficulties of understanding the nature of
Roman law and of defining its importance to history. In this essay he lucidly
traces the growth, development, and nature of Roman law during classical*

Source: F. H. Lawson, "Roman Law," in J. P. V. D. Balsdon, ed., *The Romans*
(New York: Basic Books, 1965), Chap. 6, pp. 102–128. Copyright © 1965 by
Basic Books, Inc. Reprinted by permission of Basic Books, Inc., New York and Pit-
man Publishing, Ltd., London.

antiquity and indicates precisely how Roman law has left its imprint on subsequent institutional history and legal thought. His treatment is one of the best introductions to a seminal topic, and it should help one to appreciate the extent of the Roman contribution to Western civilization in this important area, while providing an insight into the character of the Roman mind with its emphasis on the practical and on common sense. Lawson's evaluation of the importance of Roman law is a personal one, of course, and the interested student might pursue the subject by turning to the fuller treatments of B. Nicholas's An Introduction to Roman Law (1962) *or A. M. Prichard's* Leage's Roman Private Law (1961).

It is a commonplace that Roman law is the greatest contribution that Rome has made to Western civilization; and again it is often said that Roman law is one of the main structural elements in the modern world. These statements are for the most part accepted by persons who do not know what they mean and, perhaps, because they do not know. In fact it is difficult to define the historic importance of Roman law, more difficult to see what is peculiarly Roman in it and still more difficult to explain either its importance or its Roman character.

Certain statements at least can be made without much fear of contradiction.

The Roman world is a dead world existing only in the past, a mass of fragments to be dug up, seen, read, inspected, or copied. Even the Latin language no longer survives as a means of communication used naturally in ordinary intercourse, and capable of idiomatic development; its standards of correctness are all in the past. To this generalization Roman law provides a solitary exception. Less than a century ago it was completely alive in important parts of the Western world. Even now it is applied in a few places, and elsewhere it has suffered a change of name rather than of substance. Before 1900 over large parts of Germany Roman law was in active operation. In 1900 it was superseded by a Civil Code, but that code contains in scarcely modified form much that had previously existed as Roman law. Similarly in France those topics which under the *ancien régime* were governed by Roman law are still governed by the same rules and principles, though they are now integral parts of codified French law. Moreover, they remain Roman in a way that the French language does not.

Of course the Roman law in force in the modern world is not the same as that of the early city state of Rome. Such identity as Roman law has preserved throughout its history is like that of the human body, in which cells are constantly being replaced by other cells, an identity preserved by continuous development. Roman law likewise developed continuously with only one clean break at the end of the ancient world, which, however, was healed after a long interval by what was substantially a resurrection of its old self, in the condition to which it had attained before the break. Accordingly the debt which the modern world owes to Roman law cannot be understood without some knowledge of its history.

We have little direct evidence for Roman law before the time of Cicero; and indeed systematic knowledge begins in the second century A.D. with an elementary textbook written by an unknown author who went by the name of Gaius. Any attempt to describe Roman law in its earliest state must take the form of a hazardous reconstruction. There can indeed be little doubt as to its general structure, though we are probably led to think of it as neater and more logical than it really was.

The republican constitution, while it protected the citizen against the abuse of power by magistrates, conferred on him no rights which he could assert against the sovereign people. Yet it seems that although the State never admitted any limits to its power over its citizens, it interfered very little in the relations between them. A sharp distinction was always made between public law, which regulated the structure and powers of public authorities and their relations to the individual citizen, and, on the other hand, private law, which regulated the relations of citizens *inter se*. The State provided means for the settlement of their disputes and, while it allowed the administration of domestic justice by the head of a family, it had already, before historical knowledge begins, suppressed anything that may have existed in the nature of a blood feud. But although murder and treason were already crimes against the State, most of what would now be treated as criminal offences were redressed by way of civil action brought by the victim against the wrongdoer. Moreover, a person seeking justice against another person got no help from the State in bringing him before the courts. Nor was private law for the most part the product of legislation, though the Roman people could in its assemblies modify private law if it chose.

For the Roman Republic was organized on lines in many respects closely resembling, though in miniature, those regulating the federal republic of the United States. It was a group of families, each composed of a man who, having no surviving ancestors in the direct male line, exercised an unlimited jurisdiction over his slaves and his own issue in the male line, in short, a number of patriarchal families, corresponding in their main outlines to the constituent states of the American Union, the subordinate members of the family corresponding to American citizens in their capacity of citizens of their particular states. But just as the national government of the United States exercises power directly over those citizens in certain matters without the intervention of the states, so the Roman State, in matters of public law, dealt directly with all its citizens and took no notice of the subjection of some of them to a family head.

Thus we have to take account of three kinds of relations: that of the citizen to the State, that of the subordinate member of a family to its head, and that of one family head to another. That of the citizen to the State, in principle one of absolute subjection, came to be governed by public law; that of the subordinate member of a family to its head remained one of absolute subjection, tempered not by law but by public opinion and an official censorship of morals; that of one family head to another was the subject-matter of private law.

Now while the power of the State over the citizen or of the family head over his subordinates was not in fact exercised irresponsibly, each appeared too arbitrary to attract the serious attention of the jurists who turned Roman law into an object of scientific study. On the other hand, the disputes between family heads, like the disputes between nations in modern times, had to be decided on principle, with state officials doing little more than hold the ring; and this remained true even after individuals became legally important in their own right. It may be said here, once and for all, that since the Roman jurists did not subject either public law or criminal law to profound study, modern students of Roman law also have usually left them to the ancient historians and confined themselves to private law.

The rules then of private law determining a decision could not, given the essential structure of Roman society, be established by the arbitrary act of a public officer; but there had to be some persons whose business it was to "interpret" the law; those persons would have somehow or other to reduce it to a rational system; and they would be likely to find it altogether more worthy of intense study than the arbitrary commands of a superior. If we may employ a distinction familiar to students of legal theory, private law would be the product of reason, not of will. Those familiar with Roman habits of thought would doubtless prefer to speak of common sense rather than reason; and the history of Roman private law may be described as the application of organized common sense to a whole range of problems which were in principle removed from the exercise of arbitrary authority.

How that was done was in many ways very remarkable. It was for an elected magistrate, a praetor, to supervise the initial procedure under which the parties to an action arrived at an "issue," that is to say, sorted out the question to be tried. Then a private citizen, chosen by the parties from a select list and empowered by the praetor to give a binding decision, tried the action. But since he had not necessarily any knowledge of the law to be applied, he had to depend for such knowledge on others whose business it was to know the law and to interpret it. At first that function was performed by the College of Pontiffs, who kept their knowledge to themselves. In due course, partly by the enactment of the Twelve Tables in 451–50 B.C. and partly through what appears to have been a calculated indiscretion, their secrets were laid open to the general public, only to become the specialty of a few aristocrats who took a peculiar interest in studying and interpreting the law and, by discussing with their pupils the legal questions raised by actual or hypothetical cases, created a lasting tradition. These secular jurists (*jurisprudentes*) were followed by others, in an unbroken succession which lasted until the end of the third century A.D., who, directly or indirectly, did almost all the work of developing private law. As far as we can see, the secular jurists simply assumed authority to interpret the law and had no official authorization until, by an obscure provision characteristic of his general method of acquiring power, Augustus apparently authorized selected jurists to give opinions on his authority. By that time, however, the general development of Roman private law was set on permanent lines, and the jurists of the Principate seem to have done little more than fill in the necessary details and make such minor adjustments as were required by social and economic changes.

We do not know why this authority of unofficial jurists was accepted. We can only infer, first, that it was in line with the "influence" which commonly plays so great a part in an aristocratic system, and, secondly, that the general public found the quality of their work as satisfying as it has proved to later ages. For they did not trouble to give the real reasons for their opinions; at most they showed that they were consistent with pre-existing law. But no doubt another reason for their success was that they were willing to take trouble off other people's hands and were trusted as experts usually are unless they obviously go wrong.

Their influence was probably enhanced by a detachment from the actual results of litigation. They left advocacy to professional and paid orators, hoping to gain for themselves only prestige and support in a political career. Thus they did not concern themselves with the proof of facts, but gave their opinions on the assumption that the facts laid before them were correctly stated; and the outcome of litigation was, it would appear, a matter of indifference to them, a great aid to impartiality and breadth of judgement. While they cultivated the practical experience of the man of the world, they were able to see legal problems in an exceptional degree *sub specie aeternitatis* and give to their writings a universal significance applicable to far distant times and places.

So far the development of Roman private law has been indicated in such a way as to make it appear to have been entirely due to the jurists. That is an overstatement, for although legislation was resorted to on comparatively rare occasions, its intervention was important and even decisive. Thus the Twelve Tables were traditionally regarded as in some way or other the origin of most of the law, and the law of damage to property was always based in great part on the Lex Aquilia (of uncertain date). So also resolutions of the Senate (*senatusconsulta*) made important changes, especially in the law of intestate succession.

Finally, a person who had suffered loss of a novel kind might induce the praetor for the time being to afford him redress by means of a new action, not included in those authorized by the old civil law or in those promised by him in the edict he issued on entry into his praetorship; and, once the new action had been incorporated in the edicts of his successors, a new right would be seen to have come into existence by the mere fact of its having been protected by the new action. The history of private law cannot be understood without constant reference to the praetor's edict.

Nevertheless, it will not be wrong to see in the activity of the jurists the mainspring of legal change, at any rate during the six centuries from about 300 B.C. to about A.D. 300. For they alone had the necessary expert knowledge, and their services were not confined to interpreting the law. Praetors were not necessarily, perhaps seldom, learned in the law. Moreover, like other men in public positions, they were accustomed to take advice from a council, which would assuredly contain jurists. Again, the grant of a novel action would in the first instance be asked for by a litigant, who would be advised by a jurist to make the application.

In short, improvements would be sought from a praetor, from the Senate or from a popular assembly only where interpretation would not suffice, and it may fairly be inferred from all the circumstances that they would be suggested by the jurists.

We can be no less certain of their influence even when legislative power passed to the Emperor, for we know that jurists were important members of his privy council. In fact most imperial action on private law was only formally legislative and consisted of answers to questions referred to the Emperor for his decision, in much the same way as jurists gave opinions on questions submitted to them. Juristic activity persisted anonymously behind the curtain of imperial quasi-legislation.

The jurists did not create laws out of nothing; they started with certain customs, partly codified in the Twelve Tables, and modified by a few other statutes (*leges* or *plebiscita*), most of which marked settlements agreed upon between patricians and plebeians during the Struggle of the Orders. An important part of them regulated the succession on intestacy of the head of a family and accepted the principle according to which the family of a person leaving several sons was not kept intact but was divided among all the sons so as to create several new families; Roman law had already rejected the large joint family and insisted that each family should have a monarchical head exercising power over all his descendants in the male line. Otherwise the law provided a number of methods by which actions could be brought to remedy wrongs or by which heads of families could acquire property or modify their relations among themselves. The actions were all dominated by formalities, the non-observance of which rendered them invalid. So also were some contracts or modes of acquiring property, but along with them were informal acts which had a remarkable future before them.

The law may say to a person, "If you want this particular result, you must act as follows." If so, it will probably prescribe a particular formality. Or, on the other hand, it may accept what a person normally does in order to achieve a particular result and attribute to it the result that is normally aimed at; the act will then usually be informal. Where an act is required to be formal, the person doing it is made conscious of the fact that he is doing something to which the law attaches a legal consequence. If there is no such requirement, it is more than possible that he may be unaware of such a consequence and be quite without any intention of producing it. He appears to himself to be acting on the business or social, not on the legal plane. He will be like M. Jourdain in *Le Bourgeois Gentilhomme,* when he was surprised to find that he was speaking prose.

There is of course a place for both informal and formal acts. Although the modern world prefers to act informally, there may be situations where it is very important to bring to a person's notice that what he proposes to do will have a particular legal effect. Moreover, it may be necessary to be able to recognize a particular act by its outward form, especially when effect has to be given to it with extreme rapidity, as when a strictly defined form given to a cheque permits a bank cashier to pay without having to ask unnecessary questions. However, the more one requires formalities, the more one tries to canalize human activity according to preconceived ideas. There ought to be room for people to experiment, to invent ways of doing business which do not conform to predetermined forms.

The problem that then faces the jurist is one of interpreting the informal acts that are thus rendered necessary. It seems clear that the Roman jurists were more interested in solving such problems than in anything else, and moreover that this part of their activity has been of greater influence and of greater value than any other in the development of medieval and modern continental law.

It looks as though in handling these questions they made a major "break-through." Interpretation means for us elucidating the meaning of words. This task was of course one with which the Roman jurists were familiar from an early date. They were also capable of interpreting tendentiously in order to achieve a result never intended by the draftsman. But it seems that they did something quite new in accepting as valid and legally efficacious the ordinary informal acts of everyday life and in working out their legal implications on a basis of common sense. Here a few interrelated examples will do much to explain the nature of their achievement.

The Romans used the names Titius, Maevius, and Seius as English lawyers use John Doe, Richard Roe, and William Styles to denote the *dramatis personae* of legal problems. Now suppose that Titius, out of the goodness of his heart, gratuitously lends Maevius a horse for the afternoon and Maevius returns the horse in a damaged condition. Will Maevius be liable to compensate Titius for the damage? Will Maevius have a claim against Titius if the horse throws and injures him? Or again, if Seius, as a friendly act, lets Titius leave a jar of wine in his house for a short time because Titius wants to lighten the load he is carrying home, and when Titius calls for it he finds that it has been damaged and some of the wine has been lost, will Seius be liable to compensate Titius? Will Seius have claim against Titius if the wine has leaked and spoilt a valuable rug? Would the answers to any of these questions have been different if Titius had charged Maevius for the hire of the horse or Seius had charged Titius for the storage of the jar? We must assume that, as would probably have been the case, nothing had been said by any one of the parties about the possibility of damage.

It seems probable that the original answers to these questions were (1) that Maevius would be liable to Titius without proof of any fault on his part, unless indeed the damage was done by the sort of extraordinary accident which English lawyers call an act of God; (2) that Titius would be liable to Maevius only if he knew of the horse's dangerous propensity; (3) that Seius would be liable to Titius only if he had intentionally damaged the jar; (4) that Titius would be liable to Seius if he either knew or ought reasonably to have known that the jar was leaky; and (5) that if it had been agreed that the use of the horse and the storage of the jar were to be paid for, the damage would in each case have to be paid for if caused by the intentional or careless conduct of Titius, Maevius or Seius.

These are all common-sense solutions arrived at by asking what was meant by gratuitously lending or taking a thing on deposit or by letting it out on hire or storing it for reward. But although the Romans did not express themselves in that way, it has long been recognized that they constitute a mass of systematic doctrine, according to which, if both parties stood to receive reciprocal benefits, both should show reasonable diligence, but where one party alone stood to receive a benefit, that party was liable for careless or even accidental damage, whereas the other party was liable only for damage which he had caused intentionally. Many of these and similar solutions later underwent modifications, which need not be discussed here; they too were made on common-sense grounds.

Perhaps in the long run the fact that the jurists should have asked themselves what was implied in such informal acts and should have given a series of common-sense answers to the question has been of greater importance than the answers they actually gave; for they created a method of developing the law which has been a pattern for all future ages.

The republican jurists had subjected the ordinary contractual dealings of everyday life to a certain amount of analysis and classification, distinguishing, for instance, sale from hire or partnership, and, what needs to be specially mentioned, providing each of them with its own action or pair of actions if enforcement were needed. In doing so, they contrived to give to each so-called contractual figure a specific recognizable shape, while covering with only a few such figures almost the whole range of social and commercial intercourse.

It is easy to see that such a technique could be very fertile, that one solution of a problem could lead to another by a process of generalizing from a number of cases and applying the principle so arrived at to new cases, or even by mere analogy. By a cruel misfortune legal historians cannot see the republican Roman jurists at work as they made their most crucial innovations in handling private law. For the necessary steps were taken during the two or three centuries before Cicero, a period of enormous importance in the history of Roman law, but of which we can say little more than that when it started the law had hardly passed its primitive stage and it ended in an atmosphere of rationality and even sophistication.

How much of this was original and how much derived from Greek sources it is impossible to determine. We know that the Romans attributed no importance to outside influences and regarded other people's notions of law as "almost ridiculous."

The importance of informal acts was enhanced by the need to deal with the business relations of foreigners. It seems certain that Roman law at first governed only Roman citizens; we have at any rate clear evidence that early statutes did not govern foreigners. Now although the Roman people could remain indifferent to the family relations and succession rights of foreigners, they had to provide for the settlement of business disputes between Romans and foreigners. Thus by the first century B.C. all informal acts could be effectually done by foreigners as well as by Roman citizens, the most important formal contract, the *stipulatio,* was available to them, and the courts were open to them as well as to Roman citizens, the procedural stage before the praetor, which had hitherto been formalistic, having become informal.

Thus on the one hand, the law was subjected to forces which tended to make it more and more universal, and, on the other, the informal acts came to prevail over those that were formal, even when Roman citizens were dealing among themselves. In order to become universal, Roman law had to pay particular attention to informal acts, since foreigners could not be expected to know the Roman formalities; and any advantage that informality could confer on foreigners had to be accorded to Roman citizens too.

This part of Roman law available to citizens and foreigners alike became known as the *ius gentium,* in contrast to the *ius civile* available to citizens alone. It did not bear the meaning it acquired in modern times, that of International Law, for it was in no sense a law between states. There is, however, this much to be said for the transference, that what common sense prescribed for the business relations between private persons, some of whom might belong to different states, might properly govern the relations of one state to another; and indeed many of the principles of International Law were originally taken from the Roman *ius gentium.*

In the end substantially all Roman law, with the important exception of those parts which governed the family and succession on death, were made applicable to foreigners as well as to Roman citizens, and when early in the third century A.D. Caracalla extended citizenship to almost all the free inhabitants of the Empire, the whole of Roman law came to be of universal application. Moreover, such need as still survived to use the formal acts gradually disappeared and eventually those acts were themselves abolished.

The activity of the jurists culminated under the Severi in the writings of Papinian, Paul and Ulpian, all of whom served as heads of the imperial civil service. Although all of them became famous as great lawyers, Paul and Ulpian owe their prominence in part to the fact that they summed up what their predecessors had achieved. After them came the collapse of the central government known as the Anarchy, and then Diocletian's reorganization under an absolute monarchy, which historians call the Dominate. In those circumstances the summing-up of the Severan jurists proved to be final, and all subsequent legal development was by so-called *constitutiones* issued in the Emperor's name. The old law which had had its source in common sense came to be known as *ius,* or law *par excellence.* The new law emanating from the sovereign will of the Emperor usurped the title of *lex,* which had once dignified the enactments of the sovereign people. The distinction bears a rough resemblance to the English distinction between common law and statute.

The period of the Dominate is also marked by a strange phenomenon. Although the substance of the law was on the whole greatly improved by contact with the Hellenistic East, there was a serious decline in legal proficiency from the high level of intellectual mastery shown by the great jurists of the Principate. Moreover, however necessary recourse to their works might be in the practical conduct of affairs, it became increasingly difficult to consult and understand such a vast and, one may conjecture, not wholly accessible mass of legal literature, the more so because it comprised for the most part actual or hypothetical cases discussed separately and with little or no explanation of the doctrinal connexions between them.

In the sixth century Justinian decided to enact or re-enact in legislative form all the existing law, from every source, that he wished to preserve. There was no question of rewriting the law; all that could be done was to make selections from the decisions and orders of the Emperors and from the writings, the latest of which were now over two hundred years old, of the jurists, in both cases with such omissions, alterations or additions as the lapse of time had made necessary.

The various committees that Justianian appointed for this purpose produced three works, (1) the *Codex,* a new edition of the imperial constitutions, including some issued by Justinian himself, (2) the *Digest,* or *Pandects,* edited fragments from the works of the jurists, and (3) the *Institutes,* an introduction to the law for students, which was a new edition of the *Institutes of Gaius,* supplemented by extracts from similar works of roughly the same date and by new material provided by the compilers. Once promulgated by Justinian both *Codex* and *Digest* and, oddly enough, the *Institutes* also were given legislative force.

The *Institutes* are easily read and understood. They are arranged according to an order which, though it can be criticized on many grounds, is clear and perspicuous. The task of reading and understanding the *Digest* is formidable. It is of the same order of size as the Bible, and is divided into fifty books containing in all 432 titles. The titles are the important units, each of which purports to contain all the juristic material on a particular topic, such as marriage, the contract of partnership, or damage to property. The order of the titles, though unsystematic, is not in practice an obstacle to understanding. Inside each title the order is often so unintelligible that the first thing the student must do is to rearrange the various fragments of which it is composed, in the knowledge that there is quite possibly something essential to a full understanding of the topic in another, quite remote title, coupled with an apprehension that it may conflict with what he has already read. Fortunately a study of the *Institutes* greatly lightens the task of understanding the *Digest.* The *Codex,* being in a sense a supplement to the *Digest,* would be approached last, and consequently with less difficulty. In any case it is much less important for private law.

Justinian's legal activity did not cease with the publication of these three works. He continued to issue constitutions, a very few of which contained important modifications of private law. They were later collected together under the title *Novellae Constitutiones,* and are known to the modern world as the *Novels. Codex, Digest, Institutes* and *Novels* are collectively called the *Corpus Juris Civilis,* or the *Corpus Juris* for short.

With a few exceptions, far the most important of which is the *Institutes of Gaius,* contained in a palimpsest discovered in 1816, all that we know of the Roman law of the ancient world is contained in the *Corpus Juris.* It may be said that without the *Corpus Juris* later ages would have had an extremely jejune acquaintance with Roman law, and even if everything but the *Digest* had been preserved, Roman law could not have exerted much influence on the development of modern law. Whatever sins Justinian's compilers may have been guilty of in mauling the original texts of the jurists, they performed an inestimable service in transmitting the real Roman law to medieval and modern times.

The later history of Roman law in the eastern Mediterranean may be briefly dismissed. The knowledge of it was never lost, though only from time to time could the *Corpus Juris* as a whole be put to profitable use in a Greek translation. It was theoretically in force until the last generation in the Kingdom of Greece. There was, however, no substantial development apart from a slight sporadic legislation.

Roman law in the West has a much more interesting and more important history. But first came a phase of acute degeneration; a systematic and detailed body of law was inappropriate to the abject conditions of Barbarian Europe. Moreover, the new problems of a declining economy received no answer from it. It is probable that the *Digest* was never put to practical use for several centuries after its promulgation. The *Institutes* never fell out of use; they were short and simple enough to be understood. However, for the most part Roman law, where it remained in force, seems to have operated as a sort of custom, as was indeed natural in a society where hardly anyone outside the clergy was literate.

The revival of Roman law studies from about the middle of the eleventh century was therefore substantially a rebirth. It was part of an intellectual reawakening which extended also to philosophy, theology and Canon law, and for which it is impossible to assign any clear single cause. The lawyers of any country that had once been governed by Roman law must always have been under a duty to study the *Digest;* the Italian lawyers were under a special duty, for were they not subjects of the Holy Roman Empire, and was not the Emperor of their day the legitimate successor to Justinian? Why were they so slow to do their duty? A legend was once current that the Florentinus, the manuscript of the *Digest* from which all others are derived, was discovered almost miraculously at Amalfi in the eleventh century. That legend is no longer believed, and we may prefer to think that although the text of the *Digest* was always there to be read, no one before that date had enough courage and intelligence to undertake the task.

Much of the attractiveness which Roman law possessed for the men into whose hands the *Digest* now came had little relation to its inherent qualities. Almost all other law, apart from Canon law, was unwritten custom. Roman law was contained in books; and the men of the twelfth century were starved of reading matter. It is well known to medievalists that in the Middle Ages almost any book possessed some measure of authority. The Bible came first, followed by the Fathers, but Aristotle, in a Latin translation of an Arabic translation, enjoyed an authority not far behind theirs. Classical antiquity as a whole was regarded with veneration, extending even to the frivolities of Ovid. A parallel can easily be found in the tendency of uneducated people even today to believe everything they see in print; but medieval man was unaccustomed to verify statements by experiment. First, then, the *Digest* was attractive merely because it was a book.

Secondly, it was in Latin. The knowledge of Latin had never disappeared; it had survived in a sufficiently pure form alongside of the Romance languages into which it had broken down in ordinary discourse. The Western Church needed it in order to use its patristic literature, and had to maintain a means of communication intelligible to the clergy in every country. Latin remained the *lingua franca* of the literate world. Thus the *Digest* was readable to anyone prepared to take trouble.

Thirdly, there came a time when someone appeared who wanted to see what was in the *Digest*—that was probably bound to happen sooner or later—and was not put off by the difficulty of the task. There was, first of all, the difficulty of the language itself, for *Digest* Latin does not read like the simple narrative Latin of the Middle Ages. Secondly, the order in which the various topics are treated in the *Digest* is extremely unhelpful, not to say exasperating. On the other hand, to use the jargon of the present day, the *Digest* presented a challenge to anyone who wished to master its contents, and men were found who had the necessary intelligence, energy and intellectual curiosity to take it up. Moreover, the greater the difficulty, the more insistent was the challenge. For this was the age of the earlier scholastics who founded the University of Paris and were determined to employ reason to solve the riddle of the universe. Bologna produced men prepared to pit their brains against this most difficult law book, and, once a start had been made, nothing could stop the onrush of Roman law studies.

It soon became evident that, even with the help given by the more logically arranged *Institutes,* this was no task for amateurs. The men who studied the *Digest* rapidly became professionals and trained others in a professional skill. Moreover, they acquired a proprietary interest in their knowledge and skill, which they were determined to defend against all comers. Had the task of understanding the *Digest* been easy, it would have been, in the first place, intellectually unsatisfying and therefore not attractive to men of first-rate ability, and, secondly, open to all the world.

Accordingly all the cards were stacked in favour of Roman law, irrespective of its intrinsic merits. These were, however, substantial.

Not only did it provide medieval lawyers in great abundance with the detailed solutions of practical problems, but it possessed a powerful structure based on clear distinctions. It distinguished for instance between property and obligation, protecting the former against all comers, but treating the latter as a mere bond between two persons, giving the one rights only against the other or creating reciprocal rights and duties between them. In contrast to feudalism, it did not impose on the owner of a thing a duty, merely by reason of his ownership, to perform positive acts in favour of another private person. Nor did ownership of itself imply negative duties beyond a very small number which hardly diminished its economic value. An owner was indeed allowed to create rights over his property which could be enforced against anyone into whose ownership it came. Such rights exceeded merely personal rights created by obligations, but they were jealously limited so as to encumber ownership as little as possible. One variety, known as praedial servitudes, corresponded to the easements and profits of English law, more particularly rights of way or of digging lime. Since they could be exercised only by owners of neighbouring land, they were allowed in order to enhance the value of one piece of land at the expense of another. The other variety, which conferred on a person the right to the income derived from the property, could last at most for his lifetime and could not be alienated. The pattern of property rights was much simpler and more easily recognized than in customary law. Such simplicity and sharpness of outline are of immense value in teaching untutored people to think clearly about law.

Most important of all to an age of rationalists was the intensely rational character of Roman law as portrayed in the *Digest* and its freedom from relativity to any particular time or place, once such readily detachable topics as slavery and the family were put on one side. That it was law laid down by a Roman Emperor made the study of it necessary, but its sixth-century origin in no way made the doctrine contained in it out of date. Even to this day, however absorbing the study of its history may be, it is still possible to treat most of the law comprised in the *Digest* merely as good law, which H. A. L. Fisher in his little book on Napoleon described as "organized common sense."

Thus we come back by a broad circle to common sense.

Perhaps the greatest contribution made by Roman law to world civilization has been its demonstration that it is possible to construct a body of law upon a basis of common sense that can be accepted by different peoples at different stages of their development. It has been said that the difficulty with natural law is to get any detail into it. But this is what, as has already been shown, the Romans achieved by a converse process, by working out in ample detail the common-sense implications of certain institutions and gradually getting rid of the less rational elements in their law. Moreover they extended what had been the law for the citizens of a small city state to all the inhabitants of a large empire, irrespective of the language, literature or religion in which they had been nurtured. Roman law could not have become the universal law of the Mediterranean world without also becoming rational; rationalism might not have been so appealing to the jurists who imparted to the law its dominant character if they had not felt the need to extend it throughout the Empire.

We must be on our guard against exaggerating the extent of common sense, so acceptable to those who revived the study of Roman law in the Middle Ages. Not every irrational element was expelled from even the most rational parts of the law. Most Romanists would consider the law governing the contract of sale to be one of the most rational parts of Roman law, yet it contains rules the survival of which is hard to justify, however rational we might judge them once to have been did we know their history. Moreover, some of the most well-established institutions of Roman society, such as the *patria potestas,* the power exercised by a father over his issue in the male line of whatever age, continued even in the time of Justinian to resist the sapping operation of common sense; and throughout antiquity a strange inhibition prevented the Romans from admitting the legal possibility of such an indispensable part of modern life as direct agency in contract. Perhaps the need to conform to some irrational elements is necessary if law is to be obeyed as such and not merely in so far as each man considers it reasonable.

However, once medieval lawyers had seen the possibility of using common sense as a test of legal validity, there was no reason why they should always respect the inhibitions of jurists who lived a thousand years earlier. Rationalism operates by fits and starts, gaining momentum and then losing it as what is happening dawns on those with conservative prejudices and they proceed to organize their defences. But once the taste for the common-sense solution of difficult problems is acquired, it is never entirely lost.

In this connexion regard must be paid to the distinction between policy and technique. The purpose of private law being to organize civil society, effect is given to fluctuating views of what is right and proper; the determination of such views is the function of policy. How they are to be put in operation is the function of technique. Now we may say metaphorically that the law itself fixes the policy governing large portions of human intercourse; and in that department technique signifies the means afforded by the law to turn policy into rules of conduct, to ascertain those rules and to enforce them when necessary. However, over a very wide field the law has no opinion as to what ought to be done, but leaves the choice of policy to individuals acting solely or in concert; it contents itself with providing a technical apparatus of instruments or devices, the operation of which is governed by legal rules and principles, but which have for their object to enable men to act purposefully and to obtain results which would otherwise depend entirely on the goodwill of their fellow men. They are told how to act in order to attain certain ends and are guaranteed success so far as is humanly possible.

That kind of technique, dealing as it does with such matters as the making of contracts or wills, the acquisition of property and the judicial protection of rights, is what peculiarly exercises the minds of lawyers, who strive by working out its logical implications and reducing them to a system, to furnish more and more exact and efficient instruments of social intercourse. If the technique is well suited to its purpose it can be adapted and developed so as to meet new circumstances in accordance with the demands of common sense. In contrast, where the rules and principles governing conduct are the product of a policy laid down by the law itself, they can be adapted to new conditions only by a deliberate change in the law, usually a difficult and hazardous process, and one that lawyers are on the whole reluctant to undertake. Accordingly they often come to represent the common sense not of the present but of a past age.

That the Roman jurists conformed to this pattern of lawyerly activity is shown by the apparently disproportionate amount of space in the *Digest* devoted to some topics at the expense of others. Those which are most extensively discussed are precisely those on which argument on a basis of common sense is likely to be most fruitful. Thus there is a limit to what can be got out of discussing intestate succession, whereas the interpretation of wills has no end. Marriage, though it is entered into voluntarily, does not admit of variations, whereas contracts, though most of them fall into established classes, can present innumerable problems; hence the law of marriage attracted less attention than the law of contracts.

For about two hundred years the first school of medieval jurists took whatever came into their hands, and expounded it as though it was existing law, although some parts of the *Corpus Juris,* such as those dealing with slavery, marriage or intestate succession, had no relevance to the circumstances of their own time. They were concerned to understand whatever they read, and since cross-references were needed and sometimes one text had to be contrasted and if possible reconciled with another, they wrote in the manuscripts marginal notes known as *glosses;* hence they acquired the title of Glossators. The next school, that of the *Post-Glossators* or *Commentators,* which lasted in one way or another until the seventeenth century, took a more practical view of Roman law, paying attention only to what was profitable to them and reconciling it with existing practice. They carried further the process characteristic of the Roman jurists, that of working out the implications of the existing law, each generation adding new courses to what its predecessors had built. This very practical way of dealing with Roman law roused the scholarly ire of the so-called *Humanistic* school, mainly in France, who insisted, though without convincing practical lawyers, on the need to go back to the original Roman texts.

Of all the Roman law that was expounded and studied in the universities only part became "received" into the actual law of the various countries of western and central Europe. Everywhere it had to compete with varying regional and local customs and naturally with varying results. Moreover the uniform Canon law of the Catholic Church had preempted certain fields of activity. It would be dangerous to generalize; much historical research needs to be done before we can fully understand the *Reception* of Roman law in any one country. There is, however, reason to believe that by and large it was the Roman technique that was received rather than the Roman policy. It was used when people wanted to do things they had not done before and had therefore no way of doing them, or where the current ways of doing them were awkward and obviously inferior to those provided by Roman law. More often, perhaps, use was made of the Roman ways of interpreting words or acts. In countries such as England and Germany, where Roman law was refused admittance, these technical aids could not be used. In England, it has been said that the law received in the twelfth and thirteenth centuries an inoculation of Roman law that preserved it from further infection. Once Englishmen had learnt from a cursory study of Roman law how to think like lawyers they reacted against it and built up in the Inns of Court a powerful profession trained on non-Roman lines which was able to find its salvation by developing a technique of its own; and, except where a specialized group of lawyers used Roman law to administer the law of wills and maritime law, the ban remained. In Germany, where there was no such profession, use had to be made by the princes of persons who had been trained in Roman law, and who had no knowledge of any technique other than the Roman; and for that and other reasons the dam was burst and Roman law came flooding in.

This is not to say that the policy of Roman law had no influence; but there is more than a suspicion that the persons or classes dominant at any time took what they wanted of it and allowed it to lead them where they wished to go, disregarding it when it ran counter to their desires. In this they were aided by the fact that the *Corpus Juris,* by imperfectly reconciling texts from different ages, could be made to yield evidence of different and even contradictory policies. Thus some modern generations were able to use Roman technique, devised to effectuate the policy of the last centuries of the ancient world, in order to make property inalienable and keep it in a family for a long period, whereas later generations, in their desire to keep property as far as possible alienable, appealed to what was almost certainly the prevailing policy of the late republic and principate. Moreover, non-Romanized English law could favour some of the same fundamental policies as the Romanized law of France. It has, for instance, been almost an article of faith with Continental capitalists and socialists alike that Roman law was an essential factor in the emergence of modern capitalism; yet the economic changes came just as easily, and sometimes faster, in England than on the Continent.

In the end Roman law helped to dig its own grave. It has been well said that "Like the arch, Roman Law never sleeps"; it is always subject to strains and stresses. It has always strained towards the rational and the universal. Eighteenth-century lawyers on the Continent, sharing the rationalistic spirit of the age, sought to find a way out of the intolerable disorder of their laws. Their predecessors had, over many generations, attained to a sufficient mastery of the Roman texts to see that they could be purged of their remaining irrationalities and anachronisms and rearranged in a rational order together with the non-Roman elements in each country's law. And here the *Institutes of Justinian* came into their own, as showing how general principles could be detached from their detailed application. The disorder of the *Digest* could be made to yield the necessary materials, the elegant arrangement of the *Institutes* the form. The solution the jurists everywhere demanded was the creation of a common law by selecting the best elements from the regional and local customs and fusing them with the received portions of Roman law, followed by its enunciation in a civil code. The earliest such code that is still in force is the French Civil Code (the *Code Napoleon*) of 1804. It was adopted with modifications by most countries in western and central Europe, except Germany and Switzerland, each of which resisted on various grounds for about a century and then enacted a Civil Code of its own on more modern and systematic lines.

This amalgam of modernized Roman law with non-Roman elements is known to English lawyers as the "Civil Law," a term which has in due course been accepted by all who are engaged in the comparative study of law; and its practitioners and students are often called "civilians." The non-Roman elements are not always of customary origin or even of very modern development; in many countries they are a part of religion, for instance Islamic, Jewish, Hindu. What is distinguished from Civil Law under the name of Common Law has very much the same general structure, the place of Roman law being taken by a body of doctrine based mainly on cases decided by judges, at first in England and later also in countries to which English law has from time to time been taken.

If Civil Law and Common Law are understood in these broad senses, they now divide between themselves the whole world outside the Scandinavian countries, Afghanistan and Arabia. The Common Law has hardly gone outside the countries in which English is the *lingua franca,* that is to say, most of what is or was the Commonwealth and the United States. The Civil Law, with its hard core of Roman law, has the rest, including such Asian countries as Japan, Thailand, Indonesia, Iran and Lebanon, such African countries as Egypt, the Congo and the former colonies of France, and the whole of Latin America. Behind the Iron Curtain too, in the restricted sphere still governed by private law, the Civil Law prevails.

Lawyers in all these countries are conscious enough of differences which keep them apart, but to English lawyers they look very much alike, because they think in a Roman way which is alien to us; and their minds are set in such a common direction as to enable an Egyptian student to study law with profit in Paris or Rome or a Greek in Lausanne or Bonn.

An important group of countries were originally civilian, but have since been subjected to such powerful influences from England or the United States that their laws are now properly called hybrid systems. Such are Scots law, the Roman-Dutch law of South Africa, the laws of Quebec, Louisiana and the Philippines.

Reference to the original Roman texts is now almost confined to one or two countries such as South Africa, and even there is uncommon. The study of Roman law is now purely academic, though it may serve the practical purpose of introducing students to general legal ideas and, in Common Law countries, of preparing them for the study of modern Civil

Law systems. It may be doubted whether any more help can be got from Roman law in the solution of modern problems, for not only have the best parts of it already been absorbed into existing law, but the world is turning away from the kinds of society to which it has been found appropriate. We may not wish for a return of the conditions which caused the Reception of Roman law.

9. The Problem of the Historical Jesus

JOACHIM JEREMIAS

The life and teachings of Jesus Christ have had a greater influence on more people in Western history than those of any other individual. This much can be stated about Jesus, without fear of contradiction, but little else can. The major difficulty in attempting to reconstruct the life and teachings of Jesus is that the primary sources about him, the Gospels, contain very few biographical or personal details; they are for the most part collections of sayings or deeds attributed to Jesus by his followers. Compounding this problem is the fact that the Gospels as we have them represent compilations of earlier oral tradition and nonextant written records. The earliest of the Gospels in its present form was probably compiled three or four decades later than the events it purports to treat. These considerations have resulted in some difficulty in distinguishing between the "the Jesus of history" and the picture presented of him by Christian writers of the first and second centuries.

That some people may deny Jesus and his message have any significance for the Christian faith may, as Professor Jeremias observes, seem absurd, but it was an almost ineluctable conclusion of the critical scholarship of the nineteenth century. In this article Joachim Jeremias, a Lutheran and eminent New Testament scholar, traces the development of the controversy over the search for the "Jesus of history," which has played a key role in New Testa-

Source: Joachim Jeremias, *The Problem of the Historical Jesus,* trans. Norman Perrin (Philadelphia: Fortress Press, 1964), pp. 1–24. Copyright © 1964 by The Fortress Press. Reprinted by permission of the publisher. [Most footnotes omitted.]

ment studies for almost two centuries. His article is an excellent example of what the German scholars call Forschungsbericht, *a review of research. In addition to surveying the history of the problem, the article should make the reader aware of the significance of the controversy and of the nature of textual criticism. It raises questions for discussion about the nature of the books of the New Testament as historical sources; about the need for the historian to guard against distortion and modernization in an attempt to understand the past; and about the nature of Christ's message and its relation to early (and, of course, later) Christianity. For further reading, the New Testament itself, now available in several recent translations, is the fundamental source for early Christianity. A balanced account of Jesus and his ministry can be read in C. H. Dodd,* The Founder of Christianity *(1970); for Paul and his work in spreading the faith among the gentiles, A. D. Nock's* St. Paul *(1938) is still worth reading; and R. M. Grant's* Augustus to Constantine *(1970), from which the selection following this one is taken, traces the development of Christianity during the first three centuries of its existence.*

To anyone who is not aware of the controversy, the question whether the historical Jesus and his message have any significance for the Christian faith must sound absurd. No one in the ancient church, no one in the church of the Reformation period and of the two succeeding centuries thought of asking such a question. How is it possible that today this question is being asked in all seriousness, that it even occupies a central place in New Testament debate, and that in many quarters it is being answered with a decisive negative? For a widely held theological position maintains that the historical Jesus and his message have no, or at least no decisive, significance for the Christian faith. We ask: (1) Why is such a point of view possible? How has it arisen? What is its basis? (2) What can be said by way of criticism of this view? and (3) What is the relation between the good tidings of Jesus and the proclamation of the church?

131

Jeremias

THE PROBLEM
OF THE
HISTORICAL
JESUS

The Theology of the Kerygma

In order to understand the "theology of the kerygma," [1] as represented by Rudolf Bultmann and his school, it is necessary to retrace the route by which this position has been reached. We shall here attempt to sketch that route in broad outline.

HERMANN SAMUEL REIMARUS

The problem of the historical Jesus is of recent origin; the date of its birth can be precisely fixed at 1778. That date tells us that the problem of the historical Jesus is a child of the Enlightenment. Previous centuries held fast to the position that the gospels gave us absolutely reliable information about Jesus; they saw no problem here. New Testament study of

---

[1] ["Kerygma" represents a Greek term meaning "proclamation," found eight times in the New Testament.—EDITOR.]

the gospels in the two centuries before the Enlightenment essentially confined itself to the task of paraphrasing and harmonizing the four gospels. In practice New Testament exegesis was a handmaid to the study of dogmatics. It was at the end of the eighteenth century that it was first recognized that the historical Jesus and the Christ proclaimed in the gospels and by the church are not the same. The man who announced this with brutal candor was Hermann Samuel Reimarus. Born in Hamburg in 1694, he was a professor of oriental languages, i.e., he was not a theologian. He died in 1768 in his native city. At his death he left a manuscript which came into the hands of Gotthold Ephraim Lessing, who, between 1774 and 1778, published seven excerpts from it. The seventh piece bore the title *Von dem Zwecke Jesu und seiner Jünger: Noch ein Fragment des Wolfenbüttelschen Ungenannten.*[2] We must, says Reimarus, distinguish between the "aim" of Jesus, that is, the purpose which he set before himself, and the "aim" of his disciples. Jesus' purpose must be understood in the light of the cry from the cross, "My God, my God, why hast thou forsaken me?"—words which proclaimed the failure of his purpose. That is to say: Jesus was a Jewish political Messiah, who sought to set up an earthly kingdom and to deliver the Jews from a foreign yoke. His cry from the cross shows that his "aim" had not been achieved. The "aim" of his disciples was totally different. Confronted by the collapse of their dreams, what were they to do? They had no wish to return to their trade. But how were they to live? They contrived to steal the corpse of Jesus and, by inventing the message of his resurrection and return, gathered adherents. Hence it was the disciples who created the figure of Christ.

Great agitation followed upon the publication of this hate-filled pamphlet, and it rightly met with general rejection. Hate is no guide to historical truth. Nevertheless, Reimarus, the outsider, had been the first to perceive clearly a fact which had hitherto been overlooked. He had seen that the Jesus of history and the Christ preached by the church are not the same. History and dogma are two different things. The problem of the historical Jesus starts with Reimarus. Albert Schweitzer rightly entitled the first edition of his history of the study of the life of Jesus *Von Reimarus zu Wrede.*

REIMARUS TO KÄHLER

Reimarus' portrayal of the historical Jesus was clearly absurd and amateurish. Jesus was no political revolutionary. Our sources bear unambiguous and trustworthy testimony to the fact that he was sharply opposed to the nationalistic Zealot tendencies in the world of his day. Still, in his contention that the historical Jesus was different from the Christ as depicted in the gospels, notably in John, Reimarus had raised a question which could not be evaded, namely, who really was Jesus of Nazareth?

The study of the life of Jesus in which the Enlightenment now en-

---

[2] "Concerning the Aim of Jesus and his Disciples: Another Fragment by the Anonymous Author from Wolfenbüttel."

gaged sought to answer precisely this question. This study was inspired by a liberal theology and, indeed, represented a revolt against ecclesiastical dogma. This whole scholarly activity, centered on the historical Jesus, represented an attempt to break loose from dogma. The battle cry was, "Back to Jesus, the man from Nazareth!" Not christological dogma, but the personality and religion of Jesus were the decisive factors.

Under the aegis of this watchword a multitude of lives of Jesus came into being, and we smile as we read them today. These lives vary greatly. The rationalists pictured Jesus as a preacher of morality, the idealists as the ideal Man; the aesthetes extolled him as the master of words and the socialists as the friend of the poor and as the social reformer, while the innumerable pseudo-scholars made of him a fictional character. Jesus was modernized. These lives of Jesus are mere products of wishful thinking. The final outcome was that every epoch and every theology found in the personality of Jesus the reflection of its own ideals, and every author the reflection of his own views. What had gone wrong? It was that, unconsciously, dogma had been replaced by psychology and fantasy. For all these lives of Jesus have one thing in common: their delineation of the personality of Jesus had been achieved by means of these two things, psychology and fantasy. The main share of the responsibility rests, not with the sources alone, but with the modern writers' uncontrolled psychologizing. It was a real tragedy that Albert Schweitzer, who throughout his whole book had exposed with ruthless insight the true nature of this wishful thinking, should himself have been ensnared by the fallacy of psychological reconstruction when he interpreted Matthew 10:23 to mean that Jesus' disappointment concerning his expectations of the imminent parousia brought the great turning point in his life, leading him to embark upon the way of the cross as the means to force the coming of God's kingdom.

133

Jeremias

THE PROBLEM
OF THE
HISTORICAL
JESUS

At first the so-called positive theology [3] wisely confined itself essentially to warding off these attempts at reconstruction, and hence to an apologetic stance. Not until 1892 did positive theology pass over to the attack with a programmatic book by Martin Kähler, a book in advance of its time and embodying a specific thesis: *Der sogenannte historische Jesus und der geschichtliche, biblische Christus.*[4] The title of this work must be

[3] [As employed in nineteenth-century biblical studies in Germany, "positive theology" designated the position of those who, while wishing, in varying degrees, to employ the tools of historical scholarship, rejected the "negative" and often theologically liberal conclusions of many of the critical scholars. In life-of-Jesus research it opposed a "life" like that by Ernest Renan.—EDITOR.]

[4] [*The So-called Historical Jesus and the Historic, Biblical Christ.* To make a distinction in English between *historisch* and *geschichtlich* is the despair of most translators. Some challenge the distinction made even in German and feel that it is quite arbitrary in English, cf., however, *Webster's Third New International Dictionary* (Springfield, Mass.: G. & C. Merriam, 1961), p. 1073; "historical" is defined as ". . . having the character of history," and "historic" as "having . . . significance, or consequence." Professor Jeremias' explanation clarifies well what Kähler meant.—EDITOR.]

carefully examined if we wish to understand Kähler's thesis. Kähler distinguishes, on the one hand, between "Jesus" and "Christ," and, on the other hand, between *historisch* ("historical") and *geschichtlich* ("historic"). "Jesus" denoted for Kähler the man of Nazareth, as the lives of Jesus had described and were describing him, while "Christ" denoted the Savior proclaimed by the church. The term *historisch* meant for him the bare facts of the past, while *geschichtlich* meant that which possesses abiding significance. That is, he placed over against one another the so-called "historical Jesus," as the writers of the lives of Jesus had sought to reconstruct him, and the "historic, biblical Christ," as the apostles had proclaimed him. His thesis runs: only the biblical Christ can be apprehended by us, and he alone is of abiding significance for faith. Only as the gospels portray him for us, and not as the self-styled scientific reconstructions present him, does "the undeniable impression of the fullest reality" make its impact upon us. It should be noted—because it is often overlooked—that Kähler was convinced of the "reliability" of the "vivid and coherent image of a Man, an image we never fail to recognize," that confronts us in the New Testament records. At first, however, Kähler's challenge went unheard; only in our time, when Rudolf Bultmann took it up and reformulated it, has it come into its own.

MODERN CRITICAL THEOLOGY

Inaugurated by Rudolf Bultmann and under his influence a truly fascinating development has taken place in recent decades. After a hundred and fifty years of preoccupation with the historical Jesus, critical theology came to recognize that it had undertaken an impossible task; it had the courage to acknowledge this fact openly, and with banners flying went over into the enemy camp. It turned its back on its history, it endorsed Kähler's views, at least in their negative aspects, it declared its preoccupation with the historical Jesus to have been an insoluble and fruitless undertaking, and it withdrew into the invulnerable bastion of the kerygma, the proclamation about Christ.

Critical theology has based its renunciation of the historical Jesus and return to the apostolic preaching about Christ upon two considerations.

(1) It points to the peculiar character of our sources. We have no writings from the hand of Jesus, such as we possess from the hand of the apostle Paul. On the contrary, we know Jesus only from the gospels, which are not biographies but testimonies of faith. The gospels contain a great deal of material which has been extensively edited in the course of transmission, and many legends (one need refer only to the miracle stories). All four gospels picture Jesus as he is apprehended by the faith of the evangelists: Mark depicts the hidden Son of man; Matthew, the secret King of Israel; Luke, the Lord of the future church; John, the self-revealing Son of man. From this material, as a hundred unavailing attempts have shown, it is not possible to construct a life of Jesus. We must free ourselves from the subjectivity of the so-called "historical Jesus research." We must draw the full consequences of the fact that we can know Jesus

only as clad in the garb of myth. We must acknowledge that we cannot go behind the kerygma; if we attempt to do so nonetheless, we shall find ourselves on shaky ground.

(2) Now it is not as if the sources left us entirely in the lurch, says critical theology. The time is past when an unscientific skepticism could doubt whether Jesus had ever lived at all. On the contrary, we can gain considerable information about Jesus himself and also about his proclamation. But what we arrive at when we analyze the sources with the tools of historical research, says critical theology, yields nothing that would be of significance for faith. For this Jesus of Nazareth was a Jewish prophet. To be sure, he was a prophet who, since he demanded absolute obedience, saw mankind as totally sinful, and proclaimed divine forgiveness to men, had apprehended "the Jewish conception of God in its purity and consistency." He was indeed a prophet who claimed that a man's attitude toward His word determined his attitude toward God. But, for all that, he remained within the framework of Judaism. What he preached was a more radicalized form of Old Testament, Jewish faith in God. For Bultmann, the history of Jesus is part of the history of Judaism, not of Christianity. To be sure, this Jewish prophet is of historical interest for New Testament theology, but he neither has, nor can have, significance for Christian faith, since (and here we have an astonishing thesis) Christianity first began at Easter. Here a decisive point has been reached. Who would ever think of saying that Islam began after Mohammed's death, or Buddhism after the death of Buddha? If we accept the thesis that Christianity began at Easter with the proclamation about the risen Christ, then indeed the logical inference is that, since Jesus was only a Jewish prophet, he does not belong to Christianity. "The message of Jesus," so runs the opening sentence of Bultmann's *Theology of the New Testament,* "belongs to the presuppositions of the theology of the New Testament and is not a part of that theology itself." Here the plural, "presuppositions," must be especially noted. It implies that the message of Jesus is one presupposition of New Testament theology among many others, and perhaps not even the decisive one. Other factors are just as important: the Easter experiences of the disciples, the messianic expectations of Judaism, and the mythology of the pagan world which provided the garment with which Jesus of Nazareth was to be clothed. The study of Jesus and his message may be very interesting and instructive for the historical understanding of the rise of Christianity, but it has no significance for faith.

These, then, are the two bases upon which modern critical theology rests its rejection of the historical Jesus. (1) We cannot write a life of Jesus because the requisite sources are lacking, and (2) what we can regard as historical is a Jewish prophet and his message, neither of which has any significance for faith. Hence it follows that our task today is not to pursue the phantom of the historical Jesus, but to interpret the kerygma, that is, the message of the apostle Paul about the justification of sinners. Admittedly, the Christianity of the Pauline and Johannine communities is a specimen of the syncretism of the Hellenistic period, and as

135

Jeremias

THE PROBLEM
OF THE
HISTORICAL
JESUS

such reflects the religious climate of that day. But this is not an insuperable difficulty. We must demythologize the message and translate it into modern terms, with, let us say, the help of existentialist philosophy.

Gerhard Ebeling states these ideas very bluntly when he says that revelation is "not a historical datum" (*kein historisches Faktum*), nor is it "a historic event" (*ein geschichtliches Geschehen*). Revelation was not accomplished and completed during the years 1–30. Rather, it continues to take place whenever the kerygma is preached; it takes place in the act of faith.

In surveying this position we have outlined, we must first point out its positive aspects. Today critical research is very different from what it was in the previous century. It is bent on taking the entire kerygma into account and giving it its full due. The positive significance of this new stance of critical theology is of course immense. Nevertheless, I can see very grave dangers in this position. They are these: we are in danger of surrendering the affirmation "the Word became flesh" and of dissolving "salvation history," God's activity in the man Jesus of Nazareth and in his message; we are in danger of Docetism,[5] where Christ becomes an idea; we are in danger of putting the proclamation of the apostle Paul in the place of the good tidings of Jesus.

The Crucial Significance of the Historical Jesus

What can be said by way of criticism of the position which we have outlined?

THE NECESSITY OF HISTORICAL STUDY

(1) Without a doubt it is true to say that the dream of ever writing a biography of Jesus is over. It would be disastrous if we were unwilling to heed critical scholarship's salutary caution regarding uncritical use of the gospels. Nevertheless we *must* go back to the historical Jesus and his message. We cannot bypass him. Quite apart from all theological considerations, there are two circumstances which compel us to make the attempt to ascertain the character of the gospel as Jesus proclaimed it. First of all, it is *the sources* which forbid us to confine ourselves to the kerygma of the primitive church and which force us ever and again to raise the question of the historical Jesus and his message. Every verse of the gospels tells us that the origin of Christianity lies not in the kerygma, not in the resurrection experiences of the disciples, not in a "Christ-idea." Every verse tells us, rather, that the origin of Christianity lies in the appearance of the man who was crucified under Pontius Pilate, Jesus of Nazareth, and

---

[5] ["Docetism," from the Greek *dokéin*, to "appear" or "seem," refers to those types of Christian teaching where God is held to have become not really incarnate but only to have "appeared" to become man. It thus undervalues or denies the reality of the life of Jesus.—EDITOR.]

in his message. I must emphasize the last words—*and his message.* The gospel that Jesus proclaimed antedates the kerygma of the primitive community. And as uncertain as many a detail of Jesus' life may be, his message can be clearly ascertained. To be sure, the accounts of Jesus and his message were recounted by the early church as testimonies to its faith, and the gospels are, to be sure, not biographies in the sense of the Greek biographies (that much we have learned). Nevertheless there has been gross exaggeration here. It is not as though everything in the gospels is colored and shaped by the faith of the church and the evangelists. Paul wrote earlier than all four evangelists, and he was *the* great theologian in the Gentile Christian church before the composition of the gospels. But Pauline terminology is discernible only here and there in the gospels. Jesus cannot be relegated to the rank and file of an anonymous primitive community. Over and over again we come across words which unmistakably imply a situation prior to Easter. Only occasionally do we meet with traces here and there of christological overlay; and even if everything were overlaid with Christology, the study of the historical Jesus would still remain an imperative task, since the absence of primary sources should not constitute a reason for abandoning historical research.

(2) But it is not only the sources which compel us to keep on raising the problem of the historical Jesus and his message; the kerygma, too, the preaching about Christ by the early church, leads us back from itself at every turn. For the kerygma refers to a historical event. It proclaims: God was in Christ and reconciled the world to himself. God revealed himself in an event in history. The very heart of the kerygma, that "Christ died for our sins in accordance with the scriptures" (I Corinthians 15:3), represents an interpretation of a historical event: this death happened for us. But this raises the question whether this interpretation of the crucifixion of Jesus has been arbitrarily impressed upon the events, or whether there was some circumstance in the events which caused this interpretation to be attached to it. In other words, we must ask: Did Jesus himself speak of his impending death, and what significance did he attach to it? The same consideration holds good for the proclamation of the resurrection; it always refers back from itself. The risen and exalted Christ, whom the apostles preached and to whom the Christian community prayed, has features—physical characteristics and traits of character —with which the disciples were familiar, the characteristics and traits of their earthly lord. The same is true of Paul and all the rest of the preaching of the early church: they also constantly point back behind themselves. Paul fought the self-righteousness of Jewish legalism, the self-complacency of the pious and their self-glorification, against which he set the message that we are saved by faith alone, that God offers salvation, not to the righteous, but to the sinner who trusts alone in His forgiveness. But just that, although couched in other terms, is the very message of Jesus. It is clear that we cannot understand the message of Paul unless we know the message of Jesus. Whatever statements of the kerygma we may care to examine, their origins are always to be found in the message of

137

Jeremias

THE PROBLEM
OF THE
HISTORICAL
JESUS

Jesus. That the primitive church was clearly aware of this is shown by the fact that it supplemented the kerygma (the missionary preaching) with the didache (instruction for the community),[6] the precipitate of which is preserved for us in the gospels. At no time was there a kerygma in the primitive church without didache.

This, then, is the first consideration: we *must* continually return to the historical Jesus and his message. The sources demand it; the kerygma, which refers us back from itself, also demands it. To put it in theological terms, the Incarnation implies that the story of Jesus is not only a possible subject for historical research, study, and criticism, but demands all of these. We need to know who the Jesus of history was, and what was the content of his message. We may not avoid the offense of the Incarnation. And if it is objected that we fail to apprehend the essential nature of faith if we make historical knowledge the object of faith, and that faith is in this way offered up to such dubious, subjective, and hypothetical study, we can only reply that God has offered up himself. The Incarnation is the self-offering of God, and to that we can only bow in assent.

Indeed, it is precisely at this point that the latest theological developments push on beyond Bultmann's theology of the kerygma. It is now generally acknowledged that the problem of the historical Jesus must be taken seriously, and thus the situation in present-day New Testament studies is not so heterogeneous as it might seem at first sight.

BULWARKS AGAINST THE MODERNIZING OF JESUS

We must venture forth on the road to the historical Jesus and his message, no matter where it may lead us. But, and this is the second consideration, we *can* venture on it with confidence, nor need we fear that we are engaging in a perilous, fruitless adventure. The question arises, however, whether we may not be in danger of ending up once again with a subjective, modernized life of Jesus. Is there not a risk that we too, like the whole of the nineteenth century, unconsciously and unintentionally, may project our own theology back into Jesus of Nazareth? With regard to this risk, it must be said that it is certainly never wholly possible for the historian to divest himself of his own personality. We shall never be entirely able to exclude this source of danger. Nevertheless we need not give up in despair, for our position is entirely different from that of the previous century. We are in fact better equipped. Our aims have become more modest, because the mistakes of the "classical" quest of the historical Jesus serve as warnings to us not to want to know more than we can know; that is already a point of inestimable worth. The decisive point, however,

---

[6] ["Didache," a Greek term transliterated into English, means literally "teaching." It has been employed by C. H. Dodd and many others to refer to the teaching activity, especially ethical in its content, which followed after the kerygma among converts in the early church. While many scholars tend to limit the didache to ethical instruction alone, Professor Jeremias views it as reiterating and expanding the kerygma about Jesus' death and as covering all areas of Christian instruction, not just morals.—EDITOR.]

is that we today possess, if I may use a metaphor, bulwarks which will protect us from arbitrary modernizations of Jesus, that is, which will protect us from ourselves.

Here I may content myself with suggestions and briefly indicate five aspects of the case.

(1) The critical scholarship of the previous century has thrown up the first bulwark for us in the shape of the remarkable literary criticism which it developed and increasingly refined. We have been taught to distinguish sources or, more correctly (since we are becoming more and more skeptical about the assumption of written sources), strands of tradition: a Marcan tradition, a Logia tradition,[7] the special traditions of Luke, Matthew, and John. Having established this, literary criticism leads us back to the stage of oral tradition antedating our gospels. We have, moreover, been taught to recognize the style of composition of the evangelists, and hence to distinguish between tradition and redaction. We have been thus enabled to trace the tradition back into its pre-literary stage.

(2) Form criticism has led us a step further back by attempting to determine the laws which governed the shaping of the material; it has thus thrown light from another side upon the creation and growth of the tradition. It is a fact not sufficiently known or heeded that the essential significance of form criticism is that it has enabled us to remove a Hellenistic layer which had overlaid an earlier Palestinian tradition.

(3) We have been carried an important step further on the way back to Jesus himself by studies about the world of his day which have disclosed to us his environment, informing us of the religious climate and of Palestinian customs in his day. I am referring to the study of rabbinical literature and of Late Jewish apocalyptic. As one who was privileged to live in Palestine for some years, I can testify from my own experience how much new light has been thrown in this way upon the gospels. The importance of the study of both ancient and modern Palestine does not lie primarily in the fact that it has revealed to us how Jesus belonged to his own time; its main significance lies rather in the way in which it has helped us to realize afresh the sharpness of Jesus' opposition to the religiosity of his time. And this is the chief significance of the Dead Sea Scrolls for New Testament studies. The Essenism which they disclose to us enables us to realize from their own testimony to what an extent the whole of Late Judaism was imbued with a passion to establish God's holy community. We can now assess more clearly than heretofore the significance of the emphatic denial with which Jesus met all these attempts.

(4) A further result of the study of the environment of Jesus has been to force upon us the necessity of studying his mother tongue. It is barely sixty-five years ago since Dalman proved conclusively, in my estimation,

139

Jeremias

THE PROBLEM
OF THE
HISTORICAL
JESUS

---

[7] ["Logia," the Greek term for "sayings," is applied to the collection of sayings commonly called "Q" which Matthew and Luke used as a source in addition to their Marcan source. While "Q" is often thought to have been a written book, Professor Jeremias prefers to think of it as an oral stratum of tradition.—EDITOR.]

that Jesus spoke Galilean Aramaic. Since then the study of this dialect has been pursued but is still only in an early stage. We still lack critical editions of the texts and a vocabulary of Galilean Aramaic. But the studies made so far have already demonstrated how rewarding such meticulous philological research can be. It is only necessary to recall in how many cases one and the same saying of Jesus has been transmitted to us in different Greek forms. In most of these cases we are dealing with translation variants, which constitute a reliable aid in reconstructing the Aramaic form of the saying underlying the various versions. For example, the Lord's Prayer, the Greek renderings of which in Matthew and Luke show many divergences, can by this means be retranslated into Jesus' mother tongue with a high degree of probability. Anyone who has ever had anything to do with translations is aware that they can never take the place of the original, and will be able to assess how important it is that we should be able to get back with a high degree of probability to the original Aramaic underlying the Greek tradition. It must of course be remembered that the earliest Christian community spoke Aramaic too; so not every Aramaism is evidence of authenticity. At any rate, however, we are drawing nearer to Jesus himself when we succeed in rediscovering the pre-Hellenistic form of the tradition. In this connection it is of special importance to note that this kind of study reveals peculiarities in the utterances of Jesus which are without contemporary parallels. As a form of address to God the word *abba* is without parallel in the whole of Late Jewish devotional literature. Similarly there is no contemporary analogy to Jesus' use of "Amen" as an introduction to his own utterances. It may be maintained that these two characteristic features of the *ipsissima vox* of Jesus contain in a nutshell his message and his consciousness of his authority.

(5) Of special significance as a bulwark against a psychological modernizing of Jesus is the rediscovery of the eschatological character of his message. It is not only that we have learned to recognize how extensively Jesus shared the conceptions of contemporary apocalyptic and made use of its language; the decisive importance of this discovery lies elsewhere. We have seen how the whole message of Jesus flowed from an awareness that God was about to break into history, an awareness of the approaching crisis, the coming judgment; and we have seen the significance of the fact that it was against this background that he proclaimed the present inbreaking in his own ministry of the kingdom of God.

It is clear, then, that Jesus was no Jewish rabbi, no teacher of wisdom, no prophet, but that his proclamation of a God who was at the present moment offering a share in salvation to the despised, the oppressed, and the despairing ran counter to all the religiosity of his time, and was in truth the end of Judaism.

At the end of his book *The Quest of the Historical Jesus,* Albert Schweitzer has summed up graphically the outcome of the attempts to write the life of Jesus: "The study of the Life of Jesus has had a curious history. It set out in quest of the historical Jesus, believing that when it had found Him it could bring Him straight into our time as a Teacher and Saviour. It loosed the bands by which He had been riveted for centuries to the stony rocks of ecclesiastical doctrine, and rejoiced to see life and movement coming into the figure once more, and the historical Jesus advancing, as it seemed, to meet it. But He does not stay; He passes by our time and returns to His own." Such was in fact the remarkable outcome of the study of the life of Jesus begun in 1778. It had freed Jesus from fetters; he became a living figure, belonging to the present; he became a man of our own time. Yet he did not stay, but passed by our time and returned to his own. It became clear that he was not a man of our time, but the prophet of Nazareth, who spoke the language of the prophets of the old covenant and proclaimed the God of the old covenant. But we must now extend Schweitzer's metaphor. Jesus did not stay in his own time, but he also passed beyond his own time. He did not remain the rabbi of Nazareth, the prophet of Late Judaism. He receded into the distance, entered into the dim light of Easter morning, and became, as Schweitzer says in the closing sentence of his book, the One unknown, without a name, who speaks the word, "Follow thou me!"

HISTORICAL STUDY AND JESUS' CLAIM

If we travel the road thus indicated, threading our way amid the five protecting walls which guard us from modernizing Jesus and fashioning him in our own likeness, we are then confronted by a unique claim to authority which breaks through the bounds of the Old Testament and of Judaism. Everywhere we are confronted in the message of Jesus by this ultimate claim, that is to say, we are confronted by the same claim to faith as that with which the kerygma presents us. We must at this point reiterate one of the simplest and most obvious facts, since it is no longer obvious to all. Every sentence of the sources bears witness of this fact to us, every verse of our gospels hammers it into us: something has happened, something unique, something which had never happened before. The study of the history of religions has amassed countless parallels and analogies to the message of Jesus. As far as our knowledge of Pharisaic and rabbinical theology is concerned, for instance, the monumental work of Paul Billerbeck is unsurpassed and will long remain so. Yet the more analogies we amass, the clearer it becomes that there are no analogies to the message of Jesus. There is no parallel to his message that God is concerned with sinners and not with the righteous, and that he grants them, here and now, a share in his kingdom. There is no parallel to Jesus' sitting down in table-fellowship with publicans and sinners. There is no parallel to the authority with which he dares to address God as *abba*. Anyone who admits merely the fact—and I cannot see how it can be gainsaid—that the word *abba* is an authentic utterance of Jesus, is, if he understands the word correctly, without watering down its meaning, thereby confronted with Jesus' claim to authority. Anyone who reads the parable of the Prodigal Son, which belongs to the bedrock of the tradition, and observes how in this parable, which describes the unimaginable goodness of divine forgiveness, Jesus justifies his table-fellowship with publicans and sinners, is

141

Jeremias

THE PROBLEM
OF THE
HISTORICAL
JESUS

again confronted with the claim of Jesus to be regarded as God's representative, acting with his authority. One example after another could be cited, but the result would always be the same. If with utmost discipline and conscientiousness we apply the critical resources at our disposal to the study of the historical Jesus, the final result is always the same: we find ourselves confronted with God himself. That is the fact to which the sources bear witness: a man appeared, and those who received his message were certain that they had heard the word of God. It is not as if faith were made superfluous or belittled, when exegesis shows us that behind every word and every deed of Jesus lies his claim to authority. (How could faith ever become superfluous?) Indeed, the truth of the matter is that through the words and acts of Jesus at every turn the challenge to faith is presented. When we read the gospels, even when we read them critically, we cannot evade this challenge. This claim to divine authority is the origin of Christianity, and hence study of the historical Jesus and his message is no peripheral task of New Testament scholarship, a study of one particular historical problem among many others. It is *the* central task of New Testament scholarship.

The Good News of Jesus and the Proclamation of the Early Church

This brings us to one final query. If it is true that the good news of Jesus in word and deed is the origin of Christianity, then it may be asked: What is the relation between the good news of Jesus and the early church's witness of faith? What is the relation between the pre-resurrection and the post-resurrection message, between the gospel and the kerygma? With regard to these questions there are two things to be said.

(1) The good news of Jesus and the early church's witness of faith are inseparable from one another. Neither of these may be treated in isolation. For the gospel of Jesus remains dead history without the witness of faith by the church, which continually reiterates, affirms, and attests this gospel afresh. Nor can the kerygma be treated in isolation either. Apart from Jesus and his gospel the kerygma is merely the proclamation of an idea or a theory. To isolate the message of Jesus leads to Ebionitism; to isolate the kerygma of the early church leads to Docetism.[8]

(2) If, then, these two belong together, the gospel of Jesus and the early church's witness of faith, and if neither of these may be isolated, it is also of utmost importance to recognize—and this is decisive—that they are not both on the same level. The gospel of Jesus and the kerygma

---

[8] [Ebionitism was the variety of Jewish Christianity which separated from the church and became a sect emphasizing the necessity of the Law for salvation; it opposed Paul and presented only a minimal Christology, rejecting the Virgin Birth of Jesus and seeing in him only a man filled by the Spirit of God. For "Docetism," cf. note 5 above. Ebionitism severed its connection with the church of which Paul was an apostle; Docetism contested the connection of faith with the story of Jesus in all its stark reality.—EDITOR.]

of the early church must not be placed on the same footing, but they are related to one another as call and response. The life, acts, and death of Jesus, the authoritative word of him who dared to say *abba,* the one who with divine authority invited sinners to his table, and as the servant of God went to the cross—all this is the call of God. The early church's witness of faith, the Spirit-led chorus of a thousand tongues, is the response to God's call. The ancient church liked to express this relationship in pictorial representations of the cosmic liturgy, in the midst of which is depicted a gigantic figure of the Crucified, toward whom, from the right and the left, there streams a countless throng on earth and in heaven. What such representations say is that Jesus of Nazareth is God's call to his creatures; confession of him is their response. This response always has a double aspect: it is praise and adoration of God, and witness to the world. It is inspired by the Spirit of God, but it does not take the place of the call. The call, not the response, is the decisive thing. The many-sided witness of the early church—of Paul, of John, of the Epistle to the Hebrews—must be judged in light of the message of Jesus.

Underlying our protest against the equating of the gospel and the kerygma is a concern for the concept of revelation. According to the witness of the New Testament, there is no other revelation of God but the incarnate Word. The preaching of the early church, on the other hand, is the divinely inspired witness *to* the revelation, but the church's preaching is not itself the revelation. To put it bluntly, revelation does not take place from eleven to twelve o'clock on Sunday morning. Golgotha is not everywhere; there is only *one* Golgotha, and it lies just outside the walls of Jerusalem. The doctrine of continuous revelation (*revelatio continua*) is a gnostic heresy. No, the church's proclamation is, from its earliest beginnings, not itself revelation, but it does guide toward the Revelation. This, at any rate, is the way Paul conceived of the task of the kerygma when he told the Galatians that the content of his preaching had been the depiction of Christ crucified before their eyes. (Gal. 3:1; cf. I Cor. 2:2.)

Once more: according to the witness of the New Testament, the church's proclamation is not revelation, but it leads to the revelation. Jesus is the Lord. The Lord is above the one who proclaims the message. For faith, there is no other authority but the Lord. Hence, the historical Jesus and his message are not *one* presupposition among many for the kerygma, but the *sole* presupposition of the kerygma. Thus, indeed, the response presupposes the call, and the witness to the revelation presupposes the revelation. Only the Son of man and his word can give authority to the proclamation. No one else and nothing else.

143

Jeremias

THE PROBLEM
OF THE
HISTORICAL
JESUS

10. Constantine and the Church

ROBERT M. GRANT

The Christian religion, destined one day to become synonymous with Western civilization for a thousand years, had a very humble and inauspicious beginning. When Jesus of Nazareth had been crucified, his followers, already persecuted by the local Jewish authorities with the tacit consent of the Roman government, were filled with panic. After having become convinced of Jesus' resurrection and charged with his directive to "go forth and teach all nations," however, they began a proselytizing movement without parallel in history for its extent or success. At first the Christians were treated merely as a deviant, splinter group of Jews by the Roman authorities who held the world in sway; but in the course of several decades they came to be recognized as a separate, and militant, religious association.

The attitude of the Roman government toward "alien" religions was generally consistent: few found any encouragement and many were officially banned or certainly discouraged, at least in cities inhabited by Roman citizens. In practice, however, the relatively tolerant and permissive polytheism of Greco-Roman antiquity accepted the spread of several Eastern "mystery-religions" in the Roman world. Many of these shared common elements: a mystical, gratifying ritual, a promise of personal redemption and immortality, and a sense of individual importance and comradeship in cultic worship. So

Source: Robert M. Grant, *Augustus to Constantine* (New York: Harper & Row, Publishers, 1970), pp. 235–249. Copyright © 1970 by Robert M. Grant. Reprinted by permission of the publisher. [Footnotes omitted.]

*long as the devotee of Isis or Mithra also worshipped state gods, and from the
late first century onward these included the emperor himself, the Roman
government was willing to let well enough alone. This attitude perhaps represented a realization that the mystery-religions filled a need in the Roman world.
(What Marx called the "opiate of the people"?) But the Christians were unique.
Like the Jews, they were unequivocally forbidden to worship anyone but
God; thus they became suspect when they failed to perform the "patriotic"
act of offering Caesar-worship. Official opposition hardened probably because
Christianity was potentially universal, and represented, therefore, a much
more serious threat to the fabric of Roman society than the Jews who were
not charged with the same mandate to proselytize. Persecution, sporadic but
bloody, was a concomitant of the spread of Christianity during the first three
centuries of its existence as a movement.*

*In the early fourth century an event of momentous importance occurred:
a claimant to the imperial throne, Constantine son of Constantius Chlorus, decided to throw in his lot with the God of the Christians. With Constantine's
success over his rivals, Christianity ceased to be a persecuted faith and soon
became the favored, ultimately the almost universal, religion in the Roman
Empire. The conversion of Constantine had far-reaching effects, both on the
structure of the Christian church, and on the Roman world. With imperial acceptance came official sponsorship, that is, control of the church. With the
patronage of Christianity came the desire to make the church unified and universal, and to standardize worship and beliefs. Thus, the First Ecumenical
Council was held under Constantine's auspices at Nicaea in A.D. 325.*

*What was the relationship between Constantine and the church? Why did the
church accept his patronage? What effects, in organization and doctrine, did
Roman acceptance entail? And finally, what new tensions were introduced by
this change in attitude? Robert M. Grant, Professor of Early Church History
in the Divinity School of the University of Chicago, has recently explored
these and related questions in* Augustus to Constantine. *He brings a long and
intimate knowledge to the subject, revealed in several other books on early
Christianity. Grant clearly indicates the most significant contributions of Constantine to the development of the early church, and shows the directions that
later growth would take in medieval Europe.*

In 311, when Galerius issued his edict of toleration, the *de facto* ruler of
Italy was Maxentius, son of Maximian; he too issued an edict of toleration
and restored the properties of the Roman church to the bishop Miltiades.

In the following year Constantine left Gaul and moved against him.
After crossing the Alps with a fairly small army, he finally reached the
outskirts of Rome, apparently having already seen a vision of the cross
standing above the sun. On the cross were the words, "By this conquer."
Christ appeared to him and told him to place this pattern on a military
standard. Thus originated the *labarum,* a spear with the Chi Rho at the
top and a crossbar from which hung a banner with busts of Constantine
and his sons. The account of this vision, according to Eusebius, came from
the emperor himself. According to Lactantius, Constantine was outside

Rome on the night of October 26 when he dreamed that he should draw the Chi Rho on his soldiers' shields in order to win victory. These accounts presumably refer to different events.

Within the capital city Maxentius was preparing for combat by offering sacrifices and consulting the Sibylline books, where he found the enigmatic prophecy that an enemy of the Romans would perish. On October 27 he took up a position across the Tiber from Rome, with the Milvian bridge (supplemented by pontoons) behind him. In defeat he withdrew across the bridge and the pontoons collapsed; his body was found in the river the next day. The Romans enthusiastically hailed Constantine, who claimed to be restoring the Roman senate and people to their pristine glory and freedom. He was now sole ruler in the west, while Licinius, now his ally, ruled eastern Europe. His victory had been due to the power of Christ. How was he to respond?

Early in 313 Constantine met Licinius at Milan, and they agreed upon the terms of a letter concerning the Christians which was issued at once by Constantine and in May or June by Licinius, after his victory over Maximian. In addition, it would appear, the emperors agreed upon the form of a prayer to be used by Licinius' troops before encountering the enemy. Addressed to the *summus deus,* it commended the imperial cause to him and requested divine aid. The letter concerning the Christians states that the emperors had conferred about "the advantage and security of the state" and had concluded that it would be served by granting freedom of religious choice not only to Christians but to all others as well.

Under such circumstances the *summa divinitas,* now freely worshiped, might bestow his favor upon the empire and its rulers. They intended not to dishonor any religion, whatever it might be. In consequence, all confiscated churches in the possession of the treasury or of private persons were to be returned to Christians; no indemnity would be paid. Other church properties were also to be restored, and the treasury would indemnify those who had purchased church lands.

Three points deserve emphasis. First, the basic purpose of the letter was to ensure divine favor for the state by worship of the *summa divinitas.* Second, this favor was also to be elicited by the return of church properties. Third, it was assumed that there was one united body of Christians, distinguishable from adherents of other religious cults.

The Donatist Problem

The last of these assumptions was abruptly shaken soon afterward when Constantine, now master of Africa, received word from the proconsul about divisions within the Christian church. In reply he instructed the proconsul to restore the properties which belonged to "the Catholic church of the Christians." He also wrote directly to Caecilian, Catholic bishop of Carthage, providing him with a gift of 3,000 *folles* and the promise of more if necessary. Troublemakers at Carthage were to be brought before Roman judges. A month or two later he went further by directing the proconsul to exempt from civic responsibilities the clerics of "the Catholic church governed by Caecilian."

The problems in Africa had arisen as early as 305, when the election of a bishop at Cirta had been troubled by charges that an elector, the senior bishop in Numidia, had been a *traditor,* i.e., had handed over the scriptures to the authorities. The accuser, according to a later Catholic critic, was himself a confessed murderer; the bishop finally elected took bribes for ordaining men to the presbyterate. In 311 troubles broke out again. A deacon of Carthage denounced the emperor Maxentius as a tyrant, and the bishop Mensurius, ordered to surrender him, went to Rome himself but died there soon thereafter. His archdeacon Caecilian succeeded him. Unfortunately Caecilian had alienated a rich and pious woman named Lucilla by insisting that before receiving the communion she was not to kiss the bones of a martyr not recognized by the church. Lucilla provided lavish gifts (400 *folles*) for seventy Numidian bishops meeting at Carthage, and they denounced Caecilian as having been consecrated by *traditores.* The lector Majorinus, a member of Lucilla's household, was made rival bishop of Carthage. It was this situation in which Constantine intervened.

From Caecilian's opponents came a petition asking that the case be heard in Gaul where, thanks to the emperor's father, there had been no persecution. Constantine responded by ordering Caecilian to appear at Rome with twenty other bishops, evenly divided between friends and foes, and to present his case before Miltiades of Rome and three bishops from Gaul. The court, soon expanded by the addition of fourteen Italian bishops, heard testimony for three days and on October 2, 313, excommunicated Donatus of Casae Nigrae, the leader of Caecilian's opponents, and recognized Caecilian as bishop. The Donatists (whose name was derived either from this Donatus or from the next schismatic bishop of Carthage) did not accept the decision and asked the emperor for a new trial —thus appealing to the state against the church.

The synod which assembled at Arles in August 314 marked a new stage in the life of the church. Whereas the synod at Rome in 313 had been attended only by bishops from Italy, Africa, and Gaul, and had dealt only with charges brought against Caecilian by the Donatists, the synod of Arles had a much broader representation and its decisions were far more wide-ranging. Letters are still in existence from the emperor to Alafius, vicar of Africa, concerning the transportation of bishops to the synod, and to Chrestus, bishop of Syracuse in Sicily, who apparently acted as president in the absence of Silvester of Rome. No Donatist representatives were present, but the synod was attended by representatives of forty-four churches in Britain, Gaul, Spain, Sardinia, Sicily, Italy, and Dalmatia, as well as from Mauretania, Numidia, and Africa. Most of the churches were represented by bishops, some (including Rome) by presbyters and/or deacons. A few exorcists and lectors were also present. The twenty-two canons promulgated by the synod began with the question of paschal uniformity and went on to moral problems, especially those arising in consequence of the recent persecution. The questions raised by the Donatists were discussed: evidence against so-called "traditors" could be taken only from public records, while false accusations were to result in permanent excommunication. The Donatists themselves were explicitly condemned.

The Donatists immediately replied at Carthage by bringing charges against Felix, bishop of Aptunga, who had consecrated Caecilian. They presented documentary proof that he had been a "traditor" and requested an investigation of his conduct. In February 315 a trial before the proconsul of Africa ended with the demonstration that the documents were forgeries. During the year the schismatic bishop of Carthage died and was succeeded by the more famous Donatus, a man of great vigor who in 316 resisted an imperial edict expropriating Donatist churches. Bloodshed was halted in 317 by an imperial letter, and in North Africa Donatism continued to flourish. A synod held about 330 was attended by no fewer than 270 Donatist bishops.

Donatism was significant not only because of its insistence upon the attitudes and actions of those who held office in the churches but also because of its complex relationship to the state. Donatus himself asked, "What has the emperor to do with the church?" His own party, however, had once appealed to the state against a hostile Catholic community. The problem had arisen out of the recognition of the church by the emperor. Once Constantine recognized the church he had to decide what kind of church it was. Recognition led to intervention. He was the first emperor to use the power of the state against schism, and he did so without success.

On May 5, 321, Constantine issued a rescript to the vicar of Africa and informed him that no further persecution of the Donatists would take place, and around the same time he wrote to the bishops and laity of Africa, expressing his regret that the measures he had taken to promote peace and unity had not been successful. God himself would bring Donatism to an end; meanwhile the church people of Africa had to endure their trials with patience.

The emperor's concern for unity was doubtless related to the steps he was taking against Licinius. In 320 the consuls were himself and his son Constantine II; in 321 they were his sons Crispus and Constantine, both described as Caesars. Licinius, pointedly ignored, proceeded to unify his own realm on a pagan foundation. He had been willing if not eager to tolerate Christian diversity; thus in 318–319 a "synagogue of the Marcionites . . . of the Lord and Savior Jesus Christ" was built near Damascus. Now, however, he forbade the meetings of synods and, indeed, of Christians within the cities; he also insisted that men and women were not to worship together. As Eusebius suggests, he viewed Christians as supporters of Constantine.

Battles between July and September 324 left Constantine master of the Roman world. (The year is established by a papyrus rent receipt which shows that Licinius was still emperor on September 3, 324 but not on July 24, 325.) For the moment he spared Licinius' life at the request of his own sister Constantia, wife of the defeated ruler, and he issued a letter to all the people of the eastern provinces. He desired peace, concord, and tranquillity, to be ensured by equal privileges for pagans and Christians alike. Christianity alone was true, but he prayed to God that pagans might also enjoy God's blessing. It is fairly clear that he had learned the folly of enforced unity from his experiences with the Donatists.

The Arian Problem

Constantine apparently did not realize what difficulties he had acquired along with the realm of Licinius, and he was on his way from Nicomedia to the Holy Land when news of the troubles at Alexandria reached him. He then sent his ecclesiastical advisor Ossius of Cordova to the city with a letter to the bishop Alexander and the presbyter Arius, locked in combat. It would appear that the definitive break between them had occurred only about July 323.

Arius was a highly independent Christian who had been ordained deacon by Peter but twice excommunicated for defending Meletius. Advanced to the presbyterate by Peter's successor Achillas, he almost became bishop himself after Achillas died in 312. A decade later he denounced the bishop Alexander for Sabellianism and insisted that only God the Father could be called eternal and uncreated. Alexander, assisted by his young and energetic archdeacon Athanasius, demanded that Arius renounce such teaching and then summoned a synod of a hundred bishops from Egypt and Libya. The synod met in 323 and excommunicated Arius, who then sought support first in Palestine, then at Nicomedia. In this city he won the support of the bishop Eusebius, a distant relative (at a later date) of the emperor Julian and perhaps of Constantine himself. Relative or not, as bishop of the eastern capital Eusebius was one of the few eastern bishops known to the emperor, and Constantine's letter to Alexander and Arius doubtless owed something to him as well as to Ossius.

In the letter the emperor reiterated his desire for peace as the basic need of church and empire alike. The points at issue should never have been raised in public; both contestants were to recognize their ultimate unity while agreeing to differ on such minor questions. Ossius was unable to obtain agreement to the letter, and on his way back to Nicomedia he visited Antioch, where the Arian question had created difficulties. He convened a synod of bishops from the surrounding regions; almost all agreed to condemn the Arian position. Only three of them, including Eusebius of Caesarea, dissented and were excommunicated. They were given permission, however, to attend a general council which Constantine now —probably in February 325—proposed to convene at Ancyra. In March Alexander of Alexandria with some suffragans visited Nicomedia in order to appeal to the emperor. Soon thereafter the emperor transferred the proposed council to Nicaea because of its favorable climate and general accessibility. It would be not only the first council he had summoned but, indeed, the first general council of the Christian church.

On May 20 more than 250 bishops assembled at Nicaea. Only five of them were from the west; because of old age Silvester of Rome could not attend, but he was represented by two presbyters. The president of the council was Ossius of Cordova; apart from him, the most prominent bishops were Alexander of Alexandria, Eustathius of Antioch, and Macarius of Jerusalem. The emperor had made every effort to make the council representative; indeed, he had even invited the Novatianist bishop Acesius, later of Constantinople. He himself opened the proceedings by delivering a brief official address in Latin, expressing his hope that military victory over tyrants would now be followed by peace in the church of God. The sessions of the council took less than a month to complete. The three bishops excommunicated by the synod of Antioch were reinstated, and Eusebius of Caesarea presented to the council his church's traditional statement of the faith. This was generally accepted by the council members, and indeed was used as the foundation for the original "Nicene creed" itself. The emperor himself, it would appear, was responsible for making one addition: the word *homoousios,* used to indicate that the Son was "consubstantial" with the Father. Presumably the term resulted from a compromise among eastern bishops and was intended to prevent Eusebius' creed from being interpreted in Arian fashion. Constantine himself explained that it implied no corporeal substance or any division or separation of the Son from the Father, for the immaterial, spiritual, and incorporeal nature could not suffer any corporeal change. It was to be taken in a divine and mysterious sense, without analysis. "After our most wise and pious emperor made this philosophical statement," says Eusebius, the bishops accepted his amendment; they also removed any mention of the Logos from the creed and added anathemas against such Arian views as "there was a time when he was not" or "before he was begotten he was not." The council also decided to accept the date for Easter in favor at Rome and Alexandria (unfortunately in 326 the two dates were different!), tried to resolve the controversy over Melitius at Alexandria, and issued twenty canons. Most of them had to do with the organization of the ministry. The bishops of Alexandria were to rule over Christians in Egypt, Libya, and the Pentapolis; they were metropolitans like the bishops of Rome and Antioch. The bishop of Aelia (Jerusalem) had a primacy of honor not specifically differentiated from that of the metropolitan at Caesarea. Bishops were not to be chosen from recent converts; they were to be approved by all provincial bishops. No clerics were to be castrated (the case of Origen) or to live with "spiritual sisters" (the case of Paul of Samosata). The ordinations of presbyters could be invalidated on moral grounds. Presumably with regard for the turmoil of Licinius' reign, the council decided that clerics were not to be transferred from one area to another; they were not to take interest on loans; deacons were to be subordinate to presbyters. Provisions for the reinstatement of all those who had lapsed under persecution by Licinius were carefully worked out, as in the case of Novatianists and followers of Paul of Samosata returning to the church. The procedure for excommunication was regularized, and finally it was held that Christians should not kneel at services on Sundays or the days between Easter and Pentecost.

On June 19 the creed and canons were signed by almost all the bishops, and the emperor asked them to hear him once more. He spoke of peace and unity and the need for mutual forbearance, and he asked them for their prayers. On July 25 he celebrated the twentieth anniversary of his reign with a banquet for the bishops. To Eusebius of Caesarea the festivities were like a dream. They seemed to present an image of the kingdom of Christ, now almost already present. It is likely that not only the emperor but many of his bishops believed that peace had finally come to the church. Neither Eusebius of Nicomedia nor Theognius of Nicaea was present, however, for both had refused to agree to the condemnation of Arius. Two Egyptian bishops who had supported him had been exiled from Egypt, and he himself had been banished too.

The Council of Nicaea thus provided an ambiguous precedent for the east similar to the one given in the west by the emperor's intervention in the Donatist controversy. There the problem of schism had reached no solution when imperial decrees were employed. Here the question of heresy was not settled even when the emperor worked as a Christian with Christian bishops and gave guidance in their council, then endeavoring to enforce the decisions by the power of the state. In both instances the unity of the church, long precariously maintained under the threat of impending persecution, was nearly shattered once this external pressure was removed. In the west the problem of discipline, acute for nearly a century, came to the fore; in the east the unfinished business of speculative theology created violent controversy.

Soon after the council Constantine addressed a letter to the church of Nicomedia to explain his banishment of their bishop. Much is a rehearsal of political grievances. Eusebius had shared Licinius' cruelty (the execution of Licinius was thus justified) and had killed other bishops. He had brought presbyters and deacons to spy on Constantine before Licinius' defeat. At Nicaea he had sent messengers to win the emperor's favor for Arius and had thus perverted his judgment. Finally he had received ex-Christians from Alexandria after the council. This letter does Constantine small credit. Eusebius had actually been Licinius' ambassador and had not killed any bishops; the emperor himself was certainly responsible for his own decisions. To be sure, he held that "what has commended itself to the judgment of three hundred bishops cannot be other than the judgment of God," but this belief was no excuse for slander.

In 327 Arius was recalled by a second council at Nicaea, and a petition from the Bithynian bishops led to their restoration. Athanasius, bishop of Alexandria from 328, claimed that the restored Eusebius persuaded the emperor to threaten him with deposition if he did not admit Arius to communion at Alexandria.

Within a few years, perhaps in 330, troubles broke out at Antioch, where the bishop Eustathius denounced Eusebius of Caesarea as an Arian. Eusebius counterattacked by calling Eustathius a Sabellian. A synod at

Antioch then deposed Eustathius and the emperor banished him, partly because he was said to have insulted the queen mother on her visit to the east several years earlier.

Affairs at Alexandria continued to be equally chaotic. The Meletians falsely accused Athanasius of imposing an unauthorized tax on linen tunics, and he was summoned to Nicomedia. There he was also accused of having had a presbyter break the chalice used by Ischyras, and of having conspired against the emperor. Both charges were dismissed and Athanasius returned home after Easter in 332. Soon afterwards, however, the charge about the chalice was revived and it was added that Athanasius had murdered the Meletian bishop Arsenius. Athanasius was summoned to court again but was able to trace Arsenius to a monastery in Tyre, thus refuting his accusers.

In 333 Constantine made up his mind again and decided to offer a final solution to the Arian problem. The books of Arius, like those of the anti-Christian philosopher Porphyry, were to be burned; the discovery of such writings if concealed was to result in the application of the death penalty. In the same year he sent a letter of denunciation to Arius and his followers, pointing out that Arius' presence in Libya had been predicted in the *Sibylline Oracles,* three thousand years previously, and—more practically—ordering them to return to the church or suffer a tenfold increase in their poll taxes.

These actions solved nothing, and further charges brought against Athanasius led the emperor to convene a synod at Caesarea under the presidency of Eusebius. Bishops, presbyters, and others were summoned by imperial letters; a document from the Meletian monastery at Hathor shows how the monks chose their representative. The synod met on March 19, 334, to discuss "the purgation of the holy Christian body," but Athanasius refused to attend because he regarded the president as prejudiced.

The next year Constantine convened another synod, this time at Tyre, and summoned Athanasius once more. Before leaving Alexandria the bishop conducted a purge of the Meletians there, arresting and exiling bishops and having some of them scourged. In spite of this activity he was undecided about attending. The Meletians noted that emissaries came for him; he had his baggage put aboard ship, then taken off again. Finally he went. At Tyre he was once more accused of using violence and perjury to gain his ends, charges in part confirmed by the Meletian document. The synod decided against him and he was taken in custody by imperial officers. He was able, however, to reach Constantinople and appeal to the emperor himself. In response Constantine ordered the synod to meet again in the capital city. There in 336 Athanasius confronted his enemies again.

This time he was accused of threatening to place an embargo on the grain sent from Egypt to supply Constantinople. This charge was extremely grave. Constantine himself had inaugurated a dole of bread in the capital city only four years earlier. The Neoplatonist Sopater had recently been beheaded on the ground that he had used magic to stop the supply of grain. Constantine, weary of divisions within church and empire, seized the opportunity to banish Athanasius to Trier, little realizing that the bishop would now exercise his influence there as well.

By this time the emperor was concerned with arrangements for the continuance of his house. In 335 he had divided the empire among his heirs. Constantine II received Britain, Spain, and Gaul; Constantius was given Asia, Syria, and Egypt; Constans obtained Italy and Africa. Two nephews were also assigned territories: Dalmatius as Caesar received Illyricum, while Hannibalianus—in view of an impending Persian campaign—was made king of Armenia and Pontus. (Neither nephew survived a massacre soon after the emperor's death.)

Constantine's Policy

Constantine was unable to solve the complex theological and administrative problems of the Christian church. It is hard to believe that his failure was due to any lack of theological acumen. More important was the actual state of division within the church and, to some extent, the lack of understanding of its history on the part of emperor and bishops alike. If Constantine read the *Church History* of Eusebius it gave him little help. His program of tolerance and persuasion within the church was frustrated by "true believers" of various kinds, though it is worth noting that all but two of the bishops at Nicaea were willing to agree, at least verbally.

The emperor's letters to Alexander and Arius and to the churches on the Easter question show that he viewed his position in the church as like that of a bishop. On various occasions he further developed this theme. "You are bishops of those inside the church," he said, "while I have been appointed by God as bishop of those outside." By "those outside" he seems to have meant not only non-Christians but all the people of the empire, over whom God had placed him. He was responsible for Christians and non-Christians alike. Indeed, at one point he addressed a letter to the Persian king Sapor, urging him to protect Christians within his dominions. "Love them as befits your love of man." As emperor, however, he retained the old title of *pontifex maximus,* and as late as 326 he was willing to provide the Eleusinian *dadouchos* with transportation to sacred sites in Egypt. A rescript issued as late as 333 shows that he accepted religious traditions in honor of his family. The citizens of Hispellum in Umbria had asked permission to honor the Flavian house by erecting a temple, providing a priest, and holding theatrical games and gladiatorial combats. Constantine approved their proposal, but he stipulated that "the temple dedicated to our name should not be defiled by the falsehoods of any contagious superstitions." The last two words show how times had changed; two centuries earlier Pliny had applied them to Christianity.

Early in his reign the emperor was careful not to disturb traditional religious practices. Though he used the Chi Rho on official medallions, it did not appear on his coinage before the defeat of Licinius, and his triumphal arch of 315 refers to the *divinitas* as his guide, nothing more specific. A rescript of 321 stated that when public buildings were struck by lightning the *haruspices* were to be consulted for the meaning of the portent. Only private divination, regarded as dangerous by the emperor's predecessors, was forbidden. On the other hand, apparently in 331 he took the step of confiscating some temple endowments, though he did not act against the Vestal virgins or other old Roman cults. For his new imperial city he compelled Delphi to contribute its tripod, Helicon its statues of the Muses; but this was the act of an art collector, not a religious enthusiast. According to Eusebius, three important temples were finally destroyed; a healing shrine of Asclepius in Cilicia and two temples of Aphrodite, associated with ritual prostitution, in Syria. It is most unlikely that he explicitly forbade all pagan sacrifices and other rites, unless perhaps he did so at the very end of his reign.

Constantine was a Christian, however, and he was eager to provide Christian buildings equal in magnificence to the old temples. At Rome he built no fewer than seven churches, as well as others in Italy at Ostia, Albinum, Capua, and Naples. He built churches at Cirta in Africa, at Trier in Gaul, at Antioch in Syria, and at Nicomedia in Asia. He adorned his new capital city with two great churches dedicated to Peace and to the Holy Apostles. Lavish endowments were also provided for many of these churches.

His edifices in Palestine were part of his "Holy Land plan." In 324 he had been on his way there from Nicomedia when he received news of the conflicts at Alexandria and had to return. In order to unify the churches he built great churches on the holy places such as the Church of the Holy Sepulchre near Jerusalem and another at Mamre, where God had appeared to Abraham. His mother Helena built a church on the Mount of Olives to commemorate the Ascension and another at Bethlehem in honor of the Nativity. Presumably he intended to round out this program with a final dramatic celebration when he himself would be baptized in the Jordan river; but this was not to be.

The Death of Constantine

At Easter in 337 the emperor dedicated the Church of the Holy Apostles in Constantinople, but soon thereafter he was overcome by a fatal ailment. He visited the baths at Helenopolis in vain, and then proceeded to confess his sins in the Church of the Martyrs. At Ancyrona near Nicomedia, he prepared his will, leaving the empire to his three sons, and in the presence of a group of local bishops he was baptized by the bishop with whom he had fought so often, Eusebius of Nicomedia. To this prelate was entrusted the will, with instructions to deliver it to Constantius, Caesar of the east. Wearing the white robe of a neophyte, Constantine died on Pentecost, May 22.

Official mourning began at once. Soldiers placed his coffin, adorned with purple and a diadem, on a golden couch and solemnly bore it to the imperial palace in Constantinople. There generals and other officers made obeisance to the dead emperor and swore allegiance to his sons. Upon Constantius' arrival the coffin was carried to the Church of the Holy Apostles and placed among the sarcophagi dedicated to the Twelve. In the presence of a vast throng the bishops conducted an elaborate funeral with a requiem eucharist.

The dead emperor was not mourned by Christians alone. A comet announced his death to the Roman world, just as one had appeared when Augustus gave games in honor of the deified Julius Caesar. Eutropius explicitly speaks of the consecration of Constantine: *inter divos meruit referri,* "he was deservedly enrolled among the divine emperors." Eusebius does not mention it and denies that Constantine's immortality is like that of the phoenix, consumed by the flames of a pyre; the coins to which he refers, however, clearly portrayed the consecrated emperor. Inscriptions from the emperor's own time gave his father the title *divus.* Now inscriptions under his sons spoke of him as *divus Constantinus.* His body rested, however, not in any Flavian mausoleum or with any of the great pagan emperors before him but, by his own choice, among the memorials of the twelve apostles.

The story of the Christian revolutionary movement may well end at this point, for the relation of Christianity to the society in which it was now established is another matter. The acceptance for which Christians had long been seeking had been achieved. Clement of Alexandria had believed that the iron-bronze state of the Greeks was inferior to the silver of the Jews and the gold of the Christians. Now the golden age had dawned.

If we try to answer the question as to how Christianity reached this point, and how it changed as it did so, we may suggest that it could have won either by violence or by nonviolence. If it had attempted to use violence it would have contradicted its own nature in so far as it was based on the expectation of divine, not human, intervention and aid. In addition, the practical example provided by the failure of the Jewish revolts discouraged the use of arms, as did the Christian theological analysis of this failure. The nonviolent approach was obviously in harmony with the teaching of Jesus and the apostles. Practically speaking, however, it could be expected to succeed only when Greeks and Romans were convinced that Christianity was not only politically valuable but also philosophically and culturally meaningful. Such a conviction could arise in part from the observable virtue of Christians. It could also arise from the futility of continued persecution and from the power of Christian proclamation and argument. In this regard Christians necessarily laid emphasis on points of contact between their own views and those of their neighbors. A certain measure of adjustment or even compromise was inevitable. At the same time, by insisting upon the absoluteness of the Christian revelation, as understood within the church, and upon the existence of salvation only within the church, Christians were able to maintain the cohesiveness without which the movement would not have survived.

The nature of this exclusiveness and cohesiveness was not entirely religious. Indeed, we should not expect it to have been so either in ancient times or in more recent circumstances. Is anything purely religious? The good will of the Roman emperor, however, created formidable problems as he tried to solve others, and his legislation was to compound the difficulties of the church in later times as well as in his own era.

We have already mentioned the fact that in 326 he informed the vicar of the diocese of the Orient that clerical privileges were to benefit only Catholic clergy. "It is our will, moreover, that heretics and schismatics shall not only be alien from these privileges but also shall be bound and subjected to various public services." In other words, an effort to harass non-Catholic clerics was to be made. Beyond this lies an imperial letter of uncertain date in which Constantine proceeded to treat heretics just as his predecessors had treated Christians, and as Diocletian had dealt with Manichees. He spoke of the poison, the pollution, and the disease produced by Novatianists, Valentinians (Gnostics), Marcionites, Paulianists (followers of Paul of Samosata), and Cataphrygians (Montanists), and forbade their assemblies. All public meetinghouses were to be surrendered to the Catholic Church, while private houses used for meetings were to be confiscated by the state. The unity of the Christian movement was to be maintained by the power of the empire.

This cohesiveness and exclusiveness, in turn, complicated the controversies within the church, especially in the early fourth century. As we have already suggested, the uncompromising claims of Novatianists and Donatists proved to be irreconcilable with Catholic inclusiveness, even when the inclusive view was supported by the power of the state. What we may call the revolutionary rigor of the sects was not now maintained by most Christians, but it could not be suppressed. Similarly the rather archaic theological ideas of Arius, once they had been made popular at Alexandria and elsewhere, could not be put down by authority either ecclesiastical or imperial. Because of the absoluteness with which philosophical and theological ideas were maintained by almost all Christians, there was practically no room for compromise or, indeed, for conversation.

The church had finally achieved a large measure of political, social, and even cultural freedom. It had combined accommodation at some points with intransigence at many others. Whether or not it was really ready for freedom remained to be determined, but in any event the movement had succeeded. The question to which we must finally turn involves the continuity of the movement with its origins. To what extent was the church of the fourth century continuous with its earlier modes of existence?

THE
MIDDLE
AGES

PART II

B Y the middle of the first century BC the Romans had succeeded
in extending their sway over all the coastlands of the Mediterranean, and they maintained control over their empire for five
hundred years. The Romans were generous in sharing the benefits of their culture and citizenship with those who were drawn
into their empire, and they were not reluctant to benefit themselves from
contacts with older and more sophisticated peoples, particularly the
Greeks. As a consequence much of the best of thought and culture in the
Mediterranean world was brought together into a synthesis. Greco-Roman
civilization represented an accomplishment of no mean proportions, but it
had begun to lose its vitality by the second century after Christ. In the
same century the Roman government was finding it difficult to stem the
tide of Germanic tribes pressing against the northern frontiers. Christianity too was expanding and subtly impressing its own imprint on classical
civilization. By the time Roman government and administration collapsed
before Germanic pressure in western Europe in the fifth century, the empire that "fell" was in many respects hardly recognizable as that which
Augustus had founded.

Out of the chaos of the invasions, and the heritage of classical antiquity, a new order ultimately emerged. Historians discern in it several distinct elements. First, there was the speculative tradition of Greek philosophic thought, which had been absorbed into Roman culture. Second, the
Roman contribution in the example of a universal empire, governed by a

code of law that treated all alike, remained a strong influence. The third element was the Christian church, combining aspects of Hebrew thought with Greek philosophy and certain ritual practices common to other mystery cults of late antiquity. Finally, the hardy northern warriors brought their own customs and traditions and their spirit to the Mediterranean world. The impact of successive waves of migration, disrupting as they did the political, social, and economic order of the late Roman Empire, necessitated new solutions to the problems that were thus created. Over a period of centuries the mixed populations in these newly formed Western societies created new institutions: the Carolingian monarchy, the proprietary church, feudalism and knighthood, to name some of the more important ones. By the twelfth century (as Richard Southern has so well put it), a new, relatively homogeneous society had emerged in western and northern Europe: Latin Christendom.

The millennium between the dissolution of Roman power in the West and the Renaissance was hardly the static picture of decline and darkness that artists, scholars, and literati in the fourteenth and fifteenth centuries painted. Its beginning was marked by disorder and anarchic collapse of government and administration in the wake of the Germanic incursions into the European provinces in the fifth century. The expansion of Islam in the seventh and eighth centuries helped stimulate the reintegration of social and political forces, however, and in 800 Charlemagne was crowned Holy Roman Emperor, thus theoretically restoring the shattered unity of Roman power. The opposition of Byzantine emperors in the East, and a series of raids by Norse, Magyars, and Saracens from the late eighth until the tenth century retarded the Carolingian attempt to unify the West. The failure of the Carolingians led to the establishment of several feudal monarchies, which characterized social and political relationships in western Europe from the tenth to the thirteenth centuries. The Carolingian idea still held the imagination of men, however, and for three and a half centuries various German princes laid claim to the imperial title, and strove vainly to exert their control over German and Italian lands.

In the realm of culture, the destruction of barbarian raiders was made good, and significant strides were taken to preserve and advance the classical heritage in thought and letters. The chief centers of knowledge during the early Middle Ages were the monasteries where men dedicated their lives to prayer and work. Since the work was typically divided between physical labor in the fields and copying books, much was preserved from Greco-Roman culture. The monks did not merely copy, however, and attempts to educate a larger circle have prompted scholars to view various periods as times of "renaissance," or rebirth of learning: the Carolingian, in the eighth century; the Ottonian, in the ninth; the celebrated "renaissance of the twelfth century"; and the thirteenth-century achievement which saw the formal recognition of Europe's earliest universities —Bologna, Paris, and Oxford. In worship and doctrine as well the monks contributed to the development of Christianity, while in church administration and government a series of reforming popes, aided by men trained in the techniques of Roman law, advanced the claims of Rome to rule Christendom.

The selections in this section have been chosen to cast light on these developments and to further one's understanding of medieval civilization. Wallace-Hadrill's essay on the Franks brings to life the most important of the Germanic tribes and describes the way in which they established their power in Roman Gaul. The articles by Strayer and Herlihy discuss aspects of feudalism and illustrate how family structure, economic activity, and governmental functions were linked together to form a concatenated social order. Bosl's treatment of the peoples of eastern Europe in the Middle Ages reminds us of the crucial interaction between the various segments of European society in this formative period. The selections by Southern, Ullmann, and Knowles all touch on aspects of medieval Christianity: Southern's article is a brilliant view of monastic life, which points out the difficulties of the monastic ideal when pursued in the feudal world; Ullmann's argues that several popes wished to rule Christendom as temporal as well as spiritual heads, and indicates the rather surprising bases that popes and exponents of papal power pointed to in order to support their claims; and Knowles writes on the intellectual achievements of one of medieval Christianity's greatest thinkers, St. Thomas Aquinas, in whom strands of past and future, Greek philosophy and the university, came together. Finally, the last two selections provide a sort of transition to the next period. Le Patourel's discussion of the Plantagenet Dominions raises questions about the nature of medieval kingship, and anticipates the development of the state, which many scholars see as a characteristic of early modern Europe. Luzzatto's article on the development of towns and trade in Italy in the late Middle Ages also anticipates the period of the Italian Renaissance and some of the questions considered by Hay, Brucker, and others in the third part of this book. This section should elucidate some of the main developments and achievements of medieval civilization and demonstrate the complexity and richness of a period once described as an age of darkness and ignorance.

11. Clovis, King of the Franks

J. M. WALLACE-HADRILL

The most salient aspect of the decline of Roman power in the fifth century was the loss of political and military control over the western Mediterranean to numerous Germanic peoples. Italy was taken by the Ostrogoths; Spain fell before the Visigoths; Africa to the Vandals; Britain to Angles and Saxons; and Gaul, the area of modern France and Belgium, was partitioned among Visigoths, Burgundians, and Franks. Yet the political achievements of the Germanic tribes were largely negative; they destroyed Roman authority without establishing anything permanent in its place. Virtually all of these kingdoms succumbed to various pressures and disappeared within a century or two, with one notable exception. In southern Belgium and northern France, a Frankish dynasty, the Merovingians, established a kingdom in the late fifth century that was to form the core and basis of the later Carolingian Empire, the medieval kingdom of France, and the modern French nation. What was the nature of this Frankish kingdom? Why did the Franks succeed in maintaining their power where almost every other barbarian tribe failed? And what was the role and the achievement of Clovis, in whose reign the foundations of Frankish power were laid?

J. M. Wallace-Hadrill, from whose book The Long-Haired Kings *this selection is drawn, is a specialist in early medieval history and particu-*

Source: J. M. Wallace-Hadrill, *The Long-Haired Kings* (London: Methuen & Co., 1962), pp. 163–185. Reprinted by permission of the publisher. [Footnotes omitted.]

larly in Frankish institutions and history. He observes that Clovis's father was "a barbarian who had done well by the Romans; but his masters have not romanized him or converted him to their religion." At best, he was a trusted federate warrior chieftain, whose authority did not even embrace all the Franks of northern Gaul. Clovis, merely one of several reges Francorum, succeeded his father as king of the Franks around Tournai and went on to establish the most powerful political entity in Gaul. Wallace-Hadrill argues that Clovis did not create and enlarge his kingdom by design or long-range planning, but rather responded to a series of chances with "opportunism and ruthlessness." His success was due in large measure to native cunning and ability, to the willing acquiescence of Roman bishops and administrators in Gaul, to his adoption of Catholic Christianity, and to the moral support of the Byzantine emperor.

The student may wish to consider which of the influences that Wallace-Hadrill cites seems to have been the more important in the success of the Merovingians; to ask what set the Franks apart from other contemporary Germanic peoples; to evaluate Clovis's role in the evolution of the idea of kingship among the Franks; and finally, to distinguish the most significant contributions of Clovis to the formation of what would one day become France.

For those interested in pursuing this topic further, the fundamental source for Merovingian Gaul is Gregory of Tours's History of the Franks, trans. O. M. Dalton (1927). Other useful works on the period include S. Dill, Roman Society in Gaul in the Merovingian Age (reprinted 1966), F. Lot, The End of the Ancient World and the Beginnings of the Middle Ages, trans. P. and M. Leon (1931), and A. H. M. Jones, The Decline of the Ancient World (1967).

Pugnator Egregius *

The importance of Clovis to the history of the practice of kingship depends in large part on the fact that Gregory of Tours chose to write about him. Like all good historical writing, Gregory's account of the great barbarian carries that kind of conviction from which the reader can never afterwards escape. Clovis is Gregory's Clovis, whether we like it or not; he is Gregory's 'magnus et pugnator egregius', the man who brought the Salians to Catholicism and to a kind of Romanitas, the father of his dynasty. This must be accepted at the outset: there is no getting round the Bishop of Tours, however much we emend his chronology, and however often we impute to his hero motives that might have shocked him.

Childeric's successor was a youth of 15; successor, that is, to the rule of Franks, Salian and other, settled round Tournai. There were plenty more reges Francorum scattered between Tournai, Toxandria, and the Middle Rhine. There is no knowing what he made of his southern neighbour, the Rex Romanorum of Soissons, who since 476 had had no emperor he could call master, and whose legal position was thus finally exposed for the sham it was. It could have been this that brought down upon Syagrius

---

* [Pugnator egregius, mighty warrior—EDITOR.]

the warriors of a king whose title to rule was as good as his own. If it was, it took Clovis nearly five years to argue his way to this conclusion, for it was not till 486 that he attacked Syagrius in the territory of Soissons, and routed his force. When he finally laid hands on the *Rex Romanorum,* obligingly betrayed by the Visigoths, he made short work of him. Gregory paints that engagement in the colours of a personal clash, and this may reflect the actual relationship between Clovis and Syagrius, and not the romantic way of epic tradition. They may have seen each other as rivals for the floating loyalties of the warbands of *Belgica Secunda.* Some of these warbands, moreover, were Frankish and had been in the pay of the kings of Soissons since forsaking Childeric. Their natural inclination to return to the allegiance of their Frankish lord may have combined with Clovis' own wish to reclaim them, and, with them, his father's southern conquests. Yet another reason for the battle of Soissons may be found in the practical difficulty of controlling any considerable part of northern Gaul without at the same time controlling Soissons and Rheims.

Wavering loyalties had still left Syagrius ruler of what was worth fighting for. So far from collapsing before Clovis, he put up a stiff fight. Gregory's account can only mean that Syagrius thought he could win: 'sed nec iste distolit ac resistere metuit'.* His defeat was on the field of battle: there was no question of any moral disintegration of a Roman frontier-province. Except, then, in so far as he may have been an imperial official, his power and his lands fell to Clovis, who would have regarded himself as his heir. The defeated warbands would have gone to strengthen the Frankish following; and Roman notaries and the like who had served Syagrius would have been ready at hand to constitute a writing-office for the new ruler.

The chronology of the next few years cannot be determined, but it does look as if Clovis gave his energies to the affairs of the conquered province, rewarding his followers with gifts of land from the disintegrated remnants of the imperial fisc and from whatever private properties he seized. A smooth transfer of *villae* from Gallo-Roman to Frankish ownership would be too simple a way to conceive either the changing nature of the *villae* or the needs of the newcomers, whose taste for hunting-lodges in forest-clearings may have left the Romans in possession of more cultivated land than they had hoped for. A large body of warriors always remained in attendance on the king, constituting his *trustis,* the nucleus of his field-force. In Clovis' day, if not later, this *trustis* may have formed a much higher proportion of the fighting strength of the Franks than is always allowed. With its help, the king browbeat his Frankish neighbours into subservience without, however, preventing that slow, unchronicled movement of Ripuarian Franks westward from the Cologne area to colonize northern Gaul, in a way that would have been impossible for the swift-moving and less numerous Salians. Also with its help,

---

* [For he did not delay or fear to resist"—EDITOR.]

he made sallies into the chaotic Armorican region of the Loire, the home of the Bacaudae. The subsequent history of that area does not suggest that he had any more success than the Romans in making his authority felt. Little as we know about them, these operations should be interpreted strictly at their face-value. It was a time for rewarding followers and putting down rival claimants to the rule of Syagrius' rich kingdom. To see it as a 'period of consolidation' before another great advance goes contrary to the evidence. Opportunism, short-sighted and ruthless, was characteristic of every barbarian who made his way in the Roman world.

These early years were also a time for learning to know the Romans. Their tone is set by a famous letter addressed to the new king by Remigius (St. Rémi), bishop of Rheims. The bishop has learned, without being officially informed, that Clovis has taken over the administration of *Belgica Secunda:* non est novum ut coeperis esse sicut parentes tui semper fuerunt'. He goes on to speak of 'tua provincia', 'cives tuos' and praetorium tuum',* which has led some scholars to think that the letter must have been written after the defeat of Syagrius; but the case for dating it to 481 or a little after seems the stronger. It is a hortatory letter of a recognized pattern; the bishop acknowledges the effective rule of Clovis over part at least of *Belgica,* without foreseeing its extension south and without supposing that it is at all likely to be detrimental to Roman interests. The tone of the letter is patronizing: the pagan barbarian will wish to reflect on the advantages of having the Gallo-Roman Church on his side. It is not, in so many words, a warning against the Arianism of the neighbouring Visigoths and Burgundians, nor a direct appeal for conversion to Catholicism. It is rather a statement of fact: *Belgica* is Roman and is run by Roman bishops; and a prudent *rex* will wish to take note of this, since most of his subjects will be Romans. Clovis has crossed the frontier and is welcomed in, on terms. To bring about his conversion would be a matter of years: how could he think of flinging away the support of the tribal gods who had so plainly brought prosperity to him and his followers? The pagan Franks were a religious people. There is every indication that the Roman bishops also recognized this, and were much happier with a pagan overlord than they would have been with an Arian. Clovis gave them further proof of his goodwill by marrying the only Burgundian princess who was a Catholic; but however his wife and Bishop Remigius may have worked to bring him nearer conversion, he saw no reason yet to risk a breach with ancestral tradition. He took his time, as the Kentish husband of his great-granddaughter, Bertha, was to take his, a century later.

A consequence of marriage was the involvement of Clovis in Burgundian family affairs. It was the fact of kinship, not of his wife's Catholicism, that caused Clovis to intervene in the fratricidal quarrels of her un-

* ["It is not unusual that you begin to be as your ancestors always were"; "your province," "your citizens," "your headquarters."—EDITOR.]

cles. The account of the intervention given by Gregory of Tours is tricked out in the frills of saga, and this invites the historian to dismiss the whole as a latter-day invention, behind which lies the more prosaic truth that Clovis was fishing in troubled waters. But the fact is that the springs of action in these remote times lay more in kinship and its claims than in statesmanlike calculations as to the main chance. I therefore accept Gregory's statement that Clovis marched into Burgundy at the invitation of one of his kinsmen by marriage, Godigisel, caring little where it might lead. The outcome of a series of sorties into territory more romanized than any he had known was the linking, not merely of the dynasties, but of the Frankish and Burgundian peoples, in an uneasy relationship that was to last centuries. They hated each other with the hatred that barbarians reserved for barbarians; but the Franks had discovered that their new properties were exposed on the south-east frontier to a people formidably befriended by the Goths, whom they could never again afford to forget. The Merovingians were seldom astute in their handling of the Burgundians, but they had every excuse to go on trying.

Where Frankish territories approached the Upper and Middle Rhine, contact could not be avoided with the Alamans. Here, the immediate threat was to the Ripuarian Franks; but these, too, tended to fall under the kingship of Clovis, either because he was a great warrior or because he was successor of Syagrius. All the Franks looked upon the Alamans as a natural threat and as competitors for Roman territory. Though West Germans like the Franks, the Alamans were perhaps a more primitive people: their horsemen certainly struck terror into the Franks, among whom only the chieftains were mounted; they seemed to belong to another world. In addition to this antipathy, the Franks were heirs and defenders of Roman territory, even if they had it without permission. The very structure of the *regnum* of Syagrius could be overthrown by a successful Alamannic drive across the Rhine into eastern Gaul. Fear for this frontier was a constant preoccupation with Clovis, and it can hardly be doubted that Franks, whether his or those of the chieftains of *Francia Rinensis,* would have been dealing with Alamannic sorties for years before the great engagement of Tolbiac (Zülpich), when a confederation of Franks routed the Alamans, and Clovis was accepted by the Alamannic remnant as king in place of their fallen leader. We need not see Tolbiac as part of a Frankish plan to stabilize the eastern frontier and neutralize the barbarians of the Rhine and the Rhône before attempting a more ambitious push against the Goths. Such concepts belong to the sixteenth century; hardly to the sixth. Nonetheless, it is true that Tolbiac marks a turning-point in the relations of Franks with Goths. The southward flight of some at least of the Aleman host to the protection of the Ostrogoth Theodoric comes too soon after a Visigothic warning to Clovis to leave the Burgundians alone to allow any escape from the conclusion that the Arian, and equally the East German, dynasties of the West were aware that Syagrius had a successor who might endanger their own position. He had already put his own house in order to the extent that all the Frankish settlers between the Loire and the Rhine acknowledged his kingship. Here was a 'Bretwalda' if ever there was one. It seems also very probable that Clovis was already in touch with Byzantium, and that this would have been known to the Goths. Enough had happened to cause the Visigoth Alaric II to make preparations for war so extensive as to bring down a rebuke and a warning from the more prudent Ostrogoth, Theodoric. The Goths were presumably worried at news of Byzantine curiosity at the altogether unexpected success of Clovis against the Alamans. What could be done with Clovis was more interesting than what Clovis could do.

The victory of Tolbiac, whether we date it early or late in Clovis' career, was associated by Gregory with his conversion to Catholic Christianity. The pattern is familiar. Defeat stares him in the face and his gods have deserted him; his thoughts turn to his wife's god, to whom he prays in his heart for victory; and victory is his. Like Constantine in a similar predicament, Clovis knows that he must throw in his lot with the new god. This was no total conversion, for it did not imply that the myths and rituals of ancestral heathen piety were to be swept aside. The barbarian is not aware of being offered a new way of life complete with a theology of its own; at most, he sees it as an additional cult. It is a supplement, not a substitute; adhesion, not conversion. His private decision calls for no dogmatic preparation, for which indeed there is no evidence, but rather for a conviction that the territorial god of *Belgica Secunda* must be added to his people's pantheon, perhaps in a commanding position. We are still some way from the bigger decision implied by the catechumenate and by baptism: the decision to abandon, at least officially, all other gods but the Christian god. This final transition is softened by acceptance of the cultus of local saints, who must have appeared to Clovis very like demigods. But even adhesion calls for conviction of right, and it is no belittlement of Clovis' act to term it a political decision, taken after weighing Frankish pagan conservatism against the assured approval of the Gallo-Romans. We cannot tell whether the support of a Gallo-Roman episcopate, long prepared to work with Clovis without any assurance of his ultimate conversion, was at last demanding positive action. Nor can we know if he hoped that conversion would buy active imperial intervention against the Goths. The fact of conversion cannot be dissociated from the circumstances. Without Tolbiac, the proof would have been lacking that the Christian god gave victory over other Germans; there might have been no conversion, and no desire for it. Victory over enemies, victory over rebels; this, and not administrative help, is what would tempt a *rex barbarorum* to conversion. It is Christ the warrior, the defender of a chosen people, who is revealed on Frankish grave-stones in the Rhineland. The feeling is authentically conveyed in a Merovingian prayer for victory over rebels, based on Nehemiah's great invocation (2 Maccabees i. 24 ff.) beginning 'Domine, deus omnium creator, terribilis et fortis'.* Clovis

---

* ["Lord, God creator of all things, terrible and strong"—EDITOR.]

would have understood Nehemiah. The risk was great, however, and not much precision can be attached to Gregory's statement that three thousand warriors were baptized with their king: the figure comes from Acts ii. 41. A people is not converted in a generation. The hard-headed nature of the king's decision, singularly free from miraculous atmosphere, comes out well in a letter addressed to him by Bishop Avitus of Vienne. The bishop (who has one eye on his own Arian master, Gundobad of Burgundy) praises the king's *subtilitas,* as well as his courage, in abandoning the faith of his ancestors. Herein lies the miracle, that without the aid of preachers Clovis has chosen the right way, at the right time for himself. He has broken with his ancestors, so that his posterity must look back to him alone as the source of their excellence:

> Vos de toto priscae originis stemmate sola nobilitate contenti, quidquid omne potest fastigium generositatis ornare, prosapiae vestrae a vobis voluistis exsurgere. Habetis bonorum auctores, voluistis esse meliorum.*

It is the first appearance of 'le roi très chrétien': 'instituistis posteris ut regnetis in caelo'. Avitus, like Remigius, has a clear notion of what he expects a Catholic barbarian king to be, and we should not underestimate this tenacity of viewpoint in the slow evolution of Merovingian kingship. Clovis must make a sacrifice and take a risk; his heathen *fortuna* will go, and in its place he must believe that the rite of baptism will substitute a Christian *fortuna* in battle, with a fine new field of foes in God's Germanic-pagan enemies to say nothing of heretics. Avitus further compares the Frankish king with the Byzantine emperor. Clovis must now become a kind of western emperor, a patriarch to the western Germans, reigning over, though not governing, all peoples and kings:

> Quatenus externi quique populi paganorum, pro religionis vobis primitus imperio servituri, dum adhuc aliam videntur habere proprietatem, discernantur potius gente quam principe.†

One catches an echo of the tone of Remigius, writing to the young warrior twenty years earlier; there is a disposition to lecture and to patronize the child of nature, as well as some anxiety to be known for his friend. But there is also awareness of wider horizons. By the mere fact of conversion to Catholicism Clovis is a new kind of barbarian king. He stands apart from and in opposition to the Gothic kings. His natural ally and his model will be the orthodox emperor. He is Gregory's 'novus Constan-

---

* ["You, of all the stock of your ancient family, content with nobility alone, however much dignity of birth can bring honor, wished to rise up above your race by yourself. Your ancestors produced men of good stock, but you wished to produce even better ones."—EDITOR.]

† ["Since all other pagan peoples, about to devote themselves to the service of true religion for the first time because of you, while before they had a different distinguishing characteristic, are distinguished now rather by their tribe than by their king."—EDITOR.]

tinus', a figure of speech that recalls not merely the first Christian emperor but the acclamation that had for long greeted the Byzantine emperors. The break with the past is as complete as the bishops can make it; Avitus insists on it, and Remigius has nothing less in mind when he baptizes Clovis at Rheims with the words:

> Mitis depone colla, Sicamber, adora quod incendisti, incende quod adorasti! *

The mere use of 'Sicamber' with its reminder of small tribal origins, sharpens the contrast and points the moral. It is almost as if, without this emphasis, the king might have had something else, and something less, in mind. The subsequent history of the Merovingians, who owed almost nothing to Byzantine example, strongly suggests that he did. No sharp break seemed apparent to Bede's Redwald, with his prudent arrangement of a heathen and a Christian altar in one and the same building, or to Gregory's Spanish visitor, who reported that in his part of the world it was usual to pay one's respects to both heathen and Christian altars, if one happened to pass between them. Clovis presumably abandoned his heathen cultus, but the memory remained of victories, his own and his ancestor's, not won under Christ; it was a long way from Soissons to Tolbiac, as his warriors well knew, and Frankish graves of much later date than Tolbiac yield amulets and charms and offerings that are anything but Christian. At least for a time, the core of Merovingian kingship remained heathen in some indefinable way, even while it benefited from the baptism at Rheims.

Clovis fought his last campaign, against the Visigoths in 507, as a Catholic. Gregory reports that many in Gaul wanted the Franks as overlords, and gives as one example the Bishop of Rodez. We are left to infer that what the 'many' objected to were the Arian Goths, which is not quite the same thing as the Arianism of the Goths. But Gregory makes Clovis take it as a religious challenge to conquer Alaric II. Clovis set forth under the aegis of St. Martin of Tours, whose sanctuary had not long since been freed from the Visigoths; and he returned there to give thanks for his victory at Vouillé. Historians of the Church did not invent this. But there are other factors, too. Aquitaine was an indivisible part of Roman Gaul, and the peace of the new Frankish conquests south of the Seine was bound up with mastery of the Loire valley. More important still, the Goths were hereditary enemies of the Franks. Childeric had fought the Goths round Angers and Tours for years. Clovis himself had spent a decade skirmishing against them in the same area, and may even have got as far south as Bordeaux. Looked at in this way, Vouillé marks a culmination in a long series of raids and sorties in which religion can have played no part. The difference that religion made may have been more apparent after the battle than before.

---

* ["Meekly bow your head, Sicamber, adore what you have burned, and burn what you have adored." —EDITOR.]

Allowing for the fact that Vouillé did not permit Clovis to annex Visigothic Gaul, and afforded him little more than a much-needed replenishment of his treasure and relief from the threat of eclipse, he still did remarkably little with his victory if we suppose that the Mediterranean was his goal. It is not enough to see Theodoric with his Ostrogoths in Provence as too formidable to take on, especially since the Ostrogoths were themselves threatened in the rear by an imperial naval expedition to Italy, of which Clovis cannot have been ignorant. A threat had been lifted, great treasure collected, old scores wiped off, the Church delighted; and Clovis, after wintering in Bordeaux, made off north to Tours and thence to Paris. There seems never to have been any question of his transferring his headquarters from Soissons or Rheims to Toulouse. What his latest victory chiefly gave him was a free hand in the north.

The victorious Franks bestowed treasure on St. Martin's Church at Tours, for to this saint, according to Gregory's account, they thought they owed their victory. St. Martin is adopted, his cult appropriated. Henceforth this most Gallic of saints belongs to the Merovingians; his *cappa* or soldier's cloak is soon their most treasured relic, from the seventh century at latest, and probably earlier. The soldier-saint of Gaul is not the least of the Merovingian gains from the field of Vouillé, and, in the eyes of many, would be the first solid compensation for the loss of the heathen gods. The gift of treasure to his sanctuary was thus rather more than a polite way of thanking the bishops for favours received. It marked a submission. Moreover, inside St. Martin's Church, Clovis received from a representative of the Emperor Anastasius I a diploma, bestowing on him the title of consul: 'et ab ea die tanquam consul aut augustus est vocitatus'. He was then vested in a purple tunic and a chlamys, placed a diadem on his head and rode from the church into the city of Tours, scattering gold and silver among the crowd as he went. Much has been written about this incident. In general, there is a disposition to belittle it. But Gregory does not belittle it, and the facts as he states them are at least intelligible. They mean that the emperor had bestowed on Clovis an honorary title, probably of consul though possibly of patrician. He could scarcely have bestowed on him a Byzantine rank inferior to that already held by the Burgundian king; and the diploma (*codicilli consulatus*) was the essential preliminary to such an honour. The tradition of Clovis' dress is at once too exact and too misleading to be acceptable as reported by, and probably to, Gregory. It suggests rather a literary source in its details; for the *tunica blattea* and the chlamys and the diadem were all part of imperial, not of consular, ceremonial. Furthermore, a consular procession should have been in a chariot and not on horseback. Only the throwing of gold and silver was typically consular. Whatever the rank, we may be perfectly sure that Clovis and the imperial representative were not in any doubt about it. The significant point is, perhaps, not that the Byzantine envoy was on the spot with imperial approbation of the blow against Gothic power in Gaul, but that Clovis was willing to accept the public mark of that approbation. It makes him no vassal of the Byzantine court; he remains a *rex* and his own master; but he has acknowledged imperial *auctoritas,* the moral ascendency of Rome over Gaul. This is no small matter. It makes one think again of the strange tale of Childeric and Byzantium and the possible significance of the succession to Syagrius; it forewarns one of exchanges between Frankish kings and emperors; and it lends weight to the opinion of Procopius, that the Franks never felt that they held Gaul securely unless the emperor had ratified their title. Clovis would have agreed with his contemporary, Theodoric, that, leaving aside the question of function, the title of consul was supremely worth having; it was 'summum bonum primumque in mundo decus'.* No wonder that the people of Tours hailed the purple-robed barbarian as if he were a kind of Augustus; he probably felt that he was. He had received his title in a part of the world where Roman titles counted for something. The Aquitanian senators were proud of their descent. They attached importance, as did the Germans, not merely to ancestors as a class but to ancestors who were regarded as sanctified. They were confident in the future. How should they not have been, having survived the century of Visigothic rule? The Ostrogoths, moreover, were on the point of re-establishing many of the forms of imperial rule in Provence. It was the world, furthermore, of *Lex Romana Visigothorum* and *Lex Romana Burgundionum,* both of which were to leave an indelible mark upon the laws of the Franks. Thus, law and titles speak jointly for an active ideal of authority, of *imperium,* that might at any time have assumed a practical, political shape. It would be rash to assert that the investiture of Clovis had no effect upon his subsequent acts.

We have to wait three years after Vouillé for a statement of the king's relationship with the most Roman of his institutions, the Church. This is comprised in the canons of the council of Orleans, which are dated 10 July 511 and are subscribed by thirty-two bishops, who represent, largely but not exclusively, the sees of the lately-conquered region of the south. They are no manifesto of royal power. Had they been intended as such, they would surely have been promulgated immediately after Vouillé. Instead, the king waits three years, till a number of practical problems require attention. As for his choice of Orleans, it can at least be said to be further removed from Gothic influence than are the canons themselves, which at several points reflect the work of the council of Agde, summoned by Alaric II the year before Vouillé. The bishops admit that the initiative has been with the new king: he has summoned them and has directed their attention to some of the problems they have tried to solve. They have faithfully dealt with 'titulos quos dedistis'.† Which *tituli* are meant is unclear, but they probably include most of the first ten canons, which cover matters where royal authority is interested: namely, the right of asylum; royal permission for ordinations; the uses to which royal largesse to churches may be put; the frequenting of the royal court by clerics with favours to ask; the ordination of slaves; the appropriation of Arian

* ["Its honor is the highest and greatest good in the world."—EDITOR.]
† ["The charters which you granted"—EDITOR.]

churches taken from the Goths, and the employment of their ministers. To this extent, the king is exercising authority over his bishops and showing how a king may intervene; but not in a way that would have seemed excessive to bishops who remembered the voice of the Visigoth Euric. Not even the Gallo-Romans need have found it so. So powerful a prelate as St. Remigius had to consecrate a priest, at the king's wish, whom all knew to be canonically unfitted. It is an authority, moreover, that tacitly accepts that Roman Law by which the Church lived. The 'saeculari lege' of canon 23 and the 'lex romana' of canon 1 are alike the Theodosian Code. It further supposes the involvement of the Frankish king in that ferment of local loyalties, that crystallization of affection round the shrines of saints, that is the truly significant advance of the Gaulish Church in the sixth century. An aspect of this advance in which the king is necessarily involved is the rapid increase of gifts of land and money and the flow of men to churches and to monasteries. It is an increase, however, and not a beginning, since the Roman *potentes* had also been in the habit of founding churches on their estates. The grants, or some of them, involved authentication in writing; and this meant the help of Roman officials. (One such grant is the *praeceptum de rege* of *Lex Salica*, XIV, 4.) But the measures he takes to safeguard his interests say less to the historian than the fact of acquiescence, which is apparent from the moment of Vouillé and is immediately afterwards confirmed in a letter addressed to certain unknown bishops. We may detect in this letter, and in the canons of the council, a groping for a relationship, but certainly not an endeavour to theorize. The king accepts the bishops; and they accept him as yet one more *rex*. This one, indeed, is a *rex catholicus;* but there is no disposition to treat him cavalierly because of that. A king is expected to have his own way. If he believes that Tolbiac and Vouillé have made him a great Christian king, still more so do the bishops. This is perhaps as far as we can go in determining what difference his conversion made to the kingship of Clovis.

Royal authority is soon expressed in another way, if it is right to assign to these last years of his reign the promulgation of *Lex Salica*. The customary and unwritten laws of the Franks must be supposed to go back at least a century before this, and portions of them are to be seen in the *Lex*. But, as it stands in what seems to be the oldest recension, that of 65 titles, *Lex Salica* is new law; and it is royal law. Clovis was here following the example of his Visigothic and Burgundian near-contemporaries. Not long before, Euric had legislated for the Visigoths, probably following the example of predecessors; and Gundobad and Sigismund for the Burgundians. In addition, both Visigothic and Burgundian kings had legislated separately for their Roman subjects. Clovis did not legislate for his Gallo-Romans, perhaps because they were understood to live under the protection of Roman Law that needed no clarification; but he did offer his Franks the *Lex Salica*. It is a waste of time to debate how narrowly 'Salic', in a tribal sense, this law is. Perhaps it may be defined as that body of Frankish Law which any Frank choosing to acknowledge the kingship of Clovis was bound to live by. What holds it together is the king's will. Its contents are various in date, in provenance and in matter. They are largely concerned with what we should call criminal law, and hardly at all with civil. Indeed, the civil side of Frankish legal life must be supposed to have been determined by Roman practice. Predominantly, the matter of the *Lex* is Germanic, though here and there can be found certain traces of Roman legislation. The true indebtedness of *Lex Salica* to the Romans lies, however, less in specific borrowings than in the fact of composition. Only lawyers familiar with the practice of Vulgar Law in the West could have compiled *Lex Salica*. It is a compilation for barbarians, but not by barbarians. Clovis may have inherited his learned helpers from Syagrius; but there is equally the likelihood that they came to him from Burgundy; and there could have been help from Toulouse. As it originally stood, *Lex Salica* would probably have boasted some royal prefatory matter, such as figures in the Burgundian *Lex Gundobada;* and there are still traces of title-headings in the epilogue which suggest the same kind of Roman influence that moulded Visigothic law. All in all, *Lex Salica* is a fairly complex legal statement that covers a large range of the needs of Franks settled permanently among or near the properties of Christian and Latin-speaking Gallo-Romans. It accords them special privileges not because they are Franks but because they are the king's Franks; and when one considers the disparate nature of their own quite recent origins one appreciates why this protection was more important than any protection against Romans. *Lex Salica* has a practical purpose: it gathers together certain traditional Frankish practices—and these are signalized in the text by the so-called Malberg glosses, which are in the nature of scribal cross-references to aural tradition in the Frankish courts; and it adds to them other, more recent, practices that have come to be accepted on Roman soil, whether directly by the Franks themselves or indirectly, through their Germanic neighbours living in comparable circumstances; and all this matter is promulgated by the authority, the *verbum,* of the Frankish king. It has the further practical advantage of making available to the Church, and in a language it understood, the law by which the Franks chose to be judged in the criminal field. Here and there in *Lex Salica* we can see the king himself arbitrating, judging, extending his protection, when necessary over Romans as well as Franks, watching his own interests, fiscal, military, and territorial. He does not see his subjects as of one blood or appear to desire their fusion; but he is the king of them all, and a very busy man. More than this, the mere fact of his law-giving makes him more of a king. It puts him on a level with men like Alaric II, and it even recalls to his Romans, little though they benefit from *Lex Salica,* the legislative activity proper to the emperor himself. Paradoxically, Roman lawyers have helped him to be a more powerful Germanic king than he was before; they have shown him one way of drawing together his fighting-bands into a Frankish people. The kind of power that he is now able to exercise over them lies in a field where his ancestors would have had little or none; for he and his subordinates are judges in matters that would once have been left to free men in their own gatherings; and it is not to be taken for granted that the tariff fines and compositions laid down in *Lex Salica* might not be overruled by his royal will. Clovis has kept his fighting force intact about his person; he is rich enough in treasure and land to secure fidelity; his rule over Romans is acknowledged by the emperor and encouraged by the Church; and, significantly last, he has collected his Frankish followings into a people that accepts the law that he says is their own.

Clovis did not remain long at Tours. His headquarters, which it would be going too far to call his *sedes regni,* were to remain in the north. His choice was not Tournai, the family property, or Rheims or Soissons; it was Paris. Two emperors, Julian and Valentinian, had made their winter-quarters there, in the walled Île de la Cité; and it was a convenient place from which to control *Belgica Secunda* without losing touch with the Loire valley. But its greatest attraction was its position in the heart of the newly-conquered lands—Neustria—which the Franks of Clovis saw as their own particular settlement-area, as distinct from Tournai. It might, then, seem strange that the toponymy of the Paris region should show no sign of heavy Frankish settlement in the early sixth century. The picture is much more of the continuing predominance of the Gallo-Roman inhabitants of the countryside. Probably, Clovis came to Paris with no more than his private army, or *trustis,* and preferred to keep his men cantoned within the walls, as the Romans had done, and as the Visigoths did at Toulouse. Only later would they have been assimilated into the countryside of the *civitas,* where their properties lay. Two-thirds of the *civitas* were covered by forest, full of game, except where the Gallo-Romans had made clearings to grow corn and wine. Possessor by confiscation of much of this *territorium,* Clovis would have moved from one *palatium* or hunting-lodge to the next. Such movement would slowly cause some increase in population at the *villae* or *vici* concerned, and there would also follow the creation of new parishes dedicated to the tutelary saints of the dynasty. Much of this Parisian property was to go to religious houses over the succeeding three centuries. But, at the centre, lay the stronghold of Paris on the Île de la Cité and an established town on the hilly left bank of the Seine; a place, moreover, of churches where, as dedications bear witness, the cults of St. Martin and St. Marcel were flourishing before the Franks arrived. Six miles away to the north, but well within the *territorium,* was the Roman *castellum* and Christian shrine of St. Denis; the site, equally, of one of the earliest Merovingian *palatia.* We need not be concerned with the legendary story of the martyrdom of St. Denis in the third century. What does matter is that, at about the time when Clovis succeeded his father as king in Tournai, St. Genovefa (Geneviève) was building a church over the remains of St. Denis and his companions. Here, then, was another Parisian cult with which Clovis could hardly avoid contact. The earliest Merovingian associations with that cult and its shrine stretch back far behind Dagobert, to whom the abbey was to owe a new lease of life. At least one of the burials at Saint-Denis recently investigated by M. Salin could belong to the early sixth century. What part was played by the cult of St. Denis in drawing the neophyte to Paris? The biographer of St. Genovefa, writing also in the sixth century, affirms that it was at the request of his queen, Chrotechildis, that Clovis built a church on the site of what is now the Panthéon. He dedicated it to St. Peter and St. Paul, the patrons of Rome. It was further claimed that the king marked out the extent of land for the church by throwing his hatchet, according to normal Frankish practice when taking possession. It does not follow from this that the area was uninhabited or without parochial organization. The evidence is rather of flourishing life on the Rive Gauche. Perhaps the dedication betrays a directer personal submission to the papacy than any written source bears witness of; it would be quite likely, and would be in keeping with the present tendency of scholars to think that early Merovingian contacts with Rome were numerous and natural. Clovis' church was 200 feet long (longer, that is, than St. Martin's church at Tours); and it had marble columns (of which traces have been found) and mosaics representing the history of the patriarchs, the prophets and the martyrs. It may not have been completed when, in 511, Chrotechildis buried her husband there, 'in sacrario' according to Gregory of Tours, who had good reason to know of what most concerned Chrotechildis. It must have been a very different burial from that of King Childeric at Tournai, thirty years earlier. Here was a warrior of Beowulf-like stature, who yet forewent the barrow and the windy headland and was content with a Christian grave in a Parisian church. All the same, finds in later Merovingian graves would warrant the guess that the *novus Constantinus* would have been laid to rest with at least a selection of the pagan symbols dear to his race.

Clovis left behind him a Christian *regnum* that was Roman in expression. This implies that he viewed it in terms that were not wholly barbarian. It was his own conquest, his to do as he wished with; and the subsequent partition of the soil between his sons would support the view that the Franks conceived their conquests as something private to themselves. But the *regnum* itself was not divided, and there remains the possibility that Clovis had already reached an elementary concept of public law, based on his *de facto* succession to Syagrius and his control of Roman territory through Romans and with imperial sanction. But his kingship, by contrast, remained Germanic in essentials. His prestige as a warrior was what most struck the Romans about him; they admired him for being precisely that kind of shield that the Syagrii and the Visigothic kings had failed to be. He afforded them that guarantee of safety from peasant upheavals, pirates' raids and barbarian sallies that had threatened all property-owners in the fifth century, even though he himself was apparently unbound by any treaty with the Empire to respect their lands. He did not marry a Roman, as he might have done, and his children all bore Frankish names redolent of the past. Already, there is that strong Merovingian family-feeling that was to defy stress and strain in the following centuries; there is about it something that the Church was quick to foster as a mystique. Clovis summons his kindred to battle and takes vengeance on them if they fail him. He also fears that they may supplant him. Merovingian blood is fairly widely dispersed among the Frankish kinglets of the north. He does not make the mistake of some of the later Gothic kings, of appearing so Roman as to lose the sympathy of his Germanic followers. Indeed, his preoccupations were with the north, with the safeguarding of his Neustrian territory against all comers from across the Rhine. There is little enough trace of any ambition to make himself a power in the Mediterranean world.

Inevitably, one contrasts the success of Clovis in Gaul with the failure of Theodoric in Italy. The simple solution to the problem of their differing fates would lie in religion. Certainly the Arianism of the Ostrogoths, like the heathenism of the Franks, becomes a decisive factor comparatively late in the story. Both kings supposed that their Germanic and Roman subjects could in many respects live under a common law; and both were liberally served by Roman administrative skill. Laden with imperial titles, Theodoric yet seemed to have ambitions for his people in the Mediterranean world that no emperor could long approve. The effect on his prestige of the withdrawal of imperial approval was incalculable but real. Clovis, on the other hand, remained sufficiently on the fringe of the Empire to offer no threat, and obtained a mark of imperial esteem at the moment when it could most affect the sympathies of the Gallo-Romans. Each claimed a Roman victim. Clovis' was Syagrius, a forgotten marcher-lord; Theodoric's was Boethius, *anima santa* of a civilization.

12. Feudalism in Western Europe

JOSEPH R. STRAYER

*Men can never bear to remain for long in a state of anarchy. Inevitably,
in the wake of the destruction of a system of government and social order,
another will be formed to take its place. The growth of the structure called
"feudalism" in western Europe in the Middle Ages is a curious phenomenon
that shares some characteristics with analogous developments in other times
and places, but is unique in other respects. What is feudalism? What are its
origins, and how did it develop? What significance does it possess for the
course of Western history? Can we even use the term in a correct and intelligible sense?*

*Joseph Strayer addresses himself to these and similar questions in the follow-
ing essay, which was written for a general study of feudalism in world history.
Because it was written for a collection that contrasts across time and geographical areas various systems that have been described as "feudal," his
study is particularly valuable in delineating the prominent aspects of feudalism
in western European society.*

*Strayer teaches medieval history at Princeton and is primarily interested in
institutional history. His works include* The Administration of Normandy
under St. Louis *(1933),* Feudalism *(1965),* On the Medieval Origins of the
Modern State *(1970), a textbook of medieval history with D. C. Munro, and
numerous articles.*

Source: Joseph R. Strayer, "Feudalism in Western Europe," in Rushton Coul-
born, ed., *Feudalism in History.* Copyright © 1956 by Princeton University Press,
pp. 15–25. Reprinted by permission of Princeton University Press.

Strayer advances several theses in this essay, arguing that feudalism in its western European form was essentially a political phenomenon with economic aspects, in which the rights of government were attached to lordship and fiefs. It was therefore something "less than sovereignty; more than private property." He distinguishes carefully between the two stages through which Western feudalism passed, indicating what role it played in society, and how it developed as it did. For Strayer, feudalism was a positive force, a flexible one, which swept away obsolete institutions and responded to real needs. He also tries to establish its relationship with the feudal kingdoms of the Middle Ages and the early modern states. His account is a precise and succinct introduction to the subject, but it is not the final word. The interested student may well wish to pursue further the question of why feudalism followed one course of development in France and England, and another in Germany. Or he may ask what the full-blown feudal institutions owed to Germanic and to late Roman practices. C. Stephenson's brief but succinct Medieval Feudalism (1956) *provides a solid introduction to more detailed works such as M. Bloch's classic* Feudal Society, trans. L. A. Manyon (1961), *F. L. Ganshof's legal study* Feudalism, trans. P. Grierson (1961), *or Lane-Poole's* The Obligations of Society. *L. White's brilliant essay on the stirrup and the origins of feudalism in* Medieval Technology and Social Change (1962) *will reward the reader.*

Feudalism, in Western European history, is a word which has been given many meanings,* but most of them can be brought into two general categories. One group of scholars uses the word to describe the technical arrangements by which vassals became dependents of lords, and landed property (with attached economic benefits) became organized as dependent tenures or fiefs. The other group of scholars uses feudalism as a general word which sums up the dominant forms of political and social organization during certain centuries of the Middle Ages.

---

* Pollock and Maitland, *History of English Law*, 2nd edn. (Cambridge, 1923), I, 66–67: ". . . *feudalism* is an unfortunate word. In the first place it draws our attention to but one element in a complex state of society and that element is not the most distinctive: it draws our attention only to the prevalence of dependent and derivative land tenure. This however may well exist in an age which cannot be called feudal in any tolerable sense. What is characteristic of 'the feudal period' is not the relationship between letter and hirer, or lender and borrower of land, but the relationship between lord and vassal, or rather it is the union of these two relationships. Were we free to invent new terms, we might find *feudo-vassalism* more serviceable than *feudalism*. But the difficulty is not one which could be solved by any merely verbal devices. The impossible task that has been set before the word *feudalism* is that of making a single idea represent a very large piece of the world's history, represent the France, Italy, Germany, England, of every century from the eighth or ninth to the fourteenth or fifteenth. Shall we say that French feudalism reached its zenith under Louis d'Outre-Mer or under Saint Louis, that William of Normandy introduced feudalism into England or saved England from feudalism, that Bracton is the greatest of English feudists or that he never misses an opportunity of showing a strong anti-feudal bias? It would be possible to maintain all or any of these opinions, so vague is our use of the term in question."

There are difficulties with both usages. In the first category there is no agreement on the relationships which are to be considered typically feudal. Is it the act of becoming a vassal, or the act of granting a fief, or a combination of the two which makes feudalism? Retainers, clients, armed dependents of a great man—all these we have in both Germanic and Roman society from the fourth century on, but does that entitle us to speak of Late Roman or primitive German feudalism? Under Charlemagne there are vassals, and these vassals receive dependent tenures. Yet the king still keeps close control over all men and all lands, and the relationships of dependency are not necessarily hereditary. If this is feudalism, then we need another word to describe conditions in the eleventh century. In the seventeenth century, in both France and England all the technical forms of feudalism survive—most nobles are vassals and much of their land is held as fiefs. Yet it is only the form which has survived; the ideas which control the relationship of king and noble no longer conform to the feudal pattern. In short, the difficulty in concentrating on the technical aspects of feudalism is that it sets no chronological limits and provides no standards by which feudalism can be clearly distinguished from preceding and succeeding types of organization.

In the second category this difficulty is overcome by assuming at the outset that there is a "feudal age," a "feudal period" with definite chronological limits. The limits may vary, but there is general agreement on the core of the period—all authorities would admit that feudalism reached its height in the eleventh and twelfth centuries. But while this approach clears up the chronological confusion, it introduces a functional confusion by applying the feudal label to all social phenomena between the tenth and the thirteenth centuries. For example, the class structure of the late Middle Ages was very different from that of the early Middle Ages— are they both feudal? Lords used a different technique in exploiting their lands in 1200 from that in vogue in 1000—which technique should be accepted as typical of feudalism? We meet the sort of difficulties here that a modern historian would find if he assumed that the factory system were an integral part of democracy.

To obtain a usable concept of feudalism we must eliminate extraneous factors and aspects which are common to many types of society. Feudalism is not synonymous with aristocracy—there have been many aristocracies which were not feudal and there was no very clear concept of aristocracy in the early days of feudalism. Feudalism is not a necessary concomitant of the great estate worked by dependent or servile labor—such estates have existed in many other societies. Feudalism is not merely the relationship between lord and man, nor the system of dependent land tenures, for either can exist in a non-feudal society. The combination of personal and tenurial dependence brings us close to feudalism, but something is still lacking. It is only when rights of government (not mere political influence) are attached to lordship and fiefs that we can speak of fully developed feudalism in Western Europe. It is the possession of rights of government by feudal lords and the performance of most functions of government through feudal lords which clearly distinguishes feudalism from other types of organization.

This means that Western European feudalism is essentially political —it is a form of government. It is a form of government in which political authority is monopolized by a small group of military leaders, but is rather evenly distributed among members of the group. As a result, no leader rules a very wide territory, nor does he have complete authority even within a limited territory—he must share power with his equals and grant power to his subordinates. A fiction of unity—a theory of subordination or cooperation among feudal lords—exists, but government is actually effective only at the local level of the county or the lordship. It is the lords who maintain order, if they can, who hold courts and determine what is the law. The king, at best, can merely keep peace among the lords and usually is unable even to do this.

The men who possess political power also possess important sources of wealth—land and buildings, markets and mills, forests and rivers— and this wealth is naturally useful in maintaining or increasing their political authority. Yet wealth alone does not give political power—loyal vassals and courageous retainers are more important. Any sensible feudal lord will surrender much of his land in order to increase the number of his vassals, and the most powerful lords, such as the Duke of Normandy, actually possess relatively few estates. It is also true that political and economic rights do not always correspond. A lord may have rights of government where he has no land and may hold land where some other lord has superior political authority. No one finds this inconsistent, because the distinction which we have been making between political and economic rights has almost no meaning for the early Middle Ages. Public authority has become a private possession. Everyone expects the possessor of a court to make a profit out of it, and everyone knows that the eldest son of the court-holder will inherit this profitable right, whatever his qualifications for the work. On the other hand, any important accumulation of private property almost inevitably becomes burdened with public duties. The possessor of a great estate must defend it, police it, maintain roads and bridges and hold a court for his tenants. Thus lordship has both economic and political aspects; it is less than sovereignty, but more than private property.

Effective feudal government is local, and at the local level public authority has become a private possession. Yet in feudalism the concepts of central government and of public authority are never entirely lost. Kingship survives, with real prestige though attenuated power, and the Church never forgets the Roman traditions of strong monarchy and public law. The revival of Roman law in the twelfth century strengthens these traditions and by the thirteenth century most lawyers insist that all governmental authority is delegated by the king and that the king has a right to review all acts of feudal lords.

Feudal lordship occupies an intermediate place between tribal leadership and aristocratic government. It differs from tribal leadership in being more formalized and less spontaneous. The feudal lord is not necessarily one of the group whom he rules; he may be a complete stranger who has acquired the lordship by inheritance or grant. It differs from aristocracy in being more individualistic and less centralized. The feudal lord is not merely one of a group of men who influence the government; he *is* the government in his own area. When feudalism is at its height, the barons never combine to rule jointly a wide territory but instead seek a maximum degree of independence from each other. One of the signs of the decay of feudalism in the West is the emergence of the idea of government by a *group* of aristocrats.

As the last paragraphs suggest, we must distinguish between an earlier and a later stage of Western feudalism. In the early stage feudalism was the dominant fact in politics, but there was almost no theoretical explanation or justification of the fact. In the later stage feudalism was competing with and slowly losing ground to other types of political organization, and many able writers tried to explain how and why it functioned. The great law-books of the thirteenth century—the Norman *Summa de Legibus,* Bracton, Beaumanoir—fit the facts of feudalism into a logical and well-organized system of law and government. Naturally most writers of secondary works have relied on these treatises and as a result the modern concept of feudalism is largely that of feudalism in the late twelfth and thirteenth centuries—a feudalism which was much better organized, much more precise, and much less important than that of the earlier period.

The first period of feudalism is best exemplified by the institutions of northern France about 1100. In northern France the one basic institution was the small feudal state dominated by the local lord. He might bear any title (the ruler of Normandy was called at various times duke, count, or marquis) and he was usually, though not always, the vassal of a king. But whatever his title, whatever his nominal dependence on a superior, he was in fact the final authority in his region. No one could appeal from his decisions to a higher authority; no one could remain completely indifferent to his commands. His position was based on his military strength. He had a group of trained fighting men in his service; he held fortified strategic positions throughout his lands; he possessed sufficient economic resources to pay for both the army and the fortifications. There might be lesser lords within his sphere of influence who had accepted his leadership in order to gain protection or because his military power left them no choice but submission. Some of his retainers—not necessarily all—would have fiefs for which they rendered service, in which they had limited rights of government. Relations between the lord and these subordinates were still undefined. The exact amount of service to be rendered by the vassal, the rights of government which he could exercise, the degree to which these rights could be inherited by his descendants depended far more on the power and prestige of the lord than on any theory of law. It was up to the lord to defend his territory and his rights; if he failed he would either lose his lands to a stronger neighboring lord or to his more powerful subordinates. There could be great fluctuations in power and in amount of territory controlled, not merely from one generation to another, but even from one decade to another. The only thing which was relatively stable was the method of government. The customs of a region remained the same, even if the lordship changed hands, and every lord had to govern through and with his vassals. They formed his army; they made up the court in which all important acts of government were performed; they performed most of the functions of local government in their fiefs.

The second stage of feudalism—the stage described by the great lawyers of the thirteenth century—bears a closer resemblance to the neat, pyramidal structure of the textbooks. The bonds of vassalage have been tightened at the upper and relaxed at the lower level; the ruler of a province now owes more obedience to his superior and receives less service from his inferiors. Early feudalism might be described as a series of overlapping spheres of influence, each centered around the castles of some strong local lord. Later feudalism is more like a series of holding corporations; the local lord still performs important functions but he can be directed and controlled by higher authority. Appeals from the local lord to his superior are encouraged; petty vassals are protected against excessive demands for service or attempts to seize their fiefs; the central government in some cases deals directly with rear-vassals instead of passing orders down a long chain of command. Royal law-courts play a great role in this reorganization. The institution of the assizes at the end of the twelfth century in England protected the rear-vassal and brought him into direct contact with the king. The development of appeals to the king's court at Paris gave the same results in thirteenth-century France. In this much more highly organized feudalism rights and duties are spelled out in great detail. The amount of service owed is carefully stated, rules of inheritance are determined, the rights of government which can be exercised by each lord are defined and regulated. Force is still important, but only the king and the greatest lords possess sufficient force to gain by its use; the ordinary lord has to accept judicial solutions to his controversies.

There is obviously a great difference between these two stages of feudalism, and yet the transition from one to the other was made so smoothly, in many places, that it was almost imperceptible. It is true that in the later stage rulers were aided by concepts which were not derived from early feudalism, such as the revived Roman law and the Church's ideas of Christian monarchy. Yet, giving due weight to these outside influences, there must still have been some principle of order and growth in early feudalism which made possible the rapid development of relatively advanced systems of political organization in the twelfth and thirteenth centuries. Early feudal society, turbulent as it was, was never pure anarchy. There was always some government, even if rudimentary and local; there were always some centers of refuge and defense. Early feudal government, primitive as it was, was still more sophisticated and complicated than tribal government. There was a higher degree of specialization— the fighting men and the men with rights of government were clearly marked off from the rest of the group. There was a little more artificiality in political organization. Feudal government was not (necessarily) part of the immemorial structure of the community; it could be imposed from the outside; it could be consciously altered by the lord and his vassals. Early feudalism was rough and crude, but it was neither stagnant nor sterile. Flexible and adaptable, it produced new institutions rapidly, perhaps more rapidly than more sophisticated systems of government.

To understand the real vitality of feudalism we shall have to consider briefly the circumstances in which it first appeared in Europe. The Roman Empire had collapsed in the West, largely because none of its subjects cared enough for it to make any great effort to defend it. The Germanic rulers who succeeded the Emperors were not hostile to Roman civilization. They preserved as much of it as they were able; they kept together as large political units as they could. They were not entirely successful in these efforts, but they did preserve real power for the central government and they did thwart the growth of independent local lordship. The greatest of the Germanic rulers, Charlemagne, even united a large part of Western Europe in a new Empire. This was a *tour de force* which has impressed men for over a thousand years; he made his bricks not only without straw but very nearly without clay. The Latin and Germanic peoples he united had no common political tradition, no common cultural tradition and very few economic ties. Their interests were predominantly local, as they had been for centuries; only the clergy remembered with longing the peace and good order of Rome. With the moral support of the Church and the physical support of the army of his own people, the Franks, Charlemagne held his Empire together, but it was always a shaky structure. The Church profited by its existence to extend the parish system and to improve the education of the higher clergy. These developments helped to soften some of the cultural differences among Western European peoples, and to lay the foundations for a common European civilization, but the forces of localism were still stronger than those which worked for unity. Local government was in the hands of counts, men of wealth and high social position who held their authority from the king but who were not always fully obedient to him. The counts, in turn, were not always able to dominate the great landowners of their districts. Vassalage was becoming common and something very like fiefs held of the king or of lords appeared about the middle of the eighth century. Charlemagne tried to reinforce the doubtful loyalty of his subjects by making the great men his vassals, but this expedient had only temporary success. The ties between the magnates and their retainers were far closer than those between Charlemagne and the magnates, for the retainers lived with their lords while the lords visited the imperial court only occasionally. As a result the magnates had great power in their own provinces, subject only to the intermittent intervention of the king. This was not yet feudalism: there was still public authority, and the great men held political power by delegation from the king and not in their own right. But it was very close to feudalism; a strong push was all that was needed to cross the line.

The push came in the fifty years which followed Charlemagne's death. His heirs were less competent than he and quarreled among themselves. The magnates took advantage of these quarrels to gain independence; they began to consider their offices private possessions, to be inherited by their sons. Meanwhile invasions from outside threatened the security of all inhabitants of the Empire. The Saracens raided the south coast of France, the west coast of Italy, and even established a permanent fort at Garde-Frainet which interfered seriously with overland travel between France and Italy. The Magyars occupied Hungary, and from this base sent great cavalry expeditions through southern Germany, eastern France and northern Italy. Worst of all were the Northmen. For over a century their shallow-draft ships pushed up all the rivers of northern Europe and sent out raiding parties which plundered the countryside. The central government was almost helpless; it could not station troops everywhere on the vast periphery of the Empire and it could seldom assemble and move an army quickly enough to catch the fast-moving raiders. Defense had to become a local responsibility; only the local lord and his castle could provide any security for most subjects of the Empire.

It was in these conditions that feudal governments began to appear in northern France—a region which had suffered heavily from both civil war and Viking raids. We could hardly expect these early feudal governments to be well organized and efficient—they were improvised to meet a desperate situation and they bore all the signs of hasty construction. But they did have two great advantages which made them capable of further development. In the first place, feudalism forced men who had privileges to assume responsibility. In the late Roman Empire, the Frankish kingdom and the Carolingian monarchy wealthy landlords had assisted the central government as little as possible while using their position and influence to gain special advantages for themselves. Now they had to carry the whole load; if they shirked they lost everything. In the second place, feudalism simplified the structure of government to a point where it corresponded to existing social and economic conditions. For centuries rulers had been striving to preserve something of the Roman political system, at the very least to maintain their authority over relatively large areas through a hierarchy of appointed officials. These efforts had met little response from the great majority of people; large-scale government had given them few benefits and had forced them to carry heavy burdens. Always there had been a dangerous discrepancy between the wide interests of the rulers and the narrow, local interests of the ruled. Feudalism relieved this strain; it worked at a level which was comprehensible to the ordinary man and it made only minimum demands on him. It is probably true that early feudal governments did less than they should, but this was better than doing more than was wanted. When the abler feudal lords began to improve their governments they had the support of their people who realized that new institutions were needed. The active demand for more and better government in the twelfth century offers a sharp contrast to the apathy with which the people of Western Europe watched the disintegration of the Roman and the Carolingian Empires.

Feudalism, in short, made a fairly clean sweep of obsolete institutions and replaced them with a rudimentary government which could be used as a basis for a fresh start. Early feudal government was informal and flexible. Contrary to common opinion, it was at first little bound by tradition. It is true that it followed local custom, but there were few written records, and oral tradition was neither very accurate nor very stable. Custom changed rapidly when circumstances changed; innovations were quickly accepted if they seemed to promise greater security. Important decisions were made by the lord and his vassals, meeting in informal councils which followed no strict rules of procedure. It was easy for an energetic lord to make experiments in government; for example, there was constant tinkering with the procedure of feudal courts in the eleventh and twelfth centuries in order to find better methods of proof. Temporary committees could be set up to do specific jobs; if they did their work well they might become permanent and form the nucleus of a department of government. It is true that many useful ideas came from the clergy, rather than from lay vassals, but if feudal governments had not been adaptable they could not have profited from the learning and skill of the clergy.

Feudalism produced its best results only in regions where it became the dominant form of government. France, for example, developed her first adequate governments in the feudal principalities of the north, Flanders, Normandy, Anjou and the King's own lordship of the Ile de France. The first great increase in the power of the French king came from enforcing his rights as feudal superior against his vassals. Many institutions of the French monarchy of the thirteenth century had already been tested in the feudal states of the late twelfth century; others grew out of the king's feudal court. By allowing newly annexed provinces to keep the laws and institutions developed in the feudal period, the king of France was able to unite the country with a minimum of ill-will. France later paid a high price for this provincial particularism, but the existence of local governments which could operate with little supervision immensely simplified the first stages of unification.

England in many ways was more like a single French province than the congeries of provinces which made up the kingdom of France. In fact, the first kings after the Conquest sometimes spoke of the kingdom of their "honor" or feif, just as a feudal lord might speak of his holding. As this example shows, England was thoroughly feudalized after the Conquest. While Anglo-Saxon law remained officially in force it became archaic and inapplicable; the law which grew into the common law of England was the law applied in the king's feudal court. The chief departments of the English government likewise grew out of this court. And when the combination of able kings and efficient institutions made the monarchy too strong, it was checked by the barons in the name of the feudal principles expressed in Magna Carta. Thus feudalism helped England to strike a happy balance between government which was too weak and government which was too strong.

The story was quite different in countries in which older political institutions prevented feudalism from reaching full development. Feudalism grew only slowly in Germany; it never included all fighting men or all lands. The German kings did not use feudalism as the chief support of their government; instead they relied on institutions inherited from the Carolingian period. This meant that the ruler acted as if local lords were still his officials and as if local courts were still under his control. In case of opposition, he turned to bishops and abbots for financial and military aid, instead of calling on his vassals. There was just enough vitality in this system to enable the king to interfere sporadically in political decisions all over Germany, and to prevent the growth of strong, feudal principalities. But while the German kings of the eleventh and twelfth centuries showed remarkable skill in using the old precedents, they failed to develop new institutions and ideas. Royal government became weaker, and Germany more disunited in every succeeding century. The most important provincial rulers, the dukes, were also unable to create effective governments. The kings were jealous of their power, and succeeded in destroying, or weakening all the great duchies. The kings, however, were unable to profit from their success, because of their own lack of adequate institutions. Power eventually passed to rulers of the smaller principalities, not always by feudal arrangements, and only after the monarchy had been further weakened by a long conflict with the papacy. Thus the German kings of the later Middle Ages were unable to imitate the king of France, who had united his country through the use of his position as feudal superior. Germany remained disunited, and, on the whole, badly governed, throughout the rest of the Middle Ages and the early modern period.

Italy also suffered from competition among different types of government. The German emperor was traditionally king of (north) Italy. He could not govern this region effectively but he did intervene often enough to prevent the growth of large, native principalities. The Italian towns had never become depopulated, like those of the North, and the great economic revival of the late eleventh century made them wealthy and powerful. They were too strong to be fully controlled by any outside ruler, whether king or feudal lord, and too weak (at least in the early Middle Ages) to annex the rural districts outside their walls. The situation was further complicated by the existence of the papacy at Rome. The popes were usually on bad terms with the German emperors and wanted to rule directly a large part of central Italy. In defending themselves and their policies they encouraged the towns' claims to independence and opposed all efforts to unite the peninsula. Thus, while there was feudalism in Italy, it never had a clear field and was unable to develop as it did in France or England. Italy became more and more disunited; by the end of the Middle Ages the city-state, ruled by a "tyrant," was the dominant form of government in the peninsula. There was no justification for this type of government in medieval political theory, and this may be one reason why the Italians turned with such eagerness to the writings of the classical period. In any case, the Italian political system was a failure, and Italy was controlled by foreign states from the middle of the sixteenth to the middle of the nineteenth century.

There are certainly other factors, besides feudalism, which enabled France and England to set the pattern for political organization in Europe, and other weaknesses, besides the absence of fully developed feudalism, which condemned Germany and Italy to political sterility. At the same time, the basic institutions of France and England in the thirteenth century, which grew out of feudal customs, proved adaptable to changed conditions, while the basic institutions of Italy and Germany, which were largely non-feudal, had less vitality. Western feudalism was far from being an efficient form of government, but its very imperfections encouraged the experiments which kept it from being a stagnant form of government. It was far from being a just form of government, but the emphasis on personal relationships made it a source of persistent loyalties. And it was the flexibility of their institutions and the loyalty of their subjects which enabled the kings of the West to create the first modern states.

13. Land, Family and Women in Continental Europe, 701–1200

DAVID HERLIHY

According to many contemporary practicing historians, history is legitimately concerned with the achievements of mankind, and is limited in terms of its diversity and interests only by the evidence at the disposal of the historian, and his own particular capabilities and skills. Thus, where once history meant primarily the study of war and politics at the highest level, historians today are importing techniques and approaches from other social sciences like anthropology, sociology, economics, and political science to broaden their own investigations of the past. Social history in particular has become rather fashionable these days, and the study of classes in society, their composition, interests, values, and role generally is receiving a good deal of investigation. The place of women as a class in particular presently occupies the attention of many social scientists. In order to illustrate this trend, and to cover an important topic, the following selection is included.

David Herlihy is a noted medieval economic historian at the University of Wisconsin. His article on "Land, Family and Women" is a fine example of intelligent and imaginative use of sources to compile data on which theoretical speculation can be based. In an attempt to work around the paucity of direct evidence on the place of women in medieval society, Herlihy has gone to a large number of charters dealing with inheritance, bequest, and other types of

Source: David Herlihy, "Land, Family and Women in Continental Europe, 701–1200," *Traditio* XVIII (1962), pp. 89–120. Reprinted by permission of Fordham University Press. [Footnotes, graphs, and Appendix omitted.]

land transfer. The questions he poses, and the statistical evidence he compiles, are quite revealing, both about his method and the society he is studying. His conclusions clearly demonstrate the important role that many women played during the feudal period, while his analysis provides much specific information to indicate how feudal tenure operated. This information supplements the more abstract discussion by Strayer in the preceding selection.

Those who are interested in social history in the Middle Ages, and especially in the role of women, might well read Eileen Power's excellent collection of essays entitled Medieval People *(first published in 1924, but available in many subsequent editions). She was one of the first modern scholars to write about ordinary people and class history, and she made substantial contributions to the* Cambridge Economic History. *In* Medieval People *the reader will find six essays about ordinary or at least representative individuals, their daily lives and activities, which amount to an economic history of the Middle Ages.*

In reconstructing the social and economic history of the early Middle Ages, perhaps the single, most salient obstacle to our research is the scant amount of information we possess concerning the household economy of the lay family, how the family managed its lands and divided its labors among its members. Our sources, overwhelmingly ecclesiastical in provenience, tell us fairly much of the organization of Church properties, and, through a few surviving royal records, we have some information too about royal estates. But at all times in medieval Europe, non-royal lay families owned or controlled the larger portion of the soil. We must try to learn more about how these propertied families managed their estates, and how internal family structure may have been affected by, or in turn may have influenced broader economic and social changes.

In studying the management of lay patrimonies and its possible interaction with family structure, the subject of immediate interest is the woman, the position she held within the family, the role she played in the supervision of family property, and the relation between the two. For as we hope to illustrate in this article, the woman comes to play an extraordinary role in the management of family property in the early Middle Ages, and social customs as well as economic life were influenced by her prominence.

To be sure, much is already known of the legal rights of women in regards to land ownership and the administration of family property, as defined in late-Roman law and the Germanic codes. The history of Roman law is the history of progressive improvement in the legal rights of the woman. Within marriage, for example, the kind of near-parental power (the *manus mariti*) the husband exercised over his wife was not universally characteristic of Roman marriages even in the period of the Twelve Tables and by the time of the Principate had become practically non-existent. Formal tutelage (*tutela*) over adult women *sui iuris* continued longer, till about the time of Diocletian, and throughout the Imperial period a woman—as, for that matter, many men—might live under the continuing and restrictive legal authority of her father (the *patria potestas*). Still, by a variety of legal resources, the enterprising woman could, if she wished, render the tutelage more fictional than real, and even the woman under paternal power could eventually hold and manage property of her own. Within marriage, too, the property she had owned before marriage was kept distinct from her husband's, and, should the marriage be dissolved, that property and her dowry too would be returned to her. Apparently, however, late-Roman law did not yet admit of a true community property between the marriage partners, in a way that would have permitted the wife to claim, at the death of her husband and the division of family property, a share in the wealth that family enterprise might have gained. But certainly, in late-Roman legal development, progress was being made towards it.

From what we know of Old Germanic law, the woman was (as in early Roman law) similarly considered to be lacking in juridical capacity to look after her own interests. According to Lombard law (in this regard perhaps the most conservative of the Germanic codes), the woman, even as an adult, remained under the guardianship ('mundium') of a male relative (or failing such, the king), whose permission was required for any transaction involving her property. Within marriage Lombard law provided for a close union of the partners' properties under the control of the husband. The principle here seems to have been that a wife's property could neither increase nor decrease in marriage, which means she did not share in family acquests, but, should the marriage be dissolved, could claim back from it exactly what she had brought to it.

In regard to the guardianship of women and the status of their properties within marriage, the other Germanic codes are not always so clear. It is, however, certain, that by the age of the barbarian kingdoms, the traditional Germanic restrictions on a woman's capacity to inherit, own and administer property were breaking down. The famous and still somewhat mysterious title of the Salic law (62.6), prohibiting women from inheriting 'Salic' land, was modified by the Edict of Chilperic (561–84), which admitted daughters to the inheritance in the absence of direct male issue. In Frankish law too, (to judge by charters) the adult woman by Merovingian times was free of effective male tutelage. Visigothic law in particular is remarkable for the freedom it granted to the marriage partners, including the wife, to administer the respective 'capital' they possessed before marriage, and Burgundian law was similarly liberal. Moreover, in Visigothic law, acquisitions gained after marriage were considered the community property of the family, and should that family be dissolved, the wife or her heirs could claim a share in family acquests. Should the husband die, the wife retained use of and administrative control over family property and indeed over the total patrimony of her minor children. Frankish, Alemannian and Bavarian laws also provided for a close association of the partners' possessions, and the wife (though apparently not her heirs) could benefit personally from family acquests. It is, however, very

189

Herlihy

LAND, FAMILY
AND WOMEN IN
CONTINENTAL
EUROPE

difficult to judge if the often vague provisions of these codes as yet represented a true community property (as in the Visigothic law); but we may safely say again that progress was being made towards it.

Besides these contrasts among the various legal traditions, there are likewise evident certain uniformities worth pointing out. And uniformities are of course to be expected, given the all-pervasive influence of the Christian Church and given her strong notions on the proper position of the woman within the family. In unequivocally asserting that men and women shared a common spiritual destiny and dignity, the Christian Church undoubtedly helped prevent the woman from anywhere becoming a chattel of her husband; in seeking to establish the sanctity and permanence of marriage, the Church helped confirm her importance as established mistress of her household. At the same time, Christian teaching was hardly such as to allow a real social matriarchy to develop anywhere in Europe. The Church Fathers characteristically thought of the woman as a weaker vessel, and considered a prominent role in affairs outside the family unsuited for her. In other words, under the levelling influence of Christianity, the position of women throughout Europe was kept within certain limits. She was everywhere more than chattel, and everywhere less than a matriarch. Specifically in regard to property, late-Roman law and the Germanic codes were similar in recognizing that the woman could retain a personal title to property even within marriage, though the degree of freedom she possessed in administering it and the benefit she derived from further family gains differed considerably among the various legal traditions.

However, if the legal rights of women in regard to family property have already been pretty well explored, our picture still shows gaps. The laws deal largely with the great or extraordinary events in the history of medieval families: how they were created, what happened when they dissolved. They tell us rather little of the ordinary, day-by-day life of the family, how its property was administered, and the role women played in it. To investigate this, we may turn from legal codes to our so-called 'documents of practice'—donations, sales, exchanges, leases, and so forth, which constitute a detailed and precise record of early medieval agrarian life. In Italy, in Germany, in Northern France, such documents have survived in great numbers from the middle eighth century; in Southern France and Spain, from the early ninth. By 1200 they are counted by the tens of thousands.

In handling these documents, we shall try a statistical approach—not on the pretense of constructing a precise sociological survey but in an effort more effectively to survey our huge mass of material than could be done by random and impressionistic selection of a few documents out of thousands. Our statistics are directed, in other words, towards illustrating largely verbal contrasts and changes in our documents considered as a single corpus, in the hope that out of such an analysis a clearer view of woman's practical role in the family and in land administration might emerge.

Specifically, we shall construct three statistical indices, each based on a different kind of information but all reflective of the role women played in the family and in the administration of its property. Because that role varied in different parts of Europe, we shall construct these indices separately for each of the following five regions of continental Europe: Italy, Spain (including Portugal), Southern France (roughly south of the Loire River and including French Switzerland), Northern France (including the Low Countries), and Germany (including Austria, German Switzerland, Alsace and Luxemburg).

One possible indication of the importance of the woman within the family is the use, by her children, of a matronymic rather than a patronymic. We have much material with which to evaluate the importance of the matronymic in continental Europe. For the scribe of course had to identify precisely the principals in and witnesses to his charters, and to this end he often gave a parent's name: 'Petrus filius Silvestri,' simply 'Petrus Silvestri,' occasionally 'Petrus de Silvestro.' Both men and women were commonly identified by a parent's name, even after the parent's death (indicated in the charters by such words as 'quondam' or 'bone memorie'). For Italy, between the early eighth century and 1200, we can extract from the chartularies and parchment collections . . . over 80,000 patronymics. Our numbers from other regions are not so enormous, but they are still substantial. From Southern France we have close to 10,000; from Spain, nearly 19,000. In both areas, patronymics appear from the early ninth century, but remain sporadic until the eleventh. From Northern France we have over 6,000, and from Germany 700. In these regions, our series becomes threadbare from the late ninth to the eleventh centuries—a period when our northern private charters are both relatively few in number and poorly informative.

Significantly for our purposes, many persons in the charters are identified not by the name of a father but of a mother: 'Azo filius Formose,' 'Azo Formose,' 'Azo de Formosa.' We shall try to illustrate this curious popularity of the matronymic by calculating what percentage of our total identifications by parent involves female names. In calculating that percentage we take as a patro- or matronymic only the name of a male or female parent used to identify a particular individual. We do not consider as patronymics such phrases as 'heredes Iohannis,' 'filii Tancredi,' in which the 'heirs' or 'sons' are unnamed. Nor do we take as a patronymic reference to a parent who also appears in the charter; thus, in such a phrase as 'Petrus et Iohannes filius ipsius Petri,' Petrus would not be counted. In instances where both parent and grandparent are named (e.g. 'Iohannes de Petro Formose'), only the parent's name is counted. In instances where both father's and mother's names are given, only the father's is counted. In double names, the second is considered a patronymic when in the genitive case, unless it is evident from the context that it is not. Thus, 'Guillelmus' is considered a patronymic in the name 'Raimundus Gellelmi' but not in the name "Raimundus Guillelmus.' Ambiguous cases (e.g. 'in manu Raimundi Guillelmi') are excluded. Spanish second names in -z (e.g.

191

Herlihy

LAND, FAMILY
AND WOMEN IN
CONTINENTAL
EUROPE

'Petrus Lopez,' 'Iohannes Gonzalez') are counted as patronymics. However, in such Spanish names as 'Petrus Taresa' the 'Taresa' is considered a matronymic. In such hybrid names as 'Johannes Guillelmi filius Matilde' we count only the parent's name following the 'filius.' Names of kings given to date the charter are not considered. Each particular patronymic is counted only once in each charter, no matter how many individuals may bear it.

Table 1 gives the results of our count on the basis of centuries, for each of the five regions of continental Europe we are considering:

Table 1
Percentage per century of identifications by matronymic

Region	8th	9th	10th	11th	12th
Italy	2	2	5	6	5
Spain	–	–	1	6	3
S. France	–	–	9	12	10
N. France	–	0	0	6	8
Germany	3	0	–	2	8

Because of the wide regional differences in the use of patronymics and the notarial methods of expressing them, we ought not press these comparisons too closely. However, rough as our table undoubtedly is, there still emerges from it evidence of a remarkable use of matronymics in Southern France from the tenth through the twelfth century. In Spain the phenomenon is evident from the eleventh century, though Spanish matronymics are drawn, as we shall see, chiefly from particular kinds of charters. In Italy, matronymics become common from the second quarter of the tenth century and reach their peak frequency (532 out of 6062) in the early eleventh. Their relative numbers then decline, though they remain fairly plentiful through the twelfth century. In Northern Europe, the phenomenon becomes evident somewhat later than in the South, clearly so in Northern France, presumably so in Germany, though we have only few names with which to judge the incidence of matronymics before 1100 in Germany.

Graph 1, based upon our total of over 125,000 patronymics from all regions of the continent and plotted on the basis of twenty-five-year periods, affords a more accurate chronological perspective on this incidence of matronymics. It shows that the matronymic, rare from the eighth century to the middle tenth, becomes ever more common during the latter half of the tenth century and reaches its peak frequency in the early eleventh. Its incidence then falls off, though it remains relatively high through the twelfth century.*

How are we to explain this marked preference of so many individuals in our charters to identify themselves with their mothers? We cannot of course discount the influence of notarial practices upon this incidence of

* [This graph has not been reproduced here.—EDITOR.]

matronymics. Occasionally the matronymic partook of the nature of a nickname. 'Fasana the daughter of Sergius the priest,' a Neapolitan charter of 1108 reads, 'who is called de Maroccia.' In those areas where notarial tradition dictated particularly rigid formulas and strict procedures, the notary may well have suppressed such semi-popular sobriquets in favor of formal and consistent references to the father. The extreme rarity of matronymics in Milanese documents, for example, in comparison with those from other areas in Italy, may owe something to the peculiar strictness of the Lombard notarial procedures.

Still, while notarial usage may be a factor in explaining why matronymics are extremely rare in some areas, it cannot explain why they are plentiful in others. For we still need to know why, in the charters, so many men were identified with their mothers. Nor are there grounds for attributing the widespread increase in the incidence of matronymics after 950 to any evident and equally widespread change in notarial practices.

In some few instances, the matronymic seems to indicate that the father had remarried and had children by another wife. 'Petrus Vilelmi,' says a French document of 1138, 'son of Dulciana and his brother Bertrand son of Lucia.' Then too, the matronymic could be conveniently used as a means of distinguishing a son from a like-named father or grandfather. A ninth-century charter identifies Charles the Bald (d. 877) as 'son of Judith,' whether to distinguish him from other Charles's in the Carolingian line or from his half-brothers Lothar and Louis, whom his father Louis the Pious had had by earlier marriage. However, even if we could presume that substantial numbers of those bearing matronymics in our charters had half-brothers or like-named fathers, we must still explain why, in most instances, the mother's name alone was sufficiently well known in the community to identify her children. That Charles the Bald could be identified by reference to his mother Judith exclusively shows that Judith, in her own right, was a famous lady. And from what we know of her prominent role in Carolingian history, that is certain.

Occasionally, of course, the matronymic is flatly indicative of illegitimacy. 'John, natural son of Gemma,' reads a charter of 1182 from Amalfi. However, as we shall see, a careful consideration of the circumstances accompanying the use of matronymics excludes all thought that our index primarily reflects the prevalence of illegitimacy over the regions of Europe and during these centuries of its history.

More precisely, in some instances use of the matronymic reflected the fact that the person's juridic status derived from his mother. 'Tersia, the daughter of Honoria our freedwoman,' says a will of 739. In a document of 874, listing eleven serfs of the monastery of San Vincenzo al Volturno, no less than four bear a matronymic, perhaps indicating illegitimate birth, but more likely reflecting the fact the monastery's title over them came through the mother. So also, serfs appearing in the chartulary of Saint-Pierre at Ghent rather frequently bear matronymics, and sporadic examples of serfs and slaves identified with their mothers can be found widely across Europe. For typically the child of a slave-woman and a freeman re-

193

Herlihy

LAND, FAMILY
AND WOMEN IN
CONTINENTAL
EUROPE

mained a slave and the property of his mother's master. Undoubtedly liaisons between freemen and servile women were not uncommon, and the offspring who retained his mother's 'law' may also have widely borne the mother's name, at least in the records of the seigneury which owned him. Moreover, in marriages between serfs of different lords, the mother's owner typically would claim half the offspring, and this may have been reflected in the use of a matronymic. Still, marriages which broke class lines or transgressed the boundaries of the manorial community can account for only a minute fraction of our matronymics. For clearly, most individuals who figure in our charters are not the sons of serfs or persons subject to the discipline of the manorial community. They are freemen, many of them indeed representatives of the highest levels of medieval society. Nor can we satisfactorily explain the sudden and pronounced increase in the frequency of matronymics after 950 by a supposed increase in marriages of persons of different juridical status or of different manorial lords.

More important a factor behind this use and increase of matronymics is clerical marriage. It is certain that a good many of the men and women identifying themselves in the charters with their mothers were the products of clerical families. This is particularly evident in central Italy around Rome and in Tuscany, though clerics and the apparent children of clerics bearing a matronymic can be found widely in Europe. 'The sons of Benedict the cleric,' reads a charter of 1109 from Capua, 'who are called the sons of Gaita.' 'Fasana the daughter of Sergius the priest,' says the Neapolitan charter of 1108 already cited, 'who is called de Maroccia.' Ugo, son of Bishop Regembald of Florence, styled himself in a charter of *ca.* 1059 'son of Minuta.' In our central Italian and Tuscan charters, a disproportionate number of priests use a matronymic. Had they been raised in the vicinity of a church, to continue as adults their father's profession? In other words, the proliferation of matronymics after 950 would seem to some extent to measure the developing crisis in the Western Church over clerical marriage ('nicholaism'). So too, the decline in our index from the middle eleventh century to some extent shows the success of the Gregorian reform movement, which took as its supreme goal the restoration of celibacy as the fundamental rule of clerical living.

A discreet effort to conceal an uncanonical clerical marriage thus accounts for many of our matronymics. Still, such discretion cannot be the most general explanation for their use. Our charters do not give the impression of a careful reticence in regard to illegitimacy, and bastards, natural sons or children of priests are often baldly labeled in them. In many charters, the father is recognized and his name stated (prayers may be asked for his soul), but the son or daughter still uses a matronymic. Stranger still, in some instances the same individual will use a patronymic in one charter, and a matronymic in another. He changes his name as the circumstances of the contract, its locale, or the property involved in it, change. It is here evident that a matronymic is preferred because it better served to identify the principal, perhaps reflecting the fact that the mother was locally better known than the father or that her name was traditionally associated with the property involved.

Moreover, clerical marriage by itself is an insufficient explanation for this profusion of matronymics. In Northern Italy, in Germany, in Northern France, and especially in Southern France and Spain, association with the mother is most strikingly characteristic not of the clergy but of the most prominent of laymen, the nobles and knights. In Spain, in the Aragonese charters by which vassals or châtelains are invested with their tenures or oaths of loyalty taken, both the vassal and his lord will usually identify themselves by matronymics. Indeed, apart from these special (though numerous) charters, matronymics would have to be considered rare in Spanish documents. The similar acts of investiture and oath from Southern France are similarly characterized by a consistent use of matronymics to identify the principals. So strong is this tradition that in a charter from Maguelone, dated *ca.* 1155–60, a vassal designated by a matronymic, swears a feudal oath, and it later emerges that the father too (along with the mother) is physically present and 'ordering' his son so to act. Is this consistent use of matronymics in association with feudal investitures and oaths only an example of a rigidified notarial practice in those areas? Perhaps; but again, these mothers must have been well known in their communities, for their names sufficiently to identify their sons.

Moreover, in Southern France (unlike Spain), matronymics appear widely in other forms of charters too. So also in Italy, Northern France, and Germany, matronymics are found in all sorts of documents. The men who bear them are obviously socially prominent. They are often identified as knights: 'Arduinus miles, filius Joscende nobilissime mulieris,' 'Artaldus miles de Calamont, filius Alatrudis.' Most of them are appearing as witnesses to the charters of great laymen or ecclesiastics. The women whose names they bear are socially prominent too, sometimes titled, often distinguished by the term 'lady': 'Don Pedro filio de domna Cecilia,' 'Godesio Didaci de cometissa domna Geluira,' 'Guidoctus domine Navilie,' 'Iohannes de domna Maria.'

Here, there can be no question of distinguishing an illicit paternity. For several prominent families of Southern France—the Guillems of Montpellier, for example—we know quite well the genealogy of the male line. But in each generation the members characteristically identify themselves not with their fathers (from whom they principally inherited their lands and status) but with their mothers: 'Villelmus (V) filius Ermengarde,' 'Guillelmus (VI) filius Ermessendis,' 'Guillem (VII) filius Sibilie,' and the like. Was the matronymic here used primarily in order to distinguish a succession of like-named Williams? Possibly; but such a device would still presume that these mothers were well known and long remembered in Montpellier.

A Poitevin charter is dated by reference to Guillaume V Aigret of Poitou (1039–1058), seventh duke of Aquitaine: 'Lord count William, son

195

Herlihy

LAND, FAMILY
AND WOMEN IN
CONTINENTAL
EUROPE

of countess Agnes, ruling.' Guillaume's father is well known and his legitimacy unquestioned. Can we be surprised when, in the dating of a thirteenth-century Poitevin charter, Louis IX, king of France, legitimate heir to the great Capetian line, is identified as 'Louis, son of Blanche'?

Why are these knights, nobles and kings associated with their mothers? Occasionally the reason would seem that their inheritance came from their mother. Alphonse VII, 'the Emperor' (1126–1157), king of Castile, calls himself in several charters 'son of Urraca,' apparently for the reason that his Spanish inheritance devolved through her as daughter and heir of Alphonse VI rather than through his father Raymond of Burgundy. We can give an example, from Catalonia, of a son following his mother as tenant of a castle or fief, assuming, we may note, both her castle and her name. In Southern France, Mary, viscountess of Béarn, succeeded her brother Gaston V. The Béarnais revolted and forced her and her husband to abdicate in favor of one of their sons. That son (Gaston VI) is called in a charter 'son of Mary.'

Accordingly, the admissibility of women specifically to the inheritance of fiefs had some influence upon their status. In Catalonia and Southern France, it is evident from our charters that women were being widely admitted to feudal inheritances already from the tenth century. In Italy, on the other hand, the 'Edictum de beneficiis regni italici' (1037) of Emperor Conrad II expressly excluded women and cognate relatives from feudal inheritance; later emperors tried to impose a similar regimen in Germany, with indifferent success. However, even in the twelfth century, these customs governing feudal inheritance are still too amorphous and varying to have exercised a decisive influence on the prominence of women. It would be difficult to judge whether, in Southern France or Catalonia for example, such customs explain the high status of women, or the high status of women explains the development of the inheritance customs which were coming to favor them.

Moreover, the use of a matronymic in our charters does not consistently or even usually mean that the individual owed the major part of his inheritance to his mother. Guillaume V Aigret of Poitou did not inherit his lands from his mother Agnes (who was from Burgundy), nor did Louis IX receive France from his Spanish mother Blanche; yet in the charters we cited, both bear a matronymic. That Louis should be identified with Blanche of Castile would seem primarily recognition of the queen-mother's importance, of her role in the public eye, of the fact that she served as regent during her son's minority and continued to exert influence on royal policy. Agnes of Burgundy was similarly a *grande dame* of a previous century, whose role in Poitevin history was similarly prominent.

For the patronymic or matronymic served no strictly juridical purpose in the charters and was not therefore strictly reflective of juridical factors. The scribe was primarily interested in identifying particular individuals, in the way consistent with established notarial practices which would make them easily recognizable to the readers of his charters. He did this usually by naming the family from which a person came, in the sense of mentioning the parent, the father or the mother, who at the time was better known or at least well known in the community.

. . . . .

The curious and considerable reputation of women within their communities, reflected in the matronymic—this to explain is the heart of our problem. And this much at least is obvious: a woman's reputation, fame, notability, prominence, in the Middle Ages as today, could be built upon many factors. She could have sprung from a family long established in the community or of high social standing; she could have possessed in notable degree the feminine qualities of beauty, elegance, sensitivity, or simply the human qualities of intelligence, ambition or energy. According to the etiquette of courtly love, the lover or troubadour was specifically enjoined to further the repute of his lady's physical and cultural distinctions and thereby add to her fame. And in Southern France, home of courtly love, there does seem to be a correlation between the work of troubadours in lauding ladies and the kind of community reputation reflected in our matronymics.

Many things could indeed make a lady famous. We are here interested in only one factor, her economic activities. We want to inquire if there is evident any correlation between the repute of women reflected in the matronymic and the economic functions they assumed in regard to family property. This is of course to lay emphasis on one factor out of many, but that factor would seem of indisputable importance. Medieval society was land-based; the status of a family was still pretty much determined by the lands it owned. The one most prominent in managing that land, who paid or collected the rent, who sold what surpluses the farm or estate produced or bought at the market place what is lacked, who participated in the various community functions that land management entailed—he would perforce become well known to his neighbors. When and if that manager was a woman, her reputation would be widespread. Then too, prominence in economic life may have enhanced a woman's influence on those activities supported by it: court life, court entertainments, the qualities of the new vernacular literature therein developing. The possible correlation between social repute and economic functions of the lady is worth investigating.

197
Herlihy
LAND, FAMILY
AND WOMEN IN
CONTINENTAL
EUROPE

We must first note, in general terms, that the woman during the Middle Ages everywhere and always had some importance in the management of the household economy. The wife characteristically supervised the household's 'inner economy' ('Innenwirtschaft'), those activities carried on in or near the house, cooking, brewing, spinning and weaving, usually too the garden and the raising and care of yard animals. Conversely, the 'outer economy' ('Aussenwirtschaft'), principally the work in outlying fields and the tending of herds, was the man's domain. However, the precise range of the woman's inner economy was flexible, expanding or contracting in relation to whether the man had assumed other functions which might keep him from home for lengthy periods or make him disdainful of agricultural labor. If we are to believe Tacitus' picture of the family life of the Germanic freemen on the eve of the invasions, the 'best and bravest' of them left even agricultural labor to the women and made their contribution to the family fortunes by raids and wars. Tacitus elsewhere says that the Germanic warrior looked to collecting tribute from his housed slaves, but the other functions of home management, the 'officia domus,' fell to the women and children.

We need not attempt to assess the influence of the social arrangements Tacitus describes on later medieval development. For fortunately, we have a picture of household management much closer to our period of interest, dealing not with common freemen but with the greatest of propertied laymen, the king himself. In 882 Hincmar of Rheims wrote for the instruction of the Frankish king Carloman an essay on the organization of the royal household, *De ordine palatii*, substantially incorporating into his text an earlier, similar treatise written by Adalhard of Corbie and dating from the reign of Charlemagne. According to the *De ordine*, the royal treasurer, the 'camerarius,' is directly under the queen. Moreover, the queen is responsible for giving to the knights their yearly gifts, the equivalent of their salaries. This heavy responsibility falls upon the queen in order to free her husband from 'domestic or palace solicitude' and to enable him to give all his attention 'to the state of the entire kingdom.' So too, Agobard of Lyons mentions the Carolingian queen as being in a peculiar way responsible for the 'honestas' of the palace. Presumably this required too that the queen assume a similarly prominent role in supervising the economic activities which stocked the treasury, made possible the knightly gifts, and assured palatine 'honestas'—specifically the workshops ('genitia') on the royal manors and perhaps the manors themselves. Charlemagne's own *Capitulare de villis* mentions how instructions are given to manorial officials and accounts received from them by himself 'or the queen.' Why else should that phrase 'or the queen' be introduced into this administrative document, if her role in regard to manorial administration was not a real one?

We have further hints that the importance of the woman was not limited to the royal administration but extended also to other great landed households, and that that importance did not change when grants of land rather than gifts became the principal payments for dependent knights. In the marriage donation ('sponsalitium') made to Countess Adalmodis in Spain (1056), her husband specifically mentions the *mobile* or movables 'which by agreement are to be given to the châtelains every year.' Like the Carolingian palatine knights, these Spanish châtelains would be beholden for their salaries to a woman. In Spanish charters of investiture, it is also occasionally evident that a male principal is absent, as his wife must promise that he will agree to the transaction 'thirty days after Alamannus her husband comes.' The absent Alamannus, like the Carolingian king, had evidently found a way through which he could be largely relieved of 'domestic or palace solicitude.' About 1030 in Northern Italy, Waza, apparently the wife of the Margrave William III of Monferrat (d. before 1042), made a pious visit to the tomb of a saint. She went 'surrounded by knights,' and a beggar beseeched her for alms. She refused, saying that she had not wealth abundant enough to suffice for herself 'and all those seeking from me.' The verb here used, *petere*, may perhaps be reminiscent of the juridic language of numerous Italian charters of benefice and lease, introduced by a formal 'petition' for a grant of land.

Within the clerical or nicholaite family, women seem to have enjoyed a similar prominence. At Vercelli about 960, married priests ordered to put away their wives answered 'that unless they were maintained by the hands of their women they would succumb to hunger and nakedness. At Ravenna too, in 963, the priests could not live 'regularly,' i.e. celibately, 'because of hunger and nakedness,' implying that a wife assured them support not otherwise available. In the 970's when Ratherius of Verona tried to introduce celibate living among his clergy, he found: 'the excuse of almost everyone was "this can in no wise be because of our poverty".' Apparently in these nicholaite families, women had assumed economic functions of critical importance. The presence of fair numbers of available, propertied or at least economically resourceful women may have even aggravated the abuse of nicholaism within the tenth-century Church, as needy clerics sought a relief from their own poverty in advantageous liaisons. The sons of priests who use a matronymic were perhaps attempting to cover the ignominy of their fathers. But they also give illustration of the prominence and repute of their mothers within the life of the community. The important role which those women of Rome—the notorious Theodora and Marozia—played in the political history of that city in the early tenth century may perhaps be cited as further example of the prominence that women could achieve amid a largely nicholaite clergy.

. . . . .

The economic functions of women are thus clearly important, most evidently among the warriors and the married clergy, the two chief propertied classes of early medieval Europe. Can we go on to discern particular areas or periods in which the economic status of the woman loomed especially large? To attempt this, we must return again to our documents of practice.

These documents do permit us to judge approximately the distribution of land ownership in the early medieval countryside and to assess the share that women may have claimed in it. The most satisfactory way by which we can make such an assessment is through field perambulations. To identify a piece of land, the scribe would often provide the names of the owners of contiguous property: 'a field . . . which is terminated in the east by the land of Roclenus and Bernana and Bovo with his heirs . . . on the west [by the land of] Dodo and Tetuisa.' Wherever they appear, these perambulations follow pretty much a common model, and hence they permit sharper comparisons among areas and over time than that possible for our patronymics, affected as these latter are by variant notarial practices. From Italy we have over 63,000 names of contiguous lay owners, from Spain nearly 7000, from Southern France over 13,000. For reasons we have elsewhere considered, our names from the North are

199

Herlihy

LAND, FAMILY
AND WOMEN IN
CONTINENTAL
EUROPE

much fewer, in both Northern France and Germany amounting only to a few hundred. Comparisons between the North and South on the basis of contiguous owners are not possible beyond the Carolingian period, but at least for Southern Europe we have a good basis for judging the importance and extent of what we shall call women's lands.

For typically, in listing the contiguous owners, the scribe would distinguish among male owners, female owners, and unnamed sons or heirs of an earlier owner, presumably now deceased. We can calculate what percentages of our total references to contiguous owners involve women or heirs. Such phrases as 'terra Marie cum filiis suis' are counted as women's lands, but if a principal refers to the neighboring property of his own heirs, it is considered as his property.

Table 2 shows the importance of women and heirs as continguous owners for the various regions of continental Europe we are considering.

Table 2
Percentage per century of women and 'heirs'
appearing as contiguous owners

W = Women   *H = Heirs*

Region	8th		9th		10th		11th		12th	
	W	*H*	*W*	*H*	*W*	*H*	*W*	*H*	*W*	*H*
Italy	6	9	3	10	3	12	3	20	4	15
Spain	—	—	7	9	17	2	13	4	8	8
S. France	—	—	8	1	9	1	9	2	6	2
N. France	—	—	7	0	4	1	2	4	—	—
Germany	18	1	2	3	—	—	—	—	—	—

We may first of all note that German lands show a considerable proportion of women as contiguous owners in the eighth century (18 percent), though the only 300 references upon which this calculation is based may make the conclusion somewhat uncertain and the incidence seems to fall off in the ninth century. But consistently, the regions in which women appear with the greatest frequency as contiguous owners are Spain (17 percent of the total in the tenth century) and Southern France (almost 10 percent from the ninth through the eleventh centuries). In both areas, the percentages fall off in the twelfth century. It is certain that much of this land was not exclusively female property but rather belonged to a woman and her minor sons, reflecting the generous provisions of the Visigothic and Burgundian laws which left to a widow use of and control over the family patrimony. It is also possible that some of these female owners were not so much the full legal owners as the administrators of an undivided family property acting for an absent husband, though of this we cannot be certain.

These high percentages from Spain and Southern France contrast sharply with the low percentage of women's lands evident in Italy; there women constitute only 6 percent of the total owners in the eighth century, and thereafter only 3 or 4. However, in Italy we may note a proportionately greater importance of unnamed 'sons' or 'heirs' appearing as contiguous owners. This formula is unfortunately somewhat ambiguous. It could refer to an established and pretty well permanent consortery of adult owners. It could also characterize the property of minor children kept intact after the death of the father—the same kind of property which commonly figures as women's lands in French and Spanish sources. This formula seems, in other words, to mask somewhat the true extent of land in Italy under the control of women. This difference in terminology undoubtedly goes back to the contrasts between Lombard law on the one hand and Visigothic and Burgundian on the other. The widow, who in Lombard law did not enjoy a *potestas* over the patrimony of her minor children, also does not in the charters give her name to the land. Of course, within the fatherless family, the woman undoubtedly could exercise an important voice, particularly if her children were of tender years. Still, the Italian widow hardly enjoyed the prominent recognition as head of her family and arbiter of its economic fortunes conceded her in Spain and Southern France.

. . . . .

A second way by which our charters permit us to estimate the importance of women as land owners and land managers is this: the frequency with which women appear as principal donors, sellers or otherwise alienators of property within our charters. Of charters involving lay principals (excluding, however, kings and queens), we have over 20,000 from Italy, nearly 20,000 from Southern France, over 11,000 from Germany, and over 5000 from Northern France and Spain respectively. We shall count as a woman's donation those charters in which a woman alone or a woman and her children figure as principals. Charters in which a husband and wife, or an adult son (mentioned first) and his mother are the principals are considered male donations. The numerous (particularly German) charters in which only serfs are conveyed are not considered, nor do we count commercial transactions not involving land. This method based on the importance of women as principal donors is obviously crude, since it may perhaps illustrate not so much the importance of women as property owners as their higher sense of piety and greater generosity towards churches, which in most instances are receiving the land. Still, the advantage of this approach is that it offers insight into periods and areas particularly in Northern Europe poorly illuminated by our other indices.

201

Herlihy

LAND, FAMILY
AND WOMEN IN
CONTINENTAL
EUROPE

Table 3
Percentage per century of women and 'heirs'
appearing as contiguous owners

Region	8th	9th	10th	11th	12th
Italy	6	7	11	13	9
Spain	—	11	17	18	18
S. France	—	8	13	11	9
N. France	15	7	11	8	9
Germany	15	10	8	15	12

Is there a correlation between the prominence of women illustrated by our matronymics and their economic importance as owners or managers of land? We cannot of course pretend to a mechanical correspondence between our indices. Still, the increased frequency with which women appear as owners of land after 950 does seem to correspond with a similar increase in the incidence of matronymics for the same period. On a regional basis, Southern France is remarkable both for the extent of women's lands and the frequency with which the matronymic appears in our charters. In Spanish lands, matronymics are found, as we have seen, chiefly in acts involving the feudal nobility, but at least among this important propertied class, the wealth and economic role of women would seem to have contributed to their own fame and promoted the utilization of a matronymic by their sons.

· · · · ·

On the basis of our three indices and the literary texts we have cited, we may hazard a few general comments on the position of women in regard to family and land in the early Middle Ages.

Women appear with fair consistency as land owners and land managers and apparent heads of their families at all times and places in the early medieval period. Several factors explain this continuing prominence: the common principles of early medieval laws, which conceded even to the married woman a personal title to property; the influence of the Christian Church; and the practical role that the woman assumed as mistress of her own 'inner economy'—a role which helped elevate and maintain her social and legal position.

At the same time, the position of the woman varied greatly according to her class, to her region, and even to the period in which she lived.

According to class, the importance of the woman seems to advance as we ascend the social scale, becoming most pronounced among the warriors and the married clergy, the two chief propertied classes of early medieval Europe. This seems primarily attributable not to a distinctive juridical statute governing these classes but to the greater practical role the wife of a warrior or priest assumed in the economic support of her family. To fulfill their professional functions, both warrior and priest needed to some extent to be freed from what the *De ordine* calls 'domestic solicitude.' This in turn greatly enlarged the range of the woman's economic functions, increased her contacts with the world beyond her family, and gave her a social prominence frequently recognized in the matronymic borne by her sons.

Regional contrasts in the status of the woman are as pronounced as social differences. The economic role of women in Southern France and Spain, as measured by our last two indices, is particularly remarkable. Undoubtedly, a significant reason for this are the peculiarly favorable provisions of the Visigothic and Burgundian laws, which placed no juridical restrictions on her freedom to administer her own property, to share in the administration of family property or, as a widow, to assume administrative control over it. The principle of community property in Visigothic law likewise served to increase the personal wealth of the widowed woman. Conversely, in Italy Lombard law limited, though it could not entirely restrict, the freedom of the woman in the administration of land. So also, the exclusion of the woman from feudal inheritance in Lombardy, her admission to it in Southern France and Spain, are other juridical factors of importance in affecting her status.

Beyond law, we should mention the precocious development of the ideal of chivalry in Southern France, which in accentuating the professional specialization of the male as fighter simultaneously seems to have restricted his economic role within the family. Italy, on the other hand, reluctant and late in developing a true knighthood on the French pattern, does not see, within the propertied family, the same degree of specialization of the husband as fighter and his wife as largely responsible for the 'solicitude' of household management. Northern France and Germany were initially more receptive than Italy to the notions of chivalry, and the role of the woman in those regions seems to have been proportionately more prominent.

Religion, law, social customs, the continuing concerns of household management are, however, relatively stable factors, and we have yet to explain how the importance of women in regard to land and family could apparently vary markedly over time, becoming particularly pronounced after 950 and reaching a sort of apex in the eleventh century. In this, another factor seems of some significance: the physical mobility of the population. Among those social classes (such as the medieval warrior nobility) whose mode of life involves considerable travel and movement, the man is the family member most frequently absent from home, while the wife, physically less mobile, is likewise more capable of assuming a continuous supervision over the family's fixed possessions. Moreover, in a social situation involving emigration or exodus, whether permanent or temporary, from the older centers of population, men tend to leave earlier and in proportionately greater numbers than women, as they are physically and socially better able to assume the risks and face the uncertainties of often hostile frontiers.

In leaving the community, they will need to make arrangements for the administration of their properties; frequently too, they will have to sell or mortgage their lands to finance their ventures. Emigration, in other words, provides an opportunity for the more stable elements within a community to assume a greater responsibility in the management of its lands. Thus churches seem to have extended their lands considerably during periods of emigration. When the German warrior Riphwinus set forth in the 790's with Charlemagne on his Italian campaign, he gave his property to his brother who was staying home, with the proviso that it be given to the monastery of Lorsch if he did not return. The enormous increase in Church property in Carolingian times undoubtedly owed something to the extended campaigns of the great emperor, which took men like Riphwinus long and often permanently from home. So likewise, that other great age of medieval military expansion—under way by the eleventh century and most dramatically expressed in the crusades—seems similarly marked by an accumulation of lands in the hands of churches, able to extend mortgages on, or to buy outright the properties of departing warriors.

The same, largely monastic records which show against a background of military mobilization an extension of Church lands also seem to reveal an increase in the prominence of women as owners and managers of property. Sometime between 1060 and 1080, in the Vendômois in Northern France, the Lady Hersendis was forced to assume responsibility for her family's fortunes, 'her husband having gone to Jerusalem.' In company with some of her own dependent knights, she traveled to her and her husband's lord, the abbot of Marmoutier, there personally to implore the aid of St. Martin and secure the confirmation of her fief.

The history of a family in Auch in Southern France offers a clear example of the economic enterprise of women in the absence of men. Raymond Donat had three sons and two daughters. One of the sons and the heir of a second both went on crusade, and mortgaged or sold their land to their sister Saura. The other son and the male heir of Saura's sister died (we are not told how) without issue, so Saura gathered together the total inheritance of her father for herself and her own son Bertrand.

Military mobilization, its expenses, its hazards, contributed importantly to the Lady Saura's successful reconstitution of her father's possessions. Did not the frequent departures, the extended absences of males, work generally to enhance the economic position of women as administrators, as heirs of those permanently gone? Liutprand of Cremona once commented how, in a single battle against Hungarian invaders (923), so many knights were killed that to his day (he was writing *ca.* 958–62) there existed a 'permagna raritas' of knights in Lombardy. Such default of males eventually would mean an accumulation of inheritances in the hands of women, even in areas such as Lombardy where prevalent custom was unfavorable to them.

And there does seem to be a correspondence between those periods of early medieval history marked by extensive mobilization of the population, vigorous military and geographic expansion, and those periods when women come most clearly to the fore as owners and managers of land. The Carolingian charters, particularly from Northern France and Germany, show a high percentage of women as donors and as contiguous owners. Our numbers of patronymics are too few for this period to draw firm conclusions from them; but at least we may note the significant fact that matronymics were known and used apropos of warriors even before 800 in those areas. The loss of male members of the population to wars, to new lands in process of settlement, simply to the floating population, the 'army of wanderers' of which our Carolingian sources speak, seems directly related with the importance of women in the pattern of Carolingian land ownership.

From the late tenth century, a yet more vigorous wave of expansion takes shape in Europe, and this time it is Southern France and Spain which initially appear as the great centers of exodus. French chivalry in particular seems touched with a passion for wandering; French knights pour across the Pyrenees on the great highway to Compostela, frequently to participate in the wars against the Moors. Spanish knights were hardly less mobile, given (as the epic of the Cid marvellously reveals) to bold raids along the Muslim frontier in search of material and spiritual profit. This ferment blends imperceptibly with the like ferment of the crusading movement (1095), which spreads it and extends it to all corners of Europe. St. Bernard, in preaching the Second Crusade (1147), supposedly emptied Europe's castles and cities of their men. Did the largely man's world of distant pilgrimage and crusade help create a woman's world back home?—The troubadour poet Marcabru presents for us a touching lament of a 'châtelaine' weeping for her lover, not dead, simply gone with King Louis on the Second Crusade, and all her other likely beaux with him. Hers, to her sorrow, was a woman's world.

Religion, law, custom, the practical requirements of household management, and perhaps significantly too the social impact of Europe's great waves of military and geographic expansion, combined to raise the woman to a position of prominence, saluted to be sure in the charged sentiment of troubadour poetry, but as much saluted in the dry Latin of our thousand charters. The great, external, dramatic events of the day, the wars and crusades, are the work of active men. But their accomplishments were matched and perhaps made possible by the work of women, no less active. And the achievements of both are joined together in a kind of alliance of accomplishment, fascinating in itself, and profoundly influencing the Western tradition.

205

Herlihy

LAND, FAMILY
AND WOMEN IN
CONTINENTAL
EUROPE

14. Political Relations Between East and West

KARL BOSL

There has been a strong tendency in European and American historiography since the masterful German historian Leopold von Ranke wrote in the early nineteenth century to view "western civilization" at essentially Romano-German, with its focus on southern and western Europe. The political realities of nineteenth- and early twentieth-century Europe and animosities between the largely Slavic East and the Latin and Germanic West fed into this view to produce some extremely antipathetic East-West attitudes, which have not died easily. Such views as the German depiction of the Slavic East as barbaric, inferior, and a threat to Christian civilization, or the corresponding Slavic denunciation of the German expansion to the east, the Drang nach Osten, *as merciless genocidal pressure to exterminate Slavs, are a function of this state of affairs. Not only are these and similar ideas outdated and incorrect, but also they are dangerous in the postwar world where there is already sufficient mistrust between East and West. Geoffrey Barraclough, a noted medieval historian whose* Origins of Modern Germany (1946) *is an excellent introduction to medieval Germany, has assembled a group of scholars from East and West to write on East-West relations in the Middle Ages, from which this selection comes.*

Source: Karl Bosl, "Political Relations between East and West," in Geoffrey Barraclough, ed., *Eastern and Western Europe in the Middle Ages* (London: Thames and Hudson, Ltd., 1970), pp. 43–82. Copyright © 1970 by Thames and Hudson, Ltd. Reprinted by permission of Thames and Hudson, Ltd. and Harcourt Brace Jovanovich, Inc.

*Karl Bosl surveys the political relations of East and West from the first pe-
riod of Slavic movement to the west in the sixth century down to the fifteenth.
This formative period for the borderland states of Poland, Bohemia, and
Hungary comprised almost a thousand years, and witnessed varying relations
between the Western powers, especially the German Empire, and the Eastern
kingdoms. Although there were periods of hostility and warfare, for a majority
of this time relations were peaceful and much interpenetration took place between German and Slav in trade, colonization and settlement, and religion.
Bosl's chapter puts in perspective such movements as the German expansion
into Slavic lands east of the Elbe and the taking of Prussia by the Teutonic
knights. It also underscores the many positive contributions of western Europe
to the political, cultural, and economic development of the peoples who inhabited the eastern plains of Europe, while recognizing the reciprocal role
played by Czechs, Poles, and Hungarians in western European affairs. As Bosl
and his fellow contributors amply demonstrate, no picture of the development
of Western civilization is complete without an appropriate and correct appreciation of the role of the various peoples who can form a bridge between Russia in the east and Germany in the west. This chapter should provoke questions
about some of the cultural myths that are still unfortunately a part of our heritage, and be of help to increase understanding between East and West.*

Throughout the Middle Ages, for obvious geographical reasons, the peoples of eastern Europe who were in closest contact with the West were
the west, and to a lesser degree the south Slavs. This does not mean that
the Baltic provinces or the Russian empire of Kiev can be left out of account. The influence of Byzantium, which prevailed in the Kiev region,
was always important. And it was not only with their immediate neighbours, the Germans, that the Slavs were in contact. All the western peoples, including the Anglo-Saxons, had relations at one time or another
with eastern Europe; these extended from commerce to dynastic marriages. But it hardly needs demonstrating that the most intensive relations
were those between the west Slavs and their westerly neighbours: the
Germans. German-Slav relations left the most lasting mark, and here we
can distinguish four periods, or phases.

207

Bosl

POLITICAL
RELATIONS
BETWEEN EAST
AND WEST

The first begins with the westward movement of the Slav tribes in the
sixth century, against which Charlemagne organized a system of marches
on the eastern frontiers of his empire. The second stage is marked by the
rise of autonomous Slav states on the eastern flank of the Holy Roman
Empire—sometimes in loose connection with, or tributary dependence
upon it—during the ninth and tenth centuries; this period is the one
which east European historians often looked back to as the 'golden age' of
the Slav nations before their renaissance after 1918. The third period of
relations is characterized by the German eastward movement, the *Drang
nach Osten,* beginning in the second half of the eleventh century. This
German eastward movement was fundamentally different from the earlier
westward movement of the Slavs, in so far as the territories the Slavs occupied were for all practical purposes vacant, whereas the Germans came

face to face with a settled and civilized population, with which they had been in contact, sometimes friendly, sometimes hostile, for at least two or three centuries. Finally, the German eastward thrust resulted in a Slav reaction, which ushered in the fourth period. In the last century of the Middle Ages, revolts and revolutions under national kings and princes brought to an end an interval of government under foreign rulers—the Luxembourg dynasty in Bohemia, for example, or the Angevin dynasty in Hungary—whose rule had been characterized by intensive contacts, not only with Germany but also with the nations—France and Italy— west and south of the German Reich.

It was, no doubt, a consequence of the lines of historical development outlined above that the Germans stood out, in the eyes of the Slavs, as the enemies and aggressors. This attitude, anchored in the ideology of the so-called 'Slavic legend', was reinforced after the end of the Middle Ages by the fact that it was the Prussians and Austrians—joined, after the time of Peter the Great, by Russia—who became the dominant powers throughout the east European borderlands.

The Westward Movement of the Slavs

From the sixth century onwards Slav tribes immigrated into the vast territories east of the Elbe and the Saale, the Bohemian Forest and the river Enns in Austria, which the Germanic tribes had left after having settled there for many centuries. These early German tribes were different from the inhabitants of medieval Germany, just as the Anglo-Saxons were different from them, or from the Romanized Franks in Gaul. The German eastward movement of the twelfth and thirteenth centuries is therefore in no sense a resettlement of ancient German territory, for Germany as a nation did not exist before the end of the ninth century.

The original homelands of the Slavs were on the rivers Dnieper, Pripet, Bug and Vistula. They started from there in big movements westward; about AD 500 they reached the territories on the lower Danube and moved forward along the river and to the south and west into the valleys of the eastern Alps. But they lost their independence very soon, for the Avars, nomadic breeders of cattle, subjected the agrarian Slavs who moved under their pressure and influence not only into Bohemia and Moravia, but also into the lands of the Sorbs north of the Sudeten mountains and into the territory around the river Main west of the Bohemian Forest.

As these movements and settlements proceeded, corresponding types of lordship and state came into existence. In the south the states were not tribal—that is to say, built up on the foundation of family groups and family settlements—but were rather lordships, in which one leader united different tribal remnants with the aid of a group of warriors, who secured him control of market-places and highways of traffic. In the northwest, on the contrary, dominion was based on well-defined tribal groups, such as the Vilzi, Obodrites or Sorbs. We may compare these incipient states with the tribal formations of Germanic Europe, the former with the so-called war-kingdoms of the migration period, the latter with the Germanic tribal groups on the Rhine, the Weser and the Elbe, as described by Tacitus. But the Slavs who had crossed the Elbe and the Saale and the Bohemian Forest, and had settled there on the soil of the Frankish empire, failed to build up lasting political organizations and were unable to preserve their independence. They were not enslaved, but lived in a status similar to the 'Königsfreien' and other tenants (*coloni*) of the Frankish empire, not only in Thuringia and Old Saxony, but also in the upper Main valley.

It seems probable that the early lordships in the Slav lands arose under Frankish influence. Samo, founder of an empire between the Sudeten mountains and the eastern Alps, was of Frankish descent; we may surmise that he was a slave trader, for Slavs were enslaved throughout the early Middle Ages and sold at slave markets such as Venice, Verdun or Regensburg. Derwan, the duke of the Sorbs, a contemporary of Samo, had also acknowledged Frankish supremacy. Frankish influence is traceable in the ninth century among the Vilzi and the Obodrites, and Franks helped Pribina to build up his power in the region of the Plattensee in modern Hungary. But we must realize that such influences were neither strong nor continuous; only a few specifically Frankish institutions were transferred, which did not substantially alter the original Slav foundations. We should not forget, either, that our information comes from Frankish sources which present us with only one side of the picture.

. . . . .

The first Slavs to found an empire were the tribes of Moravia, united under the rule of the descendants of Moimir. The centre of their kingdom was the valley of the river March, where excavations carried out since 1945 by the archaeologists of the Czechoslovak Academies of Prague and Bratislava have yielded impressive evidence, in the form of fortifications, towns, churches and so on, of a relatively high and developed civilization. We can trace the beginnings of this so-called Great Moravian empire before Charlemagne, who decisively defeated the Avars by a concentric attack on their central position on the river Theiss. The ancient Roman province of Pannonia, comprising western Hungary and modern Yugoslavia, was a vast field for the interplay of cultural and ecclesiastical movements from east, south and west, and here the Moravian rulers tried to build up an independent position between the powers of their age, the Byzantine empire, the Carolingian empire in the west, and the Roman church. The arrival of the Magyars in the ninth century destroyed the domination of the descendants of Moimir in the eastern part of modern Czechoslovakia. But it seems that, as late as the end of the ninth century, Prague and its rulers still obeyed the last Moravian ruler, Svatopluk, and so the influence of Moravian civilization persisted in this region and was still an effective force in medieval Bohemia, for instance in the monastery of Sázava.

In the eastern Alps the Slavs succeeded in erecting an autonomous 'state', which was called later Carantania, or Carinthia. We do not yet

209

Bosl

POLITICAL
RELATIONS
BETWEEN EAST
AND WEST

know exactly what role the Croats played in this development. Carinthia was later incorporated into the duchy of Bavaria and so into the Carolingian empire. The Croats were the first Slavs to build up a strong autonomous 'state' in the southern parts of central Europe, in Pannonia and Dalmatia. Their rulers Ljudevit and Borna were dangerous opponents of the western empire and the Croats preserved their independence until 1091.

The political independence of eastern Europe, and the formation of a distinctive society there within the framework of medieval Christian civilization was largely the result of the development of three states in the ninth, tenth and eleventh centuries: Bohemia and Poland, both Slav, and Hungary, the main element in the population of which was not Slav, but Finno-Ugrian and Turco-Tatar. The Czechs, first named in 806 in a Frankish source, gained control over Bohemia under the rule of the Přemyslids, who subjected or eradicated the minor lords and castellans throughout the country. This process was completed by 995, when the Slavnikids, their chief rivals, were eliminated by murder. The castle of Prague was the centre of Přemyslid dominion and became the capital of the country for a thousand years.

This Czech or Bohemian 'state' was characterized by strong internal cohesion, a sign of effective rulership. Although Franks and Germans influenced its development and although its territory was included in the Bavarian bishopric of Regensburg as a missionary district, none of this was decisive and it did not interfere with the individual shaping of this extraordinary kingdom. Modern Czech nationalist historians have rejected the fact that Bohemia was more or less closely linked with the German empire since the tenth century; but such a linkage did occur and was the consequence of the organization of a Bohemian territorial church about 973, when the bishopric of Prague was founded and united with the German imperial church as part of the metropolis of the archbishopric of Mainz. It was Charles IV, German emperor and king of Bohemia in the middle of the fourteenth century, who secured the elevation of Prague into an independent archbishopric and gave his country a short, but virtually complete independence for a period of one and a half centuries. Slav Bohemia became one of the most highly developed 'territorial states' in advance of all other German territories, and it is equally significant that, as in Hungary and Poland, the crown came to symbolize an objective and impersonal idea of the state earlier than in Germany. This fact indicates the inherent statesmanlike qualities of the west Slavs. In spite of being a nominal member of the Empire, Bohemia never became merely one among the many territorial states of which the Empire was composed.

Poland and Hungary, the two other leading states of east central Europe, stood for only a very short time under the suzerainty of the German emperors of the Saxon line. Both quickly succeeded in gaining complete independence. The Magyars, nomadic horsemen who terrorized Europe for half a century and devastated parts of Saxony, France, Italy and the Byzantine empire, were compelled by their defeat in 955 at the battle of the Lech to change their way of living and to settle down in the plains along the Danube and the Theiss where they ruled over an indigenous population of Slavs. The fact that they did not accept the Christian faith from Byzantium, but adopted the western and Roman liturgy and ritual, was of decisive importance, although they postponed their final decision for some decades. The Magyars celebrate Stephen I as the founder and hero of the Hungarian state; although the details are not very clear, it is beyond dispute that he was proclaimed king by both emperor and pope.

In the second half of the tenth century Mieszko I united a number of Slav tribes east of the Oder under his rule and in this way founded the original Polish state. The centre of his realm was round Kruszwica, Gniezno and Poznań; from here he began to expand his political dominion over Bohemia, Cracovia and Silesia, and after 990 over Pomerania also. By formally placing his territories under the suzerainty of St. Peter he won the acknowledgment of his position by the Holy See. Significantly the account of this transfer, called 'Dagome iudex' from its opening words, sets out exactly the frontiers of the territories under Mieszko's rule, thus indicating that in Poland also the concept of a territorial state with fixed borders existed from the beginning. Mieszko acknowledged the supremacy of the German kings, but he pursued a completely independent policy, not least of all in his relations with the Roman church, and this policy was continued by his son Boleslav I Chrobry, 'the Mighty' (992–1025). Whether the ruling family of Piasts was of Viking descent or not, cannot be confirmed or disproved. But the newly founded Polish archbishopric of Gniezno (AD 1000) became an independent metropolitan province of the universal church and this act simultaneously opened the way for political independence.

211

Bosl

POLITICAL
RELATIONS
BETWEEN EAST
AND WEST

The German emperor Otto III (983–1002) and his clerical advisers saw the need to establish some sort of order among the newly rising states in eastern Europe. One of the objects of Otto III's policy of 'Renovatio', or the renewal of the ancient Roman empire, it has been suggested, was to make a place for western Slavs as members of the Empire with equal rights under the suzerainty of the German king. This particularly affected the Poles who apparently were thought to hold the dominant position in this area. But with the early death of Otto III the rather vague idea of a universal Christian empire over the whole of central and eastern Europe collapsed. Boleslav Chrobry pursued an independent policy of his own. In his eyes the foundation of the archbishopric of Gniezno and his designation as the emperor's 'cooperator mundi' and 'associate and friend' did not mean the inclusion of Poland in a universal Christian empire ruled by the Roman-German emperor, but liberation of the Polish church from the control of a German metropolitan and full freedom of action for the growing Polish state. When in 1002, after the death of Otto III, Boleslav launched an attack on the Empire and temporarily occupied the march of Meissen, the ruler of the young Polish state made clear that he was not willing to accept a situation which prevented him from attacking his neighbours, particularly Bohemia, and attempting to unite the Slav peoples of the area in a strong state under Polish leadership. The policy of Otto III had failed.

Nevertheless, although asserting their political independence, the new powers in the east of central Europe—Poland, Hungary, Bohemia— were all influenced in one degree or another by contact with the Empire. They had peaceful as well as hostile relations with their neighbours in the West. Although the rising states of eastern Europe were overshadowed by the Empire, Slavs and Germans not only fought, but also compromised and co-ordinated their interests. In particular, the Christianization and ecclesiastical organization of the three eastern European states prevented the West from waging missionary war against them; as a result of their conversion they obtained equal religious rights and equal status as autonomous members of Christendom. Although the missionaries came from outside, especially from German bishoprics, Christianization was not carried out by the sword but took place in agreement with the native princes and magnates. This voluntary religious decision prepared the way for a voluntary integration into the political system of medieval Europe.

The invasion of the Magyars and their settlement in the plains of Hungary had separated the world of the Slavs into a western and a southern group. The south Slavs in the Balkans and in the Danube area and the eastern Alps reacted in the same way as their western brothers against pressure from the West; that is to say, they voluntarily accepted the Christian faith. The Slav tribes between the Elbe, the Saale and the Oder, on the other hand, had a different fate. Many of them were later forcibly converted to Christianity from Germany, others—especially in the regions south of the Baltic Sea—from Poland. They were subjected to German domination, though only after bitter struggles with Poland for control of the area. The archbishopric of Magdeburg had been established as a missionary centre for the Slavs beyond the Elbe in the time of the emperor Otto I. In this early period no clear distinction was drawn between religion, politics and missionary activities; and it is undeniable that missions were frequently used as an instrument of policy, not only by the Germans but also by the Poles under Boleslav I. But the classic instances of the use of religion to enforce political control came later with the so-called 'crusade' or German missionary war against the Wends in 1147 and the subjection of the heathen Prussian tribes on the Baltic by the Teutonic knights in the thirteenth century.

The Slav tribes in this area also had to face growing pressure from the marches which Charlemagne had organized along the eastern borders of his empire, and which were later extended. The German ruler Henry I (919–36) conquered Brandenburg and established the march of Meissen. His son Otto I organized new marches east of the Elbe and the Saale. The Magyar onslaught had shattered the defences along the Carolingian frontier in the south-east; so the same ruler took measures here also to restore the frontier system under new margraves or 'marchiones'. In this area the German bishoprics continued to control the territory beyond the frontier; but in the north-east new bishoprics were erected in the newly created marches.

Otto I's aggressive policy in the eastern marches of Saxony and the forced Christianization which accompanied it, provoked the great rebellion of the Slavs in 983, which had even more serious repercussions than the invasion of the Magyars in the south. German domination between the Elbe and the Oder north of Magdeburg broke down completely and could not be restored in spite of many military campaigns. A number of small Slav principalities were set up in the liberated areas and managed to survive for a short period without being Christianized. The majority of the tribes stubbornly resisted missionary activity. Since bishoprics had once been established here and then destroyed, these people were not pagans in the eyes of rulers and clergy; they were therefore declared renegades, who were to be guided back to the true faith by force. But in the area south of Magdeburg, in the so-called Middle Germany of today, the Germans succeeded in maintaining their hold over the inhabitants, mostly Slavs, but scarcely Christians. The Slavs in the southeastern territories of the Empire, in the eastern Alps and along the Danube also lost their independence. Ever since Carolingian times, but particularly after Otto I's defeat of the Magyars in 955, there was a continuous admixture of German settlers and the native population was intensively Christianized. In Bohemia, on the other hand, there were only a few German settlers; the Czech character of the people was untouched and native dukes ruled the country virtually independently, although formally Bohemia was a member of the western empire.

Acceptance of the Christian faith made the Slavs a part of the growing Christian society of Europe. By adopting the progressive institutions of the greater powers and by imitating their standards of civilization and accepting the Christian faith, the Slav princes built up their reputation at home, reinforced their power abroad, and secured their political independence. The strength and genius of individual rulers and their decision to follow the model of western institutions in state and church definitely united the Slav tribes in effective states. This was the case not only with the Czechs, Poles and Magyars, but also with the eastern Slavs in the empire of Kiev during the tenth century. Here also western influences were stronger than is often allowed, and it was not yet certain in the tenth century whether Kiev would follow the Byzantine or the Roman ritual and liturgy. It was no accident that in the Gospel of Otto III, in the famous miniature in which figures representing the four parts of the Empire do homage to the emperor, 'Sclavinia' took its place beside 'Roma', 'Gallia' and 'Germania' as the fourth member of the western Christian community. By the end of the first millennium the Slavonic East was an integral part of the European world.

Another consequence of these events was that none of these nations ever again lost its individuality and its distinctive character. The Croats lost their national dynasty shortly before 1100 and from that time forward were ruled by the Hungarian dynasty and associated with Hungary in a personal union. On the other hand, the Serbs, living in the central mountains of the Balkans, succeeded in spite of many political fluctuations in building up a wall consisting of their own and other peoples around their

213

Bosl

POLITICAL
RELATIONS
BETWEEN EAST
AND WEST

often endangered state. Under the leadership of Stefan Dušan (1331–55), Serbia entered on a period of great achievement and importance, shortly before the Turks invaded the Balkan peninsula. And native dynasties ruled Bohemia, Poland, Hungary and Russia until the fourteenth century or later. These dynasties, the Přemyslids and Piasts, the Arpads and the Rurikids, had major achievements to their credit. It was due to them that, from the beginning of the second millennium, their kingdoms were able to stand on their own feet and keep back the political pressures and cultural penetration of foreign powers. They rejected the universal pretensions of the German emperors, took over the tasks of civilizing their subjects and set about improving the living standards of their own people.

The western emperor had lost his commanding position in eastern Europe by the close of the eleventh century; the Byzantine empire was also losing its influence in the Slav world. From the time of Boleslav Chrobry the pagan Baltic tribes came under missionary influence from Poland. Much the same happened in the area inhabited by the south Slavs, which the Hungarian rulers tried to annex to their dominions, organizing a system of marches along the frontiers and south of the Danube against invasions from outside. In the pagan Baltic area Polish and Russian rulers cooperated from the eleventh century onwards.

Ecclesiastical and political developments in the new states of eastern Europe bear witness to steady cultural interchange between East and West, especially between the western Slavs and Hungary on the one side, and Germany on the other. But there were also direct communications with France and Italy, which indicate the independent position and reputation of these nations within the Christian society of Europe.

There is no better example of the progress of culture in the eastern world than Kiev. Russian literature developed under Byzantine and Bulgarian influence during the eleventh century, and many important literary documents—among them we find testimonies of the missionary activities of Cyril and Methodius and their pupils in Moravia—came to Kiev from the West. Kiev was linked with the West by relatively intensive trade and commercial relations. Regensburg in Bavaria and its citizens continued to trade with Kiev and its empire for more than two hundred years. There were also intensive commercial relations between Kiev, Prague and Poland. The Rurikids showed special interest in the fields of architecture, literature, historiography and legislation. The 'Paučenije' of Prince Vladimir Monomach (1113–25) is an impressive testimony of human and political wisdom.

The German Eastward Movement

The end of the early Middle Ages and the supersession of the primitive society of early medieval Europe was marked in the eleventh century by a rapid growth of social mobility. This new mobility ushered in a period of expansion beyond the old frontiers of Europe, both in the Mediterranean and east of the Empire, as well as a vast process of internal colonization, the clearance of forests and the draining of swamps, in the old areas of settlement. The crusades in the south and the eastward thrust of the Germans in the north were the two outstanding events in this process of change which was taking place in the whole of Europe. The archaic feudal society was not dissolved, but its character was changed and broadened in essential ways by the rise of a new middle class, the citizens, and the structure of European society was enriched by a new kind of urban civilization.

Human, social, commercial, and political life was concentrated in the new towns and cities, developed from pre-urban settlements, which we find among the Slavs as well as in the Latin and German parts of Europe. The new social and economic movements, themselves a consequence of a population surplus, the new settlements and a progressive urban civilization initiated the third period of political relations between East and West. The centres of this movement were Italy, Flanders and south and west Germany. There is no doubt that the East gained new impulses and strength from the new movements, the power of the east European states was intensified, East and West drew closer together, and an intensive assimilation of standards took place. The Danes and Swedes, heirs of Viking tradition, also participated in this movement, but the Germans played the most important part.

This process of assimilation was a decisive development in European history; but for the Slavs, at least up to recent times, its negative aspects have loomed larger than the positive ones. The reason, of course, is that during this period not only were vast Slav territories in the western border zone lost to the Germans, but also a new political order was established between the Baltic Sea and the Danube valley which fundamentally altered the situation of the east European states. In the West, on the other hand, especially among the Germans and German historians, the conviction gained ground that it was only at this time and as a result of 'Germanization' that the Slavs acquired the foundations of higher civilization, by the assimilation of the more progressive techniques of the West, by the acceptance of western standards in social, economic, legal and spiritual life, and especially by the penetration into the Slav lands of the urban civilization of Germany.

215

Bosl

POLITICAL
RELATIONS
BETWEEN EAST
AND WEST

If such views could prevail, it was in part at least because vast territories in the east of the Slav world were lost to sight by the West as a result of the establishment of Tatar or Mongol domination in the thirteenth century and the rise of the centralized state of Moscow. In reality, the German eastward movement in the thirteenth and fourteenth centuries was successful only because the Slavs were already Christians and already had civilized standards; reluctant, hostile and pagan barbarians would not have been able or willing to accept the new progressive way of life. The rulers of eastern Europe were interested in reforming the economy and the social structure of their countries, in order to be able to compete with the West, and for this purpose they invited western settlers, artisans, miners and traders to settle in their kingdoms.

Poland is the best example of these trends. The growing population surplus in Poland made it possible, even necessary, to cultivate new land, especially to open up the forests within the Polish frontiers. With this land policy the princes combined large-scale efforts to increase the military and financial power of their country by internal colonization and urbanization. But the effects of internal colonization were limited if carried out according to existing Polish law. What was necessary, if the legal and economic situation were to be improved, was a shift in balance between rights and duties, between the rights of the urban and rural classes involved in the colonizing movement and those of the government; and this could not be secured by any measures available in Slav legal tradition. Hence the Polish rulers turned to German methods of colonization, inviting western settlers into the country and granting them privileges. Colonization was carried out according to German law; and the success of this method in solving the difficulties and meeting the requirements of the situation is indicated by the fact that the privileges of German law were also granted to Slav peasants and settlers.

In this way the economic, social and legal order of eastern Europe was improved and reformed. Later, in the fifteenth century, the same methods were applied in the Russian-settled territories of the Polish-Lithuanian Union. Colonization and the opening up of new land were successful, because the application of German law and methods enabled the Slav nations to introduce a new measure of social differentiation and a broader cultural base. Looked at from this point of view, we can see that the effects of the so-called German eastward movement were not confined only

to the extension of German national territory, but had important consequences for the internal development of the Slav states, and played their part in the shaping of European civilization. They helped to secure economic stability and a balanced social order not only in Poland, but also in Bohemia and Hungary. On this foundation rulers such as Přemysl Otakar II and Charles IV of Bohemia, Casimir the Great of Poland and the Angevin kings of Hungary won a high reputation for statesmanship throughout Europe.

The resistance of the western Slavs and Hungarians, who could not be defeated by force and war, prevented the German kings from conquering their territories by direct assault. In part this failure was a result of the swampy terrain of north-east Europe. But it was also a proof of the material and moral strength and of the spirit of freedom of the small and often mutually hostile Slav tribes between the Elbe and the Oder. But the medieval German settler movement beginning at the end of the eleventh century, an event comparable with the American westward movement and settlement of the nineteenth century, eventually Germanized this area. The immediate result was expansion of German domination and the dissemination of western political, legal and economic institutions in a German form, as well as of western science, poetry and art. But it was the assimilation of these institutions by the countries involved that has shaped the cultural face of central and eastern Europe from that time down to the present day.

The settlement of German townsfolk and peasants was not met by force by the Slavs as the earlier military attacks had been. Kings, dukes and princes in Hungary, Bohemia, Silesia, Mecklenburg, Pomerania and Poland all supported the colonizing movement, and the German immigrants were given effective aid by the crown, which resisted the opposition of the native nobility and clergy to the foreigners. The settlers brought with them methods of cultivation which had already been used, particularly by the Carolingian emperors, for opening up and colonizing the Frankish lands, and which had proved to be an effective instrument in developing the powers of government. Now in the East these methods were improved, developed and used on a large scale, and often combined with the existing east European procedures, which they transformed and sometimes replaced. In this way the German element prevailed, the Slav inhabitants were Germanized, and a 'German East' was built up. But it is vitally important to distinguish between this 'German' or 'Germanized' East—confined to the territories of the small west Slav tribes, such as the Vagrians, the Obodrites, the Sorbs, the Wends and the Lusatians— and eastern Europe proper. The German or Germanized East exercised pressure on the lands between the German and the Russian borders, but the latter never lost the will and capacity to shape their own independent history.

The eastern frontier of the area of German domination was, of course, for a long time fluctuating. Down to the middle of the twelfth century it was marked by the territories ruled by the dynasties of Babenberg, Wettin and Ascania. After this time the colonizing movement spread out beyond the frontiers of the Empire and reached the mountainous country of Siebenbürgen in Hungary and the Baltic lands. In the south, Germans served under foreign rulers, but they were incorporated and privileged; in the north they established a strong dominion over a non-German population and connected it with the Empire. In Silesia, Germans had no special status, but they put pressure on the Slavs simultaneously from above and from below.

The independent states of eastern Europe profited from this movement, which helped them to reach a level of civilization equal to that of the West. Some, such as fourteenth-century Bohemia, even surpassed it. In the occupied and Germanized territories of the 'German East', on the other hand, only a few remnants of the original Slav population survived, for instance in the so-called 'Lausitz', where a Slav idiom was preserved, although for centuries the people regarded themselves as German. Linguistic and political boundaries did not coincide in this area until very recent times. The early wars between Slavs and Germans were savagely fought on both sides; but the process of infiltration and cultural intermixture after these wars took place without force. Nevertheless Christian missions were often accompanied by force; it was, after all, St. Bernard of Clairvaux who summoned the Germans to the crusade against the Wends in 1147. The Teutonic knights also used the idea of crusade as a justification for their pitiless attacks on the heathen Prussians; but these ideas came

217

Bosl

POLITICAL
RELATIONS
BETWEEN EAST
AND WEST

from western Europe. Nevertheless it is significant that a Germanizing melting process took place not only in areas subjected and conquered by force, where German marcher lords and other nobles ruled over both the native and the immigrant population—for example, the east march south of the river Danube from which Austria developed, or the marches of Meissen or Brandenburg—but even in such countries as Pomerania and Mecklenburg, where Slav princes and noblemen continued to rule although they were attached to the Empire by feudal bonds. The same is true of Silesia, which only became linked to the Empire in 1335 as a dependency of Bohemia, although it had become a country of German character long before that.

The chief agents of this melting process were the ruling dynasties, their nobility and the clergy. Gradually, by birth, by free decision, by custom or by marriage, the nationality of these groups changed. After that, a broad peasant class could be formed by the settling of immigrants and the assimilation of the native population. This brought the process of Germanization to a conclusion. On the other hand, German townsfolk and peasants were not able to retain their identity in a non-German environment, still less to give the Slav state a German character, in spite of their economic and cultural importance. In the Baltic lands the nobility gave them support, and the territorial princes were German.

The Czechs are justly proud of having preserved their national character, in spite of the fact that Bohemia and Moravia were members of the Empire, which more than once played a decisive part in shaping the course of events in Germany. Many factors helped the Czechs to maintain their national identity and gave them the strength to withstand German infiltration and assimilation. In the first place, German settlement was confined to the frontier regions of Bohemia and Moravia, where the Slavs themselves had not settled or had settled only in very small numbers. Thus considerable areas in the mountains on the borders of Bohemia— the Sudeten mountains, the Erzgebirge and the Bohemian Forest— became German-populated country as forests and swamps were opened up and cultivated. But the central area of Bohemia remained in the hands of the Czechs and Slavs, although in the cities and towns a German majority prevailed for a longer time and the countryside was infiltrated by islands of German language. Slavs and Germans in the towns were assimilated, and in a number of places the German citizens adopted the Czech language and nationality.

The German failure to assimilate the central region of Bohemia and Moravia was a decisive factor in checking and halting the process of Germanization in the independent Slav and Hungarian states further east. Nevertheless the Germanized territories in the East steadily gained momentum, power and weight in the later Middle Ages. The centre of gravity of the Empire shifted from West to East, as a result of German expansion. Not only did German territory increase by about a third as a result of the Germanization of the East, but bigger and more effective territorial states were created in the eastern areas, including Prussia, a union of the march of Brandenburg and the lands of the Teutonic knights, and Austria—the two powers which played a dominant part in German history down to the nineteenth century. Thereafter the centre of gravity moved back to the West under the influence of economic and social changes involving the whole of Europe. Nevertheless the significance of the German eastward movement in the Middle Ages is indicated by the fact that the two capitals of Berlin and Vienna were both situated in the newly colonized German East.

Apart from the expansion of German power and dominion, another basic feature was the assimilation of many peoples of Slav and Baltic descent. The tribes along the Elbe and other west Slav peoples lost their political identity as a result of German and Polish pressure, but their national substance was not destroyed. In the twelfth century a German eastward drive coincided with a Polish westward drive. Their rivalry was most clearly expressed in the field of ecclesiastical politics. The Poles founded the bishoprics of Włocławek, Lebus and Wollin-Cammin before the old German bishoprics of Brandenberg and Havelberg, which had perished in the Slav revolt of 983, were re-established, and before Henry the Lion, duke of Saxony and Bavaria from 1139 to 1180, began to found new ones. The archbishop of Magdeburg, Norbert of Xanten (d. 1134), famous as the founder of the Premonstratensian Order, was aware of the plans of the Poles, but failed to frustrate them at Rome. The Slavs on the Baltic Sea and on the Elbe and Oder, who preserved their pagan faith, were compelled to fight on two fronts. Not surprisingly they were unable to withstand this twofold pressure.

Politically, the defeat of Polish aspirations in this region was the result of the actions of German kings, princes and noblemen, and of the Teutonic Order; but socially it was the German peasants and settlers who Germanized the area in co-operation with German townsmen and German nobles. Living together with the native Slavs, these rural settlers assimilated them in process of time. By and large the German immigrants settled in areas of forest and swamp, which they cultivated, but they are also found in older settlements, where the islands of German immigrants became centres of the melting process. In the Baltic states, on the other hand, German infiltration was not successful, in spite of German political domination, because of the lack of German rural settlers. And Germanization was also frustrated in countries such as Bohemia and Poland, where the nobility and clergy resisted the movement; here the process of assimilation had a contrary effect and resulted in the absorption of the newcomers into the native population.

The Obodrites and Liutizi, the Pomeranians and Sorbs, the Slav tribes of Silesia, the Baltic Prussians, and last but not least the Slavs of the Alpine regions were not destroyed, but rather were integrated into a new mixed German-Slav population. They made a vital contribution to the formation of the 'Neustämme', or new ethnic groups, of eastern Germany. The strong Slav admixture in the population of the eastern areas of the Empire—and later, as a new melting process got under way, in the

219

Bosl

POLITICAL
RELATIONS
BETWEEN EAST
AND WEST

population of western Germany—was one of the most far-reaching consequences of the political relations between eastern and western Europe during the Middle Ages. The east Germans are born of a mixture of native Slavs and German immigrants from the West, themselves the descendants of the older tribes of southern and western Germany, which were a mixture of pre-Germanic and other peoples, who came with the Romans into the areas around the Rhine and the Danube.

In the eyes of the Poles the knights of the Teutonic Order and their successors were invaders and aggressors, who pretended to be carrying out a Christian mission in order to conquer Slav territories and who ruthlessly used the power of the sword to plunder and subjugate peaceful people. Only united national resistance could overcome this inhuman onslaught. In this way both Poles and Germans came to see their history in the later Middle Ages as one of continuous national struggle. In reality, however, political relations between the German emperor and the Polish king were relatively peaceful during this period. Both powers were weakened by internal dissension and their interests had changed. When the Poles were again united, under Casimir the Great (1333–70), the main field of Polish political activity was in the East, where Galicia was occupied in the middle of the fourteenth century. Casimir's attitude towards the West was defensive, and he was even willing to sacrifice territory there in order to safeguard his rear. These were the circumstances in which Silesia, now divided into seventeen separate lordships under princes of the Silesian Piast dynasty, passed out of Polish hands and became part of Bohemia. The Silesian Piasts rendered homage to John of Bohemia, son of the German emperor, Henry VII, and the first ruler of the Luxembourg dynasty. And it is significant that it was the dukedoms of Upper Silesia where the Poles were in the majority that first accepted the feudal lordship of the Bohemian king, whereas the dukedoms of Lower Silesia with their strong German minority remained subject to the Polish crown for a longer period. These facts do not suggest that Silesia was Germanized by force.

It was a Polish duke, Conrad of Masovia, who in 1225 invited the Teutonic Order and its grand master, Hermann of Salza, to come into his country, which had suffered heavily from the incursions of the pagan 'Pruzzi' or Prussians, a Baltic tribe of Lithuanian descent living between Poland and the Baltic Sea, from whom the name 'Prussia' is derived. Hermann of Salza succeeded in getting a privileged position from both emperor and pope, which made him for practical purposes independent of the territorial prince of Masovia. The Teutonic knights quickly conquered the Prussian lands, forced the Prussians to accept Christianity and freed the Masovians from the perilous attacks from the north. But this was only a beginning. The initial successes were exploited, after 1230, and a rapid expansion of the Order began. Towns were founded, German peasants settled on the land, and the knights soon built up a very progressive territorial state, independent of the Polish king; indeed, their militant, expansive state drew ahead of neighbouring Poland not only in administration and finance, but also in commerce and agriculture, and most of all in military power.

The knights had no hesitation about exploiting their preponderance. Though it is undeniable that the Teutonic Order disseminated western and Christian civilization in Prussia and Livonia, it is also undeniable that this was done by the sword rather than by preaching. Inevitably, the thrusting, aggressive policy of the Order produced a reaction, which came to a head after the death of the grand master, Winrich of Kniprode, in 1382. The dynastic union of Poland and Lithuania by the marriage between the Polish heiress, Hedwig, and Jagiello, the prince of Lithuania, in 1387, set up a barrier to further expansion. It also resulted in the conversion of the Lithuanians, the last pagans in Europe, and with this conversion the missionary task of the Order ceased to make sense. At the same moment the ambiguity of its position became apparent. Enthusiasm for the crusade had disappeared; the influx of knights from the Empire declined; the citizens and other inhabitants of the Order state resented the heavy burden of clerical domination, which was becoming increasingly anachronistic. Hence the defeat of the Teutonic knights at Tannenberg in 1410 was a not unexpected military disaster, although the political situation still remained fluid. But the Poles definitely asserted their superiority in the peace treaty of Thorn (1466), when the territories of the Order were partitioned, the western part, with the port of Gdańsk (Danzig), passing to Poland. Half a century later the Teutonic state lost its clerical character when the grand master, Albrecht of Hohenzollern, became a vassal of the Polish king for the diminished territories which the Teutonic Order still retained.

The defeat and decay of the Teutonic Order was not the result of a national or racial conflict. The thirteen years' war, which ended in 1466, was waged by the Prussian Union, a federation of the cities of Gdańsk and Toruń (Thorn) with the rural gentry, who were laymen and not members of the Order. This was a German revolt against the territorial domination of the knights. Of course it is evident that the united strength of Poland and Lithuania was an important factor in weakening the position of the Order in the Baltic countries; unification with Lithuania made Poland a leading European power. But relations with the West played a secondary role in Polish policy at this stage. In the second half of the fifteenth century Poland's efforts were directed mainly against the rising power of Moscow in the East, although Jagiellons also ruled in Bohemia and Hungary.

It is undeniable, in summary, that the Teutonic knights pursued an aggressive policy. But it would be a mistake to judge the whole movement of German eastern colonization by this standard. The eastward movement of German settlers brought many Germans into Poland, but not according to a planned policy of expansion; their settlement was much more a consequence of measures of economic planning on the Slav side. Moreover, this movement did not harm the bulk of the Polish people. It was only in

221

Bosl

POLITICAL
RELATIONS
BETWEEN EAST
AND WEST

a few areas near the western frontier of Poland, especially in Silesia, that Germanization later took place; further east the German settlers, lacking any direct connection with their German homeland, were absorbed into the Polish nation after the close of the fifteenth century.

The Rule of Foreign Dynasties and the Rise of Nationalism

The fourth period in the political relations between East and West is characterized by the rule of foreign kings in Bohemia and Hungary and by a national reaction in the fifteenth century, especially the Hussite revolution in Bohemia, which quickly became an event of European significance.

Hungary had defended its leading position in the Danube valley in the first half of the thirteenth century. Its mighty nobility was privileged in 1222 by a charter similar to that obtained by the English barons in 1215. But the invasion of the Mongols and Tatars in 1241 disturbed the course of development both in Hungary and in Poland. After the Babenberg dynasty died out in Austria, in 1246, the Austrian nobility elected as successor the son of king Wenceslaus I of Bohemia. He was Přemysl Otakar II, who was elected king of Bohemia in 1253 after the death of his father. The Hungarians and the majority of the Polish dukes opposed this expansion of Bohemian power, particularly when, as a result of the defeats of king Béla IV of Hungary at the hands of the Mongols, Otakar also occupied the dukedoms of Styria, Carinthia and Carniola and united the territories of the Slovenes in Austria with his Bohemian kingdom. For a moment the territorial union of the south and west Slavs seemed a possibility. But Otakar's policy was not national and still less racial. Like his predecessors, he summoned German artisans, merchants, miners and settlers into his realm. The Czechs did not support him, and aided his rival, Rudolf of Habsburg, while the Polish princes formed a common Slav defensive alliance against the Germans.

Otakar's aim was the imperial German crown, which he hoped to win with the aid of the pope. Had he succeeded, Bohemia would no doubt have been linked more closely to Germany than it already was, and the character of the Empire would have undergone substantial changes under the rule of a Slav emperor. When the German princes elected Rudolf of Habsburg in 1273, Otakar had to defend his Austrian acquisitions against the new German king, who aspired to develop a strong territorial state in this area. The issue was decided in 1278 at the battle of the Marchfeld, north of Vienna, in which Otakar lost his life. The Habsburg dynasty was now free to pursue a policy of expansion beyond the frontiers of the Empire and the Danube area. The immediate result of the defeat of 1278 was a serious weakening of Czech power, and German and imperial influence in Bohemia and Moravia increased steadily. However, Wenceslaus II, Otakar II's son, was elected king of Poland in 1300, and in the following year his son was crowned king of Hungary, on the death of Andrew III, last representative of the Arpad dynasty. Thus Bohemia, Poland and Hungary were united for a short time, but only by dynastic union.

This did not last long. With the murder of Wenceslaus III in 1306 the old Czech royal family of the Přemyslids died out. This event released the Polish Piasts from the continuous pressure of the Přemyslid kings and secured the complete independence of their country. It also set up rivalry for the thrones of Bohemia and of Hungary. Both the Habsburg dynasty and the Wittelsbach dukes of Bavaria competed for the crowns of St. Wenceslaus and St. Stephen. Neither succeeded. With the help of the pope, Charles Robert, a scion of the French Angevin dynasty, was elected king of Hungary in 1308. This foreign dynasty preserved the traditions of Hungarian independence and blocked the growing German influence. In Bohemia Přemyslid rule was followed by that of the western house of Luxembourg, which also was strongly influenced by French connections and attitudes. John of Luxembourg, who succeeded in 1310, was the son of the emperor, Henry VII, and both he and his son Charles IV, German emperor and king of Bohemia, followed the French style of education and a French way of life during the whole of their careers. Working in co-operation with the Teutonic Order, they became very dangerous rivals of Poland. At the end of the fourteenth century they also won the Hungarian crown.

These developments in Bohemia and Hungary, taken together with the rise of Moscow and the invasion of the Balkans by the Turks, marked a climax in the history of eastern and central Europe. The reign of Charles IV was both a turning-point in German history and a period of extraordinary progress in the Bohemian lands. Prague became the capital of the Empire and Bohemia played a leading part both in politics and in culture. The foundation of the first university of central Europe in Prague by Charles IV in 1348 indicates the momentum Bohemia had gained under his rule. Shortly afterwards universities were established, more or less simultaneously, at Cracow in Poland, at Pécs (Fünfkirchen) in Hungary, and at Vienna in Austria.

It is true that this flourishing civilization and the close contacts with the West, particularly with Germany, had to be paid for by stricter dependence on the Empire, which threatened loss of independence and of liberty of decision. On the other hand, the Bohemian lands were organized ecclesiastically in 1344 as a single independent archbishopric; the kingdom of Bohemia now had its own autonomous territorial church. After having occupied the whole of Lausitz, Charles acquired the march of Brandenburg for his son Sigismund; the Ascanian and Wittelsbach dynasties had already made this territory a strong German bulwark, menacing the independence of Poland. The emperor also arranged a dynastic marriage between his son and Mary, the heiress of Hungary, daughter of the last Angevin king of that country, Louis the Great, who died in 1382. Thus the idea of a union of Bohemia and Hungary, going back to the time of Otakar II, was revived.

The Angevins had come to Hungary from Italy, and at their courts at

223

Bosl

POLITICAL
RELATIONS
BETWEEN EAST
AND WEST

Buda or Wissegrad there was a flourishing French and Italian civilization with elements of early Renaissance culture. Charles Robert co-operated with the Polish king very closely and married Elisabeth of Poland, daughter of Wladisław Łokietek, in 1320. Louis the Great, son of Charles Robert, had to face the hostility of the biggest commercial power in the region, the republic of Venice; but he was able to reoccupy Dalmatia in 1358. After 1370 he was also king of Poland following the death of the last of the Piasts. But he had no sons, and his heritage fell to his daughters. The marriage of Hedwig with William of Habsburg was intended as a first step towards union between Hungary and Austria. But after Louis the Great's death a national reaction intervened and the plan came to nothing. As in Poland and a little later in Bohemia, a national revolution swept away the foreign influences which had prevailed under the foreign kings.

Meanwhile Serbia had made great progress under the rule of Stefan Dušan, the greatest monarch of his time, who planned to build a Serbian empire, which should replace the Byzantine empire of the Paleologues in the Balkans. Dušan was named 'imperator Daciae et Romaniae'. But Serbian power and independence collapsed completely on the battlefield of Kossovo in 1389 under the blows of the Turkish general, Murad I. Bulgaria also was conquered and occupied by the Turks after the destruction of its capital Trnovo in 1393, and national life and civilization were extinguished in the Balkans for half a millennium.

The fifteenth century in eastern Europe was characterized by the rise of national kingdoms in Bohemia and Hungary and by expansion on the eastern frontiers of the united Polish-Lithuanian state by the Jagiellonian kings. It was Sigismund, son of Charles IV and ruler of Germany since the forced abdication of his brother Wenceslaus (or Vaclav) in 1400, who lit the spark which kindled the nationalism of Bohemia. By summoning the Czech reformer Jan Hus before the Council of Constance (1414–18), and condemning him to death because he refused to renounce his religious views, Sigismund provoked a national reaction in the Bohemian lands. The Hussite revolution was the first social movement in Europe with an explicit will to change the whole order of society. It was also a rebellion for Czech independence. Against this revolt, backed by the estates of Bohemia, the idea of crusade, invoked by pope and emperor, proved ineffective. The Hussites under the military leadership of Jan Žižka and Procop launched attacks on the neighbouring countries; but all German counter-attacks were defeated, and the Taborites became a military power. The Poles also had already strongly resisted the concept of imperial supremacy at the Council of Constance.

Meanwhile Bohemia was suffering from the ravages of war, and the Council of Basel, which convened in 1431, made peace with the moderate wing of the Hussites. Both sides agreed in 1433 to sign the so-called Compacts of Prague, which approved the minimal demands of the Czech reform movement, and the radical Hussite wing of the movement was defeated in 1434 at the battle of Lipany. The emperor Sigismund was then acknowledged as king of Bohemia. Finally, therefore, he succeeded in uniting the crowns of the Empire, Bohemia and Hungary. But this success was precarious and short-lived. When Sigismund died in 1437 without a son, he transferred his three kingdoms to Albrecht of Habsburg, the husband of his daughter Elisabeth. But Albrecht also died in 1439, leaving a posthumous son, Ladislaus, as heir to Bohemia and Hungary. His claims were never effective; Bohemia and Hungary were riddled with civil war, and when Ladislaus died in 1457, national kings were elected in both realms, for the representatives of the estates were very strong and effective in both countries. George of Poděbrad, a Czech nobleman of Utraquistic confession, became king of Bohemia; Matthias Corvinus, son of the Hungarian national hero, John Hunyadi, was elected king of Hungary. But Casimir Jagiello of Poland, husband of Albrecht II's daughter, Elisabeth, also laid claim to the crowns, as did the Habsburg emperor, Frederick III. Eventually, but not until the next century, the Habsburg claims proved successful, and Hungary and Bohemia passed under Habsburg rule, which lasted until 1918.

The Slav nations of eastern Europe, no less than the Romano-Germanic nations of the West, are constituent elements of European society and civilization. The political relations between western and eastern Europe in the Middle Ages, underpinned and supported by Christian missions and ecclesiastical organization, as well as by trade, commerce, urban development, law and science, brought both parts into contact, inaugurated a process of assimilation, and introduced similar standards in both regions. These relations, it is true, were often hostile; many wars and much fighting took place; but the traditional emphasis of historians on wars and assassinations too easily obscures the fact that most of the time relations were peaceful. To a large extent political relations were made up of dynastic marriages between the ruling families, of legations of all kinds, of the exchange of gifts and privileges, of treaties, agreements, conferences and meetings, and they assumed a wide variety of forms of association, not all of them implying subjection. In all these ways the tribes and nations of eastern Europe were not only able to establish more or less independent states of their own, but also became fully fledged members of the Christian society of medieval Europe.

225

Bosl

POLITICAL
RELATIONS
BETWEEN EAST
AND WEST

15. The Monasteries

R. W. SOUTHERN

As in most religious movements that have become institutionalized, there were several tensions in early Christianity. On the one hand, Christ had commanded his faithful to love one another, to share what they had, and to go among those who did not know him, spreading his message. Thus there was a strong impulse for the radically committed Christian to involve himself in society and to do Christ's work in that way. On the other hand, personal salvation was an essential element of Christianity, and the church taught that salvation was to be achieved by a life of good works, prayer, devotion, and withdrawal from the temptations of secular life. In the third century, in Egypt and Syria, some had gone off to seek a life of solitude and seclusion in order to avoid the distractions of the world, and to serve God more perfectly through contemplation of his mysteries and dedication to his worship. As conditions became more and more unsettled in the West, largely as a result of the inroads of Germanic marauders from the fourth century on, many turned to the earlier example of the East and sought refuge in a solitary life of asceticism as monks.

The most influential man in Western monasticism, St. Benedict of Nursia, found himself surrounded by men who wished to follow his example, and consequently he composed a "Rule" to govern the lives of those who would live as monks. The Rule stressed poverty, obedience to the superior of the

Source: R. W. Southern, *The Making of the Middle Ages* (New Haven: Yale University Press, 1953), pp. 125–127, 154–169. Reprinted by permission of the publisher. [Footnotes omitted.]

order, and humility. Benedict's wording proved flexible and adaptable enough for his Rule to become the basis of all later monastic charters, and it has remained the fundamental document in Western monasticism up until the present. This is not to say that there were not difficulties in the development of the idea.

The tension between the monk's ideal of withdrawal and the priests' commitment to working in the world played a major role in the medieval church. Another significant factor affecting monastic life was the unavoidable involvement of the monastery in the world. The monastery usually possessed fields and serfs with which to support itself. In the course of time, many monastic establishments became part of the structure of feudal Europe, with the result that abbots, whose primary duties were supposed to be concerned with the religious welfare of their subordinates, found themselves obligated to render justice or even to provide military service to feudal overlords. A similar situation developed in a great many bishoprics as these centers of church administration acquired more and more land with attendant military and social obligations. In response to this increasing complexity, various reform movements arose which attempted to purify the monasteries.

R. W. Southern, in his much acclaimed The Making of the Middle Ages, *is concerned with change in society, especially from the tenth to the late twelfth century. In the following selections, he gives a brilliant picture of the Gregorian reform movement of the eleventh century in the description of the Council of 1049, and discusses the complicated structure of the monasteries and their involvement with secular society. Writing with great knowledge and feeling, Southern skillfully describes the problems of the monastic ideal in this formative period and sketches some of the principal attempts made to solve the difficulties that contemporaries saw. The student who wishes to read further on the subject might consult Southern's* Western Society and the Church in the Middle Ages *(1970).* The Rule of St. Benedict *is available in several translations, and is also worth reading for an understanding of monastic ideals.*

Only five years after Benedict IX sold the papacy, in the year before Count Wilfred of Cerdaña died leaving his sons so firmly entrenched in the episcopacy, an event took place at the other end of Europe which struck a great blow at the manner in which he had provided for his family. In 1049 Pope Leo IX made a tour through his native land, along the Rhine and up the Moselle. The final stage of his journey brought him to the city of Rheims, where he was engaged to consecrate the newly built church of the monastery of St. Remigius, and to transfer to the high altar the bones of its patron saint. Here the Pope had summoned a large concourse of bishops and abbots to meet him. The response to the Pope's summons had been disappointing. There were no more than twenty bishops present—one from England, five from Normandy, but only a handful from the great provinces of Rheims and Sens, which should have provided most. From these unpropitious beginnings, however, there developed an awe-inspiring scene, and we are fortunate in having from a contemporary a day-to-day account of a Council which men later remembered as a landmark in the history of the Church.

The Feast of St. Remigius, 1 October, had been fixed for the ceremony of translation, and the Pope arrived in Rheims on 29 September. The King of France had refused to be present, and he was largely responsible for the poor attendance of bishops. But the vast concourse of people who filled the town formed a striking and instructive contrast to the sparse gathering of notabilities. The 30 September was spent in rest; then, on the appointed day, amid scenes of immense popular enthusiasm and excitement, the bones of St. Remigius were carried round the town. The time had now arrived for the Pope to place them in their new resting place, but instead of doing so, he had them laid on the high altar of the church in which the Council was to be opened on the following day. The awful presence of the apostle of the Franks appeared from that moment to dominate the meeting. When the Council opened, the Pope—through the mouth of his chancellor, the cardinal deacon Peter, who was in charge of the business—made an unusual demand: before proceeding to the business of the meeting, each bishop and abbot was enjoined to rise and declare whether he had paid any money to obtain his office. The proposal caused considerable consternation. The Archbishop of Rheims asked for a personal interview with the Pope; the Bishops of Langres, Nevers, Coutances and Nantes remained silent. Of the abbots, only a few seem to have made the necessary declaration: the silence of the remainder expressed their embarrassment or guilt. Apparently the case against the abbots was allowed to drop; but during the remaining two days of the Council, in the intervals of the humdrum business of ecclesiastical disputes, the Papal Chancellor relentlessly pressed the bishops who had not dared to make the required declaration. The position of the Archbishop of Rheims, who was the host, was delicate: he was spared to the extent of being ordered to appear at Rome in the following year to make his explanation at the Council to be held in the middle of April. The full weight of the Chancellor's attack fell on the Bishop of Langres, a somewhat learned man, who, we notice, had just written a pamphlet against the heresy of Berengar of Tours. He asked for counsel: two archbishops undertook his defence, but one of them (the archbishop of Besançon) found some difficulty in speaking when his turn came, and the other (the archbishop of Lyons) made a partial admission of guilt on behalf of his client. The matter was adjourned, and came to climax on the following day. The Bishop of Langres was found to have disappeared in the night. He was excommunicated; and his counsel, the archbishop of Besançon, revealed that he himself had been struck dumb on the previous day when he attempted a defence of his guilty colleague. The assembly felt the influence of the awful presence on the altar, and a wave of excitement ran through the church. The Pope rose with the name of St. Remigius on his lips, and the business was interrupted while they all sang the antiphon *Sancte Remigi.* After these excitements, the case against the other bishops was quickly disposed of. The Bishop of Nevers confessed that his parents had paid a high price for his bishopric, but declared that he was ignorant of this at the time. He laid down his pastoral staff at the Pope's feet, and the Pope restored him to office, giving him (the symbolism is significant) another staff. The Bishop of Coutances then said that his bishopric had been bought for him by his brother without his knowledge; and that when, on discovering the transaction, he had tried to flee, he had been brought back and forcibly invested with the bishopric. He was declared innocent and he lived to be one of the builders of the Anglo-Norman state and one of the most magnificent prelates of his age. The Bishop of Nantes fared worse: he confessed that his father, who had been bishop before him, had obtained for him from the count the reversion of the bishopric, and that he himself had been obliged to pay a large sum to enter into his inheritance. He was deprived of his episcopal ring and staff, and allowed only to retain the status of a priest.

The business of the Council was now rapidly brought to an end. Various excommunications were pronounced against absent or contumacious bishops, decrees were promulgated which were long remembered for their disciplinary vigour, and a number of sentences and prohibitions were directed against laymen. On the day after the dissolution of the Council, the Pope raised the body of St. Remigius from the high altar and bore it on his own shoulders to its new resting place. He had been in Rheims just a week, and during this time, he had left a mark on the affairs of the Church which would not easily be effaced. The Pope had appeared in a more commanding position than at any time in living memory; out of the handful of bishops present at the Council, a quarter had confessed to simony, and had been judged as if they had committed a crime; an archbishop had been summoned to Rome. The promptings of conscience of men like Reginald of Liège were being stiffened by the sterner voice of authority.

. . . . .

The religious life, throughout our period,* meant pre-eminently the life of monastic discipline. But the monasteries were neither static institutions, nor were they remote from the lay world. Indeed, it was a cause of complaint that they were not remote enough, that the monks had their ears too close to the ground for news and rumours of wars, and that they could listen from their windows to the busy chattering of the world. And no amount of effort could really remedy this defect—if it was a defect. The monks were too much in the public eye to escape attention; they were moreover a costly institution, and it is scarcely putting it too strongly to say that their benefactors expected value for their money. Nor, even physically, was seclusion from the world easy to obtain; there was no Mount Athos in the Western Church dedicated to the religious life; the monks of the West were found in the greatest numbers where population and wealth accumulated. They were not town dwellers like the friars who were appearing at the end of our period, but they were seldom far from the centres of feudal government and social life.

This mingling of monastic and secular life did not please everyone, and

* [The eleventh and twelfth centuries—EDITOR]

it was certainly not foreseen in the Rule which St. Benedict had drawn up in the sixth century. But the intercourse was too engrained in the society of the tenth and eleventh centuries to be easily disturbed. We have already seen that there was, in the later eleventh century, a great reaction against the tendency to treat the Church as a branch of government under the control of the lay ruler; we shall see that the history of monasticism is deeply marked by a similar reaction against the type of monastery created by tenth- and eleventh-century rulers—but this reaction, though it caused much bitterness in monastic circles, did not affect the close relations between monasteries and their lay patrons. The monasteries were a force making for peace in a world which was rudely shaken by the controversies of the Hildebrandine age. The insistence that clerks were not to be treated as other folk came as a shock, and threatened to upset many well-established arrangements, especially in the field of law and government. But the parallel insistence that monks should be less concerned with the world had no troublesome secular reactions and threatened no man's rights. It was a point of view which found ready support among the laity.

Nevertheless this challenge threatened the peace of mind and questioned the vocation of many conscientious monks who had felt their lives safe in the routine of a well-ordered system. So far as the monastic life was concerned the century following the death of Gregory VII was an age of controversy, as the previous century had been one of steady conforming to a pattern admired by all. It was not one controversy but many—was the solitary life superior to the monastic life? Should monks exercise secular jurisdiction? How closely should they follow the Rule of St. Benedict? Should they introduce a greater simplicity into their church services? But all these controversies resolved themselves into the one all-important question—were the ideas which had guided the monastic reformers of the tenth and eleventh centuries to be thrown over or not? In the end, the work of these centuries proved extraordinarily solid, and it set the tone not only for the monastic life but also for much of the secular religion and private devotion of the whole Middle Ages. The corporate and institutional sense which formed Cluny was less logical and, in a sense, less spiritual than that which later formed Cîteaux or which, later still, informed the Franciscan way of life, but like the society itself which grew up in those hard times it was made to last.

In what follows we shall first say something about the relations between lay society and the monasteries, and secondly about the monastic ideal of the tenth and eleventh centuries, and the reasons why it came under criticism.

Lay Society and the Monasteries

The first contact between lay society and a monastic community was in the act of foundation. We have a great number of documents describing the foundation of monasteries in the period from the late tenth to the early twelfth century, and they show very clearly the sustained corporate effort which was needed to bring a monastery into being. The initiative generally lay with a great baron who gave the site, provided an endowment of land and revenues, granted jurisdictional immunities, decided the affiliations of his monastery and regulated the future relations of his family to the community. But close on the heels of the baron came his vassals: they also contributed lands and rights, and claimed a share in the spiritual benefits of the monastery. The charters of foundation gave full weight to the part played by the vassals. More than any other documents of the age they symbolize the unity of a baron and his knights, and the social solidarity of the feudal unit. The religious foundations of the Carolingian age had rested on the precariously narrow basis of royal or semi-royal munificence; their large and compact estates proclaimed the generosity of a very few with very much indeed to give. But the strength of the later monasteries, like the strength of the new social order itself, lay in their widespread and intricate connexion with the countryside; their possessions were scattered, generally in small parcels, among the lands of the neighbouring aristocracy to whom they owed their origin. Like the society which produced them, these monasteries were intensely local in their interests and independent in their government. If they stand in strong contrast to the monasteries of a previous generation in the range of their social connexions, they are even more sharply divided from the religious orders of the thirteenth century in their localism and in the solidity of their economic foundations. The thirteenth-century houses of friars were merely the local offshoots of a great organization; starting from small beginnings and needing very little initial equipment, they were able to find lodgement in corners where no monastery could have supported itself. The eleventh-century monastery was a cumbrous and costly organism, but it was so well rooted in the soil that only Reformation or Revolution could uproot it.

The intimate association of lay benefactors with the monastery did not cease when the foundation was complete. The lay magnate who was also a connoisseur in matters of religious observance is a familiar figure at least from the time of Charlemagne till the seventeenth century. Charlemagne played the autocrat in church with as much confidence as in the council chamber, pointing, as one of his biographers tells us, with his finger or a stick to the person whom he wished to read the lessons, and peremptorily bringing the lesson to an end with a cough. No one in a later age could compete with Charlemagne in the control of his clerks, but our period is rich in secular rulers of both sexes and all degrees of wealth, whose interest in the highly elaborate routine of religious observance in the monasteries was an important factor in the life of the time.

The Dukes of Normandy illustrate very well the persistent interest which men of different characters, in the midst of crushing practical difficulties, showed in the latest developments of monastic life wherever they might be found. We have already mentioned the periodic visits of the monks of Mount Sinai to Rouen, and the interest of the Dukes in fostering the pilgrimage to Jerusalem. But their first interest in religion lay in the ordering of the monastic life. The English Chronicler, who had reason to know of Duke William's fierce and primitive love of the red gold, noted that he was nevertheless mild to the good men who loved God— that is, to the monks; and men were astonished to see that the dreadful old man became gentle and affable in the presence of the Abbot of Bec. After William's funeral, when the company were sitting round the Great Hall at Caen, they remembered this trait in his character, and the talk turned on his admiration for St. Richard, the great Abbot of Verdun, who had been his father's friend. Someone told how William had maintained his father's generosity to this distant monastery, and how, after a period of silence, being anxious to continue his alms in a good cause, he had made enquiries about the community; but he received a poor account of the state of discipline, and kept his gifts to himself.

Without a background of interest of this kind, the whole story of monastic foundations and reform during our period would be unintelligible. The laity not only watched the interior discipline of the monasteries with observant eyes, they also learnt from what they saw. We know little about the religious practices of the ordinary layman in the eleventh and twelfth centuries; but what is quite clear is that those who set themselves a standard higher than the ordinary looked to the monasteries for their examples. It was from the monasteries that the countryside learnt its religion. From their liturgical experiments and experiences there grew up a body of devotional practices which became part of the inheritance of every pious layman.

The influence of the monasteries on the lay religion of the later Middle Ages was deep and lasting, and in some ways surprising. Few expressions of devotion could seem less nearly allied to the complex routine of a tenth- or eleventh-century monastery than those Books of Hours which became the main instrument of lay piety in the centuries before the Reformation. On the one hand we have the extreme elaboration of corporate services; on the other, a series of devotional forms which are short, simple, and full of emotional tenderness. Yet it has been amply demonstrated that the Books of Hours simply contain those additions to the monastic services which had been introduced into the monasteries in the period from the ninth to the eleventh century. In their monastic context they were merely additions—at first private and later corporate—to an already heavy round of liturgical duties; in their later form they had an independent existence and met the needs of people whose lives were mostly occupied with secular affairs. The process of disentanglement was a long one, but it is surely a striking indication of the power of the monastic innovators to express the spiritual impulses of their own age and to form those of the future, that their novelties survived almost unaltered into times so different and among people so far removed from the life of monastic observance.

It argues a very sensitive relationship between the monasteries and the community that this transference of monastic usages to the world at large happened by a natural sympathy and without a struggle, despite a strong reaction within the monasteries themselves against the habits of mind which had produced the additional services in the first place. The channels of communication with the world which made this transference possible were almost infinite. Most obviously, there was the slow process of infiltration from the monasteries to the great collegiate and cathedral churches, and from them to the parish churches and the homes of the laity. More spasmodic but equally clear, there were individual laymen who, by an intense personal effort, adopted some part of the monastic routine in private life. Such a person was Queen Margaret of Scotland who died in 1093. Already, her biographer tells us, she had seized on those additions to the monastic offices which made up the major part of the later Books of Hours, and she began her day by reciting the Offices of the Holy Trinity, the Holy Cross, and the Blessed Virgin, and the Office of the Dead. Then there was a third channel by which monastic influence was communicated to the world, less clear-cut but perhaps no less powerful than these others: the channel of the ordinary lay magnate, illiterate himself and confined by this fact to a somewhat external view of monastic developments, who could nevertheless observe, admire and encourage with his wealth and protection. Such a man was King Malcolm, the husband of Queen Margaret, who (says her biographer) was unable to read, but turned over in his hands, kissed and fondled the books from which his wife prayed and—having found out which she admired most— had it bound in gold and precious stones. Such a man, in his own way, was William the Conqueror, with his far-flung yet judicious benefactions. Such, in varying degrees, were very many barons, who, having in solemn state been admitted to the fraternity of a monastic house, found there a centre of family interest: here they might end their days; here they would be buried with their fathers; and here, however little they knew of the liturgical innovations of the tenth century, they would know they could rely on the aid of the daily Office of the Dead. Even those who are known in general history as despoilers of monasteries seem to have been glad to know that there was some monastery where they stood on this footing and might expect these benefits.

The Monastic Ideal of the Tenth and Eleventh Centuries

What did men expect to find in a great monastery in the eleventh century?—what, for example, did William the Conqueror look for at Verdun and fail to find? Briefly, they expected to find a busy, efficient, orderly community, maintaining an elaborate sequence of church services, which called for a high degree of skill and expert knowledge. They did not expect to find a body of ascetics or contemplatives, and they would have thought it a poor reward for their munificence if they had found marks of poverty in the buildings, dress or equipment of the monks. For them, monasticism was not a flight into desert places undertaken by individuals under the stress of a strong conviction; it was the expression of the corporate religious ideals and needs of a whole community.

This was a situation which could scarcely have been envisaged by the founder of the monastic rule in the sixth century. St. Benedict might have welcomed or deplored the circumstances in which new communities sprang up under the shelter of his Rule during the eleventh century, but clearly the Rule could not mean the same to his later followers as it did to his first companions. The Rule had assumed a more inward religion, a more sustained power of meditation, a greater self-discipline, than the reformers of the tenth and eleventh centuries could expect to find in their monks. It had *not* assumed the existence of highly developed social conventions and ideals, from which the monasteries were not a refuge, but of which they were rather an expression. The zeal of founders had made the monasteries less centres of private religious exercise, than centres of public intercession and prayer, performing a necessary service for the well-being of founders, benefactors and of society in general. The point of view of founders, made articulate by the churchmen who stood at their elbow, found expression in the communities which they established. Here is King Edgar founding his new monastery at Winchester in 966:

> Fearing lest I should incur eternal misery if I failed to do the will of Him who moves all things in Heaven and Earth, I have— acting as the vicar of Christ—driven out the crowds of vicious canons from various monasteries under my control, because their intercessions could avail me nothing . . . and I have substituted communities of monks, pleasing to God, who shall intercede for us without ceasing.*

For all we know, the secular clerks who were driven out were no worse than the clergy who in their turn took the place of the monks six centuries later: but for the purpose King Edgar had in mind, they were inefficient. He required not spontaneity, but a ceaseless penitential work, proceeding with tide-like regularity.

This ideal set a delicate problem to the spiritual guides and leaders of the age. On the one hand, the monasteries were too numerous to be filled by voluntary recruitment—and they had no desire to see them filled with men from the plough. It became a duty to provide the men, as well as the means of support for the monasteries. Good birth lost none of its attraction by being in a monastery. But how were sufficient men of good birth to be attracted? Partly by providing a noble and colourful life. Partly also by bringing them up in the monastic profession from childhood. To a naturally community-minded age, there seemed nothing outrageous in offering children to perform a necessary and dignified function for the rest of their lives. There were abuses: "When they have got their houses full of sons and daughters, if any of them is lame or infirm, hard of hearing or short of sight, they offer them to a monastery", wrote an eleventh-century Cluniac monk about the nobility of his day.† But we may be more im-

---

* *The Liber Vitae of New Minister and Hyde Abbey*, ed. W. de Gray Birch (Hampshire Record Soc., 1892), p. 237.
† Udalricus, *Consuetudines Cluniacenses*, P. L., vol. 149, 635–6.

pressed by the number of outstanding men who found their vocation by being offered as children to a monastic house. This was not the only method of recruitment—the number of those who came to the monastic life as adults was never negligible; but it remains true that the proportion of the monastic population of the eleventh century, which had adopted the life by their own volition, was probably no greater than the proportion of volunteers in a modern army.

The monasteries were filled with a conscript army. It was not an unwilling or ineffective army on that account: the ideal of monastic service was too widely shared for the conscription to be resented. But the circumstance that many men and women in the monasteries had no special aptitude for the life presented a further problem. Communal effort, at the best of times, is easily dissipated, and readily evaporates in a multitude of trivial channels. Sickness, absence, the necessary offices of daily life call men away from the main task—the 'parade strength' is very different from the paper strength. This is a problem of discipline, and this was something to which the monastic leaders of the tenth and eleventh centuries devoted much of their attention. The Rule of St. Benedict laid down a framework of daily life, but it left many details unclear. If we attempt to regulate the activities of a community for each day in a year punctuated by frequent saints' days and revolving in methodical variety through the seasons of the church year we shall find that a great deal of regulation is necessary. Only so, in the circumstances of the time, could the ideal of a rich, varied and efficient service be fulfilled. So it came about that the eleventh century is the century of the fully articulated monastic customaries—books several times the length of the ancient rule, in which the activities of the community were set forth in minute detail. It was by means of these books, often informally circulating from one monastic house to another, that the standard of meticulous, highly organized and elaborate Benedictine life spread throughout western Europe. In the tenth century, such a life had been a wonder, confined to a few centres, to be sought out and learnt by painful steps: a century later, this life was —with infinite local variations, and differences of emphasis between one community and another—taken for granted in the family of Benedictine monasteries.

This phase of monastic development will always be associated with the name of Cluny. It was the active centre of Europe in the days before Gregory VII, when Rome with its great reserves of power was still quiescent. When men thought of religion, they thought of Cluny. They might doubt whether it was the place for them—St. Anselm for instance thought it would give him too little time for study—but it stood above all conflicts, and almost above criticism. In the noble surroundings of the Burgundian hills it offered, for those who could understand, all that the age knew to dignify and exalt the daily round of religious duties: the daily recital of large parts of the Bible in a regular sequence, obstinately maintained in the face of other claims which were beginning to make themselves felt; the leisurely absorption of the learning of the past; familiarity with works bringing memories of all ages of Christian history; the constant companionship of noble buildings, the solemnities of elaborate rites, the company of distinguished men, and that elevation and excitement of feeling which comes from the sense of being at once pioneers in the art of living, and yet firmly established in the esteem and respect of the world. It was a majestic life, incomparable perhaps in this respect to any form of the Christian life developed before or since. It is a far cry from the fastnesses of Subiaco where the Benedictine life was born, to the rich hills of Burgundy with Cluny in their midst; but the monks of Cluny felt firmly rooted in the Rule which they were doing so much to interpret afresh.

Just as the small monastic foundations of obscure barons made for social unity in a disordered local society, so in the larger world of the eleventh century Cluny was a link between men all over Europe. Abbot Odilo, whose rule lasted from 994 to 1049, was the one man of his day of truly European stature. Fulbert of Chartres called him the "archangel among monks", and the phrase had in it the recognition of a peculiar authority. Odilo was as much at home in Pavia as in Paris, at both of which he had the task of directing important monasteries. He was the friend of the 'unreformed' popes, Benedict VIII and John XIX, of the King of France and of three successive German Emperors. The kings of Hungary and Navarre, though they had never seen him, sent him letters and gifts, and solicited his prayers. More than any other man of his time he moved in a large world; yet at its centre was the ordered routine of Cluny. We have a picture of him, much occupied in the affairs of the world, hurrying back to the fellowship of the monastery for the great festivals. His biographer gives an account of him on one of these occasions. He was trying to get back to the monastery for Christmas, and his party was drenched and wearied after a long and hazardous journey. At length, late at night, they reached the monastery at Chalon where they were to lodge, and sat round the fire warming themselves and changing their clothes. The Abbot's heart was moved when he thought of all they had been through together and, to raise their spirits, he declaimed the lines,

O quondam fortes per multa pericula fratres,
Ne vestra vestris frangatis pectora rebus;
Per varios casus, per tot discrimina rerum
Tendimus ad regnum coeli sedesque beatas.
Durate et haec olim meminisse juvabit.*

The words were an adaptation of some lines of Virgil in the first book of the Aeneid (lines 198–207) where Aeneas was encouraging his storm-tossed followers as they lay exhausted and disheartened on the coast of Africa. The allusion was characteristic of Odilo's large and far-ranging mind. He used to say—looking round on the changes which had been wrought at Cluny in his day—that he had found it wood and left it marble, after the example of Augustus who found Rome brick and left it marble. He took pride in the comparison. Marble pillars, no doubt from

* P. L., 142, 921.

ancient Roman ruins, were sought out and brought by water up the Rhône and Saône to decorate the new cloisters which he built towards the end of his life—and this was only the last work of a life-time's delight in making Cluny resplendent. In every way he was a big man, blending with singular harmony the traditions of a pagan and a Christian past, the corporate grandeur of the new monasticism and the simplicity of a monk. In outward things he helped to build up the massive structure of Cluniac greatness and splendour, but in private he felt forward to the new and intimate forms of devotion which captured the imagination of the succeeding generation.

This large and unfanatical spirit was the contribution of Cluny, and in their own degree of the many monasteries which embraced the same ideals of discipline, to a harsh and warlike age. The influence of Cluny had never seemed more secure than in the last quarter of the eleventh century; the expansion of its influence through the foundation of daughter houses was more remarkable than ever—they came to Spain in the wake of active and successful papal legates, and to England in the wake of the Norman conquerors. But there was an uneasiness in the air. Men who fifty years earlier would have found their peace in the established routine of monastic life, seemed bent on making some new experiment.

The most influential of these restless spirits of the late eleventh century was a runaway English monk whose name in his native tongue must have been something like Hearding, and in its Latin form was Hardingus. He had been dedicated as a child to the monastic life in the monastery of Sherborne at about the time of the Norman Conquest, but when he came to manhood he cast aside the cowl, abandoned the religious life and set out on his travels. Any competent authority would have been bound to condemn his action in leaving the monastery to which he had been finally though involuntarily committed. The clue to his purposes at this time is entirely lost, but he was evidently not an ordinary rebel. After a good deal of wandering, he found his way (in the eighties or early nineties of the eleventh century) to a recently founded monastery at Molesme in Burgundy, which, under a remarkable abbot, Robert, was the scene of a vigorous controversy. On the one hand there were those who with their abbot were working towards a simpler and more rigorous life, in keeping, as they believed, with the primitive spirit of the Benedictine Rule; on the other there were those who stood firm for the innovations which had stamped the reforms of the last two centuries. The new arrival, who now, it seems, changed his name to Stephen, threw in his lot with the abbot and his supporters, and from this association there arose first the monastery (1098) and then the order of Cîteaux. Our earliest informant, the English historian William of Malmesbury, who from his nearby monastery knew Sherborne well and was evidently familiar with the Sherborne side of the story, says that it was Harding who began the controversy at Molesme. In this he may be mistaken, but it is certain that Stephen Harding, as he is known to later historians (though his contemporaries knew him only by one or other of these names according as they were French or English), had an extraordinary talent for giving legislative form to a spiritual ideal. He was the author of the two great documents of early Cistercian history, the *Carta Caritatis* and the *Exordium Cisterciensis Coenobii;* and it was during his abbacy (1110–33) that what had been an obscure experiment became the most stimulating source of religious life in Europe. The Cistercians challenged the accepted ideals of monastic life with peculiar force because they sprang from the older order—all the founders of Cîteaux, like Harding himself, had experienced the established monastic routine—and they confronted the immediate past with a past more ancient and more authoritative. Nor was Cîteaux simply a return to the past; it claimed also to be a revolt of reason and sound authority against the shackles of custom. It is striking that the earliest accounts of Cîteaux emphasize the atmosphere of debate in which it started; and the debate continued, though with dying force, for nearly a century. Just as Gregory VII and the circle of which he was the most eminent member focused the controversy about the ordering of the life of the Church as a whole, so the Cistercians became the centre of the controversy about the ordering of the monastic life. The Hildebrandine Reform of the Church has often been associated with the name of Cluny; but, considered as a principle—in its return to the ancient, Roman, pre-Germanic, past; in its appeal to reason and ancient authority against custom; and in its challenge, not simply to corruption, but to a recognized ideal—the kinship is rather with Cîteaux.

Just as the Hildebrandine Reform would not have succeeded unless it had been supported by widespread practical needs and spiritual enthusiasms, so the Cistercian controversy would have fallen on deaf ears unless it had reflected an uneasiness and expressed aspirations shared by many beyond the walls of the monastery. At the time when Harding was coming to his early manhood of discontent, there was in the Forest of Craon —that bone of contention between the monks of Angers and Vendôme —a group of hermits who were exploring in solitude the foundations of the monastic life. These were men of local influence in the religious life of the Loire valley, but two hundred and fifty miles away, at Rheims, there were discussions which led to an experiment of wider interest. Three scholars of varied origin—Master Bruno of Cologne, Ralf Green (Radulfus Viridis), later Archbishop of Rheims, and Fulcius of Beauvais— were sitting in the garden of Bruno's lodgings making plans to leave the "false lures and perishable riches of this world" and follow a monastic life. This must have been about the year 1080. Of the three men only one remained firm in his resolve: Ralf became an archbishop and Fulcius an archdeacon, but Bruno became the founder of the Carthusian order, the most solitary of all the forms of organized religious life produced in this period, and the most withdrawn from the world. After twenty-five years of life at Chartreux, from his solitude in Calabria he wrote to remind Ralf of their discussion of long ago, and he sketched in a few words the circumstances of his own life:

I live the life of a hermit far from the haunts of men on the borders of Calabria, with my brethren in religion—some of them learned men—who await the Lord's return in holy watching, that, when He knocketh, they may open to Him immediately. What words can describe the delights of this place—the mildness and wholesomeness of the air—the wide and fertile plain between the mountains, green with meadows and flowering pastures—the hills gently rising all around—the shady valleys with their grateful abundance of rivers, streams and fountains, or the well-watered gardens and useful growth of various trees? But why should I linger over these things? The delights of the thoughtful man are dearer and more profitable than these, for they are of God. Yet the weak spirit, which has been tired by the harder discipline of spiritual endeavour, is often refreshed and renewed by such things. For the bow which is kept at a stretch becomes slack and less apt for its work. But only they who have experienced the solitude and silence of a hermitage know what profit and holy joy it confers on those who love to dwell there.*

In varying degrees, all these men represented a movement back to simplicity and solitude. They sought to let light and air into an atmosphere heavy with the accumulation of customs, and to give freedom to men burdened with a multiplicity of duties. The intricate and dazzling solemnities, supported by every contrivance of art, and witnessing to a long period of communal growth, weighed heavily on the individual. There was —men came to feel—something lacking in all this: they wanted more time and room for privacy, for a more intense spiritual or intellectual effort, for the friendship of kindred spirits. Meditation and spiritual friendship: these things had never been lacking even in the most busily ordered monastic life, but they had existed in the interstices of scanty leisure; the system, at its most rigorous, had not provided for them. By the end of the twelfth century it is difficult to find any enthusiasm for that ornate and crowded life which a hundred and fifty years earlier had seemed like the doorway to Paradise. "What sweetness or devotion will you find among those whose mumbling and confused reiteration and long drawing-out of Psalms is repeated *ad nauseam?*" † This was the language of a scholar about 1185, and he was a man of moderation. Others spoke more harshly, and if any still regarded the monasteries as places of heroic struggle against the Devil, they kept the thought to themselves.

For better or worse, society had in the tenth and eleventh centuries espoused the cause of Benedictine monasticism. Whether it would have

---

* The letter of St. Bruno is printed in A. Wilmart, *Deux lettres concernant Raoul le Verd, l'ami de saint Bruno,* in Revue Bénédictine, 1939, LI, 257–74.

† This passage from a letter of Peter of Blois is the starting point of an intensely vivid meditation on the difference between Cluniacs and Cistercians by Edmund Bishop, printed posthumously in the *Downside Review,* 1934, lii, 48–70.

done so at the end of the twelfth century with equal fervour, it is useless to enquire. The monasteries were there; there was much criticism of them but no one proposed that they should be abolished. In a later chapter we shall be concerned with some aspects of the spiritual enthusiasm which refashioned the forms of religious devotion in the twelfth century; but the enthusiasms of an age have to work for the most part within institutions which were formed to meet quite different needs and as a result of quite different enthusiasms. It is very probable that there was more happiness, more largeness of life and recreation of spirit in a great Benedictine house in the year 1200 than there had been in 1050, but the fact did not seem worth recording. The monasteries were accepted as part of the order of things, as most people now accept the House of Lords or the Universities of Oxford and Cambridge, as objects of interest and even of pride and affection, but not as tremendous facts in their society.

16. The Hierocratic Doctrine in Its Maturity

WALTER ULLMANN

In contrast to most of the ancient civilizations of the Near East, there has generally been a distinction and separation of religious and secular power throughout most of European history. In the Roman Empire, the trend toward autocracy was associated with attempts to consider the emperor a god, and subjects were, therefore, required to worship him as a god. This produced a conflict with Christianity, as we have previously noted, but the tendency seems to have been much more a matter of politics or patriotism than one of spirituality. With the triumph of Christianity under Constantine, the problem of the relations between religion and the state took a new turn. Generally emperors who claimed the right to rule universally recognized their obligations to their subjects in religion, but few made any claims to absolute control, either in religion or politics, over Christendom. The same was not true of the spiritual heads of Christendom.

The popes, Bishops of Rome who claimed to be the lineal successors of St. Peter, upon whom Christ himself had conferred special authority, came to be regarded as the supreme heads of the church by many in the eleventh century. The problem was complicated when reforming popes, anxious to impose stricter discipline upon their subordinates, found that many abbots and bishops were also feudal lords whose possessions included fiefs for which ser-

Source: Walter Ullmann, *A History of Political Thought: The Middle Ages* (Harmondsworth, Eng.: Penguin Books, 1965), pp. 100–115. Copyright © 1965 by Walter Ullmann. Reprinted by permission of Penguin Books Ltd.

vices were due to feudal kings or even to the emperor. A conflict over the appointment and control of ecclesiastical dignitaries erupted between Pope Gregory VII and Henry IV in 1073, and continued in one form or another until the defeat of the claims of Boniface VIII by Philip the Fair of France in the early fourteenth century. In the meanwhile, papal claims to absolute control of Christendom, extending even to the right to depose kings or emperors, grew up and were elaborated.

How did the church, apparently intended by Christ to occupy itself with the salvation of souls and otherworldly affairs, come to be involved in struggles for power with secular rulers? What claims were put forth by papal extremists in this contest? What rationale was advanced to justify these claims?

Walter Ullmann, an authority on the medieval papacy and medieval political thought at Cambridge University, discusses the hierocratic theory, that doctrine whereby the pope was supposed to represent Christ on earth and could, by reason of his obligation to care for men's souls, intervene in secular matters of government and administration. His thesis, first stated in Medieval Papalism *(1949), holds that some popes, aided by tradition and canon law, sought to rule Christendom absolutely. This view has been very vigorously challenged by several historians, notably F. Kempf in* Papsttum und Kaisertum bei Innocenz III *(1954) and A. Stickler in a series of articles. These scholars argue that the medieval papacy inclined to a view called dualistic, in which secular and papal power were legitimate and independent, each in its own sphere. The evidence is often ambiguous, but Ullmann writes forcefully and clearly about the basis of the extremist claims for the pope. His work indicates also the tensions in society that are produced by the interpenetration of forces and ideals, and the difficulties of neatly segmenting one's loyalties in a concatenated social order.*

Main Characteristics

It may be helpful to state here the essence of the hierocratic ideology, according to which the pope as successor of St. Peter was entitled and bound to lead the community of the faithful, the Church. The means for the pope to do so were the laws issued by him in his supreme jurisdictional function, which claimed universal validity, and concerned themselves with everything that affected the vital interests and structural fabric of the Christian community. Obviously, from this hierocratic point of view, the judge of what was in the interests of that community, what facts, circumstances, actions, or situations touched its vital concerns, was the pope. He was the 'judge ordinary' and claimed to possess the specific knowledge of when legislation was required. The function of the pope was that of a true monarch, governing the community that was entrusted to him. A further essential feature of this theory was the hierarchical gradation of offices, which ensured what was called order and smooth working of the whole community. This order was said to be maintained if everyone remained within his functions which were assigned to him. Bishops had their special functions, and so had kings. If either king or bishop intervened in, or rather interfered with, the other's functions, order would suffer and disorder would follow. The limitation of functional action was the hallmark of the hierocratic thesis, or, in other words, the principle of division of labour was a vital structural element of the thesis. Supreme directive control, the supreme authority (sovereignty), remained with the pope, who, standing as he did outside and above the community of the faithful, issued his directions as a 'steersman', as a *gubernator*.

While considering the theory, the allegorical manner of expressing the relationship between priesthood and laity deserves consideration. The metaphor constantly used was that of the soul and body. The *anima-corpus* allegory was adduced a hundredfold to show the inferiority of the laity and the superiority of the clergy, to show that, just as the soul ruled the body, in the same manner the clergy ruled the laity, with the consequence that, as for instance Cardinal Humbert in the mid-eleventh century stated, the kings were the strong arms of the clergy, for the clergy were the eyes of the whole Church who knew what was to be done. In interpreting this antithesis one should not be misled by pure allegory. What the metaphorical use of soul and body attempted to express was that, because faith in Christ was the cementing bond of the whole Church and the exposition of the faith the business of the clergy, the law itself as the external regulator of society was to be based upon the faith. Faith and law stood to each other in the relation of cause and effect. The 'soul' in this allegory was no more and no less than the pure idea of right and law, the uncontaminated Christian idea of the right way of living. What legal or legislative action faith required could be discerned only by those who had the eyes to see, the clergy. Differently expressed, since every law was to embody the idea of justice, and since justice was an essential ingredient of the Christian faith, the 'soul' in this allegory meant the Christian idea of justice. There can be little doubt that this thesis was the medieval idea of the 'rule of law', and manifested the idea of the supremacy of the law. For the body of the faithful could, so it was said, be held together only by the law based on (Christian) justice, which on the one hand externalized the faith and on the other hand reflected the teleological thesis, for the law was considered the appropriate vehicle by which the body of the faithful was enabled to achieve its end. In short, the law was the soul which ruled the body corporate of the Christians. The legalism of the Middle Ages and quite especially of the hierocratic form of government, found its ready explanation. It was said often enough that only through the law could a public body live, develop, and reach its end.* Within the hierocratic thesis the king was subjected to sacerdotal rulings, the basic idea being that

243

Ullmann

THE
HIEROCRATIC
DOCTRINE IN
ITS MATURITY

* It should not be too difficult to understand on this basis also the meaning of the Ruler as 'the living law' (*lex animata*). This whole cluster of ideas could of course only exist within the descending theory of government, in which the 'will of the prince' formed the material ingredient of the law. It was this will that, so to speak, breathed life into, or animated, the body corporate. This thesis was actually of Hellenistic origin, where the Ruler was known to be the *nomos empsychos,* of which the expression *lex animata* was a literal translation.

the king was not qualified enough to lay down the law in those matters which touched the essential fabric of Christian society. Fundamentally, this thesis of soul and body expressed simply the idea of governing a body public and corporate by means of the law.

As a consequence, the hierocratic ideology which emerged in its full maturity from the pontificate of Gregory VII onwards (1073–85) also laid particular stress upon the law. In fact, this pope went so far as to state dogmatically that it was 'legal discipline' that had led kings onto the path of salvation. After all, they were distinguished by divinity to be the trustees of their kingdoms and had therefore all the more grounds for showing themselves 'lovers of justice' (*amatores justitiae*), and justice, as an ingredient of the Christian faith, could be expounded only by the Roman Church, which was consequently called the 'seat of justice'. The king's duty was obedience to papal commands: he was a subject of the pope, to whom all Christians in any case were subjects. The teleological argumentation received its precision, notably by reference to the accumulated body of knowledge and learning as well as to the interpretation of the coronation orders: the purpose of God granting power to the king in the public sphere was to repress evil. If there had been no evil, there would have been no need for the power of the physical sword. Hence the pope claimed to exercise a 'universal government' (*regimen universale*) by means of the law which made no distinction between matters or persons. The Petrine powers were comprehensive, exempting no one and nothing from the pope's jurisdiction. With exemplary unambiguity for instance Gregory VII declared:

> If the holy see has the right to judge spiritual things, why then not secular things as well?

On another occasion he stated:

> For if the see of St. Peter decides and judges celestial things, how much more does it decide and judge the earthly and secular.

From the papal standpoint it was true to say that the pope bore a very heavy burden, not only of spiritual tasks, but also of secular business, for he considered himself responsible for the direction of the body of the faithful under his control and in his charge. Obviously, the governmental power of the popes referred specifically to kings, because they disposed of the means of executing papal orders and decrees. Moreover, the king, for the reason already stated, was an 'ecclesiastical person', whose office concerned itself with the repression of evil. Both the kingdom and the king's soul were, as the popes repeatedly declared, in their power. But the developed hierocratic programme did make the qualification that the pope considered papal jurisdiction to come into play only when the basic and vital interests of the body of the faithful called for his intervention. None expressed this principle better than Innocent III (1198–1216) in his usual concise language. He stated that feudal matters as such were of no concern to the pope's jurisdiction, which came into full operation however when sin was involved. *Ratione peccati* (by reason of sin) was the technical expression to denote the overriding papal jurisdiction. Evidently, the judge of when sin was involved was the pope himself.

The process of monopolizing the Bible had meanwhile made great strides. The popes applied to themselves the passage in Jeremiah i, 10: 'I have set thee over the nations and kingdoms . . .', because this was, according to Innocent III, a 'prerogative' (the term occurs here for the first time) of the pope: this was nothing but the explicit expression of the monarchic principle. The same Innocent III declared that he was less than God but more than man, a statement that brings into clearest possible relief the very essence of the papal thesis, namely the superior status of the pope, his sovereignty, standing outside and above the community of the faithful. And it was precisely by virtue of his 'superior' status that the papal Ruler gave the law. The development in the twelfth century leading to the concept of the pope as the vicar of Christ only underlined this point of view. The papal vicariate of Christ in itself changed nothing in the papal function. It attributed no more powers to him than he already had. What the concept of the vicariate of Christ focused attention on were the vicarious powers which Peter was said to have been given by Christ: it was these which, by way of succession, came to be wielded by the pope. The concept considerably clarified the function of the pope, with the consequence that a number of biblical passages which referred to Christ were now directly applied to the pope, so, for instance, the Matthean passage: 'All power is given unto me . . .' The vicariate of Christ in the pope demonstrated the pope as the point of intersection between heaven and earth. Hence it was that Innocent III said that what he had decreed was decreed by Christ Himself. And Innocent IV (1245–54) stated that the pope figured as Christ's 'corporal presence'. It was quite in keeping with this theory that the government of the pope was considered to be a true *monarchatus,* because, as the canon lawyers taught, in his hands the 'keys of the kingdom of heaven' had changed into the 'keys of the law'. This monarchic theory was succinctly expressed by Gregory IX (1227–41) thus:

245

Ullmann

THE
HIEROCRATIC
DOCTRINE IN
ITS MATURITY

> When Christ ascended into heaven, He left one vicar on earth, and hence it was necessary that all who wished to be Christians were to be subjected to the government of the vicar.

By virtue of the thesis that God was the creator of everything on earth, the claim was raised by Innocent IV that every human creature (and not merely Christians) were subjects of the pope (who in the doctrine of the canon lawyers was *de jure,* but not *de facto,* the universal monarch). Indeed, the pope possessed—or at least claimed to possess—supreme overlordship over both bodies and souls of all men, as the same Gregory IX asserted. And before him a similar theory was expressed by Innocent III who held that the princes of the world had power over the body only, whilst the priests had power on earth as well as in heaven and over the souls also.

Because the pope functioned as the monarch of the body of the faithful, he claimed that his laws had reference to anyone and anything. Wherever the line of distinction between spiritual and temporal matters might have been drawn, for papal governmental ideology the distinction had no operational value. Since the end of the body of the faithful governed by the pope lay in the other world, anything that might be called temporal was subjected to that spiritual end. St. Paul had often enough declared the superiority of the spiritual over and above the mundane, the visible, the corporeal, or the secular. And by the process of monopolization the papacy made these Pauline views its own. Some statements of Gregory VII have already been quoted, but there were dozens of similar views expressed by other popes in the twelfth and thirteenth centuries. There was also the actual government of the popes who intervened in what might well have appeared, to the less sophisticated contemporaries, purely temporal matters. In the final resort the papal standpoint was based on the view that Christianity seized the whole of man and the whole of his activities without splitting them up into different compartments, which view led to the 'totalitarian' system of government. If, indeed—and as we shall see, it was the royal opposition which argued in this way—the temporal was to be exempt from papal jurisdiction, this would not only have contradicted the all-embracing character of the Petrine powers of binding and loosing, but also the very essence of Christianity, at least as the papacy saw it. Neither things temporal nor the temporal Ruler could have had an autonomous, independent, autogenous standing in the papal scheme of government. Each was a means to an end. The pope, as monarchic sovereign, stood indeed outside and above the body of the faithful,* a body that was one—'we are one body in Christ' according to St. Paul—and which suffered no division. In brief, unity of the body demanded unity of government, which manifested itself in the monarchy of the pope as the 'overseer' (*speculator*) over all matters of basic concern to the well-being of the body.

The correctly understood monarchic point of view also made understandable the unaccountability of the pope for his actions and decrees. The maxim 'The pope cannot be judged by anyone' was, as we have said, the medieval manner of expressing his sovereignty. He was the final arbiter and judge on appeal; to appeal from his court to a council drew the charge of suspected heresy. His plenitude of power was, however, thoroughly juristically conceived. His powers had nothing to do with any divine omnipotence. The anti-papal charge, 'if the pope is the vicar of Christ, why does he not work miracles?'—mainly raised by the French in the early fourteenth century—was really beside the point. No pope

---

* It should be made clear, perhaps, that this thesis—that the pope did not belong to the Church and that he stood outside and above it—had reference only to his capacity as a governor. In what doctrine called the pope's private capacity, that is, as a Christian, he was of course a member of the Church, and, therefore, had his own confessor.

had at any time asserted that the Petrine powers were anything but juristic powers which did not suppose any 'divine' or divinely omnipotent powers. In the papal monarchy one found the classic expression of the descending thesis of government. The material ingredient that gave the papal law the character of an enforceable rule was the pope's will: it was the application of the ancient principle of the 'will of the prince' (*voluntas principis*) as the element that imparted enforceability to the law. Given as it was to the subjects, they had the duty of obedience. And Gregory VII laid down that only he who accepted unquestioningly the decrees of the pope could call himself a catholic.

The distinction, so clearly elaborated by Leo I between the person of the pope and the office of the pope, was perhaps the most useful governmental doctrine that any institution had ever possessed, for thereby considerations concerning the person, character, or bearing of the individual pope were relegated to the background. What stood in the foreground was the office, and the law or decree that flowed from the office. The validity of a decree or law was not in the least dependent upon the personality of the pope: any charge levelled at the pope's personal bearing could be (and was) dismissed as irrelevant. The sovereign status of the pope showed itself, finally, in the full freedom of the pope to change the law which any of his predecessors might have issued. No pope could bind his successor (just as no parliament can today bind its successor), and that seems to be the test of monarchic sovereignty of the pope. The idea underlying it was that no pope followed a predecessor in his function as pope, but succeeded Peter directly without any intermediaries. In the pope, Peter's powers continued (temporal succession was, of course, necessary for the pope's episcopal status). This immediate continuation of Peter's status and office in the pope was in the last resort the explanation why each medieval pope so studiously avoided saying that any of his predecessors had committed an error. For that admission would have been tantamount to saying that St. Peter himself had erred, he who was credited with Christ's vicarious powers.

The application of any monarchic form of government necessitates a firm control of subordinate officers. For the papal monarchy this meant the control of the episcopacy. Without its control neither the king nor the pope could hope to exercise governmental powers effectively, hence the ferocious conflict between the papacy and the kings, predominantly the German king, during the Investiture Contest, the main phases of which occurred in Gregory VII's pontificate. The governmental, that is jurisdictional, subordination of the bishops to the pope proceeded only in stages. It began with the episcopal oath which the bishops had to take to the pope, and the payment of regular visits to the pope, and ended with the quite significant designation of the bishops as 'Bishop by the grace of God and that of the apostolic see' (*episcopus Dei et apostolicae sedis gratia*). The implementation of a worthwhile control presupposed the elaboration of the constitutional relationship that existed—or was held to exist— between the pope and the bishops. Again, the working out took a long

247

Ullmann

THE
HIEROCRATIC
DOCTRINE IN
ITS MATURITY

time, though it visibly began in Gregory VII's pontificate and was, to a large extent, foreshadowed in the pseudo-Isidorian forgeries. It culminated in the assertion that the bishop received his power to govern the diocese from the pope, a thesis which left the sacramental standing of the bishop intact. Hence a deposition or suspension of a bishop by the pope referred to the former's governing powers which were withdrawn or suspended: he still remained bishop, though he was unable to exercise government in his diocese. This thesis was strenuously opposed by the episcopacy, because the bishops stressed the identity of their sacramental function with that of the pope, relying furthermore on the interpretation of Matthew xviii, 18 (as opposed to the papal reliance on Matthew xvi, 18), and consequently were extremely reluctant to acknowledge the papal standpoint. The episcopalist thesis was not destroyed, but only driven underground from the twelfth century onwards, and it began to emerge in a different guise as conciliarism in the late fourteenth century. The papal standpoint was that governmental powers of the bishop were derived from the pope who possessed the plenitude of power, in which the bishops merely partook.

Similarly, the logical pursuit of the papal governmental programme also necessitated the claim to exercise control over the temporal Rulers. This control was basically different in the case of the emperor of the Romans and the other kings. The German king—papal ideology was firm on this—had no right to the imperial crown, which was an 'apostolic favour'. By the late twelfth century the theory of the so-called 'Translation of the Empire' was evolved, according to which the pope had transferred the imperial crown from the 'Greeks' to the Germans: this was simply an attempt to interpret the Donation of Constantine in the light of history. The papal doctrine concerning the empire was classically expressed by Innocent III, who maintained that, because no one had a right to a favour, the German king could have no claim to emperorship. The king had to be approved by the pope as well as confirmed and crowned, for, if there were a right to emperorship, Innocent argued, he would not only have no choice, but would in fact be forced to crown a heretic, a tyrant, an imbecile, and the like. Before the pope put the crown on him, he was no emperor of the Romans, but merely a candidate. What papal doctrine was always insistent upon was to examine the suitability of the king for emperorship, because he was to be the strong arm of the papacy.

Moreover, from the ninth century onwards, the papacy had taken great pains to distil its governmental ideas into the imperial coronation orders. The official (and last medieval) imperial coronation order was made by Innocent III, who in precise and unsurpassable manner managed to incorporate papal doctrine into the liturgical symbolism of the coronation. Once again, purely abstract thought was presented in physical and easily understandable gestures and actions. Each symbol—ring, sword, sceptre, orb, crown—was conferred with an accompanying prayer-text which left no doubt as to the meaning. The imperial unction was, in fact, liturgically on a lower level than the royal unction, because not chrism, but an inferior kind of oil was used, which was applied not to the head (as in the case of the king), but between the shoulderblades and on the right arm (with which he was to wield the sword). Another significant feature was the oath of the emperor-elect to the pope, promising fidelity, protection, and defence. It was no less significant that the emperor-elect was made a cleric by the pope: he was given the right to wear tunic, dalmatic, and mitre. In general, the imperial coronation order, made by Innocent III, combined Byzantine and Western royal features.

But what was most significant was the absence of any enthronement of an emperor: there was no throne. Perhaps in no other way did the medieval papacy manage so clearly to convey its views on the function of the emperor as in this: the emperor was an (exalted) officer, and no officer ever sat on a throne. The coronation rite also made clear that the power of the emperor as an officer or assistant of the pope on a universal scale came from God—no pope ever deviated from this Pauline principle —but it was the pope who acted as the mediary between God and the king to be made emperor. Autonomous powers the emperor had not. If he had had them, there would have been no need, so Innocent III was adamant in his repeated declarations, to supplicate for the papal favour. Nevertheless, the same Innocent was equally insistent that he did not wish to interfere in the elections of the German king as king—not, however, without also declaring that the German princes had received the right to elect their king from the pope. It was mainly in regard to imperial matters that Innocent III often repeated that he had both regal and sacerdotal powers in the fashion of Melchisedek, the Old Testament king and priest. And hence in the creation of the emperor this combined power of the pope showed itself most fully. The *factor proprius* of the emperor, the organ that brought him into being, was the pope, as Gregory IX stated.

Innocent III's thesis owed a good deal to St. Bernard of Clairvaux who, a generation before, had introduced the hierocratically orientated Two-Sword theory into the discussion, a theory that was alleged to have had its origin in Luke xxii, 38, and which had been used in a different sense already by Charlemagne's adviser, Alcuin, as well as by Henry IV. But, according to the doctrine of St. Bernard the pope possessed both swords, that is, the spiritual and the temporal (material), the one signifying the pope's priestly coercive power, the other the regal coercive power. During the coronation the pope gave the latter to the emperor, who was then said to wield the sword at the bidding of the pope (*ad nutum*). This Two-Sword theory was to signify that the actual physical power the emperor possessed was derived from the pope, or rather from God through the mediating organ of the pope. The ancient Isidorian doctrine was given its allegorical clothing. Gregory IX explicitly stated that the Lord had given the pope both swords, one of which the pope retained and wielded, the other he gave away. Or, as his successor Innocent IV stressed, the power of the material sword belonged potentially to the pope, but actually to the emperor. This Two-Sword allegory had reference to the emperor only. What therefore at the end of the thirteenth century Boniface VIII asserted in his *Unam sanctam* could barely be squared with the actual development, for he applied the allegory also to the kings who had never been crowned, nor had ever expressed an intention to be crowned, as emperors: a characteristic extension of a suggestive allegory. What, however, is significant is that the relevant decrees of the popes, especially Innocent III and IV and Gregory IX, were appropriately enough incorporated in the official canon law books under the title 'Of majority and obedience', which seems very important in view of the (medieval) meaning of 'majority', that is, sovereignty and the corresponding obedience on the part of the subjects.

Although the papal thesis concerning the empire logically led to the fourteenth-century view of the pope as temporary administrator and vicar of the empire during a vacancy, the papacy never established— doctrinally at any rate—such close control over 'mere' kings. For, unlike the emperor, kings were rarely crowned by the pope; he never in theory at least claimed to intervene in royal elections; few of the arguments developed in regard to the emperor could be applied to the kings. Nevertheless, Innocent III stated that 'by reason of sin' he could intervene in purely royal matters as well as 'upon examination of certain causes' (*certis causis inspectis*). This Innocentian standpoint brought out clearly the underlying idea of papal governmental principles, that is, to act when the well-being of the whole Christian commonwealth in his view demanded his intervention, because the pope was the 'Overseer'. The idea of *utilitas publica,* that is, the concern for the public weal and its well-being, was an ever-present conception of papal ideology and was in fact raised to the level of a governmental principle by Innocent III, according to whom private interests had to yield to the demands of the public interest. That, in the overwhelming majority of cases, there was no friction between the kings and the popes should not lead to the assumption that, in papal theory, the papacy had no jurisdiction over kings, for in borderline cases and disputes (and they usually were the crucial ones) it was the pope who asserted the claim to overriding jurisdiction. In other words, the principle of division of labour was to be fully applicable in the relations between papacy and kings.

The royal view itself—the 'King by the grace of God'—played into the hands of the papal doctrine. For in the old Gelasian view the popes had to render an account of how the kings discharged their trust. If therefore the kings, in the papal view, misused their trust, the popes considered themselves bound to take action and either to remove the king altogether or to inflict ecclesiastical censures upon him. The principle of suitability or of usefulness became especially operative. Gregory VII was very insistent on the operation of this principle, and this was one of the reasons why the German King Henry IV was first suspended from his kingship (in 1076) and four years later finally deposed. The deposition of kings was decreed when the pope had reached the conclusion that the king in question was unsuitable for his office, as again Gregory VII made clear. But just as the removal of a king was claimed to be the pope's right and duty, so was at times the making of a king his right and duty. Innocent III, for instance, declared in setting up the king of Bulgaria, Joannitza, that thereby he 'wished to ensure the spiritual and temporal well-being of the Bulgarian kingdom'. In any case, the king was an 'ecclesiastical person', which facilitated the emergence of papal doctrine and assisted its application. But whilst deposition of a king was the final sanction the pope could employ, the excommunication of a king was based on different criteria. He could be excommunicated, not so much because he was useless as because he showed himself a disobedient son of the Roman Church. The effects of excommunication were, however, equally stringent, for doctrine had developed the view (which later became also the law) that the excommunicate person was infected with a contagious disease and that therefore nobody was permitted to have any intercourse or contact with him. Consequently, if only his immediate family circle could be in touch with him, government was extremely difficult for a king. Deposition affected the king's title-deed to rule; excommunication entailed his exclusion from the Christian community.

By virtue of his sovereign function within the Christian society, the pope furthermore claimed the right—of which the papacy made significant use—to declare treaties between kings null and void; to annul secular laws, such as Magna Carta or, later in the thirteenth century, the German lawbook, *The Mirror of the Saxons;* to decree ecclesiastical censures against those who exacted unjust tolls or fees on the highways and rivers; to order the king to despatch armed troops in support of another king or against pagans and heretics; to sanction territories obtained by military conquest as legitimate possessions; to compel belligerent parties to stop hostilities and to enter into peace negotiations; to force by interdict or excommunication the population of a kingdom not to obey a king; and so on. The papal plenitude of power enabled the pope, as Gregory VII professed on the occasion of deposing King Henry IV, to take away kingdoms, empires, principalities, and in fact the possessions of all men (*possessiones omnium hominum*), as the case merited. This view was partly based on the thesis that private ownership of goods was an issue of divine grace: because the owner had shown himself unworthy of this divine good deed, the pope considered himself entitled to take away property.

Partly by reason of the demands of public interest, partly by reason of safeguarding the bond that cemented the universal Christian society, partly by reason of the papacy's duty to protect the faith from corrosion, the doctrine was advanced in the early thirteenth century (it became law by the middle of the century) that special tribunals should be set up which were to deal with aberrations from faith. The inquisitorial machinery as laid down by Gregory IX and Innocent IV was the mechanism which was to bring to book those who had shown themselves disobedient rebels to the papal law. The mechanics of this machinery does not belong to the development of governmental thought. What does belong to it is

251

Ullmann

THE
HIEROCRATIC
DOCTRINE IN
ITS MATURITY

(1) the concept of heresy as a crime construed (by Innocent III) as high treason against the divine majesty, committed through aberration from the faith as laid down by the papacy, and as such had the appropriate, fearful sanctions attached, including confiscation of property of the descendants, even if yet unborn; (2) the duty of the secular Ruler to exterminate heretics from his domains. If he were remiss, he himself was to be declared a heretic, his subjects were to be released from their obligation by the pope, and his kingdom was to be occupied by an orthodox catholic prince. This was actually the ruling of the Fourth Lateran Council (1215), which remained the basic decree for the rest of the Middle Ages, and to some extent also beyond.

The governmental ideology underlying these measures, however unfamiliar to modern readers, was nevertheless one that embodied a great many concepts, maxims, and topics which at a later age were to be evaluated as 'political'. From the historical angle one should not forget that these concepts—such as sovereignty, the law, the subject, obedience, and so on—were worked out exclusively within an ecclesiological framework, and it was only later, from the late thirteenth century onwards, that ecclesiology and politology became two distinct branches of thought. Then indeed all of these concepts were to become the working tools of the new science of politology. It was one of the anachronistic feats of the papacy that it solemnly proclaimed in pithy and concise form its own governmental doctrine, at a time when the peak of practical application of papal governmental thought had long been passed.

The decree *Unam sanctam* by Boniface VIII, issued in 1302, was an able and succinct summary of the papal doctrine, culled as it was from a variety of sources which were nevertheless skilfully stitched together. He made great use of the Bible in its papal interpretation, of Cyprian, Pseudo-Denys, St. Bernard, Hugh of St. Victor, Thomas Aquinas, and so on, and though not a single point was new, the significance of *Unam sanctam* was that it presented a summary of papal governmental thought at this late hour. Boniface set out from the ancient idea of the Church as an indivisible body and that no salvation was possible outside it (this was originally Cyprian's thesis and was a century earlier stressed by Innocent III). The principle of oneness manifested itself in that there was one Lord, one faith, one baptism (this was of Augustinian origin). The papal monarchic government was based, according to Boniface, upon this principle: the Church needed one head. A body with two heads was a monster, and that head was Christ Himself and on earth Christ's vicar (this had been put forward by the English canonist Alan in the early thirteenth century). Whatever Greeks and others had asserted, all Christians belonged of necessity to the 'sheep of Christ', and hence were subjected to the pope (this was the thesis of Thomas Aquinas, expounded in his booklet *Against the Errors of the Greeks*). But—by virtue of the principle of division of labour—the two swords possessed by the pope were not wielded by him, but one only, whilst the other was to be used by the kings (and not merely emperors) 'at the bidding and sufferance of the pope' (an extension of Bernard's thesis.) * In his exposition of the hierarchical gradation he relied on Pseudo-Denys and went on to declare that the inferior must be ruled by the superior or the 'supreme power', the latter denoting the sovereign, to whom everybody was subjected. This had with singular clarity been expressed a generation before by the eminent canon lawyer, Cardinal Henry of Susa (Hostiensis), who maintained that, since the pope was concerned with the law, the king's duty was to enforce the papal law: for the smooth working of Christian society it was necessary, the Cardinal said, that the law issued by a 'majority' of the pope was to be followed and obeyed by the royal power. For, as Boniface himself said, on the model of Hugh of St. Victor (who assumed the authority of the Holy Scriptures: *nam testante scriptura*) the spiritual power had to institute royal power (clearly a reference to the coronation proceedings) which remained at all times subjected to the pope (this was derived from Gregory VII). Anyone therefore resisting the papal law, resisted the divine power itself—an application of St. Paul (Romans xiii, 4). He concluded that in order to achieve salvation it was necessary for every human creature to be subjected to the Roman pontiff.†

* John of Salisbury's theory was not unlike Boniface's. Writing in the mid-twelfth century he said that the sword as the symbol of coercive power was wielded by the prince, because the priesthood was forbidden to shed blood and had therefore conferred the sword on the prince, who however remained subjected to the priesthood. The prince for John was in a sense an 'executioner'.

† It should be noted that the phrase 'every human creature' was, in the re-issue of *Unam sanctam* by the Fifth Lateran Council in the early sixteenth century, expunged and 'every Christian' substituted.

253

Ullmann

THE
HIEROCRATIC
DOCTRINE IN
ITS MATURITY

17. St. Thomas Aquinas

DAVID KNOWLES

*The medieval period has often been described as an "age of faith," and such an
appellation at least implicitly suggests an opposition to human reason. It is
simply not true, however, that the medieval mind was closed to rational
thought as a means of solving problems and advancing knowledge. Among
the works directly preserved by monastic activity from late antiquity were
several dealing with logic, or the art of correct reasoning. By the twelfth
century, Peter Abelard demonstrated the absurdity of unthinking reliance
on authority, that is, religious authority or that of the classical writers,
to discover truth. In his* Sic et Non, *Abelard listed contradictory authorities on
a whole series of propositions and suggested that the way to reconcile the di-
vergent views was to appeal to reason. It should be noted that Abelard was in
advance of his time, and he suffered repeated censure and attack from various
ecclesiastical superiors for his views. By the twelfth century, however, many
in the West were reacting to the introduction of the corpus of ancient writings
on science, medicine, and mathematics, which the Arabs had transmitted, and
it was becoming clear that some attempt at a synthesis of knowledge was
necessary.*

*One of the greatest medieval intellectuals, who was associated with several
of the recently established universities, St. Thomas Aquinas produced a system*

Source: David Knowles, *The Evolution of Medieval Thought* (London: Longmans, Green & Co., 1962), pp. 225–268. Copyright © 1962 David Knowles. Reprinted by permission of Longmans, Green & Co., London.

*of thought that reconciled material that had often been considered mutually
exclusive and contradictory: Greek speculative thought, principally Aristotelianism, and Christian doctrine. In his own day, Aquinas's synthesis was but
one of several; its sophistication may perhaps be judged by the fact that it
received official acceptance in the sixteenth century, and in many respects
remains the foundation for Catholic metaphysics today. What is the essential
core of Thomism? Where does St. Thomas belong in the development of
medieval thought? And what is his contribution to Western thought generally?*

*Dom David Knowles, a Catholic clergyman who has had a long and dis-
tinguished career in medieval studies, discusses these questions in the following
article on St. Thomas. He has written widely on medieval thought and culture,
and his works include* The Monastic Order in England *(1963),* The Historical
Context of the Philosophical Works of St. Thomas Aquinas *(1958), and*
Christian Monasticism *(1969). In Knowles's view, the most significant contribution of Aquinas is that he produced the first original philosophical system
that Christianity had known, and demonstrated that faith and reason were not
necessarily in conflict. An interesting account of the life of many medieval
scholars is to be found in H. Waddell,* The Wandering Scholars *(1934). C. H.
Haskins's* The Rise of the Universities *(1959) provides a brief introduction
to the standard work on the subject. Also of interest is H. Rashdall's* The Universities of Europe in the Middle Ages *(1929).*

St. Thomas Aquinas has been hailed by common consent in the modern
world as the prince of scholastics, not only the *doctor angelicus,* but also,
as he was acclaimed soon after his death, the *doctor communis.* To Tho-
mists of pure blood, as to many others besides, he appears as the authentic
voice of reason, interpreting and defending tradition, as the greatest medieval representative of the *philosophia perennis,* the way of thinking that
is ever ancient and ever new.

The newcomer to Aquinas who is unacquainted with the language and
preoccupations of medieval theology, or whose reading in philosophy has
lain among the ancients or the moderns, will probably be dismayed or
frustrated by the form of his writings. He will find none of the literary
charm that the writer of the dialogue or treatise can diffuse; the great
doctor goes remorselessly forward through things great and small, following for the most part an invariable sequence of objection, solution and argument; there is no emphasis, no high lighting, no difference between
points that seem trivial or otiose and the supreme problems of existence.
All is settled by a personal assertion, with little apparent distinction between what is substantial and of common belief, and what is only a possibility or an opinion. It is this apparent lack of discrimination that repels
or confuses many readers of to-day, and it must be admitted that some of
the admirers and followers of St. Thomas have done him a real disservice
by their failure to realize themselves, and to communicate to others, the
fundamental characteristics of the spirit and doctrine of the master. A
rigid and unspiritual Thomist can be the worst of guides to St. Thomas.

For the greatness is there. The judgment of his contemporaries and posterity has not been false. As we read, with sympathy and a receptive mind, on and on in the two great *Summmae,* the pattern unfolds and the cardinal principles of thought recur and are used, like keen knives, to separate the truth from all else. We come to expect, and never fail to find, a justice and lucidity of thought and expression that thrills and stimulates by the impression it creates that a veil has fallen away and that the pure light of reason and reality is streaming into our minds.

The peculiar greatness of Aquinas, as a master of technical method, lies in his combination of fearless strength of reasoning with an entire absence of personal bias, and in his ability to recognize and produce harmony and order—to recognize them in the universe, and to produce them in his own thought—to a degree without parallel among the great philosophers of the world. The two *Summae* have been compared, not inaptly, to the whole mass of the medieval fabric and furnishings of such a building as Salisbury cathedral, their exact contemporary. The design, the symmetry, the sublimity and the beauty flow from the genius of Aquinas; the basis upon which the soaring structure rests is in the main the work of Aristotle.

St. Thomas stands apart from all the other scholastics to the modern world. He is not only recognized by all as a figure of importance, one who can stand alongside of Dante as a representative of medieval genius at its height, but he has stood, ever since his lifetime and never more than now, as a master to a large body of thinking men. As such, he has, during the past eighty years, broken clean out of the scholastic framework. This creates difficulties for the historian. Thomism, the philosophico-theological system derived from the writings of St. Thomas, and itself divided into what may be called its integral and its eclectic subdivisions, may well be a logical and legitimate derivation, but it is not in all respects and unquestionably to be found in the writings of Aquinas, which alone are of interest to the historian. Philosophers and theologians have rarely been historians. They have tended to treat the works of St. Thomas as a single timeless text-book, from which the desired answer can be extracted, as from a dictionary, by a use of the elaborate indices provided by editors. Only in the past fifty years, largely owing to the work of Martin Grabmann, have the works of St. Thomas come to be regarded historically, as a series of writings conditioned by all kinds of local, intellectual and chronological circumstances, and as the work of a mind always ready to modify an opinion or an argument in the face of new information or valid criticism. While it is true that the writings of Aquinas present considerably less evidence of change or development than do those of a Plato or a Russell, they are not a monolith; there is a distance between the *Sentences* and the Second Part of the *Summa Theologica,* and those who study his thought on, e.g. the eternity of the world, or the Immaculate Conception, will find that it changes, and sometimes returns yet again to its starting-point. Here we are concerned only with the Aquinas of history. As such, his significance appears in two principal achievements. He integrated Aristotelian philosophical principles with traditional speculative theology, and he created, by remoulding and rethinking existing materials and old problems, a wholly new and original Christian philosophy.

As a follower of Albert who outran his master he accepted human reason as an adequate and self-sufficient instrument for attaining truth within the realm of man's natural experience, and in so doing gave, not only to abstract thought but to all scientific knowledge, rights of citizenship in a Christian world. He accepted in its main lines the system of Aristotle as a basis for his own interpretation of the visible universe, and this acceptance did not exclude the ethical and political teaching of the Philosopher. By so doing, and without a full realization of all the consequences, St. Thomas admitted into the Christian purview all the natural values of human social activity and, by implication, a host of other activities such as art. All these activities were indeed subordinated by him to the supernatural vocation of man, and were raised to a higher power by the Christian's supernatural end of action, but they had their own reality and value, they were not mere shadows or vanities.

Aquinas did not merely adopt and 'baptize' or 'Christianize' Aristotle. He had, indeed, no hesitation in extending his thought, in filling gaps within it and in interpreting it in accord with Christian teaching. He also took many elements from elsewhere. But he did more than this: and Aristotle, had he been restored to life to read the *Summa contra Gentiles,* would have had difficulty in recognizing the thought as his. For indeed Aquinas stood the system of Aristotle on its head or, to speak more carefully, supplied the lack of higher metaphysics in Aristotle by framing a conception of the deity which was in part drawn from Judeo-Christian revelation and which when proposed in Thomist terms embodied all that was most valuable in the metaphysic of Platonism. While Aristotle, the empiricist, looked most carefully at the universe of being as it was displayed to the senses and intelligence, and explored in his *Metaphysics* the veins and sinews of substance, he became imprecise when he rose to consider mind and soul, and hesitant when he looked up towards the First Cause of all things. His God is a shadow, an unseen, unknown, uncaring force and reason necessary to give supreme unity to the universe. In the Aristotelian system reality, existential reality, is strongest in the world of everyday experience; the loftier the gaze, the weaker the reality. With Thomism, on the other hand, the infinitely rich, dynamic existential reality is God, the creator and source of all being, goodness and truth, present in all being by power and essence, holding and guiding and regarding every part of creation, while as the one subsistent Being, the uncaused cause, the *ens a se* in whom alone essence and existence are one, He takes the place of the Platonic forms and exemplars as the One of whose Being all created being, its essence perfected by its God-given existence, is a reflection and (according to its mode as creature) a participant. It is only on a lower level that the Aristotelian universe of being is found, but the two visions of reality are fused by Aquinas under the light of the unifying principles, first proposed by the Greeks, of cause, reason and order.

Thomas, a younger son in the large family of the count of Aquino, and related through his mother to the Emperor Frederick II, was born in the castle of Roccasecca, in the broad valley above Cassino, in 1225 or 1226. Of his life, as of Shakespeare's, we know surprisingly little. His personal letters, if he wrote them, have not been preserved; there is not a single personal reminiscence in his voluminous works, nor a single expression of personal taste or feeling, if we except a rare word of disapproval in one of his last works, and, what is stranger still, the greatest thinker and theologian of his age, recognized as a saint by all who knew him, found no adequate biographer.

His parents offered Thomas in 1230 as a child of the cloister at Monte Cassino; no doubt he was destined for the monastic life and perhaps for the abbacy; he was in any case bereft of what many would think the most gracious memories of childhood, though he remained throughout life in close contact with his family. The monks were expelled from Cassino by Frederick II in 1239, and Thomas became a student at the newly founded university of Naples, where he is known to have been taught by a devotee of Aristotelian thought. Taking the Dominican habit in 1244 he was destined for Paris, but like St. Clare of Assisi thirty years previously he was kidnapped by his brothers and held in confinement for a year. When released he proceeded to Paris and Cologne; at the former he may have been, at the latter from 1248 he certainly was, a pupil of St. Albert. From 1252–5 he taught as bachelor at Paris, and in 1256 he became licentiate, but could not proceed master on account of the conflict then raging between the mendicants and the university, though he acted as regent in the Dominican house from 1256–9. In 1257 he was admitted to his degree by papal command, along with St. Bonaventure. From 1259–68 he was in Italy, teaching and writing while following the papal court at Anagni, Orvieto, Viterbo and Rome; St. Albert was with him for part of the time, and he formed a friendship with another fellow-Preacher, the Greek scholar William of Moerbeke, whom he interested in the translation of Aristotle. He returned to Paris for another regency in January 1269, and soon became a rock of scandal to the conservative theologians who engaged him in dispute, while with the other hand he was occupied in attacking Siger and his friends; these years were a time of great literary activity. Called away from Paris in 1272, perhaps on account of mounting opposition, he organized studies at the university of Naples, and died on 7 March 1274, at the age of 48/9, at the Cistercian abbey of Fossanuova, on his way to the Council of Lyons. Few personal details are known of him: he was corpulent and silent—the 'dumb ox'—and a celebrated anecdote shows him preoccupied with speculation even in company with St. Louis. Other stories recall his simplicity and gentleness in disputation, even when provoked. The Office and Mass of Corpus Christi, surely the most admirable liturgical service ever composed to order (1264), show him not only as an exact theologian and a scriptural anthologist of peculiar felicity, but also as a master of prosody. The hymn *Adoro Te,* if his, touches a note of deep emotion which is still nearer to great poetry.

Aquinas, in common with all the great scholastics, was a tireless and voluminous writer, and every treatise, however small, bears the mark of his luminous and penetrating genius. Careful modern criticism has shown that he willingly and often modified his opinions on reflection, and that he applied critical methods to his authorities and abandoned a text (such as the pseudo-Augustinian *De spiritu et anima*) if he had convinced himself that it was not authentic. While many of his shorter works, such as *De Ente et Essentia, De Veritate* and *De Unitate Intellectus* show all his superior qualities present to an eminent degree, pride of place must be taken by his three large works, the early *Commentary on the Sentences* (1253–7), the *Summa contra Gentiles* (1261–4), probably written for the use of Dominican controversialists in Spain, and the *Summa Theologica* I and II (1266–71) and III (1272), left unfinished at his death. Of these the *Sentences* is of interest as showing the early stages in the development of his thought, with the main lines already firmly drawn; the *Contra Gentiles,* a work of maturity, is of especial importance by reason of the very full development of his metaphysical positions: the arguments of natural religion and apologetics are forcefully developed and subjected to a more detailed criticism than was to be possible in the *Summa Theologica.* Nevertheless, the last-named has always been recognized as his masterpiece —a masterpiece of architectonics, of logical thought, and of deep and genial pronouncements, in which almost every question of theology and morality is touched upon.

The qualities which give Aquinas individuality as one of the very greatest of the world's thinkers are perhaps his exquisite lucidity, which is derived not from an impoverishment or dilution of thought, but from the domination and diffusion of light over a whole landscape of ideas; his sense of proportion; and his ability to construct a great edifice which is a perfect whole and is informed by a few simple but pregnant leading principles. This is not the place to attempt a survey of his system of thought; several good studies exist, though no single account can be described as perfectly satisfactory. We shall merely glance, as historians, at a few of the most significant ideas and characteristics.

St. Thomas followed his master, Albert, in a resolute separation of the spheres of reason and revelation, the natural and the supernatural. While on the one hand this recognized the autonomy of human reason in its own field, it also limited its competence severely. Pure mysteries, such as the Trinity and the Incarnation, were no longer susceptible of proof, of comprehension, or even of adequate explanation. The human mind was now bounded by its contacts with the external world, according to the axiom *nihil est in intellectu, nisi prius fuerit in sensu.*[1] It was from observation of external reality, not through the soul's direct consciousness of its own or of God's existence, that a proof of the First Cause could be found. It was from contact with external reality, not from a divine illumination or contact with the divine ideas, that a knowledge of truth came. This was in harmony with a key proposition of Aquinas: *quicquid recipitur,*

[1] 'The mind can perceive nothing that has not previously been perceived by the senses.'

secundum modum recipientis recipitur, which in the field of epistemology became: *cognitum est in cognoscente per modum cognoscentis*[2]—God is known from His works not in Himself—but it might well seem to theologians of the traditional Franciscan school a despiritualization of religious thought. Yet it gave a new dignity to the human reason by lending philosophical support to a conviction common to all men, viz., that our knowledge comes to us directly or indirectly from the universe of being around us, and that neither our senses nor our reason play us false when they function normally. In other words, the activity of the human mind is as much a factor in the dynamics of the universe as are purely material or mechanistic activities. The human reason is a perfectly adequate precision instrument for perceiving all truth in the world of matter and spirit around it, within the limits of its range. Aquinas thus set his face both against any kind of 'double truth' and against the Platonic conception of the world as a mere shadow and symbol of true reality. The realms of reason and revelation became separate, and the bounds of theology and philosophy, faith and natural knowledge, stood out sharp and clear. There is only one truth, but there are realms of truth to which the unaided human mind cannot attain; there is only one truth, and we can recognize it when we see it; it is therefore not possible for a man to have faith and natural certainty about one and the same proposition, still less can faith and natural certainty be in opposition. Moreover, all being and therefore all truth comes from a single source; there is therefore an order and harmony in all the parts. In the celebrated and characteristic phrase of Aquinas: 'Grace does not destroy nature; it perfects her.' [3]

Yet though Aquinas followed Aristotle he also went beyond him with new intuitions and principles, such as the unicity of form in all beings, man included, and the distinction between essence and existence. How novel these principles appeared to contemporaries can be seen clearly enough in the words of two contemporaries. The one, Guglielmo da Tocco, the earliest and most reliable biographer of the saint, who had lived with him during his last years at Naples, wrote: 'in his lectures he propounded *new* theses, and discovered a *new* manner of proof, bringing forward *new* reasons, so that no one who heard him teaching these *new* doctrines and settling doubts by these *new* reasons could doubt that God was illuminating him with a *new* light, that he to whom *new* inspiration was given should not hesitate to teach and write *new* things.' [4] John Pecham, the Franciscan archbishop of Canterbury, who had been regent at the Paris house of his order—the 'opposite number' to St. Thomas—

---

[2] 'Whatever is received, is received according to the mode of being of the receiver', as for example, the sound of a clock striking is heard merely as a sound by an animal, but as a time-signal by a man. 'What is known is in the mind of the knower according to his mode of being.'

[3] *Gratia non tollit sed perficit naturam.* (*Summa Theologica* I 8 ad 2, and elsewhere.)

[4] *Acta Sanctorum,* March I 7. Vita S. Thomae n. 15.

was equally convinced of the novelty, though less inclined to attribute it to divine inspiration.[5]

One of these new doctrines was undoubtedly his metaphysic of being. The leading idea running through his whole system is that every finite being is made up of act and potency, essence and existence. Existence brings the potency of an essence into act, but is itself limited by that potency. This distinction between essence and existence is vital; it is the shibboleth of Thomism. It is because God alone is subsistent being, without distinction between His essence and existence, that He is all-perfect, and it is ultimately from contingent being that we deduce the existence of God. Nothing of which we have experience is a self-caused being, an *ens a se;* [6] it must therefore depend on a cause which exists of itself. In other words, a contingent uncaused being is a contradiction in terms. This conception of being throws light also on the nature of God. Subsistent being is above all created natures, it is therefore supernatural being, unattainable by any created or creatable intelligence. God is therefore in essence transcendent, though He is also, by essence, power and presence immanent. But if God is a supernatural being, how can we have any knowledge of Him by natural powers?

Aquinas answers this question by his profound doctrine of analogy, which again depends upon the distinction between essence and existence. The qualities or perfections of creatures, such as being, truth, goodness, beauty and the rest, are in God not only virtually, as the source of creative power, but, as the technical phrase goes, *formaliter eminenter:* that is, they are really present in the Godhead, but in a manner inconceivable and inexpressible by the human mind—beyond its limit, as one might say. Goodness, for example, is not predicated of God and ourselves univocally—men are not good as God is good—nor is it predicated merely equivocally—the same word with a different meaning—but analogically. It is thus that Aquinas avoids both agnosticism and anthropomorphism.

Indeed, the thought of Aquinas, if considered from one point of view, is almost always a mean between two extremes, though the mean is not a compromise between the extremes, but a summit which overlooks them. Thus in the oldest of all metaphysical controversies, typified in ancient Greece by the systems of ceaseless flux (Heraclitus) and static monism (Parmenides), Aquinas adopts the philosophy of 'becoming', of potency and act, of indeterminate matter and determinant form, of essence and existence. We shall see that his epistemology is a moderate realism, between Plato and the Nominalists. In another field he holds the mean between a mechanistic and dynamistic analysis: the universe is neither the sum of col-

---

[5] Peckam (Pecham), *Registrum Epistolarum,* ed. C. T. Martin (Rolls Series 77) III 901–2, cp. dcxlv. 'Illa novella doctrina . . . quasi tota contraria . . . doctrinae patris Bonaventurae.' ["That new teaching . . . almost completely opposed . . . to the teaching of our founder Bonaventura". Editor]

[6] *Ens a se* = 'a being which is its own cause and origin'.

liding and pressing atoms, nor of immaterial energy, but a compound of both, with energy as form gradually assuming greater and greater importance in vegetable, animal and rational shape, for in contradiction to the materialists Aquinas sets his axiom that form, energy, determines all: action follows being (*agere sequitur esse*). Finally, in the great controversy of ethics he stands between determinism and moral agnosticism. The will is determined by the good; it cannot choose evil as such; but it is not determined by individual good things or designs; it can choose at the bidding of reason, but its choice is always, really or apparently, good.

St. Thomas's theory of knowledge is that of Aristotle, rendered somewhat more explicit. The mind is a *tabula rasa*. External things impinge upon the senses, which present the individual object to the mind; this strips off all that is individual and accidental, and grasps the essence or nature. We see Smith, and recognize in him manhood, the nature of a rational animal, man. The essence of the individual abstracted by the mind is in one way less real than it is in the individual himself, for it only exists fully and in its own right in the individual. But in another sense it is more real, for to Aquinas, as to the Neoplatonists, immaterial being, spirit and thought, is more real than physical, material being; it is a higher mode of being and is logically prior to anything physical. By reaching the essence we reach the formal cause of a being, the expression in rational shape of the spiritual idea which is ultimately its constitutive agency.

We have alluded to the thorough acceptance of Aristotle by Aquinas. This leads him to assert, or rather to assume, what has been called the primacy of the intellect. Reason and order throughout the universe reflect the unchanging mind and law of God. Hence the celebrated doctrine of the various kinds of Law. Just as with man nothing can be willed before it is known (*nil volitum quin praecognitum*), and therefore reason is of the essence of freedom, so with God it is His knowledge, His unalterable law, that logically precedes His decrees. Consequently Aquinas, like Avicenna and Aristotle before him, has a strong bias towards determinism, and in one of the bitterest of all theological controversies his interpreter, the great Bañez, was accused of near-Calvinism.

Yet Aquinas's acceptance of Aristotle, though thorough and epoch-making, is neither uncritical nor absolute. He accepts his metaphysics almost in entirety, but his world-system only with reservations, and for all the higher levels of Christian life he repeatedly asserts Aristotle's incompetence. Similarly, while taking over bodily from the Jewish Maimonides much of his natural theology, he takes only part (and that with cautious reservation) of his and others' Jewish and Neoplatonist teaching on the information of the heavenly spheres by intelligences or angels, and he firmly rejects the series of creative causes posited by Avicenna, and the emanations of the Neoplatonists. At the same time, Aquinas admits far more from non-Aristotelian sources than appears at first sight. Thus the Platonic ideas, resolutely banished in their familiar form from epistemology and metaphysics, remain 'in the heavens' (to use a Platonic phrase) where Augustine had seen them, as the eternal, exemplary, creative ideas in what we call 'the mind of God'. Moreover, as we have seen, the 'exemplary' and participatory function of the ideas is assumed by the Thomist doctrine of essence and existence. Similarly in ethics, alongside the everday virtues of Aristotle are the four cardinal virtues taken from Plato and the Plotinian specification of all the virtues on the three levels of ordinary life, proficiency in virtue, and the state of perfection. These many undertones and overtones in the thought of Aquinas are important; they give it a richness and a flexibility which it might not otherwise possess.

Indeed, Aquinas makes so much use of ways of thought that are ultimately Platonic that it may almost be said of him that he achieves that fusion of the Academy and the Lyceum that so many of his predecessors and contemporaries were attempting. He accomplishes this, however, not by a synthesis, but by using elements from Platonism mainly in the higher levels of metaphysics. Thus by his use of the principle that all creatures participate in being, though in varying measure, by his use of exemplarism in which the creature reflects the creator, by his doctrine of metaphysical composition, and by his assertion of the self-sufficing being of God, he makes of God the centre and cause of a universe of manifold being, and in ethics the creator, lawgiver and providential Father of each human soul, thus placing the centre of gravity, so to say, at the summit of being, and revealing a radiating centre, a living principle and a final goal where Aristotle points merely to an abstract postulate. In this way he adds all that is true in Plato's idealism, otherworldliness and spirit of love to the common-sense, rationalistic empiricism of Aristotle.

To this copious fund of material taken from older thinkers, and to the many, and as yet not fully catalogued, debts which Thomas owed to his immediate predecessors and masters, another rich source must be added, the self-revelation of God in the Old and New Testaments. This revelation is not indeed philosophy, but, as M. Gilson has finely shown, it gives a clear and simple answer to several of the problems that all philosophers must face; it directs attention to the sovereign importance of others which they might neglect; and it brands as false many conclusions to which some thinkers in every age are prone. In all these ways the Christian religion, in a mind profoundly receptive of its influence, must present the philosopher with a view of the universe different in many respects from that of Plato and Aristotle. Whether this view, and the intuitions and axioms it encourages, are fuller and more true than any purely natural outlook could be, is of course a matter on which universal agreement will never be reached, but it is undoubtedly a constitutive element, and not mere colouring matter, in a philosophical system.

From all these constituents of Aquinas's thought there emerged the first original philosophical system that Christianity had seen—neither Platonism, nor Aristotelianism, nor Augustinism, but Thomism. Henceforward this presentation of the universe of reality could be regarded, not only as a phase in the ever-changing outlook of thinking man, and as a phenomenon of thirteenth-century intellectual life, but as a system to which men could return to study, to adopt and to amend. It is still a common belief, and a common error, that the teaching of Aquinas, besides being the most complete and coherent and in the opinion of many the most intellectually satisfying system of the middle ages, was in addition the most characteristic and the most influential. This belief has been considerably strengthened by the great, though often misrepresented, influence exerted by Aquinas over the single supreme poet of the middle ages. Dante knew his *Summa* well enough, and could apply it to any situation he wished, but he is even less of a pure Thomist than Thomas is a pure Aristotelian. Moreover, Dante speaks for himself, not for his world. When he began to write, and still more when he died, the academic climate had changed from that of the decade of his birth. Thomism, from 1290 to the early sixteenth century, was only a unit, and at times a small unit, in the European pattern of thought. It was only with the counter-Reformation, and still more with the nineteenth century, that the thought of Aquinas came to be regarded as in some respects synonymous with Catholic philosophy. As Gilson remarks with great felicity, at the end of his review of Aquinas, in the thirteenth century 'St. Thomas may not have been fully acclaimed by his age, but time was on his side: "These things shall be written in another generation than ours, and a people yet to be created shall praise the Lord".' [7]

The preceding observations, as indeed the whole tenor of the modern presentation of St. Thomas, have stressed his significance as a philosopher to the detriment, or at least to the overshadowing, of his wider reputation. We must not forget that St. Thomas was also, indeed was primarily, a great theologian. Though, true to his own principles, he uses philosophical arguments to defend and to explain some of the most obscure mysteries of the faith, such as the trinity, the personal union of the divine and human natures in the Incarnate Word, and the real presence in the Blessed Sacrament, while his methods were later applied by others to the problems of Grace and Predestination, the careful reader of the *Summa* becomes aware of other qualities in the philosopher, of a wide and living knowledge and an unusually felicitous use of Scripture wholly different from that of St. Bernard, but no less impressive; of an unexpected tolerance of Dionysian elements of thought, and of a clarity of exposition which makes many of the Trinitarian articles unrivalled as precise statements of the Christian faith. It is not uncommon for those writing on St. Thomas to point to his hymns in the office of Corpus Christi as evidence that the Angelic Doctor joined devotion to his metaphysics. Even the sympathetic Rashdall could write of 'the cold, rationalistic orthodoxy of Thomas'.[8] St. Thomas, it is true, eschews the purple patch of piety and his words have on their surface less unction than have those of St. Bonaven-

[7] Psalm 101 (Vulgate), v. 19. *'Scribantur haec in generatione altera, et populus qui creabitur laudabit Dominum.'*

[8] *The Universities of Europe in the Middle Ages,* ed. Powicke and Emden, III, 260.

ture. But still waters run deep, and if he uses the language of cold human reason in matters where rational argument suffices, he does not thereby leave out of the reckoning a higher and entirely supernatural light that directs the purified mind to a higher truth. In the words of an eminent modern Thomist, he distinguishes the various degrees of knowledge only to unite them without confusion.[9] We speak of the dialectical aridities of the schools, but for St. Thomas there is a knowledge more perfect than dialectic. Hear him speak of wisdom, the noblest of the Gifts of the Holy Ghost:

> Wisdom by its very name implies an eminent abundance of knowledge, which enables a man to judge of all things, for everyone can judge well what he fully knows. Some have this abundance of knowledge as the result of learning and study, added to a native quickness of intelligence; and this is the wisdom which Aristotle counts among the intellectual virtues. But others have wisdom as a result of the kinship which they have with the things of God; it is of such that the Apostle says: 'The spiritual man judges all things.' The Gift of Wisdom gives a man this eminent knowledge as a result of his union with God, and this union can only be by love, for 'he who cleaveth to God is of one spirit with Him'. And therefore the Gift of Wisdom leads to a godlike and explicit gaze at revealed truth, which mere faith holds in a human manner as it were disguised.[10]

The pages from which these words are taken are perhaps among the most eloquent in the whole of the works of Aquinas, though they occur at no climax, and show no difference in formal arrangement, from any other page in the vast work. We feel as we read them that he is speaking of what he knows, and we can understand why, some months before his death, he ceased from his occupation with academic theology, and we can believe him when he said, only a few days before his death, that all that he had written of divine things was mere trash compared with the truth of which he now enjoyed another and a more direct and certain vision.

[9] *Distinguer pour unir* (1932) is the title of M. Jacques Maritain's great book, translated into English with the title *The Degrees of Knowledge*.
[10] *Commentary on the Sentences*, D. 35, q. 2, art. 1.

18. The Plantagenet Dominions

JOHN LE PATOUREL

Since the nineteenth century when nationalism became a force in the world, many historians have tended to write "national" histories. While such a tendency may well have served the interests of patriotism, and may have been a useful corrective to the attempts of various dynastic powers to curb dissident elements within their empires, it is a dangerous way to approach the study of medieval European history. In the Middle Ages there were no political entities corresponding to the modern national state, nor did there exist a sense of nationalism as we understand it today. Rather, medieval thinkers were taken up either with universalist ideas, such as fitted the church or the empire, or local or particularistic concerns, limited to one's natal region. Loyalties were to Normandy or Bavaria, not to France or Germany.

Le Patourel argues strongly in this article that it is wrong for historians to speak of that collection of territories known as the Angevin Empire as English; to the extent that such national epithets are applicable at all, it was much more a French creation. His paper raises many interesting questions of governmental organization and administration: What are the origins of those territorial expressions that would become France and England? What relationship did they bear to each other, and to the ruling dynasty? What reference did they have to later ideas of nationalism and sovereignty?

Source: John Le Patourel, "The Plantagenet Dominions," *History*, Vol. 50 (1965), pp. 289–308. Reprinted by permission of the editor, *History*, and the author. [Footnotes omitted.]

For Le Patourel, the Angevin ruler was faced with one overriding problem: how to govern and administer a collection of territories quite distinct in terms of traditions and customs, and that owed allegiance only to him. The problem was solved by three means: first, by personal visits of the ruler to his various domains; second, by the creation of new officials, responsible to the ruler, and recipients of delegated authority to perform certain functions such as the administration of justice; and third, by the naming of successors to the throne as regents for parts of the domain.

This article provides an excellent introduction to the problems of state-building in the Middle Ages and is full of valuable information about the various component segments of the Angevin Empire. Above all it makes clear the strength of local loyalties and the absence of the sense of commitment to a larger unit that would characterize the emergent nation-states some two centuries later. Three excellent books that will provide further information on these topics are R. Fawtier, The Capetian Kings of France, *trans L. Butler and R. H. Adams (1960), G. O. Sayles,* The Medieval Foundations of England *(1948), and a comparative study by C. Petit-Dutaillis* The Feudal Monarchy in France and England: From the Tenth to the Thirteenth Century, *trans. E. D. Hunt (1964).*

The title of this lecture has been a matter of some difficulty, and it might be well to begin by saying what is meant by it. I am using the term 'Plantagenet' as a conventional name for the family of the counts of Anjou. There is not much contemporary justification for this. 'Plantegenêt' was only one of the soubriquets given to Geoffrey, the father of King Henry II, and it was not treated as an hereditary surname until the fifteenth century. From that time, however, it has been wished on to the family retrospectively; historians have used it in this sense and it is convenient. The word 'dominion' is used in the general sense in which it appeared until lately in the royal style, that is, signifying political units, distinct in law and administration, ruled together by one monarch. In the twelfth century the word 'land' would generally have been used in this context; but 'dominium' was also used, certainly in the fourteenth century. It would have been possible to call this lecture simply 'The Angevin Empire'; and I shall often have occasion to use the word 'empire' in the general sense of an assemblage of 'lands' or 'dominions' under one ruler. But 'The Angevin Empire' as a title could have been misleading; though it is part of the present argument that the term has a much wider significance than is generally given to it.

The subject of this lecture, then, is the government of all those lands which in one way or another, and at one time or another, came into the possession or in some way under the authority of this family—Anjou, Touraine, Maine; Normandy, Aquitaine, England; Brittany, Ponthieu, Calais; the Celtic countries of the British Isles. The government of these countries in the Middle Ages has been the subject of an enormous volume of historical writing; but that they formed a governmental unit, or a unit of any kind over a considerable length of time, has not often been suggested. The argument that follows may be a little clearer if I say briefly how I arrived at it. The starting point was a study of the medieval administration of the Channel Islands, a useful starting point since the history of the Islands, local history by the usual criteria, has to be seen against a background of the history not only of England but of France as well. In attempting to define this background, the 'whole' of which the history of the Islands must form a part, the notion of some sort of a 'Medieval British Empire' emerged, in which Normandy and Aquitaine and the rest appeared as dependencies of England. This is, after all, how they appear in most of our histories, at least by implication; sometimes explicitly, as in a well-known title, *Gascony under English Rule*. But as soon as it is seen that the relationship between England and Aquitaine, for example, as it was in the thirteenth and fourteenth centuries, grew naturally and continuously out of their relationship in the twelfth century, and that England was not at the centre of the Plantagenet dominions in the time of Henry II or Richard I, any such notion collapses; and so indeed does any conception of the matter that puts England at the centre all the time. In its place, the idea of a 'greater Angevin empire', of a complex of 'Plantagenet dominions', retaining its identity through periods of growth, transformation and decline, has been forming; and that is the idea that is set out here.

There is one final point of definition. I shall argue incidentally that the Plantagenets and their empire were French, at least for much of their history. It has been pointed out that while it is reasonable to say that they were not 'English,' to call them 'French' only introduces a new confusion; for the adjective 'French' has as many nationalistic and other anachronistic overtones as 'English'. There is a real difficulty of language here. In this lecture, when referring to the Middle Ages, the term 'French' is used in the sense that Normandy, Anjou and the rest were 'French' at that time.

The beginnings of the subject do not lie in England. They lie in the feudal empires that were built up on the ruins of Carolingian government in West Francia, and, in particular, in the feudal empire that was built up from the Carolingian county of Anjou, *pagus Andecavorum*.

The family that established itself in possession of this county during the course of the tenth century descended from a half-legendary Enjeuger. It seems that he had been entrusted with the eastern half of the county on the understanding that he would drive the Bretons out of the western half. By the time of Hugh Capet's accession in 987, Enjeuger and his successors had not only done this, but they had made themselves the hereditary counts of Anjou, seized the remaining royal properties and prerogatives there, and had already acquired important properties in the neighbouring county of Touraine to the south-east and in the Pays des Mauges to the south-west. They found themselves surrounded by families which were doing much the same thing, the counts of Blois-Chartres, of Poitou, of Rennes, of Nantes and of Maine. To maintain their local preeminence, based ultimately upon wealth, they had to attract men to their service and vassalage, and continually invest their property in service; thus they had to be extending their possessions all the time. Under the two great counts of the eleventh century, Fulk Nerra and Geoffrey Martel, they conquered the Touraine, acquired a large interest in Aquitaine (not only the castles of Loudun and Mirebeau pointing towards Poitiers, but Saintes and neighbouring castles, perhaps the whole of Saintonge), and made themselves suzerains of the small county of Vendôme and the vast county of Maine. By 1060 the first Angevin empire was already in being.

For a while, after 1060, this empire went through a time of troubles during which some of the outlying possessions were lost. Yet the counts were strong enough still to maintain their hold on Maine, even though this brought them into direct confrontation with the dukes of Normandy. Fulk 'le Réchin' married his heir to the heiress of Maine; and thus Geoffrey Plantagenet, Fulk's grandson, inherited both Maine and Anjou and so absorbed Maine into the possessions of his family.

The really phenomenal expansion of Anjou, however, took place after 1128, the year in which Geoffrey Plantagenet married Matilda, daughter and heiress of Henry I, king of England and duke of Normandy. This expansion took a familiar form, the acquisition of rights by marriage, inheritance or in other ways, and their enforcement by war. Principalities at that time were treated as property by princely families. The marriage of Geoffrey and Matilda is generally considered from an Anglo-Norman point of view, in terms of Henry I's desperate search for an heir who would continue to rule England and Normandy together. But if it is looked at from the Angevin point of view, it appears as the culminating point of a century of warfare between Anjou and Normandy, when the heir of Anjou married the heiress of Normandy, and so brought Normandy, and England with it, into the family. Henry I was somewhat furtive over this marriage; in Angers it was a triumph. As it turned out, Geoffrey and Matilda had to fight for Henry's inheritance. Geoffrey had won Normandy by 1144; but he never made any attempt, personally, to secure England, and Matilda failed. It was not until their son Henry was a more powerful man, potentially at any rate, than his father had ever been, that he was able to make a satisfactory agreement with Stephen regarding the succession to England, and this after a good deal more than a show of force. For Henry had taken over the government of Normandy early in 1150, had succeeded to Geoffrey in Anjou and its annexes in 1151, and, in the next year, he married Eleanor, the divorced wife of King Louis VII of France and heiress to the duchy of Aquitaine. Though Henry did not take the ducal title at once, and though it might be some time before he could enjoy such wealth as Aquitaine might bring, he could not but be regarded, after his marriage, as the greatest baron in France. And it was this prestige which, together with Stephen's recent misfortunes, at last gave force to his claims in England. From the end of the year 1154, he was 'King of the English, Duke of the Normans and Aquitanians, Count of the Angevins'.

During this phase of the accumulation of lands into what it is customary to call the 'Angevin Empire', Henry had taken over two other feudal empires. The duchy of Aquitaine, the first of these, was in its formation not unlike greater Anjou. In spite of memories of a Roman province and a Carolingian kingdom, Aquitaine in the twelfth century was simply the 'empire' of the counts of Poitou, built up in much the same way as the empire of the counts of Anjou. Between 850 and 950 three lines of counts had in turn established a hegemony in what was then understood as Aquitaine, and had called themselves 'duke', sometimes 'duke of Aquitaine', as a decorative title to mark this hegemony. First it was the counts of Auvergne, then the counts of Poitou, then briefly the count of Toulouse, finally, and permanently, the counts of Poitou. From 987 the title 'duke of Aquitaine' was official in the sense that it was used by the chancery of the king of France; but this 'duchy' simply consisted of Poitou together with other counties which the family of the counts of Poitou had inherited or acquired (e.g. Limousin and Auvergne), together with others over which they had established their suzerainty (e.g. Périgord and Angoulême); and the alternative title 'count of Poitou' persisted through to Richard I's time and even into the thirteenth century. In the middle of the eleventh century, the dukes of Aquitaine acquired the duchy of the Gascons in ways that are obscure but which seem to have involved inheritance, purchase and warfare. It is difficult to say what Gascony could have meant to them, for the Gascon counts and *vicomtes* who were nominally the duke's vassals were in practice independent, and there seems to have been very little ducal domain left. At all events, the dukes of Aquitaine saw no reason to move their chief residence south from Poitiers. When Henry married Eleanor, therefore, he put himself in the way of annexing the empire of the counts of Poitiers to the empire of the counts of Anjou. Aquitaine was not so large or so monolithic as it appears in most historical atlases; but it represented an immense accession of prestige, if no more.

Two-and-a-half years after his marriage, when he was crowned king of England, Henry completed his acquisition of another feudal empire, the empire of the dukes of Normandy. This Norman empire, apart from its first seventy years or so when it was little more than a Viking state living on plunder, had likewise been built up in the way which must now be familiar. By the usual methods of aggression, marriage and exploiting any opportunity to impose feudal suzerainty, the counts of Rouen, as the dukes were originally styled, not only acquired the lands that made up the historic duchy, but prepared the way to take possession of, or at least to acquire a considerable interest in Brittany, Maine, the Vexin, Ponthieu, perhaps Flanders—and England. At the same time, Normans were fighting in Spain and carving out principalities for themselves in South Italy. The feudal empire that William built up (though it was by no means all his own work) was basically of the same character as the feudal empires we have already considered. Even the fact that it had crossed the Channel and extended beyond the bounds of the kingdom of France was in no way exceptional. The counts of Flanders, and many other seigneurs down the eastern frontier, had similarly extended their possessions beyond the kingdom.

In one respect, however, this Norman empire was indeed exceptional. The conquest of England had been accompanied by a colonization of the country by the nobility, clergy and merchants of Northern France, Normandy in particular. The families that took estates in England mostly continued in possession of their lands in France, giving to England and Normandy one single aristocratic society, a French aristocracy which was a powerful force, with the interests of the royal-ducal family itself, for the maintenance of a union between the two countries. There seems to be no parallel to this elsewhere in the Plantagenet dominions, save in the Celtic countries of the British Isles, where the same men continued the work of colonization they had begun in England. It may also be argued that the conquest of England differed from other acquisitions in that it made William a king; and it is certainly true that he was very conscious of his new dignity and enhanced status. But England still did not take the place of his patrimony. He continued to give as much time and attention to his interests on the Continent as to those of his kingdom, and he had to recognize that Normandy should descend to his eldest son. England's chief value to him and to his French followers was not the status she conferred, but her wealth in money as well as in land.

Thus in the years from 1150 to 1154 the empire of the counts of Anjou had absorbed two other similar empires, the empire of the counts of Poitou and the empire of the dukes of Normandy. But the momentum of its expansion was not yet exhausted. Henry successfully asserted his feudal suzerainty over the king of Scots (King William the Lion, indeed, became his liege man for Scotland), and a similar, if less strictly feudal authority over the Welsh princes. Having planned a conquest of Ireland in 1155, he took charge of the conquest begun there in 1169 by the Norman marcher lords of South Wales, securing a share of the land for his own domain, the homage of the conquerors and the submission of the surviving Irish kings. As duke of Normandy he had long-standing claims to suzerainty over Brittany which were made the basis of what amounted to a conquest in 1166. As duke of Aquitaine, he strove unsuccessfully to recover what his predecessors had lost in Berry and Auvergne; and although his attempt to conquer the huge county of Toulouse was a failure, the count nevertheless did homage in 1173. Henry even made a marriage treaty with the count of Maurienne which, if the marriage had taken place, might have led him into Italy.

At this point, about the year 1180, the Plantagenet dominions stood at their widest extent. A very great deal has been written about them, from one point of view and another; and the latest work to offer a general description, during Henry's reign only, is a book of nearly 700 pages. What follows are some of the considerations necessary to the present argument, and those alone.

We tend to use abstract expressions like 'the expansion of Anjou'. These are, it goes without saying, no more than a convenient shorthand. To describe the process with any approach to realism would take a long time; but such 'expansion' was clearly the work of men, of ambitious, greedy and forceful men, the most successful and the most ruthless among other ambitious, greedy and forceful men. William of Normandy did not undertake the conquest of England nor Geoffrey Plantagenet the conquest of Normandy for the greater good of England, or Normandy or Anjou, but to increase their own wealth and power and glory, to gain control over more lands and more men; and those who joined them did so out of loyalty, in part, but also for what they could gain for themselves. Apply these considerations to the history of the formation of the Angevin Empire and the obvious point must appear—obvious, but its implications are often overlooked—that this empire was made by the family of the counts of Anjou, partly directly and partly by taking over the feudal empires already made by the counts of Poitou and the dukes of Normandy. The point may be demonstrated visually by a glance at the genealogical table. The succession was continuous in the male line, father to eldest surviving son, from Fulk 'le Réchin' to Richard 'Cœur-de-Lion'.

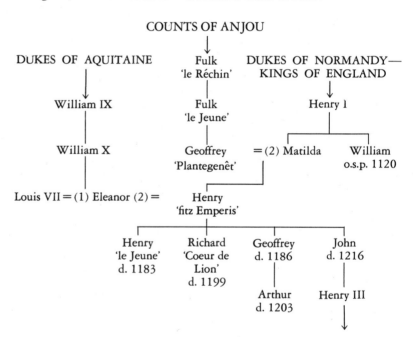

An important implication of this for us in this country is that the Angevin Empire was 'made in France'. In the sense in which the term is used in this lecture, Henry and his immediate descendants were Frenchmen, as French, certainly, as the Geoffreys and the Fulks and the Williams in their ancestry. Though Henry might be campaigning in Wales or in Ireland, the centre of his interests and ambitions lay in France. He was born at Le Mans, he died at Chinon and he is buried at Fontevrault. Even after he became king of England, he spent much more time in France than in England, more in Normandy alone. England had in fact been gathered into a French feudal empire. It would be interesting to know how strong the suggestive power of our historical atlases has been. Just as Britain and the British Empire of modern times are coloured in red, so are the Plantagenet dominions in the British Isles and in France. The suggestion, intended or not, is that England was at the centre of an empire in medieval as in modern times; and the preconception that underlies it has led to the incautious use of phrases like 'Gascony under English Rule', or 'la domination anglaise' when referring to Angevin rule in Aquitaine or Brittany. This is quite wrong. England was then a conquered country. It had been colonized by Frenchmen and it was exploited by its Norman and Angevin rulers for their continental ambitions. The Angevin Empire was a French empire.

But this empire, this vast accumulation of property and authority over men, had to be governed and administered if its wealth and the power that its possession could give were to be enjoyed by its lords. Here there was a problem. Each of the major units of the empire, England, Normandy, Anjou, Brittany and (with some reservations) Aquitaine, were already, at the moment of their acquisition, principalities with their own systems of law and their own traditions of government, and in each of them government was still essentially the personal rule of count, duke or king. Yet no ruler could be everywhere at once. This problem was not peculiar to the Angevin Empire, and it was not new within the empire in 1154. It had faced William of Normandy after 1066 and Henry I after his conquest of Normandy in 1106; it faced Louis VII when, as duke of Aquitaine, he succeeded to the throne of France in 1137, and Geoffrey Plantagenet after he had conquered Normandy in 1144.

To some extent the problem was met by itineration. Rulers of this time were accustomed to move constantly about their lands, taking their 'household' with them and holding their court at convenient places. The acquisition of a new land simply extended the itinerary. The possibility of governing their lands from a fixed centre, impracticable in any case, did not arise. Thus William the Conqueror and Henry I circulated about England and Normandy, and Geoffrey Plantagenet spent some part of every year in Normandy between 1144 and his death in 1151. In part they had to do this from military necessity and the need for what we might call police action, but not entirely; it was also a means of government. But by itself it was not sufficient. Any but the most primitive financial system, for example, required that the accounts of local officers should be rendered at regular intervals and if possible at a fixed place; judicial affairs could not always await the king-duke-count's next visit or attend him on his wanderings; and in any case, if he could not be present in person some substitute for his presence had to be found in each of his dominions or his authority would diminish.

There had been many experimental solutions of this part of the problem. William had appointed *ad hoc* regents to represent him during his absences from either England or Normandy; and this practice continued, beside others, for a long time. On the other hand, Henry I developed the role of the officer who came to be known as the justiciar and made him almost a standing viceroy. In his time there was a justiciar of England and a justiciar of Normandy, in substance if not very certainly in name. Louis VII, when he became king, converted the personal, domestic seneschal of the dukes of Aquitaine into a territorial officer, virtually his viceroy in Aquitaine, quite distinct from the seneschal of the royal household. Geoffrey Plantagenet did much the same in Anjou after 1144. At that point the 'count's seneschal' became the 'seneschal of Anjou'; and Geoffrey had a 'seneschal of Normandy' as well. Seneschal or justiciar, these officers were developing into standing representatives of the king-duke-count in each land. There was a third possibility. The counts of Anjou had, for some generations, associated their successor with them in the work of government during their declining years, much as the kings of France did. In 1150 Geoffrey Plantagenet adapted this idea by making his son Henry duke of Normandy while he himself remained count of Anjou; and it seems most probable that this is what Henry in turn was doing when he made the Young Henry king of England and duke of Normandy, Richard duke of Aquitaine and Geoffrey duke of Brittany. The troubles which followed were those most naturally to be expected in such a situation.

All these means of supplying the king-duke's presence were employed, and it would take a great deal of working-out to define their relative importance at any one time; but by the end of the twelfth century it was the vice-regal justiciar or seneschal on whom the king-duke chiefly relied. In each country this officer was at the head of the administration, working with an exchequer in England, Ireland and Normandy, and with far less developed but still discernible institutions in the other continental dominions.

The government of the Plantagenet dominions, by the end of the twelfth century, thus appears as a three-tiered structure. At the top, the king-duke-count, with his chamber, chancery and other household offices, itinerating ceaselessly over the length and breadth of his dominions, repressing disorder, defending the rights of churches, holding court and delivering justice, accessible to those who must bring their cases to the king and to the king alone. In the middle, the localized administrations organized and directed by justiciar or seneschal according to the laws and governmental traditions of each land; dealing with routine financial and judicial and sometimes military business on their own (delegated) authority and, on the king's order, with anything at all. At the bottom, the local administration of sheriff, reeve, *bailli, vicomte, prévôt* and so on, entirely the product of regional circumstances and history. It seems to make a rational system, and to give to the Angevin Empire that degree of coherence that makes it reasonable to argue that it was this empire, though still fundamentally the family estate of the Plantagenets, that constituted the political reality of the day, rather than any part of it. And it follows from this that the government of England was not a complete and autonomous system in the twelfth century, but part of a larger whole. Local institutions, the administration of justiciar, exchequer and the justices were specific to England; but the itinerant part of the government, king and household, were shared with the other Plantagenet dominions, and England's share was not disproportionately large.

Although few say it in so many words, the implication of most historical writers on the subject is that the Angevin Empire came to an end in John's reign. Certainly there were great changes at that time. As the result of John's condemnation in 1202, the king of France attacked and quickly overran Normandy and Poitou. The king of Castile saw his opportunity and invaded Gascony. The defections were equally serious. The count of Toulouse withdrew his allegiance immediately after the sentence; the barons of Brittany and greater Anjou rebelled in 1203; many of the more important barons in Aquitaine, like the vicomte of Limoges and the count of Périgord, changed sides several times, but eventually adhered to the king of France. But all this, though in the end it seriously reduced the territorial extent of the Plantagenet dominions and deprived them of their original nucleus, did not amount to dissolution. The French, accepting the unity of the Angevin Empire, pursued their aim of destroying Plantagenet power by invading England, but they were soon driven out and the lands and lordships in the British Isles were territorially unaffected; John quickly recovered his position in Gascony and Poitou; the duke of Brittany, anxious to recover Richmond, was soon negotiating with John and actually did homage for his duchy to King Henry III; the vicomte of Béarn did homage to Henry in 1242, and this was the first time in a hundred years that he had recognized the suzerainty of a duke of Aquitaine; there were loyalists in Normandy for many years, and no real need to despair of what had been lost until the 1240's. King Henry III continued to use the titles 'duke of Normandy' and 'count of Anjou' until 1259. There was no breach of continuity.

Yet in the end there was a great transformation, but a slow transformation going on throughout the thirteenth century. These are some of the changes that were brought about in the course of this transformation:

First: although allegiances and territorial holdings in France fluctuated during the century, yet by the Treaty of Paris of 1259 Henry had to renounce his title to Normandy, Anjou and Poitou; and although this in itself involved no break in the government of the Plantagenet dominions as a whole, it did change the whole territorial balance. In Henry II's time these dominions formed a French feudal empire, the political centre of gravity of which was in France; but with the loss of much of the French lands, including the ancestral county of Anjou, England soon became by far the most important part of what was left. The political centre of gravity was shifting from France to England.

Second: in the time of Henry, Richard and John the Plantagenet dominions were governed by an itinerant monarch, who divided his time between his various lands as interest and policy directed. But in the thirteenth century, when departments of government generally were beginning to settle down, the ruler of the Plantagenet dominions, after he had lost the greater part of his lands in France, would naturally choose England for his normal residence. Significantly, the justiciarship of England was abolished, for practical purposes, in 1234. Even so, government by itineration did not come to an end all at once. King John was in Aquitaine in 1206 and 1214 and in Ireland in 1210; Henry III was in Aquitaine in 1230, 1242–3 and 1253–4; Edward I was king-duke in 1273–4 and 1286–9. And these were not the purely military expeditions they have often been made out to be. A good deal of normal governmental business was transacted on each occasion. For the time, the king-duke was 'in residence', available for whatever had to be done, taking homages, settling disputes, calling assemblies, surveying the administration, refreshing loyalty. Moreover the fuller records of the thirteenth century enable us to see something, on these occasions, of the practical relationship between the itinerant and the localized parts of Plantagenet government. But these visits were growing more infrequent; and after 1289 there were none. It was one thing to cross the Narrow Seas and progress through Normandy, Anjou and Poitou to Bordeaux; it was quite another proposition to fit out an expedition which would take the king and his court and his army to Bordeaux by sea. Consequently the form of government in the remaining continental lands had to be adapted to deal with the king-duke's lengthening and ultimately permanent absence, just as in England it had to be adjusted to his more or less permanent presence.

Third: not all the major changes affecting the Plantagenet dominions were taking place within their borders. Before about 1150 the counts of Anjou and dukes of Normandy were indeed vassals of the king of France, but in a personal sense and in a way that did not affect their government of their lands. If this had not been so, the formation of the Angevin and Norman empires would have been impossible. After about 1150 the king of France began slowly to revive the idea of his sovereignty and to acquire the means to make it effective. The great vassals began to do their homage for specified lands, and then to describe it as liege; and the king was able, in course of time, to deduce from the relationship so created a right to require service, to legislate generally, to hear appeals, to levy taxation and so forth. Technically, King John's condemnation in 1202 was based on an appeal from certain vassals to the court of his lord, the king of France. When the duchy of Aquitaine was reconstituted by the treaty of 1259, it was reconstituted on the basis of liege homage, and the acknowledgement of sovereignty in its mid-thirteenth-century sense which that had come to imply. In this respect Edward I's or Edward II's position as duke of Aquitaine was very different from that of Henry II.

Fourth: the Plantagenet dominions of the twelfth century, though they were beginning to acquire some of the elements of a unitary political structure, could still be treated as a family assemblage. They had been accumulated for the benefit of a family, and they might be distributed in the interests of the members of that family. Geoffrey Plantagenet may have willed the division of his lands between two of his sons; in 1155 Henry contemplated the conquest of Ireland to make provision for his youngest brother William; the association of his sons Henry, Richard and Geoffrey in the government of England-cum-Normandy, Aquitaine and Brittany respectively implied a divided inheritance; and in fact, when Richard died in 1199, the empire did indeed fall apart momentarily—Aquitaine rallying to the Queen-Mother Eleanor, Brittany and Anjou to Arthur, Geoffrey's son, and England and Normandy to John. This happened because the rule of succession was still not defined in the circumstances of such an occasion; different solutions might find acceptance in the different dominions; and there was as yet no law to hold them together.

When, however, Henry III constituted an appanage for his eldest son, the Lord Edward, he gave him Ireland, the Channel Islands, Oléron and Gascony, among other possessions, 'in such manner that the said lands . . . may never be separated from the crown and that no one, by reason of this grant made to the said Edward, may have any claim to the said lands . . . , but that they should remain to the kings of England in their entirety for ever'. This was in 1254; and by this act the Plantagenet dominions were in effect given a constitution. Henceforth, whoever was the lawful king of England was, by that fact alone, the lawful duke of Aquitaine, lord of Ireland, and lord of the Channel Islands, at least in the eyes of English lawyers.

Taken together, these changes represent a great transformation. In the twelfth century, the Plantagenet dominions had been a family assemblage, governed by an itinerant 'central' government and localized administrations in each dominion under a justiciar or seneschal, and with the ruler's centre of interest in France. In the thirteenth century the monarchy was settling in England, and was coming to govern the other dominions more and more from England (a late symptom and landmark was the order of 1293 that the accounts of Ireland and Aquitaine should in future be audited at the English exchequer instead of by local commissions). Yet in all this change there was continuity. This is so in the forms of government in England and Ireland; it is equally so in the forms of government in Aquitaine and the Channel Islands, though these had to be built up extensively to take account of the new political conditions and their phenomenal economic development; and it was so in the Plantagenet dominions as a whole. Although English and French interpretations of the treaty of 1259 might differ and the changes it brought about were in any case very important, Edward I could claim to be duke of Aquitaine and lord of the Channel Islands just as much by right and inheritance as he was king of England.

In the English Chancery rolls of the fourteenth century the term *dominia transmarina* is occasionally used to denote the king's lands other than England. The use of the word *overseas* is significant; the Plantagenet dominions, in their transformed shape, were centred on England. The change-over was now complete from the Angevin Empire of the twelfth century, centred on France, to a political complex which could be described as England and 'the king's dominions overseas', centred on England. This phase may be dated, approximately, from the middle of the thirteenth to the middle of the fourteenth century. The territories now concerned were England, Wales, part of Ireland and, though briefly, Scotland, in the British Isles; and, in France, the duchy of Aquitaine reconstructed in accordance with the Treaty of Paris of 1259, the county of Ponthieu inherited by Queen Eleanor in 1279, the Channel Islands (a relic of the duchy of Normandy) and what may be described, perhaps, as a 'special relationship' with the duchy of Brittany—this last a very valuable asset.

During this phase the king-duke was no longer itinerant as he had been in the twelfth century. He never went to Ireland; his visits to Wales and Scotland were essentially military; Edward I, it is true, spent some time in Aquitaine, but his successors never went there. In 1286, Edward still took the Great Seal with him to Gascony, and the wardrobe; but the chancery staff was divided, and more and more the household offices would be identified with England, as the seal, originally used by the king-duke in all his dominions, eventually became the Great Seal of England. The king, and what had been the itinerant part of Angevin government, that is to say, was coming more and more to be identified with England, and thus the administration of Gascony was being subordinated to what were primarily English institutions. The accounts of Aquitaine and Ireland were, as we have seen, ordered to be audited in the English exchequer; Gascon petitions were brought before the parliament of England. It can be little more than a suggestion at present, but what seems to be developing is a sedentary, 'metropolitan' government at Westminster, or at any rate one identified with England, with corresponding delegated, dependent governments in Aquitaine, Ponthieu, the Channel Islands, Ireland, and in any other lands that might come under the rule of the king-duke, capable of functioning in a situation in which his absence was normal.

In Aquitaine, so far as can be seen at present, the building-up of ducal government to meet this situation was very largely the work of Edward I, though the process was a gradual one as the situation developed. First, the administration was unified. At the end of the twelfth century there were normally two seneschals, a senseschal of Poitou and a seneschal of Gascony; and in the thirteenth, as lands came into the hands of the king-duke, a seneschal was appointed for each of them, in John's reign for Périgord, the Limousin and the Angoumois, and, after 1259, for the 'Three Dioceses', Saintonge and the Agenais. But, from 1280, there was one chief seneschal, often styled the 'seneschal of Aquitaine', and the others were made subordinate to him. Then, since the duties of the chief seneschal, originally embracing almost everything, were growing beyond the capacity of one man, his office was departmentalized, giving finance (the organization of which had been centralized at the same time) to the constable of Bordeaux and the controller, much of the seneschal's judicial responsibilities to professional judges, and some of his military and judicial duties to a lieutenant who ranked above him. Finally he was given a professional council. Such an administration, under the direction of the king and his council in England, and the exchequer later on, could cope with anything short of an emergency. In the Channel Islands the office of warden (similar in function to that of the seneschal of Gascony) was likewise departmentalized—justice to the bailiffs of Jersey and Guernsey, finance to the receivers, and some military responsibilities to the constables of the royal castles. What needs to be emphasized is that in the French lands these developments were characteristically French in form. The connection with England gave urgency to governmental developments in Aquitaine on account of the king-duke's absence, just as his commitments in France and consequent financial needs hastened institutional and constitutional developments in England; but it was the same sort of development, though speeded up, as would have taken place if the king-duke had been a normally resident ruler. The law remained purely native, and analogies in financial organization and judicial administration were with contemporary Brittany, Burgundy or Toulouse, for example, not with England; just as in the Channel Islands the law remained Norman and continued to develop on Norman lines for centuries after their political separation from the Norman mainland.

This is partly because, though Gascony and the Channel Islands were in English law annexed to the crown of England, in French law the duke of Aquitaine, the count of Ponthieu and the lord of the Channel Islands was the liege vassal of the king and a peer of France, his lands in France an integral part of the kingdom. Therefore, like any other French baron, he owed homage on the usual occasions, military service and attendance at the king's court on summons, and loyalty—loyalty above all. He must submit to the fact that his courts in Aquitaine and Ponthieu were not sovereign, that his subjects there could appeal from them to the Court of France, the *Parlement de Paris,* and that French legislation might apply to his lands and even French royal taxation be levied in them. Thus a large part of the king-duke's administration of his French lands was made up of the professional council which he, like other French barons, maintained in Paris to watch his interests in the Court of France; and one reason why the seneschal of Aquitaine had to delegate so many of his duties was the amount of time he had to spend in French courts defending appeals against the decisions of courts held by him or in his name. Yet, although he had to watch his interests very carefully, there is nothing to show that Edward I regarded this situation as anything but the natural order of things during the first twenty years of his reign. But the war of 1294 changed much; and from 1300 at any rate the king-duke was endeavouring, as a matter of both doctrine and practice, to oppose a concept of ducal sovereignty to royal sovereignty in his French lands. In this he was only a few decades and a few degrees ahead of his peers in the higher

French baronage—the dukes of Brittany, for example. One quite possible interpretation of the fourteenth-century phase of the Hundred Years' War is that it was a revolt of the greater French barons against royal centralization, a revolt led by the greatest of their number, one who had immense resources outside the kingdom, that is, the duke of Aquitaine. This heavy commitment in France, indeed the extent to which they were 'Frenchmen' still, does much to explain the continental activities of Edward I and Edward III (much of which had little relevance to purely English interests) and the failure of Edward II.

Another reason why the institutional development of Aquitaine and the Channel Islands was French (Ponthieu remained purely French) rather than English was simply that the kings of England were dukes of Aquitaine and lords of the Channel Islands by inheritance and tradition as ancient and well-established as that which gave them their kingdom. They were the lawful descendants of earlier native rulers; in a sense they were native rulers themselves. Though their kingdom conferred a higher status, their French lands provided resources and prestige that were not to be despised, and there was no reason why Edward I, for example, should not still feel himself to be as much a French baron as an English king. It was one of the traditions of the Angevin empire that customs were not transported from one dominion to another, that the government of each dominion should proceed according to its own laws and customs; and this tradition still held in the French lands and in England. But the policy of the Angevin rulers towards the Celtic countries was in complete contrast. There, their rule was based upon conquest rather than upon inheritance; and thus the institutions of government in Ireland, after the 'Anglo-Norman' conquest, were a reproduction of institutions in England, and there was at least a partial introduction of the law then obtaining in England. In Wales and in Scotland, after a long period during which the Norman and Angevin rulers of England had been satisfied with a recognition of suzerainty and the colonizing of the 'Anglo-Norman' nobility, Edward I was driven to attempt conquest and the introduction of some laws and institutions from England. In Wales he was reasonably successful; in Scotland he and his successors failed.

There is an epilogue which can only be touched upon briefly. In 1337 the king of France, in his court and in accordance with the law and procedure of the time, declared the lands of 'the king of England, duke of Aquitaine, peer of France, count of Ponthieu' in France to be confiscate. Since Edward III resisted, and advanced counter-claims of his own, this precipitated what we call the Hundred Years' War. Two-and-a-half years later, for reasons which we can only deduce but which, in great part, must have been implicit in all the long history of the Plantagenet dominions, Edward assumed the title 'king of France'. Together, these two events mark a break with the past; for they ended the feudal relationship which had hitherto existed, in its varying forms, between the ruler of the Angevin lands in France and the Capetian or Valois king of France. Yet in many respects there was continuity still. The lands in France which Edward III occupied or received by treaty during the course of the war, in Brittany, Normandy, the county of Guînes and Calais (for some time even in Calais town, from which most of the French property-owners had been expelled), and in the lands ceded by the treaty of 1360, were governed for him as though he had been the lawful heir or representative of the native ruler; and in Normandy he actually assumed the ducal title for a few years. Local law and institutions were respected, and military exactions apart, the revenues collected were customary. Care was taken that Edward's assumption of the French royal title should do nothing to prejudice the laws and customs of Aquitaine; and though its effect on the constitutional position of the Channel Islands is obscure, it is hard to see that it had any influence on their laws and institutions though prolonged war conditions naturally did influence them. In short, Edward III, heir to all the traditions of the Plantagenet dominions, was still very much a French prince; the Angevin Empire, transformed and still in course of transformation, had not yet completely lost its identity.

The conclusion I should like to be able to draw is that what I have called 'the Plantagenet Dominions' or (though in a wider sense than is customary) 'the Angevin Empire' was a continuous political phenomenon, a historical entity, and sufficiently coherent to make it, rather than any of the units of which it was composed, the political reality of its day. As far as continuity in time goes, the case is perhaps made in dynastic terms (and it was men and families, more than impersonal forces, more even than ideas, that made states in the Middle Ages); the case may even have been made, to some extent at any rate, in territorial terms, for if the territorial content changed over the centuries, the Plantagenet dominions were by no means unique in that respect; but although I have suggested that in its political organization, and in the face that it presented to the rest of the western world, it was an effective unity, there is still much to be done on that score.

Supposing, however, that the case were fully made, there is one big implication which must be apparent but which still needs to be emphasized. As historians we tend to project the present into the past. We give courses of lectures and write books and series of books on 'English history from the earliest times to the present day', as though there was a kind of history that was 'English', as opposed to a French kind of history or a German kind of history, as though there had always been something fundamentally identical with the England of today, and as though all the 'history of England' were leading naturally and inevitably to the England we know. The French do the same with the history of France; and so 'English history' and 'French history' tend to be two separate and distinct subjects *at all times*. The implication of the argument in this lecture, on the other hand, is that the effective political units from 1066 until some time in the fourteenth century were not England and France as we ordinarily think of them, but a Norman empire and an Angevin empire and a kingdom of

France (the 'Capetian empire'), overlapping and interpenetrating; and there are many economic, cultural and social considerations that would support this idea. Only gradually, and certainly not by 1340, did England and France crystallize out as truly independent kingdoms. Before that happened, the French possessions of the men who were kings of England cannot be treated as appendages to England or as parts of France under alien rule, to be brought to mind only when their affairs happen to impinge upon the conventional narrative of national history; they must be regarded, with England, as part of the matrix from which England and France were eventually shaped. 'English History' in the twelfth and thirteenth centuries, as it is commonly understood, is provincial history.

19. Italian Towns and Trade

GINO LUZZATTO

*One of the most important developments of the later Middle Ages (the twelfth
to the fourteenth centuries) was the revival of large-scale trade and the growth
of towns. The closed economy of the early Middle Ages, in which the manor,
ideally self-sufficient, formed the basic unit of social and economic life, was
coming to an end. Long-distance commerce and the rise of self-governing
municipalities meant many changes for Europe: greater diversification within
society; a somewhat better distribution of wealth, with more opportunity for
more people; the gradual erosion of feudal organization; and, what seemed to
some scholars to be most significant, the evolution of new forms of government and the birth of a new civic spirit.*

*The principal centers in which these developments took place were the com-
munes of north Italy and Tuscany, and the trading and manufacturing towns of
Flanders and the Netherlands. How did municipal life develop in Italy? What
forces were at work? What obstacles were there to the process? What were the
new economic activities in which people engaged? And what were the effects
of these new endeavors on society, both in the local sense and also on the wider
European scene?*

*Gino Luzzatto, a specialist on Italian economic history, has written several
books on this subject. In these selections from his* Economic History of Italy,

Source: Gino Luzzatto, *An Economic History of Italy,* trans. Philip Jones (New
York: Barnes & Noble, 1961), pp. 79–85, 98–121. Reprinted by permission of
Barnes & Noble, Inc., New York, and Routledge & Kegan Paul Ltd., London.

*he underlines the peculiar situation of Italy in the feudal world. While tech-
nically Italy belonged to the Holy Roman Empire, it had been left very
largely in a state of salutary neglect, especially after the eleventh century. The
result was that feudalism, which had never struck the same deep roots in Italy
as it had in France or Germany, tended to give way before vague stirrings
in the various Italian communes. These centers then came to assume a greater
and greater measure of independence and autonomy, until they were in practice
sovereign entities in their own right. With the invitation to trade that the sea
afforded, and a surplus in production, many cities began to turn to manufacture
and commerce. This in turn stimulated the rise of a new class, the bourgeoisie,
who unlike serfs or landed nobles were not bound by feudal ties.*

*Luzzatto sketches the main lines of development in the formative period of
the eleventh and twelfth centuries, and then goes on to describe economic
activities in the great period of the thirteenth and fourteenth centuries. In this
selection he makes plain the numerous inventions and contributions of Italy to
the development of what would become common practices in business and
commerce later on throughout Europe. His work contains some provocative
ideas about the relationship of political vitality, social mobility and opportunity,
and economic vigor, illustrated, for example, in the development of the guilds.*

Economic Progress in the Great Inland Communes and the Development of the Bourgeoisie

The revival of urban life, of which we were able to study the early phases
in the eleventh-century towns of Lombardy, and which was probably common to other towns of the Po valley and Tuscany, had also spread during
the eleventh and twelfth centuries into southern Italy. Not only had many
southern towns risen to great prosperity; they had also become self-governing, with officially recognized customs and even codes of municipal
law, and with the privilege of exercising jealously guarded sovereign
rights such as the right to coin money and conclude commercial and political treaties. This rapid movement towards municipal liberties was
brought to a stop by the unifying and centralizing policy of Roger II, and
then in the thirteenth century suppressed outright by Frederic II, who
would tolerate no privileges of town or class incompatible with royal authority. But even without opposition from the Crown it may be doubted
whether urban autonomy could have flourished much longer in the south,
for by the time of the early Angevin rulers the evidence suggests that economic conditions had ceased to favour the development of an urban class
wholly supported by trade and industry. In strictly formal terms, no doubt,
the urban commune was a creation of feudal society; it came into existence with the transfer of certain public rights, by sovereign concession,
from a feudal lord to a group of vassals associated for the purpose. In reality, however, this transfer of rights was accompanied by a revolutionary
change in society: the formation and entry into politics of a bourgeois
class.

The bourgeoisie emerges as a class in the first century of the urban commune, or what is generally called the "consular" period. During that time two complementary movements are evident. On the one hand the commune invaded the countryside (*contado*) in order to protect its interests, and began to extend its authority beyond the walls and suburbs of the town; on the other a massive migration from the countryside invaded the town. The immigrants were of every kind. Some were minor feudal lords or simple landowners who, partly of their own free will but more often under duress, came to settle in the city, or engaged at least to build a house there and reside for certain months of every year, simultaneously renouncing all jurisdiction over their "subjects" (*homines*) in favour of the commune. More numerous were the free tenants (*libellarii*) and vassals of feudal lords in the *contado* who came without condition or constraint, either attracted by the nearby urban market or impatient to be free of feudal obligation. Immigrants of this class, it must be noted, did not normally sever all relation with their former life; most of them retained their land and connexions in the countryside. The case was otherwise with the class of dependent cultivators, the praedial serfs and slaves. For them the city, with its growing population and developing trades, offered not only increasing opportunities of work but also the promise of personal freedom, which most urban statutes were ready to grant at the end of a few years' residence. Migration for them, in short, meant greater security and the chance of a better paying occupation and more tolerable condition of life.

Before 1300 neither chronicles nor other sources permit us to measure even roughly the size of urban population. But they do offer unanimous proof of a very rapid increase in numbers, which between 1100 and 1250 must have raised the population of many Italian towns from a mere 5,000 or 6,000 souls to 30,000 and even more. An increase of this order is suggested particularly by the repeated extension of city walls, which in certain places came to include an area ten times larger than that within the original perimeter; and even then the space was often too narrow to contain the whole population, part of which spread outside into crowded suburbs. In these conditions the towns took on an entirely changed appearance. What had once been open field and pasture, swamp and waste, sparsely covered with huts of clay, wood, or wattle, an occasional rustic chapel and the barest scattering of public and ecclesiastical buildings, now became congested with the lowly wood and stone houses of the urban multitude, dominated here and there by the towered dwellings of immigrant nobles, majestic Romanesque churches, and austere public palaces, which bore witness to the energy and ambition of the new burgess classes.

No less radical were the changes in society and economic life. In the early days of the communal regime the economic links between town and country were still unbroken. The urban population was still quite small, and beside a few artisans and merchants, urban society was still composed of a certain number of clerks, justices, and notaries, and a group of middle-class landowners who had joined together and brought their dependent tenants under the control of the commune. At this time no doubt it was the custom of the humbler inhabitants, whether long-established residents or recent settlers, to go out each morning to work in the fields and come back each night, as people still do today in many towns of southern Italy. The proprietors and peasants whose home was in the towns lived mainly on the produce of their land, which they stored in warehouses, cellars, and stables inside the walls. Only a part of their produce was intended for exchange with merchants and artisans in return for goods the land could not supply and household industry no longer provided insufficient quantity. But conditions were very different after the communes had subdued the lords of the *contado*. The economic unity of the manor, already compromised by the break-up and alienation of demesne, was now completely destroyed. Steadily the urban market extended its range and importance, manorial workshops disappeared or decayed, and even country people turned to the town for the goods they could not make at home. The growing demand of town and country for manufactured wares attracted a large number of immigrant countrymen into urban crafts; and in a short time slaves and serfs were transformed into free artisans. The final result of this process, at least in the more important places, was a sharp division of labour between country and town. The primary function of the country was to produce food and raw materials while the town became the centre of industry and trade.

At the same time immigration from the country had the effect of developing class distinctions in the towns. On the one hand an aristocracy grew up composed of great landowners; these men were wedded to the past and had no wish to sacrifice their traditional immunities, their share in public revenues, or the rights they enjoyed over subject *homines* who had now become members of the commune. On the other hand were all those men who had entered some urban trade or profession and cut the ties which bound them to the court of their feudal lord; their wish was to be free of all ancient claims to rent and services and to exercise their chosen trade in peace. The merchant class occupied an intermediate position, formed as it was not of simple shopkeepers retailing goods from stalls in the town square, but of citizens who travelled long distances to foreign fairs and markets and imported merchandise from abroad. In a few towns, where commerce had developed most rapidly, we find the merchants owning land and taking part in communal government from the very beginning, alongside the landed aristocracy. But more often we find them leading the urban artisans in their movement of association, resistance, and revolt, and providing the main strength of the new middle class, or what was then called "The People" (*popolo*).

Origin, Character, and Purpose of the Craft and Merchant Guilds

During the second half of the twelfth century we begin to hear of artisans and merchants being organized in what today are usually described as trade and professional guilds, but in the towns of medieval Italy were variously known as *arti, fraglie, paratici,* and so on. The guilds included not only the masters of each trade but also, in a subordinate position, their working companions (*socii, laborantes*) and apprentices (*discipuli*).

In recent times, as we have seen, and especially since the publication of the *Honorantiae civitatis Papiae,* most historians have accepted the conclusion that, at least in certain towns of medieval Italy both Byzantine and Lombard, some kind of guild organization had continued to exist in a number of trades which engaged in work of importance to the state; such guilds paid dues to the government and were granted rights of monopoly in return. But, in spite of these relics from the past, the evidence leaves no doubt that the twelfth-century guilds were new institutions, created by conditions which only developed in the urban communes after their first foundation and after the influx of people from the country. One sign of this is the sudden and rapid rise of guilds in the second half of the twelfth century. Another is the form, which the guilds first assumed, of perfectly free associations. A final proof is the growth of similar corporations, about the same time, in towns of central and north-west Europe which had never been more than faintly influenced by the ancient Roman world. Indeed if the few artisans and merchants who lived in the towns of the tenth and earlier centuries had all been combined in close, monopolistic guilds of the kind revealed by the *Honorantiae,* they would surely have put up a bitter fight to keep out new competitors from their trades and organization. It is far more likely that the initiative came from the former feudal subjects (*homines*) of lords in the *contado,* who after moving to the town and adopting some new craft or trade, felt the need to draw together in common defence against their ancient masters. It is no doubt possible that they were influenced by surviving Roman traditions and by the example of guilds already established in the town. Nor can it be said for certain that the new corporations were quite unaffected by the long tradition of manorial workshops, where slaves were divided into groups under masters (*magistri*) according to their several crafts (*ministeria*). But more than anything they were governed by the universal impulse of their time to unite in sworn associations of defence and defiance, like the clan federations of nobles (*consorterie, Società delle Torri*), the armed companies of commoners (*compagnie armate del popolo*), the religious confraternities of pious laymen, and—most important of all—the urban commune itself. From the commune, specifically, the craft and merchant guilds borrowed their form of organization.

Economic causes, however, were hardly less important. The very custom of the urban market encouraged combination, for by ancient tradition all tradesmen practising the same craft produced and sold their goods in shops on the same street. This is why so many streets, especially round the markets of old Italian towns, bear the name of particular trades: Smith St. (Via dei Fabbri), Baker St. (Via dei Pistori), Weaver St. (Via dei Tessitori), and so on. Guilds in fact were not established simply to protect artisans from the insolence of aristocratic *consorterie;* for this purpose they could probably rely on the armed companies, which were formed about the same time in the ranks of the urban *popolo*. The function of the guilds was economic as much as social. In particular they met the needs of an urban economy which could only command a closed and limited market. The market was limited because the communes were so numerous. One after another, in the space of a few decades, all the ancient Roman cities which had survived the ruin of the Empire, as well as many of the larger *castelli,* developed into self-governing communes, bent on asserting their political and economic supremacy throughout the surrounding countryside. The number of towns all over north and central Italy which achieved practical autonomy in the course of the twelfth century was astonishingly high. As a result the average distance separating one commune from another never exceeded 20 to 25 miles, so that even after the *contado* had been wholly subjugated, the conquered territory never reached much further than 10 to 12 miles from the city walls. To go beyond was to enter foreign and unfriendly country. For, despite occasional treaties of good neighbourship, which may have encouraged reciprocal trade, most communes lived in a state of undeclared or open warfare with bordering states. Only in the season of fairs, when special safe-conducts were in force, could the citizens of any commune venture across the frontier for purposes of trade; otherwise they might forfeit their goods and often their liberty as well.

In these conditions it was natural to try to organize production in such a way that town and country could provide as far as possible for all their basic and reciprocal needs. And so it became a matter of policy to maintain inside the city a multitude of small specialized industries, each of which was restricted to so small a clientele that they would infallibly have gone out of business had not measures been introduced to check competition between men of the same trade and prevent any fatal crisis of overproduction. Rules were therefore adopted to govern the relations of masters and workmen, limit the number of apprentices, and fix their period of training. Sharp penalties were imposed on masters who hired runaway workers or raised wages above the statutory limit. Outsiders were inhibited from practising established trades but tempted with favours to introduce trades that were new. The acquisition and use of raw materials was minutely regulated to ensure high quality. Methods of sale were controlled and price-lists circulated. And many days of the year were set aside for compulsory rest.

By its very nature a system so nicely balanced that every petty trader and artisan could calculate the exact demand of his few, unchanging customers, was certain to break down as soon as economic enterprise in some of the larger towns outgrew the narrow limits of the early commune. But this development, which was destined to transform the social and economic structure of the larger cities, only took place during the second period of communal history, especially after the first decades of the thirteenth century and in the first half of the fourteenth, when the urban economy of medieval Italy may be said to have entered its prime.

. . . . .

Agriculture, Industry, and Trade
in the Age of the Communes

AGRICULTURE

The rise to predominance of the urban communes was accompanied by profound, indeed revolutionary, changes in the state of rural property; and these changes reacted in turn upon agriculture. The very vicinity of the towns, with their rapidly growing population, industry, and trade, was enough to disturb and disrupt the old manorial organization. Little by little were relaxed the ties of common interest which bound subject holdings to the lord's demesne and maintained cohesion and balance in the working of the great estates. The demand for labour rose, as more land was needed for tillage and tracts of waste were cleared which hitherto had only provided men with game or fish, wild marsh grasses, or a little rough grazing for pigs and other animals. Between the eleventh and the thirteenth centuries vast areas in the lowlands of the Po valley were drained, dyked, and reclaimed from wood, swamp, and waste. In the territory of Mantua, which has been studied in particular detail, the northward advance of the Po down to about 1100 necessitated the construction of elaborate embankments to protect the land abandoned by the river; the works are mentioned in many leases of the period, which require tenants to keep the banks in good repair. At the same time a spirited attack was begun on the woodland, pasture, and fen, which before the eleventh century had occupied most of Mantuan territory (in 1072 one large estate in the lowlands of Mantua comprised no less than 3,000 *jugera* of wood, beside a mere 32 *jugera* of cultivated land). It appears that the most effective means of carrying out this work, was to break up the greater properties into small holdings and tenures. We find the same in the Polesine, the lowlands of Verona, and all the country lying along the Po and Adige: land at one time undivided and almost wholly desolate now became covered with farms. In some cases the transformation was the result of intensive and systematic colonization. Thus, during the years 1077 to 1091, the margrave Boniface of Canossa parcelled out his property into 233 separate holdings (*mansi*) of 10 *jugera* each, and let them to families of peasants on terms designed to promote the clearance of wood, the reclamation of waste, and most of all the planting of vines. The effect of such works on the countryside was well summed up in 1233 by the provost of Mantua cathedral, when he said that in less than a hundred years the lands of his church had been entirely "cleared, ploughed, redeemed from wood and marsh, and converted to the production of food (*ad usum panis reductae*)".

In cases like these the interests of landlords and peasants combined to hasten the break-up and disappearance of the old demesne; labour services were abandoned, and in their place tenants were required to co-operate in building dykes, developing new crops, and making other improvements. In other cases, however, the owners of great estates, especially church estates, were obliged to grant out land or demesne, which they could no longer work themselves, to tenants who were neither peasants nor cultivators. The grants were variously made by fief, emphyteusis, or *libellus* for 29 years; but whatever their type, they were all in reality concealed alienations: *dominium utile* became quite separate from *dominium directum,* and the tenant obtained unrestricted control of the land in return for payment of an insignificant rent.

Not all changes in the rural order were so obedient to the forms of law. Peasants in particular adopted more revolutionary methods. Often they simply refused to go on rendering dues and services which hindered them from giving full time to their holdings and exploiting the growing market for agricultural produce. Their resistance was usually successful and led to the conclusion of written agreements, which fixed the relations of landlord and tenant, suppressed all arbitrary exactions, and reduced all services to a minimum. These collective contracts served as the basis of later village statutes. All the same, collaboration did not cease between peasants and proprietors; sufficient proof of this is the steady diffusion of partiary tenure, which in most of central Italy and much of the Po valley came to assume the form of strict *métayage* or *mezzadria*. At the same time, the social character of landownership was itself largely transformed by the rise of a bourgeois class of landlords. This was partly the result of migration to the town by large numbers of rural proprietors, but partly due also to the tendency of merchants, grown rich by trade, to invest a proportion of their profits in land, for reasons of security or social prestige.

It was long believed that the Italian communes caused far more radical changes than these in the agrarian regime. In particular, they were said to have reformed the legal and social condition of the peasantry so completely that, five hundred years before the French Revolution, the labouring classes became perfectly free. With very good reason this opinion has been frequently criticized, or at any rate seriously qualified. To be sure, it was almost a general rule for rustics, who settled and lived in the city for a specified length of time, to be treated as free by the law; but the measures of collective enfranchisement which certain communes enacted were simply conceived as a means of fighting feudatories in the *contado,* and were never designed to overturn the foundations of rural society. While slavery disappeared entirely from the countryside, the ties which bound dependent peasants to the land were never effectively suppressed. The ties were no longer legal, but in practice most peasant cultivators (now called *villani, manentes,* or *residentes*) were perpetual tenants of their holdings. Farms passed from father to son for many generations, and we often find them described in deeds of sale, inheritance, and partition, by the tenant's own personal name.

The persistence of the same families on the same farms for generations and even centuries, and the survival of land divisions going back as far as Roman times, seem to suggest that, although waste land may have been cleared and drained in the Middle Ages, there can have been very little progress in agricultural technique. Land lost to cultivation during the decay of Rome, the barbarian invasions, and the depopulation of the countryside, was certainly brought back into use; but as far as we can judge (and our knowledge is admittedly slight), no advance was made beyond the agricultural practice described by Cato, Varro, and Columella.

The same crops were grown as before. The cereals still were wheat, spelt, barley, oats, millet, and also probably rye in the Alpine valleys. There is no evidence for the introduction of maize, frequently confused by historians with sorghum (*meliga, saggina*), which was in fact cultivated in many places. Of tree crops far the most widespread was the vine; and most of the leases for development, which survive in growing numbers from the ninth century on, were addressed to extending viticulture. Olive cultivation was much more restricted, but even so we find it practised during the Middle Ages in many parts of the Po valley and the Venetian plain. The mulberry was probably brought to Sicily by the Arabs. It then spread particularly to the coasts overlooking the Straits of Messina and later on, after the twelfth century, to the territory of Lucca and certain districts in northern Italy. But its progress was very slow, and down to the sixteenth century the Italian silk industry had to rely for its raw material on imports from the East.

The oldest Italian treatise on agriculture composed in the Middle Ages is that of the Bolognese jurist, Pietro dei Crescenzi. For the materials of his book, Crescenzi drew extensively upon the Roman agronomists; but he was also a shrewd and enthusiastic observer of the methods of cultivation used in the various districts of the Marche, Tuscany, Emilia, Piedmont, and Lombardy, which he had to visit in the course of his judicial activities. So for example, when discussing the vine, he describes the forms of cultivation current in Lombardy, Romagna, Modena, the March of Ancona, Pistoia, and Cortona. In one particular chapter, which is quite independent of his Latin authorities, he records the varieties of grape grown, not only in these regions, but also in the countryside of Padua, Pisa, Asti, and Ferrara; elsewhere, in a passage devoted to the pruning of vines, he turns for illustration to Asti, Crema, Milan, Bergamo, Verona, Bologna, Modena, and Forli. Among other crops he gives special attention to sorghum and hemp, plants which the ancients had disregarded almost entirely; and he pauses to investigate the various uses to which hemp may be put, indicating the places and methods of cultivation appropriate to the manufacture of rope, nets, sacking, and so on. We may conclude that, if a writer so attentive to actual conditions was normally content to reproduce the statements of Latin writers, he must have found what they had to say in general agreement with the practice of his time. This means that, despite the formation of a wealthy class of urban proprietors, Italian agriculture in the period of greatest communal prosperity was still mainly governed by the legacy of ancient Rome. Not before the mid-sixteenth century do we begin to hear of isolated attempts to discard traditional principles for more rational and scientific methods.

Industries are nourished by markets and can only thrive in the neighbourhood of markets. It is not surprising therefore that during the age of the
communes most industries were located in the towns.

The only exception to this, for obvious reasons, was the mining and
smelting industry. Italy is notoriously poor in minerals, but this deficiency
was much less acutely felt in the Middle Ages, when the great difficulty
and cost of importing gold and silver from central and eastern Europe,
and later on from Africa, encouraged exploitation of the most unreward-
ing resources. Thus the sands of certain Alpine streams were washed for
gold, and silver was dug from mines in the Trentino and Cadore, Tuscany
and Sardinia, which today have either been abandoned or are simply
worked for lead and copper pyrites or iron. Gold-washing made little
claims on labour or techniques. But mining was carried on during the
communal period by fairly advanced methods, as we learn quite early
from a Trentine codex of 1193. Galleries were made to follow the seams
of ore; they were approached by inclined or vertical shafts, and had to be
ventilated with special air-holes and drained with special pumps or tun-
nels. The ore itself was extracted with picks or by kindling large wood
fires, which were set alight on non-working days to make the harder rocks
more easy to dig. The miners worked a five-day week, each day being divided into two twelve-hour shifts. The work was complex, and the many
operations in and round the mine not only employed a great variety of instruments, but also imposed a division of labour among the workmen
themselves. Most of the workmen, particularly those with special skill in
mining, were immigrants from Germany. Frequent migration, indeed, was
part of the trade. It was a consequence of mining methods, by which each
group of miners was only granted limited workings (*fosse*) to dig—
according to the statutes never more than fifteen paces apart. As a result
the seams were soon exhausted and the miners had to go in search of
other concessions, often far away. The *fosse* were divided (in just the
same way as merchant ships) into lots, 32 in all, which were shared in
various proportions by the partners (*partiarii*) and represented a corresponding number of individual claims upon the total output of the group.
But since the claims were heritable and alienable, they often passed in
practice to persons wholly unconnected with mining, who lived for the
most part in the towns and employed skilled men, unprovided with capital, to work their claims. So we find two distinct groups already formed in
the thirteenth century: the partners (*partiarii*) and the workers (*labora-
tores*). As a general rule the entire mining concession was sub-let to a
company of workers, who either took two-fifths of the metal extracted or
kept it all to themselves and paid a rent to the various partners. In some
places, however, particularly the Maremma, the partners chose one of the
more expert workmen to serve as master, and he then hired other labourers by the week or the day and paid them with a share of the mineral.

Closely related to mining was the iron-smelting industry. This was especially well developed in the valleys behind Bergamo and Brescia, where

iron of the purest quality, highly valued in arms manufacture, was produced in small lots from numbers of tiny forges.

All the other industries of Italy were by this time located in the cities. They may be divided into two classes, of which the first, the most numerous, provided for the daily needs of the local town and country population, and the second, the more specialized, produced goods for a much wider market. Industries of the former kind were composed of artisans in the strict sense, working for a small number of customers, whose tastes and needs they understood and could easily assess in advance. Such men clearly avoided risks, but they also avoided profits. To them at least, and the petty merchants like them, it is proper to apply Sombart's definition of medieval business as a system organized for immediate consumption and not for profit. But side by side with the small local industries medieval Italy was quick to develop other, far larger enterprises, which often commanded vast international markets.

In the Middle Ages, unlike today, the leading place in industry was occupied, not by the so-called heavy industries, but by the manufacture of textiles, in particular woollens. The growth of woollen industries was obviously favoured wherever wool of suitable quality was in plentiful supply; but this was not an indispensable condition of development. The Mediterranean countries which grew the finest fleeces, the so-called *Garbo* wool and the wool of the Castilian tableland, were content for centuries to send their product abroad in the raw state. Even fifteenth-century England still exported more wool than cloth. On the other hand the major centres of the medieval woollen industry—Flanders, Brabant, and northern France, certain towns of southern France, Lombardy, Venetia, and Tuscany—did not derive their superiority from local flocks or pastures so much as from their trade, which enabled them to import choice wools easily, even from a distance.

It would certainly be absurd to claim that Italy ever attained supremacy in the manufacture of woollen cloth; this distinction belongs unquestionably to the countries of north-west Europe. But in the marketing of woollen cloth Italy was second to none. In the large-scale export of northern cloth to the south and south-east, either from the centres of production or through the fairs of Champagne, Italian merchants were the most active and enterprising agents; and it was mainly due to them that northern draperies (the so-called "French" cloth) were able to reach the principal markets of the Mediterranean. From the eleventh century onwards, a growing number of "Lombard" merchants frequented the markets of France and the Low Countries, and this they did for the primary purpose of buying cloth. Indeed, the whole class of greater merchants in Italy built up their business and economic power on the local sale and re-export of foreign textiles. The Florentine Calimala guild is the most brilliant example of success in this lucrative trade, but the basis of mercantile activity was not substantially different in Lucca, Siena, Piacenza, Milan, or the other large communes of northern Italy.

In most of these communes, as we shall presently see, the cloth trade eventually stimulated the growth of a local woollen industry, also producing for export. But in certain places it acted rather as a check to local manufacture. At Genoa and Venice, at least, this was not simply due to pressure from the importers of foreign cloth. Not only the interests of a group were at stake, but the prosperity and even the survival of all maritime trade, especially trade with the Levant, where fine fabrics represented one of the few western products in great demand. We have clear proof of this in two Venetian tariffs of the thirteenth century, which mention cloth from only six Italian towns (Lucca, Florence, Milan, Como, Bergamo, Brescia), as against thirty different grades of woollen cloth, mostly of expensive quality, from twenty different towns of France, the Low Countries, and (in one case) England. It is obvious that any policy which might have favoured local industry at the expense of such invaluable imports would have impeded very seriously the flow of Oriental goods to Venice.

The position was different in the greater communes of the interior. In these towns the merchant class itself came to realize the advantages of combining home-produced with foreign cloth. The inland communes also commanded much more territory than either Genoa or Venice, from which a growing textile industry could draw supplies of raw material and labour. The actual extension of cloth production was the effect of various influences, both at home and abroad. At home, the rapid rise in urban population increased the demand for cheap inferior fabrics; while abroad, the decline of the fairs of Champagne, the repeated restrictions imposed on Italian trade, especially in France, and finally the improvement of shipping services, which made it easy to import high-grade wools from foreign countries like England, all encouraged Italian wool manufacturers to raise the quality of their products for purposes of export. Thus in Florence, according to Giovanni Villani, there were 300 workshops at the beginning of the fourteenth century producing yearly 100,000 pieces of cloth (i.e. one piece per shop per day), whereas thirty years later there were only 200 shops producing 70,000–80,000 pieces; but if the number of pieces had fallen, their value had also doubled, reaching a total of 1,200,000 gold florins or an average of 15 florins a piece, and this transformation, Villani explains, was mainly due to the recent introduction of English wool. As regards prices at least, Villani's figures are abundantly confirmed by the records of Venetian trade, which show that towards the middle of the fourteenth century the best Florentine cloth equalled or surpassed in value the most favoured fabrics of Flanders. It should be noted all the same that, while production flourished in the Florentine woollen industry, the twenty companies of the Calimala guild still found demand enough in the local market to justify the import of 10,000 pieces of foreign cloth, valued at 300,000 florins; and this was apart from other stocks, undefined but certainly large, which were destined for re-export.

Outside Florence the woollen industry also made rapid progress during the fourteenth century in the Lombard towns and certain towns of Venetia. Here too use was made of foreign wool, especially Spanish wool, imported by way of Pisa, Genoa, and Venice. And here too great strides were made in the technical organization and management of textile manufacture.

The organization of the woollen industry was controlled by the various technical processes, some fifteen in all, which were necessary for turning raw and dirty wool into finished cloth. Each of these processes was entrusted to special groups of workers who, apart from the spinners, were not allowed to sell the product of their industry, but only to pass it on to the men in charge of the next operation. This arrangement was enough by itself to create the need for entrepreneurs, who would buy raw material and pay for each successive stage of manufacture. But certain operations in particular demanded a complex organization and a substantial advance of capital; these were the finishing operations, applied to the woven cloth—cleansing, fulling, tentering, raising, shearing, dressing, and dyeing. In very small places, with a limited market for cloth, it is possible that all these processes were undertaken by one master craftsman, normally a weaver or dyer, and that customers were expected to pay part of the cost in advance. But in big towns, where production was largely for export and a fairly long period was bound to elapse between the purchase of the raw materials and the sale of the finished goods, the whole organization was inevitably dependent on capitalist entrepreneurs, who could pay all or most of the cost in advance, and also market the cloth. These men, as we have said, might be actual workers in the industry, such as weavers or dyers; but mostly they were merchants, the so-called drapers or *lanaiuoli* (wool manufacturers), who apart from selling cloth retail also engaged in the export trade. Technically they were still artisans, but in practice they performed the functions of the merchant entrepreneurs, who often disposed of insufficient resources and were obliged to enter into partnership with other capitalists. At the other extreme stood the workers employed in the preliminary operations of cloth manufacture, who were wage-labourers, usually hired by the day.

Of the metal industries the only one about which we have any information (apart from what is contained in guild regulations) is the arms industry, which reached the peak of perfection and production in fourteenth-century Milan. The industry was favoured by the command of excellent raw material from the ironworks of the Alpine valleys and Lombardy, and was also greatly stimulated by the rapid increase in demand for weapons which accompanied the replacement of urban militias by mercenary troops after the middle of the thirteenth century. About that time, according to Bonvesin della Ripa, Milan alone possessed over one hundred workshops producing body armour, apart from numerous other shops which turned out weapons of every kind. Even today, in the centre of the city, there is an "Armourer St.", "Swordsmith St.", and "Spurrier St." In the later fourteenth century, during the most critical period of the War of Chioggia, one of the most eminent citizens of Venice was sent on an urgent mission to Milan to buy up arms, and in very little time he was supplied with 1,230 corselets, 1,492 helmets, and 180,000 crossbow bolts, costing in all 7,200 gold ducats. This Milanese arms industry, which acquired an international reputation by manufacturing corselets of the finest steel mail, owed its excellence to the personal skill of the craftsmen. For this reason production was never centralized but was carried on by individual masters in their own shops, with the help of a few companions and apprentices. Generally they worked on their own account and dealt directly with their clients.

A more distinctly capitalist structure is evident, from the thirteenth century on, in the shipbuilding industry, at least at Genoa and Venice. The *Annals* of the chronicler Caffaro show that, from quite an early date, private and public enterprise collaborated in the building of galleys at Genoa, and that the government often made use of merchant shipping. Shipbuilding was financed in the case of private vessels by the shipowners themselves, and was organized on a basis of contracts and sub-contracts, whereby the work was first entrusted to a master shipwright, who then shared it out among various specialized craftsmen employing wage-labour. At Venice, shipbuilding was carried on in two forms, public and private. The public industry was located in the famous Arsenal, while private shipbuilding was dispersed in a large number of smaller shipyards or *squeri*, at Venice itself, Chioggia, and on various islands of the estuary. As a rule the state looked after the navy, and private industry took care of the merchant marine; but quite often private shipyards also were commissioned to build galleys and other warships. The workers in the Arsenal, even skilled workers qualified as masters, were all wage-labourers. Private shipbuilding, by contrast, retained more the forms of an artisan organization, to the extent at least that every process of construction was assigned to separate master craftsmen, each of whom was assisted by a small group of workers and apprentices and was inscribed as a member of the guild of caulkers (*calafati*) or carpenters (*marangoni*). But essentially most of these masters, like most of the masters of the Arsenal, were nothing more than trained workmen, drawing a daily or weekly wage and their keep from an entrepreneur. Only a very small number formed a kind of aristocracy apart, the so-called *protomaestri,* who took contracts for particular jobs of construction or repair and directed the work of groups of masters. At Venice, as at Genoa, the actual risks and costs of construction were covered by the shipowners. Not even the owners of the shipyards, the *squeraroli,* normally did more than make occasional repairs or build a few light craft for inland traffic; their activity was generally limited to letting out sections of their yard for shipowners to build in.

Quite different from this, and entirely individualistic in character, were the art industries which started to develop in various Italian cities during the fourteenth century. These industries, however, only attained their fullest splendour after the fifteenth century, and we must therefore postpone all treatment of them.

The Range of Italian Commerce. If industry made great advances in the communal age, and even agriculture, which is slow to change, recovered the ground once lost during the decline of Rome and the barbarian invasions, it was commerce more than anything that raised Italy to undisputed supremacy in the economy of the medieval world. Indeed, it was to satisfy the needs of international commerce that technology and legal institutions were improved and business organization put upon a rational basis, that the spirit of initiative and enterprise was developed to the highest degree, and a new social type, the modern entrepreneur, was brought into being. There were no boundaries for the merchants of medieval Italy; their activities traversed the entire known world and penetrated into unfamiliar regions with which westerners had had no direct contact before the thirteenth century. The best-known commercial manual of the time, the *Pratica della mercatura,* written in the first half of the fourteenth century by Francesco Pegolotti, a representative of the great Bardi company of Florence, passes in review an astonishing number of trading centres in the Old World, extending far beyond the limits of the ancient Roman Empire. Not only the Mediterranean and the Black Sea towns find a place in this treatise, but also many countries further east: Armenia and Persia, the Caspian coastlands, Turkestan, Mongolia, and China. Clearly the voyages undertaken by the Polo family had not been isolated ventures, the disregarded exploits of ardent pioneers; other merchants from other towns had followed in their footsteps, enticed by the prospect of profitable business. Such journeys may not have been frequent, for the distances involved were enormous, and Pegolotti himself calculates that 250 days were needed to get from Caffa (Feodosia) in the Crimea to Peking; but relations with the East were evidently close enough to justify his giving detailed information about the coinage and paper money, the weights and measures, and the commercial practices of these remote places.

In Africa, Italian merchants travelled no further south than Cairo and the Atlantic coast of Morocco. But in the fifteenth century a number of enterprising navigators, Venetians and still more Genoese, were enlisted by the Portuguese court in voyages of discovery southward from Morocco. In the Iberian peninsula the Italians frequented the Mediterranean ports of the Balearics, Barcelona, Valencia, and Almeria, and the Atlantic ports of Lisbon and Cadiz; after the middle of the thirteenth century they also began to invade the great commercial centre of Seville. In France and the Low Countries Italians travelled everywhere; in England they were mostly to be met with in London and Southampton.

Apart from the cities which Pegolotti lists, we have clear and abundant evidence of Italians trading in many other towns which he ignores, possibly because the Florentines did not go there. If we add these to the reckoning, then we must include in the range of Italian commerce all the countries of central Europe, in particular the Rhineland and the upper

297

Luzzatto

ITALIAN TOWNS
AND TRADE

and middle Danube, from which Italian merchants passed to Poland and the Baltic.

Transport and Communications. This enormous expansion in the range of commerce was not matched by any comparable improvement in the means of transport and communication. Considerable progress was made, to be sure, in the building of roads and canals, but this was confined to the territory of particular communes or, later on, to particular regions, mainly in Tuscany and the Po valley. Across the Apennines and Alps the roads were such that goods could only be carried on the backs of men or pack-animals or at best on tiny carts. In the lowlands a great deal of traffic moved by waterway. Thus in Tuscany the Arno was used for navigation, though this was possible only at certain times of the year and along the stretch between Signa and Pisa; from Pisa to Porto Pisano and from the Arno to the Serchio, numerous canals had to be cut for the convenience of traffic between Lucca, Pisa, and the sea. River navigation had far greater importance in the valley of the Po, especially on the lower reaches between Piacenza and the coast. The Venetian lagoon was connected by canal with the Adige and the Po. In 1220, when the Mantuans were threatening to divert all traffic on the Po to their city, the communes of Cremona and Reggio combined to defeat the design by building a grand navigation canal some forty miles long, which after leaving the Po at Guastalla, where the river turns north, re-entered it at the mouth of the Panaro. Even towns which did not lie along the Po, in particular Milan, Bergamo, Lodi, Brescia, Parma, Reggio, Modena, and Bologna, were all connected with it by rivers or canals and all maintained their tiny ports.

Conditions of travel were far worse in those parts of Italy which possessed no great communes or wealthy business class. The journey from Florence to Naples, which merchants sometimes managed to complete in eleven or twelve days by riding from morning to night and travelling via Terni, Aquila, Sulmona, and Teano, bristled with difficulties and dangers. The only way across the Abruzzi was by rough country track, and the borders of Campania were infested with brigands. The shortest route from Rome to Naples, the road through Terracina, had such an evil reputation that only troops and public officials dared to use it, while all trade went round by sea. Beyond Naples, the only major highway was the ancient road leading from Campania to Foggia and Manfredonia (Siponto): this could carry small carts and was used extensively by merchants.

Even greater difficulties had to be faced by Italians travelling overland to the fairs of Champagne, to Paris, and to Flanders. Politics often played a part, and so forbidding were the hazards that merchants commonly preferred to go by sea to the ports of Provence and then proceed by way of the Rhône and Saône to their northern destinations. Even so, the shorter Alpine route was never entirely neglected, in spite of serious obstacles. There were numerous passes over the Alps, from the Little St. Bernard in the west to the Pontebba in the east, but the tracks were rough and steep and the carriage of all goods had to be entrusted to local people, since every tiny Alpine commune held a monopoly of transport through its territory. These privileges, which made it necessary to change the carriers (*vetturali*) at every stage, only served to make the journey longer. Six days were needed to make the relatively short crossing from Chiavenna to Chur.

But if transport was slow, postal services by land were comparatively quick. During the communal period, from about 1300 onward, increasing use was made of couriers by all kinds of institutions: monasteries and universities, the governments of the greater communes, and most of all the merchant guilds. Couriers usually travelled on horseback, riding either the whole journey or between established stages, where post-horses were kept. By such means, with a little luck, the entire route from Venice to Bruges could be covered in seven or eight days.

Incomparably cheaper and safer than movement overland was movement by river. In Italy, however, river-transport was only practicable in certain regions and over relatively short distances. And so throughout the Middle Ages much the most active highway of communication was the sea.

Sea transport also had its perils, some of them natural, some contrived by men. Thus the danger of shipwreck, to which the small craft of the time were frequently exposed, was aggravated by the survival of the right of wreck (*jus naufragii*), by which lords and communes were permitted to seize all goods thrown up on the shores of their territory. But the greatest menace to merchant shipping was piracy, which some maritime communities made their principal occupation. Even when the use of the compass facilitated long-distance navigation in the open sea, the lack of security, especially in waters far from home, maintained the habit of travelling in convoy with naval escort. All these dangers explain the custom of dividing the ownership of vessels among several partners, who shared the risks in proportion to their holdings. Similar reasons lay behind the widespread popularity of the sea loan, which not only increased the amount of money invested in one enterprise, but also extended the risks of navigation to a capitalist who owned no part of the ship. Frequent recourse to loans of this kind, it is plausibly suggested, eventually encouraged the development of marine insurance, which after the early years of the fourteenth century we begin to find in fairly general use.

In spite of the dangers, however, sea communication was still much the most preferred method of travel, even for journeys that could be made by land, because it offered the means of transporting heavy, bulky, and inexpensive goods. It is true that even merchant ships were of very small tonnage in the Middle Ages, though after the thirteenth century they tended to increase in size, especially those which braved the Atlantic or were destined for the distant Black Sea. According to the maritime laws of Venice, compiled in the first half of the thirteenth century, merchant ships varied in capacity from 200 to 1,000 *libbre grosse,* or from 94 to 470 tons. But in the centuries following, the galleys and other vessels (*cocche*), which plied the three routes to Flanders, Syria, and Constantinople (with the

Black Sea), were conspicuously larger: by the early fifteenth century the Flanders boats exceeded 750 tons, while the others ranged from 600 to 800 tons.

The Volume of Trade. If we were lucky enough to possess trade statistics relating to the ports of Genoa and Venice during the period of their greatest prosperity and placed them beside similar figures of our own day from New York, London, Antwerp, Rotterdam, or Hamburg, we should be immediately struck by the comparative insignificance of medieval trade. Such a comparison, however, even if it were possible, would not provide decisive proof that commerce was negligible in the communal age, because modern statistics are enormously distended by the trade in such extremely cheap and bulky goods as mineral oils and coal, iron ore, phosphates, cement materials, and so on, all of which were quite unknown in the Middle Ages. At that time, admittedly, the demand for foreign wares was very small in volume, because the population was much less dense than now and the lower orders of society, both in the country and to a great extent also in the town, had no share in it whatever. This is well shown by the simple case of the woollen industry, which spread to many small towns, and even to *castelli,* precisely in order to supply the needs of humble people, who had to be content with second-rate cloth woven from local wool. The top-grade wools, imported from Morocco, Spain, and England, were reserved for upper-class needs.

All the same, the flourishing state of the Italian towns between the thirteenth century and the first half of the sixteenth was not built exclusively on trade in high-quality merchandise; in practice much the greater part of the goods which Italians shipped by sea consisted not of gold or silver or slaves, or the precious products of the East, but of wool, cotton, silk, salt, wheat, sugar, wine, timber, iron, copper, dye-stuffs, and alum. Sombart has challenged Villani's well-known figures for Florentine industry on the grounds that a yearly production of 100,000 pieces of cloth is hardly compatible with an import of only 4,000 sacks of English wool, which would yield at most 12,000 pieces. But he overlooked the fact that not only English wool was used in the production of the best Florentine fabrics, but also *Garbo* wool, Spanish wool, and wool from the Apennines and other parts of Italy, which may all have been imported in far larger quantity.

Markets and Fairs. Small Merchants and Great Merchants. In the Italian towns of the Middle Ages which played most part in international trade, we find two types of merchants living side by side, differing profoundly in their form of activity, manner of life, and business outlook. There was first of all the small merchant, the shopkeeper, who as an economic figure was hardly distinguishable from the artisan. This man spent the day behind his shop-counter, selling miscellaneous wares to a small and barely changing group of customers, and exercised his trade subject to regulation and inspection by his guild and by the government officials charged with control of the market. He earned enough to support his family, but could rarely hope to widen the range of his affairs or multiply his profits.

Much of the business done by small traders of this kind was transacted in daily and weekly markets where people from the country round about exchanged their produce for the manufactures of urban craftsmen. The infrequent mention of annual fairs in both documents and chronicles is probably due to the fact that in the greater commercial cities trade in all commodities, whether local or foreign, went on all through the year. The only exceptions, outside the March of Ancona, the Abruzzi, Apulia, and a few other southern districts, were certain towns in the valleys of the Po and Adige (Piacenza, Bologna, Ferrara, Trent, Bolzano) which, mainly for geographical reasons, were the meeting-place of important fairs throughout the Middle Ages and beyond. Best known are the fairs of Ferrara, a town situated at the intersection of the Po and the highways from Romagna, Tuscany, Mantua, and Verona. They were held twice a year, at Easter and Martinmas, and were frequented by merchants from Bologna, Mantua, Milan, and other Lombard towns, as well as by Tuscans and occasional foreigners, who were attracted by the trade in cloth, skins, metalwork, and other goods.

With the Italian fairs, limited though their function may have been, we begin to leave the small world of local trade for the wider horizons of inter-regional and international trade on the grand scale. This was the exclusive concern of the great merchants, who in the Italian towns of the Middle Ages formed a class entirely separate from the petty shopkeepers. In places where commerce was most intense and throve in combination with industry, we do not find a single comprehensive merchant guild but rather a number of different corporations, each representing a particular branch of trade and sometimes associated with a corresponding branch of industry. Instead of the merchant guild there existed a board of magistrates, a public commission called the *Mercanzia*. At Genoa and Venice, where the commune itself formed the corporation of the commercial aristocracy, the great merchants did not feel any need to combine in professional guilds, but preferred to use the guild organization, especially in Venice, as a means of control and domination over the much more numerous class of artisans. The very fact that there were guilds of haberdashers, grocers, and second-hand dealers (*rivenduglioli*), and none at all of money-changers and bankers, cloth merchants, and shipowners, is enough to show how radical and universally acknowledged was the difference between the shopkeeper, who was treated much like an artisan, and the merchant, in the loftier sense of the word, who invested his time and capital in international trade and enjoyed full political rights. Even when the greater merchants—like those of the Calimala guild at Florence—combined big business with shopkeeping, their mode of training and *curriculum vitae,* which varied very little from one large commercial town to another, still marked them off emphatically from the petty local tradesmen. After taking a course in grammar and arithmetic (including com-

301

Luzzatto

ITALIAN TOWNS
AND TRADE

mercial arithmetic), they began their career at a very early age with a number of protracted journeys over land and sea. Often they spent long periods in foreign countries, representing the family business or the firm in which members of their family were the leading partners, and transacting other affairs on behalf of relatives and friends. A few even finished up their wanderings from one great town to another by settling permanently abroad. But most of them came home after reaching middle age, though not in order to retire; on the contrary, they now took charge of operations at the centre, maintaining close contact with the foreign agencies and branches of their business, even when invested with high offices of state.

As for the quantity of business done, though it may be true that merchants were often ready to devote unlimited time and patience to obtaining a few pieces of cloth, or write numerous letters and engage in prolonged litigation for the sake of a few dozen ducats, there is still plenty of evidence of larger transactions, which even in our own day would be judged important. When the books of the Bardi company were balanced on 1 July 1318, they registered a total turnover of 873,638 gold florins. Even when the figures for individual transactions seem pitifully small, it must always be remembered that most great merchants dealt in a wide variety of goods. To take just one example: the merchandise, in store or still at sea, which was sold up by the executors of the Venetian, Pietro Soranzo, on his death in the second half of the fourteenth century consisted of pepper, valued at 3,000 ducats, nutmegs, cloves, tin, lead, and iron, valued at much the same amount, gold from Russia worth 1,478 ducats, raw silk worth 3,810 ducats, and Russian skins worth 1,900 ducats, together with a quantity of Syrian and Cypriot sugar, wax, honey, and pearls, of which the value, though not precisely stated, was certainly high. About the same period the brothers Cornaro entered into partnership with a certain Vito Lion, gentleman of Verona, to carry on trade with Cyprus; their joint capital amounted to 83,273 ducats and their imports for a single year were worth 67,000 ducats.

Beyond a doubt the pace of medieval business was very slow. Thus, it took four months, on an average, to transport a bale of cloth from Flanders to Florence. But before the age of steam and the telegraph, the speed of communications was never much increased, yet this did not prevent the Fuggers and other business houses from amassing gigantic fortunes in the sixteenth century. To big firms, with branches in all the main markets of the world and a substantial turnover of business in every one, the slow rate of each transaction scarcely mattered; and it certainly did not stop them from making very large total profits, even though the average return from commercial investments was relatively small (according to Sapori between 10 and 15 per cent). At the time of his death, early in the fourteenth century, the total patrimony of Bartolo di Jacopo Bardi amounted to no more than 17,240 florins in movable goods and 8,400 florins in landed property. Less than forty years later his sons had increased the family fortune to 129,142 florins, and this they accomplished entirely by trade and banking.

But the magnitude and modernity, so to speak, of large-scale Italian commerce during the thirteenth and still more the fourteenth centuries is most clearly displayed in the complex and systematic organization of business houses. In the space of thirty-six years, between 1310 and 1345, the Bardi company employed altogether 346 agents (*fattori*). Since each agent remained in the service of the firm for an average of eleven to twelve years, it follows that every year the company must have had between 100 and 120 employees on its books. The members of this staff received various rates of pay, ranging from 5 to 7 gold florins per annum for apprentices, to 200 florins for branch-managers in Flanders and England, and 300 florins for directors in charge of accounts at the centre. All these agents were distributed over 25 different branches: 12 in Italy, 4 in the Levant, and 9 in France, the Low Countries, England, Spain, and Tunis.

With firms of this complexity and size to manage, Italian merchants were bound to develop entirely new methods of organization, administration, and accounting; and it was thanks to them if rapid progress in the sciences of reckoning and bookkeeping, commercial technique and law, made Italy the business school of Europe during the fourteenth and fifteenth centuries.

The Forms of Investment in International Trade. It appears, then, that the great merchant of medieval Italy was preeminently a man of enterprise and resource, generously endowed with the spirit of initiative and organization, who was ready to engage in all kinds of affairs: foreign and domestic trade, both wholesale and retail, dealings in cloth or raw wool, grain, spices, salt, or metals, the financing of industry and the business of exchange, loans to private citizens and princes, communes, or despots, and the farming of customs and taxes. But the personal capital with which the merchant first ventured on these various activities was generally insufficient; gradually therefore, as the scope of his business widened, he sought among his relatives and friends, or among other merchants at home and abroad, men who were prepared to entrust him with their capital for some particular enterprise, or join with him as partners in all his undertakings for a stated length of time. The forms of capital investment and partnership varied. In particular, those employed in maritime trade differed from those developed in trade by land.

The two forms of contract most generally favoured in the maritime towns between the twelfth and the fourteenth centuries were the sea loan and the *commenda*, or what was called in Venice the *colleganza*. The sea loan was an advance of money by a capitalist to a merchant or ship's captain at the start of a trading voyage; the money travelled at the lender's risk, and was repaid with interest (generally very high interest) on arrival at the port of destination or return to the port of embarkation. In many, perhaps the majority of cases, a clause was inserted requiring restitution in a different coinage from that of the original payment, which converted the loan into a contract of exchange (*a cambio marittimo*). Widespread though it was, the sea loan was much less common a form of investment in overseas trade than the *commenda*, a type of contract admirably designed for granting people in all walks of life a chance to share in the expected profits of maritime commerce, without the dangers and discomforts of a voyage by sea. *Commenda* contracts were of two kinds, bilateral and unilateral, and these survive in roughly equal numbers in the records. In the case of the bilateral *commenda* (which the Genoese called a *societas*), the partner who stayed at home (the *stans*) contributed two-thirds of the capital, while the seafaring merchant who managed the venture (the *procertans* or *tractator*) contributed only a third. By the unilateral *commenda*, or *commenda* proper, the *stans* provided all the capital and reserved three-fourths of the profits. In practice, however, both types of agreement were probably unilateral in character, and the fiction of bilateral investment may have been introduced into the contract to justify the division of the risks, which were not assumed entirely by the lender, as in the sea loan, but were shared in the proportion of two-thirds and one-third by the *stans* and the *procertans*. The relationship of merchant and capitalist was essentially one between debtor and creditor, with the simple but significant difference that the merchant was bound not only to repay the borrowed money with all agreed interest, but also to render account of the business transacted with the money or merchandise entrusted to him "in commenda", and justify any failure to repay the full sum invested. The German historian Sombart, determined at all costs to minimize the volume of traffic in the communal age, makes fun of the merchants who set off on "great" trading enterprises with a mere hundred Genoese pounds commended to them; but he overlooks the numerous surviving *commenda* contracts for much larger sums, and forgets that the same merchant would normally receive a dozen or several dozen commissions of the kind at one time. Both at Genoa and at Venice the *commenda* became the most favoured and frequent type of investment during the thirteenth century. To quote one example: at the time of his death in 1268, the Venetian doge Ranieri Zeno still had pending 132 contracts of *colleganza*, representing 22,935 *lire* out of a total personal estate of 38,848 *lire*. Not only this; the same doge accompanied the legacies granted in his will to relatives and religious, churches and monasteries, with a recommendation, and often a stipulation, that the same form of investment should continue to be used. This attitude was not peculiar to the Venetians, but was equally common among the merchants of Pisa, Genoa, Marseilles, and Barcelona.

Profoundly different from these seafaring partnerships were the forms of commercial partnership which prevailed in the towns of the interior and which began to spread, after the thirteenth century, to the coastal cities as well. The capital for a commercial company was subscribed, in varying proportions, by a whole group of people, most of whom belonged to one family, so that companies were generally known by a family name. Unlike the seafaring partnerships, which were formed for the duration of only one trading venture and then dissolved, commercial companies were established to carry on business of many different kinds during a specified length of time. At the end of the period the firm was dissolved, but in normal circumstances a new company was immediately formed, either with the same partners as before or with some fresh members added. Liability for debts was the collective responsibility of all the partners, and profits were divided, on liquidation, in proportion to each partner's initial investment.

Accounting. The merchants of medieval Italy were not obliged by law to keep accounts, but as business expanded in range and complexity, they found it increasingly convenient to do so; and once partnerships became the rule in the larger commercial enterprises, systematic bookkeeping was unavoidable. At first, no doubt, the main object in bookkeeping was simply to preserve a record of transactions which had not been promptly settled in cash; later on, however, these rough memoranda were supplemented by a complete, co-ordinated set of books, which made it possible to trace every stage of the firm's business. The practice now began of keeping a day-book, recording each day's operations, and a ledger (*libro mastro*), in which every person dealing regularly with the firm was entered, with a separate account, on a separate page, under his own name, with the debit column (*dare*) on the left side and the credit column (*avere*) on the right. At the same time we begin to encounter the system of double-entry bookkeeping, in which every transaction is entered twice in the same register, once on the debit side and once on the credit side; it was possible to give this double character to each transaction by representing things as well as persons as creditors and debtors. The invention of the double-entry system was long attributed to Luca Paciolo of Borgo San Sepolcro, who in his *Summa de Arithmetica,* published at Venice in 1494, described this method of accounting in great detail. The truth is, however, that the learned friar invented nothing; all he did, as he says himself, was give an accurate exposition of accounting methods which had long been used in the business houses of Venice (whence the name *scrittura alla Veneziana*), Florence, Genoa, and Milan.

EARLY
MODERN
EUROPE

PART III

The period roughly from 1400 to 1700 has frequently been viewed as a time of change, which ushered in the "modern world." This attitude stems from the feeling of many scholars and writers in Italy in the fourteenth and fifteenth centuries who saw their age as one of rediscovery of classical antiquity and of rebirth of culture and learning. Although the concept of the Renaissance originated with contemporary thinkers who consciously modeled many of their activities on the remote past of Greco-Roman antiquity and felt that they had broken decisively with their immediate past, the seminal work of Jacob Burckhardt, a noted Swiss historian of the nineteenth century, gave an even more forceful expression to the idea of a new age dawning with the Renaissance. His theses, emphasizing such ideas as the autonomy of the state, the importance of the individual as against the corporateness of medieval society, and the preponderance of secular over spiritual values, were presented over a hundred years ago in *The Civilization of the Renaissance in Italy* and have had a fundamental impact on subsequent historians' views of this period. Few today subscribe to all of Burckhardt's ideas, but there is general recognition that much change occurred in European society between 1400 and 1700. One object of the following section is to ask, What is modern about this period, and what is medieval?

To begin with, two of the most salient characteristics of medieval civilization, the ideal of a unified Christian church and that of a universal empire, were dispelled by the Reformation of the sixteenth century and by the emergence of autonomous states, which owed no allegiance to the emperor and even fought against him to further their own interests. And yet, although the old ideal of society united in obedience to the Roman church was shattered by the successes of Luther, Calvin, and other reformers, sixteenth- and seventeenth-century Europe was deeply conscious of and motivated by religion. In this respect society was much closer to medieval attitudes than to the secular, often agnostic outlook of the twentieth century. Likewise, the huge Hapsburg Empire struggled to combat separatist tendencies in its various component parts and relied heavily on medieval theories of universal empire in maintaining itself for most of the sixteenth century.

These centuries witnessed many advances in science and technology, such as the invention of printing and of the sextant, of gunpowder for military purposes, and of refined methods for observation of natural phenomena. These discoveries contributed to the European discovery and settlement of the Americas; to a revolution in the techniques of warfare; and to the foundations of modern science. Despite these advances, life for the millions of ordinary people in these centuries was not appreciably different from what it had been for a millennium before. Plague and starvation continued to take their toll of populations, and the lot of the common man hardly changed. Egalitarian ideals had to await the French Revolution; elitism still ruled men's minds. When the peasants of Swabia rose in revolt against the oppressive feudal dues and obligations of their masters, misinterpreting Luther's defiance of the authority of Rome as a general call for rebellion against tyrannical exploitation, Luther condemned them in horrified tones and lent his support to the local nobility in quelling the disturbances. While one cannot deny the elements in what Denys Hay calls the Early Modern period that point to future developments, one should not ignore those that reflect the past as well.

In the first selection in this part, Denys Hay deals with the concept of the Renaissance as a period and offers some very interesting ideas about the nature of the early modern period in general. The next six selections are all concerned with various aspects of change, discovery, and innovation in society. Some, like Garrett Mattingly's selections and Elizabeth Eisenstein's article on the impact of printing, deal with practical or technological discoveries, while those by Gene Brucker, D. B. Davis, and Isaiah Berlin treat social and intellectual change and probe the meaning of the conflicts in thought and values occasioned by changes in society. The articles by Erik Erikson, J. H. Hexter, and H. G. Koenigsberger center on the medieval themes of a universal church and a universal empire, and trace their history in the sixteenth century.

For the seventeenth century, six readings have been chosen to illustrate the nature and problems of several states that would play a dominant role in European society for the next centuries. The first, by Hobsbawm, discusses the late sixteenth and early seventeenth centuries as a period of general crisis in Europe, and J. H. Elliott, C. R. Boxer, Austin Woolrych, Pierre Goubert, and Vasili Klyuchevsky study particular problems in, respectively, Spain, the Netherlands, England, France, and Russia against this background of crisis and emerging statism. Finally, the last two selections are concerned with the growth and development of the modern view of science, which has come to be almost as characteristic of modern Western civilization as was the notion of Christendom in the Middle Ages. Joseph Ben-David's article discusses the general formation of a scientific attitude, while A. Rupert Hall's centers on the work of Newton, probably the most important figure in Western science between 1400 and 1700.

In sum, the readings in this section will provide much material for discussion about the peculiar formation of what has come to be called the modern world, and about the way society changes gradually over time. They present much that is new and provocative from eminent historians and can introduce the reader to recent trends in historical thought about the early modern period.

20. The Renaissance as a Period in European History

DENYS HAY

One of the operations that the historian must perform if he is to write good history is abstraction, or generalization. Unless he provides a theme for his subject, it will be difficult to distinguish what is important from what is trivial in the mass of detailed information available to him. Of course, there is always the danger of bias or preoccupation, usually unconscious in the historian, distorting his writing to some degree; the student of history must therefore be especially alert for traces of "nonobjectivity" in historical writing. As a corollary of the necessity to generalize in order to avoid a meaningless string of facts, the historian must "periodize" his subject, that is, he must divide "the seamless web of History, of durée*" in Professor Hay's phrase. What then is a historical period? Is it merely the artificial creation of the working historian, devised for convenience and ease of writing? Or can one speak of historical periods as having an inner unity of coherence which sets them off, one from another?*

It is particularly appropriate to raise these questions in connection with the following selections on the Renaissance, for the intellectuals and men of letters of the Renaissance wrote frequently about the ages or periods of history. For them the world of the early fourteenth century was one such period, and an especially critical period of "rebirth" or "renaissance." The human spirit, they felt, had rediscovered the high culture of Greco-Roman antiquity and had

Source: Denys Hay, *The Italian Renaissance in Its Historical Background* (London: Cambridge University Press, 1961), pp. 10–25. Reprinted by permission of the author and publisher. [Footnotes omitted.]

risen above the stagnation, gloom, and backwardness of the long "Dark Ages"
which separated their age from the Roman world. Thus Renaissance scholars in-
vented the value judgment that the Middle Ages were a time of intellectual
decline, followed by a rebirth of learning and creativity on classical models in
the fourteenth and fifteenth centuries. However much we may correct or re-
dress this wrong and oversimplified view, it seems that we are tied to period-
ization as devised by Renaissance men.

Denys Hay, Professor of History at the University of Edinburgh, is a specialist
in Renaissance history and historiography, and has published numerous books
including Europe: The Emergence of an Idea *(1957, rev. ed. 1968) and* Europe
in the Fourteenth and Fifteenth Centuries *(1966), and he edited* The Age of
the Renaissance *(1967).* The Italian Renaissance in its Historical Background
(1961), from which this selection is taken, treats many aspects of this period, and
especially the entire question of the legitimacy of writing about such a thing as
the "Renaissance." Hay accepts the necessity of keeping the time-honored names,
and in addition he feels that in many respects—in politics, with the develop-
ment of parliamentary monarchy; in economics, with the transition from land-
based to cash values; and in culture, with a world that is lay, yet still Christian
—it is legitimate to speak about these centuries as a distinct period of transi-
tion from medieval to early modern history. Italy especially is for him the
source of many ideas and practices that later become characteristic of the "mod-
ern world." Is he correct in his judgment? Was Renaissance society one of in-
novation and a harbinger of modern times? Whether or not one agrees with
Professor Hay's theses, his essay is a splendid introduction to the problem of
periodization and to the Renaissance as a historical period, and it demonstrates
the need for broad acquaintance with the sweep of history if one is to make valid
judgments about the course and divisions of history.

As used in the title of these lectures and in the text of the book, the
word 'Renaissance' means a period of time and certain characteristics associated with the period. It is on all fours with Middle Ages, Victorian
and other similar labels. It is perhaps more liable to beget confusion than
these for two reasons. It is a term which was more or less invented at the
time and not, as with most such names, a great deal later. And it implies
by itself a key idea—that of rebirth—which may lead the unwary
into feeling that it has an inevitability denied to other categories; that
one can, so to speak, handle its pure gold while 'Middle Ages' and 'Victorian' are mere monies of account. We are, it appears to me, thus faced
at the outset with two questions: how does the term Renaissance emerge
and how valid a notion is it? are we justified in identifying for separate
treatment a period—whether or not called 'Renaissance'—in the centuries lying between the medieval and the modern?

The history of the notion of rebirth is a long one and it has been much
written about. From our point of view the significant steps were taken by
Italians, and especially Florentines, when reflecting on their own history
and especially on their own cultural history. It is in the field of Latin let-

ters and the fine arts that, from the fourteenth century onwards, an increasing number of statements are to be found which condemn the trough of time between the end of the ancient world and the Trecento as a period of darkness, where there is no eloquence, no poetry, no great sculpture or painting. We find this attitude in Petrarch and Boccaccio, in Salutati and Bruni, and in the artists and architects of the great age—Ghiberti and Alberti. As an example of this kind of awareness, here are some remarks by the Florentine Matteo Palmieri (1406–75), whose *Vita Civile* will often be quoted in later pages:

> Where was the painter's art till Giotto tardily restored it? A caricature of the art of human delineation! Sculpture and architecture, for long years sunk to the merest travesty of art, are only today in process of rescue from obscurity; only now are they being brought to a new pitch of perfection by men of genius and erudition. Of letters and liberal studies at large it were best to be silent altogether. For these, the real guides to distinction in all the arts, the solid foundation of all civilization, have been lost to mankind for 800 years and more. It is but in our own day that men dare boast that they see the dawn of better things. For example, we owe it to our Leonardo Bruni that Latin, so long a bye-word for its uncouthness, has begun to shine forth in its ancient purity, its beauty, its majestic rhythm. Now, indeed, may every thoughtful spirit thank God that it has been permitted to him to be born in this new age, so full of hope and promise, which already rejoices in a greater array of nobly-gifted souls than the world has seen in the thousand years that have preceded it.

This rhapsody, the fervour of which we shall have to account for in later pages, was written in the mid 1430's.

The turn for the better in letters was variously ascribed to Dante, to Petrarch and his contemporaries, or (as in the passage just quoted from Palmieri) to Bruni; in the fine arts Cimabue and Giotto were regarded as pioneers. At the same time the historians, and especially Leonardo Bruni and Flavio Biondo, proceeded as though the break between antiquity and what followed occurred with the barbarian invasions culminating in the sack of Rome in A.D. 410. Biondo in a passage of his *Italia illustrata* discussed later in this book linked together fourteenth-century innovations in letters and politics, making this a fresh general turning-point. In this way the *middle* ages were born. A sense of historical distance was achieved both with regard to the ancient world, for which the artists and writers of fourteenth- and fifteenth-century Italy felt affinity, and with regard to the centuries when, as they felt, art and letters had been neglected. In this way also was born a new sense of style—the *maniera* of the critics from Ghiberti onwards—which enabled the artist to distinguish as never before what was appropriate to given periods of architecture and painting. These processes reach their ultimate point of development in the *Lives* of

313

Hay

THE
RENAISSANCE
IN EUROPEAN
HISTORY

the artist Giorgio Vasari. From this point onwards Italians and Europeans in general came to accept a Gothic period of the arts associated with a 'medieval' period of history, followed by 'modern' art and history.

The victory in Italy of the new styles, and the occasion for their rapid assimilation outside Italy, are the theme of this study and we may anticipate the outcome by noting now that one of the most remarkable results has been a general division of European history into medieval and modern. Each country has its own boundary for this, adapted to its own development. For France 'modern' history dates from the invasion of Italy in 1494; for England it starts with the advent of the Tudors in 1485; in Spain is is the union of Castile and Aragon in 1479 and in Germany the election of Charles V as emperor in 1519. In this way the Renaissance has been treated as ushering in the modern world—a doctrine which was elaborated in the second half of the nineteenth century, above all by Jacob Burckhardt in his *Civilization of the Renaissance in Italy* (1860).

Criticisms of these attitudes to the past have been frequent and often acrid. In particular the Renaissance condemnation of medieval barbarism has been challenged during the last hundred years by many historians. It has been shown how original as well as beautiful are the buildings and decorations of Gothic Christendom, how vigorous were its social and political institutions, how strong and noble the researches of its philosophers and scientists. Moreover the very field of literary revival or rebirth has been asserted to belong to the medieval North: we have been reminded that a love of letters, an eager cultivation of the Latin classics, is as characteristic of France and England in the twelfth century, of the court of Charlemagne in the ninth, as of the Italian cities in the time of Petrarch and his successors. With much of this any dispassionate person must agree. It is no longer possible to talk, as humanists did, of medieval darkness and obscurantism. And if one feels that the handful of scholars who constitute the 'Carolingian Renaissance', the coteries—who lacked all public patronage—in Chartres and Paris in the days of John of Salisbury, are somewhat esoteric as they were certainly uninfluential, this is not to refuse to the middle ages its own unique and invaluable contributions to literature and art. One further denunciation—that 'Renaissance' is a misnomer because what was being done in letters and art was original and in no sense a revival of antiquity—is not worth bothering about. Time and again (especially in cultural and religious history) we find new wine being poured from old bottles.

What seems to many nowadays to be indefensible in the older approach is its attempt to make the Renaissance the herald of what we now regard as our world. What has the Renaissance contributed to the railway engine, the aeroplane, mass education and the ideal of popular government? We live in a world where Latin letters are remote from our present anxieties and pleasures, where even our art and architecture have left the norms set up in the sixteenth century. Beyond that we live, for better and for worse, in *one* world: Africa, Asia, the Americas are daily present, politically and economically and culturally, in our Europe; as Europe is present elsewhere: this is all very different from earlier ages when the traditional geographical limits of Europe represented the furthest bounds of most European activity. This modern world emerged out of its predecessor. Are we justified in treating the preceding epoch as a unit, whether or not we accept for it the term Renaissance? To my mind the answer must be yes, and the justification for accepting as useful a period embracing what we clumsily call at present 'late-medieval, early modern' can be provided in a brief survey of the main evidence—in politics, economics and in intellectual development.

As far as the political structure of Europe is concerned, it will surely be agreed that the fifteenth and sixteenth centuries were the age of kings. This is obvious enough for the sixteenth century. But the upheavals in France in the early fifteenth century and a little later in England are strong evidence of the power of monarchy, for in both cases the contending magnates sought not to destroy monarchy, but to dominate it for their own purposes. This is clear too from the virtually uninterrupted accretion of power to the English crown from Edward I onwards, so that the machinery taken over by Henry VII was stronger, not weaker, than anything of the kind before, while in France, from Philip IV and Charles V later sovereigns such as Charles VII and Louis XI inherited an administration which again was growing daily in tenacious penetration into all spheres of French public life. Is it not from the later middle ages, so called, that the strong German principates must be dated, the Golden Bull of 1356 offering a convenient date for the start of the process? Does it not seem improbable that the sixteenth-century monarchy *par excellence,* that of Spain, should have resulted merely from a happy marriage in 1469 rather than from the preceding century of growing bureaucratic centralization in the as yet separate kingdoms? Professor Herbert Butterfield has written: 'It does seem that before the Reformation some wind in the world had clearly set itself to play on the side of kings.' This 'wind in the world' was blowing strongly through the fourteenth, fifteenth, sixteenth and seventeenth centuries, reaching hurricane force at times. From Philip the Fair to Louis XIV, France and the monarchy are interchangeable terms, however one looks at the political history of the period: and more especially in foreign policy is this the case—dynasticism is the only key.

The practice of monarchy in the fourteenth and succeeding centuries had a theory to reinforce it. Notions of sovereignty were in the air at the end of the thirteenth century, as Dr. W. Ullmann and others have shown. Paradoxically, it was the Church which hit on the first water-tight formula: 'Porro subesse Romano pontifici omni humanae creaturae declaramus, dicimus, et definimus, omnino esse de necessitate salutis.' This categorical statement in *Unam Sanctam* (1302) is more revolutionary than its expropriation, in a secular sense, by Marsilio of Padua twenty years later. Marsilio's *Defensor Pacis* was too academic for the rough and tumble empiricism of fourteenth-century monarchs, though we may note that Henry VIII of England took an interest in a suitably doctored version of a

315

Hay

THE
RENAISSANCE
IN EUROPEAN
HISTORY

book which seemed to offer a justification of the omnipotence of Tudor monarchy. Far more useful to the contemporaries of Marsilio was the virtual stranglehold which kings had over popes: the first of the concordats is really implicit in the Statutes of Provisors and Praemunire (1351, 1353 and subsequent reissues) which finally made the king, not the pope, master of the hierarchy in England. And in the fifteenth century there grew up that doctrine of Divine Right (first in Germany and Spain, be it noted) which was to be a more congenial prop to monarchs than the ambiguous arguments of Aristotelians and Averroists. In defining papal sovereignty the Papacy made, however, only one of its contributions to the strengthening of lay monarchy. The papal court of the thirteenth and fourteenth centuries was an object lesson in administrative efficiency; the bureaucracy of curia and camera, the use of international banking houses, the employment of mercenary armies—these were all devices which kings could borrow from the pope and develop on a vastly grander scale. Even before the end of the thirteenth century St. Thomas Aquinas wrote: 'The pope has a plenitude of pontifical power *like a king in a kingdom*'; it was soon to be the case that kings, being their own popes in both Catholic and Reformed communities, could laugh at claims expressed in terms so curiously flattering to themselves. Of course the most impressive evidence for the ubiquity of monarchy lies in the country where the strongest republican and municipal tradition existed—Italy. Here, where oligarchic rule had flourished unchecked, the fourteenth century witnessed the rise of indigenous principates, as we shall see later.

The urban middle class of the fourteenth to seventeenth centuries was, generally speaking, not averse to strong monarchy. On the contrary, one of the most significant features of the period I am trying to describe is the understanding which existed between town and crown. Tacit, for the most part, even concealed beneath courtly contempt and municipal servility, this alliance was the product of an overwhelming community of political and economic interest. Another group is rising in importance, also (for the most part) in association with the crown: the gentry. All over Europe from the fourteenth century onwards the lesser landholder is becoming more noticeable, more literate, more politically ambitious.

With this all-too-brief picture of 'late medieval' and 'early modern' politics, contrast for a moment what had gone before, what was to come later. Earlier we are in a world of landed magnates, power is decentralized, 'feudalism' totally devoid of a political theory. The king, it is true, survives this twilight of monarchy: he is often himself a great baron; he is hedged by a divinity of sorts. But real power lies with the independent magnates, supreme, when they care, in the king's *entourage,* supreme in that 'manorial system' which fed and clothed themselves and their followers. If we turn to the later period, the world we live in ourselves, we find it dominated by middle-class values in politics, as in economics and art; we live, so to speak, in a parliamentary world; this is true of the monarchies, and it is true of the dictatorships. The theory of republicanism is now universal, socialism and even communism becoming (at any rate in large areas) the refuge of the humdrum and the respectable. The kings have departed in all but name.

In the realm of economic and social structures the evidence for continuity in the period I am discussing seems to me to be overwhelming. The European world of the fourteenth, fifteenth, sixteenth and seventeenth centuries saw an extraordinary balance between cash values and land values. It was a world of banks yet without banknotes; of commerce without industry; of enormous financial operations in an atmosphere almost devoid of financial security; where one had capital, so to speak, without capitalism; where town and country were almost evenly matched in economic importance; where money might be made in a hundred and one ways, but where the only long-term investment was land. Even the revolutionary movements which mark the period are significant: they are almost entirely agrarian, for social liberty had been identified, yet they were nearly all in urbanized areas, for it was in the towns that the identification of social liberty had been realized.

Again, we find a marked contrast between earlier and later periods. In the 'early middle ages' land, as has often been said, was virtually the only source of wealth; there were no peasant risings worth the name before 1200. Money and merchants always existed, it seems, even in the darkest part of the Dark Ages, but they were insignificant. Looking on the other hand at the modern period proper we find that land, though still a source of social prestige, is little else, except when operated industrially. Above all, for over a century the main pace-maker in social and economic affairs has been industry rather than commerce; and the social upheavals in the modern world have arisen from the claims of a proletariat, faintly foreshadowed in fourteenth-century Flanders and Florence, which is fundamentally urban, not agrarian.

Finally we come to the religious, intellectual, literary and artistic features of the 'later medieval—early modern' period. The most obvious characteristic of the intellectual situation (to use an awkward phrase) of these centuries is that it is essentially *lay* and yet essentially *Christian*. The agnostics and atheists are so few that we may forget about them: they are heralds and harbingers, no more. The bulk of the intelligentsia was Christian and yet the impetus to devotion had certainly passed out of the hands of the clergy. The mystical movements of the period are predominantly lay both in composition and leadership, from the Brethren of the Common Life to the Jansenists. What is there *priestly* about Gerard de Groot, Erasmus or Pascal? They reflect, indeed, that preoccupation with the world which is found in the friars: Giuseppe Toffanin has said, with some justice, that the Counter-Reformation begins with St. Francis and St. Dominic. Certainly no one could accuse the Jesuits (might one not describe them as the most secular of the religious?) in the sixteenth and seventeenth centuries of neglecting this world, in their gallant battle to make the hereafter palatable here below. As a result of the lay direction of Christian spirituality, this epoch is also marked by a series of heresies and schisms: both seem endemic between the fourteenth and the seventeenth

317

Hay
THE
RENAISSANCE
IN EUROPEAN
HISTORY

centuries, the very instruments designed to meet them, like the friars and the sixteenth-century reformers, leading to further division. Above all, it is a period when reform, real reform of the morality of the clergy, seems incapable of achievement, save for the briefest periods and the most restricted localities. What Luther, Calvin and the fathers at Trent accomplished was definition of dogma; pluralism, ignorance, immorality seem as common in all confessions in the seventeenth century as they had been in the undivided Church of the fifteenth. The laymen who were setting the pace in religion were equally setting it in scholarship: the omnivorous honest gentry for whom so many short cuts to universal knowledge were provided, from Pastrengo to Pierre Bayle. For this public the existing university had no relevance as a centre of active scholarship, and consequently in these centuries the universities of Europe enter on a relatively sterile phase of their history.

In literature the period is marked by a striking balance between the new vernaculars and a classical Latin whose revival is discussed in later pages. We are apt to write down the Latin writings produced between the fourteenth and the seventeenth centuries, although practically every important work of scholarship was written in Latin and though its profound influence is still commemorated, at any rate in Europe, in an exceedingly large number of teachers of Latin (who, alas! tend to scorn all the literature written after the second century A.D.). Revived classical Latin gave the vernaculars more than a few merely formal devices: it forced a development of orthography and grammar and vocabulary which might else have taken three or four centuries to accomplish; it gave a characteristic patina to most European literature in the sixteenth and seventeenth centuries. Nor, I believe, is the evidence of art history out of step with the general picture. The late-thirteenth and fourteenth centuries see over all western Europe a new concern for both realism and decoration—the main ingredients of the 'international Gothic' as the style has been christened. This has its influence even in Italy where another style was to be born destined by the seventeenth century to be accepted throughout the continent, but which spread along paths already in some sense explored, towards destinations already familiar.

Given the secular leadership in religion and literature, given (with the help of Latin) increasingly mature and competent vernaculars, it is not surprising that this period sees a remarkable growth of patriotic sentiment which at times verges on nationalism: the Italians felt themselves superior to the Greeks, let alone to the Barbarians in the north; the French and English began to evolve mythologies about each other; the Germans at Paris objected to being termed the English Nation in the early fifteenth century, while at Constance the claim of Greater Britain to be a leading nation was hotly debated. One characteristic feature which, in different guises, runs through the period from start to finish is known under the name it acquired in the seventeenth century: the Battle of the Books. Yet—and here we are faced with a phenomenon similar to the lay but Christian attitude I have mentioned—this world of separate principates, divided politically and religiously, remained throughout loyal to the old notion of Christendom. As Franklin Le Van Baumer has reminded us, Protestant Englishmen rejoiced at the victory of the Papists at Lepanto, and the very word 'Christendom' put up a long fight against its successful rival 'Europe'. Consciousness of a larger grouping during the period is, in fact, an amalgam of the two notions, of Europe and of Christendom, similar to the amalgam of town and crown, of land values and cash values, already noted.

When comparison is made with the earlier period, what a different world we find! Christianity then is the business of the clergy, regular and secular. Lay piety has only two distinguishable outward forms—the endowment of the Church and the retreat from the world into the Church. This society, where only clerks were required to be literate, could and did sustain a living Latin literature, but the furtive and despised vernaculars were almost entirely oral. The Latin literature which then flourished was, however, corrupted year by year by contact with inchoate Romance and Teutonic dialects, while a great and fatal division cut across literature: for the serious work was a Latin work and the vernaculars were secular, ephemeral, frivolous; the fine arts, like serious literature, appear almost solely in religious contexts. As against the widely held patriotism I have just mentioned the early middle ages held no loyalties larger than those which sprang from local leadership, except those fugitive and grandiose concepts the Universal Church and the Universal Empire. In such an environment heresy could scarcely flourish, and in fact there is scarcely any before 1200 in the provinces which looked to the Roman pope.

Equally, 'modern' history is cut off, in the matters I have been touching on, from the era that starts in the fourteenth century. As against the widespread but secular interest in Christianity as a moral guide, we have the abandonment of organized religion as an inspiration in the intelligentsia during the nineteenth century. As against the classical norms so universally accepted up to the Enlightenment, and the identification of scholarship with literature, we have romanticism, a subjective approach, a candid specialism in scholarship (aided by the revived universities), and an encyclopaedism which, unlike its predecessor, caters not for the man who seeks to know all, but for the man who knows he can never know anything. Nationalism, once the decent emotion of responsible men, restricted in scope and elevating in its effects, has become in the last hundred and fifty years the sordid catchword of the masses. Above all, in the modern period proper we are confronted with the universal presence of science. By science today we mean what the earlier period termed Natural Philosophy, and the change in terminology is instructive. For us, all knowledge is essentially scientific in the new sense: our modern heresies are scientific. No doubt the roots of science in this sense go far back: to the Paduan Averroists and Aristotelians, to Ockham's brand of Nominalism, and further still. But we must admit that, before genuinely modern times, science was singularly uninfluential.

Divisions of the seamless web of History, of *durée,* are, I repeat, bound to falsify, for they mean drawing boundaries, however broad and ill-de-

319

Hay

THE
RENAISSANCE
IN EUROPEAN
HISTORY

fined, where no boundaries were felt to exist at the time: contemporaries at any moment consider themselves to be 'modern'. But for practical purposes such frontiers must be created. No formal discussion of any subject can be conducted save by cutting it up somehow—into courses of lectures or chapters in a book. All that I am urging is that our old twofold division of European history (medieval, modern) should be replaced by a threefold division (medieval, the new period, modern).

Just as the characteristic features of the medieval period—the fief, Gothic architecture, scholastic philosophy—were ultimately to be the pattern for Christendom as a whole but were first and most purely expressed in northern France, so in the succeeding age nearly all that was to be most unique about it was first and most purely expressed in Italy. The morality, the intellectual and artistic styles, and some aspects of politics and economic activity which were in the sixteenth century to provide Europe with a new cultural and social unity, comparable to that of the twelfth century, all these were largely Italian in origin as I hope to show in later pages. Hence it seems not unreasonable to call the new 'middle' ages, the 'late medieval–early modern' of our present arrangements, by the name Renaissance.

21. Renaissance Diplomacy

GARRETT MATTINGLY

One of the most striking features of modern Western interstate relations is the existence of permanent diplomatic representatives. Interestingly, permanent exchange of ambassadors or other representatives was not known in antiquity, nor in the medieval period; it spread to the rest of the world largely through European influence after the sixteenth century. Modern diplomacy, centering on permanent representatives abroad, is thus a creation of the Renaissance. What was the role of Italy in the evolution of political forms and practices for the rest of Europe? What precise innovations and contributions did she make to diplomacy and interstate relations, and why?

Garrett Mattingly, who is well known for his works on European politics in the fifteenth and sixteenth centuries, especially The Armada (1959) *and* Catherine of Aragon (1941), *wrote a ground-breaking book entitled* Renaissance Diplomacy, *from which the following selection comes.*

The invention of diplomatic techniques was a crucial element in the establishment of the balance of power created by the Treaty of Lodi in 1454; the balance of power concept in turn was widened to embrace continental Europe in the sixteenth century, and it has played a fundamental role in international relations until the twentieth century. Mattingly's study, as the first modern attempt to trace the course of these developments, remains an outstanding contribution to an understanding of modern Europe.

Source: Garrett Mattingly, *Renaissance Diplomacy* (Boston: Houghton Mifflin Company, 1955), pp. 55–70. Reprinted by permission of the publisher. [Footnotes omitted.]

His major thesis is that political power in the Italian communes was fundamentally illegitimate, since in theory Italy belonged to the Holy Roman Empire. The communal governments were therefore pragmatic, provisional, and amoral and were in need of means to secure some semblance of legitimacy for themselves. War, as a means both of insuring the viability of the small Italian states of the Renaissance, and of increasing the power of one state at the expense of another, became accepted practice and a characteristic of Italian politics. As a counter-measure to the ever constant threat of warfare, diplomatic practices, including the permanent resident ambassador who was on the scene and could act for his state at once, grew up. For Mattingly, Renaissance diplomatic practice, the forerunner of our modern diplomacy, was almost a natural and pragmatic response to common problems. He further emphasizes the essential balance of power in Italy among five large states which prevailed until the French invasion of 1494, and adumbrated the "balance of power" concept that was to dominate the larger European scene from 1700 on. Finally, Mattingly describes the evolution of the resident ambassador from the temporary legal or commercial agents required by the exigencies of Italian commerce to the full-time and permanent diplomatic representative.

Mattingly's absorbing study raises some further questions which cannot be dismissed. How much of institutional history develops in such a pragmatic, haphazard manner? Is there a fundamental and necessary correlation between permanent ambassadors and the threat of war? Why have we in the West continued to employ diplomatic practices which were formed in an age now far different from our own; especially in light of the substantial technological changes that have occurred in transportation, communication, and similar areas? Does this system of diplomacy still serve the best interests of modern states, or have the inventions of Renaissance diplomacy outworn their usefulness?

The Renaissance Environment

Diplomacy in the modern style, permanent diplomacy, was one of the creations of the Italian Renaissance. It began in the same period that saw the beginnings of the new Italian style of classical scholarship and in the same areas, Tuscany and the valley of the Po. Its earliest flowering came in the same decade in which Massacio announced a new art of painting on the walls of the Brancacci Chapel and Brunelleschi began the first Italian Renaissance building in the cloister of Santa Croce. Its full triumph coincided with the full triumph of the new humanism and of the new arts, and under the same patrons, Cosimo de'Medici, Francesco Sforza and Pope Nicholas V. Thereafter, like other creations of the Italian Renaissance, the new diplomacy flourished in Italy for forty years before it was transplanted north of the Alps, and acclimatized in one country after another of Western Europe.

The new diplomacy was the functional expression of a new kind of state. It is simple and easy to say that this new kind of state, 'the state as a work of art', was in turn a primary expression of the creative spirit of the Renaissance. That classic generalization has supplied the foundation for most of what has been written in the last century about Renaissance diplomacy. It does make easy a vivid distinction between the newer style of diplomacy and the older; otherwise it is not very useful. What we see when we look at Italy between 1300 and 1450 is the rise of a number of new institutions and modes of behaviour, among them a new style of diplomacy, all leading to something like a new concept of the state. To label this bundle of ways of acting and thinking and feeling 'the Renaissance State' is unobjectionable. To treat the label as if it were an entity, and say that it was generated by another entity, the spirit of the Renaissance, is explanation only in terms of mythology. It might make better sense to say that the spirit of the Renaissance (whatever that might be) had, among its causes, the evolution of the new state. In this gradual evolution, separate institutional adaptations to changes in the political climate, and consequent acceptance of appropriately changed modes of feeling certainly preceded the finished concept.

The political climate of Italy began to change in the eleventh century. Some of the institutional adaptations, then, are far older than anything we usually call the Renaissance. When the reformed and reforming papacy first defied the German emperors, forces were set in motion which finally burst for Italy the feudal ties in which all the rest of Europe long remained entangled. The energies of the new Lombard and Tuscan communes were set free By the aid of those energies the papacy tamed the violence of Barbarossa and survived its mortal struggle with Frederick II. By their aid the popes triumphed, and the Guelph party shattered with revolutionary violence the last props of German feudal and imperial dominance. Except for the overshadowing papal and Angevin power, the burghers of Lombardy and Tuscany were left masters of their own political future. By the early fourteenth century, the decline of the Neapolitan kingdom and the failure and humiliation of the papacy cleared the board.

After the popes withdrew to Avignon, Italy was a political vacuum, a gap in the medieval system of hierarchically ordered duties and loyalties. The vacuum had to be filled by the political inventiveness of Italians. After the Emperor Charles IV's subsidized excursion to Rome to collect the imperial crown like a tourist's souvenir, the party war-cries of Guelph and Ghibelline lost meaning. When, in another twenty years, the legates of Avignon re-established the temporal sway of the papacy in central Italy, it was the great Guelph republic Florence which, with eloquence and gold, with hired arms and the new weapons of diplomacy, fought the papal forces to a standstill. The temporal authority of the popes could only be re-admitted to Italy if it accepted equality with those purely temporal powers which had grown up under its shadow.

It was one of the paradoxes of the papal revolt against the emperor that it produced the first, and for a long time the only, purely secular states in Christendom. Everywhere else temporal powers were masked and sanctified by religious forms, by priestly consecrations and unctions with holy oil, just as they were at once buttressed and confined by fundamental laws and ancient constitutions, and elevated and immobilized by their position as keystones in the intricately interlocking arches of European feudalism. But in Italy, power was temporal in the strictest sense of the term. It was naked and free, without even the most tenuous connection with eternity. Fundamentally it was illegitimate, the unanticipated by-blow of a clerical revolt and thus an anomaly in the ordered hierarchy of divinely legitimated rights. Its theorists might dream of republican and imperial Rome. Its custodians might occasionally buy themselves an imperial or a papal title to turn an immediate profit. But they knew that the key to power was force. Thus, in Italy the struggle between the two heads of Christendom cleared the ground for the planting of the first omnicompetent, amoral, sovereign states.

The pragmatic and provisional nature of power made all temporal authority quite literally temporary authority. It depended on the ability of the rulers to compel by force an unhabitual obedience, and on the voluntary allegiance of enough citizens to permit the use of force against the rest. The insecurity of their tenure made the rulers, whether tyrants or oligarchs or dominant factions of the burgher class, alert, uneasy, self-conscious. They had to be sensitive to every threat from within or without. Just 'to maintain the state', just, that is, to keep the current government from being overthrown, was a grave, continuous problem. Because the state, in the realistic sense in which Renaissance Italians used the term, that is, the government, the persons or party actually in power, was always beset by enemies. There were implacable exiles, the leaders of the faction out of power, prowling just beyond reach. There were rival cities, eager to make the profit out of a neighbour's difficulties. And there were usually secret enemies conspiring within the gates.

Therefore the state, depending for its survival on power, was compelled constantly to seek more power. It was ruthless to anomalies and inconsistencies which a more stable, traditional authority might have seen with indifference. And it widened its boundaries when it could. Because the state (that is, the government) could not count on the automatic, customary allegiance of its citizens, it had to win and hold that allegiance by intensifying the community's self-consciousness. It had to serve, or appear to serve, at least some of the interests of at least some of its people.

The shortest way to these objectives was by war. War dramatized the state. War focused loyalty by identifying opposition with treasonable comfort to those who were plotting to plunder the city's treasures and bring low her liberties. War, if it injured the trade of the competitor, strengthened a monopoly, or cleared away an obstructive toll, might actually benefit the interests of the merchants who were always worth conciliating, even when they were not themselves in power. And successful war, if it resulted in the conquest of a neighbour, or the wiping out of some enclave within one's boundaries, actually increased the power of a machine which fed on power.

So warfare between city and city became endemic all over northern and central Italy. Only commercial giants like Venice and Genoa could afford to wage their wars on the sea lanes and shake half the peninsula with their quarrels. Mostly the war was with the nearest independent city, a convenient day's journey or so away. Thus Perugia warred with Arezzo, Florence with Siena, Verona with Padua. But whether the distances were more or less, whether the cities were tyrannies or republics, great or small, war became the health of the state.

It was also its most dangerous disease. More even than the factional quarrels of the ruling classes and the mounting unrest of the urban proletariat, the endemic wars of Italy threatened its communes with the loss of their hard-won liberties. Even the richest and strongest cities found long-continued wars debilitating. And in the end, victory and defeat were almost equally dangerous. If defeat threatened the return of the exiles, victory risked the seizure of power by a successful general.

The chief danger, however, was complete subjugation. Big cities ate smaller ones. The boundaries of the victors widened ominously towards one another. From 1300 on, the number of independent communes dwindled. Florence took Arezzo and then Pisa, Milan absorbed Brescia and Cremona, Venice annexed Verona and Padua. And these victims had been powerful cities, the conquerors of their smaller neighbours before they were conquered in their turn. Unlikely as it seemed that any one of the rivals could succeed in devouring all the others, no city was strong enough to feel really secure. Under jungle law, the price of survival was incessant alertness. One method of providing for this alertness and of countering the dangers of constant war was found in a new style of diplomacy. It was one of the most characteristic adaptations of the Italian cities to their growing pressure upon one another.

These pressures were intensified, just as the internal development of each state was hastened, by the scale of the peninsular environment. The growth of states of a new kind in Italy was fostered by a favourable ratio between the amount of social energy available and the amount of space to be organized. In any attempt to account for the precocity of Italian Renaissance political institutions, and particularly for their precocity in diplomacy, this point is second in importance only to the peculiarity of the psychological environment of which we have been speaking.

At the beginning of the fifteenth century Western society still lacked the resources to organize stable states on the national scale. On the scale of the Italian city-state it could do so. Internally the smaller distances to be overcome brought the problems of transport and communication, and consequently the problems of collecting taxes and maintaining the central authority, within the range of practical solution. The capital wealth and per capita productivity of the Italian towns may not have been very much greater (it was certainly somewhat greater) than that of the more prosperous regions north of the Alps. But the relative concentration of population and the restricted area to be administered enabled the Italian city-states to find the means necessary for the ends of government to an extent long impossible to the sprawling, loose-jointed northern monarchies. In consequence, not only was the natural pull of each capital intensified by the regular activities of paid officials, but the whole state was able to mobilize its forces with rapidity and ease rarely possible beyond the Alps.

In external relations, scale had a double effect. The comparative efficiency of the new Italian states (in part a function of their limited areas) enabled them to pursue the objectives of their foreign policy with greater continuity and agility than Europe could show elsewhere. At the same time, the presence within the limited space of upper Italy of armed neighbours, equally efficient, agile and predatory, made continuous vigilance in foreign affairs a prime necessity.

North of the Alps the greater spaces to be overcome made the clash of foreign policies less continuous and less menacing. A Philippe le Bel, an Edward III, a Henry V might be just as aggressive, ambitious, and unscrupulous as any Italian tyrant, and such a king might be capable of summoning from his realm a spurt of energy comparable in intensity to the best Italian effort and, of course, enormously more formidable in size. But such bursts of energy proved sporadic. Because they had not yet succeeded in organizing their own internal space, the feudal monarchies were incapable of really sustained exertions, and the more they were driven towards it, the more likely they were to sink back into regional indifference and factional strife. Meanwhile, the relatively vast and unorganized spaces of transalpine Europe cushioned political conflicts.

'Vast spaces' is scarcely an exaggeration. We are accustomed to thinking of space as having shrunk in our day. We are vaguely aware that Moscow is nearer to Chicago now than London was to Paris in Napoleon's time. But we are not so aware that space has been shrinking, though at a slower rate, for a good many centuries and that in terms of commercial intercourse, or military logistics, or even of diplomatic communication, European distances were perceptibly greater in the fourteenth century than in the sixteenth, and remained greater in the sixteenth than they were to become by the eighteenth. In the fourteenth and fifteenth centuries, the continental space of Western Europe still impeded any degree of political organization efficient enough to create a system of continuous diplomatic pressures. Rulers might indulge themselves in foreign adventures out of vainglory or greed or spite; they were not yet compelled to continuous vigilance and continuing action beyond their own frontiers by constant, unavoidable pressures.

It was otherwise in Italy. In upper Italy, by about 1400, space was becoming completely organized; political interstices were filling up; the margins and cushions were shrinking, and the states of the peninsula were being obliged by the resulting pressures to a continuous awareness of each other. Italy was beginning to become such a system of mutually balanced parts in unstable equilibrium as all Europe was to be three hundred years later, a small-scale model for experiments with the institutions of the new state.

For this model to work freely, one other condition was necessary: a relative isolation. For more than a century, from about 1378 to 1492, Italy did enjoy that condition. The schism of the papacy, the impotence of the Empire, the long misery of the Hundred Years War, the recurrent anarchy of the Iberian realms, produced all round Italy a series of crises and conflicts which diverted European pressures from the peninsula. Not that Italy was ever long free from the intrusion of some foreign adventurer in quest of a crown, a lordship or a subsidy. Not that there was ever a decade in which some Italian power was not intriguing to call in a foreigner in order to gain for itself some local advantage. But the foreign intrusions were all on what one may call an Italian scale. None of them threatened more than briefly to become unmanageable, or to alter radically the peninsular balance.

The final result of this long immunity from serious foreign threats was to make Italian statesmen insensitive to the difference in scale between their system and that of Europe, blind to the fact that the tallest giants among the Italian states were pigmies beside the monarchies beyond the Alps. They grew rashly confident of their ability to summon the barbarians when they might be useful and send them home if they became embarrassing. Thus, in the end they failed to understand the catastrophe that overwhelmed them. But the immediate result of the absence of severe outside pressures was to set the states of Italy free for their competitive struggle with one another, and so to intensify their awareness of the structure and tensions of their own peninsular system.

Mainly it was these tensions that produced the new style of diplomacy. Primarily it developed as one functional adaptation of the new type of self-conscious, uninhibited, power-seeking competitive organism. But relatively secondary factors had some influence: the character of Italian warfare and the trend of upper class Italian culture.

Warfare in Italy had changed as busy, pecuniary-minded citizens turned over more and more of the actual fighting to professional soldiers. These were recruited from the more backward regions of the peninsula and commanded by generals who were, in effect, large-scale contractors. Wars waged by mercenary troops under generals mainly zealous for their own professional reputation tended to be less bloody and less decisive than the earlier clashes of citizen militias, though still painfully expensive. War became more rational and, therefore, if less glorious, more civilized. But for this very reason, as campaigns became more and more a series of manoeuvres for political advantage, conducted by relatively small bodies of not always trustworthy professionals, the management of wars made increasing demands upon statesmanship. Success now depended less upon the brutal shock of massed force than upon vigilant and agile politics. The diplomat was needed to supplement the soldier.

At the same time the dominant elements in Italian society began to set a higher value on a form of contest in which their leading citizens, not mercenary strangers who might change sides for the next campaign, were the champions. Business men were delighted by the skills of the diplomat, the nimble anticipation of the next move on the chess board, the subtle gambit which could trip a stronger opponent, the conversion of an enemy into a partner against some common rival, the snatching of victory from defeat by bluff and persuasion and mental dexterity. These qualities were surely more admirable than the brute valour of the condottiere. Diplomacy was for rulers; war for hired men.

It was also natural for the ruling groups—merchants and professional men—most of them with some legal or notarial training (the practical basis of a humanistic education) and most of them experienced in the haggling of the forum and the market place—to believe that words might be as potent as swords. The faith of the merchants and the politicos in the efficacy of diplomatic and forensic persuasion as an auxiliary to or substitute for military force was probably heightened by the reviving interest in classical literature. In turn, no doubt, this faith strengthened the new humanism and helped to give it its prevailing bias towards public rhetoric. The real effectiveness of this form of psychological warfare no one can hope to estimate now. Certainly public opinion among the educated classes was more or less susceptible to propaganda, and certainly, from the time of Petrarch and Cola de Rienzi onward, there was an increasing tendency to try to manipulate this opinion by literary means.

One may be permitted to doubt that an oration by Coluccio Salutati really fell into the scales of political decision with the weight of a thousand horses, but the straight-faced ascription of such a remark to Salutati's most formidable antagonist reminds us of the norm of Renaissance judgment. In that judgment the importance to the state of the diplomat's power of public persuasion, of his ability to deliver a moving formal speech or compose an effectively argued state paper, was at least equal to his utility as an observer, reporter and manipulator of events. In both his aspects, as public orator and as secret negotiator, the fifteenth-century Italian tended to value the successful diplomat with or above the successful general. Not because 'the business of an ambassador is peace', but because the diplomat, like the general, was an agent of the preservation and aggrandizement of the state.

Precedents for Resident Embassies

The pressures of the Italian system led to the invention of a new kind of diplomatic officer, the resident ambassador. Before the end of the fifteenth century, resident ambassadors, unknown elsewhere in Europe, were common throughout Italy. They had become the chief means by which Italian statecraft observed and continually readjusted the unstable equilibrium of power within the peninsula. They were at once the agents and the symbols of a continuous system of diplomatic pressures. And they had proved their worth as one of the most potent weapons of the new states in their unremitting struggle for survival and for the power on which they fed.

As weapons in the struggle for power, resident ambassadors began to be employed by the other states of Europe in about 1500. They have been the most characteristic officers of Western diplomacy ever since. They differentiate our system strikingly from any other we know about elsewhere. Naturally, therefore, scholars have inquired what prior suggestions could be found for this striking invention, and not unnaturally, the answers have been various.

Perhaps it would be as well to say here what is meant by a resident ambassador. He is, to put Wotton's wry epigram into English and disregard its English pun, 'a man sent to lie abroad for his country's good.' He is a regularly accredited envoy with full diplomatic status. But he is sent—this is the significant departure—not to discharge a specific piece of business and then return, as Bernard du Rosier assumed all ambassadors would be, but to remain at his post until recalled, in general charge of the interests of his principal. For the period before 1648 it is not sensible to impose any third requirement. Not all resident embassies were reciprocal. And not all residents were called 'ambassadors,' though whenever there are enough documents it is easy to tell whether they enjoyed that status.

Most sixteenth-century writers about diplomacy were still puzzled and embarrassed by the mere fact of resident ambassadors. When, towards the end of the century, the humanists finally agreed on an account of their origins, the genealogy was fanciful. Some of the provisions of Roman law concern those *legati* sent by the provinces to represent them at the capital. Some of these *legati* were obliged by their business to remain in Rome for years. 'Certainly,' said the humanists, who thought no institution respectable unless it had a classical ancestor, 'anyone can see what happened. When the empire fell, the barbarian kings of the succession states continued to maintain the *legati* of their provinces at the papal court. These were the first resident ambassadors.'

The explanation has not the slightest basis in historical fact, but it continued to survive in the textbooks for a long time. Even today most writers walk warily around it by excluding Rome from any generalization about the history of residents. In many respects, of course, the diplomatic relations of the papacy were quite unlike the relations of secular states with one another. But resident embassies are a secular institution, and the Roman curia played only a slight rôle in their development. There were no resident ambassadors at the Holy See before the 1430's, or at least there is no discernible trace of any. Their appearance at Rome in the fifteenth century was a consequence of the general development.

Two more recent suggestions connect the origin of the system with Rome. A nineteenth-century German canonist thought he had found the first resident ambassadors in the resident representatives maintained by the popes at Constantinople from the sixth to the middle of the eighth century. These officers, called *apokrisiarii* or *responsales,* were in charge of the business which the see of Rome still had with its then temporal overlords, the Eastern emperors. During the same period the patriarchs of Alexandria, Antioch and Jerusalem maintained similar representatives at Constantinople, also for ecclesiastical business. The popes stopped sending any before 750. Certainly nobody in the eighth century thought of such officers as ambassadors. Probably nobody in the fifteenth century remembered them at all.

In the early 1900's another German scholar pointed out that the procurators sent by James II of Aragon to Rome at the end of the thirteenth century actually discharged most of the duties later expected of resident ambassadors. This seems a more plausible precedent. Besides performing their normal legal function, the Aragonese procurators negotiated diplomatic business, and regularly reported to the king the latest developments in Italian politics. For at least a decade they constituted a continuous series. More recently a brilliant study has drawn attention to a whole line of procurators representing the kings of England at Paris in the early 1300's. It suggests that these procurators were prototypes of the resident ambassador, and that similar procurators at the papal court at Avignon, 'became the first permanent diplomatic representatives.'

These instances are interesting for their parallelism in certain respects to the first phase of the establishment of resident embassies, and for their differences in others. Both thirteenth-century examples show a prolonged period of negotiation between two powers with common interests, between the king of Aragon and Pope Boniface VIII, because of their alliance against Frederick of Sicily, and between the English and French kings because of their efforts to solve the problems of their feudal ties without resort to war. Both the Aragon of James II and the England of Edward I and Edward II displayed an unusual degree of diplomatic activity. Both left in their archives evidence of the precocious development of record-keeping and other foreign office techniques necessary for the conduct of continuous diplomacy. These are among the conditions which, nearly a century and a half later, seem to have favored the development of resident embassies. Both England and Aragon, by maintaining procurators at the courts of their partners, did take what looks like the first step in such a direction.

The differences, however, are equally striking. In both countries the burst of diplomatic activity flagged and died away. After the transfer of the papacy to Avignon, the kings of Aragon were not always represented at the curia, and, when they were, their procurators rarely had any but the usual ecclesiastical business. After the 1330's England had no procurators in Paris, and a little later none at Avignon either. There is no evidence that the early experiment was remembered two hundred years afterwards, or that it had any influence as a precedent.

It scarcely could have had, since the very act of sending a legal procurator meant the acknowledgment of a superior legal jurisdiction. Legal procurators were officers attached to a court of law, representing the interests of clients with suits at its bar. If the king of England had not been, in his dignity as duke of Aquitaine, subject to the jurisdiction of the *Parlement de Paris,* he would have sent no legal procurators to France. Of course, not only kings but cities or corporations or individuals sometimes sent such procurators to the papal court. In the English and Aragonese instances confusion is easy because both groups of documents mention two kinds of procurators, legal ones, residing near a court of law, and envoys with powers to conclude diplomatic transactions. But the diplomatic procurators were not residents, and the resident ones were not diplomats.

This does not deny that resident legal procurators were sometimes useful to royal diplomacy. Apparently the Aragonese ones were in the 1290's, and later, after 1450, when most of the major powers were beginning to maintain permanent resident procurators at Rome, some of these church lawyers had occasion to report political news to their clients and even to meddle in diplomacy. In the 1480's England and Spain were represented at Rome by individuals who were accredited both as ambassadors and as procurators. So it is fair enough to say that their procurators at Rome gave transalpine powers their first experience of permanent diplomatic representation and, in a sense, their first resident ambassadors. But by the 1480's resident ambassadors were commonplace among the secular states of Italy. Whatever really influential precedents for the new institution there may have been, must have been available, therefore, in previous Italian experience.

One of the chief functions of the resident ambassador came to be to keep a continuous stream of foreign political news flowing to his home government. Long before 1400 the Italian city-states had the opportunity to appreciate the value of such news to makers of policy. It came to them from two sources, from the consuls of their merchant communities abroad, and from the resident foreign agents of their bankers.

From the twelfth century onward Italian merchants began to cluster in colonies in the chief commercial cities of the Levant and to organize themselves under the jurisdiction of consuls. The consuls were often elected by the members of the community and were primarily judges or arbiters of disputes among its members and the official representatives of its interests before the local authorities. From the first, however, the home governments of the colonists participated in this colonial organization and sent out officers with various titles to supervise and direct it. Later the consuls themselves acquired a more official standing and were frequently appointed by the governments of their native cities and directly responsible to them. In a sense they represented not just the interests, say, of the Pisan merchants at Acre, the Genoese at Constantinople or the Venetians at Alexandria, but the whole power and dignity of the Pisan, Genoese and Venetian Republics.

Strictly speaking, consuls were not diplomats. Their status depended not on the general principles of international law but on special treaties with the powers on whose territory they were. But they did in fact perform some of the services later performed by resident ambassadors. Although any really important message or negotiation would be entrusted to a special embassy, consuls did sometimes deliver messages on behalf of their governments to the local authorities, sometimes, therefore, to reigning princes. Sometimes they did negotiate on behalf of their governments. In some places they had positions assigned to them at public functions. And the consuls of some republics, those of Genoa and Venice, at least, were expected to report regularly news of political as well as of commercial interest.

For Venice, anyway, a case might be made for her consuls having been the precursors of her resident ambassadors. One Venetian representative abroad, the *bailo* at Constantinople, performed both consular and diplomatic functions in the fifteenth century. Other consuls were sometimes given special diplomatic credentials. And all the surviving evidence indicates that by the latter part of the fifteenth century regular consular reports to the Venetian Senate had become a long established custom. Apparently the Venetians themselves thought there was a close connection between the two institutions. When, in 1523, the Venetian ambassador was recalled from England, the Senate voted that, until he could be replaced, the interests of the republic should be confided to the Venetian consul at London, 'according to the custom of former times.'

Even before Venetian consuls appeared in European cities, the merchant bankers of Lombardy and Tuscany had begun to maintain permanent resident representatives, the medieval equivalents of branch managers, at the courts or in the commercial centres where they did most business. Since much of that business was loans to sovereigns, the access of banking agents to the prince and his council could be as easy as that any diplomat enjoyed. In the correspondence of these agents the political news must often have been the most profitable part of the letter. When the bankers thus represented were members of the ruling oligarchy of their city, or the trusted clients of its tyrant, the reports of their agents could supply the basis for political action, and the conduct of the agents themselves might be guided, by political motives. When the banker reported to was himself the actual, if unofficial, ruler of his city—when, for example, he was Cosimo de'Medici—the diplomatic function of his foreign branch managers might become very considerable indeed. After 1434 it was progressively harder to distinguish between the resident representatives of the Medici bank and the political agents of the Florentine state. But this is a late instance.

Before 1400, the tyrants and oligarchs of northern Italy must already have learned all that experience with consuls and branch banks had to teach. The earliest Italian resident diplomatic agents are to be found well before that date. They were not called 'ambassadors' at first or entitled (as we shall see) to diplomatic honours and immunities. But they were received in the cities where they resided as the actual agents of their masters, and were charged with most of the duties later discharged by resident ambassadors. In northern and central Italy between 1380 and 1450 this kind of semi-official resident agent became increasingly common. Towards 1450 several of the earliest official residents of whom we have any certain notice began their careers as members of this ambiguous class, among them that Nicodemus of Pontremoli upon whom the consensus of recent writers has thrust, on somewhat slender grounds, the distinction of being the first resident ambassador.

We shall probably never be able to lay down with certainty every step in the period of transition before 1455. Many records have vanished. Those which survive are largely unpublished and inadequately explored.

Nor is it likely that any number of documents would enable us to assign with confidence respective weights to the influence of such antecedents as procurators, consuls and banking agents on the invention of resident ambassadors. But the main outline of the story is clear. The new institution was Italian. It developed in the hundred years before 1454. And whatever suggestions, possible antecedents, and analogies may have been offered, the development was, in the main, an empirical solution to an urgent practical problem. Italy first found the system of organizing interstate relationships which Europe later adopted, because Italy, towards the end of the Middle Ages was already becoming what later all Europe became.

22. The Florentine Patriciate

GENE BRUCKER

Marvelous energy and creative activity in the arts, literature, trade, commerce, and political life were characteristic of northern Italy, and especially of Florence, during the Renaissance. Who were the people who composed this fabulous society? What were their goals, dreams, and ideals? What values and traditions ordered their lives and undertakings? What was the structure of their society, and the relationships within it? These questions are of importance, and of great interest to anyone who would appreciate the spirit of the Italian Renaissance. Gene Brucker has examined them in his recent Renaissance Florence, *which was written especially for the* Historical Cities *series. Brucker brings a familiarity with Florence and a good deal of new information based on personal research in Florentine archives to this study.*

Brucker asserts that there was a basic contradiction within the structure of the Florentine patriciate, the well-off upper classes. The principle of aristocratic status, which tended to keep the social strata more or less static, was forced to give way to that of egalitarianism, a fluid measurement that admitted to the patriciate those who by hard work, marriage, or plain good fortune could improve their material position. Florence did not possess a completely "open society" however, and the fundamental contrast between a relatively stable, wealthy patriciate and a majority of depressed, and sometimes oppressed, wage laborers should be kept in mind.

Brucker distinguishes another basic contradiction besetting the upper classes in

Source: Gene Brucker, *Renaissance Florence* (New York: John Wiley & Sons, 1969), pp. 89–92, 101–109. Copyright © 1969. Reprinted by permission of John Wiley & Sons, Inc.

four distinct and often opposite traditions, each with its own value system. The Christian tradition demanded renunciation of material concerns and attention to spiritual values; it was opposed by the mercantile, which stressed success in business, as measured by the acquisition of wealth and the improvement of family fortunes. The feudal tradition, which had a particular importance for many older noble families, emphasized independence and often egotistic self-reliance, while the communal tradition demanded subordination of the individual to the common good of the municipality. The contrasts and interpenetration of these varying strains in Florentine society produced much change, and were apparently largely responsible for the vitality and energy of Florentine society.

Brucker's study is a fresh and very interpretive view of Florence, based on a wide variety of sources: civic records, diaries, journals, business correspondence, public documents, etc. His approach is challenging, and even if his conclusions have not yet all received the certification of orthodoxy, they will provide a point for discussion for some time to come. One may ask if the pluralistic Florentine social heritage is a prime causal factor in the Florentine achievement? And, if so, should we generalize from this to infer that one can expect to find a correlation between pluralism and creative achievement?

The Structure of Patrician Society

The . . . analysis of the Florentine economy has focused particularly upon the activities of those merchants and industrialists who owned a major portion of the city's capital resources and who controlled the large business firms. This concentration on "big business" has neglected other important dimensions of the economy: the small, local enterprises of retailers and artisans, the activities of workers in cloth factories and building projects, the unremitting toil of the peasantry upon whose labor the city's existence and survival literally depended. To justify this emphasis, it is not sufficient to claim that the activities of rich bankers and merchants are more fully documented (although this is true), or more varied and interesting than those of a pork butcher or a cloth shearer. It can be argued, however, that the scale and magnitude of Florence's international trade and banking, and of her cloth production, was a distinctive feature of this economy, which set the city apart from smaller towns like Pistoia or Parma or Forlì. A similar argument is used to justify the focus of this chapter upon the social behavior and values of those families that constituted Florence's patriciate, her aristocracy. By virtue of their wealth, pedigree, and prestige, these houses formed the most powerful and influential "class" in the community. Moreover, they possessed certain distinctive qualities and traits, a particular outlook, which distinguished them from the rest of Florentine society and, to a certain degree, from the aristocracies of other major Italian cities. In a literal sense, these patricians were the creators of the Renaissance: its style of life, its values, its modes of thought and perception. The remaining chapters of this book [*Renaissance Florence*] are devoted to the analysis of this new style and these values: in politics, religion, education, and art.

Two important attributes of this social order were the critical importance of wealth as a determinant of status, and the survival, from the city's medieval past, of a corporate structure and ethos. These qualities, which were blended in the Florentine crucible, were fundamentally irreconcilable. A capitalistic economic order is characterized by risk, uncertainty, flexibility, and sharp fluctuations. It fosters individualism and contributes to social mobility and dislocation through perpetual redistribution of wealth. Conversely, a corporate social order stresses group action; its goals are stability, security, conformity. It gives its members a sense of identity, of "belonging"; it teaches them to accept the principles of a hierarchic social structure, a sense of social place. It is instructive to visualize Florentine history during its most dynamic period as a perpetual conflict between these two contradictory elements. The tension created by their juxtaposition may have been a source of vitality and creativity. It also explains some peculiar features of this society in the early Renaissance: the coexistence of cosmopolitanism, a by-product of Florence's international economic and political role, and of parochialism, an attitude encouraged by the corporate social order.

The family constituted the basic nucleus of Florentine social life throughout the Renaissance, and the bond existing between family members was the strongest cement in the city's social structure. One of its sources of vitality was tradition, the collective memory of a past when family members were forced to unite and act as a group in order to survive. The strong kinship sense of such prominent families as the Cavalcanti and the Buondelmonti was nourished by memories of the roles these houses had played in the city's history—the street fights against rival clans, the exploits of their ancestors in battles against Florence's enemies. Physical evidence of this cohesiveness was the concentration of a family's households in one district, along a single street, or surrounding a square. Other kinds of evidence survive in written form: in the list of offices and dignities held by members of a family, in the proud claims to family antiquity and distinction recorded in private diaries. As early as 1350, a member of one prominent mercantile house, the Alberti, commissioned an agent to search for documents which would throw light upon his family's origins. Sixty-five years later, Doffo Spini expressed surprise that no member of his family had ever written about their ancestors; he then recorded all of the data he could recall pertaining to the early Spini. Most diarists had rather inflated views of the wealth and social status of their ancestors; few were as modest as the merchant Giovanni Morelli who wrote in 1400 that his forebears were poor but honorable folk who had migrated into Florence from the countryside in the thirteenth century. Morelli justified the composition of his family history by stating that he wished to instruct his sons concerning their past, and he added: "For everyone today pretends a family background of great antiquity, and I want to establish the truth about ours." No genealogical tree, however, was so fanciful as that created for the Medici by a court historian of the sixteenth century, who traced that family's origins to one of Charlemagne's captains who had accompanied the emperor into Italy in the eighth century.

It was to the family that the individual owed his primary obligation; the rank and condition of the family largely determined the course which his own life was to take. The family's status (and this was carefully weighed and measured) established the individual's position in society. The family provided wealth, business and political connections, the opportunity for public office. Not only was a man's bride normally chosen by his father but the paternal choice was limited to those houses similar in rank to his own. Even after a son was legally emancipated from his father, he was bound to his relatives by many ties. A head of a household who planned to marry his daughter would invariably consult with his kin about the choice of son-in-law. Any important decision—the purchase of land, a marriage contract, the making of a will—was made with the advice and consent of father, uncles, cousins. From this system, which restricted the individual's actions, he received certain positive benefits. He could normally expect his relatives to assist him in case of grave financial need, and to give him support in lawsuits. Although the vendetta was slowly disappearing as a social institution, a scion of a large and powerful family could be secure in the knowledge that only a very bold man would deliberately court the hostility of his kin by attacking him.

In a society thus organized around the family, the marriage contract was a document of supreme significance. First, it was an important financial transaction. The size of the dowry was an indication of the economic status of the contracting parties. In 1400, a dowry of 1000 florins was common in patrician marriages. In his account book, the silk merchant Gregorio Dati described how he invested dowry money in business enterprises and received substantial profits from his wife's capital. Marriage connections also had political implications. It was customary for families belonging to the same party or faction to intermarry. Conversely, an alliance contracted with a family in political disfavor was a dangerous and foolhardy enterprise.

Marriages were also indices of social status, and of the rise and decline of particular families. In 1396 a merchant from a family of middling rank, Francesco Davanzati, wrote to his father in Venice of a marriage arranged with the socially prominent Peruzzi: "Bartolomeo has taken a bride and has made a great and noble marriage alliance. . . . Truly none of our ancestors have ever made so honorable a marriage." But families which had suffered misfortune were often forced to marry beneath them. One of the city's most prominent houses, the Strozzi, lost influence and status in 1434 when their political enemies, the Medici, came to power. In 1448 Alessandra Strozzi wrote to her exiled son in Naples about a marriage which she had negotiated between her daughter and a young silk manufacturer named Giovanni Parenti who (she wrote) "possessed a little status." The phrase contains a hint of irony, for Parenti's grandfather had been an artisan. Giovanni's marriage with a Strozzi was a clear sign that the Parenti had "arrived," and also that the fortunes of one Strozzi household had declined.

Social Values and Their Inner Contradictions

The behavior patterns and values of the Florentine patriciate represented a blend of four distinct traditions, often incompatible and frequently irreconcilable. In order of antiquity but not necessarily of vitality, these traditions were Christian, feudal, mercantile, and communal. In his behavior and his ideals, each patrician was a composite of these traditions. Frequently, one element predominated over the others, and gave a distinctive and unique cast to the individual's personality. No one escaped the tensions and contradictions of this pluralistic social heritage.

The discords of these traditions are significant. Like all Europeans, the Florentine's values were influenced by his religious beliefs. From childhood he was instructed in the Christian virtues of love, charity, humility, and poverty. In sermons and devotional literature, he was warned against the sins of pride and avarice, of gluttony and lechery. He was taught to shun wealth, to be content with his lot in this vale of tears, to be humble in his demeanor, and to turn the other cheek to his enemy. The values which he inherited from the feudal past were quite different. These were largely the ideals of Europe's warrior nobility; they emphasized such qualities as honor, pride, glory, and generosity, and such bellicose military virtues as aggressiveness and valor. At variance with both of these traditions, the Christian and the feudal, were the values derived from those business pursuits upon which the city's wealth and power were established. Finally, the civic values derived from membership in, and loyalty to, the political community often conflicted with these older traditions. The tensions arising from this particular category of disharmony will be examined in the next chapter, which focuses upon politics.

Some of these value conflicts are revealed by Florentine attitudes concerning occupations. The two most respected professions in the city were the law and international trade. Lawyers enjoyed the high prestige which Florentines (and all Europeans) accorded to men with university degrees. But knowledge of the law was particularly valued in Florence, where social and economic relations were governed by a complex and sophisticated legal code, and where the lawyer's talents were useful in politics. The prominent status granted to the international merchant distinguished Florence from other cities which did not engage so extensively in European commerce. Gregorio Dati was stating a commonly held opinion when he wrote: "A Florentine who is not a merchant, who has not traveled through the world, seeing foreign nations and peoples and then returned to Florence with some wealth, is a man who enjoys no esteem whatsoever."

This exaltation of the merchant was not the simplistic approbation of a commercial society for the activity from which it derived much of its wealth. The attitude was more complex, and it reflects the evolution of the city's social structure. Gregorio Dati was probably correct in his claim (made in 1410) that the international merchant was universally respected, but his statement would not have been so valid a half-century earlier, when there still survived among the families which descended (or pretended to descend) from feudal nobility a conviction that commerce was an unworthy and degrading occupation. Luca da Panzano, a descendant of an old noble house which had received a baronial title in the twelfth century from the Holy Roman Emperor, commented on his selection to the Merchants' court that "since we were old nobility, no one from our house . . . ever held this office, since they were not merchants." A scion of another noble family, Bernardo da Castiglionchio, drew a finer distinction between the categories of mercantile pursuits. He noted with pride that no member of his family had been forced by poverty to engage in a lowly trade or occupation. Some of his ancestors had been merchants, he admitted, but they had engaged in "noble and honest not base merchandise, voyaging to France and England and trading in cloth and wool as do all the greater and better men of the city."

In the professional hierarchy established by Florentine preferences and prejudices, cloth manufacturers and bankers ranked immediately below the lawyers and international merchants. As late as 1400, the stigma of usury—illegal gain—still attached to the banking profession. The Prato merchant Francesco Datini was advised in 1398 to abandon his plan to establish a bank by one of his associates on the grounds that banking was less profitable, less honorable and less pleasing to God, "for there is not one [banker] who does not make usurious contracts." Farther down on the scale were businessmen who participated in local trade (druggists, goldsmiths, used-clothes dealers), and then the petty shopkeepers and artisans: masons, carpenters, winesellers, blacksmiths, and bakers. Physicians occupied a median position in this hierarchy, below the great merchants and industrialists but above the shopkeepers. University professors were accorded respect and deference, as were the humanist scholars who dominated Florentine intellectual life in the fifteenth century. But grammar school teachers possessed as little social status and wealth as their modern counterparts. The tax assessments of *maestri di grammatica* were among the lowest in the city, and they were not permitted to organize into a guild and thus be eligible for public office.

A lucid exposition of the social values of the Florentine patriciate is found in the memoirs of Giovanni Morelli, written between 1393 and 1421. Morelli was a wealthy merchant of solidly respectable (but not distinguished) lineage. His memoirs reflect his mercantile background and orientation, and his ethics are essentially those of the successful business entrepreneur. Thrift, sobriety, caution, restraint are the supreme virtues. Morelli considered the conservation of the family patrimony to be a primary goal of life. So fearful was he of business failure that he advised his sons to operate alone, and never to employ factors or agents. He warned against the practice of usury less through fear of divine retribution than for concern about legal penalties. Recognizing that business talent was not inherited by everyone, he counseled those without it to abandon trade, to invest their money in land and live as rentiers. He repeatedly warned his sons to trust no one, not business associates, peasants, or factors and employees in one's shop. This obsessive fear of betrayal might seem to be a manifestation of Morelli's paranoid personality, but similar sentiments were expressed by several of his fellow-citizens. He was articulating the economic insecurity of the whole society.

Morelli's values are expressed with greatest clarity in his judgment of others. His father Paolo was a man of supreme talent and worth (in his son's opinion), who triumphed over many obstacles and difficulties to achieve success. He had been tricked out of part of his inheritance by his brothers, but rather than harbor resentment he continued to treat them with Christian affection. "He maintained close relations with them, demonstrating his great love by helping them as much as possible, by advising them on their affairs, and thus demonstrating his faith and hope in them." Disaster struck the family in 1363, when the plague killed his brother, and Paolo was forced to work hard to save the family patrimony. Then he too died of the plague in 1374, when he was forty. Had he lived another ten years, Giovanni wrote, "he would have achieved a great fortune of 50,000 florins."

The qualities stressed in this biography are astuteness in economic affairs, family loyalty, and sociability. These traits were also lauded in Morelli's description of his cousin, Giovanni di Bartolomeo. As a young man, Giovanni was "very obliging, almost prodigal, so that his expenditures were frivolous and not very honorable." But marriage sobered him: "He became the most thrifty man in the world and an excellent administrator of his property." Morelli also wrote approvingly of his cousin's social demeanor: "He was an agreeable man, very lighthearted, eager to converse, astute, affectionate, friendly, a fine storyteller." From other sources, it is clear that these gregarious qualities, the ability to forge warm and intimate human relationships, was a prized asset in Florence, and one that did not derive from the business ethic. Another trait which Morelli praised was liberality. Of his father Paolo he wrote: "He was a great giver of alms, and he never refused anything asked of him by rich or poor, and particularly money." Yet Morelli also emphasized the virtues of parsimony and austerity in living habits. Unconsciously, he was expressing a conflict between the burgher impulse toward thrift and the aristocratic trait of open-handed generosity.

This conflict between mercantile and noble values was also reflected in other dimensions of social behavior. In the distant past, the Florentine bourgeoisie had created an image of the feudal magnate as a violent, lawless figure, who habitually exploited and maltreated peaceful merchants and artisans. As the old feudal nobility became domesticated and practically indistinguishable from the urban bourgeoisie, this image bore less relation to reality. Yet the myth persisted into the fifteenth century. It found expression in countless accusations against members of magnate families, who were described as *grandi e possenti,* as in this secret denunciation delivered to a judge in 1394: "You should know that the Bardi are a great and arrogant family and they have no concern for anyone, and every day they use violence against everyone [whom they encounter]." This sentiment also was articulated in the petitions for family divisions, in which the appellants invariably characterized themselves (as did the Velluti family in 1395) as "pacific and tranquil men who seek to maintain peaceful relations with everyone," and who described their relatives as men "who seek to offend others and who do not pursue peaceful ways." Yet the manners of the feudal nobility were not universally despised, even by the peace-loving merchants. Displays of strength and force, even aggressive and arrogant manifestations of power, still commanded respect, fear, and admiration.

The Florentine patrician was very troubled by the gulf between Christian norms and the realities of social behavior. In three particular areas, the conflict was acute: in the conception of "honor," in sexual mores, and in the problem of wealth. The stress upon honor, derived in large part from the chivalric code of the feudal nobility, permeated the whole system of patrician values. To live honorably meant to act according to the standards of one's class, and to be imbued with a sense of personal dignity and responsibility. Dishonorable behavior comprised any act that lowered or demeaned the status and prestige of the individual or his family. In a capsule biography of a distant relative, Piero di Ciore Pitti, the lawyer Donato Velluti (d. 1370) described a man who had plumbed the depths of dishonor. After wasting his paternal inheritance, Pitti earned his livelihood as a soldier and then as a day laborer in a cloth factory. "He was wounded by one of the Machiavelli and never engaged in a vendetta. He took for a wife Monna Bartolomea, the grand-daughter of Bongianni, the wine seller, who had been the whore of other men, and with whom he lived in a miserable state." When Pitti died in a hovel near the church of S. Giorgio, none of his relatives attended his funeral. Florentines displayed little charity or pity for the fallen, even those who were not wholly responsible for their fate. One unfortunate member of a prominent family, Giovanni Corsini, was described by a chronicler as "so immersed in a brimming expanse of misery and poverty that . . . he was even despised by his own relatives." The church's exaltation of humility, its denunciation of pride, made very little impression upon the Florentine patriciate.

The sexual mores of the upper class coincided with the Christian ethic in a single respect: in the universal concern for the chastity of its women, before and after marriage. Women of good family were closely guarded from contacts with strange men; they left their houses rarely, and then to go to mass or to family celebrations. The intimate relations between young men and women which Boccaccio describes in his *Decameron* are fictional; even the crisis of the Black Death would not have led to such free contact between the sexes. Boccaccio certainly exaggerated the extent of illicit love and infidelity within the patriciate, but his descriptions of licentious behavior had some basis in fact. Paolo Sassetti, a merchant of respectable family, recorded in his diary the fallen state of his cousin Letta, the daughter of Federigo Sassetti, who died in 1383 in the house of her paramour, Giovanni Porcellini. "May the devil take her soul, for she has brought shame and dishonor to our house." Sassetti reconciled himself to this situation by commenting that men could not repair what God had decreed in punishment for their sins, but then he added: "We will launch such a vendetta [against Porcellini] that our pride will be assuaged."

No social stigma attached to the male for sexual relations with other women, so long as he did not bring dishonor to his family by marrying a mistress of lowly birth. Florentine men took their pleasure with women whenever opportunity and inclination permitted, and this was not infrequent. Common targets of their affection were the domestic servants and slaves of the household, although it was not unusual for alliances to be formed with women of the lower classes in city and countryside. Giovanni Morelli's account of his cousin's extramarital relations is not untypical. "He had no children from his wife Simona, although he did have several illegitimate offspring, some from a woman of good family, and some from a slave who was very beautiful, and whom he later married to someone from the Mugello." With uncharacteristic reticence, he added: "I don't wish to name her husband, since it would not be proper [to identify] this family, for it is of quite good condition." The offspring of these illicit alliances were not ostracized by society, but they did suffer discrimination. Normally, they did not inherit a full share of their father's property, although they frequently received a monetary bequest. The commune would occasionally approve petitions to legitimize a bastard child, but only if the father had no male heirs.

The problem of wealth, its acquisition and its use, created the sharpest discord in the ethical and moral system of the Florentine patriciate. The traditional Christian hostility to riches was constantly reiterated in the sermons of friars, in devotional literature, and in the writings of theologians. Efforts to bridge the gap between belief and practice, between word and deed, constitute one of the most significant themes in the history of this city, and, indeed, in the history of late medieval Europe. Every Florentine felt some guilt for living in a society whose material existence conflicted so sharply with its spiritual ideal.

Florentines responded to this dilemma in two ways, either by admitting guilt and seeking to assuage it, or denying it by justifying the acquisition of wealth. Evidence for the open and candid admission of guilt is most abundant in the testaments of fourteenth-century merchants, who specifically admitted that their fortunes were increased by usury. The grandfather of Cosimo de' Medici, Bicci (d. 1363), stipulated in his will that 50 *lire* should be set aside to compensate those from whom he had taken money illicitly. Society equated the practice of usury with damnation, and the souls of manifest usurers were believed to be lost irretrievably. They were not allowed to make wills, nor were they given Christian burial. After 1437, only Jews were permitted to operate pawnbroking shops; thus the authorities could not be accused of permitting Christian souls to suffer eternal damnation. Although usury was strictly defined, and strenuous efforts were made to distinguish between licit and illicit gain, the failure of the theologians to agree upon these distinctions sowed doubts in men's minds which were never entirely dispelled. The tacit admission of guilt was usually expressed by large bequests to charitable or religious foundations. Vespasiano da Bisticci was describing the mental state of many businessmen when he noted that Cosimo de' Medici "had prickings of conscience that certain portions of his wealth . . . had not been righteously [i.e., licitly] gained," and Cosimo's decision to rebuild the monastery of S. Marco was one of many similar acts made by troubled men. The artistic creations of medieval and Renaissance Florence are the result, in large part, of the guilt feelings of the patriciate.

Two random examples will illustrate specific ways in which some individuals responded to the tensions between the Christian ideal and the realities of the business world. Donato Velluti described a strange interlude in the life of his cousin Bernardo, who had followed the normal routine of the merchant class by entering a cloth factory as an apprentice, and then establishing a partnership. During Lent in the year 1350, he experienced a religious crisis and fled to the monastery of Certosa. There he spent a year as a novice, rejecting all appeals from his relatives to return to the world, and he remained "as firm as a rock [in his determination] to stay there and die." While settling his temporal affairs before taking final vows, he became involved in a controversy with his uncle over a disputed inheritance. Fearful that his orphaned brothers and sisters would lose their patrimony, he abruptly changed his mind and informed the prior that he was leaving the monastery. Ignoring the monk's pleas and warnings that he was jeopardizing his soul, Bernardo returned to his shop in Florence and picked up the strings of his abandoned mercantile career.

The solution adopted by Gregorio Dati to placate his conscience was less drastic, but no less revealing of the tensions under which the merchant lived and worked. In his "secret book," Dati lamented his failure to abide by the precepts of his religion. "For our sins," he wrote, "we are subjected to many tribulations of spirit and to many bodily passions in this miserable life, and if it were not for the aid of divine grace . . . we would perish daily." He confessed that during his lifetime he had regularly disobeyed God's commandments, and then added: "Since I do not trust myself to reform my habits to their proper state, I must begin slowly, step by step." Dati promised that he would refrain from any business activity on feast days, and that he would not allow others to labor on his behalf "for gain or temporal benefit." But the merchant realized that the flesh was weak, and that circumstances might force him to break his resolution. Thus he promised to give 1 florin to the poor whenever he violated this rule, "and I have written this down to keep it firmly in mind for my embarrassment, if I contravene it." Dati also sought to protect himself from religious penalties by stipulating that these resolutions were not, strictly speaking, vows, "but I make them to encourage myself to observe these good practices, insofar as it is possible for me." As befits a sensible merchant, he limited his commitments and obligations, and sought to steer a prudent course between the demands of the world and of the spirit. He recognized and accepted the dangers of this temporizing course, which required both courage and faith.

23. Some Conjectures About the Impact of Printing

ELIZABETH L. EISENSTEIN

Modern technology has moved at such a rapid, dizzying pace in the last few decades that many a contemporary student has had his sense of awe and wonder at new inventions jaded beyond redemption. How difficult it must be for someone who can watch instantaneous communication between astronauts on the moon and their control station on earth to become excited about anything as mundane as the invention of movable type! And yet, for untold millennia, communication among men was limited by very practical and inescapable considerations. To possess a book, before printing had been invented, meant to be rich and fortunate enough to commission someone to copy, laboriously and by hand, the book one wanted. The risk of errors in transcription was enormous; the delay in waiting for one's book could be great, and annoying. Most of all, it was virtually impossible for someone with novel or revolutionary ideas to reach a mass audience quickly and effectively. With the invention of printing, all this changed.

In the following selection Elizabeth L. Eisenstein, who has devoted much effort recently to consideration of the role that printing has played in Western history, offers some new perspectives. She exhibits a great deal of originality in suggesting a number of areas in which further research should be carried out.

Source: Elizabeth L. Eisenstein, "Some Conjectures about the Impact of Printing on Western Society and Thought: A Preliminary Report," *The Journal of Modern History,* XL (1968), pp. 1–56. Reprinted by permission of the University of Chicago Press and the author. [Footnotes omitted.]

Her article is a good example of seminal work likely to have a significant effect on historical research for some time to come; a panel on this subject held at the 1971 meeting of the American Historical Association is testimony to this view. This article should stimulate thought and discussion about several questions. What use was made of the new invention at first? What market did it serve? What effects did it have on other areas of knowledge? Interested students may wish to read the final part of this article on "The Rise of the Reading Public," or Professor Eisenstein's "The Advent of Printing and the Problem of the Renaissance," Past and Present, *No. 45 (1969).*

We should note the force, effect, and consequences of inventions which are nowhere more conspicuous than in those three which were unknown to the ancients, namely, printing, gunpowder, and the compass. For these three have changed the appearance and state of the whole world.—FRANCIS BACON, Novum organum, *Aphorism 129*

This paper presents portions of a work that is still in progress. It deals with "the force, effect, and consequences" of the first invention singled out by Bacon. Much has been written about how the way was paved for Gutenberg's invention and about the problem of defining just what he did invent. There are few studies, however, of the consequences that ensued once the new process had been launched. Explicit theories as to what these consequences were have not yet been framed, let alone tested or contested. To develop such theories is much easier said than done. Still, I think the effort should be made. Consequences entailed by a major transformation have to be reckoned with whether we pay attention to them or not. In one guise or another they will enter into our accounts and can best be dealt with when they do not slip in unobserved.

To dwell on the reasons why Bacon's advice ought to be followed by others is probably less helpful than trying to follow it oneself. This task clearly outstrips the competence of any single individual. It calls for the pooling of many talents and the writing of many books. Collaboration is difficult to obtain as long as the relevance of the topic to different fields of study remains obscure. Before aid can be enlisted, it seems necessary to develop some tentative hypotheses and to suggest how they relate to particular historical problems. This is the purpose of my work in progress, some samples of which I am offering here. Speculations that are possibly unfounded and certainly still shaky will be presented to stimulate thought and encourage further study.

Defining the Initial Change of Phase: An Invisible Revolution in the Fifteenth Century

As you may have noted, I have already reformulated Bacon's advice by taking it to pertain, not to a single invention that is coupled with others, but rather to the launching of a new process and to a major transformation. Indecision about what is meant by the advent of printing has, I think, helped to muffle concern about its possible consequences and made them more difficult to track down. It is difficult to find out what happened in a particular Mainz workshop in the 1450's. When pursuing other inquiries, it seems almost prudent to bypass so problematic an event. This does not apply to the appearance of new occupational groups, workshops, techniques, trade networks, and products unknown anywhere in Europe before the mid-fifteenth century and found in every regional center by the early sixteenth century. To pass by all that when dealing with other problems would seem to be incautious. For this reason, among others, I am skipping over the perfection of a new process for printing with movable types and will take as my point of departure, instead, the large-scale utilization of this process.

By the advent of printing, then, I mean the establishment of presses in major urban centers throughout Europe during an interval that coincides, roughly, with the era of incunabula. So few studies have been devoted to this point of departure that no conventional label has yet been attached to it. One might talk about a basic change in a mode of production, or a communications revolution, or (most explicitly) a shift from scribal to typographical culture. Whatever label is used, it should be understood to cover a large cluster of relatively simultaneous, closely interrelated changes, each of which needs closer study and more explicit treatment —as the following quick sketch may suggest.

First of all, the marked increase in the output of books and the more drastic reduction in the number of man-hours required to turn them out deserve stronger emphasis. At present there is a tendency to think of a steady increase in book production during the last century of scribal culture followed by a steady increase during the first century of printing. An evolutionary model of change is applied to a situation that seems to call for a revolutionary one. A hard-working copyist turned out two books in little less than a year. An average edition of an early printed book ranged from two hundred to one thousand copies. Chaucer's clerk longed for twenty books to fill his shelf; ten copyists had to be recruited to serve each such clerk down to the 1450's, whereas one printer was serving twenty before 1500. The point is that references to "enormous numbers" of scribal books are deceptive. With regard to quantitative output, an abrupt change, not a gradual one, probably occurred.

Similarly, qualitative changes affecting the nature of the book itself —its format, arrangement of contents, page layouts, and illustrations— need to be underlined. That late manuscripts resembled early incunabula, that scribes and printers copied each others' products for several decades, should not distract attention from changes that occurred when the single text was replaced by a first edition and the manuscript became "copy" that was edited and processed before duplication. Even before 1500 such changes were being registered. Title pages and running heads were becoming common, and texts were being illustrated by "exactly repeatable pictorial statements" designed by woodcarvers and engravers. Not only were products from artisan workshops introduced into scholarly texts, but the new mode of book production itself brought metalworkers and merchants into contact with schoolmen. A most interesting study might be devoted to a comparison of the talents and skills mobilized within printers' workshops with those previously employed in scriptoria.

Other changes associated with the shift from a retail trade to a wholesale industry also need to be explored. Early crises of overproduction and drives to tap new markets could be contrasted with the incapacity of manuscript dealers and copyists to supply existing demands. The movement of centers of book production from university towns and patrician villas to commercial centers, the organization of new trade networks and fairs, competition over lucrative privileges and monopolies, and restraints imposed by new official controls have all been covered in special accounts. But the implications of such changes need to be spelled out. If it is true that the main bulk of book production was taken out of the hands of churchmen, who ran most large scriptoria, and was lodged in those of early capitalists, who established printing plants, this is surely worth spelling out. If such a statement will not hold up or merely needs to be qualified, then this too is something we need to be told.

We also need to hear more about the job printing that accompanied buok-printing. It lent itself to commercial advertising, official propaganda, seditious agitation, and bureaucratic red tape as no scribal procedure ever had. A new form of silent publicity enabled printers not only to advertise their own wares but also to contribute to, and profit from, the expansion of other commercial enterprises. What effects did the appearance of new advertising techniques have on commerce and industry? Possibly some answers to this question are known. Probably others can still be found. Many others aspects of job printing and the changes it entailed clearly need further study. The calendars and indulgences issued from the Mainz workshops of Gutenberg and Fust, for example, warrant at least as much attention as the more celebrated Bibles. Indeed the mass production of indulgences illustrates very neatly the sort of change that often goes overlooked so that its consequences are more difficult to reckon with than perhaps they need be.

In contrast to the changes sketched above, those that were associated with the consumption of new printed products are more intangible, indirect, and difficult to handle. A large margin for uncertainty must be left when dealing with such changes. Many of them—those associated with the spread of literacy, for example—also have to be left for later discussion, since prolonged transformations were entailed. Yet relatively abrupt changes belonging to my original cluster *were* experienced by already literate sectors. More thought might be given to the social composition of these sectors. Although rigorous analysis is impossible on the basis of scribal records, useful guesses could be made. Did printing at first serve an urban patriciate as a "divine art" or more humble folk as a "poor man's friend"? Since it was described in both ways by contemporaries, possibly it served in both ways. If we think about Roman slaves or later parish priests, lay clerks, and notaries, it seems that literacy was by no means congruent with elite social status. The new presses, therefore, probably did not *gradually* make available to low-born men what had previously been restricted to the high born. Instead, changes in mental habits and attitudes entailed by access to printed materials affected a wide social spectrum from the outset. In fifteenth-century England, for example, mercers and scriveners engaged in a manuscript book trade were already catering to the needs of lowly bakers and merchants as well as to those of lawyers, aldermen, and knights. The new mode of book production also left many unlettered nobles and squires untouched for some time.

While postponing until later conjectures about social and psychological transformations, certain points should be noted here. One must distinguish, as Altick suggests, between literacy and habitual book-reading. Even down to the present, by no means all who master the written word become members of a book-reading public. Learning *to read* is different, moreover, from learning *by reading*. Reliance on apprenticeship training, oral communication, and special mnemonic devices had gone together with mastering letters in the age of scribes. After the advent of printing, however, learning by doing became more sharply distinguished from learning by reading, while the role played by hearsay and memory arts diminished. Since they affected the transmission of all forms of knowledge, such changes seem relevant to historical inquiries of every kind. Issues pertaining to shifts in book-reading habits go far beyond the special concerns of literary historians. They have a direct bearing on economic, legal, technological, and political developments as well. Last but not least, the most important members of the new book-reading public in the age of incunabula are most often overlooked. They belonged to the new occupational groups created by the new mode of production. Those who processed texts or presided over the new presses were the first to read the products that came off them. In particular, early scholar-printers themselves registered most forcefully the consequences of access to printed materials. It is possibly because of this kind of "feedback" that the infant industry was so rapidly modernized. As early as the 1480's, "modern" workshops had already displaced "medieval" ones, and several "large capitalist firms" had already been launched.

Relating the Typographical Revolution to Other Developments

Granted that some sort of revolution did occur during the late fifteenth century, how did this affect other historical developments? Since the consequences of printing have not been thoroughly explored, guidance is hard to come by. Most conventional surveys stop short after a few remarks about the wider dissemination of humanist tomes or Protestant tracts. Several helpful suggestions—about the effects of standardization on scholarship and science, for example—are offered in works devoted to the era of the Renaissance or the history of science. By and large, the effects of the new process are vaguely implied rather than explicitly defined and are also drastically minimized. One example may illustrate this point. During the first centuries of printing, old texts were duplicated more rapidly than new ones. On this basis we are told that "printing did not speed up the adoption of new theories." But where did these new theories come from? Must we invoke some spirit of the times, or is it possible that an increase in the output of old texts contributed to the formulation of new theories? Maybe other features that distinguished the new mode of book production from the old one also contributed to such theories. We need to take stock of these features before we can relate the advent of printing to other historical developments.

I have found it useful, in any case, to start taking stock by following up clues contained in special studies on printing. After singling out certain features that seemed peculiar to typography, I held them in mind while passing in review various historical developments. Relationships emerged that had not occurred to me before, and some possible solutions to old puzzles were suggested. Conjectures based on this approach may be sampled below under headings that indicate my main lines of inquiry.

A CLOSER LOOK AT WIDE DISSEMINATION: VARIOUS EFFECTS PRODUCED BY INCREASED OUTPUT

Most references to wide dissemination are too fleeting to make clear the specific effects of an increased supply of texts directed at different markets. In particular they fail to make clear how patterns of consumption were affected by increased production. Here the term "dissemination" is sufficiently inappropriate to be distracting. Some mention of cross-fertilization or cross-cultural interchange should be included in surveys or summaries. More copies of one given text, for instance, were "spread, dispersed, or scattered" by the issue of a printed edition. For the individual book-reader, however, different texts, which were previously dispersed and scattered, were also brought closer together. In some regions, printers produced more scholarly texts than they could sell and flooded local markets. In all regions, a given purchaser could buy more books at lower cost and bring them into his study or library. In this way, the printer provided the clerk with a richer, more varied literary diet than had been provided by the scribe. To consult different books it was no longer so essential to be a wandering scholar. Successive generations of sedentary scholars were less apt to be engrossed by a single text and to expend their energies in elaborating on it. The era of the glossator and commentator came to an end, and a new "era of intense cross referencing between one book and another" began. More abundantly stocked bookshelves increased opportunities to consult and compare different texts and, thus, also made more probable the formation of new intellectual combinations and permutations. Viewed in this light, cross-cultural interchanges fostered by printing seem relevant to Sarton's observation: "The Renaissance was a transmutation of values, a 'new deal,' a reshuffling of cards, but most of the cards were old; the scientific Renaissance was a 'new deal,' but many of the cards were new." Combinatory intellectual activity, as Koestler has recently suggested, inspires many creative acts. Once old texts came together within the same study, diverse systems of ideas and special disciplines could be combined. Increased output directed at relatively stable markets, in short, created conditions that favored, first, new combinations of old ideas and, then, the creation of entirely new systems of thought.

Merely by making more scrambled data available, by increasing the output of second-century Ptolemaic maps and twelfth-century *mappae mundi,* for instance, printers encouraged efforts to unscramble these data. Hand-drafted portolans had long been more accurate, but few eyes had seen them. Much as maps from different regions and epochs were brought into contact, so too were diverse textual traditions previously preserved by specially trained groups of schoolmen and scribes. It should be noted that cross-cultural interchange was not solely a consequence of augmented output. For example, texts were provided with new illustrations drawn from artisan workshops instead of scriptoria. Here again, different traditions were brought into contact. In this case, words drawn from one milieu and pictures from another were placed beside each other within the same books. When considering new views of the "book of nature" or the linking of bookish theories with observations and craft skills, it may be useful to look at the ateliers of Renaissance artists. But one must also go on to visit early printers' workshops, for it is there above all that we "can observe the formation of groups . . . conducive to cross-fertilization" of all kinds.

Cross-cultural interchange stimulated mental activities in contradictory ways. The first century of printing was marked above all by intellectual ferment and by a "somewhat wide-angled, unfocused scholarship." Certain confusing cross-currents may be explained by noting that new links between disciplines were being forged before old ones had been severed. In the age of scribes, for instance, magical arts were closely associated with mechanical crafts. Trade skills were passed down by closed circles of initiates. Unwritten recipes used by the alchemist were not clearly distinguished from those used by the apothecary or surgeon, the goldsmith or engraver. When "technology went to press," so too did a vast backlog of occult lore, and few readers could discriminate between the two.

The divine art or "mystery" of printing unleashed a "churning turbid flood of Hermetic, cabalistic, Gnostic, theurgic, Sabaean, Pythagorean, and generally mystic notions." Historians are still puzzled by certain strange deposits left by this flood. They might find it helpful to consider how records derived from ancient Near Eastern cultures had been transmitted in the age of scribes. Some of these records had dwindled into tantalizing fragments pertaining to systems of reckoning, medicine, agriculture, mythic cults, and so forth. Others had evaporated into unfathomable glyphs. All were thought to come from one body of pure knowledge originally set down by an Egyptian scribal god and carefully preserved by ancient sages and seers before becoming corrupted and confused. A collection of writings containing ancient lore was received from Macedonia by

Cosimo de' Medici, translated by Ficino in 1463, and printed in fifteen editions before 1500. It seemed to come from this body of knowledge—and was accordingly attributed to "Hermes Trismegistus." The hermetic corpus ran through many more editions during the next century before it was shown to have been compiled in the third century A.D. On this basis we are told that Renaissance scholars had made a radical error in dating. But to assign definite dates to scribal compilations, which were probably derived from earlier sources, may be an error as well.

The transformation of occult and esoteric scribal lore after the advent of printing also needs more study. Some arcane writings, in Greek, Hebrew or Syriac, for example, became less mysterious. Others became more so. Thus hieroglyphs were set in type more than three centuries before their decipherment. These sacred carved letters were loaded with significant meaning by readers who could not read them. They were also used simply as ornamental motifs by architects and engravers. Given baroque decoration on one hand and complicated interpretations by scholars, Rosicrucians, and Freemasons on the other, the duplication of Egyptian picture writing throughout the Age of Reason presents modern scholars with puzzles that can never be solved. In brief, when considering the effects produced by printing on scholarship, it is a mistake to think only about new forms of enlightenment. New forms of mystification were entailed as well.

It is also a mistake to think only about scholarly markets when considering the effects of increased output. Dissemination as defined in the dictionary does seem appropriate to the duplication of primers and ABC books, almanacs, and picture Bibles. An increased output of devotional literature was not necessarily conducive to cross-cultural interchange. Catechisms, religious tracts, and Bibles would fill some bookshelves to the exclusion of all other reading matter. A new wide-angled, unfocused scholarship had to compete with a new single-minded, narrowly focused piety. At the same time, guidebooks and manuals also became more abundant, making it easier to lay plans for getting ahead in this world—possibly diverting attention from uncertain futures in the next one. It is doubtful whether "the effect of the new invention on scholarship" was more important than these other effects "at the beginning of the sixteenth century." What does need emphasis is that many dissimilar effects, all of great consequence, came relatively simultaneously. If this could be spelled out more clearly, seemingly contradictory developments might be confronted with more equanimity. The intensification of both religiosity and secularism could be better understood. Some debates about periodization also could be bypassed. Medieval world pictures, for example, were duplicated more rapidly during the first century of printing than they had been during the so-called Middle Ages. They did not merely *survive* among the Elizabethans. They became *more available* to poets and playwrights of the sixteenth century than they had been to minstrels and mummers of the thirteenth century.

In view of such considerations, I cannot agree with Sarton's comment:

"It is hardly necessary to indicate what the art of printing meant for the diffusion of culture but one should not lay too much stress on diffusion and should speak more of standardization." How printing changed patterns of cultural diffusion deserves much more study than it has yet received. Moreover, individual access to diverse texts is a different matter than bringing many minds to bear on a single text. The former issue is apt to be neglected by too exclusive an emphasis on "standardization."

CONSIDERING SOME EFFECTS PRODUCED BY STANDARDIZATION
Although it has to be considered in conjunction with many other issues, standardization certainly does deserve closer study. One specialist has argued that it is currently overplayed. Yet it may well be still under-stressed. Perhaps early printing methods made it impossible to issue the kind of "standard" editions with which modern scholars are familiar. Certainly press variants did multiply, and countless errata were issued. The fact remains that Erasmus or Bellarmine could issue errata; Jerome or Alcuin could not. The very act of publishing errata demonstrated a new capacity to locate textual errors with precision and to transmit this information simultaneously to scattered readers. It thus illustrates, rather neatly, some of the effects of standardization. However fourteenth-century copyists were supervised, scribes were incapable of committing the sort of "standardized" error that led printers to be fined for the "wicked Bible" of 1631. If a single compositor's error could be circulated in a great many copies, so too could a single scholar's emendation. However, when I suggest that we may still underestimate the implications of standardization, I am not thinking primarily about textual emendations or errors. I am thinking instead about the new output of exactly repeatable pictorial statements, such as maps, charts, diagrams, and other visual aids; of more uniform reference guides, such as calendars, thesauruses, dictionaries; of increasingly regular systems of notation, whether musical, mathematical, or grammatical. How different fields of study and aesthetic styles were affected by such developments remains to be explored. It does seem worth suggesting that both our so-called two cultures were affected. Humanist scholarship, belles lettres, and fine arts must be considered along with celestial mechanics, anatomy, and cartography.

Too many important variations were, indeed, played on the theme of standardization for all of them to be listed here. This theme entered into every operation associated with typography, from the replica casting of precisely measured pieces of type to the subliminal impact upon scattered readers of repeated encounters with identical type styles, printers' devices, and title-page ornamentation. Calligraphy itself was affected. Sixteenth-century specimen books stripped diverse scribal "hands" of personal idiosyncrasies. They did for handwriting what style books did for typography itself; what pattern books did for dressmaking, furniture, architectural motifs, and ground plans. In short the setting of standards—used for innumerable purposes, from cutting cloth to city-planning—accompanied the output of more standardized products.

Here, as elsewhere, we need to recall that early printers were responsible not only for issuing new standard reference guides but also for compiling many of them. A subsequent division of labor tends to divert attention from the large repertoire of roles performed by those who presided over the new presses. A scholar-printer himself might serve as indexer-bridger-lexicographer-chronicler. Whatever roles he performed, decisions about standards to be adopted when processing texts for publication could not be avoided. A suitable type style had to be selected or designed and house conventions determined. Textual variants and the desirability of illustration and translation also had to be confronted. Accordingly, the printer's workshop became the most advanced laboratory of erudition of the sixteenth century.

Many early capitalist industries required efficient planning, methodical attention to detail, and rational calculation. The decisions made by early printers, however, directly affected both toolmaking and symbolmaking. Their products reshaped powers to manipulate objects, to perceive and think about varied phenomena. Scholars concerned with "modernization" or "rationalization" might profitably think more about the new kind of brainwork fostered by the silent scanning of maps, tables, charts, diagrams, dictionaries, and grammars. They also need to look more closely at the daily routines pursued by those who compiled and produced such reference guides. These routines were conducive to a new *esprit de système*. "It's much easier to find things when they are each disposed in place and not scattered haphazardly," remarked a sixteenth-century publisher. He was justifying the way he had reorganized a text he had edited. He might equally well have been complaining to a clerk who had mislaid some account papers pertaining to the large commercial enterprise he ran.

SOME EFFECTS PRODUCED BY EDITING AND REORGANIZING TEXTS:
CODIFYING, CLARIFYING, AND CATALOGUING DATA

Editorial decisions made by early printers with regard to layout and presentation probably helped to reorganize the thinking of readers. McLuhan's suggestion that scanning lines of print affected thought processes is at first glance somewhat mystifying. But further reflection suggests that the thoughts of readers are guided by the way the contents of books are arranged and presented. Basic changes in book format might well lead to changes in thought patterns. Such changes began to appear in the era of incunabula. They made texts more lucid and intelligible. They involved the use "of graduated types, running heads . . . footnotes . . . tables of contents . . . superior figures, cross references . . . and other devices available to the compositor"—all registering "the victory of the punch cutter over the scribe." Concern with surface appearance necessarily governed the handwork of the scribe. He was fully preoccupied trying to shape evenly spaced uniform letters in a pleasing symmetrical design. An altogether different procedure was required to give directions to compositors. To do this, one had to mark up a manuscript while scrutinizing its contents. Every scribal text that came into the printer's hands, thus, had to be reviewed in a new way. Within a generation the results of this review were being aimed in a new direction—away from fidelity to scribal conventions and toward serving the convenience of the reader. The competitive and commercial character of the new mode of book production encouraged the relatively rapid adoption of any innovation that commended a given edition to purchasers. In short, providing built-in aids to the reader became for the first time both feasible and desirable.

The introduction and adoption of such built-in aids, from the 1480's on, has been traced and discussed in special works on printing but has been insufficiently noted in other accounts. We are repeatedly told about "dissemination," occasionally about standardization, almost never at all about the codification and clarification that were entailed in editing copy. Yet changes affecting book format probably contributed much to the so-called rationalization of diverse institutions. After all, they affected texts used for the study and practice of law—and consequently had an impact on most organs of the body politic as well. This has been demonstrated by a pioneering study of the "englishing and printing" of the "Great Boke of Statutes 1530–1533." I cannot pause here over the many repercussions, ranging from statecraft to literature, that came in the wake of Tudor law-printing according to this study. To suggest why we need to look at new built-in aids, I will simply point to the introductory "Tabula" to the "Great Boke"; "a chronological register by chapters of the statutes 1327–1523." Here was a table of contents that also served as a "conspectus of parliamentary history"—the first many readers had seen.

This sort of spectacular innovation, while deserving close study, should not divert attention from much less conspicuous but more ubiquitous changes. Increasing familiarity with regularly numbered pages, punctuation marks, section breaks, running heads, indexes, and so forth helped to reorder the thought of *all* readers, whatever their profession or craft. Hence countless activities were subjected to a new *esprit de système*. The use of arabic numbers for pagination suggests how the most inconspicuous innovation could have weighty consequences—in this case, more accurate indexing, annotation, and cross-referencing resulted. Most studies of printing have quite rightly singled out the provision of title pages as the most important of all ubiquitous print-made innovations. How the title page contributed to the cataloguing of books and the bibliographer's craft scarcely needs to be spelled out. How it contributed to a new habit of placing and dating in general does, I think, call for further thought.

On the whole, as I have tried to suggest throughout this discussion, topics now allocated to bibliophiles and specialists on printing are of general concern to historians at large—or, at least, to specialists in many different fields. The way these fields are laid out could be better understood, indeed, if we opened up the one assigned to printing. "Until half a century after Copernicus' death, no potentially revolutionary changes occurred in the data available to astronomers." But Copernicus' life (1473–1543) spanned the very decades when a great many changes, now barely visible to modern eyes, were transforming "the data available" to all book-readers. A closer study of these changes could help to explain why systems of charting the planets, mapping the earth, synchronizing chronologies, and compiling bibliographies were all revolutionized before the end of the sixteenth century. In each instance, one notes, ancient Alexandrian achievements were first reduplicated and then, in a remarkably short time, surpassed. In each instance also, the new schemes once published remained available for correction, development, and refinement. Successive generations of scholars could build on the work of their sixteenth-century predecessors instead of trying to retrieve scattered fragments of it.

The varied intellectual revolutions of early modern times owed much to the features that have already been outlined. But the great tomes, charts, and maps that are now seen as "milestones" might have proved insubstantial had not the preservative powers of print also been called into play. Typographical fixity is a basic prerequisite for the rapid advancement of learning. It helps to explain much else that seems to distinguish the history of the past five centuries from that of all prior eras—as I hope the following remarks will suggest.

CONSIDERING THE PRESERVATIVE POWERS OF PRINT: HOW FIXITY
AND ACCUMULATION ALTERED PATTERNS OF CULTURAL
AND INSTITUTIONAL CHANGE

Of all the new features introduced by the duplicative powers of print, preservation is possibly the most important. To appreciate its importance, we need to recall the conditions that prevailed before texts could be set in type. No manuscript, however useful as a reference guide, could be preserved for long without undergoing corruption by copyists, and even this sort of "preservation" rested precariously on the shifting demands of local elites and a fluctuating incidence of trained scribal labor. Insofar as records were seen and used, they were vulnerable to wear and tear. Stored documents were vulnerable to moisture and vermin, theft and fire. However they might be collected or guarded within some great message center, their ultimate dispersal and loss was inevitable. To be transmitted by writing from one generation to the next, information had to be conveyed by drifting texts and vanishing manuscripts.

When considering developments in astronomy (or geography or chronology) during the age of scribes, it is not the slow rate of cognitive advance that calls for explanation. Rather, one might wonder about how the customary process of erosion, corruption, and loss was temporarily arrested. When viewed in this light, the "1,800 years" that elapsed between Hipparchus and Copernicus seem less remarkable than the advances that were made in planetary astronomy during the 600 years that elapsed between Aristotle and Ptolemy. With regard to all computations based on large-scale data collection, whatever had once been clearly seen and carefully articulated grew dimmed and blurred with the passage of time. More than a millennium also elapsed between Eratosthenes and Scaliger, Ptolemy and Mercator. The progress made over the course of centuries within the confines of the Alexandrian Museum seems, in short, to have been most exceptional. To be sure, there were intermittent localized "revivals of learning" thereafter, as well as a prolonged accumulation of records within certain message centers. Ground lost by corruption could never be regained, but migrating manuscripts could lead to abrupt recovery as well as to sudden loss. Yet a marked increase in the output of certain kinds of texts resulted generally in a decreased output of other kinds. Similarly, a "revival" in one region often signified a dearth of texts in another.

The incapacity of scribal culture to sustain a simultaneous advance on many fronts in different regions may be relevant to the "problem of the Renaissance." Italian humanist book-hunters, patrons, and dealers tried to replenish a diminished supply of those ancient texts that were being neglected by scribes serving medieval university faculties. Their efforts have been heralded as bringing about a "permanent recovery" of ancient learning and letters. If one accepts the criteria of "totality and permanence" to distinguish prior "revivals" from the Renaissance, then probably the advent of the scholar-printer should be heralded instead. He arrived to cast his Greek types and turn out grammars, translations, and standard editions in the nick of time—almost on the eve of the Valois invasions.

Once Greek type fonts had been cut, neither the disruption of civil order in Italy, the conquest of Greek lands by Islam, nor even the translation into Latin of all major Greek texts saw knowledge of Greek wither again in the West. Instead it was the familiar scribal phrase *Graeca sunt ergo non legenda* that disappeared from Western texts. Constantinople fell, Rome was sacked. Yet a cumulative process of textual purification and continuous recovery had been launched. The implications of typographical fixity are scarcely exhausted by thinking about early landmarks in classical scholarship and its auxiliary sciences: paleography, philology, archeology, numismatics, etc. Nor are they exhausted by reckoning the number of languages that have been retrieved after being lost to all men for thousands of years. They involve the whole modern "knowledge industry" itself, with its mushrooming bibliographies and overflowing card files.

They also involve issues that are less academic and more geopolitical. The linguistic map of Europe was "fixed" by the same process and at the same time as Greek letters were. The importance of the fixing of literary vernaculars is often stressed. The strategic role played by printing is, however, often overlooked. How strategic it was is suggested by the following paraphrased summary of Steinberg's account:

> Printing "preserved and codified, sometimes even created" certain vernaculars. Its absence during the sixteenth century among small linguistic groups "demonstrably led" to the disappearance or exclusion of their vernaculars from the realm of literature. Its presence among similar groups in the same century ensured the possibility of intermittent revivals or continued expansion. Having fortified language walls between one group and another, printers homogenized

what was within them, breaking down minor differences, standardizing idioms for millions of writers and readers, assigning a new peripheral role to provincial dialects. The preservation of a given literary language often depended on whether or not a few vernacular primers, catechisms or Bibles happened to get printed (under foreign as well as domestic auspices) in the sixteenth century. When this was the case, the subsequent expansion of a separate "national" literary culture ensued. When this did not happen, a prerequisite for budding "national" consciousness disappeared; a spoken provincial dialect was left instead.

Studies of dynastic consolidation and/or of nationalism might well devote more space to the advent of printing. Typography arrested linguistic drift, enriched as well as standardized vernaculars, and paved the way for the more deliberate purification and codification of all major European languages. Randomly patterned sixteenth-century typecasting largely determined the subsequent elaboration of national mythologies on the part of certain separate groups within multilingual dynastic states. The duplication of vernacular primers and translations contributed in other ways to nationalism. A "mother's tongue" learned "naturally" at home would be reinforced by inculcation of a homogenized print-made language mastered while still young, when learning to read. During the most impressionable years of childhood, the eye would first see a more standardized version of what the ear had first heard. Particularly after grammar schools gave primary instruction in reading by using vernacular instead of Latin readers, linguistic "roots" and rootedness in one's homeland would be entangled.

Printing helped in other ways to permanently atomize Western Christendom. Erastian policies long pursued by diverse rulers could, for example, be more fully implemented. Thus, the duplication of documents pertaining to ritual, liturgy, or canon law, handled under clerical auspices in the age of the scribe, was undertaken by enterprising laymen, subject to dynastic authority, in the age of the printer. Local firms, lying outside the control of the papal curia, were granted lucrative privileges by Habsburg, Valois, or Tudor kings to service the needs of national clergies. The varied ways in which printers contributed to loosening or severing links with Rome, or to nationalist sentiment, or to dynastic consolidation cannot be explored here. But they surely do call for further study.

Other consequences of typographical fixity also need to be explored. Religious divisions and legal precedents were affected. In fact, all the lines that were drawn in the sixteenth century (or thereafter), the condemnation of a heresy, the excommunication of a schismatic king, the settling of disputes between warring dynasts, schisms within the body politic— lines that prior generations had repeatedly traced, erased, retraced— would now leave a more indelible imprint. It was no longer possible to take for granted that one was following "immemorial custom" when granting an immunity or signing a decree. Edicts became more visible and irrevocable. The Magna Carta, for example, was ostensibly "published" (i.e., proclaimed) twice a year in every shire. By 1237 there was already confusion as to which "charter" was involved. In 1533, however, Englishmen glancing over the "Tabula" of the "Great Boke" could see how often it had been repeatedly confirmed in successive royal statutes. In France also the "mechanism by which the will of the sovereign" was incorporated into the "published" body of law by "registration" was probably altered by typographical fixity. Much as M. Jourdain learned that he was speaking prose, monarchs learned from political theorists that they were "making" laws. But members of parliaments and assemblies also learned from jurists and printers about ancient rights wrongfully usurped. Struggles over the right to establish precedents probably became more intense as each precedent became more permanent and hence more difficult to break.

On the other hand, in many fields of activity, fixity led to new departures from precedent marked by more explicit recognition of individual innovation and by the staking of claims to inventions, discoveries, and creations. By 1500, legal fictions were already being devised to accommodate the patenting of inventions and the assignment of literary properties. Upon these foundations, a burgeoning bureaucracy would build a vast and complex legal structure. Laws pertaining to licensing and privileges have been extensively studied. But they have yet to be examined as by-products of typographical fixity. Both the dissolution of guild controls and conflicts over mercantilist policies might be clarified if this were done. Once the rights of an inventor could be legally fixed and the problem of preserving unwritten recipes intact was no longer posed, profits could be achieved by open publicity, provided new restraints were not imposed. Individual initiative was released from reliance on guild protection, but at the same time new powers were lodged in the hands of a bureaucratic officialdom. Competition over the right to publish a given text also introduced controversy over new issues involving monopoly and piracy. Printing forced legal definition of what belonged in the public domain and clear articulation of how one sort of literary product differed from another. When discussing the emergence of a new kind of individualism, it might be useful to recall that the eponymous inventor and personal authorship appeared at the same time and as a consequence of the same process.

The emergence of uniquely distinguished, personally famous artists and authors out of the ranks of more anonymous artisans and minstrels was also related to typographical fixity. Cheaper writing materials encouraged the separate recording of private lives and correspondence. Not paper mills but printing presses, however, made it possible to preserve personal ephemera intact. As an expanding manuscript culture found its way into print, formal compositions were accompanied by intimate anecdotes about the lives and loves of their flesh-and-blood authors. Was it the "inclination" to "publish gossip" that was new in the Renaissance, or was it, rather, the possibility of doing so? The characteristic individuality of Renaissance masterpieces surely owes much to the new possibility of preserving the life-histories of those who produced them. As art historians have shown, the hands of medieval illuminators or stone-carvers were, in fact, no less distinctive. Their personalities remain unknown. Vestiges of their local celebrity have vanished. They must therefore be portrayed as faceless master guildsmen in terms of the garb they wore or the life-style they shared with colleagues. What applies to personality may also apply to versatility. Alberti probably was not the first architect who was also an athlete, orator, scholar, and artist. But he *was* the first whose after-dinner speeches, boasts about boyhood feats, and "serious and witty sayings" were collected and transmitted to posterity along with the buildings he designed and formal treatises he composed. He may be displayed at home and in public, as an athletic youth and elderly sage, moving through all the ages of man, personifying earlier archetypes and collective roles. Possibly this is why he appears to Burckhardt in the guise of a new ideal type, *homo universalis.*

Similar considerations are also worth applying to authors. The personal hand and signature of the scribe was replaced by the more impersonal type style and colophon of the printer. Yet, by the same token, the personal, private, idiosyncratic views of the author could be extended through time and space. Articulating new concepts of selfhood, wrestling with the problem of speaking privately for publication, new authors (beginning, perhaps, with Montaigne) would redefine individualism in terms of deviation from the norm and divergence from the type. The "drive for fame" itself may have been affected by print-made immortality. The urge to scribble was manifested in Juvenal's day as it was in Petrarch's. But the *insanabile scribendi cacoethes* may have been reoriented once it became an "itch to publish." The wish to see one's work in print (fixed forever with one's name, in card files and anthologies) is different from the urge to pen lines that could never get fixed in a permanent form, might be lost forever, altered by copying, or—if truly memorable—carried by oral transmission and assigned ultimately to "anon." When dealing with priority disputes among scientists or debates about plagiarism among scholars, the advent of print-made immortality has to be taken into account. Until it became possible to distinguish between composing a poem and reciting one or between writing a book and copying one, until books could be classified by something other than incipits, how could modern games of books and authors be played?

Many problems about assigning proper credit to scribal "authors" may result from misguided efforts to apply print-made concepts where they do not pertain. The so-called forged book of Hermes is a good case in point. But countless other scribal works are too. Who *wrote* Socrates' lines, Aristotle's works, Sappho's poems, any portion of the Scriptures? Troublesome questions about biblical composition, in particular, suggest how new forms of personal authorship helped to subvert old concepts of collective authority. Veneration for the wisdom of the ages was probably modified as ancient sages were retrospectively cast in the role of individual authors —prone to human error and possibly plagiarists as well. Treatment of battles of books between "ancients and moderns" might profit from more discussion of such issues. Since early printers were primarily responsible for forcing definition of literary property rights, for shaping new concepts of authorship, for exploiting best sellers and trying to tap new markets, their role in this celebrated quarrel should not be overlooked. By the early sixteenth century, for example, staffs of translators were employed to turn out vernacular versions of the more popular works by ancient Romans and contemporary Latin-writing humanists. This might be taken into account when discussing debates between Latinists and the advocates of new vulgar tongues.

It is also worth considering that different meanings may have been assigned terms such as "ancient" and "modern," "discovery" and "recovery," "invention" and "imitation" before important departures from precedent could be permanently recorded. "Throughout the patristic and medieval periods, the quest for truth is thought of as the *re*covery of what is embedded in tradition . . . rather than the *dis*covery of what is new." Most scholars concur with this view. It must have been difficult to distinguish discovering something new from recovering it in the age of scribes. To "find a new art" was easily confused with retrieving a lost one, for superior techniques and systems of knowledge *were* frequently discovered by being recovered. Probably Moses, Zoroaster, or Thoth had not "invented" all the arts that were to be found. But many were retrieved from ancient giants whose works reentered the West by circuitous routes. The origins of such works were shrouded in mystery. Their contents revealed a remarkable technical expertise. Some pagan seers were believed to have been granted foreknowledge of the Incarnation. Possibly they had also been granted a special secret key to all knowledge by the same divine dispensation. Veneration for the wisdom of the ancients was not incompatible with the advancement of learning, nor was imitation incompatible with inspiration. Efforts to think and do as the ancients did might well reflect the hope of experiencing a sudden illumination or of coming closer to the original source of a pure, clear, and certain knowledge that a long Gothic night had obscured.

When unprecedented innovations did occur, moreover, there was no sure way of recognizing them before the advent of printing. Who could ascertain precisely what was known—either to prior generations within a given region or to contemporary inhabitants of far-off lands? "Steady advance," as Sarton says, "implies exact determination of every previous step." In his view, printing made this determination "incomparably easier." He may have understated the case. *Exact* determination must have been impossible before printing. Given drifting texts, migrating manuscripts, localized chronologies, multiform maps, there could be no systematic forward movement, no accumulation of stepping stones enabling a new generation to begin where the prior one had left off. Progressive refinement of certain arts and skills could and did occur. But no sophisticated technique could be securely established, permanently recorded, and stored for subsequent retrieval. Before trying to account for an "idea" of progress, we might look more closely at the duplicating process that made possible a continuous accumulation of fixed records. For it seems to have been permanence that introduced progressive change. The preservation of the old, in brief, launched a tradition of the new.

The advancement of learning had taken the form of a search for lost wisdom in the age of scribes. This search was rapidly propelled after printing. Ancient maps, charts, and texts once arranged and dated, however, turned out to be dated in more ways than one. Ordinary craftsmen and mariners appeared to know more things about the heavens and earth than were dreamt of by ancient sages. More schools of ancient philosophy than had previously been known were also uncovered. Scattered attacks on one authority by those who favored another provided ammunition for a wholesale assault on all received opinion. Incompatible portions of inherited traditions were sloughed off, partly because the task of preservation had become less urgent. Copying, memorizing, and transmitting absorbed fewer energies. Some were released to explore what still might be learned. Studying variant versions of God's words gave way to contemplating the uniformity of His works. Investigation of the "book of nature" was no longer undertaken by studying old glyphs and ciphers. Magic and science were divorced. So too were poetry and history. Useful reference books were no longer blotted out or blurred with the passage of time. Cadence and rhyme, images and symbols ceased to fulfil their traditional function of preserving the collective memory. The aesthetic experience became increasingly autonomous, and the function of works of art had to be redefined. Technical information could be conveyed more directly by plain expository prose and accurate illustration. Although books on the memory arts multiplied after printing, practical reliance on these arts decreased. Scribal schemes eventually petrified, to be ultimately reassembled, like fossil remains, by modern research. The special formulas that had preserved recipes and techniques among closed circles of initiates also disappeared. Residues of mnemonic devices were transmuted into mysterious images, rites and incantations.

Nevertheless, scribal veneration for ancient learning lingered on, long after the conditions that had fostered it had gone. Among Rosicrucians and Freemasons, for example, the belief persisted that the "new philosophy" was in fact very old. Descartes and Newton had merely retrieved the same magical key to nature's secrets that had once been known to ancient pyramid-builders but was later withheld from the laity or deliberately obscured by a deceitful priesthood. In fact, the Index came only after printing and the preservation of pagan learning owed much to monks and friars. Enlightened freethinkers, however, assigned Counter-Reformation institutions to the Gothic Dark Ages and turned Zoroaster into a Copernican. Similarly, once imitation was detached from inspiration and copying from composing, the classical revival became increasingly arid and academic. The search for primary sources was assigned to dry-as-dust pedants. But the reputation of ancient seers, bards, and prophets was not, by the same token, diminished. Claims to have inherited their magic mantle were put forth by new romanticists who reoriented the meaning of the term "original" and tried to resurrect scribal arts in the age of print. Even the "decay of nature" theme, once intimately associated with the erosion and corruption of scribal writings, would be reworked and reoriented by gloomy modern prophets who felt that regress, not progress, characterized their age.

AMPLIFICATION AND REINFORCEMENT: ACCOUNTING FOR
PERSISTENT STEREOTYPES AND
INCREASING CULTURAL DIFFERENTIATION

Many other themes imbedded in scribal writings, detached from the living cultures that had shaped them, were propelled as "typologies" on printed pages. Over the course of time, archetypes were converted into stereotypes, the language of giants, as Merton puts it, into the clichés of dwarfs. Both "stereotype" and "cliché" are terms deriving from a typographical process developed three and a half centuries after Gutenberg. They point, however, to certain other features of typographical culture in general that deserve closer consideration. During the past five centuries, broadcasting new messages has also entailed amplifying and reinforcing old ones. I hope my use of the terms "amplify" and "reinforce" will not distract attention from the effects they are meant to designate. I am using them simply because I have found no others that serve as well. Some such terms are needed to cover the effects produced by an ever-more-frequent repetition of identical chapters and verses, anecdotes and aphorisms drawn from very limited scribal sources. This repetition is not produced by the constant republication of classical, biblical, or early vernacular works, although it undoubtedly sustains markets for such works. It is produced by an unwitting collaboration between countless authors of new books or articles. For five hundred years, authors have jointly transmitted certain old messages with augmented frequency even while separately reporting on new events or spinning out new ideas. Thus, if they happen to contain only one passing reference to the heroic stand at Thermopylae, a hundred reports on different military campaigns will impress with a hundredfold-impact Herodotus' description on the mind of the reader who scans such reports. Every dissimilar report of other campaigns will be received only once. As printed materials proliferate, this effect becomes more pronounced. (I have encountered several references to Thermopylae in the daily newspaper during the past year.) The same is true of numerous other messages previously inscribed on scarce and scattered manuscripts. The more wide ranging the reader at present, the more frequent will be the encounter with the identical version and the deeper the impression it will leave. Since book-writing authors are particularly prone to wide-ranging reading, a multiplying "feedback" effect results. When it comes to coining familiar quotations, describing familiar episodes, originating symbols or stereotypes, the ancients will generally outstrip the moderns. How many times has Tacitus' description of freedom-loving Teutons been repeated since a single manuscript of *Germania* was discovered in a fifteenth-century monastery? And in how many varying contexts—Anglo-

Saxon, Frankish, as well as German—has this particular description appeared?

The frequency with which all messages were transmitted was primarily channeled by the fixing of literary linguistic frontiers. A particular kind of reinforcement was involved in relearning mother tongues when learning to read. It went together with the progressive amplification of diversely oriented national "memories." Not all the same portions of an inherited Latin culture were translated into different vernaculars at the same time. More important, entirely dissimilar dynastic, municipal, and ecclesiastical chronicles, along with other local lore, both oral and scribal, were also set in type and more permanently fixed. The meshing of provincial medieval *res gestae* with diverse classical and scriptural sources had, by the early seventeenth century, imbedded distinctively different stereotypes within each separate vernacular literature. At the same time, to be sure, a more cosmopolitan *Respublica litterarum* was also expanding, and messages were broadcast across linguistic frontiers, first via Latin, then French, to an international audience. But messages received from abroad were not amplified over the course of several centuries in the same way. They only occasionally reinforced what was learned in familiar tongues at home.

On the other hand, the fixing of religious frontiers that cut across linguistic ones in the sixteenth century had a powerful effect on the frequency with which certain messages were transmitted. Passages drawn from vernacular translations of the Bible, for example, would be much more thinly and weakly distributed throughout the literary cultures of Catholic regions than of Protestant ones. The abandonment of church Latin in Protestant regions made it possible to mesh ecclesiastical and dynastic traditions more closely within Protestant realms than in Catholic ones—a point worth noting when considering how church-state conflicts were resolved in different lands. Finally, the unevenly phased social penetration of literacy, the somewhat more random patterning of book-reading habits, and the uneven distribution of costly new books and cheap reprints of old ones among different social sectors also affected the frequency with which diverse messages were received within each linguistic group.

24. Navigator to the Modern Age

GARRETT MATTINGLY

25. The Justification of Slavery

DAVID BRION DAVIS

*Among the many discoveries, advances, and revolutions in thought and society
that mark the beginning of the early modern period in European history, perhaps
none was more fateful than the discovery of the New World. The Western Hemisphere has been there for ages; how was it that Europeans "discovered" its existence only in the fifteenth century? Put differently, why had there been no earlier
period of expansion and exploration similar to that of the fifteenth century? Was
it mere chance that Portuguese, Spanish, and Italian seamen suddenly dared to
go where men had not gone before? (The Vikings of course had reached North
America about the year 1000, but little was known of this in southern Europe
in the fifteenth century.) Or were there forces leading to the navigational voyages that opened America and the Far East to European penetration? If so, what
were they?*

*In this article, Mattingly discusses the career of Henry, Prince of Portugal, the
man often credited with opening the great period of European exploration. It was
not for commercial gain, nor for military or political power that Henry pushed
his captains to sail further and further south until they had begun the trek past the
Cape of Good Hope into the Indian Ocean, but rather in the pious medieval
hope that he could find the kingdom of the legendary "Prester John," and join
him in a crusade against the forces of Islam. The role of Prince Henry's youthful*

Source: Garrett Mattingly, "Navigator to the Modern Age," *Horizon*, III (November 1960), pp. 73–83. Copyright © 1960 by American Heritage Publishing Co.,
Inc. Reprinted by permission from *Horizon*.

desire to go on a crusade, which led to the accidental capture of Ceuta; the scientific inventions and nautical improvements that rendered Portuguese ships ocean-worthy; the lure and romance of the unknown or half-known—these and other factors in the development of European exploration are vividly discussed by Mattingly. The discovery of the New World was hardly inevitable, and Prince Henry played a crucial role in preparing the way for it.

Soon after Columbus had "discovered" the existence of land to the west of Europe, which was not the Indies, a great scramble began among the European powers, principally Spain and Portugal, to expropriate and colonize this new world. For many it was a land of new hope, of promise, primitive and unspoiled. Yet from the very beginning European explorers brought human slaves to work the land and produce wealth for the Old World. The importation of the institution of slavery in the early sixteenth century is somewhat puzzling, for it was declining in Europe at this time, and was frowned upon by many. It is clear that both Europeans and Africans found the trade in slaves lucrative, and that slave labor proved to be a cheap and profitable source of gain in the Americas. But what did contemporary European thought say about this development? How, if at all, was it explained or justified? What traditions lay behind slavery in the European past?

David Brion Davis published in 1966 a stimulating study, The Problem of Slavery in Western Culture, which was awarded a Pulitzer Prize. Although his principal concern was to trace the rise and development of antislavery or abolitionist thought through the colonial period, Davis went on to explore the origins of Western thought about slavery, its nature, origins, and basis. In the selection reprinted here, he raises the question of why slavery was accepted by sixteenth-century Europeans as perfectly suitable in the New World at a time when it was on the wane in the Old. His discussion of the debate on the subject is particularly informative about the underlying traditions that conditioned men to adopt and employ slavery on a massive scale. As so often in human history, part of the problem was a dichotomy between what men held to in theory and what they did in practice. But there was more to it than this. Davis finds deep roots for the tradition of slavery in Western culture, and it seems we must recognize that our heritage is hardly one of unblemished humanitarianism.

Some other recent works that offer stimulating views of the impact of discovery on European thought and society include Donald Lach's multivolume work Asia in the Making of Europe (1965–), and J. H. Elliott's The Old World and the New 1492–1650 (1970).

GARRETT MATTINGLY

Five hundred years ago there died in a storm-battered little castle, perched on a cliff at the extreme southwestern corner of Europe, a medieval prince who was the father of the modern world. We have come to call him "Henry the Navigator," although he never sailed farther than the coast of Morocco just across from Portugal, and probably never navigated anything. He gave his father's house and the cheerful, comfortable, slightly backward little nation his father ruled, one of the most far-flung empires and one of the richest overseas trades the world had ever seen; but no progeny of his succeeded to that empire, and it seems doubtful whether trade or empire had much place in his plans. We can only guess at what those plans were, and what forces drove him to change the whole picture of the world.

We find him baffling, inscrutable. So did his contemporaries. The face which looks out from the "panel of Prince Henry" in the famous reredos at Lisbon is different from all the surrounding faces, not just because it is swarthier, not because the eyes are more brooding and the forehead more lined with thought, but because the whole countenance is marked by a deliberate stillness; withdrawn, aloof, it looks as if no one else existed, as if there was nothing at all except the vision or puzzle on which his attentive eyes are fixed. All we can be sure of is that he is seeing something no one else can see.

What it was he saw, he never said. His was a voluble, mercurial, self-dramatizing family, given to noisy quarrels and tearful reconciliations, to violence and rhetoric (after all, he and his brothers were half Plantagenets), to childishly magnificent display and childishly cunning political charades. Amidst all this uproar, Prince Henry moved like an abstracted adult through the noisy play of children. Even his generosity had something absentminded about it, so that while men respected him and served him gladly, it seems unlikely that many loved him. His family was literate, even literary, and for men of their time, unusually self-explanatory, but Henry wrote nothing, except perhaps a few prayers, that was not strictly utilitarian. His letters, for the most part, are as dry and businesslike as if he were the bailiff of his own estates. Nowhere is there a line to tell us what he hoped and dreamed. The clues to that are in what happened.

What happened began like a tale in a romance of chivalry. The three eldest sons of King John I of Portugal—Duarte, Pedro, and Henrique (Edward, Peter, and Henry)—had grown up during an uneasy truce with Castile which only the year before had been converted into a permanent peace. Now, in 1411, they were respectively, twenty, nineteen, and seventeen, and it was high time they should be knighted. But there was no enemy against whom they might win their spurs; so their father planned a series of magnificent tournaments to which all the best knights of Europe would be invited and where the three princes might exhibit their prowess at the risk of nothing more than a few bumps and bruises. The king had no more than begun his plans when his sons sought an audience and knelt at his feet. Let not the wealth of the kingdom, they implored, be squandered on vain displays and mock battles. Let them, instead, flesh their swords on the enemies of Portugal and of the Christian faith. Portugal had been born of the Crusade. With their new dynasty, let the Crusade begin again. And since the lands of Castile lay athwart the way to the nearest infidels, the Moors of Granada, let them require the old insults of past invasions and strike at the paynims, this time on their own African soil. Let them attempt the conquest of Ceuta.

It was a surprising suggestion. People still talked about the Crusade but seldom did anything about it. Crusading had gone out of fashion. The princes' uncle, Henry IV of England, said often enough that he hoped one day to lead an army to liberate the Holy Land and lay his bones at last somewhere near the sepulcher of his Saviour, but the nearest he got to doing so was to die amidst his ill-gotten gains in the Jerusalem Chamber at Westminster. As for his son, the future Henry V, he found a nearer and richer enemy more attractive, and would soon be setting out to demonstrate his superior claim to the crown of France by burning the wretched villages of his prospective subjects. In general, throughout Europe, Christian princes preferred to pursue their vendettas with one another while they wrangled over which of the three current popes best deserved their allegiance. Christendom seemed to be shrinking and breaking up. The Ottoman Turks, quickly recovering from the awful blow dealt them by Tamerlane, pressed forward again on its eastern flank. Even in Portugal, which from one end to the other had been carved out of Moslem territory by the swords of crusaders, nobody had done any serious crusading for a hundred and fifty years.

Nevertheless, when he came to think of it, King John could see merits in his sons' suggestion. Ceuta, lying just across the straits from Gibraltar, was the chief port of the Barbary corsairs. It could watch all the shipping that went to and fro in the strait. From Ceuta swooped the swift galleys to seize Italian merchantmen making for Lisbon or to raid the little villages of the Portuguese Algarve and carry off men, women, and children to the slave markets of Africa. Moreover, Ceuta was the favorite staging area and jumping-off-place for the hordes of desert fanatics who from time to time had swept into Spain. To hold it was to hold one of the chief keys to the whole peninsula. Finally, Ceuta was the chief terminus west of Algiers for the caravan trails which came up across the great desert from the wealthy Negro kingdoms of the south. The bazaars and warehouses would be stuffed with monkeys and parakeets, ostrich plumes and elephants' tusks, rare woods and Guinea pepper, and there would be leather bags of gold dust and wedges of reddish-yellow gold tucked away in the strong rooms of every prosperous merchant. At the very least there would be rich spoil, and if the caravans would keep coming, the trade of Africa might fill the coffers of Portugal. When his spies reported that Ceuta might prove vulnerable to determined assault, King John began to make his preparations.

There was a great deal to do. Portugal had to buy cannon and gunpowder abroad, and even ordinary arms and armor. It had to hire ships. And it was impossible in a poor little kingdom to keep these expensive preparations secret; so all of Portugal's neighbors got justifiably nervous. There was grave danger that Castile might take alarm and, thinking these preparations were meant against her, strike first. There was even graver danger that Ceuta might smell the threat and strengthen her defenses. A properly prepared Ceuta would be, against any possible Portuguese effort, impregnable. But by an elaborate comedy of misdirection, King John actually succeeded in persuading observers that what he was preparing was an invasion of—of all places—Holland, so that when the Portuguese armada turned south from Lisbon, the watchful Moors were astonished and dismayed. Even though a tempest blew the invasion fleet off station before a surprise attack could be mounted, Moorish vigilance and Moorish valor could not stop the wild rush of the Portuguese who came boiling off their little ships and splashing through the shallows with Prince Henry at their head. There was savage fighting in the narrow, twisty streets, but before nightfall the last Moorish defenders had fled, and King John was able to knight his three sons in the first city, outside Europe, taken from the infidels in almost three hundred years.

The loot of Ceuta was richer even than had been anticipated. This was a city as stuffed with treasure as Venice, and though most of the gold and precious stones seem to have vanished into the pockets of seamen and archers and men-at-arms, the immediate profit to the crown made the venture a success. But for the long pull, Ceuta was a liability. No more caravans brought the wealth of Ghana across the Sahara to its bazaars. No more merchants from Cairo came with the silks and spices of the East. The wooded hills behind Ceuta were full of Moorish partisans, and the place was under virtual siege except when its former ruler found enough allies to make the siege close and actual. In either case, a strong Portuguese garrison had to be maintained, and the whole town, Christians and Moors alike, had to be fed by sea by convoys escorted by war galleys. For a little country like Portugal, the drain of such an outpost was heavy and the advantage doubtful. No one expected in 1415, when the eyes of Europe were fixed on Agincourt and Constance and on all the internal squabbles which were weakening Christendom against the advancing Turk, that the capture of Ceuta marked the reversal of a trend and that, henceforward, instead of contracting, as it had done for the past two hundred years, Europe would begin to expand again until its civilization circled and dominated and began to unite the globe. It was for no such reason that the Portuguese hung on to Ceuta; they did so simply because it seemed shameful to abandon a city won from the infidels.

The burden of its defense was laid on Prince Henry. Some months after the taking of the city, when he was only twenty-two, his father appointed him Governor of Ceuta and, a little later, Lieutenant-General of the Kingdom of the Algarve, the southernmost province of Portugal, and Grand Master of the crusading Order of Christ. Entrusting the actual command of the garrison at Ceuta to a deputy, the prince himself undertook the harder task of maintaining the line of supply. At first he lived mostly near the sleepy little port of Lagos on the south coast. Later he spent more and more time on the wind-swept headlands of Cape St. Vincent looking out south and west over the tumbling Atlantic. And sometime in those years he saw the vision and accepted the mission to which, with monklike dedication, he devoted the rest of his life. In an ominous waxing crescent, the great world of Islam, stretching from the Russian steppes to the Atlantic coast of Morocco, hemmed in and threatened the smaller Christian world. But beyond the barrier of Islam to the east and south were non-Islamic peoples, some of them (nobody knew how many) Christians. If Islam could be outflanked, the old enemy could be taken in the rear and the Crusade resumed. There was only one way to do it— by sea.

The thing to do was to sail south down the African coast. Henry's earliest chronicler, Zurara, sets forth the prince's objectives as if they had been analyzed by a staff for a command decision. The date, he implies, was about 1419, when Henry was first setting up his court at Sagres. A scientific objective: to explore the coast of Africa beyond the Canary Islands and Cape Bojador because at that time nothing was known by experience, or from the memories of men, or from books, of the land beyond that cape. An economic objective: to seek beyond the cape countries with whom it would be possible to trade. A military objective: to find out by reconnaissance how far south the country of the Moors extended, since a prudent man tries to learn the strength of his enemy. A political objective: to seek a Christian kingdom as an ally. A religious objective: to extend the faith. More than thirty years later, Duarte Pacheco told a somewhat different story. "One night," he said, "as the Prince lay in bed it was revealed to him that he would render a great service to our Lord by the discovery of the Ethiopians . . . that many of them could be saved by baptism . . . and that in their lands so much gold and other riches would be found as would maintain the king and people of Portugal in plenty and enable them to wage war on the enemies of our holy Catholic Faith." There is at least a poetic truth in Pacheco's version, for what turned out to be the greatest series of scientific experiments ever conducted up to that time by Western man, a series which changed the face of the globe and introduced the modern age, began in the haze of a medieval dream. The dream is explicit in the fourth of Zurara's dryly stated objectives: to seek a Christian kingdom as an ally. That could only be the kingdom of Prester John.

Probably the first Prester John heard of in Europe was some Turkish chieftain of the Eastern steppes, some sort of Buddhist or, perhaps, Nestorian Christian, a priest and king at enmity with neighboring Moslems. Later, Prester John became identified with the Coptic Christian overlord of the Abyssinian highland, some of whose priests had chapels at Jerusalem and Bethlehem and some of whose envoys, or persons representing themselves as his envoys, occasionally found their way to Rome and the courts of the West. Medieval Europe was able to transfer the same king, with the same legend, from central Asia to northeast Africa with a minimum of trouble, for both lands lay "somewhere toward the Indies" on the borders of myth and fable. Here unicorns strayed and griffins guarded gold. Here were cannibals, and men whose heads did grow beneath their shoulders, and other men who hopped about on one leg with an enormous foot which, when they took a noonday siesta, they used as an umbrella. Here was a nation of giants who hunted dragons, using lions as hunting dogs. In the midst of these wonders, Prester John dwelt in a high-perched impregnable castle, its moat a constantly flowing river, not of water but of precious stones, and in its throne room a magic mirror in which the Priest King could see at will any part of the world. Seven kings served at his court, sixty dukes, and three hundred and sixty counts. Seventy-two kings obeyed him. Thousands of war elephants marched at his command and hundreds of thousands of horsemen, to say nothing of a special division mounted on ostriches and another on camelopards. His foot soldiers were as innumerable as the sands of the sea. The legends of Prester John vary. In one he was John, the Beloved Disciple, who could not die before the Second Coming and so sat, meditating on his mountain, guarded by hosts of the faithful, awaiting the day of the Last Judgment. But however the legends vary, there is one common factor: in all, the Priest King is very wealthy and very powerful, a reputation which, one may be sure, such subjects of the Ethiopian emperor as reached the West did nothing to diminish. To reconnoiter the Moorish left flank, and perhaps to divert to Portugal the trade which the Moors had diverted from Ceuta, to increase knowledge and convert the heathen, these were all worthy objectives, but the grand objective was to find Prester John and reunite the broken halves of Christendom in a renewal of the Crusade.

The only way to get in touch with Prester John was by sea. And by sea there were, geographically, two possibilities. Either Africa was a peninsula, almost an island, or it was not. Herodotus said it was and that a bold crew of Punic seamen had once sailed down its west coast and emerged, after three years, at the head of the Red Sea. Nobody was known to have repeated their feat since, and certainly not all of Herodotus's geographical information was thoroughly reliable; but some Greek, some Arabic, and some Western geographers spoke of Africa as a peninsula, though they differed about how far it might extend to the south. The contrary opinion, however, was sustained by the great authority of Ptolemy, an authority never greater than in the first years of Prince Henry's mission, for the first complete Latin translation of Ptolemy's geography had just been published in 1410. Ptolemy was sure that the land masses north and south of the equator must be roughly equal, otherwise the globe would be overbalanced. So the great world map constructed from his gazetteer shows Africa curving round until it joins with Asia, making the Indian Ocean a vaster Mediterranean.

Nevertheless, Prince Henry thought the best chance of reaching Prester John was to sail south past Cape Bojador. For even if Ptolemy were right, and the way by sea was blocked, there might be another way to the fabled kingdom. Some Arab sages said that the Nile which flowed through Egypt rose in a great lake amidst the Mountains of the Moon. And out of that same lake, they said, flowed another mighty river, the Western Nile, which took its course through the land of the Negroes and emptied into the Atlantic. At least one fourteenth-century map showed both rivers with, right between them and near the shores of the lake in the Mountains of the Moon, the magic castle of Prester John. Now it was well known that through wealthy Ghana flowed a great river (the Niger, really) with rich cities on its banks. It was not unreasonable to assume that the kings of these cities, like the Ethiopians farther east, were the subjects and vassals of the Priest King, and that the ascent of their River of Gold might lead directly to the Priest King's court. So Prince Henry said to his captains, "Go south!"

Nevertheless, for fourteen years none of them got south of Cape Bojador. Their resources were somewhat limited. Most years, there were at sea in the prince's service not more than two or three *barcas,* the kind of ships the Portuguese used in fishing for tunny or hauling wine and grain along the coast—half-decked vessels shaped like butter tubs with one stubby mast and one clumsy great square sail amidships, commanded by daring, impecunious *fidalgos* and manned by fishermen from the neighborhood of Lagos. They were not afraid of blue water, however, and they knocked about a good deal in the Atlantic, perhaps looking for the islands, real or imaginary, with which all medieval maps dotted the Ocean Sea, perhaps testing Ptolemy's hypothesis that India was, after all, not very far west of Spain. In the course of their voyages they touched the Canaries and discovered, or rediscovered, the Madeiras and the Azores. And every year one or more of them went down to Cape Bojador, took a good look, and came away again. In spite of Prince Henry's repeated exhortations to go farther south, that was as far as any of them went.

It is not that it is so hard to round Cape Bojador. It's an insignificant little bump on the coast of Africa, and once you have reached it, the difficulty is *not* to round it. Most of the time a wind blows steadily from the northeast—the wind Yankee sailors called, hundreds of years later, "the Portygee Trades"—a wind capable of shoving even a tubby Portuguese *barca* along at a stiff clip while the current tugs at her keel with a force of another knot and a half. But out to seaward, as far as the eye can see, there is brown shoal water with here and there a tumble of breakers. Once past this cape, with no sea room to maneuver and the wind and current against you, how would you ever get back? Rounding Cape Bojador was like entering the mouth of a trap. That is what men were convinced it was, a death trap, for the wind and current would be thrusting you on into the Green Sea of Darkness.

The legend of the Green Sea of Darkness begins with the theories of the Greek geographers. Basically, they said, the globe was divided into five zones. At either pole there was a Frigid Zone, where men could not live because it was too cold. Its outer ring was merely inhospitable, gradually becoming incapable of supporting life. Nearer the pole, the air was so mixed with frozen water that it was opaque and unbreathable. One Greek traveler actually claimed to have seen this interesting phenomenon. Then there was the Temperate Zone, with the best climate, of course, in Greece, getting gradually too hot in Egypt and too cold in Scythia. In the Southern Hemisphere there was another Temperate Zone, the Antipodes, where, some said, everything in the north Temperate Zone was exactly reproduced. But it would be impossible to find out because between the two lay the Torrid Zone. In it the heat of the sun grew so fierce that no man could hope to cross the Torrid Zone and live.

To this symmetrical Greek picture, the Arabs added horrors of their own to describe the sea beyond Cape Bojador. As the sun grew hotter, the steaming sea became a thickening broth coated with a scum of green weed and infested with loathsome monsters. Near the equator the sea boiled, the tar would boil in a ship's scams, and the brains would boil in a man's skull. But it was unlikely that any ship could get that far. Long before, it would have been dragged to the bottom by the huge sea serpents which abounded in the region, or crunched up like a biscuit by a crocodile bigger than the biggest whale. Allah had placed the Green Sea for a barrier across the southern ocean. Even to attempt to enter it was blasphemy.

Only the most ignorant believed that the world was flat and that men who sailed too far would fall off the edge, but geographers, Arab and Latin, took the Green Sea of Darkness seriously. Nobody knew just where it began, and many must have rejected its more spectacular terrors, but there was considerable agreement that the ocean south of Cape Bojador was dangerous. At least no one had sailed it and returned. In 1291 two Genoese brothers had rounded Bojador, making for India by sea. They were never heard of again. Half a century later, an adventurous Catalan expedition on the same course, looking this time for the River of Gold (the Western Nile?), also disappeared without a trace. Understandably, even brave Portuguese *fidalgos* hung back. But Prince Henry still said, "Go farther south."

Then, in 1434, after these probes into the vast spaces of the ocean had gone on for fourteen years, one of the prince's captains, Gil Eannes, rounded Cape Bojador and returned. The sea and the wind and the sandy desert shore seemed much the same on one side of the cape as on the other, and the next year Eannes went farther, and the next year one of his companions went farther still, four hundred miles into an unexplored ocean along an unexplored coast. Then came a pause. A disastrous campaign in Morocco and serious domestic disorders distracted Henry's attention, and without the prince's driving will nobody went exploring.

In that interval a great step forward must have been taken in the development of the vessel which made possible the conquest of the ocean. According to Zurara, Gil Eannes rounded Bojador in a *barca*. Nobody says what ships made the next two voyages, and no record survives of how the new type was developed; but when exploration was resumed in 1441, only caravels were used, caravels built in Prince Henry's port of Lagos, expressly, one assumes, for the prince's captains. Caravels continued to carry the explorers until almost the end of the century. They were longer, narrower, more graceful ships than *barcas,* with lateen sails—the primitive form of the fore and aft rig—on two or three masts. They could lie close to the wind and were capital for inshore work. "The best ships in the world and able to sail anywhere," wrote the Venetian Cadamosto after he had commanded one for Prince Henry. For some years, only the Portuguese built caravels, and they sedulously cultivated the legend that no other type of ship could make the African voyage.

We know nothing, except by inference, of Prince Henry's role in the development of the caravel. And we know almost as little of the famous "school" which he set up at his villa at Sagres. He early drew there Jaime of Majorca, prince of cartographers and instrument makers, a man learned in everything that concerned the stars and the sea, the son of the great Abraham Cresques who designed the Catalan Atlas, and possessor, probably, of his father's books and maps. But Henry was always drawing learned men to Sagres, and experienced pilots and far-wandering travelers. It was not so much a school, really, as a sort of scientific congress in continuous session, working out for the first time the problems of navigating the trackless ocean and of charting unknown coasts by using what the northerners knew of tides and the lead line, what the Italians knew of stars and compass piloting, what could be learned from the Arabs, and what from the ancient Greeks—all to be tested by continuous experiment at sea.

Henry died in 1460, just as his captains began reporting that the African coast was trending to the east. He must have died hoping that Prester John and the fabulous Indies were now not far off. They were more than a generation off, actually, but the back of the problem was broken. By compass and quadrant, Portuguese pilots were finding their way across the trackless ocean, standing boldly out from the Cape Verdes to make a landfall at the Azores, harnessing the great wind systems of the Atlantic— the trades and the westerlies—confidently to their purpose. The African coast was mapped as far as the beginning of the Gulf of Guinea. So were the islands. And sugar from Madeira and cargoes of slaves from Negroland were helping to finance the exploring voyages. Men had seen a new heaven and a new earth, the lush green land beyond the Sahara and the rising constellations of the Southern Hemisphere. And, best of all, the superstitious terrors of the Sea of Darkness, the scientific terrors of the Torrid Zone had been dispersed forever. The ocean south of Cape Bojador was like the ocean north of it. There were no clinging weeds, no horrendous monsters, and a man on the deck of a ship off Sierra Leone, less than ten degrees from the equator, was no more uncomfortably hot than he might have been on a July day in the streets of Lagos. To the south, anyway, there were no unnavigable seas, no uninhabitable lands.

More than forty years of patient, probing experiment had at last made Europeans free of the ocean. From this the voyages of Vasco da Gama and Columbus and Magellan, the European settlement of the Americas, the European commercial dominance of Asia and Africa necessarily followed, and with these things followed too the revolutions, in men's ways of thinking and of making a living, which ended the Middle Ages. The monkish ardor of a medieval prince, his long quest for a mythical kingdom, made inevitable the modern world.

DAVID BRION DAVIS

In subsequent chapters* we shall have occasion to discuss Protestant sources of antislavery thought, as well as early Catholic protests against the African trade. For our present discussion, however, it is sufficient to note that the Reformation brought no immediate change in the traditional ideas of servitude. When Swabian serfs appealed for emancipation in 1525, holding that Christ had died to set men free, Martin Luther was as horrified as any orthodox Catholic. Such a total distortion of Scripture would make Christian liberty "gantz fleisschlich." The peasants' demands would make all men equal and convert Christ's spiritual kingdom into a worldly, external thing. As Saint Paul had shown, masters and slaves must accept their present stations, for the earthly kingdom could not survive unless some men were free and some were slaves.

But if Luther's traditionalism is hardly surprising, we might well expect to find a growing hostility to perpetual bondage in the writings of jurists and humanists of the Renaissance, who took an increasingly secular view of human institutions, and who arrived at an enlarged estimate of man's creative powers and inherent nobility. Such a trend toward liberalism would have been in conformity with the actual erosion of slavery and serfdom in Western Europe. As early as the fourteenth century an eminent Italian jurist, Bartolo de Sassoferrato, noted that Europeans had long since abandoned the custom of enslaving one another in war. By 1608 Antoine Loisel could say that in France all men were free. One might suppose that this progress in the accepted rules of warfare had discredited the leading justification of slavery inherited from the Justinian Code. From the perspective of the nineteenth century, it would have been only natural if such beneficent changes had been accompanied by stirring protests against human bondage in any form.

Yet one could not lightly challenge an institution approved not only by the Fathers and canons of the Church, but by the most illustrious writers of antiquity. Men who showed increasing respect for Plato, Aristotle, and Roman law would not be likely to condemn slavery as an intrinsic evil. Hence the revival of classical learning, which may have helped to liberate the mind of Europe from bondage to ignorance and superstition, only reinforced the traditional justifications for human slavery.

Consider, for example, the *Utopia* of Thomas More. Because More permitted both war and slavery in his imaginary society, scholars have long debated whether he proposed an ideal of true social perfection. Certainly

Source: David Brion Davis, *The Problem of Slavery in Western Culture* (Ithaca, N.Y.: Cornell University Press), pp. 106–121. Copyright © 1966 by Cornell University. Used by permission of Cornell University Press. [Footnotes omitted.]
    * [Reference is to *Slavery in Western Culture*—EDITOR.]

More was bold enough to criticize many injustices, such as enclosure and a barbarous penal code. If he felt that man could never achieve absolute perfection on earth, he suggested that natural reason could create a society in which the individual and common good would merge to produce the maximum possible happiness. In the words of R. P. Adams, his utopia offered "a concrete vision of a good life perhaps attainable." And yet he would allow the "vyle drudge" who was "a poore laborer in an other cowntreye" to become a bondsman in utopia. Persons convicted of atrocious crimes would be excommunicated from society and would be enslaved, "For there commeth more profite of theire laboure, then of theire deathe." Like later Americans, More showed faith in the criminal justice of less perfect countries, since utopia's slaves would include those who "in the Cytyes of other landes for greate trespasses be condemned to deathe." And while the foreign perpetrators of wars would be killed, their troops would be captured and enslaved. The stigma of bondage would not be passed on to subsequent generations, but the fact remains that More embraced a fully developed slave system. In part this was a logical extension of his sharp dichotomy between the children of virtue and the criminals and aliens who refused to live by the highest standards of reason. But it was also a reflection of his dependence upon previous thinkers, such as Duns Scotus, Plato, and the Stoics. The problem of slavery in *Utopia* is put in better perspective when we note that no protest against the traditional theory emerged from the great seventeenth-century authorities on law, or from such philosophers and men-of-letters as Descartes, Malebranche, Spinoza, Pascal, Bayle, or Fontenelle.

But the fact that slavery had declined in Europe and yet was being revived in a deadly form in America gave a peculiarly abstract character to discussions governed by the Justinian Code. Throughout Europe scholars debated the relation of slavery to divine and natural law as an exercise in dialectic; it was as if the learned volumes on law and statecraft had been produced in a different world from that which contained the Negro captives awaiting shipment at Elmina Castle, the disease and sickening stench of the slave ships, and the regimented labor of colonial plantations. Even in sixteenth-century Spain the theories of such imposing figures as Covarruvias and Luis Molina regarding legal enslavement of prisoners of war had little relevance to the actual slaving raids of African chieftains. The inherent contradiction of human slavery had always generated dualisms in thought, but by the sixteenth and seventeenth centuries Europeans had arrived at the greatest dualism of all—the momentous division between an increasing devotion to liberty in Europe and an expanding mercantile system based on Negro labor in America. For a time most jurists and philosophers met this discrepancy simply by ignoring it, and by adhering to classical theories of slavery that were thought to have universal application.

Nevertheless, the polarities of geography and race were matched by a widening division in the jurisprudence of slavery which arose from changing attitudes toward natural law. Traditionally, philosophers had assumed a direct correspondence between human institutions, the law of nations, and the fundamental rules of equity as established by nature and right reason. Jurists searched for the concrete applications of a law that was at once transcendent and written on the hearts or in the consciences of men. In the fifteenth century Bartolomeo Coepolla could assume that slavery was authorized not only by civil law and the *jus gentium,* but by natural and divine law as well. But increasingly there was a weakening of the link of relative natural law that had connected the world of human institutions with the ideal realm of nature. This was particularly true in Protestantism. Luther's profound separation of inner liberty from outward obedience to established authority transformed every subject into a divided being who resembled, to some extent, the Stoic picture of the slave. For Melanchthon, as for the Stoics, there was no incompatibility between bondage and true liberty. By shifting the ground of religion from meritorious works to an inward faith, Protestantism moved away from the idea of an organic society in which rights and duties are intricately balanced, and tended to free worldly authority from the restraints of natural law.

But even Francisco Suarez, who followed Saint Thomas in many respects, accepted a sharp dualism between the eternal law of nature and a law of nations governed by expediency and conditioned by circumstance. Slavery, like private property, could not be justified by the highest moral law; yet its *expediency* had been revealed by the almost universal practice of nations. According to Suarez, it was unnecessary that an institution sanctioned by utility and common practice be shown as conformable to the absolute ideal of nature. Similarly, when the Protestant Pierre Jurieu used the traditional Christian argument that slavery, though a consequence of sin, was contrary to nature, Jacques Bossuet based his reply on the practical ground that one could not reject the institution without rejecting both war and the law of nations. Citing slavery as an example of a dominion unlimited by compact, Bossuet argued that all authority, regardless of its origin, became legitimate with time and common acceptance. Anarchy was the worst of all evils, for it made everyone both master and slave. And if slavery was often seen as a necessary instrument for discipline and secular statecraft, needing no further sanction of natural or divine law, circumstances might justify it in one country and not in another. François Delaunay, whom Louis XIV appointed to the chair of French law at Paris, could affirm that colonial slavery was in no way contrary to Christianity, and yet take satisfaction from the fact that in France all men were free.

The inclination to discuss slavery as a matter of public policy was of course strengthened in the seventeenth century, when the slave trade and colonial plantations became increasingly important in international contest for economic and military power. As attention shifted from original sin and natural rights to more practical questions of national self-interest and the best means of procuring and governing a colonial labor force, the moral grounds of slavery receded from view. We shall treat these questions in some detail later on, but first we need to ask whether the trends in secular political thought, at the highest level, provided an intellectual basis for challenging the decisions of judges and statesmen, and for demanding a reversal in the policy of nations.

That Jean Bodin should show a marked hostility to human bondage, and originate what may properly be called an antislavery philosophy, presents a perplexing problem. His mind was medieval enough to be obsessed with witches and demons. He so exalted the rights of private property that he would require the consent of owners to all taxation. He would give to fathers, in the interest of proper discipline, the right of life and death over their children. But of all Renaissance political thinkers he was in some ways the most original and modern. He did much to create the idea of sovereignty as a supreme political authority which responds to change by constructive legislation. His views on slavery were no more anomalous than were his views on the state, and in the last analysis must be regarded as the product of a uniquely independent mind.

Bodin's mind, however, did not work in a historical vacuum. Apparently while he was a student of civil law at the University of Toulouse, a Genoese merchant visited the province with a slave. When the merchant's host persuaded the slave to demand his freedom, the magistrates discovered records proving that any slave who entered Toulouse was automatically free. The merchant, who was on his way from Spain to Genoa, could not see why he should be bound by French law, but he reluctantly manumitted his slave after making a contract for lifetime service. Bodin was impressed by the incident, and used it as evidence that the laws of France did not permit slavery. And for Bodin such legal precedent was vaguely associated with a higher law which guided and limited even the sovereign, free as he might be from all human authority.

We should note that in the 1570's, when the *Republic* was written, France had not yet committed herself to the slave trade, and a supporter of Henry III would not lose favor by exposing the barbarity of the Spanish. Bodin's religious unorthodoxy, which verged on Protestantism, had caused him to be imprisoned for a year and a half. In an age of the cruelest religious warfare, he looked to an all-powerful sovereign as the best means for fashioning a rational social order. If his independence of mind and religious unorthodoxy equipped him to perceive the injustice of widely accepted institutions, he did not arrive at his antislavery position through a belief in the natural equality of mankind. His chief disciple in England was not John Locke, but Sir Robert Filmer. For Bodin it was unthinkable that any group of men, no matter how base or degraded, should be excluded from the body politic and thus deprived of being subjects of an absolute sovereign. His concept of an organic state would not permit the dualism of slavery and freedom. One of his analogies was given heightened significance by the traditional association between slaves and sex: "There be in mans bodie," he discreetly suggested, "some members, I may not call them filthie (for that nothing can so be which is naturall) but yet so shamefull, as that no man except he be past all shame, can without blushing reveale or discover the same: and doe they for that cease to be members of the whole bodie?"

But what of the opinions of philosophers and the precedents of antiquity? Bodin took obvious delight in assaulting Aristotle and the entire tradition of scholastic reasoning, and his key weapon in this demolition was the logic of Petrus Ramus. The disciples of Ramus assumed that truth, which was eternal but frequently obscured by fallacious reasoning, could be revealed most simply and directly by reducing a question to one or more dichotomies, and discarding those parts which seemed to violate common sense. As applied to the problem of slavery the process appears obviously simple, but it represented a radical departure from the traditional discussions of natural law and the law of nations. Bodin was content to summarize arguments for and against slavery, and to ask which of the two was the better. In each argument the final test was expediency and common sense. Hence the Aristotelian case for natural slavery would hold only if the brutal, rich, and ignorant obeyed the wise, prudent, and humble. The Augustinian theory of slavery as punishment for sin would be valid only if masters were agents of the divine will and invariably obeyed God's laws. The provisions of the *jus gentium* for enslaving prisoners of war were impractical as well as inhumane, for it was no charity to spare a man's life only to exploit his labor; and if examples were wanted to deter future aggressors, it would be more effective to kill all captives. The appeal to precedent and to the common practice of nations was groundless, since every kind of wickedness, including human sacrifice, had been regarded as virtuous at some time in history.

Of cardinal importance was Bodin's belief that mankind could err through centuries in both thought and practice, but that social and political truths were knowable if one used the correct process of reasoning. While this implied a rejection of historical precedent, the gravamen of his case against slavery rested on historical evidence. With great learning he showed that slavery had always brought cruelty, corruption, conspiracy, and rebellion. Even the mitigating regulations of Jews, Moslems, and Christians had seldom been observed. It was a catastrophe that slavery had ever been introduced into the world, let alone reintroduced into America after Europe had progressed so long toward freedom. Yet bondage seemed to be creeping back into the continent from its outer boundaries. The Tarters had enslaved many Christians in eastern Europe; bondsmen had appeared again in Italy; in Spain and Portugal they were openly sold as if they were beasts. Though Bodin placed considerable blame on the latter two countries, he did not really explain how this retrogression had come about. He implied that it was simply the result of a spirit of boldness and insubordination which could not be controlled even by benevolent monarchs like Charles V. Bodin was more interested in positive legislation that would prevent slavery from spreading across Europe, or that would modify it for the good of the commonwealth. The wise legislator, who could anticipate problems, would destroy a possible source of bondage by providing public houses where the poor could learn useful trades. In nations where slavery already existed, it could best be eradicated by a very gradual process of emancipation, "having before their enfranchisement taught them some occupation whereby to releeve themselves." Unless they were "strangers," by which Bodin apparently meant men of different nationality, the liberated slaves should become full citizens. To many ears these cautious arguments and proposals would still sound radical after some two centuries had passed.

If Bodin has often been pictured as a defender of absolute power and hence as an enemy of freedom, Hugo Grotius has been classed as a liberal humanist who, along with Jacobus Arminius, helped free the human will from a theoretical bondage imposed by Augustine and revived by Calvin. It was Grotius who also loosened natural law from the confining web of theology and raised it as a supreme authority above not only the will of every earthly sovereign but above the will of God. Ernst Cassirer has said that Grotius accomplished for law what Galileo did for natural science. By making law independent of both divine revelation and the transitory conditions of life, and thus as autonomous and self-evident as mathematics, he created a standard which might at once bind the capricious will of tyrants and help shape the world of men into a more rational and purposeful order.

But did this transcendent law, revealed to man by natural reason, secularized by its divorce from the doctrine of sin, necessarily exclude the practice of slavery? Was it legal for Dutch captains, sailing in increasing numbers while Grotius wrote, to purchase Negroes on the coast of Africa and transport them to the New World? Here we arrive at a seeming paradox. Where Bodin would use the will of the sovereign to abolish slavery in the most expedient fashion, Grotius, who would subordinate all sovereign power to the rules of reason, saw slavery as harmonious with natural justice. His intimate knowledge of classical authorities could be used to create a secular philosophy of law and constitutional power; but it could also be turned to a secular defense of slavery at a time when the prosperity of Holland was closely linked to the African trade.

Few of his contemporaries could have possessed so wide a knowledge of the history of slavery. His discussion was studded with references to the views of Aristotle, Philemon, Seneca, Saint Paul, Gaius, Ulpian, Augustine, and Clement of Alexandria. He gave lip service to the traditional belief that slavery, being unknown in man's primeval state, was not a product of nature. But Grotius made no attempt to bridge the gap between slavery and nature by appealing to original sin or to man's fall from a better condition. For how could an institution supported by so many authorities and sanctioned by the general custom of nations be intrinsically unjust or repugnant to natural reason?

In attempting to construct a rational and secular defense of slavery Grotius betrayed at moments a profound uncertainty. If one chose as a criterion the actual practice of nations, he must conclude that the subjects of an enemy could be enslaved, even when they had committed no delict. The utility of slavery as a means of sparing the lives of prisoners seemed self-evident; a soldier would be more likely to preserve the life of a captive if he knew that he could later sell such property or claim the progeny that would never have been born had he killed a female prisoner. Yet Grotius had to admit that Christians and Moslems did not enslave members of their own faiths. The example of Christians in ransoming captives showed that slavery was not always necessary to prevent wholesale slaughter. Grotius appeared to feel more confident in arguing that masters who provided sustenance to the children of slaves had a right to their perpetual service; there could be nothing shocking, he said, about such an exchange of bondage for a perpetual certainty of food. Parents, after all, had a natural right to sell children who could be provided for in no other way. But it was precisely when Grotius turned to the rights of masters that his assumed harmony between general custom and natural reason broke down. The custom of endowing a master with absolute power could be justified on the utilitarian ground that a more limited power might not have been sufficient inducement for sparing the life of the original captive. Yet absolute power was repugnant to Grotius's entire philosophy of law, and accordingly he drew a distinction between external right, derived from utility, and intrinsic justice as revealed by natural reason. And since a slaveowner might have a legal right to do that which was intrinsically unjust, there were certain limits to the slave's duty of obedience. It was Grotius's "probable opinion" that it was lawful for a slave subjected to extreme cruelty to seek refuge in flight. Similarly, the slave or the descendant of a slave who had been unjustly captured would not be morally guilty of theft if he should escape, provided that he did not owe anything to his master.

Despite these reservations, which were necessary to preserve the supremacy of a higher law, Grotius tended to associate slavery with the entire fabric of social discipline and authority. Without reference to original sin, he quoted Augustine on the necessity of people bearing with their princes, and of slaves submitting to their masters. The most telling reason why slaves could not disobey or resist their masters was that the latter's external rights, though originating in utility and only *permitted* by natural reason, were protected and supported by judicial tribunals. Thus to resist the master was to challenge the authority of the magistrate. While Grotius helped to free the subject of slavery from the doctrine of original sin, he saw it as an integral part of a system of authority and discipline that was an expression of the world's rational order.

The lingering uncertainties which Grotius felt over intrinsic justice and external right disappear entirely in the writings of Thomas Hobbes. For Hobbes slavery was an inevitable part of the logic of power. It raised no questions of sin or natural inferiority, except in the sense that all authority rested on a natural force restraining man from his anarchic and aggressive individualism. While Hobbes retained the traditional view that slavery was a component in the world's system of subordination and authority, he felt no sense of tension between this worldly state of obedience and discipline and an ideal state of natural freedom. He also abandoned completely the Stoic and Christian distinction between external bondage of the flesh and internal liberty of the soul. Indeed, for Hobbes the slave's will was so utterly subordinated to that of his master that he could only will whatever his master willed. It was therefore impossible for an owner to do injury to his slave.

It is true that Hobbes recognized, as had Dio Chrysostom many centuries before, that when a man was captured in war there was nothing to prevent him from attempting to escape or from continuing the war by trying to kill his captor. Presumably, such a prisoner would be physically bound, which for Hobbes was the only true meaning of deprivation of liberty. Up to this point the relation of captor to captive was purely one of physical power. But when the bonds were broken and the prisoner accepted obedience in return for corporal freedom, the dominion of the master was sanctioned by compact. This model of slave-making resembled in many respects Hobbes's concept of the social compact. Hobbes stated quite explicitly that the only difference between the free subject and the "servant" was that one served the city and the other served a fellow subject. Hence the "servant" had no cause to complain of oppression or lack of liberty, when he was only kept from hurting himself and was provided with sustenance in exchange for being governed. By "compact," however, Hobbes did not imply reciprocal rights and obligations. The "servant" had no rights whatsoever and was obliged to obey every command of his lord. For disobedience he might even be killed with impunity. He could be sold or conveyed as his master wished.

Since the time of Plato and Aristotle there had been few justifications of such unmitigated power of one man over another. Nevertheless, it was precisely this unmitigated power that made the "compact" between master and slave a meaningless fiction, and opened the way for the bondsman's legitimate escape or rebellion. The master could use all the power at his command to prevent such resistance from a slave who felt that continued bondage was not in his own self-interest, but in Hobbes's theory there was no legal basis for challenging successful revolt. Indeed, in a paradoxical way Hobbes may be seen as one of the prime sources of antislavery thought. By sweeping away traditional distinctions based on supposedly natural merit and wisdom, and by reducing all social relations to fear and self-interest, he undermined both the classical and Christian justifications for human bondage.

Insofar as Hobbes linked the defense of slavery with the defense of an absolutist state, departing from the Hellenic distinction between domestic bondage and constitutional government, he also made it easier for future writers to move from an attack on absolutism to an attack on slavery. In France, the same can be said of Bossuet. Yet Hobbes's views on servitude were adopted at least in part by men like Samuel Pufendorf, whose philosophies of natural law and social compact inspired eighteenth-century defenders of liberty. Though Pufendorf did not follow Hobbes to the extreme of maintaining that a master could do no injury to his slave, he agreed that the institution was founded on compact and was in accord with natural law. Moreover, since the majority of men lived by selfish impulse, he thought that slavery was highly useful as an instrument of social discipline, comparable to monogamous marriage or to the coercive functions of the state. Believing that it would reduce the number of idlers, thieves, and vagabonds, Pufendorf had no objection to its being revived in Europe.

For John Locke, on the other hand, "Slavery is so vile and miserable an Estate of Man, and so directly opposite to the generous Temper and Courage of our Nation; that 'tis hardly to be conceived, that an *Englishman,* much less a *Gentleman,* should plead for 't." This ringing challenge was directed to Sir Robert Filmer's contention that all authority was like that of master over slave, and that regal power, beginning with Adam, was absolute, arbitrary and unlimited. Yet John Locke, who was certainly an Englishman and a gentleman, had in 1669 transcribed, as secretary to Lord Ashley, the Fundamental Constitutions of Carolina, which provided that church membership would have no effect whatever on the status of slaves, and that "every freeman of Carolina, shall have absolute power and authority over his negro slaves." There is no evidence that he found these provisions objectionable; indeed, he was to become an investor in the Royal African Company, and clearly regarded Negro slavery as a justifiable institution.

But how can it be that so great a defender of the inalienable rights of man was not at heart a determined enemy of slavery? It was Locke, after all, who sought to free the individual from authority based on revelation, precedent, or sheer might. It was Locke who held that even after an individual had voluntarily subjected himself to the social compact, his fundamental rights should always be protected from "the inconstant, uncertain, unknown, Arbitrary Will of another Man." It was of the very essence of Locke's philosophy of inalienable rights that no man could sell himself to another. And regardless of his station in life, every man, in Locke's eyes, should have a right to his own person and labor, and to the property which resulted from mixing his labor with nature. Surely this is the very antithesis of the proslavery views of Pufendorf, Hobbes, and Grotius. Since slavery was so utterly repugnant to the spirit of Locke's social contract, there could be no question of its being justified as a useful or necessary link in society's chain of authority.

But we have already noted the curious capacity of slavery for generating or accommodating itself to dualisms in thought. We have seen that American colonists were not the first to combine a love of political liberty with an acceptance of chattel slavery. And ironically, it was precisely the same opening in Locke's theory of social contract that allowed both a justification of slavery and the preservation of natural rights. For in Locke's view, the origin of slavery, like the origin of liberty and property, was entirely outside the social contract. When any man, by fault or act, forfeited his life to another, he could not complain of injustice if his punishment was postponed by his being enslaved. If the hardships of bondage should at any time outweigh the value of life, he could commit suicide by resisting his master and receiving the death which he had all along deserved: "This is the perfect condition of *Slavery*," Locke wrote, "which *is* nothing else, but *the state of War continued, between a lawful Conquerour, and a Captive*." Hence the relationship was one in which the obligations of the social compact were entirely suspended. Like the murderer, the slave had abrogated the compact and forfeited his natural rights. But whereas the relatives of the murderer's victim were required to surrender to the state their natural right of retaliation, the continuing war between master and slave carried over into society, and was presumably outside the jurisdiction of the state.

Though it may be objected that these views had little subsequent influence, they raise a number of interesting implications. First of all, in Locke's world men would be either entirely free or entirely slave, and the condition of the latter would not be mitigated by the influence of natural reason or intrinsic justice. The master's authority would be as unlimited as it had been for Hobbes, but even Hobbes thought of slavery as part of the social order and as having at least the form of a compact; in theory it could be regulated or abolished by the sovereign. But the elemental struggle between two enemies—which Hobbes took as only the natural condition which made slavery necessary as a social institution—Locke took as slavery's continuing and essential character. This meant that he had turned the traditional Stoic and Christian conception of slavery upside down, for instead of picturing bondage as a product of sinful society, he found its origins and justification outside the limits of a free and rational society. It followed, though Locke did not press the point, that slavery was in conformity with natural law and was as universally valid as private property. And since slaves were private property, and the title of owners was based on natural right, it would presumably be the duty of any state to protect the rights of slaveholders.

Locke's entire argument was highly legalistic and abstract. Unlike Bodin and Grotius, he generally ignored historical precedent. Unlike Suarez, he appealed to principle rather than to expediency or the common practice of nations. He wrote as if no one had ever questioned the right to enslave prisoners of war. And whereas servants were subject only to limited and contractual duties, slaves, "being Captives taken in a just War, are by the Right of Nature subjected to the Absolute Dominion and Arbitrary Power of their Masters." Locke assumed that the authority of West Indian planters was like that of the Biblical patriarchs, but argued that in both cases dominion derived from the purchase of legitimate captives rather than from the inheritance of divinely instituted rights. Like Hobbes, Locke narrowed the ground on which slavery could be justified; and obviously his theory of natural liberty could become a vital component of abolitionist thought. But his unquestioning acceptance of colonial slavery shows how remote abolitionism was from even the more liberal minds of the late seventeenth century.

We must conclude, then, that the thought of Grotius, Hobbes, Pufendorf, and Locke, while preparing the way for the secular theories of the

Enlightenment, provided little basis for criticizing Europe's policy of supporting and extending slavery in the New World. The ancient Stoic dualism of slavery and nature, which had been embodied in Christian doctrine, might have served as a foundation for antislavery thought as soon as men sought to develop a theory of politics on natural principles. But despite the early lead of Jean Bodin, political thought in the seventeenth century did not move in the direction of abolitionism. To be sure, the most original minds no longer justified human bondage as the dark fruit of sin or as a disciplinary force in the divine government of the world. But for Grotius, Hobbes, and Pufendorf the divine order had been at least partly replaced by a system of law or power in which slavery was a rational and harmonious element. This, after all, was in the great tradition of Plato, Aristotle, and Aquinas. For Locke, on the other hand, original sin had been replaced by a supposedly willful act which required that the slave be forever excluded from the paradisial compact and worked, in the sweat of his brow, for the benefit of others. And from this secular hell there was apparently no redemption.

26. The Question of Machiavelli

ISAIAH BERLIN

In 1513 Niccolò Machiavelli wrote a small pamphlet entitled The Prince, *which shocked many of his contemporaries and has continued to shock and puzzle until today. In* The Prince *Machiavelli presumably does no more than offer pragmatic advice to monarchs who would be successful in ruling principalities. Yet in this treatise Machiavelli says things that have caused some scholars to consider him amoral, cynical, immoral, or anti-Christian, whereas others see him as a sincere patriotic Italian, and still others merely as an uninspired writer reflecting contemporary morality in a well-worn literary genre. What is the essence of Machiavelli's political thought? Why have his ideas caught the attention of so many, and caused so much debate, often acrimonious, for over three centuries? In short, what nerve in Western man's corporate consciousness did Machiavelli touch, and touch so deeply?*

Isaiah Berlin, in a trenchant and searching analysis, has recently explored these questions. He has drawn fresh and original conclusions, which not only put Machiavelli in a new perspective but also singularly demonstrate the traumatic nature of his contribution to Western political thought. Professor Berlin argues very persuasively that Machiavelli had deliberately and necessarily chosen between two competitive and mutually exclusive moral systems, that of pagan, classical antiquity and that of Christian medieval Europe. The choice

Source: Isaiah Berlin, "The Question of Machiavelli," *The New York Review of Books,* 4 November 1971, pp. 20–32. Reprinted with permission from *The New York Review of Books.* Copyright © 1971 NYREV, Inc. [Footnotes omitted.]

was ineluctable, for Christian values and Christian morality, in Berlin's analysis of Machiavelli, cannot lead to a stable and successful political community here on earth. On this view, much of the apparent cynicism, amorality, and ambiguity in Machiavelli's thought disappear. But a further conclusion of even greater import emerges. Machiavelli's thought represents an invincible attack on one of the most fundamental propositions of Western political thought, namely, that the world and all in it is directed toward a single, overarching ultimate good, and that eventually human endeavor will discover that social and political order which conforms to this final end. This truth, if truth it is, accounts for so much of the distress and dissatisfaction with Machiavelli's ideas.

Berlin's essay is a brilliant and provocative piece of interpretive writing that touches on issues of fundamental importance to modern man, as he grapples in search of a better world with forces sometimes not yet understood. It is an essay that can be read and understood without a close acquaintance with Machiavelli's thought, although it must be read carefully and thoughtfully. Nonetheless it will prove rewarding both for the light it throws on a crucial and influential European thinker who has been described as "the father of modern politics," and whose dicta were quoted by statesmen and politicians from Frederick the Great to Napoleon and Mussolini, and for the statement it provides of a central contemporary problem.

I

There is something surprising about the sheer number of interpretations of Machiavelli's political opinions. There exist, even now, over a score of leading theories of how to interpret *The Prince* and *The Discourses*—apart from a cloud of subsidiary views and glosses. The bibliography of this is vast and growing faster than ever. While there may exist no more than the normal extent of disagreement about the meaning of particular terms or theses contained in these works, there is a startling degree of divergence about the central view, the basic political attitude of Machiavelli.

This phenomenon is easier to understand in the case of other thinkers whose opinions have continued to puzzle or agitate mankind—Plato, for example, or Rousseau or Hegel or Marx. But then it might be said that Plato wrote in a world and in a language that we cannot be sure we understand; that Rousseau, Hegel, Marx were prolific theorists and that their works are scarcely models of clarity or consistency. But *The Prince* is a short book: its style is usually described as being singularly lucid, succinct, and pungent—a model of clear Renaissance prose. *The Discourses* are not, as treatises on politics go, of undue length and they are equally clear and definite. Yet there is no consensus about the significance of either; they have not been absorbed into the texture of traditional political theory; they continue to arouse passionate feelings; *The Prince* has evidently excited the interest and admiration of some of the most formidable men of action of the last four centuries, especially our own, men not normally addicted to reading classical texts.

There is evidently something peculiarly disturbing about what Machiavelli said or implied, something that has caused profound and lasting uneasiness. Modern scholars have pointed out certain real or apparent inconsistencies between the (for the most part) republican sentiment of *The Discourses* (and *The Histories*) and the advice to absolute rulers in *The Prince*. Indeed there is a great difference of tone between the two treatises, as well as chronological puzzles: this raises problems about Machiavelli's character, motives, and convictions which for three hundred years and more have formed a rich field of investigation and speculation for literary and linguistic scholars, psychologists, and historians.

But it is not this that has shocked Western feeling. Nor can it be only Machiavelli's "realism" or his advocacy of brutal or unscrupulous or ruthless politics that has so deeply upset so many later thinkers and driven some of them to explain or explain away his advocacy of force and fraud. The fact that the wicked are seen to flourish or that wicked courses appear to pay has never been very remote from the consciousness of mankind. The Bible, Herodotus, Thucydides, Plato, Aristotle—to take only some of the fundamental works of Western culture—the characters of Jacob or Joshua, Samuel's advice to Saul, Thucydides' Melian dialogue or his account of at least one ferocious but rescinded Athenian resolution, the philosophies of Thrasymachus and Callicles, Aristotle's more cynical advice in *The Politics,* and, after these, Carneades' speeches to the Roman Senate as described by Cicero, Augustine's view of the secular state from one vantage point, and Marsilio's from another—all these had cast enough light on political realities to shock the credulous and naïve out of uncritical idealism.

The explanation can scarcely lie in Machiavelli's tough-mindedness alone, even though he did perhaps dot the i's and cross the t's more sharply than anyone before him. Even if the initial shock—the reactions of, say, Pole or Gentillet—is to be so explained, this does not account for the reactions of one who had read or even heard about the opinions of Hobbes or Spinoza or Hegel or the Jacobins and their heirs. Something else is surely needed to account both for the continuing horror and for the differences among the commentators. The two phenomena may not be unconnected. To indicate the nature of the latter phenomenon one may cite only the best known interpretations of Machiavelli's political views produced since the sixteenth century.

According to Alberico Gentile and the late Professor Garrett Mattingly, the author of *The Prince* wrote a satire—for he certainly cannot literally have meant what he said. For Spinoza, Rousseau, Ugo Foscolo, Signor Ricci (who introduces *The Prince* to the readers of the Oxford Classics), it is a cautionary tale; for whatever else he was, Machiavelli was a passionate patriot, a democrat, a believer in liberty, and *The Prince* must have been intended (Spinoza is particularly clear on this) to warn men of what tyrants could be and do, the better to resist them. Perhaps the author could not write openly with two rival powers—those of the Church and of the Medici—eying him with equal (and not unjustified) suspicion. *The Prince* is therefore a satire (though no work seems to me to read less like one).

For Professor A. H. Gilbert it is anything but this—it is a typical piece of its period, a mirror for princes, a genre exercise common enough in the Renaissance and before (and after) it, with very obvious borrowings and "echoes"; more gifted than most of these, and certainly more hard-boiled (and influential), but not so very different in style, content, or intention.

Professors Giuseppe Prezzolini and Hiram Haydn, more plausibly, regard it as an anti-Christian piece (in this following Fichte and others) and see it as an attack on the Church and all her principles, a defense of the pagan view of life. Professor Toffanin, however, thinks Machiavelli was a Christian, though a somewhat peculiar one, a view from which Marchese Ridolfi, his most distinguished living biographer, and Father Leslie Walker (in his English edition of *The Discourses*) do not wholly dissent. Alderisio, indeed, regards him as a passionate and sincere Catholic, although he does not go quite so far as the anonymous nineteenth-century compiler of *Religious Maxims faithfully extracted from the works of Niccolo Machiavelli* (referred to by Ridolfi in the last chapter of his biography).

For Benedetto Croce and all the many scholars who have followed him, Machiavelli is an anguished humanist, and one who, so far from seeking to soften the impression made by the crimes that he describes, laments the vices of men which make such wicked courses politically unavoidable— a moralist who wrings his hands over a world in which political ends can only be achieved by means that are morally evil, and therefore the man who divorced the province of politics from that of ethics. But for the Swiss scholars Wälder, Kaegi, and von Muralt, he is a peace-loving humanist, who believed in order, stability, pleasure in life, in the disciplining of the aggressive elements of our nature into the kind of civilized harmony that he found in its finest form among the well-armed Swiss democracies of his own time.

For the great sixteenth-century neo-Stoic Justus Lipsius and later for Algarotti (in 1759) and Alfieri (in 1796) he was a passionate patriot who saw in Cesare Borgia the man who, if he had lived, might have liberated Italy from the barbarous French and Spaniards and Austrians who were trampling on her and had reduced her to misery and poverty, decadence and chaos. The late Professor Mattingly could not credit this because it was obvious to him, and he did not doubt that it must have been no less obvious to Machiavelli, that Cesare was incompetent, a mountebank, a squalid failure; while Professor Vögelin seems to suggest that it is not Cesare, but (of all men) Tamerlane who was hovering before Machiavelli's fancy-laden gaze.

For Cassirer, Renaudet, Olschki, and Sir Keith Hancock, Machiavelli is a cold technician, ethically and politically uncommitted, an objective analyst of politics, a morally neutral scientist, who (K. Schmid tells us) anticipated Galileo in applying inductive methods to social and historical material, and had no moral interest in the use made of his technical discoveries—being equally ready to place them at the disposal of liberators and despots, good men and scoundrels. Renaudet describes his method as "purely positivist," Cassirer, as concerned with "political statics." But for Federico Chabod he is not coldly calculating at all, but passionate to the point of unrealism. Ridolfi, too, speaks of *il grande appassionato* and De Caprariis thinks him positively visionary.

For Herder he is, above all, a marvelous mirror of his age, a man sensitive to the contours of his time, who faithfully described what others did not admit or recognize, an inexhaustible mine of acute contemporary observation; and this is accepted by Ranke and Macaulay, Burd, and, in our day, Gennaro Sasso. For Fichte he is a man of deep insight into the real historical (or super-historical) forces that mold men and transform their morality—in particular, a man who rejected Christian principles for those of reason, political unity, and centralization. For Hegel he is the man of genius who saw the need for uniting a chaotic collection of small and feeble principalities into a coherent whole. His specific nostrums may excite disgust, but they are accidents due to the conditions of their own time, now long past. Yet, however obsolete his precepts, he understood something more important—the demands of his own age—that the hour had struck for the birth of the modern, centralized, political state, for the formation of which he "established the truly necessary fundamental principles."

The thesis that Machiavelli was above all an Italian and a patriot, speaking above all to his own generation, and if not solely to Florentines, at any rate only to Italians, and that he must be judged solely, or at least mainly, in terms of his historical context is a position common to Herder and Hegel, Macaulay and Burd. Yet for Professors Butterfield and Ramat he suffers from an equal lack of scientific and historical sense. Obsessed by classical authors, his gaze is on an imaginary past; he deduces his political maxims in an unhistorical and a priori manner from dogmatic axioms (according to Professor Huovinen)—a method that was already becoming obsolete at the time at which he was writing. In this respect his slavish imitation of antiquity is judged to be inferior to the historical sense and sagacious judgment of his friend Guicciardini (so much for the discovery in him of inklings of modern scientific method).

For Bacon (as for Spinoza, and later for Lassalle) he is above all the supreme realist and avoider of utopian fantasies. Boccalini is shocked by him, but cannot deny the accuracy or importance of his observations; so is Meinecke for whom he is the father of *Staatsraison*, with which he plunged a dagger into the body politic of the West, inflicting a wound which only Hegel would know how to heal. (This is Meinecke's optimistic verdict half a century ago, implicitly withdrawn after the Second World War.)

But for Koenig he is not a tough-minded cynic at all, but an aesthete seeking to escape from the chaotic and squalid world of the decadent Italy of his time into a dream of pure art, a man not interested in practice who painted an ideal political landscape much (if I understand this view correctly) as Piero della Francesca painted an ideal city. *The Prince* is to be read as an idyl in the best neoclassical, neo-pastoral, Renaissance style. Yet De Sanctis in the second volume of his *History of Italian Literature* denies *The Prince* a place in the humanist tradition on account of Machiavelli's hostility to imaginative visions.

For Renzo Sereni it is a fantasy indeed but of a bitterly frustrated man, and its dedication is the "desperate plea" of a victim of "severe and constant misfortune." A psychoanalytic interpretation of one queer episode in Machiavelli's life is offered in support of this thesis.

For Macaulay he is a political pragmatist and a patriot who cared most of all for the independence of Florence, and acclaimed any form of rule that would ensure it. Marx calls *The Discourses* a "genuine masterpiece," and Engels (in the *Dialectics of Nature*) speaks of Machiavelli as "one of the giants of the Enlightenment," a man "free from *petit-bourgeois* outlook. . . ." Soviet criticism is more ambivalent.

For the restorers of the short-lived Florentine republic he was evidently nothing but a venal and treacherous toady, anxious to serve any master, who had unsuccessfully tried to flatter the Medici in the hope of gaining their favor. Professor Sabine in his well-known textbook views him as an anti-metaphysical empiricist, a Hume or Popper before his time, free from obscurantist, theological, and metaphysical preconceptions. For Antonio Gramsci he is above all a revolutionary innovator who directs his shafts against the obsolescent feudal aristocracy and Papacy and their mercenaries. His *Prince* is a myth which signifies the dictatorship of new, progressive forces: ultimately of the coming role of the masses and of the need for the emergence of new politically realistic leaders—*The Prince* is "an anthropomorphic symbol" of the hegemony of the "collective will."

Like Jakob Burckhardt and Friedrich Meinecke, Professors C. J. Friedrich and Charles Singleton maintain that he has a developed conception of the state as a work of art. The great men who have founded or maintain human associations are conceived as analogous to artists whose aim is beauty, and whose essential qualification is understanding of their material—they are molders of men, as sculptors are molders of marble or clay. Politics, in this view, leaves the realm of ethics and approaches that of aesthetics. Singleton argues that Machiavelli's originality consists in his view of political action as a form of what Aristotle called "making"—the goal of which is a non-moral artifact, an object of beauty or use external to man (in this case a particular arrangement of human affairs)—and not of "doing" (where Aristotle and Aquinas had placed it), the goal of which is internal and moral, not the creation of an object, but a particular kind—the right way—of living or being.

This position is not distant from that of Villari, Croce, and others, inasmuch as it ascribes to Machiavelli the divorce of politics from ethics. Professor Singleton transfers Machiavelli's conception of politics to the region of art, which is conceived as being amoral. Croce gives it an independent status of its own: of politics for politics' sake.

But the commonest view of him, at least as a political thinker, is still that of most Elizabethans, dramatists and scholars alike, for whom he is a man inspired by the Devil to lead good men to their doom, the great subverter, the teacher of evil, *le docteur de la scélératesse,* the inspirer of St. Bartholomew's Eve, the original of Iago. This is the "murderous Machiavel" of the famous 400 references in Elizabethan literature.

His name adds a new ingredient to the more ancient figure of Old Nick. For the Jesuits he is "the devil's partner in crime," "a dishonorable writer and an unbeliever," and *The Prince* is, in Bertrand Russell's words, "a handbook for gangsters" (compare with this Mussolini's description of it as a *"vade mecum* for statesmen," a view tacitly shared, perhaps, by other heads of state). This is the view common to Protestants and Catholics, Gentillet and François Hotman, Cardinal Pole, Bodin, and Frederick the Great, followed by the authors of all the many anti-Machiavels, the latest of whom are Jacques Maritain and Professor Leo Strauss.

There is prima facie something strange about so violent a disparity of judgments. What other thinker has presented so many facets to the students of his ideas? What other writer—and he not even a recognized philosopher—has caused his readers to disagree about his purposes so deeply and so widely? Yet I must repeat, Machiavelli does not write obscurely; nearly all his interpreters praise him for his terse, dry, clear prose.

What is it that has proved so arresting to so many?

II

Machiavelli, we are often told, was not concerned with morals. The most influential of all modern interpretations—that of Benedetto Croce, followed to some extent by Chabod, Russo, and others—is that Machiavelli, in E. W. Cochrane's words, "did not deny the validity of Christian morality, and did not pretend that a crime required by political necessity was any the less a crime. Rather he discovered . . . that this morality simply did not hold in political affairs, and that any policy based on the assumption that it did, would end in disaster. His factual objective description of contemporary practices is a sign not of cynicism or detachment but of anguish."

This account, it seems to me, contains two basic misinterpretations. The first is that the clash is one between "this [i.e., Christian] morality" and "political necessity." The implication is that there is an incompatibility between, on the one hand, morality—the region of ultimate values sought after for their own sakes, values recognition of which alone enables us to speak of "crimes" or morally to justify and condemn anything; and on the other, politics—the art of adapting means to ends, the region of technical skills, of what Kant was to call "hypothetical imperatives," which take the form "If you want to achieve x, do y" (e.g., betray a friend, kill an innocent man) without necessarily asking whether x is itself intrinsically desirable or not. This is the heart of the divorce of politics from ethics which Croce and many others attribute to Machiavelli. But this seems to me to rest on a mistake.

If ethics is confined to, let us say, Stoic or Christian or Kantian, or even some types of utilitarian ethics, where the source and criterion of value are the word of God, or eternal reason, or some inner sense or knowledge of good and evil, of right and wrong, voices which speak directly to the individual consciousness with absolute authority, this might have been tenable. But there exists an equally time-honored ethics, that of the Greek *polis,* of which Aristotle provided the clearest exposition. Since men are beings made by nature to live in communities, their communal purposes are the ultimate values from which the rest are derived, or with which their ends as individuals are identified. Politics—the art of living in a *polis*—is not an activity that can be dispensed with by those who prefer private life: it is not like seafaring or sculpture which those who do not wish to do so need not undertake. Political conduct is intrinsic to being a human being at a certain stage of civilization, and what it demands is intrinsic to living a successful human life.

Ethics so conceived—the code of conduct or the ideal to be pursued by the individual—cannot be known save by understanding the purpose and character of his *polis;* still less be capable of being divorced from it, even in thought. This is the kind of pre-Christian morality that Machiavelli takes for granted. "It is well-known," says Benedetto Croce, "that Machiavelli discovered the necessity and autonomy of politics, which is beyond moral good and evil, which has its own laws against which it is useless to rebel, which cannot be exorcised and made to vanish by holy water." Beyond good and evil in some non-Aristotelian, religious, or liberal-Kantian sense; but not beyond the good and evil of those communities, ancient or modern, whose sacred values are social through and through. The arts of colonization or of mass murder (let us say) may also have their "own laws against which it is useless to rebel" for those who wish to practice them successfully. But if or when these laws collide with those of morality, it is possible, and indeed morally imperative, to abandon such activities.

But if Aristotle and Machiavelli are right about what men are (and should be—and Machiavelli's ideal is, particularly in *The Discourses,* drawn in vivid colors), political activity is intrinsic to human nature, and while individuals here and there may opt out, the mass of mankind cannot do so; and its communal life determines the moral duties of its members. Hence, in opposing the "laws of politics" to "good and evil" Machiavelli is not contrasting two "autonomous" spheres of acting— the "political" and the "moral": he is contrasting his own "political" ethics with another ethical conception which governs the lives of persons who are of no interest to him. He is indeed rejecting one morality —the Christian—but not in favor of something that is not a morality at all but a game of skill, an activity called political, which is not concerned with ultimate human ends and is therefore not ethical at all.

He is indeed rejecting Christian ethics, but in favor of another system, another moral universe—the world of Pericles or of Scipio, or even of the Duke Valentino, a society geared to ends just as ultimate as the Christian faith, a society in which men fight and are ready to die for (public) ends which they pursue for their own sakes. They are choosing not a realm of means (called politics) as opposed to a realm of ends (called morals), but opt for a rival (Roman or classical) morality, an alternative realm of ends. In other words the conflict is between two moralities, Christian and pagan (or as some wish to call it, aesthetic), not between autonomous realms of morals and politics.

Nor is this a mere question of nomenclature, unless politics is conceived as being concerned (as it usually is) not with means, skills, methods, technique, "knowhow" (whether or not governed by unbreakable rules of its own), but with an independent kingdom of ends of its own, sought for their own sake; unless politics is conceived as a substitute for ethics. When Machiavelli said (in a letter to Guicciardini) that he loved his country more than his soul, he revealed his basic moral beliefs—a position with which Croce does not credit him.

The second implausible hypothesis in this connection is the idea that Machiavelli viewed the crimes of his society with anguish. (Chabod in his excellent study, unlike Croce and some Croceans, does not insist on this.) This entails that he accepts the dire necessities of the *raison d'état* with reluctance, because he sees no alternative. But there is no evidence for this: there is no trace of agony in his political works, any more than in his plays or letters.

The pagan world that Machiavelli prefers is built on recognition of the need for systematic guile and force by rulers, and he seems to think it natural and not at all exceptional or morally agonizing that they should employ these weapons wherever they are needed. Nor does he seem to think exceptional the distinction he draws between the rulers and the ruled. The subjects or citizens must be Romans too: they do not need the *virtù* of the rulers, but if they also cheat, Machiavelli's maxims will not work; they must be poor, militarized, honest, and obedient; if they lead Christian lives, they will accept too uncomplainingly the rule of mere bullies and scoundrels. No sound republic can be built of such materials as these. Theseus and Romulus, Moses and Cyrus did not preach humility or a view of this world as but a temporary resting place for their subjects.

But it is the first misinterpretation that goes deepest, that which represents Machiavelli as caring little or nothing for moral issues. This is surely not borne out by his own language. Anyone whose thought revolves round central concepts such as the good and the bad, the corrupt and the pure, has an ethical scale in mind in terms of which he gives moral praise and blame. Machiavelli's values are not Christian, but they are moral values.

On this crucial point Professor Hans Baron's criticism of the Croce-Russo thesis seems to me correct. Against the view that for Machiavelli politics were beyond moral criticism Professor Baron cites some of the passionately patriotic, republican, and libertarian passages in *The Discourses* in which the (moral) qualities of the citizens of a republic are favorably compared with those of the subjects of a despotic prince. The last chapter of *The Prince* is scarcely the work of a detached, morally neutral observer, or of a self-absorbed man, preoccupied with his own inner personal problems, who looks on public life "with anguish" as the graveyard of moral principles. Like Aristotle's or Cicero's, Machiavelli's morality was social and not individual: but it was a morality no less than theirs, not an amoral region, beyond good or evil.

It does not, of course, follow that he was not often fascinated by the techniques of political life as such. The advice given equally to conspirators and their enemies, the professional appraisal of the methods of Oliverotto or Sforza or Baglioni spring from typical humanist curiosity, the search for an applied science of politics, fascination by knowledge for its own sake, whatever the implications. But the moral ideal, that of the citizen of the Roman Republic, is never far away. Political skills are valued solely as means—for their effectiveness in re-creating conditions in which sick men recover their health and can flourish. And this is precisely what Aristotle would have called the moral end proper to man.

This leaves still with us the thorny problem of the relation of *The Prince* to *The Discourses*. But whatever the disparities, the central strain which runs through both is one and the same. The vision, the dream—typical of many writers who see themselves as tough-minded realists—of the strong, united, effective, morally regenerated, splendid, and victorious *patria*, whether it is saved by the *virtù* of one man or many, remains central and constant. Political judgments, attitudes toward individuals or states, toward *Fortuna* and *necessità*, evaluation of methods, degree of optimism, the fundamental mood—these vary between one work and another, perhaps within the same exposition. But the basic values, the ultimate end—Machiavelli's beatific vision—does not vary.

His vision is social and political. Hence the traditional view of him as simply a specialist in how to get the better of others, a vulgar cynic who says that Sunday school precepts are all very well, but in a world full of evil men, a man must lie, kill, and betray if he is to get somewhere, is incorrect. The philosophy summarized by "eat or be eaten, beat or be beaten"—the kind of worldly wisdom to be found in, say, Lappo Mazzei or Giovanni Morelli, with whom he has been compared, is not what is central in him. Machiavelli is not specially concerned with the opportunism of ambitious individuals; the ideal before his eyes is a shining vision of Florence or of Italy. In this respect he is a typically impassioned humanist of the Renaissance, save that his ideal is not artistic or cultural but political, unless the state—or regenerated Italy—is considered, in Burckhardt's sense, as an artistic goal. This is very different from mere advocacy of tough-mindedness as such, or of a realism irrespective of its goal.

Machiavelli's values, I should like to repeat, are not instrumental but moral and ultimate, and he calls for great sacrifices in their name. For them he rejects the rival scale—the Christian principles of *ozio* and meekness, not, indeed, as being defective in themselves, but as inapplicable to the conditions of real life; and real life for him means not merely (as is sometimes alleged) life as it was lived around him in Italy—the crimes, hypocrisies, brutalities, follies of Florence, Rome, Venice, Milan. This is not the touchstone of reality. His purpose is not to leave unchanged or to reproduce this kind of life, but to lift it to a new plane, to rescue Italy from squalor and slavery, to restore her to health and sanity.

The moral ideal for which he thinks no sacrifice too great—the welfare of the *patria*—is for him the highest form of social existence attainable by man; but attainable, not unattainable; not a world outside the limits of human capacity, given human beings as we know them, that is, creatures compounded out of those emotional, intellectual, and physical properties of which history and observation provide examples. He asks for men improved but not transfigured, not superhuman; not for a world of angelic beings unknown on this earth, who, even if they could be created, could not be called human.

If you object to the political methods recommended because they seem to you morally detestable, if you refuse to embark upon them because they are, to use Ritter's word, "*erschreckend*," too frightening, Machiavelli has no answer, no argument. In that case you are perfectly entitled to lead a morally good life, be a private citizen (or a monk), seek some corner of your own. But, in that event, you must not make yourself responsible for the lives of others or expect good fortune; in a material sense you must expect to be ignored or destroyed.

In other words you can opt out of the public world, but in that case he has nothing to say to you, for it is to the public world and to the men in it that he addresses himself. This is expressed most clearly in his notorious advice to the victor who has to hold down a conquered province. He advises a clean sweep: new governors, new titles, new powers, and new men; "He should make the poor rich and the rich poor, as David did when he became king . . . who heaped riches on the needy and dismissed the wealthy empty-handed." Besides this, he should destroy the old cities and build new ones, and transfer the inhabitants from one place to another. In short, he should leave nothing unchanged in that province, so that there should be "neither rank, nor grade, nor honor, nor wealth that would not be recognized as coming from him." He should take Philip of Macedon as his model, who "by proceeding in that manner became . . . master of all Greece."

Now Philip's historian informs us—Machiavelli goes on to say—that he transferred the inhabitants from one province to another "as shepherds move their flocks" from one place to another. "Doubtless," Machiavelli continues, "these means are cruel and destructive of all civilized life, and neither Christian nor even human, and should be avoided by everyone. In fact, the life of a private citizen would be preferable to that of a king at the expense of the ruin of so many human beings. Nevertheless, whoever is unwilling to adopt the first and humane course must, if he wishes to maintain his power, follow the latter evil course. But men generally decide upon a middle course which is most hazardous; for they know neither how to be wholly good nor wholly bad, and so lose both worlds."

This is plain enough. There are two worlds, that of personal morality and that of public organization. There are two ethical codes, both ultimate; not two "autonomous" regions, one of "ethics," another of "politics," but two (for him) exhaustive alternatives between two conflicting systems of value. If a man chooses the "first, humane course," he must presumably give up all hope of Athens and Rome, of a noble and glorious society in which human beings can thrive and grow strong, proud, wise, and productive. Indeed, he must abandon all hope of a tolerable life on earth: for men cannot live outside society; they will not survive collectively if they are led by men who (like Soderini) are influenced by the first, "private" morality; they will not be able to realize their minimal goals as men; they will end in a state of moral, not merely political, degradation. But if a man chooses, as Machiavelli himself has done, the second course, then he must suppress his private qualms, if he has any, for it is certain that those who are too squeamish during the remaking of a society, or even during its pursuit and maintenance of its power and glory, will go to the wall. Whoever has chosen to make an omelette cannot do so without breaking eggs.

Machiavelli is sometimes accused of too much relish at the prospect of breaking eggs—almost for its own sake. This is unjust. He thinks these ruthless methods are necessary—necessary as means to provide good results, good in terms not of a Christian, but of a secular, humanistic, naturalistic morality. His most shocking examples show this. The most famous, perhaps, is that of Giovanpaolo Baglioni, who caught Julius II during one of his campaigns, and let him escape, when in Machiavelli's view he might have destroyed him and his cardinals and thereby committed a crime "the greatness of which would have overshadowed the infamy and all the danger that could possibly result from it."

Like Frederick the Great (who called Machiavelli "the enemy of mankind" and followed his advice), Machiavelli is, in effect, saying *"Le vin est tiré: il faut le boire."* Once you embark on a plan for the transformation of a society you must carry it through no matter at what cost: to fumble, to retreat, to be overcome by scruples is to betray your chosen cause. To be a physician is to be a professional, ready to burn, to cauterize, to amputate; if that is what the disease requires, then to stop halfway because of personal qualms, or some rule unrelated to your art and its technique, is a sign of muddle and weakness, and will always give you the worst of both worlds. And there are at least two worlds: each of them has much, indeed everything, to be said for it; but they are two and not one. One must learn to choose between them and, having chosen, not look back.

There is more than one world, and more than one set of virtues: confusion between them is disastrous. One of the chief illusions caused by ignoring this is the Platonic-Hebraic-Christian view that virtuous rulers create virtuous men. This, according to Machiavelli, is not true. Generosity is a virtue, but not in princes. A generous prince will ruin the citizens by taxing them too heavily, a mean prince (and Machiavelli does not say that meanness is a good quality in private men) will save the purses of the citizens and so add to public welfare. A kind ruler—and kindness is a virtue—may let intriguers and stronger characters dominate him, and so cause chaos and corruption.

Other writers of "Mirrors for Princes" are also rich in such maxims, but they do not draw the implications. Machiavelli's use of such generalizations is not theirs; he is not moralizing at large, but illustrating a specific thesis: that the nature of men dictates a public morality that is different from, and may come into collision with, the virtues of men who profess to believe in, and try to act by, Christian precepts. These may not be wholly unrealizable in quiet times, in private life, but they lead to ruin outside this. The analogy between a state and people and an individual is a fallacy: "The state and people are governed in a different way from an individual." "It is not the well-being of individuals that makes cities great, but of the community."

One may disagree with this. One may argue that the greatness, glory, and wealth of a state are hollow ideals, or detestable, if the citizens are oppressed and treated as mere means to the grandeur of the whole. Like Christian thinkers, or like Constant and the liberals, or like Sismondi and the theorists of the welfare state, one may prefer a state in which citizens are prosperous even though the public treasury is poor, in which government is neither centralized nor omnipotent, nor, perhaps, sovereign at all, but the citizens enjoy a wide degree of individual freedom; one may contrast this favorably with the great authoritarian concentrations of power built by Alexander or Frederick the Great or Napoleon, or the great autocrats of the twentieth century.

If so, one is simply contradicting Machiavelli's thesis: he sees no merit in such loose political textures. They cannot last. Men cannot long survive in such conditions. He is convinced that states that have lost the appetite for power are doomed to decadence and are likely to be destroyed by their more vigorous and better armed neighbors; and Vico and modern "realistic" thinkers have echoed this.

III

Machiavelli is possessed by a clear, intense, narrow vision of a society in which human talents can be made to contribute to a powerful and splendid whole. He prefers republican rule in which the interests of the rulers do not conflict with those of the ruled. But (as Macaulay perceived) he prefers a well-governed principate to a decadent republic, and the qualities he admires and thinks capable of being welded into—indeed, indispensable to—a durable society are not different in *The Prince* and *The Discourses:* energy, boldness, practical skill, imagination, vitality, self-discipline, shrewdness, public spirit, good fortune, *antiqua virtus, virtù*—firmness in adversity, strength of character, as celebrated by Xenophon or Livy. All his more shocking maxims—those responsible for the "murderous Machiavel" of the Elizabethan stage—are descriptions of methods of realizing this single end: the classical, humanistic, and patriotic vision that dominates him.

Let me cite the best known of his most notoriously wicked pieces of advice to princes. One must employ terrorism or kindness, as the case dictates. Severity is usually more effective, but humanity, in some situations, brings better fruit. You may excite fear but not hatred, for hatred will destroy you in the end. It is best to keep men poor and on a permanent war footing, for this will be an antidote to the two great enemies of obedience—ambition and boredom—and the ruled will then feel in constant need of great men to lead them (the twentieth century offers us only too much evidence for this sharp insight). Competition—divisions between classes—in a society is desirable, for it generates energy and ambition in the right degree.

Religion must be promoted even though it may be false, provided it is of a kind that preserves social solidarity and promotes manly virtues, as Christianity has historically failed to do. When you confer benefits (he says, following Aristotle), do so yourself; but if dirty work is to be done, let others do it, for then they, not the prince, will be blamed and the prince can gain favor by duly cutting off their heads: for men prefer vengeance and security to liberty. Do what you must do in any case, but try to represent it as a special favor to the people. If you must commit a crime do not advertise it beforehand, since otherwise your enemies may destroy you before you destroy them. If your action must be drastic, do it in one fell swoop, not in agonizing stages. Do not be surrounded by overpowerful servants—victorious generals are best got rid of, otherwise they may get rid of you.

You may be violent and use your power to overawe, but you must not break your own laws, for that destroys confidence and disintegrates the social texture. Men should either be caressed or annihilated; appeasement and neutralism are always fatal. Excellent plans without arms are not enough or else Florence would still be a republic. Rulers must live in the constant expectation of war. Success creates more devotion than an amiable character; remember the fate of Pertinax, Savonarola, Soderini. Severus was unscrupulous and cruel, Ferdinand of Spain is treacherous and crafty: but by practing the arts of both the lion and the fox they escaped both snares and wolves. Men will be false to you unless you compel them to be true by creating circumstances in which falsehood will not pay. And so on.

These examples are typical of "the devil's partner." Now and then doubts assail our author: he wonders whether a man high-minded enough to labor to create a state admirable by Roman standards will be tough enough to use the violent and wicked means prescribed; and, conversely, whether a sufficiently ruthless and brutal man will be disinterested enough to compass the public good which alone justifies the evil means. Yet Moses and Theseus, Romulus and Cyrus combined these properties. What has been once can be again: the implication is optimistic.

These maxims have one property in common: they are designed to create or resurrect or maintain an order that will satisfy what the author conceives as men's most permanent interests. Machiavelli's values may be erroneous, dangerous, odious; but he is in earnest. He is not cynical. The end is always the same: a state conceived after the analogy of Periclean Athens, or Sparta, but above all the Roman Republic. Such an end, for which men naturally crave (of this he thinks that history and observation provide conclusive evidence), "excuses" any means. In judging means, look only to the end: if the state goes under, all is lost. Hence the famous paragraph in the forty-first chapter of the third book of *The Discourses* where he says:

> When the very safety of the country depends upon the resolution to be taken, no considerations of justice or injustice, humanity or cruelty, not of glory or of infamy, should be allowed to prevail. But putting all other considerations aside, the only question should be "What course will save the life and liberty of the country?"

The French have reasoned thus, and the "majesty of their King and the greatness of France" have come from it. Romulus could not have founded Rome without killing Remus. Brutus would not have preserved the republic if he did not kill his sons. Moses and Theseus, Romulus, Cyrus, and the liberators of Athens had to destroy in order to build. Such conduct, so far from being condemned, is held up to admiration by the classical historians and the Bible. Machiavelli is their admirer and faithful spokesman.

What is there, then, about his words, about his tone, which has caused such tremors among his readers? Not, indeed, in his own lifetime— there was a delayed reaction of some quarter of a century. But after that it is one of continuous and mounting horror. Fichte, Hegel, Treitschke "reinterpreted" his doctrines and assimilated them to their own views. But the sense of horror was not thereby greatly mitigated. It is evident that the effect of the shock that he administered was not a temporary one: it has lasted almost into our own day.

Leaving aside the historical problem of why there was no immediate contemporary criticism, let us consider the continuous discomfort caused to its readers during the four centuries that have passed since *The Prince* was placed upon the Index. The great originality, the tragic implications of Machiavelli's theses seem to me to reside in their relation to a Christian civilization. It was all very well to live by the light of pagan ideals in pagan times; but to preach paganism more than a thousand years after the triumph of Christianity was to do so after the loss of innocence—and to be forcing men to make a conscious choice. The choice is painful because it is a choice between two entire worlds. Men have lived in both, and fought and died to preserve them against each other. Machiavelli has opted for one of them, and he is prepared to commit crimes for its sake.

In killing, deceiving, betraying, Machiavelli's princes and republicans are doing evil things not condonable in terms of common morality. It is Machiavelli's great merit that he does not deny this. Marsilio, Hobbes, Spinoza, and, in their own fashion, Hegel and Marx did try to deny it. So did many a defender of the *raison d'état,* Imperialist and Populist, Catholic and Protestant. These thinkers argue for a single moral system, and seek to show that the morality which justifies, and indeed demands, such deeds is continuous with, and a more rational form of, the confused ethical beliefs of the uninstructed morality which forbids them absolutely.

From the vantage point of the great social objectives in the name of which these (prima facie wicked) acts are to be performed, they will be seen (so the argument goes) as no longer wicked, but as rational—demanded by the very nature of things, by the common good, or man's true ends, or the dialectic of history—condemned only by those who cannot or will not see a large enough segment of the logical or theological or metaphysical or historical pattern; misjudged, denounced only by the spiritually blind or short-sighted. At worst, these "crimes" are discords demanded by the larger harmony, and therefore, to those who hear this harmony, no longer discordant.

Machiavelli is not a defender of any such abstract theory. It does not occur to him to employ such casuistry. He is transparently honest and clear. In choosing the life of a statesman, or even the life of a citizen with enough civic sense to want his state to be as successful and splendid as possible, a man commits himself to rejection of Christian behavior. It may be that Christians are right about the well-being of the individual soul, taken outside the social or political context. But the well-being of the state is not the same as the well-being of the individual—"they cannot be governed in the same way." You have made your choice: the only crimes are weakness, cowardice, stupidity which may cause you to draw back in midstream and fail.

Compromise with current morality leads to bungling, which is always despicable, and when practiced by statesmen involves men in ruin. The end "excuses" the means, however horrible these may be in terms of even pagan ethics, if it is (in terms of the ideal of Thucydides or Polybius, Cicero or Livy) lofty enough. Brutus was right to kill his children: he saved Rome. Soderini did not have the stomach to perpetrate such deeds, and ruined Florence. Savonarola, who had sound ideas about austerity and moral strength and corruption, perished because he did not realize that an unarmed prophet will always go to the gallows.

If one can produce the right result by using the devotion and affection of men, let this be done by all means. There is no value in causing suffering as such. But if one cannot, then Moses, Romulus, Theseus, Cyrus are the exemplars, and fear must be employed. There is no sinister satanism in Machiavelli, nothing of Dostoevsky's great sinner, pursuing evil for evil's sake. To Dostoevsky's famous question "Is everything permitted?" Machiavelli, who for Dostoevsky would surely have been an atheist, answers, "Yes, if the end—that is, the pursuit of a society's basic interests in a specific situation—cannot be realized in any other way."

This position has not been properly understood by some of those who claim to be not unsympathetic to Machiavelli. Figgis, for example, thinks that he "permanently suspended the *habeas corpus* of the human race," that is to say, that he advocated methods of terrorism because for him the situation was always critical, always desperate, so that he confused ordinary political principles with rules needed, if at all, only in extreme cases.

Others—perhaps the majority of his interpreters—look on him as the originator, or at least a defender, of what later came to be called *"raison d'état," "Staatsraison," "Ragion di Stato"*—the justification of immoral acts when undertaken on behalf of the state in exceptional circumstances. More than one scholar has pointed out, reasonably enough, that the notion that desperate cases require desperate remedies—that "necessity knows no law"—is to be found not only in antiquity but equally in Aquinas and Dante and other medieval writers long before Bellarmine or Machiavelli.

These parallels seem to me to rest on a deep but characteristic misunderstanding of Machiavelli's thesis. He is not saying that while in normal situations current morality—that is, the Christian or semi-Christian code of ethics—should prevail, yet abnormal conditions can occur, in which the entire social structure in which alone this code can function becomes jeopardized, and that in emergencies of this kind acts that are usually regarded as wicked and rightly forbidden are justified.

This is the position of, among others, those who think that all morality ultimately rests on the existence of certain institutions—say, Roman Catholics who regard the existence of the Church and the Papacy as indispensable to Christianity, or nationalists who see in the political power of a nation the sole source of spiritual life. Such persons maintain that extreme and "frightful" measures needed for protecting the state or the Church or the national culture in moments of acute crisis may be justified, since the ruin of these institutions may fatally damage the indispensable framework of all other values. This is a doctrine in terms of which both Catholics and Protestants, both conservatives and communists have defended enormities which freeze the blood of ordinary men.

But it is not Machiavelli's position. For the defenders of the *raison d'état,* the sole justification of these measures is that they are exceptional —that they are needed to preserve a system the purpose of which is precisely to preclude the need for such odious measures, so that the sole justification of such steps is that they will end the situations that render them necessary. But for Machiavelli these measures are, in a sense, themselves quite normal. No doubt they are called for only by extreme need; yet political life tends to generate a good many such needs, of varying degrees of "extremity"; hence Baglioni, who shied from the logical consequences of his own policies, was clearly unfit to rule.

The notion of *raison d'état* entails a conflict of values which may be agonizing to morally good and sensitive men. For Machiavelli there is no conflict. Public life has its own morality, to which Christian principles (or any absolute personal values) tend to be a gratuitous obstacle. This life has its own standards: it does not require perpetual terror, but it approves, or at least permits, the use of force where it is needed to promote the ends of political society.

Professor Sheldon Wolin seems to me right in insisting that Machiavelli believes in a permanent "economy of violence"—the need for a consistent reserve of force always in the background to keep things going in such a way that the virtues admired by him, and by the classical thinkers to whom he appeals, can be protected and allowed to flower. Men brought up within a community in which such force, or its possibility, is used rightly will live the happy lives of Greeks or Romans during their finest hours. They will be characterized by vitality, genius, variety, pride, power, success (Machiavelli scarcely ever speaks of arts or sciences); but it will not, in any clear sense, be a Christian commonwealth. The moral conflict which this situation raises will trouble only those who are not prepared to abandon either course: those who assume that the two incompatible lives are, in fact, reconcilable.

But to Machiavelli the claims of the official morality are scarcely worth discussing: they are not translatable into social practice. "If men were good . . ." but he feels sure that they can never be improved beyond the point at which power considerations are relevant. If morals relate to human conduct, and men are by nature social, Christian morality cannot be a guide for normal social existence. It remained for someone to state this. Machiavelli did so.

One is obliged to choose: and in choosing one form of life, give up the other. That is the central point. If Machiavelli is right, if it is in principle (or in fact: the frontier seems dim) impossible to be morally good and do one's duty as this was conceived by common European, and especially Christian, ethics, and at the same time build Sparta or Periclean Athens or the Rome of the Republic or even of the Antonines, then a conclusion of the first importance follows: that the belief that the correct, objectively valid solution to the question of how men should live can in principle be discovered is itself, in principle, not true. This was a truly *erschreckend* proposition. Let me try to put it in its proper context.

One of the deepest assumptions of Western political thought is the doctrine, scarcely questioned during its long ascendancy, that there exists some single principle that not only regulates the course of the sun and the stars, but prescribes their proper behavior to all animate creatures. Animals and subrational beings of all kinds follow it by instinct; higher beings attain to consciousness of it, and are free to abandon it, but only to their doom. This doctrine in one version or another has dominated European thought since Plato; it has appeared in many forms, and has generated many similes and allegories. At its center is the vision of an impersonal Nature or Reason or cosmic purpose, or of a divine Creator whose power has endowed all things and creatures each with a specific function; these functions are elements in a single harmonious whole, and are intelligible in terms of it alone.

This was often expressed by images taken from architecture: of a great edifice of which each part fits uniquely in the total structure; or from the human body as an all-embracing organic whole; or from the life of society as a great hierarchy, with God as the *ens realissimum* at the summit of two parallel systems—the feudal order and the natural order— stretching downward from Him, and reaching upward to Him, obedient to His will. Or it is seen as the Great Chain of Being, the Platonic-Christian analogue of the world-tree Ygdrasil, which links time and space and all that they contain. Or it has been represented by an analogy drawn from music, as an orchestra in which each instrument or group of instruments has its own tune to play in the infinitely rich polyphonic score. When, after the seventeenth century, harmonic metaphors replaced polyphonic images, the instruments were no longer conceived as playing specific melodies, but as producing sounds which, although they might not be wholly intelligible to any given group of players (and even sound discordant or superfluous if taken in isolation), yet contributed to the total pattern perceptible only from a loftier standpoint.

The idea of the world and of human society as a single intelligible structure is at the root of all the many various versions of Natural Law —the mathematical harmonies of the Pythagoreans, the logical ladder of Platonic Forms, the genetic-logical pattern of Aristotle, the divine *logos* of the Stoics and the Christian churches and of their secularized offshoots. The advance of the natural sciences generated more empirically conceived versions of this image as well as anthropomorphic similes: of Dame Nature as an adjuster of conflicting tendencies (as in Hume or Adam Smith), of Mistress Nature as the teacher of the best way to happiness (as in the works of some French Encyclopaedists), of Nature as embodied in the actual customs or habits of organized social wholes; biological, aesthetic, psychological similes have reflected the dominant ideas of an age.

This unifying monistic pattern is at the very heart of traditional rationalism, religious and atheistic, metaphysical and scientific, transcendental and naturalistic, which has been characteristic of Western civilization. It is this rock, upon which Western beliefs and lives had been founded, that Machiavelli seems, in effect, to have split open. So great a reversal cannot, of course, be due to the acts of a single individual. It could scarcely have taken place in a stable social and moral order; many besides him, ancient Skeptics, medieval nominalists and secularists, Renaissance humanists, doubtless supplied their share of the dynamite. The purpose of this paper is to suggest that it was Machiavelli who lit the fatal fuse.

If to ask what are the ends of life is to ask a real question, it must be capable of being correctly answered. To claim rationality in matters of conduct was to claim that correct and final solutions to such questions can in principle be found.

When such solutions were discussed in earlier periods, it was normally assumed that the perfect society could be conceived, at least in outline; for otherwise what standard could one use to condemn existing arrangements as imperfect? It might not be realizable here, below. Men were too ignorant or too weak or too vicious to create it. Or it was said (by some materialistic thinkers in the centuries following *The Prince*) that it was technical means that were lacking, that no one had yet discovered methods of overcoming the material obstacles to the golden age; that we were not technologically or educationally or morally sufficiently advanced. But it was never said that there was something incoherent in the very notion itself.

Plato and the Stoics, the Hebrew prophets and Christian medieval thinkers, and the writers of utopias from More onward had a vision of what it was that men fell short of; they claimed, as it were, to be able to measure the gap between the reality and the ideal. But if Machiavelli is right, this entire tradition—the central current of Western thought— is fallacious. For if his position is valid then it is impossible to construct even the notion of such a perfect society, for there exist at least two sets of virtues—let us call them the Christian and the pagan—which are not merely in practice, but in principle, incompatible.

If men practice Christian humility, they cannot also be inspired by the burning ambitions of the great classical founders of cultures and religions; if their gaze is centered upon the world beyond—if their ideas are infected by even lip-service to such an outlook—they will not be likely to give all that they have to an attempt to build a perfect city. If suffering and sacrifice and martyrdom are not always evil and inescapable necessities, but may be of supreme value in themselves, then the glorious victories over fortune, which go to the bold, the impetuous, and the young, might neither be won nor thought worth winning. If spiritual goods alone are worth striving for, then of how much value is the study of *necessità* —of the laws that govern nature and human lives—by the manipulation of which men might accomplish unheard-of things in the arts and the sciences and the organization of social lives?

To abandon the pursuit of secular goals may lead to disintegration and a new barbarism; but even if this is so, is this the worst that could happen? Whatever the differences between Plato and Aristotle, or of either of these thinkers from the Sophists or Epicureans or the other Greek schools of the fourth and later centuries, they and their disciples, the European rationalists and empiricists of the modern age, were agreed that the study of reality by minds undeluded by appearances could reveal the correct ends to be pursued by men—that which would make men free and happy, strong and rational.

Some thought that there was a single end for all men in all circumstances, or different ends for men of different kinds or in dissimilar historical environments. Objectivists and universalists were opposed by relativists and subjectivists, metaphysicians by empiricists, theists by atheists. There was profound disagreement about moral issues; but what none of these thinkers, not even the Skeptics, had suggested was that there might exist ends—ends in themselves in terms of which alone everything else was justified—which were equally ultimate, but incompatible with one another, that there might exist no single universal overarching standard that would enable a man to choose rationally between them.

This was indeed a profoundly upsetting conclusion. It entailed that if men wished to live and act consistently, and understand what goals they were pursuing, they were obliged to examine their moral values. What if they found that they were compelled to make a choice between two incommensurable systems? To choose as they did without the aid of an infallible measuring rod which certified one form of life as being superior to all others and which could be used to demonstrate this to the satisfaction of all rational men? Is it, perhaps, this awful truth, implicit in Machiavelli's exposition, that has upset the moral consciousness of men, and has haunted their minds so permanently and obsessively ever since?

Machiavelli did not himself propound it. There was no problem and no agony for him; he shows no trace of skepticism or relativism; he chose his side, and took little interest in the values that this choice ignored or flouted. The conflict between his scale of values and that of conventional morality clearly did not (*pace* Croce and the other defenders of the "anguished humanist" interpretation) seem to worry Machiavelli himself. It upset only those who came after him, and were not prepared, on the one hand, to abandon their own moral values (Christian or humanist) together with the entire way of thought and action of which these were a part; nor, on the other, to deny the validity of, at any rate, much of Machiavelli's analysis of the political facts, and the (largely pagan) values and outlook that went with it, embodied in the social structure which he painted so brilliantly and convincingly.

Whenever a thinker, however distant from us in time or culture, still stirs passion, enthusiasm, or indignation, any kind of intense debate, it is generally the case that he has propounded a thesis that upsets some deeply established *idée reçue,* a thesis that those who wish to cling to the old conviction nevertheless find it hard or impossible to dismiss or refute. This is the case with Plato, Hobbes, Rousseau, Marx.

I should like to suggest that it is Machiavelli's juxtaposition of the two outlooks—the two incompatible moral worlds, as it were—in the minds of his readers, and the collision and acute discomfort that follow that, over the years, has been responsible for the desperate efforts to interpret his doctrines away, to represent him as a cynical and therefore ultimately shallow defender of power politics; or as a diabolist; or as a patriot prescribing for particularly desperate situations which seldom arise; or as a mere time server; or as an embittered political failure; or as a mere mouthpiece of truths we have always known but did not like to utter; or again as the enlightened translator of universally accepted ancient social principles into empirical terms; or as a crypto-republican satirist (a descendant of Juvenal, a forerunner of Orwell); or as a cold scientist, a mere political technologist free from moral implications; or as a typical Renaissance publicist practicing a now obsolete genre; or in any of the numerous other roles that have been and are still being cast for him.

Machiavelli may have possessed some of these attributes, but concentration on one or other of them as constituting his essential, "true" character seems to me to stem from reluctance to face and, still more, discuss the uncomfortable truth that Machiavelli had, unintentionally, almost casually, uncovered: namely, that not all ultimate values are necessarily compatible with one another—that there might be a conceptual (what used to be called "philosophical"), and not merely a material, obstacle to the notion of the single ultimate solution which, if it were only realized, would establish the perfect society.

IV

Yet if no such solution can, even in principle, be formulated, then all political and, indeed, moral problems are thereby transformed. This is not a division of politics from ethics. It is the uncovering of the possibility of more than one system of values, with no criterion common to the systems whereby a rational choice can be made between them. This is not the rejection of Christianity for paganism (although Machiavelli clearly prefers the latter), nor of paganism for Christianity (which, at least in its historical form, he thought incompatible with the basic needs of normal men), but the setting of them side by side with the implicit invitation to men to choose either a good, virtuous private life or a good, successful social existence, but not both.

What has been shown by Machiavelli, who is often (like Nietzsche) congratulated for tearing off hypocritical masks, brutally revealing the truth, and so on, is not that men profess one thing and do another (although no doubt he shows this too) but that when they assume that the two ideals are compatible, or perhaps are even one and the same ideal, and do not allow this assumption to be questioned, they are guilty of bad faith (as the existentialists call it, or of "false consciousness," to use a Marxist formula) which their actual behavior exhibits. Machiavelli calls the bluff not just of official morality—the hypocrisies of ordinary life—but of one of the foundations of the central Western philosophical tradition, the belief in the ultimate compatibility of all genuine values. His own withers are unwrung. He has made his choice. He seems wholly unworried by, indeed scarcely aware of, parting company with traditional Western morality.

But the question that his writings have dramatized, if not for himself, then for others in the centuries that followed, is this: what reason have we for supposing that justice and mercy, humility and *virtù*, happiness and knowledge, glory and liberty, magnificence and sanctity will always coincide, or indeed be compatible at all? Poetic justice is, after all, so called not because it does, but because it does not, as a rule, occur in the prose of ordinary life, where, *ex hypothesi*, a very different kind of justice operates. "States and people are governed in a different way from an individual." Hence what talk can there be of indestructible rights, either in the medieval or the liberal sense? The wise man must eliminate fantasies from his own head, and should seek to dispel them from the heads of others; or, if they are too resistant, he should at least, as Pareto or Dostoevsky's Grand Inquisitor recommended, exploit them as a means to a viable society.

"The march of world history stands outside virtue, vice and justice," said Hegel. If for the march of history you substitute "a well governed *patria*," and interpret Hegel's notion of virtue as it is understood by Christians or ordinary men, then Machiavelli is one of the earliest proponents of this doctrine. Like all great innovators, he is not without ancestry. But the names of Palmieri and Pontano, and even of Carneades and Sextus Empiricus, have left little mark on European thought.

Croce has rightly insisted that Machiavelli is not detached nor cynical nor irresponsible. His patriotism, his republicanism, his commitment are not in doubt. He suffered for his convictions. He thought continually about Florence and Italy, and of how to save them. Yet it is not his character, nor his plays, his poetry, his histories, his diplomatic or political activities that have gained him his unique fame. Nor can this be due only to his psychological or sociological imagination. His psychology is often excessively primitive. He scarcely seems to allow for the bare possibility of sustained and genuine altruism, he refuses to consider the motives of men who are prepared to fight against enormous odds, who ignore *necessità* and are prepared to lose their lives in a hopeless cause.

His distrust of unworldly attitudes, absolute principles divorced from empirical observation, is fanatically strong—almost romantic in its violence; the vision of the great prince playing upon human beings like an instrument intoxicates him. He assumes that different societies must always be at war with each other, since they have conflicting purposes. He sees history as one endless process of cutthroat competition, in which the only goal that rational men can have is to succeed in the eyes of their contemporaries and of posterity. He is good at bringing fantasies down to earth, but he assumes, as Mill was to complain about Bentham, that this is enough. He allows too little to the ideal impulses of men. He has no historical sense and little sense of economics. He has no inkling of the technological progress that is about to transform political and social life, and in particular the art of war. He does not understand how either individuals, communities, or cultures develop and transform themselves. Like Hobbes, he assumes that the argument or motive for self-preservation automatically outweighs all others.

He tells men above all not to be fools: to follow a principle when this may involve you in ruin is absurd, at least if judged by worldly standards; other standards he mentions respectfully, but takes no interest in them: those who adopt them are not likely to create anything that will perpetuate their name. His Romans are no more real than the Stylized figures in his brilliant comedies. His human beings have so little inner life or capacity for cooperation or social solidarity that, as in the case of Hobbes's not dissimilar creatures, it is difficult to see how they could develop enough reciprocal confidence to create a lasting social whole, even under the perpetual shadow of carefully regulated violence.

Few would deny that Machiavelli's writings, more particularly *The Prince,* have scandalized mankind more deeply and continuously than any other political treatise. The reason for this, let me say again, is not the discovery that politics is the play of power—that political relationships between and within independent communities involve the use of force and fraud, and are unrelated to the principles professed by the players. That knowledge is as old as conscious thought about politics—certainly as old as Thucydides and Plato. Nor is it merely caused by the examples that he offers of success in acquiring or holding power—the descriptions of the massacre at Sinigaglia or the behavior of Agathocles or Oliverotto da Fermo are no more or less horrifying than similar stories in Tacitus or Guicciardini. The proposition that crime can pay is nothing new in Western historiography.

Nor is it merely his recommendation of ruthless measures that so upsets his readers. Aristotle had long ago allowed that exceptional situations might arise, that principles and rules could not be rigidly applied to all situations; the advice to rulers in *The Politics* is tough-minded enough. Cicero is aware that critical situations demand exceptional measures; *ratio publicae utilitatis, ratio status* were familiar in the thought of the Middle Ages. "Necessity is not subject to law" is a Thomist sentiment; Pierre d'Auvergne says much the same. Harrington said this in the following century, and Hume applauded him.

These opinions were not thought original by these, or perhaps any, thinkers. Machiavelli did not originate nor did he make much use of the notion of *raison d'état.* He stressed will, boldness, address, at the expense of the rules laid down by the calm *ragione,* to which his colleagues in the *Pratiche Fiorentine,* and perhaps the Oricellari Gardens, may have appealed. So did Leon Battista Alberti when he declared that *fortuna* crushes only the weak and propertyless; so did contemporary poets; so, too, in his own fashion, did Pico della Mirandola in his great apostrophe to the powers of man the creator, who, unlike the angels, can transform himself into any shape—the ardent image that lies at the heart of European humanism in the North as well as the Mediterranean.

Far more original, as has often been noted, is Machiavelli's divorce of political behavior as a field of study from the theological world picture in terms of which this topic was discussed before him (even by Marsilio) and after him. Yet it is not his secularism, however audacious in his own day, that could have disturbed the contemporaries of Voltaire or Bentham or their successors. What shocked them is something different.

Machiavelli's cardinal achievement is his uncovering of an insoluble dilemma, the planting of a permanent question mark in the path of posterity. It stems from his *de facto* recognition that ends equally ultimate, equally sacred, may contradict each other, that entire systems of value may come into collision without possibility of rational arbitration, and that not merely in exceptional circumstances, as a result of abnormality or accident or error—the clash of Antigone and Creon or in the story of Tristan —but (this was surely new) as part of the normal human situation.

For those who look on such collisions as rare, exceptional, and disastrous, the choice to be made is necessarily an agonizing experience for which, as a rational being, one cannot prepare (since no rules apply). But for Machiavelli, at least in *The Prince, The Discourses, Mandragola,* there is no agony. One chooses as one chooses because one knows what one wants, and is ready to pay the price. One chooses classical civilization rather than the Theban desert, Rome and not Jerusalem, whatever the priests may say, because such is one's nature, and—he is no existentialist or romantic individualist *avant la parole*—because it is that of men in general, at all times, everywhere. If others prefer solitude or martyrdom, he shrugs his shoulders. Such men are not for him. He has nothing to say to them, nothing to argue with them about. All that matters to him and those who agree with him is that such men be not allowed to meddle with politics or education or any of the cardinal factors in human life; their outlook unfits them for such tasks.

I do not mean that Machiavelli explicitly asserts that there is a pluralism or even a dualism of values between which conscious choices must be made. But this follows from the contrasts he draws between the conduct he admires and that which he condemns. He seems to take for granted the obvious superiority of classical civic virtue and brushes aside Christian values, as well as conventional morality, with a disparaging or patronizing sentence or two, or smooth words about the misinterpretation of Christianity. This worries or infuriates those who disagree with him the more because it goes against their convictions without seeming to be aware of doing so—and recommends wicked courses as obviously the most sensible, something that only fools or visionaries will reject.

If what Machiavelli believed is true, this undermines one major assumption of Western thought: namely, that somewhere in the past or the future, in this world or the next, in the church or the laboratory, in the speculations of the metaphysician or the findings of the social scientist or in the uncorrupted heart of the simple good man, there is to be found the final solution of the question of how men should live. If this is false (and if more than one equally valid answer to the question can be returned, then it is false) the idea of the sole true, objective, universal human ideal crumbles. The very search for it becomes not merely utopian in practice, but conceptually incoherent.

One can surely see how this might seem unfaceable to men, believers or atheists, empiricists or apriorists, brought up on the opposite assumption. Nothing could well be more upsetting to those brought up in a monistic religious or, at any rate, moral, social, or political system than a breach in it. This is the dagger of which Meinecke speaks, with which Machiavelli inflicted the wound that has never healed; even though Professor Felix Gilbert is right in thinking that he did not bear the scars of it himself. For he remained a monist, albeit a pagan one.

Machiavelli was doubtless guilty of much confusion and exaggeration. He confused the proposition that ultimate ideals may be incompatible with the very different proposition that the more conventional human ideals—founded on ideas of Natural Law, brotherly love, and human goodness—were unrealizable and that those who acted on the opposite assumption were fools, and at times dangerous ones; and he attributed this dubious proposition to antiquity and believed that it was verified by history.

The first of these assertions strikes at the root of all doctrines committed to the possibility of attaining, or at least formulating, final solutions; the second is empirical, commonplace, and not self-evident. The two propositions are not, in any case, identical or logically connected. Moreover he exaggerated wildly: the idealized types of the Periclean Greek or the Roman of the old Republic may be irreconcilable with the ideal citizen of a Christian commonwealth (supposing such were conceivable), but in practice—above all in history, to which our author went for illustrations if not for evidence—pure types seldom obtain: mixtures and compounds and compromises and forms of communal life that do not fit into easy classifications, but which neither Christians nor liberal humanists nor Machiavelli would be compelled by their beliefs to reject, can be conceived without too much intellectual difficulty. Still, to attack and inflict lasting damage on a central assumption of an entire civilization is an achievement of the first order.

He does not affirm this dualism. He merely takes for granted the superiority of Roman *antiqua virtus* (which may be maddening to those who do not) over the Christian life as taught by the Church. He utters a few casual words about what Christianity might have become, but does not expect it to change its actual character. There he leaves the matter. Anyone who believes in Christian morality regards the Christian Commonwealth as its embodiment, but at the same time largely accepts the validity of Machiavelli's political and psychological analysis and does not reject the secular heritage of Rome—a man in this predicament is faced with a dilemma which, if Machiavelli is right, is not merely unsolved, but insoluble. This is the Gordian knot which, according to Vanini and Leibniz, the author of *The Prince* had tied, a knot which can only be cut, not untied. Hence the efforts to dilute his doctrines, or interpret them in such a way as to remove their sting.

After Machiavelli, doubt is liable to infect all monistic constructions. The sense of certainty that there is somewhere a hidden treasure—the final solution to our ills—and that some path must lead to it (for, in principle, it must be discoverable); or else, to alter the image, the conviction that the fragments constituted by our beliefs and habits are all pieces of a jigsaw puzzle, which (since there is an a priori guarantee for this) can, in principle, be solved; so that it is only because of lack of skill or stupidity or bad fortune that we have not so far succeeded in discovering the solution whereby all interests will be brought into harmony—this fundamental belief of Western political thought has been severely shaken. Surely in an age that looks for certainties, this is sufficient to account for the unending efforts, more numerous today than ever, to explain *The Prince* and *The Discourses,* or to explain them away?

This is the negative implication. There is also one that is positive, and might have surprised and perhaps displeased Machiavelli. So long as only one ideal is the true goal, it will always seem to men that no means can be too difficult, no price too high, to do whatever is required to realize the ultimate goal. Such certainty is one of the great justifications of fanaticism, compulsion, persecution. But if not all values are compatible with one another, and choices must be made for no better reason than that each value is what it is, and we choose it for what it is, and not because it can be shown on some single scale to be higher than another. If we choose forms of life because we believe in them, because we take them for granted, or, upon examination, find that we are morally unprepared to live in any other way (although others choose differently); if rationality and calculation can be applied only to means or subordinate ends, but never to ultimate ends; then a picture emerges different from that constructed round the ancient principle that there is only one good for men.

If there is only one solution to the puzzle, then the only problems are first how to find it, then how to realize it, and finally how to convert others to the solution by persuasion or by force. But if this is not so (Machiavelli contrasts two ways of life, but there could be, and, save for fanatical monists, there obviously are, more than two), then the path is open to empiricism, pluralism, toleration, compromise. Toleration is historically the product of the realization of the irreconcilability of equally dogmatic faiths, and the practical improbability of complete victory of one over the other. Those who wished to survive realized that they had to tolerate error. They gradually came to see merits in diversity, and so became skeptical about definitive solutions in human affairs.

But it is one thing to accept something in practice, another to justify it rationally. Machiavelli's "scandalous" writings begin the latter process. This was a major turning point, and its intellectual consequences, wholly unintended by its originator, were, by a fortunate irony of history (which some call its dialectic), the basis of the very liberalism that Machiavelli would surely have condemned as feeble and characterless, lacking in single-minded pursuit of power, in splendor, in organization, in *virtù*, in power to discipline unruly men against huge odds into one energetic whole. Yet he is, in spite of himself, one of the makers of pluralism, and of its—to him—perilous acceptance of toleration.

By breaking the original unity he helped to cause men to become aware of the necessity of making agonizing choices between incompatible alternatives, incompatible in practice or, worse still, for logical reasons, in public and private life (for the two could not, it became obvious, be genuinely kept distinct). His achievement is of the first order, if only because the dilemma has never given men peace since it came to light (it remains unsolved, but we have learned to live with it). Men had, no doubt, in practice, often enough experienced the conflict that Machiavelli made explicit. He converted its expression from a paradox into something approaching a commonplace.

The sword of which Meinecke spoke has not lost its edge: the wound has not healed. To know the worst is not always to be liberated from its consequences; nevertheless it is preferable to ignorance. It is this painful truth that Machiavelli forced on our attention, not by formulating it explicitly, but perhaps the more effectively by relegating much uncriticized traditional morality to the realm of utopia. This is what, at any rate, I should like to suggest. Where more than twenty interpretations hold the field, the addition of one more cannot be deemed an impertinence. At worst it will be no more than yet another attempt to solve the problem, now more than four centuries old, of which Croce at the end of his long life spoke as *"una questione che forse non si chiuderà mai: la questione de Machiavelli."* *

* ["A question which perhaps will never be closed: the question of Machiavelli"—EDITOR.]

27. Young Man Luther

ERIK H. ERIKSON

There are in history certain individuals whose acts have far-reaching, even cataclysmic effects, and Martin Luther was one of these. His revolt against Rome began simply to protect certain abuses in religious practices, such as the "sale of indulgencies"; these abuses were obvious to many humanists like Erasmus who also wanted ecclesiastical reform. But Luther would not draw back before official censure, and he became intransigent and convinced that he was in the right; that, in his famous utterance, "he could not do otherwise." The question of why nearly half of Christian Europe was prepared to follow Luther's example in repudiating the moral authority of Rome is complex, and social, economic and political motives probably have as much to do with it as religious ones. What though are we to make of the man who set the example, of Luther himself?

Historians have long debated this question, and have seen Luther in various lights: as misguided reformer, religious fanatic, megalomaniac, schemer and opportunist, inspired leader, and so on. Recently the problem has been studied afresh from a new viewpoint by the eminent psychoanalyst Erik Erikson. In Young Man Luther, *Erikson attempts to use psychoanalytic methods to explain Luther's actions. It is particularly in what he calls the "crisis of adolescence" that Erikson finds the source of much of Luther's difficulties—in his search for identity, and in his relationship with his two fathers, heavenly and biological.*

Source: Erik H. Erikson, *Young Man Luther* (New York: W. W. Norton & Co., 1958), pp. 14–17, 36–40, 137–140, 144–145. Copyright © 1958, 1962 by Erik H. Erikson. Reprinted by permission of W. W. Norton & Company, Inc.

In the following selection, Erikson describes the identity crisis and discusses two early incidents that manifest Luther's struggle and his rebellious spirit. The reader must judge how convincingly Erikson has put his case, but he cannot escape certain other implications of the argument. What limitations does the historian see in such a method? Should we attempt to explain the careers of great men through this approach? If so, how much weight should one give to the psychoanalytic approach? Is it legitimate to employ such a technique to people long dead, who can be studied only through their writings and those of others? Is Erikson's a sufficient explanation of a complex man and a complex career?

There has been much vigorous debate among historians concerning the validity of psychoanalytic techniques to reconstruct the past, and two recent works treat these problems: B. Wolman, ed., The Psychoanalytic Interpretation of History *(1971) and B. Mazlish, ed.,* Psychoanalysis and History *(1971). For a quite recent and stimulating example one might read O. Pflanze, "Toward a Psychoanalytic Interpretation of Bismarck,"* American Historical Review, *LXXVII (1972). Whatever the problems with Erikson's method, it is a fascinating and interesting one which has already found much favor with one school of historians.*

I have called the major crisis of adolescence the *identity crisis;* it occurs in that period of the life cycle when each youth must forge for himself some central perspective and direction, some working unity, out of the effective remnants of his childhood and the hopes of his anticipated adulthood; he must detect some meaningful resemblance between what he has come to see in himself and what his sharpened awareness tells him others judge and expect him to be. This sounds dangerously like common sense; like all health, however, it is a matter of course only to those who possess it, and appears as a most complex achievement to those who have tasted its absence. Only in ill health does one realize the intricacy of the body; and only in a crisis, individual or historical, does it become obvious what a sensitive combination of interrelated factors the human personality is— a combination of capacities created in the distant past and of opportunities divined in the present; a combination of totally unconscious preconditions developed in individual growth and of social conditions created and recreated in the precarious interplay of generations. In some young people, in some classes, at some periods in history, this crisis will be minimal; in other people, classes, and periods, the crisis will be clearly marked off as a critical period, a kind of "second birth," apt to be aggravated either by widespread neuroticisms or by pervasive ideological unrest. Some young individuals will succumb to this crisis in all manner of neurotic, psychotic, or delinquent behavior; others will resolve it through participation in ideological movements passionately concerned with religion or politics, nature or art. Still others, although suffering and deviating dangerously through what appears to be a prolonged adolescence, eventually come to contribute an original bit to an emerging style of life: the very danger which they have sensed has forced them to mobilize capacities to see and say, to dream and plan, to design and construct, in new ways.

Luther, so it seems, at one time was a rather endangered young man, beset with a syndrome of conflicts whose outline we have learned to recognize, and whose components to analyse. He found a spiritual solution, not without the well-timed help of a therapeutically clever superior in the Augustinian order. His solution roughly bridged a political and psychological vacuum which history had created in a significant portion of Western Christendom. Such coincidence, if further coinciding with the deployment of highly specific personal gifts, makes for historical "greatness." We will follow Luther through the crisis of his youth, and the unfolding of his gifts, to the first manifestation of his originality as a thinker, namely, to the emergence of a new theology, apparently not immediately perceived as a radical innovation either by him or his listeners, in his first Lectures on the Psalms (1513). What happened to him after he had acquired a historical identity is more than another chapter; for even half of the man is too much for one book. The difference between the young and the old Luther is so marked, and the second, the sturdy orator, so exclusive a Luther-image to most readers, that I will speak of "Martin" when I report on Luther's early years, which according to common usage in the Luther literature include his twenties; and of "Luther" where and when he has become the leader of Lutherans, seduced by history into looking back on his past as upon a mythological autobiography.

Kierkegaard's remark * has a second part: ". . . of very great import for Christendom." This calls for an investigation of how the individual "case" became an important, an historic "event," and for formulations concerning the spiritual and political identity crisis of Northern Christendom in Luther's time. True, I could have avoided those methodological uncertainties and impurities which will undoubtedly occur by sticking to my accustomed job of writing a case history, and leaving the historical event to those who, in turn, would consider the case a mere accessory to the event. But we clinicians have learned in recent years that we cannot lift a case history out of history, even as we suspect that historians, when they try to separate the logic of the historic event from that of the life histories which intersect in it, leave a number of vital historical problems unattended. So we may have to risk that bit of impurity which is inherent in the hyphen of the psycho-historical as well as of all other hyphenated approaches. They are the compost heap of today's interdisciplinary efforts, which may help to fertilize new fields, and to produce future flowers of new methodological clarity.

Human nature can best be studied in the state of conflict; and human conflict comes to the detailed attention of interested recorders mainly under special circumstances. One such circumstance is the clinical encounter, in which the suffering, for the sake of securing help, have no other choice than to become case histories; and another special circumstance is history, where extraordinary beings, by their own self-centered maneuvers and through the prodding of the charismatic hunger of mankind, become (auto)biographies. Clinical as well as historical scholars have much to

* [Erikson has referred to this in an earlier passage—EDITOR]

learn by going back and forth between these two kinds of recorded history. Luther, always instructive, forces on the workers in both fields a special awareness. He indulged himself as he grew older in florid self-revelations of a kind which can make a clinical biographer feel that he is dealing with a client. If the clinician should indulge himself in this feeling, however, he will soon find out that the imaginary client has been dealing with him: for Luther is one of those autobiographies with a histrionic flair who can make enthusiastic use even of their neurotic suffering, matching selected memories with the clues given to them by their avid public to create their own official identities.

I intend to take my subtitle seriously. This "Study in Psychoanalysis and History" will re-evaluate a segment of history (here the youth of a great reformer) by using psychoanalysis as a historical tool; but it will also, here and there, throw light on psychoanalysis as a tool of history. At this point I must digress for a few pages from the subject of my main title in order to attend to the methodological subtitle.

Psychoanalysis, like all systems, has its own inner history of development. As a method of observation it takes history; as a system of ideas it makes history.

I indicated in the preface that whenever a psychoanalyst shifts the focus of his interest to a new class of patients—be they of the same age, of similar background, or the victims of the same clinical syndrome— he is forced not only to modify his therapeutic technique, but also to explain the theoretical rationale of his modification. Thus, from a gradual refinement of therapeutic technique, the perfection of a theory of the mind is expected to result. This is the historical idea psychoanalysis lives by.

The treatment of young patients who are neither children, adolescents, nor adults is characterized by a specific exaggeration of trends met with in all therapies. Young patients (as well as extraordinary young people) make rather total demands on themselves and on their environment. They insist on daily confirming themselves and on being confirmed either in their meaningful future or in their senseless past; in some absolute virtue or in a radical state of vice; in the growth of their uniqueness or in abysmal self-loss. Young people in severe trouble are not fit for the couch: they want to face you, and they want you to face them, not as a facsimile of a parent, or wearing the mask of a professional helper, but as the kind of over-all individual a young person can live by or will despair of. When suddenly confronted with such a conflicted young person the psychoanalyst may learn for the first time what facing a face, rather than facing a problem, really means—and I daresay, Dr. Staupitz, Martin's spiritual mentor, would know what I have in mind. . . .

The limitations of my knowledge and of the space at my disposal for this inquiry preclude any attempt to present a new Luther or to remodel an old one. I can only bring some newer psychological considerations to bear on the existing material pertaining to one period of Luther's life. As

I indicated . . . the young monk interests me particularly as a young man in the process of becoming a great one.

It must have occurred to the reader that the story of the fit in the choir attracted me originally because I suspected that the words "I am *not!*" revealed the fit to be part of a most severe identity crisis—a crisis in which the young monk felt obliged to protest what he was *not* (possessed, sick, sinful) perhaps in order to break through to what he was or was to be. I will now state what remains of my suspicion, and what I intend to make of it.

Judging from an undisputed series of extreme mental states which attacked Luther throughout his life, leading to weeping, sweating, and fainting, the fit in the choir could well have happened; and it could have happened in the specific form reported, under the specific conditions of Martin's monastery years. If some of it is legend, so be it; the making of legend is as much part of the scholarly rewriting of history as it is part of the original facts used in the work of scholars. We are thus obliged to accept half-legend as half-history, provided only that a reported episode does not contradict other well-established facts; persists in having a ring of truth; and yields a meaning consistent with psychological theory.

Luther himself never mentioned this episode, although in his voluble later years he was extraordinarily free with references to physical and mental suffering. It seems that he always remembered most vividly those states in which he struggled through to an insight, but not those in which he was knocked out. Thus, in his old age, he remembers well having been seized at the age of thirty-five by terror, sweat, and the fear of fainting when he marched in the Corpus Christi procession behind his superior, Dr. Staupitz, who carried the holy of holies. (This Dr. Staupitz, as we will see, was the best father figure Luther ever encountered and acknowledged; he was a man who recognized a true *homo religiosus* in his subaltern and treated him with therapeutic wisdom.) But Staupitz did not let Luther get away with his assertion that it was Christ who had frightened him. He said, *"Non est Christus, quia Christus non terret, sed consolatur."* (It couldn't have been Christ who terrified you, for Christ consoles.) This was a therapeutic as well as a theological revelation to Luther, and he remembered it. However, for the fit in the choir, he may well have had an amnesia.

Assuming then that something like this episode happened, it could be considered as one of a series of seemingly senseless pathological explosions; as a meaningful symptom in a psychiatric case-history; or as one of a series of religiously relevant experiences. It certainly has, as even Scheel suggests, *some* marks of a "religious attack," such as St. Paul, St. Augustine, and many lesser aspirants to saintliness have had. However, the inventory of a total revelation always includes an overwhelming illumination and a sudden insight. The fit in the choir presents only the symptomatic, the more pathological and defensive, aspects of a total revelation: partial loss of consciousness, loss of motor coordination, and automatic exclamations which the afflicted does not know he utters.

In a truly religious experience such automatic exclamations would sound as if they were dictated by divine inspiration; they would be positively illuminating and luminous, and be intensely remembered. In Luther's fit, his words obviously expressed an overwhelming inner need to deny an accusation. In a full religious attack the positive conscience of faith would reign and determine the words uttered; here negation and rebellion reign: "I am *not* what my father said I was and what my conscience, in bad moments, tends to confirm I am." The raving and roaring suggest a strong element of otherwise suppressed rage. And, indeed, this young man, who later became a voice heard around the world, lived under monastic conditions of silence and meditation; at this time he was submissively subdued, painfully sad, and compulsively self-inspective—too much so even for his stern superiors' religious taste. All in all, however, the paroxysm occurred in a holy spot and was suggested by a biblical story, which places the whole matter at least on the borderline between psychiatry and religion.

If we approach the episode from the psychiatric viewpoint, we can recognize in the described attack (and also in a variety of symptomatic scruples and anxieties to which Martin was subject at the time) an intrinsic ambivalence, an inner two-facedness, such as we find in all neurotic symptoms. The attack could be said to deny in its verbal part ("I am not") what Martin's father had said, namely, that his son was perhaps possessed rather than holy; but it also proves the father's point by its very occurrence in front of the same congregation who had previously heard the father express his anger and apprehension. The fit, then, is both unconscious obedience to the father and implied rebellion against the monastery; the words uttered both deny the father's assertion, and confirm the vow which Martin had made in that first known anxiety attack during a thunderstorm at the age of twenty-one, when he had exclaimed, "I want to be a monk." We find the young monk, then, at the crossroads of obedience to his father—an obedience of extraordinary tenacity and deviousness—and to the monastic vows which at the time he was straining to obey almost to the point of absurdity.

We may also view his position as being at the crossroads of mental disease and religious creativity and we could speculate that perhaps Luther received in three (or more) distinct and fragmentary experiences those elements of a total revelation which other men are said to have acquired in one explosive event. Let me list the elements again: physical paroxysm; a degree of unconsciousness; an automatic verbal utterance; a command to change the over-all direction of effort and aspiration; and a spiritual revelation, a flash of enlightenment, decisive and pervasive as a rebirth. The thunderstorm had provided him with a change in the over-all direction of his life, a change toward the anonymous, the silent, and the obedient. In fits such as the one in the choir, he experienced the epileptoid paroxysm of ego-loss, the rage of denial of the identity which was to be discarded. And later in the experience in the tower, . . . he perceived the light of a new spiritual formula.

The fact that Luther experienced these clearly separate stages of religious revelation might make it possible to establish a psychological rationale for the conversion of other outstanding religionists, where tradition has come to insist on the transmission of a total event appealing to popular faith. Nothing, to my mind, makes Luther more a man of the future—the future which is our psychological present—than his utter integrity in reporting the steps which marked the emergence of his identity as a genuine *homo religiosus*. I emphasize this by no means only because it makes him a better case (although I admit it helps), but because it makes his total experience a historical event far beyond its immediate sectarian significance, namely, a decisive step in human awareness and responsibility. To indicate this step in its psychological coordinates is the burden of this book.

Martin's general mood just before he became a monk, a mood into which he was again sliding at the time of the fit in the choir, has been characterized by him and others as a state of *tristitia*, of excessive sadness. Before the thunderstorm, he had rapidly been freezing into a melancholy paralysis which made it impossible for him to continue his studies and to contemplate marriage as his father urged him to do. In the thunderstorm, he had felt immense anxiety. Anxiety comes from *angustus*, meaning to feel hemmed in and choked up; Martin's use of *circumvallatus*—all walled in—to describe his experience in the thunderstorm indicates he felt a sudden constriction of his whole life space, and could see only one way out: the abandonment of all of his previous life and the earthly future it implied for the sake of total dedication to a new life. This new life, however, was one which made an institution out of the very configuration of being walled in. Architecturally, ceremonially, and in its total world-mood, it symbolized life on this earth as a self-imposed and self-conscious prison with only one exit, and that one, to eternity. The acceptance of this new frame of life had made him, for a while, peaceful and "godly"; at the time of his fit, however, his sadness was deepening again.

As to this general veil of sadness which covered the conflicts revealed so explosively in the choir, one could say (and the psychiatrist has said it) that Martin was sad because he was a melancholic; and there is no doubt that in his depressed moods he displayed at times what we would call the clinical picture of a melancholia. But Luther was a man who tried to distinguish very clearly between what came from God as the crowning of a worthwhile conflict, and what came from defeat; the fact that he called defeat the devil only meant he was applying a diagnostic label which was handy. He once wrote to Melanchthon that he considered him the weaker one in public controversy, and himself the weaker in private struggles— "if I may thus call what goes on between me and Satan." One could also say (and the professor has said it) that Martin's sadness was the traditional *tristitia*, the melancholy world mood of the *homo religiosus;* from this point of view, it is a "natural" mood, and could even be called the truest adaptation to the human condition. This view, too, we must accept to a point—the point where it becomes clear that Martin was not able in the long run to embrace the monastic life so natural to the traditional *tristitia;* that he mistrusted his sadness himself; and that he later abandoned this melancholic mood altogether for occasional violent mood swings between depression and elation, between self-accusation and the abuse of others. Sadness, then, was primarily the over-all symptom of his youth, and was a symptom couched in a traditional attitude provided by his time. . . .

Soon after his profession, Martin was told that he was destined for the priesthood. This was to be expected in the case of an M.A. of such caliber, as was also his later selection for a lectureship. In neither case could he, personally, have chosen his course, nor could he have decided against it. This was the first step beyond being a simple monk, and thus beyond his original vow. Obedience had once again brought him face to face with an authority's ambitious scheme for a new graduation for him, with other graduations in store.

He was at this point as free from temptations as he would ever be, and at the same time, unquestionably a part of a minutely scheduled life. It makes psychiatric sense that under such conditions a young man with Martin's smouldering problems, but also with an honest wish to avoid rebellion against an environment which took care of so many of his needs, would subdue his rebellious nature by gradually developing compulsive-obsessive states characterized by high ambivalence. His self-doubt thus would take the form of intensified self-observation in exaggerated obedience to the demands of the order; his doubt of authority would take the form of an intellectualized scrutiny of the authoritative books. This activity would, for a while longer, keep the devil in his place. However, neither Martin nor Hans could leave well enough alone for long.

The preparation for priesthood included the study of works on the basic concepts of Catholicism. Outstanding among these was Gabriel Biel's interpretation of the Canon of the Mass, a book by which Martin was deeply moved and soon deeply troubled: reading it made "his heart bleed." He immersed himself in the dogma: but the Canon of the Mass was disquieting to him because it became obvious to what an extent he would have to assume the supreme worthiness of the priest who transfers to others the very presence of Christ, and the very essence of His blood sacrifice. Martin's tendency toward obsessive rumination seized on the fact that the priest's supreme worthiness depended on the inner status with which he approached the ceremony and on his attentiveness to the procedure itself. Interestingly enough, slips of the tongue or involuntary repetitions of words or phrases were considered to mar the effectiveness of the prescribed words. Biel makes it very clear, however, that only a reasonable suspicion of an unconfessed deadly sin could prevent the priest, on any given day, from approaching the Mass; only conscious contempt of its rules should keep him from conducting it. Once he had started celebrating it, however, not even the sudden thought of a not-previously-remembered deadly sin should interfere with its completion. This liberal interpretation was quite in keeping with the general tone of the other authority on clerical procedure, Jean Gerson of the University of Paris, an Occamist like Biel. However, to Martin, all rules had gradually become torment. Monastic rules in themselves were a ritual elaboration of the scrupulousness which belongs to the equipment of our conscience; and for this reason, a monastic priest, protected as he was from many of the world's evils, and equipped as he was with special avenues of grace by confession, was expected to master them, not to be obsessed by them. Special vestments to be worn during Mass had to be complete and correct; thoughts could not stray; important phrases had to be completed without halting, and, above all, without repeating—all of these simple rules became potential stumbling blocks for Martin's apprehensions.

A priest's first Mass was a graduation of unique import. Therefore a celebration was planned, and his family, according to custom, was invited to attend. "There," Luther later said in a strange table talk, "the bridegroom was invested in the light of torches with *horas canonicas;* there the young man had to have the first dance with his mother if she was alive, even as Christ danced with his mother; and everybody cried."

The books do not say whether or not Luther's mother was invited; it may well be that only male relatives were expected to attend. Martin did invite his father, who wrote back that he would come if the monastery would suit his schedule. It did. Hans arrived on the appointed day, leading a proud cavalcade of twenty Mansfeld citizens, and bringing twenty *Gulden* as a contribution to the monastery's kitchen. "You must have a good friend there," one of the marveling onlookers is said to have remarked.

There are a number of versions of the two decisive events of that day: Martin's anxiety attack during the Mass, and Hans' attack of loud anger during the following banquet. In regard to both instances the more dramatic versions claim public commotions: they say that Martin was about to flee the ceremony, but was restrained by a superior, and that during the banquet the father denounced the assembled staff of the monastery. Luther himself later often contributed to the embellishment of the events, reporting things which had taken place only in conversation or entirely in his own mind. This is owing partially to the folksy exaggeration of his table-talk vocabulary, partially to the literalism of his listeners, and partially to his distinct tendency to retrospective dramatization, which I will call *historification* in order to avoid calling one more process "projection." I mean by this that Luther may honestly have remembered as a detailed event in time and space what actually occurred only in his thoughts and emotions. It is clear that his upbringing in the miner's world, with its reifications and rumors, facilitated this tendency, which came to full bloom when Luther had to accept his final identity as a historical personality.

First, then, the Mass. Luther may or may not have meant it literally when he said later that he had felt like fleeing the world as a Judas, and had actually made a motion to run away when he read the words, *Te igitur clementissime Pater,* which appeal "to the most merciful Father"; he suddenly felt that he was about to speak to God directly, without any mediator. The professor finds this incredible, because Luther must have known that these words are followed by the phrase, *Per Jhesum Christum filium tuum Dominum nostrum supplices rogamus et petiamus,* which refers to God's Son as the transmitter of our supplications to His Father. But however it came to pass that Luther ignored this phrase, we must accept his assurance that he "almost died" from anxiety because he felt no faith (*weil kein Glaube da war*). No witness, however, reports that he really made a move to leave the altar.

As is so often the case with Luther, exaggerations and conjectures can neither enhance nor destroy the simple dramatic constellations which characterized his moments of fate. In this moment he had the presence of the Eucharist in front of him—and the presence of the father behind him. He had not yet learned to speak with God "without embarrassment," and he had not seen his father since the visit home before the thunderstorm. At this moment, then, when he was to mediate between the father and The Father, he still felt torn in his obedience to both. I would not be willing to give exclusive precedence to the theological conflict (as the professor does) or to the personal-neurotic one (as the psychiatrist does) in this condensed, intensive experience. Martin, at this moment, faced the Great Divide of his life, as every young man must sooner or later—the divide which separates, once and for all, the contributaries to the future from the regressive rivulets seeking the past. In front of him was the Eucharist's uncertain grace; behind him his father's potential wrath. His faith at that moment lacked the secure formulation of the nature of mediatorship which later emerged in the lectures on the Psalms. He had no living concept of Christ; he was, in fact, mortally afraid of the whole riddle of mediatorship. Because of all this, he may well have been morbidly sensitive to some theological problems which only much later did he have the courage to face and challenge as true moral problems.

The Eucharist's long history had served to confuse its meaning more than to clarify it. It had started in Paulinian times as a highly devotional meal to commemorate that Passover which had turned out to be the last supper. As a ritual meal, it is a supremely sublimated version of a long series of blood sacrifices and rituals culminating in the devouring of flesh, first human, then animal, for the sake of magic and spiritual replenishment. In the original *Eucharistia* the community "gave thanks": they ate bread from the same loaf and drank wine from the same cup, thus remembering, as Christ had asked them to do, his sacrificial death. This is a sublimated act because Christ had not only made the supreme sacrifice, self-chosen and human ("I am the lamb"); he had also made each man's responsibility inescapably personal: "Let a man examine himself, and so let him eat of that bread, and drink of that cup . . . for if we would judge ourselves, we should not be judged." True, Paul had berated those earliest communities for not being quite able to keep competitive voraciousness out of this rite; but, alas, they were simple folk. . . .

We have quoted Luther's statement that as he celebrated his first Mass he was overcome by the feeling that he had to face God directly without a mediator. We must now discuss his other impending encounter: the one with his earthly father. Is it not astonishing that the biographers who have tried to account for Luther's anxiety have not considered it worth emphasizing that he had not seen his father since his impulsive visit home; and that he had not, as yet, faced him to see—yes, in his face —the result of that extracted permission? Could not Martin foresee that his father would be essentially unreconstructed and ready to remind Martin of the obedience due him, knowing, in turn, quite well that the son had never wholly relinquished his filial obedience—and that he never would, never could? In Martin's first Mass the paradox of paternal obediences was fully propounded. Martin, who had sought the identity of a monk, had been ordered to become a priest, a dispenser as well as a partaker of the Eucharist. There is no use saying he should have been glad: like other great young men, Martin never felt worthy of the next step in his career. Later he thought and said he would surely die when he was ordered to become a professor; and still later, after his unexpectedly triumphant entrance into Worms, when it was clear that he could not escape being the people's reformer, he stood most meekly before the emperor and was hardly audible. As always, he first had to grow into the role which he had usurped without meaning to. And this first and anxious anchorage of his future identity as a responsible churchman had to be witnessed by the father, who cursed it (and said so presently) as his son's final escape from the identity of being most of all Hans' son. The attempt of the biographers to separate the mystic presence of the Eucharist and the oppressive presence of the father is invalid in view of what happened later that day, and forever after.

It cannot be denied that Martin asked for it—he could not let his father go any more than the father could let him go. Martin knew that he had not won his father's *gantzen Willen,* his whole will. But during the meeting which they had after the ceremony, "as we sat at the table, I started to talk with him with a childish good comportment, wanting to put him in the wrong and myself in the right, by saying: 'Dear father, why did you resist so hard and become so angry because you did not want to let me be a monk, and maybe even now you do not like too much to see me here, although it is a sweet and godly life, full of peace?' But there [the father] carried on, in front of all the doctors, magisters and other gentlemen: 'You scholars, have you not read in the scriptures that one should honor father and mother?'" And as others started to argue with him, Hans Luder said what was as good as a curse: "God give that it wasn't a devil's spook" (*Satanae praestigium, Teuffel's Gespenst*)— referring, of course, to the thunderstorm on the road to Erfurt, Martin's "road to Damascus." As Luther wrote to his father publicly when he had become a great man: "You again hit me so cleverly and fittingly that in my whole life I have hardly heard a word that resounded in me more forcefully and stuck in me more firmly. But," he added—putting the father in his place more than a decade after the event—"but I, secure in my justice, listened to you as to a human being and felt deep contempt for you; yet belittle your word in my soul, I could not."

What would not some of us give if, in certain decisive moments, we could have felt clearly and said calmly to a parent what the great man could write only after many years: "I listened to you as to a human being" (*Te velut hominem audivi et fortiter contempsi*)? But at the time, Martin, too, fell silent. As he confessed later, he heard God's voice in his father's words, which helped to make the fusion of presences fatefully permanent. His father, he felt, had not given his benediction "as to a betrothal," and God had denied him the experience of the Eucharist. But for less, Martin (Hans' son) could not settle and remain whole; he would yet find the right word "to speak to God directly."

He was alone now; alone against his temperament, which his father had predicted would refuse submission to celibacy; and alone against his wrath, which his father had shown was indomitable in the Luders. Incredible as it seems, at this late date Martin was thrown back into the infantile struggle, not only over his obedience toward, but also over his identification with, his father. This regression and this personalization of his conflicts cost him that belief in the monastic way and in his superiors which during the first year had been of such "godly" support. He was alone in the monastery, too, and soon showed it in a behavior that became increasingly un-understandable even to those who believed in him. *To be justified* became his stumbling block as a believer, his obsession as a neurotic sufferer, and his preoccupation as a theologian.

28. Utopia and Geneva

J. H. HEXTER

In the decades after Luther's break with Rome, it became apparent that wide areas of Europe were ready to deny the authority of the pope at Rome. All of Scandinavia, large segments of Germany and Bohemia, and areas of France, Switzerland, and the Netherlands embraced varying forms of the "new Christianity." England, as so often, was a case apart, but ultimately there too the supremacy of Rome was denied in favor of that of the crown. Ironically, the various champions of Protestant thought proved in many instances to be even more intolerant and authoritarian than Rome had been. The principle of cuius regio eius religio, *adopted at Augsburg (1555) in order to put an end to fighting, recognized the legitimacy of Catholicism and Lutheranism only. Instead of granting the right of an individual to follow his conscience in matters of worship, this stipulation forced the subjects of a ruler to accept his faith, or to leave his territory and usually their ancestral homes, relatives, and livelihoods.*

Of the various churches that were formed in the wake of Luther's original revolt, none was more militant or aggressive, and in a sense more successful, than Calvinism, despite the provisions of Augsburg. What elements in Calvin's thought helped his religion to overcome the opposition of Catholic and Lu-

Source: J. H. Hexter, "Utopia and Geneva," in Theodore K. Rabb and Jerold E. Siegel, eds., *Action and Conviction in Early Modern Europe: Essays in Memory of E. H. Harbison* (Princeton: Princeton University Press, 1969), pp. 77–89. Copyright © 1969 by Princeton University Press. Reprinted by permission of Princeton University Press. [Footnotes omitted.]

*theran officialdom? What made this austere and rigorous creed attractive to so
many in Europe?*

*J. H. Hexter, Professor of History at Yale, elucidates several points of sim-
ilarity between Calvin's Geneva and the ideal community depicted by the
Catholic humanist St. Thomas More. Hexter's careful study of More's* Utopia
*suggests many reasons for the appeal of Geneva to reform-minded Christians,
and is a model of detailed textual analysis. His essay should also help to explain
the intense involvement of the sixteenth-century mind with matters of religion
and the preoccupation with personal sin and salvation, so essential to understanding events in that period. A further note on Calvinism and Geneva
should include Robert M. Kingdom's recent volumes on Geneva and the religious wars in France, and E. William Monter's* Calvin's Geneva *(1966).*

Like many of the noblest men of the early decades of the sixteenth century, Thomas More was deeply concerned with the problem of bringing
about a fundamental spiritual change in Europe. But in *Utopia* he did not
suggest a strategy for achieving that change. Rather, he revealed two
daunting obstacles which any such strategy must encounter and had but
little chance to overcome: first, the inability of reformers to serve with
good conscience as advisors to the rulers of Europe; and second, the fundamental character of Europe's institutions, especially its institutions of
property. Scarcely a decade after More's death, a Christian humanist reformer in some ways very unlike More, in others somewhat like him, obliterated the first obstacle, circumvented the second, and established in a
town in the heart of Europe a Hagnapolis—a holy community almost
as austere as Utopia. That reformer wrought mightily for almost two decades, his successors for several more, and by the end of the sixteenth century the town had become under resolute pressure "peaceful, well-ordered,
pious, literate, learned, poised, cultured, when before it was nothing but a
big uncivilized village." The transformed "village" was Geneva; the reformer was John Calvin.

The curious similarities between Utopia and Geneva have been unduly
obscured by the undeniable differences between More and Calvin, between
the Roman Catholic martyr and the hero of the Reformation. Calvin, of
course, wrought under limitations with which More did not have to concern himself, and Calvin's materials were considerably more intractable.
More worked with pens and paper, Calvin with men and a social order. It
is easier to impress one's aspirations with pens on paper than with men
on a social order; men are more balky, a social order less readily receptive
to new imprints. Consequently, compared with some of Utopia's iron ordinances, the law of Calvin's Geneva was mild. Idle pastimes and evil re-
sorts, prohibited in Utopia, were regulated in Geneva. In the Swiss city
no law reduced to bondage a citizen who twice left town without permission, as Utopia's law did; nor was criminal intent punished as heavily as
criminal act, as it was on More's blessed island. And, real flesh being
somewhat harder to tame than paper flesh, the Utopian penalty for
adultery—bondage for the first offense, death for the second—was,

despite Calvin, too stern for Calvin's Geneva, where the reformer's own sister-in-law and stepdaughter so offended and where, as late as 1556, a citizen reckoned that rigorous proceedings against adulterers and fornicators might cost the town half its population. Unlike King Utopus, Calvin did not fall heir to what every radical reformer dreams of—a submissive and ductile people like the conquered Utopians. Only slowly and with frequent setbacks was he gradually able to mold the tough, late medieval institutions of the Genevan urban patriciate into something closer to his heart's, and therefore (as he saw it) to God's desire.

Granted all the differences, the similarity both in detail and in spirit between Utopia and Geneva is nevertheless noteworthy, even when the instruments and institutions for working out the details and for maintaining the spirit diverge. This similarity is evident in the rules of More's "best ordered commonwealth" and of Calvin's New Jerusalem with respect to dress, leisure, and privacy. Consider the apparently trivial matter of costume. Sumptuary legislation dealing with dress was an old medieval story. But in the Middle Ages the purpose of such legislation was to maintain social hierarchy—in effect, to maintain the status value of aristocratic, conspicuous consumption by denying bourgeois crows the right to noble peacock feathers. Utopia and Geneva, too, had rules about what the inhabitants might wear, but they differed markedly, and in a similar way, from the medieval rules. In Utopia plainness of dress was so much a matter of course and good custom that a Utopian, seeing a finely decked-out ambassador from another land, mistook him for the ambassador's fool. The Utopians wore plain, undyed grey garments; and when, some weeks after he had sent his book to Erasmus to have it printed, More dreamed of being a prince in Utopia, he imagined himself wearing the habit of Franciscan grey that was standard there. For a Utopian there was nothing else to wear; the law allowed no finery, not so much as variety in the color of men's clothing, even to the magistrates. Similarly, and at considerable risk, on the rather odd issue of slashed breeches for the local soldiery, Calvin faced down the chief of the citizen militia, who was also the spearhead of the patrician opposition to the reformer. Geneva's law and Utopia's were much alike; Calvin's attitudes and More's stood squarely and precisely opposed in purpose to medieval sumptuary legislation and precisely identical to each other. The Utopians despised men who felt that the more spendidly they dressed, the higher was the honor due them. Or, as Calvin succinctly put it, slashed breeches, like other unnecessary adornments, ministered to pride. Therefore, "it is against God and of the devil, and a disorder such as ought not to be tolerated at any price."

As on the matter of dress, so on the question of leisure, the views of More and Calvin were much alike. In both Utopia and Geneva mere idleness lay under a ban. The aristocratic-courtly conception of a pastime as something to fend off *accidia,* or boredom, was offensive to both More and Calvin. Time is God's gift to men, not to be destroyed, but to be used to glorify Him through righteous, useful doing in the world, whether with hands or with mind. In both Utopia and Geneva the courtly pastime is replaced by the scholar's recreation, that respite which does not kill time but saves it by renewing a man's energies for the activity or study to follow.

As with dress and leisure, so with privacy. In Utopia, with its extended families, multiple-unit houses without locks on the doors, and common meals, privacy had little place. Nor was this an accident. The open and common way of life in Utopia was designed to maintain a common standard of conduct, to foster a common ethic. In the ecclesiastical ordinances for his New Jerusalem, Calvin created a new kind of church officer whose authority over morals obliterated the customary line between private affairs and public life almost as effectively as Utopian institutions did. The lay elders had the duty *"to watch over the life of everyone,* to admonish in a friendly way those who fell short or led ill-ordered lives." Such elders were to be chosen for every section of the city, *"in order to have an eye everywhere."* In a startling way Calvin's language echoes More's description of Utopia. There, too, men have no "license to waste time nor pretext to evade work, . . . no lurking hole . . . being under the eyes of all."

By making sin very public indeed, Calvin succeeded in achieving some of the ends of Utopian society without resorting to Utopian means—community of property, destruction of the market, abolition of money. As a very practical man with a series of very knotty problems to solve in his relentless drive to create in Geneva a model Christian commonwealth, Calvin did not consider means as far beyond his reach as the Utopian social order was. He had a system, however, which in a measure served the same purpose. And that system is curiously prefigured in detail in *Utopia* itself. Describing the Utopian clergy, Hythlodaeus says that they

> are censors of morals. It is counted a great disgrace for a man to be summoned or rebuked by them as not being of upright life. It is their function to give advice and admonition, but to check and punish offenders belongs to the governor and the other civil officials. The priests, however, do exclude from divine services individuals whom they find to be unusually bad. There is almost no punishment which is more dreaded: they incur very great disgrace and are tortured by a secret fear of religion. Even their bodies will not long go scot free. If they do not demonstrate to the priests their speedy repentance, they are seized and punished by the senate for their impiety.

It was precisely such a refurbished and sharpened instrument of ecclesiastical discipline that Calvin established in Geneva. The institution he created to suit his purpose was the Consistory, the assembly of ministers and lay elders. The weapon was excommunication, with restoration to the holy community contingent on public repentance. And the cutting edge was condemnation to exile by the civil magistrates of those who long failed to repent. Using its disciplinary power, the Consistory "intervened to re-establish peace and union in families, to recall individuals to their duty; it took in hand . . . reforms favorable to the weak and the lesser folk, it summoned and censured the lazy and the idle, over-hard fathers and creditors; it was pitiless to usurers, monopolists and engrossers. It combatted the coarse manners of the age, the brutality of men." Thus the expression of brotherhood was achieved, not through community of property, but by the spiritual communion of those who shared in the holy sacrament of the Lord's Supper and by the exclusion from it of the unworthy. Through the disciplinary instrument provided by the Lord's Supper, too, the Reformed Church at Geneva was able to express the profound leveling implicit in the Calvinist sense of God's majesty and man's depravity and in Calvin's doctrine of the calling. So worthless and shriveled was sinful man beside the greatness of God that the scale of earthly rank was as nothing to Him or to the ministers of His Word. To those entrusted with earthly authority who glorified God by earnest service in their calling, praise was due, as it was to all men who served God well; to men who did otherwise, whatever their rank, censure was due. Accordingly, with no respect of person or station, the Consistory brought to book the big folk of the city—councillors, the wife of the captain-general, the city treasurer, his wife and his mother, the wife of Calvin's own brother. Thus, by means less than Utopian, Calvin came close to achieving in his City of Saints an equality of austere men not unlike that found in More's Hagnapolis.

Moreover, like Utopia, Geneva was dedicated not only to education but to the principle that sound education helps to make righteous citizens. That it was is not surprising, since Calvin was an admirer of Erasmus and, more than Luther, perhaps even more than Zwingli, a Christian humanist. In his inaugural address at the founding of the Academy of Geneva, Theodore Béza, the first rector, chosen by Calvin, spoke to the students who, "instructed in the *true religion* and *the knowledge of good literature,* have come in order to *work for the glory of God.*" It would be hard to find in so few phrases a more perfect expression of the religious aspiration which the Utopian commonwealth reflected.

Except of course that the religion Béza called true, and loved, More, had he known it, would surely have called false, and hated. Between Utopia and Geneva, between More in 1516 and Calvin, after all, lies the thundering torrent of religious revolution. All the better reason then, lest we lose our bearings in a flood that destroyed many landmarks, for us to recognize continuities, however unexpected, indeed however unlikely, they may seem at first glance. Those continuities exist as elements in a vast stratum of events—the Christian Revival, a stratum that stretched across to both sides of that conspicuous historical watershed, the year 1517. The part which preceded 1517 has been called the Pre-Reformation and the Religious Revival. Part of what followed 1517 has been called the Protestant Reformation (or, simply, the Reformation), the Protestant Revolt, or the Protestant Revolution; the other part, the Catholic Reformation, the Catholic Counter-Reformation, or the Catholic Counter-Revolution. And this may not be an exhaustive inventory of the current nomenclature. To add yet another name to the many already in use may seem a supererogatory contribution to an already more than adequate confusion. The addition, however, may be warranted because historians have no single covering phrase to describe the intensification of religious sentiment and concern that began long before 1517 and extended long afterward, that in its full span had room for Ximenes and Savonarola, Luther and Loyola, the Reformed Churches and the Jesuits, John of Leyden and Pope Paul IV, Thomas Cranmer and Edmund Campion, and Michael Servetus. Only if amid the upheavals of the following century we discern the continuity provided by the Christian Revival can we find clues to render intelligible some of the varieties of human conduct during the Age of Reformation, varieties otherwise hard to understand. They become intelligible as partial consummations of some of the durable aspirations of that Revival. It thus may seem improbable that the nearest men came in the sixteenth century to realizing More's dream of a sober, disciplined commonwealth, ruled in its daily life by the teaching of Christ, was the Calvinist capital at Geneva. But it is a fact, and, unless we grasp that fact, it is hard to explain a considerable group of other facts about the history of Europe in the sixteenth century.

Of these facts the most significant is the survival and resilience of Protestantism in the century after the death of Luther. In the generation between the posting of the ninety-five theses on indulgences and Luther's death, the religious movement that took his name had lost most of its momentum in the heart of Europe and advanced only in murky struggles in the backward northlands—Scandinavia and the Baltic regions. Toward the end of that same generation the Roman Church began to rally its forces of defense and soon launched a counter-attack. When Mary Tudor became Queen of England in 1553, there was not a single great Protestant realm in Europe, only a few low-grade German and northern principalities whose princes were all too likely to make a deal and return to the Roman obedience if the going got rough, as it looked to be doing. Yet, for better or worse, Protestantism was still very much alive and kicking in 1600; it did not fold up in face of the Catholic Counter-Revolution. And that it did not do so was unmistakably the result of the initiative of the followers of Calvin.

What were the resources of the Calvinists that enabled them to resist the Catholic counter-attack so effectively? No doubt they had a certain amount of luck, but no more than their share, and in almost all the more obvious equipage of combat they were absurdly deficient, compared with their Catholic adversaries. Their military resources were trivial. The other side had all the best generals—the Duke of Guise, Alva, Parma—and by far the best soldiers, the Spanish *tercios,* as well as *most* of the soldiers. Since the Calvinists did not control the political apparatus in a single important European state, their military recruiting was always hand-to-mouth. And, of course, compared to the enemy, they were bone poor. Even when Elizabeth was dragged kicking and screaming into Europe's religious wars, the gross financial resources available to the Calvinists came far short of those commanded by the Pope, the Catholic League, and Philip II. Before the half-hearted accession of Elizabeth to support of their cause, the Calvinists had been *gueux* indeed—Sea Beggars, Land Beggars, beggars in every way. And, finally, the Calvinists were enormously outnumbered. At a very rough guess, there were from ten to thirty Catholics for every Calvinist, and perhaps even more.

Under such adverse circumstances, how were the Calvinists able not only to hold their own but to enjoy a more secure position in 1600 than they had held in 1564 at Calvin's death? Part of the answer is suggested by a letter sent in the 1560's from a Catholic *gouverneur,* or stadholder of a province in the Netherlands to his masters in Brussels. With something between petulance and patience, he explains to the council in Brussels why he is not enthusiastically uprooting heresy in his territory, as ordered. Unfortunately, he observes, all the ablest people in the province are heretics—which makes matters difficult. The heretics in question were, of course, Calvinists. Any explanation of the survival of Protestantism that leaves out of account what the stadholder was pointing to, however unprecisely, is deficient. Most students of the sixteenth century would probably agree with this rephrasing of his insight: in the later sixteenth century, compared with other religious creeds, Calvinism had a very high proportion of adherents who combined keen intelligence with deep dedication and zeal, and among such adherents was a high proportion of laymen.

This insight suggests that Calvinism somehow drew on a reservoir of talents that had hitherto remained untapped. The reservoir consisted of men of a kind that had begun to come to the fore in the Christian Revival. This kind of man was well-read in classical literature, deeply pious, convinced that there was a hideous gap between what Christ demanded of Christians and the way professed Christians lived, and sure that to narrow that gap was part of the duty of a true Christian. The difficulty for such a man lay in the fact that, though he believed himself called by God to action, he did not find in the world he lived in any channels into which he could pour forth his energies in the conviction that he was making the full and right use of the talents God had given him. Drawn to the monastic life by its theoretical rigor and discipline, by the renunciation of avarice and sloth and pride which it demanded, he was repelled by the actualities of that life in his time—the rules relaxed, the monks resistant to reform, study at a halt, an existence marked by idleness and tedium instead of learning and labor. And though taking the vows of an order did not necessarily prevent a man from working for God's kingdom on earth, still, by subjecting his freedom of action to a religious superior of dubious zeal, it well might do so. Nor, outside Italy, did the universities offer great attraction, since in the main they were still devoted to the old learning, which to such a man was not merely old but bad. Rightly or wrongly, like More, this kind of man found the scholastic questions which were the formal basis of that learning empty and stultifying. What drove him was zeal for the Christian commonwealth, the desire to employ as instruments to draw men toward the *regnum Christi* such powers as God gave him. Consequently, as More observed, he did not regard it as the pinnacle of human achievement and godly doing to "squat with the monks," in the ill-warranted belief that "to reside forever in the same spot like a clam or sponge, to cling eternally to the same rock is the last word in sanctity."

Of course, some men of the Christian Revival did go to the cloister and some to the schools, but probably not without qualms of conscience and the sense that they had left half their work behind them in a world in which they belonged.

There was another way to go—the way of the court. "Mere" humanists, proficients in the classical languages with little Christian concern and no commitment to reform, paddled merrily—and some, indeed, wallowed—in courtly pleasure and courtly rackets, hitherto mainly the perquisites of the legists and the military élite. But to the men most deeply engaged by the religious resurgence there was bound to be about the courts of most Renaissance princes the stench of a moral pigsty, rather than the odor of sanctity. Of course, the man at the very heart of the resurgence, Erasmus, became a councillor to his native ruler, Charles, Prince of Castile and, among other things, Count of Holland. But Erasmus's councillorship was what in academic circles today would be called a "prestige appointment," with a concomitant absence of responsibilities. Erasmus received the post, as he put it, with "my liberty reserved by the vote of the Council." The terms were, indeed, such as any man might have found gratifying—no duties and a regular stipend. But Erasmus was unique. Such a tidy and sanitary arrangement was not offered to lesser men; they had to get right down into the courtly muck. The better the man, the worse his lot at court; it was not a place for one with a demanding conscience. Others with such a moral constitution had learned the same lesson before the Renaissance, and more were to do so afterward. In earlier centuries medieval authors, quite unaffected by deep religious feelings, had produced a considerable literature on the falseness of court life and recommended retreat to the country to avoid its pitfalls. Some men touched by the Christian Revival doubtless pursued this course; but it, too, had its frustrations—the frustrations of village Hampdens or mute inglorious Miltons ready to serve the Christian commonwealth with all their heart, all their soul, and all their mind, but finding nothing in their rustic retirement to engage even half their talents. Christian reformers were not endowed with either the temperament or the intricate egoism of Michel de Montaigne.

From the 1540's on, a number of men whose response to their historical milieu was similar to the one that inspired *Utopia* found in Calvin's Geneva the resolution in action of dilemmas that More resolved only in imagination in his well-ordered commonwealth. They poured into the Savoyard town in thousands from France, from the Netherlands, from Italy, from Spain, from Germany, from England, and from Scotland. And there they believed they found what they sought: "the most perfect *school of Christ* that ever was in the earth since the days of the apostles," "the miracle of the whole world" where men of many nations "being coupled with the only yoke of Christ . . . live . . . lovingly and friendly, and monks, laymen, and nuns . . . dwell together like a spiritual and Christian congregation." What gave Geneva its magnetic attraction for men who had felt the impulse toward a Christian Revival John Knox explained very succinctly. Christ was truly preached in other places, "but manners and religion to be so sincerely reformed, I have not yet seen in any other place." It was the "manners . . . sincerely reformed" that drew monks and nuns from their cloisters, well-to-do laymen from town and country, "to live in poverty" in Geneva in enjoyment of "the holy discipline." In the Middle Ages successive waves of religious fervor, the impulse toward dedication, toward living wholly for God and by His rule, flowed into new or revitalized forms of monastic life and an *ausserweltliche Askese,* an otherworldly asceticism. In the sixteenth century, as a consequence of the holy discipline in Geneva, many of those waves flowed into the *innerweltliche Askese* of a City of Saints. The layman official in the councils or Consistory of Geneva had no need to feel the compunction which afflicted Hythlodaeus and the author of Utopia over a life spent in serving the wicked appetites of vainglorious princes. He could find fulfillment in the austere joy of ruling in a holy commonwealth, in a realization, partial at least, of More's dream of being a prince in Utopia.

In the later sixteenth century this emancipation from scruple of pious Calvinist laymen, which brought the full range of their abilities into action in the political arena, spread from Geneva to the lands where Calvinism penetrated, especially to France, the Netherlands, England, and Scotland. It was able to spread because Geneva remained an example to Calvin's followers of how a community could be transformed by the holy discipline. In France Calvinist laymen provided zealous support for Henry of Navarre, in the Netherlands for William of Orange, and in England for Elizabeth. Henry eventually became a Roman Catholic. William, baptized as a Roman Catholic, raised as a Lutheran in his nonage, and living as a Roman Catholic thereafter, did not become a Calvinist until 1573, when he was forty—with what degree of conviction it is hard to know. And Elizabeth never made any bones about her opposition to the Genevan Church order. Yet men touched by the Calvinist aspiration to see that God's will, as they conceived it, was done on earth could serve Henry and William and Elizabeth, because God not only walked in mysterious ways but occasionally chose rather odd instruments, His wonders to perform; and again, as they saw it, Henry and William and Elizabeth were clearly such instruments. Through them the society of saints might yet bring Christ's kingdom on earth. Thus able and religious laymen, among whom Francis Walsingham, Philippe de Mornay, and St. Aldegonde are perhaps the most eminent, men who might have turned away from political action under other circumstances, provided invaluable aid to their princes during Europe's religious civil wars in the later sixteenth century.

Most remarkable was a cluster of Elizabeth's councillors—Mildmay, Sadler, Knollys, Wilson, Walsingham. They brought to the Queen's service a sobriety, honesty, and zeal not common in princely courts, accompanied by a continuing and unpunished personal alliance with the elements in the country intent on subverting her too-worldly religious settlement. This almost accidental materialization in More's country of a situation in which men similar to him, not in creed but in moral temper, were drawn toward the service of their ruler did not last. Even before the accession of the Stuarts, the curious symbiosis had broken down. Lay religious zeal gradually went out of the court when Archbishop Whitgift won his struggle against the Puritans. The dilemmas of *Utopia* reasserted themselves again—the dilemma of the intellectual in a bureaucracy, the dilemma of a Christian servant of worldly power, the dilemma of the prophet and the Prince.

Those dilemmas were in the cards for men with their hearts and minds set on the attainment of the Christian commonwealth, on having God's will done on earth as it is in heaven, who tried to reach that goal through service in the courts of Renaissance princes. Indeed, More had already well read those cards in 1516, when he wrote *Utopia*.

> At court . . . one must openly approve the worst counsels and subscribe to the most ruinous decrees. He would be counted a spy and almost a traitor, who gives only faint praise to evil counsels. Moreover there is no chance for you to do any good because you are brought among colleagues who would easily corrupt even the best men before being reformed themselves. By their evil companionship either you will be seduced yourself or, keeping your own integrity and innocence, you will be made a screen for the wickedness and folly of others.

The conjuncture of the aims and aspirations of zealous Calvinists directed toward the *regnum Christi* with the aims and aspirations of rulers with eyes hard fixed on the earthly kingdom was both fortuitous and short.

For a while, however, Calvin's Geneva and international Calvinism provided psychic fulfillment for a number of men steeped in the spirit of Christian humanism. And the curious similarities of Utopia and Geneva help us understand how this could have been. Yet, as we have seen, in one most important matter Utopia was not at all like Geneva. Calvin tried to infuse into all citizens a sense of their obligation to serve God and do His will unremittingly, and to this end he forced a remodeling of the Church in doctrine, government, and discipline. But it was the Church alone that he sought directly to remodel. In Geneva, and wherever else Calvinists planted a Reformed Church, they accepted in the main the existing structure of rules about property and power. They sought to permeate that structure with the spirit of the holy community generated by the Church. More, too, recognized how essential it was that good teaching permeate the structure of society. But not for a moment in Utopia does he accept the notion that merely by good teaching (or good preaching), or even by ecclesiastical discipline and censure, can a corrupt commonwealth be transformed into a good one. Such a transformation is only possible through a transmutation of the *forma reipublicae,* the structure of the commonwealth, of the *maximum totius institutiones fundamentum,* the principal foundation of the whole structure, of the *vitae instituta,* the institutions of life, of the *reipublicae fundamenta,* of the foundations of the commonwealth. For these sixteenth-century Latin phrases the nearest present-day English equivalent is "the social order," and the nearest present-day English equivalent for the transformation More wrote about is "social revolution."

435

Hexter

UTOPIA
AND GENEVA

29. The Empire of Charles V in Europe

H. G. KOENIGSBERGER

By the late fifteenth century Europe was beginning to look something like the political map with which we are familiar in the twentieth century. In the west especially national monarchies were emerging and the foundations of the important nation-states, France, England, and Spain, were being laid. The last claims of English kings to rule parts of France were laid to rest at the end of the Hundred Years' War, and the Valois kings turned their energies to consolidating their power on the continent. The marriage of Ferdinand and Isabella brought the crowns of Castile and Aragon together in a personal union and paved the way for the unification of Spain, already aided by the long process of warfare to drive out the Moorish invaders. Italy seemed to have reached a kind of stability, divided among Venice, Milan, Florence, the Papal States, and the kingdom of Naples. Only Germany remained fragmented into a host of political entities, small and large, secular and ecclesiastical and united only by the vague traditions of the Holy Roman Empire, which, as Ranke observed, was neither holy, Roman, exclusively German, nor an empire! Into this picture came the meteoric rise of Charles V, Holy Roman Emperor, king of Spain, hereditary duke of Burgundy and the Netherlands and of Hapsburg Austria, and of a variety of lesser principalities. Such a vast concentration of power altered the political relation-

Source: H. G. Koenigsberger, *The Habsburgs and Europe, 1516–1660* (Ithaca, N.Y.: Cornell University Press, 1971), pp. 1–2, 4–16, 25–27. Copyright © 1971 by Cornell University Press. Reprinted by permission of Cornell University Press.

ships of Europe and remained central to the state system of the European hege-
mony at least through the First World War.

The position of Charles V was the creation of a process, part accident and
part design, of dynastic consolidation and expansion through marriage, inheri-
tance, purchase, and conquest. The questions that faced Charles were several,
and difficult. What objects should he pursue with the vast power at his disposal?
How was he to govern his composite and diverse realm? What traditions
would best help him form imperial policy?

Professor Koenigsberger, a modern Europeanist at Cornell University, has
attempted to set the Hapsburgs within the wider European context, and to evalu-
ate their effects on the sixteenth and seventeenth centuries. Excellent studies
exist on more specific topics, such as K. Brandi's biography The Emperor
Charles V, *trans. C. V. Wedgwood (1939) and J. H. Elliott's* Imperial Spain,
1469–1716 *(1964), but Koenigsberger suggests that Charles V and Hapsburg*
power should be viewed in broader perspective. The following selection presents
his analysis of the nature and problems of Charles's empire.

The sixteenth century was an age of prophets. Luther, Zwingli, and Calvin interpreted the Word of God, challenging the claim of the Roman
Church to its own uniquely valid interpretation. These prophets found
their armed champions in Knox, Coligny, and William of Orange. The
Catholic Church countered them with her own arms, with Loyola, with
Philip II and the Inquisition. But for more than a generation, before the
religious conflicts erupted into open war, the political and religious life of
Europe was dominated by a very different fighter for God: the Habsburg
emperor Charles V, the last medieval emperor to whom the religious and
political unity of Christendom was both the ideal purpose of his life and a
practicable object of policy. "Caesar is not a doctor of the gospels," wrote
Erasmus in his dedication to Charles of his paraphrase of St. Matthew;
"he is their champion." "God's standard bearer," the emperor called himself when, in June 1535, he weighed anchor at Barcelona to wrest Tunis
from the Turks.

The Formation of the Habsburg Empire

Charles had good reasons for his belief. "God has set you on the path toward a world monarchy," said the grand chancellor Gattinara, in 1519.
Marriage alliances and inheritance had given Charles this unique opportunity. In the fifteenth century, the houses of Austria and Burgundy had become united in northern Europe, those of Aragon and Castile in the
south; but the marriage of Philip of Burgundy and Joanna of Castile, at
the beginning of the sixteenth century, produced a similar union between
the northern and southern houses only through a series of unexpected
deaths. As a result, Charles inherited the Habsburg possessions of Austria,
Tyrol and parts of southern Germany, the Netherlands and Franche-
Comté, and, south of the Alps, Spain with her new American colonies and

the Spanish dominions in Italy, Sicily, Sardinia, and Naples. To Charles V, this inheritance was a sacred trust, the evidence of a divine intention as well as the material means to carry out this intention. Others had jealously claimed some of his provinces without just title; but, with God's help and his own unceasing efforts, he had always managed to preserve his inheritance undiminished for an heir. Thus wrote Charles to his son in his secret instructions and testaments. At one time or another during his reign, Charles himself or a member of his family sat as ruler or consort on nearly every royal throne of Europe. Dynastic alliances had appeared as the effective instrument of God's will, and dynastic alliances remained the emperor's favorite policy throughout his life, the only type of policy he chose freely for the enhancing of his power in Europe. "For that which God most commends [to princes] is peace," he admonished his son in 1548. All wars which he had waged against Christian princes had been forced on him.

Only against the infidel was offensive warfare justified. Charles saw his task as the divinely appointed one of leading a united Christendom against the external enemy, the Muslim Turk and, later, against its internal enemies, the Lutheran heretics.[1] To this end the houses of Burgundy, Austria, and Spain had been raised and united in his person. To this end Charles supported the legitimate rights of its members, even against the dictates of reason of state; he refused to accommodate Henry VIII in the divorce of Catherine of Aragon and pressed for decades the impracticable claims of his niece Dorothea to the Danish throne. To this end, too, he insisted that the members of his family sacrifice themselves to his imperial policy just as he sacrificed himself; for thus he wrote to his sister, Mary of Hungary, who had protested against the proposed marriage of their barely twelve-year-old niece, Christina of Denmark, to the duke of Milan in 1535.

For most of Charles's contemporaries, his imperial position had no such transcendental significance, least of all for the men responsible for the young prince's smooth entry into the inheritance of his many lands. Charles had lost his father in 1506 at the age of six and had inherited from him the possessions of the house of Burgundy: Franche-Comté with the claim to the duchy of Burgundy (since 1477 in French hands) and the provinces which were then called *les pays de pardeça* and which came to be known as the Netherlands (*les pays d'embas*) only from the 1530's. These were the duchies of Luxemburg and Brabant, and the counties of Flanders, Holland, Zeeland, Hainault, and Artois, together with a number

[1] This is substantially the view of P. Rassow, *Die Kaiser-Idee Karls V* (Berlin, 1932); *Die Politische Welt Karls V* (Munich, 1947). E. Armstrong, *The Emperor Charles V,* 2nd ed. (London, 1910), argued that the emperor's policy was purely defensive, with all his actions forced on him by others. K. Brandi, *Kaiser Karl V,* vol. 1 (Munich, 1937), trans. C. V. Wedgwood (London, 1939); vol. II, *Quellen und Erörterungen* (Munich, 1941), in the fullest modern biography and an exhaustive critical bibliography, maintained that Charles's policy was more positive, with the increased greatness of the house of Habsburg as its ultimate aim.

of smaller counties and lordships. Charles's mother, Joanna of Castile, who survived until 1555, was insane and incapable of government. In consequence, the regency for the child was undertaken by his grandfather, the emperor Maximilian I, acting through his daughter, Margaret of Austria, dowager duchess of Savoy. Margaret's regency was brought to an end in January 1515 when the estates bribed Maximilian to have the young prince declared of age.

Within a year of this event, Ferdinand of Aragon was dead (January 23, 1516). The whole inheritance of the Catholic kings, Ferdinand and Isabella, now fell to Charles of Burgundy. To Guillaume de Croy, lord of Chièvres, the effective head of Charles's government, the problem was neither new nor unexpected. Little more than ten years before, the Burgundian nobility had accompanied Charles's father, Philip, to Spain and had helped him to make good his claims to the crown of Castile. Since then, Spanish grandees had lived at the Burgundian court and had been admitted to the Order of the Golden Fleece. Spanish merchants were familiar figures in Bruges and Antwerp. For Chièvres and the great seigneurs in his council the question of whether or not to accept the Spanish succession never arose; it was only a question of how to achieve it. Chièvres was the leader of the old Walloon nobility. By culture, family ties, and the possession of estates near or even across the French border they were traditionally francophile. Now, Chièvres had to reconcile the "English" party with whose help Margaret had governed. He had to win over Maximilian and Henry VIII into full co-operation and induce Francis I to maintain a benevolent neutrality (Treaty of Noyon, December 3, 1516).

Having none of Gattinara's or Charles's sense of imperial mission, Chièvres could afford to leave France in control of northern Italy if this meant peace and amity with his powerful neighbor. When finally, in September 1517, he concluded a truce with the old enemy of the Habsburgs, Charles of Guelders, Burgundian diplomacy had won its major objectives —peace in Europe and freedom from all interference with the Spanish succession.

The situation in Spain itself was much more problematical. The union of the Spanish crowns had not meant the union of the Spanish kingdoms, and there were still powerful forces in each which would gladly have seen a return to separate rulers. The Castilians would not suffer the appointment of an Aragonese as Spanish ambassador in Rome; the men of Navarre said they would rather see a Turk than an Aragonese as commander of the fortress of Pamplona. In Castile, despite the efforts of Isabella, the power of the crown was still far from firmly established. At every royal death, the old antagonism between grandees and towns broke out into open strife. Since Isabella's death, the regency of Castile had been in the hands of her old minister, Cardinal Ximenes de Cisneros, archbishop of Toledo. After Ferdinand's death, Ximenes was well aware that only the early arrival of Charles in Spain could assure him a smooth succession. The nobles, trying to profit by the interregnum, were attempting to regain their old control over the towns. Toledo and Valladolid were in revolt against their corregidors, the royal representatives in the city administration. The cardinal's attempt to raise a militia of thirty thousand was sabotaged by both towns and grandees who feared for their own power. Ximenes had to give way for fear of more serious trouble. Most difficult of all, and most embittering, was the problem of royal appointments. The Spaniards accused the Netherlanders of greed and place-hunting. In fact, the court at Brussels was careful to hold its hand in all but a few cases; but, in Spain itself, Ximenes's secretary wrote that government was impossible without giving benefices and rewards (*mercedes*) and that the Flemings were hated even before they had arrived.

The eighteen months which it had taken Chièvres to prepare for Charles's departure had been too long an interregnum for Spain. When Charles landed there, in September 1517, his supporters were already disillusioned, while nobles and towns were sullenly apprehensive of the expected rule of the foreigner. The cardinal regent lay dying, for joy at the king's arrival, as Charles's court jester maliciously said. Charles himself, young, ugly, and inexperienced, speaking no Spanish and surrounded by Burgundian councilors and courtiers, did not initially make a good impression. The Spaniards contrasted the magnificence of the Burgundian court, its tournaments and balls, with the sober and inexpensive habits of the Catholic kings. Only three bishoprics were given to foreigners, but these included the see of Toledo, for Chièvres's nephew, and it was easy to regard this as plunder for the Burgundians. Moreover, it appeared that those Spaniards who had been in the Netherlands were preferred to those who had served the king's cause in Spain. In February 1518, the cortes of Valladolid presented Charles with far-reaching demands and much pointed counsel as a condition of the country's homage and of a grant of 600,000 ducats payable over three years. The court was accommodating and, if relations were not cordial, Charles was now the acknowledged king of Castile.

The estates of the realms of the crown of Aragon had preserved even greater liberties than those of Castile. It took much longer than in Castile to come to terms with the cortes of Saragossa and Barcelona and to obtain from them 200,000 and 100,000 ducats respectively. Chièvres preferred not to repeat this delay in Valencia. With the crown of Aragon, Charles had now inherited the old Aragonese empire, the Balearic Islands, Sardinia, Sicily, and Naples. It was a union of kingdoms each with its own history, its own traditions, obligations, and enmities. The necessity of defending southern Italy from the Turks inevitably brought Charles V's empire into collision with the Ottoman empire, quite apart from Charles's view of himself as the champion of Christendom. The rival Aragonese and Angevin claims to Naples brought Charles into collision with France, a collision which the purely Burgundian policy of Chièvres had at least temporarily been able to avoid. Defense against the Turks inevitably turned into a struggle for the control of the central Mediterranean. Defense against the French inevitably turned into a struggle for the control of Italy and hence, as the emperor's advisers Gattinara and Granvelle were later to argue, into a struggle for the dominant position in Europe. Even without Charles's election as emperor, Castile's traditional friendship with France (maintained despite the francophobia of the Castilians) was now irretrievably broken, and similarly broken was the Walloon nobility's policy of Franco-Burgundian amity.

There remained the final step in Charles's succession, the succession to the Austrian and South German dominions of the Habsburgs and his election as king of Germany, which carried with it the crown of the Holy Roman Empire. Even before Maximilian's death, January 12, 1519, the Habsburg courts in Spain, the Netherlands, and Austria were busy with their preparations for the election. When Francis I entered the field as a candidate, the rivalry between the two rulers appeared for the first time openly, and with Charles took that curiously personal and moral flavor based on his conviction of the divinely ordained nature of his claims. With the pope supporting Francis I and the electors still undecided, Margaret of Austria suggested that both pope and electors might be more easily induced to accept Charles's younger brother, Ferdinand, than the powerful ruler of the Netherlands, Spain, and half of Italy. Charles's sharp reaction from Barcelona reads like a program for his reign. "It seems to us," he wrote to his aunt, "that if the said election is conferred on our person . . . we will be able to accomplish many good and great things, and not only conserve and guard the possessions which God has given us, but increase them greatly and, in this way, give peace, repose and tranquillity to Christendom, upholding and strengthening our holy Catholic faith which is our principal foundation." Experience had shown, he continued, that even such a virtuous and victorious prince as the emperor Maximilian had been in constant trouble to safeguard his patrimony and imperial rights; but he, Charles, with the power of all his great kingdoms and dominions, would be feared and esteemed among other princes, would obtain true obedience from the subjects of the Empire and defeat the enemies of the faith. This would be greater glory for both Ferdinand and himself than acquiring dominion over Christians. Charles promised, however, to work for Ferdinand's election as king of the Romans, that is as heir presumptive to the imperial title. In the end, Charles was elected unanimously by the German electors (June 28, 1519).

The election was peculiarly the triumph of the new grand chancellor, the Piedmontese Mercurino Arborio di Gattinara who had been appointed to his office in 1518. A brilliant lawyer and superb administrator, an enthusiastic humanist and admirer of Erasmus, he had risen in the service of Margaret of Austria. For the next twelve years he did more than any other person to shape the development of his master's political ideas, then still in the youthful stage of the chivalrous quest for personal glory in the tradition of the Burgundian court. In his own memoirs, in speeches to the Spanish cortes and the Netherlands states general, in memoranda for the emperor and his council, Gattinara reiterated his belief that the imperial title gave Charles authority over the whole world, for it was "ordained by God himself, foretold by the prophets, preached by the apostles and approved by the birth, life and death of our Redeemer Christ." It was Dante's imperial idea revived. Like Dante, Gattinara, his learned and historically conscious compatriot, saw the center of imperial power in Italy. Not the personal possession of Milan or of other territories, but the friendship and support of the Italian states and all Christian princes (guaranteed, no doubt, by Habsburg military power) were to assure the emperor his position as moral and political leader of the world. In time Charles made these views his own, with little of the Italian's humanist learning, but with an even greater emphasis on the religious and dynastic aspects of his position. When Gattinara died in 1530, Charles had grown up to intellectual and moral independence. From thenceforth he dispensed with a grand chancellor. Long years of power had heightened his sense of responsibility and had developed his slow and unoriginal mind to self-assurance and mastery of politics, making him tower over his contemporaries both in the constancy of his ideals and in the flexibility and shrewdness of his tactics. At thirty-four he wrote to his younger sister Mary, dowager queen of Hungary and recently appointed regent of the Netherlands, to console her over the troubles of her task: when she had had as much experience as he, she would no longer despair over difficulties. Years later, Mary was to complain to their brother, Ferdinand, "that the emperor is difficult and does not always think well of a matter if it does not come from him." Thus, self-assured and masterful, in his later years a little skeptical, the emperor appears in Titian's famous portraits.

Not all contemporaries, not even those in his own dominions, could accept Charles's and Gattinara's view of the empire as standing for peace among Christians and the defense of Christianity against Muslims and heretics. Gattinara's Italian policy was ascribed to his possession of estates in the duchy of Milan. His policy of moral leadership for the emperor became suspect when, after the battle of Pavia, he urged the annexation of Dauphiné and Languedoc. With an imperial niece married to the duke of Milan and imperial troops in control of its fortresses, the emperor's claim that he was preserving the independence of the duchy had a hollow ring to the Venetians and the French. Europe saw Charles V's empire primarily in terms of power, and in this view originated the permanent hostility of the only other European power of comparable strength, France, and the intermittent hostility or at best cool friendship of the lesser independent powers, England, Denmark, and the Italian states. Moreover, Charles's very insistence on his religious aims and their fusion with his political ends helped to make insoluble two problems which were difficult enough in any case: his relations with the German princes and his relations with the pope. To the Protestant German princes, the emperor's policy represented the double threat of imperial and religious coercion; and since the Catholic princes were equally alarmed about the emperor's political power, they never gave him the political support which alone would have enabled him to solve the religious question.

The pope seemed to be the natural ally of "God's standard bearer," and

Charles never ceased to hope that such he would prove to be. But Clement VII and Paul III, in their capacity of Italian princes, were as alarmed as their twelfth- and thirteenth-century predecessors at seeing Naples and Milan united in one hand. They therefore never stopped intriguing with France against the imperial power in Italy. Of this fact Charles was fully aware. What he never fully understood was that the popes, as spiritual heads of the Christian Church, could never entertain the emperor's claim to be the ultimate arbiter of the religious troubles which afflicted Christendom. It was unacceptable that at Augsburg and Regensburg the emperor's theologians should attempt to reach a compromise with the Protestants binding on all Christians; it was intolerable that a secular prince should take the initiative in reforming the Church and should threaten to summon a general council. The threat of the Turks and Protestants held pope and emperor together in uneasy alliance and only once, in 1527, did the underlying hostility break out into open and disastrous warfare; but the emperor's inability to induce the Papacy to co-operate whole-heartedly in his policies was one of the major weaknesses of his position.

Imperial Administration and Imperial Policy

The very existence of Charles V's empire—the uniting of a number of countries under the rule of one person—thus raised problems which the individual countries either would not have had to face at all, or, as the histories of France and England demonstrated, would have had to face in a much more tractable form. Added to these difficulties was the unprecedented problem of governing this diverse collection of states. In the last analysis, the empire of Charles V existed only in the person of the emperor. It was not even called an empire. That name was reserved for the old Holy Roman Empire, here distinguished by a capital letter from the empire of Charles V, a term which should be clearly understood as a purely modern designation; when Charles V's contemporaries used a collective name for his dominions at all, it was *monarchia*. There was much confusion in the minds of contemporaries as to the significance of even that venerable institution, now that it had suddenly acquired such a powerful head. To Gattinara, at least, it was clear that the personal union of the states of the empire must be matched by a functional union. By training and experience, Gattinara belonged to the school of Roman lawyers, mostly natives of Franche-Comté, who had helped the dukes of Burgundy to weld the Netherlands into a functional union by establishment of the councils and courts through which they governed the provinces. His authority as Burgundian grand chancellor was now extended to cover all of Charles's dominions. The Council of State, the only one of the councils to which great nobles were admitted and which advised the emperor on all imperial matters, was extended to include Spanish and Italian members, as well as the Burgundians. Characteristically, Gattinara saw his emperor as legislator for the whole world, "following the path of the good emperor Justinian," reforming the laws and simplifying legal procedures, so that all the world would want to use them and that "it would be possible to say that there was one emperor and one universal law."

Nothing came of this vision. Nor did anything come of Gattinara's plan for a treasurer general to whom the treasuries of all the emperor's dominions should render account. After Gattinara's death and the abolition of his own office of grand chancellor, the other all-imperial institutions regressed even from the very modest level they had attained. The central control of the empire became more and more a matter of personal control by Charles and those advisers whom he chose to consult on any particular issue. The enormous amount of paper work (of which only a small part has been published) was handled by two distinct institutions: a Spanish secretariat of state, continuing traditions inaugurated by the Catholic kings and responsible for the affairs of Spain, Italy, and the Mediterranean; and a French secretariat, based on Burgundian traditions and responsible for all affairs north of the Alps. The old German imperial chancellery continued to function independently in purely technical matters, but politically it was dependent on the Franco-Burgundian secretariat. Inevitably, these developments led to a great increase in the power of the secretaries of state. Both the Spanish secretary, Francisco de los Cobos, and the Franco-Burgundian secretary, Nicolas Perrenot, seigneur de Granvelle, another Franche-Comtois, were men of great ability; but neither their functions nor their personalities made their position and influence comparable to that of Gattinara before 1530.

More than ever Charles, and Charles only, represented the empire. He governed it like the head of one of the great sixteenth-century merchant houses where the junior members of the family served as heads of the foreign branches of the firm. There were great advantages in having members of the Habsburg family as governors general, regents, or even kings in his dominions. They were locally more acceptable than even the greatest nobles of nonroyal blood and much less likely to be involved in local feuds; their employment as his personal representatives accorded with Charles's own views of the central role of the dynasty in his whole position. The Netherlands, the Empire, and Spain after 1529 were always, at least nominally, entrusted to a Habsburg or his consort. Only for the Italian dominions had nonroyal viceroys to be appointed. In the event, the emperor's policy proved a success in all but one disastrous case, and his family served him loyally and, in the persons of his two governors general of the Netherlands, his aunt Margaret of Austria (1518–1530) and his sister Mary of Hungary (1531–1555), with more than common skill and devotion.

. . . . .

Within the different parts of the empire there were powerful forces willing to support Charles and his imperial policy. The Burgundian high nobility who had done so much to secure their prince the effective succession to his kingdoms remained loyal to the end even if, for most of them, Gattinara's and Charles's Christian ideals meant little more than the fashionable commonplaces of their knightly upbringing at the Burgundian court. When Philibert de Chalon, prince of Orange and Charles's viceroy of Naples, appealed to him for support against the French invasion of Naples in 1528, he wrote, "The king of France is sparing no effort. It would be very shameful and damaging to you, Sire, if you did not do your utmost; for it is by this that the world will see which one of you two will remain the master." There was no imperial ideal here. Chalon and many of his fellow nobles saw the emperor's policy as simply a quest for personal honor and reputation. It was enough for them to serve the most powerful prince in Christendom and to have the opportunity of appointments to provincial governorships or even viceroyalties, or to win fame by leading his armies against Frenchman, Turk, or heretic. Thus, too, thought the Spanish nobility. Their early hostility to Charles soon changed to enthusiastic support. More than the Netherlanders, they were in sympathy with Charles's crusading and imperial ideals. Had not the Castilians fought the Moors on their own soil? Had not the Aragonese achieved power and renown by their Italian conquests and wealth by the easy acquisition of Sicilian and Neapolitan estates or ecclesiastical benefices? The double lure of knight-errantry and plunder made the Spaniards imperialists in Europe as it made them *conquistadores* in America. Nor did the chances of promotion and high office hold less attraction for the Italian nobility. As king of Sicily and Naples, the emperor was their own prince as much as he was ruler of Spain and Germany. The Gonzaga, the Pescara, the del Vasto preferred the role of an imperial viceroy or captain general to that of a provincial condottiere.

Next to the high nobility, the lawyers were the emperor's most enthusiastic supporters. Trained in Roman law with its imperial and absolutist traditions, many of them humanists and Erasmians, they found it easy to combine their sympathy for Charles V's imperial claims with the prospect of dazzling careers in the imperial councils. For the rest of the populations of the emperor's dominions the advantages of belonging to a world empire appeared more doubtful. There were those, especially among the merchant class, who were able to take advantage of the political connections between Italy, Spain, and the Netherlands. But, as we have seen, the economic links between the parts of the empire depended little on its political structure or on the emperor's policies. The Spanish hidalgos, the lower nobility, who flocked in their hundreds to serve under the emperor's standards in the Spanish *tercios*, represented a Spanish, rather than a universal, imperialism. For the mass of the population, the empire seemed to be the last chance of peace within Christendom—that passionate longing which had attached itself for centuries to the name of the Roman Empire. Now, in Charles V, it seemed to find its fulfilment. Or so it appeared to the crowds who cheered the emperor's, or his son's, entry into their city on his journeys from country to country; and so it was presented on the triumphal arches which greeted him—arches on which local Latinists displayed their learning and enthusiasm for the "restorer of the Roman Empire" and the "future ruler of the whole globe." But it was just this longed-for peace which the emperor failed to give his subjects. When the court had passed on its way, the taxes remained to pay for wars which often seemed no concern of the single provinces. If loyalty to the emperor seldom wavered, his governors, foreign or native, were often hated, and the ruler's absence on his imperial duties was deeply resented. Ultimately, local interests and loyalties remained predominant in every case; the feeling of imperial solidarity never developed sufficiently to become an effective political force.

30. The Crisis of the Seventeenth Century

E. J. HOBSBAWM

31. The Decline of Spain

J. H. ELLIOTT

In the past fifteen years a number of studies have appeared that emphasize a general crisis in Europe during the seventeenth century; population decline, economic stagnation or regression, popular revolts, and a check to overseas expansion are among the most prominent factors cited for this crisis. The following article by Professor Hobsbawm, originally published in Past and Present *and reprinted in* Crisis in Europe, 1560–1660, *was one of the first papers to appear on the subject and it has been very influential in the ensuing debate among historians over the nature and causes of what has now been generally recognized as a crisis in Europe.*

Professor Hobsbawm finds evidence for several kinds of decline or trouble in Europe's economy, and although the sometimes incomplete nature of our evidence precludes absolute proof of all of his areas of generalization, most historians accept the main aspects of the crisis as correct. The chief indicators of this crisis are a general decline or at best leveling off of population; a decline in production in many European industries; a check in commerce, followed only much later by changes in the nature of commercial enterprise and a consequent upsurge; a transition in the nature of overseas expansion; and numerous social revolts, in England, France, Spain, and Germany most notably. While the exis-

Source: E. J. Hobsbawm, "The Crisis of the Seventeenth Century," *Past and Present*, No. 5, 1954, reprinted in *Crisis in Europe, 1560–1660,* ed. Trevor Aston, pp. 5–27. Copyright © 1965 by Routledge & Kegan Paul, Ltd. Reprinted by permission of author and publishers.

tence of a crisis has been accepted by many, the explanation of this crisis that Hobsbawm suggests has found less favor. His interpretation is avowedly Marxist, and his main thesis is that to discuss the crisis is to ask the fundamental question about capitalism: why did the expansion of the fifteenth and sixteenth centuries not lead directly into the epoch of the industrial revolution of the eighteenth and nineteenth centuries? In Hobsbawm's view, the primary obstacle was the feudal structure, which still predominated in much of Europe. The difficulties with this explanation, as Professor Trevor-Roper has observed in another essay reprinted in Crisis in Europe, is that it is virtually unsubstantiated. What evidence does Hobsbawm adduce in support of his hypothesis? What does he mean by the term "feudal structure," and how does his usage compare with that given by Professor Strayer in his article on European feudalism? Finally, what are the dangers to historical writing in any aprioristic approach to the past?

The second article in this section also comes from Crisis in Europe, but in it Professor Elliott is concerned to explore the background of the particular crisis in the Spanish Monarchy, which reached a peak in 1640, against the general setting of European developments. In his view, the troubles of the Spanish Crown stemmed not from any pan-European failure of nascent capitalism to overcome the resistance of a moribund feudal structure, but rather from several critical failures within the kingdom of Castile itself, the core of the Spanish Monarchy. By a meticulous and creative examination of work in many areas of social and economic history, he argues persuasively that the period 1590–1620 saw a fundamental breakdown in three sectors in which Castile had contributed materially to Spanish power in the preceding century: population, economic productivity, and overseas wealth. Professor Elliott's study is an elegant piece of sociological analysis, and it demonstrates the need for detailed investigation rather than mere hypotheses in historical explanation. The reader interested in exploring these areas further might well begin with Crisis in Europe (1965), and with J. H. Elliott's Imperial Spain, 1469–1716 (1964).

E. J. HOBSBAWM

In the first part of this essay I wish to suggest that the European economy passed through a 'general crisis' during the seventeenth century, the last phase of the general transition from a feudal to a capitalist economy. Since 1300 or so, when something clearly began to go seriously wrong with European feudal society,[1] there have been several occasions when parts of Europe trembled on the brink of capitalism. There is a taste of

[1] E. Perroy, R. Boutruche, R. H. Hilton have discussed this in recent years in *Annales E.S.C.,* and elsewhere. See also the discussion among M. Dobb, P. M. Sweezy, H. K. Takahashi, R. H. Hilton and C. Hill in *Science and Society,* xiv–xvii (1950–3), and the general survey by M. Malowist in *Kwartalnik Historiczny,* i (1953). (I am indebted to the Polish Institute, London, for a translation of this.)

'bourgeois' and 'industrial' revolution about fourteenth-century Tuscany and Flanders or early sixteenth-century Germany. Yet it is only from the middle of the seventeenth century that this taste becomes more than a seasoning to an essentially medieval or feudal dish. The earlier urban societies never quite succeeded in the revolutions they foreshadowed. From the early eighteenth century, however, 'bourgeois' society advanced without substantial checks. The seventeenth century crisis thus differs from its predecessors in that it led to as fundamental a solution of the difficulties which had previously stood in the way of the triumph of capitalism, as that system will permit. In the first part of this essay I propose to marshal some of the evidence for the existence of a general crisis, which is still disputed by some, and to suggest an explanation of it. In the second part I propose to discuss some of the changes it produced, and how it was overcome. It is very probable that a great deal of historical work will be done on this subject and period in the next few years. Indeed, lately historians in various countries have tentatively suggested something like that 'general check to economic development' or general crisis with which this paper deals.[2] It may therefore be convenient to take a bird's eye view of the field, and to speculate about some sort of working hypothesis, if only to stimulate better ones, or further work.

The 'General Crisis'

A good deal of evidence for the 'general crisis' is available. We must, however, be careful to avoid the argument that a general crisis equals economic retrogression, which has bedevilled much of the discussion about the 'feudal crisis' of the fourteenth and fifteenth centuries. It is perfectly clear that there *was* a good deal of retrogression in the seventeenth century. For the first time in history the Mediterranean ceased to be a major centre of economic and political, and eventually of cultural influence and became an impoverished backwater. The Iberian powers, Italy, Turkey were plainly on the downgrade: Venice was on the way to becoming a tourist centre. With the exception of a few places dependent on the north-western States (generally free ports) and the pirate metropolis of Algiers, which also operated in the Atlantic,[3] there was little advance. Farther north, the decline of Germany is patent, though not wholly unrelieved. In the Baltic Poland, Denmark and the Hanse were on the way

449

Hobsbawm

THE CRISIS
OF THE
SEVENTEENTH
CENTURY

[2] F. Braudel, *La Méditerranée . . . au temps de Philippe II* (Paris, 1949), p. 1097. R. Romano, 'Industries textiles et conjoncture à Florence au XVIIᵉ siècle'; *Annales E.S.C.,* viiᵉ année (1952), p. 510. French historians regard the 'phase de contraction du XVIIᵉ siècle' as 'un fait maintenant établi' (P. Chaunu in *Rev. Hist.,* ccx [1953], p. 379). In what follows I owe a great deal to discussion with J. Meuvret who confirmed many of my non-specialist guesses. However I doubt whether he would agree with much of this paper.

[3] C. A. Julien, *Histoire de l'Afrique du Nord* (Paris, 1931), pp. 538 ff; the 'industrial revolution' in piracy, due to the introduction of northern sails by English and Dutch after 1604 may be noted.

down. Though the power and influence of Habsburg Austria increased (perhaps largely because others declined so dramatically), her resources remained poor, her military and political structure rickety even at the period of her greatest glory in the early eighteenth century. On the other hand in the Maritime Powers and their dependencies—England, the United Provinces, Sweden, and in Russia and some minor areas like Switzerland—the impression is one of advance rather than stagnation; in England, of decisive advance. France occupied an intermediate position, though even here political triumph was not balanced by great economic advance until the end of the century, and then only intermittently. Indeed an atmosphere of gloom and crisis fills the discussions there after 1680, though conditions in the previous half-century can hardly have been superior. (Possibly the huge catastrophe of 1693–4 accounts for this.[4]) It was in the sixteenth not the seventeenth century that invading mercenaries marvelled at how much there was to loot in France, and men in Richelieu's and Colbert's era looked back on Henry IV's as a sort of golden age. It is indeed possible that, for some decades in the middle of the century, the gains made in the Atlantic did not replace the losses in the Mediterranean, central Europe and the Baltic, the total proceeds from both stagnating or perhaps declining. Nevertheless what is important is the decisive advance in the progress of capitalism which resulted.

The scattered figures for European *population* suggest, at worst an actual decline, at best a level or slightly rising plateau between the mounting slopes of the population curve in the later sixteenth and eighteenth centuries. Except for the Netherlands, Norway and perhaps Sweden and Switzerland and some local areas, no major increases in population appear to be recorded. Spain was a byword for depopulation, southern Italy may have suffered, and the ravages of the mid-century in Germany and eastern France are well known. Though Pirenne has argued that Belgian population increased, figures for Brabant do not seem to bear him out. Hungarian population fell; that of Poland even more. English population growth probably slowed down rapidly and may actually have ceased after 1630.[5]

[4] J. Meuvret in *Mélanges d'Histoire Sociale*, v (1944), pp. 27–44; in *Population*, i (1946), pp. 643–50 and an unpublished paper on the effects of the 1693–4 and 1709–10 famines on French diplomacy.

[5] There are, of course, no reliable statistics and not always good indirect indices. This paragraph is based, in particular, on: K. Larsen, *History of Norway* (Princeton, 1948) (figures only for 1665 and after); K. Mayer, *The Population of Switzerland* (New York, 1952), and Patavino's estimate for 1608 which is as great as Mayer's for 1700, in H. Nabholz, Muralt, Feller, Bonjour, Dürr, *Gesch. d. Schweiz* (Zurich, 1932–8), ii, p. 5; H. Wopfner, *Gueterteilung u. Uebervoelkerung* (Berlin 1938), pp. 202 ff; H. v. z. Muehlen, 'Entstehung d. Gutscherrschaft in Oberschlesien', in *Vierteljahrschrift f. Soz.- und Wirtschaftgesch.*, xxxviii, pp. 334–60; E. Beloch, *Bevoelkerungsgeschichte Italiens* (Leipzig, 1937), i, pp. 153, 225 ff; E. Keyser, *Bevoelkerungsgesch. Deutschlands* (Leipzig, 1941), pp. 304 ff, 361 ff; G. Roupnel, *La Ville et la campagne dijonnaises au xviie siècle* (Paris, 1922); P. Goubert, 'Problèmes démographiques du Beauvaisis au 17e s.' (*Annales, E.S.C.*, viie année [1952], pp. 452–68), for an area which seems to have suffered rather less; G. De-

In fact it is not easy to see why Clark concludes that 'the seventeenth century in most of Europe saw, like the sixteenth, a moderate increase in population'.[6] Mortality was certainly higher than in either the sixteenth or eighteenth. No century since the fourteenth has a worse record for epidemic disease and recent work has demonstrated that its ravages cannot be dissociated from those of famine.[7] While a handful of court and administrative metropoles or centres of international trade and finance grew to great size the number of great cities, which had risen in the sixteenth century, remained stable and small and medium towns frequently declined. This appears to apply in part even to the maritime countries.[8]

What happened to *production?* We simply do not know. Some areas were plainly de-industrialized, notably Italy which transformed itself from the most urbanized and industrialized country of Europe into a typical backward peasant area, most of Germany, and parts of France and Poland.[9] On the other hand there was fairly rapid industrial development in some places—Switzerland, and, in the extractive industries, England and Sweden, and an important growth of rural out-work at the expense of urban or local craft production in many areas which may or may not have meant a net increase in total output. If prices are any guide we should not

bien, *En Haut-Poitou; Défricheurs au Travail (XV–XVIII siècles)*, and for absence of forest-clearing and recovery of forests, *Bull. Soc. Hist. Mod.*, lvii (1953), pp. 6–9; H. Pirenne, *Hist. de Belgique* (Bruxelles, 1900), iv, pp. 439–40; A. Cosemans, *Bevolkering v. Brabant en de 17e eeuw* (Brussels, 1939), pp. 224–4; G. N. Clark, *The Seventeenth Century* (Oxford, 1929); J. Rutkowski, *Hist. Econ. de la Pologne avant les Partages* (Paris, 1927), pp. 91–92; L. Stone in *IX Congrès International des Sciences Historiques*, ii (1951), pp. 49–50; W. G. Hoskins, "The Rebuilding of Rural England 1570–1640', *Past and Present*, no. 4 (Nov. 1953).

[6] Op. cit., p. 6. The same criticism may be made of the estimates of Urlanis, *Rost nasielenia v. Jemropie* (Moscow, 1941), p. 158, which seem rather optimistic. I am indebted to Mr. A. Jenkin for drawing my attention to these figures.

[7] S. Peller, 'Studies in Mortality since the Renaissance', *Bull. Inst. Hist. of Medicine*, xiii (1943), pp. 443, 445, 452, and esp. p. 456; ibid., xvii (1947), pp. 67, 79. Meuvret and Goubert, op. cit. and the literature quoted in H. J. Habakkuk, 'English Population in the Eighteenth Century', *Econ. Hist. Rev.*, 2nd ser., vi (1953). For the epidemiology of the century, in addition to innumerable local studies, H. Haeser, *Gesch. d. Medizin u. d. epidem. Krankheiten* (Jena, 1882); C. Creighton, *Hist. of Epidemics in Britain* (Cambridge, 1891, 1894); L. F. Hirst, *The Conquest of Plague* (Oxford 1953); L. Prinzing, *Epidemics Resulting from Wars* (Oxford, 1916); J. Brownlee, 'Epidemiology of Phthisis in Great Britain and Ireland', *Medical Research Council* (London, 1918); Campbell, 'The Epidemiology of Influenza', *Bull. Inst. Hist. Medicine*, xiii (1943); W. J. Simpson, *A Treatise on the Plague* (Cambridge, 1905).

[8] W. Sombart, *Luxus u. Kapitalismus*, pp. 26–27; G. F. v. Schmoller, *Deutsches Staedtewesen in älterer Zeit* (Bonn and Leipzig, 1922), pp. 60–95; B. Bretholz, *Gesch. Boehmens u. Maehrens* (Reichenberg, 1924), iii, pp. 61–63; E. Baasch, *Hollaendische Wirtschaftsgeschichte* (Jena, 1927), pp. 24–25.

[9] C. M. Cipolla, 'The Decline of Italy', *Econ. Hist. Rev.*, 2nd ser., v (1952); Roupnel, op. cit., for reversion of Burgundy to autarky; R. Reuss, *Hist. de Strasbourg* (Paris, 1922), pp. 280–6; P. Boissonade, 'La Crise de l'industrie languedocienne 1600–1660', *Annales du Midi*, xxi (1909); G. Aubin and H. Kunze, *Leinenerzeugung . . . im oestl. Mitteldeutschland* (Stuttgart, 1940).

451
Hobsbawm
THE CRISIS
OF THE
SEVENTEENTH
CENTURY

expect to find a general decline in production, for the deflationary period which followed the great price-rise of the pre-1640 era is more easily explained by a relative or absolute falling-off in demand rather than by a decline in the supply of money. However, in the basic industry of textiles there may have been not only a shift from 'old' to 'new' draperies, but a decline of total output for part of the century.[10]

The crisis in *commerce* was more general. The two main areas of established international trade, the Mediterranean and the Baltic, underwent revolution, and probably temporary decline in the volume of trade. The Baltic—the European colony of the western urbanized countries—changed its staple exports from foodstuffs to products like timber, metals and naval stores, while its traditional imports of western woollens diminished. Trade as measured by the Sound tolls reached its peak in 1590–1620, collapsed in the 1620s, and declined catastrophically after some recovery until the 1650s, remaining in the doldrums until 1680 or so.[11] After 1650, the Mediterranean became like the Baltic an area exchanging locally produced goods, mainly raw materials, for the Atlantic manufactures and the oriental goods now monopolized by the north-west. By the end of the century the Levant got its spices from the north, not the east. French Levantine trade halved between 1620 and 1635, sank almost to zero by the 1650s and did not really recover from depression levels until after the 1670s. Dutch Levantine trade did poorly from about 1617 to about 1650.[12] Even then the French hardly exceeded pre-depression levels much before 1700. Did the British and Dutch sales drive in the south make up for losses in the Baltic markets? Probably not. It may barely have made up for the decline in previous sales of Italian products. The international trade in foodstuffs—Baltic corn, Dutch herrings and Newfoundland fish—did not maintain its Jacobean levels. The international trade in woollen cloths may have shrunk; nor was it immediately replaced by other textiles, for the great centres of exportable linen, Silesia and Lusatia, seem to have declined somewhat after 1620. In fact it is not unlikely that a general balance of rising and declining trade would produce export figures which did not rise significantly between 1620 and 1660. Outside the maritime states it is unlikely that sales on the home markets made up for this.

As we know from the nineteenth century, the malaise of business cannot be measured simply by trade and production figures, whatever these may be. (It is nevertheless significant that the whole tone of economic dis-

[10] For figures of the Dutch and Florentine production, N. W. Posthumus, *Gesch. v. d. Leidsch. Lakenindustrie* (Hague, 1932); Romano in *Annales,* loc. cit.

[11] N. E. Bang and K. Korst, *Tabeller over Skibsfart* (København and Leipzig, 1930–53); A. Christensen, *Dutch Trade and the Baltic about 1600* (Copenhagen, 1940).

[12] G. Tongas, *Relations entre la France et l'Empire Ottoman durant la première moitié du XVII* ^{e} *siècle* (Toulouse, 1942); P. Masson, *Le Commerce français dans le Levant au XVII* ^{e} *siècle* (Paris, 1896), esp. pp. 130–4, App. xv, p. 236; H. Wätjen, *D. Niederländer im Mittelmeergebiet* (Berlin, 1909), pp. 145, 149.

cussion assumed stable markets and profit opportunities. Colbertian mercantilism, it has often been said, was a policy of economic warfare for large slices of a world trade-cake of fixed size. There is no reason why administrators and traders—for economics was not yet an academic subject—should have adopted views which were greatly at variance with appearances.) It is certain that even in countries which did not decline there were secular business difficulties. English East India trade languished until the Restoration.[13] Though that of the Dutch increased handsomely, the average annual dividend of their East India Company fell for each of the ten-year periods from the 1630s to the 1670s (including both), except for a slight rise in the 1660s. Between 1627 and 1687 sixteen years were without dividend; in the rest of the Company's history from 1602 to 1782 none. (The value of its goods remained stable between 1640 and 1660.) Similarly the profits of the Amsterdam Wisselbank reached a peak in the 1630s and then declined for a couple of decades.[14] Again, it may not be wholly accidental that the greatest messianic movement of Jewish history occurred at this moment, sweeping the communities of the great trading centres—Smyrna, Leghorn, Venice, Amsterdam, Hamburg—off their feet with special success in the middle 1660s as prices reached almost their lowest point.

It is also clear that the *expansion of Europe* passed through a crisis. Though the foundations of the fabulous colonial system of the eighteenth century were laid mainly after 1650,[15] earlier there may actually have been some contraction of European influence except in the hinterlands of Siberia and America. The Spanish and Portuguese empires of course contracted, and changed character. But it is also worth noting that the Dutch did not maintain the remarkable rate of expansion of 1600 to 1640 and their Empire actually shrank in the next thirty years.[16] The collapse of the Dutch West India Company after the 1640s, and the *simultaneous* winding-up of the English Africa Company and the Dutch West India Company in the early 1670s may be mentioned in passing.

It will be generally agreed that the seventeenth century was one of *social revolt* both in western and eastern Europe. This clustering of revolutions has led some historians to see something like a general social-revolu-

453

Hobsbawm

THE CRISIS
OF THE
SEVENTEENTH
CENTURY

[13] Bal Krishna, *Commercial Relations between India and England 1601–1757* (London, 1927), chaps. ii–v; S. A. Khan, *East India Trade in the Seventeenth Century* (London, 1923), pp. 74 ff.

[14] C. de Lannoy and H. Van der Linden, *Hist. de l'Expansion des Peuples Européens, Néerlande et Danemark (XVII et XVIII siècles)* (Bruxelles, 1911), pp. 334, 344–5, 363. The indebtedness of the Company was also higher than before or after; J. G. Van Dillen, *Bronnen tot d. Geschiedenis d. Wisselbanken* (Hague, 1925), ii, pp. 971 ff.

[15] Barbados began to export sugar in 1646, Jamaica started planting in 1664, Haiti re-established plantation in 1655, Martinique began it in the same year, St. Kitts's sugar exports passed its indigo exports in 1660: E. O. v. Lippman, *Gesch. d. Zuckers* (Leipzig, 1890).

[16] For a comparison of its size in 1641 and 1667, J. Saintoyant, *La Colonisation Européenne* (Paris, 1947), pp. 271–3.

tionary crisis in the middle of the century.[17] France had its Frondes, which were important social movements; Catalan, Neapolitan and Portuguese revolutions marked the crisis of the Spanish Empire in the 1640s; the Swiss peasant war of 1653 expressed both the post-war crisis and the increasing exploitation of peasant by town, while in England revolution triumphed with portentous results.[18] Though peasant unrest did not cease in the west—the 'stamped paper' rising which combined middle class, maritime and peasant unrest in Bordeaux and Brittany occurred in 1675, the Camisard wars even later [19]—those of eastern Europe were more significant. In the sixteenth century there had been few revolts against the growing enserfment of peasants. The Ukrainian revolution of 1648–54 may be regarded as a major servile upheaval. So must the various 'Kurucz' movements in Hungary, their very name harking back to Dozsa's peasant rebels of 1514, their memory enshrined in folksongs about Rakoczy as that of the Russian revolt of 1672 is in the song about Stenka Razin. A major Bohemian peasant rising in 1680 opened a period of endemic serf unrest there.[20] It would be easy to lengthen this catalogue of major social upheavals—for instance by including the revolts of the Irish in 1641 and 1689.

Only in one respect did the seventeenth century as a whole overcome rather than experience difficulties. Outside the maritime powers with their new, and experimental bourgeois régimes most of Europe found an efficient and stable form of government in *absolutism* on the French model. (But the rise of absolutism has been taken as a direct sign of economic weakness.[21] The question is worth exploring further.) The great age of *ad hoc* devices in politics, war and administration vanished with the great world empires of the sixteenth century, the Spanish and Turkish. For the first time large territorial States seemed capable of solving their three fundamental problems: how to have the orders of government obeyed directly over a large area, how to have enough cash for the large lump-sum payments they periodically needed, and—partly in consequence of this —how to run their own armies. The age of the great independent financial and military subcontractors faded with the Thirty Years' War (1618–48). States still had to subcontract, as the practice of selling of-

[17] B. Porshnev in Biryukovitch, Porshnev, Skazkin, *et al., Novaya Istoriya, 1640–1789* (Moscow, 1951), p. 444. This follows a suggestion of Marx in 1850 (*Sel. Essays,* ed. Stenning [London, 1926], p. 203). The coincidence has often been noted, e.g. Merriman, *Six Contemporaneous Revolutions* (Oxford, 1938).

[18] Merriman, op. cit.; B. Porshnev, *Narodnie vosstaniya vo Frantsii pered Frondoi 1623–1648* (Moscow, 1948); O. Schiff, 'D. deutschen Bauernaufstaende 1525–1789', *Hist. Zeitschrift,* cxxx (1924), pp. 189 ff; R. Feller, *Gesch. Berns,* ii (Bern, 1953), chaps. iv and v.

[19] J. Lemoine, *La Révolte du Papier Timbré* (Paris, 1898), prints numerous documents.

[20] H. Marczali, *Hungary in the Eighteenth Century* (Cambridge, 1910), p. xxxvii; Bretholz, op. cit., pp. 57–61.

[21] A. Nielsen, *Daenische Wirtschaftsgeschichte* (Jena, 1933), pp. 94–95.

fices and farming taxes bears witness.[22] However, the whole business was now officially controlled by governments, not merely controlled in practice by the fact that, as the Fuggers and Wallenstein had found to their cost, the monopoly buyer can dictate terms as much as the monopoly seller. Perhaps this obvious political success of the absolutist territorial states with their pomp and splendour has in the past distracted attention from the general difficulties of the age.

If only part of this evidence holds water, we are justified in speaking of a 'general crisis' in the seventeenth century; though one of its characteristics was the relative immunity of the States which had undergone 'bourgeois revolution'. It is probable—though here we venture on the complex territory of price history [23]—that the crisis began about 1620; perhaps with the slump period from 1619 into the early 1620s. It seems certain that, after some distortion of price movements by the Thirty Years' War, it reached its most acute phase between 1640 and the 1670s, though precise dates are out of order in the discussion of long-term economic movements. From then on the evidence is conflicting. Probably the signs of revival outweigh those of crisis, not only (obviously) in the Maritime States but elsewhere. However, the wild oscillations of boom and depression, the famines, revolts, epidemics and other signs of profound economic trouble in 1680–1720 should warn us against antedating the period of full recovery. If the trend was upwards from, say, the 1680s—or even earlier in *individual* countries—it was still liable to disastrous fluctuations.

It may, however, be argued that what I have described as a 'general crisis' was merely the result of seventeenth-century wars, particularly of the Thirty Years' War. In the past historians have in fact tended to take (or rather to imply) this view. But the crisis affected many parts of Europe not ravaged by generals and quartermasters; and conversely, some traditional 'cockpits of Europe' (e.g. Saxony and the Low Countries) did notably better than more tranquil regions. Moreover, there has been a persistent tendency to exaggerate the long-term and permanent damage done by seventeenth-century wars. We now know that (other things being equal) the losses of population, production and capital equipment of even twentieth-century wars, whose destructive capacities are much greater, can be made good within a matter of twenty to twenty-five years. If they were not in the seventeenth century, it was because wars aggravated already existing tendencies of crisis. This is not to deny their importance, though their effects were more complex than appears at first sight. Thus against the ravages of the Thirty Years' War in parts of central Europe we must set the stimulus it gave to mining and metallurgy in general, and the temporary booms it stimulated in non-combatant countries (to the temporary benefit of Charles I in the 1630s). It is also proba-

455

Hobsbawm

THE CRISIS
OF THE
SEVENTEENTH
CENTURY

[22] R. Mousnier, *La Vénalité des offices sous Henri IV et Louis XIII* (Rouen, 1946); K. W. Swart, *Sale of offices in the Seventeenth Century* (Hague, 1949).

[23] See the note on Price History, below p. 28; [omitted here].

ble that, but for it, the great 'price-rise' would have ended in the 1610s and not the 1640s. The war almost certainly shifted the incidence of the crisis and may, on balance, have aggravated it. Lastly, it is worth considering whether the crisis did not to some extent produce a situation which provoked or prolonged warfare. However, this point, which is not essential to the argument, is perhaps too speculative to be worth pursuing.

The Causes of the Crisis

In discussing the seventeenth-century crisis we are really asking one of the fundamental questions about the rise of capitalism: why did the expansion of the later fifteenth and sixteenth centuries not lead straight into the epoch of the eighteenth- and nineteenth-century Industrial Revolution? What, in other words, were the obstacles in the way of capitalist expansion? The answers, it may be suggested, are both general and particular.

The general argument may be summarized as follows. If capitalism is to triumph, the social structure of feudal or agrarian society must be revolutionized. The social division of labour must be greatly elaborated if productivity is to increase; the social labour force must be radically redistributed from agriculture to industry while this happens. The proportion of production which is exchanged in the supra-local market must rise dramatically. So long as there is no large body of wage-workers; so long as most men supply their needs from their own production or by exchange in the multiplicity of more or less autarkic local markets which exist even in primitive societies, there is a limit to the horizon of capitalist profit and very little incentive to undertake what we may loosely call mass production, the basis of capitalist industrial expansion. Historically, these processes cannot always be separated from one another. We may speak of the 'creation of the capitalist home market' or the divorce of the producers from the means of production which Marx called 'primitive accumulation': [24] the creation of a large and expanding market for goods and a large and available free labour force go together, two aspects of the same process.

It is sometimes assumed that the development of a 'capitalist class' and of the elements of the capitalist mode of production within feudal society automatically produces these conditions. In the long run, taking the widest view over the centuries from 1000 to 1800, this is no doubt so. In the

[24] V. I. Lenin, *The Development of Capitalism in Russia,* chap. i (conclusions), chap. ii (conclusions), chap. viii (the formation of the Home Market). *Capital,* i (1938 edn.), pp. 738, 772–4. That Marx did not think primarily of the actual accumulation of resources is shown, I think, by a preparatory draft to the Critique of Political Economy: 'Eigen ist dem Kapital nichts als die Vereinigung von Haenden und Instrumente, die es vorfindet. Es agglomeriert sie unter seiner Botmaessigkeit. Das ist sein wirkliches Anhaeufen; das Anhaeufen von Arbeitern auf Punkten nebst ihren Instrumente' (*Formen die der kapitalistichen Produktion vorbergeben* [Berlin, 1952], pp. 49–50).

shorter run it is not. Unless certain conditions are present—it is by no means yet clear what they are—the scope of capitalist expansion will be limited by the general prevalence of the feudal structure of society, that is of the predominant rural sector or perhaps by some other structure which 'immobilizes' both the potential labour-force, the potential surplus for productive investment, and the potential demand for capitalistically produced goods, such as the prevalence of tribalism or petty commodity production. Under those conditions, as Marx showed in the case of mercantile enterprise,[25] business might adapt itself to operating in a generally feudal framework, accepting its limitations and the peculiar demand for its services, and becoming in a sense parasitic on it. That part of it which did so would be unable to overcome the crises of feudal society, and might even aggravate them. For capitalist expansion is blind. The weakness of the old theories which ascribed the triumph of capitalism to the development of the 'capitalist spirit' or the 'entrepreneurial spirit' is that the desire to pursue the maximum profit without limit does not automatically produce that social and technical revolution which is required. At the very least there must be mass production (that is production for the greatest aggregate profit—large profits, but not necessarily large profits per sale) instead of production for the maximum profit per unit sale. Yet one of the essential difficulties of capitalist development in societies which keep the mass of the population outside its scope (so that they are neither sellers of labour-power nor serious buyers of commodities) is that in the short view the profits of the really 'revolutionary' types of capitalist production are almost certainly less, or look less attractive, than those of the other kind—especially when they involve heavy capital investment. Christian Dior then looks a more attractive proposition than Montagu Burton. To corner pepper in the sixteenth century would seem much sounder than to start sugar plantations in the Americas; to sell Bologna silks than to sell Ulm fustian. Yet we know that in subsequent centuries far vaster profits were achieved by sugar and cotton than by pepper and silk; and that sugar and cotton contributed far more to the creation of a world capitalist economy than the other two.

Under certain circumstances such trade could, even under feudal conditions, produce large enough aggregate profits to give rise to large-scale production; for instance if it catered for exceptionally large organizations such as kingdoms or the Church; if the thinly spread demand of an entire continent were concentrated into the hands of businessmen in a few specialized centres such as the Italian and Flemish textile towns; if a large 'lateral extension' of the field of enterprise took place, for example by conquest or colonization. A fair amount of social re-division was also possible without disturbing the fundamentally feudal structure of society—for instance the urbanization of the Netherlands and Italy on the basis of food and raw materials imported from semi-colonial territories. Neverthe-

457

Hobsbawm

THE CRISIS
OF THE
SEVENTEENTH
CENTURY

[25] *Capital,* iii, pt. iv (Merchant's Capital); and esp. vol. ii, p. 63. See also R. H. Hilton, 'Capitalism, What's in a Name?', *Past and Present,* no. 1 (Feb. 1952).

less the limits of the market were narrow. Medieval and early modern society was a good deal more like 'natural economy' than we care to recall. The sixteenth- and seventeenth-century French peasant is said hardly to have used money except for his transactions with the State; retail trade in German towns was unspecialized, like that in village shops, until the late sixteenth century.[26] Except among a small luxury class (and even there changing fashion in the modern sense probably developed late) the rate of replacement of clothes or household goods was slow. Expansion was possible and took place; but so long as the general structure of rural society had not been revolutionized it was limited, or created its own limits; and when it encountered them, entered a period of crisis.

The expansion of the fifteenth and sixteenth centuries was essentially of this sort; and it therefore created its own crisis both within the home market and within the overseas market. This crisis the 'feudal businessmen'—who were the richest and most powerful just because the best adapted for making big money in a feudal society—were unable to overcome. Their unadaptability intensified it.

Before analysing these things further, it may be worth stressing that the purely *technical* obstacles to capitalist development in the sixteenth and seventeenth centuries were not insuperable. While the sixteenth century may not have been capable of solving certain fundamental problems of technique, such as that of a compact and mobile source of power which so baffled Leonardo, it was quite capable of at least as much innovation as produced the eighteenth-century revolution. Nef and others have made us familiar with the innovations which actually occurred, though the phrase 'Industrial Revolution' seems less apt for the period 1540–1640 than for the Germany of 1450–1520 which evolved the printing press, effective fire-arms, watches, and the remarkable advance in mining and metallurgy summarized in Agricola's *De Re Metallica* (1556). Nor was there a crippling shortage of capital or capitalist enterprise or of labour, at least in the advanced areas. Sizeable blocks of mobile capital anxious for investment and, especially in the period of rising population, quite important reservoirs of free wage-labour of varying skill existed. The point is that neither were poured into industry of a potentially modern type. Moreover, methods for overcoming such shortages and rigidities of capital and labour supplies might have been utilized as fully as in the eighteenth and nineteenth centuries. The seventeenth-century crisis cannot be explained by the inadequacies of the equipment for industrial revolution, in any narrowly technical and organizational sense.

Let us now turn to the main causes of the crisis.

[26] J. Meuvret, 'Circulation monétaire et utilisation économique de la monnaie dans la France du XVIe et du XVIIe siècle', *Etudes d'Histoire Moderne et Contemp.*, i (1947), pp. 14–29; R. Latouche, *La Vie en Bas-Quercy* (Toulouse, 1923); E. Koehler, *Der Einzelhandel im Mittelalter* (Stuttgart and Berlin, 1938), pp. 55–60.

THE SPECIALIZATION OF 'FEUDAL CAPITALISTS':
THE CASE OF ITALY

The decline of Italy (and the old centres of medieval commerce and manufacture in general) was the most dramatic result of the crisis. It illustrates the weaknesses of 'capitalism' parasitic on a feudal world. Thus sixteenth-century Italians probably controlled the greatest agglomerations of capital, but misinvested them flagrantly. They immobilized them in buildings and squandered them in foreign lending during the price-revolution (which naturally favoured debtors) or diverted them from manufacturing activities to various forms of immobile investment. It has been plausibly suggested that the failure of Italian manufacture to maintain itself against Dutch, English and French during the seventeenth century was due to this diversion of resources.[27] It would be ironic to find that the Medici were Italy's ruin, not only as bankers but as patrons of the expensive arts, and Philistine historians are welcome to observe that the only major city-State which never produced any art worth mentioning, Genoa, maintained its commerce and finance better than the rest. Yet Italian investors, who had long been aware that too large cathedrals harm business,[28] were acting quite sensibly. The experience of centuries had shown that the highest profits were not to be got in technical progress or even in production. They had adapted themselves to business activities in the comparatively narrow field which remained for them once one left aside the majority of the population of Europe as 'economically neutral'. If they spent vast amounts of capital non-productively, it may have been simply because there was no more room to invest it progressively on any scale within the limits of this 'capitalist sector'. (The seventeenth-century Dutch palliated a similar glut of capital by multiplying household goods and works of art [29] though they also discovered the more modern device of a speculative investment boom.) Perhaps the Italians would have been shocked into different behaviour by economic adversity; though they had made money for so long by providing the feudal world with its trade and finance that they would not have learned easily. However, the general boom of the later sixteenth century (like the 'Indian summer' of Edwardian Britain) and the suddenly expanded demands of the great absolute monarchies which relied on private contractors, and the unprecedented luxury of their aristocracies, postponed the evil day. When it came, bringing decay to Italian trade and manufacture, it left Italian finance still upright, though no longer dominant. Again, Italian industry might well have maintained some of its old positions by switching more

459

Hobsbawm

THE CRISIS
OF THE
SEVENTEENTH
CENTURY

[27] A. Fanfani, *Storia del Lavoro in Italia dalla fine del secolo XV agli inizii del XVIII* (Milan, 1943), pp. 42–49.

[28] R. S. Lopez, 'Economie et architecture médiévales', *Annales E.S.C., viie* année (1952), pp. 443–8.

[29] G. Renier, *The Dutch Nation* (London, 1944), pp. 97–99.

completely from its old high-quality goods to the shoddier and cheaper new draperies of the north. But who, in the great period of luxury buying from 1580–1620, would have guessed that the future of high-quality textiles was limited? Did not the Court of Lorraine, in the first third of the century, use more textiles imported from Italy than from all other non-French countries put together? [30] (One would like to reserve judgment on the argument that Italy lost ground because of higher production costs for goods of equal quality, until stronger evidence for it is brought forward or until we have a satisfactory explanation for the failure of Italian production, after promising beginnings, to shift as wholeheartedly from towns to countryside as did the textile industries of other countries.[31])

The case of Italy shows why particular countries went down in the crisis, not necessarily why it occurred. We must therefore consider the contradictions of the very process of sixteenth-century expansion.

THE CONTRADICTIONS OF EXPANSION: EASTERN EUROPE

The comparative specialization of west-European towns on trade and manufacture was to some extent achieved in the fifteenth and sixteenth centuries by the creation of a sizable surplus of exportable food in eastern Europe and perhaps by ocean fisheries.[32] But in eastern Europe this was achieved by the creation of serf agriculture on a large scale; that is a local strengthening of feudalism. This, we may suggest, had three effects. It turned the peasant into less of a cash customer than he had been or might have been (or else it forced him off good-quality western textiles into cheap locally produced cloth). It diminished the number and wealth of the minor nobility for the benefit of a handful of magnates. In Poland the former controlled 43.8 per cent of ploughs in the mid-fifteenth century, 11.6 per cent in the mid-seventeenth; the share of the latter rose from 13.3 to 30.7 per cent in the same period. Lastly, it sacrificed the livelier market of the towns to the free trade interests of exporting landlords, or else seized much of what trade was going for the benefit of the already bloated lords.[33] The expansion thus had two results. While creating the conditions for the expansion of manufactures in western Europe, it cut

[30] H. Roy, *La Vie, la mode et le costume au XVIIe siècle* (Paris, 1924), prints a full list of all the types of textile used at this Court.

[31] Cipolla, 'The decline of Italy' (cited above n. 9), for the high-cost argument.

[32] M. Malowist in Report of *IX Congrès International des Sciences Historiques*, i (1950), pp. 305–22.

[33] For the extent of this increasing exploitation, J. Rutkowski, 'Le Régime agraire en Pologne au XVIIIe siècle', *Rev. Hist. Econ. and Soc.*, xix, xx (1926 and 1927), esp. 1927, pp. 92 ff; J. Rutkowski, 'Les Bases économiques des partages de l'ancienne Pologne', *Rev. d'Hist. Moderne*, N.S., iv (1932); R. Rosdolsky, 'The distribution of the Agrarian Product in Feudalism', *Jl. of Econ. Hist.*, xi (1951), pp. 247 ff. For the unimportance of cash payments, Rutkowski, op. cit., 1927, p. 71 and 1926, p. 501; Malowist, op. cit., pp. 317 ff. For an example of town impoverishment due to this, F. Tremel, 'Handel d. Stadt Judenburg im 16 Jh.', *Ztschr. d. hist. Vereins fuer Steiermark*, xxxviii (1947), pp. 103–6.

down, for a time at least, the outlets of these manufactures in the Baltic area—perhaps its most important market. The desire to cash in rapidly on the growing demand for corn—the Baltic now began to feed not only northern Europe but also the Mediterranean—tempted serf-lords into that headlong expansion of their demesnes and intensification of exploitation which led to the Ukrainian revolution, and perhaps also to demographic catastrophes.[34]

THE CONTRADICTIONS OF EXPANSION: OVERSEAS AND COLONIAL MARKETS

Much of the trade between Europe and the rest of the world had, as we know, been passive throughout the ages, because Orientals did not need European goods to the same extent as Europe needed theirs. It had been balanced by bullion payments, supplemented from time to time by such exports as slaves, furs, amber or other luxuries. Until the Industrial Revolution the sales of European manufactures were not important. (African trade, which was not deficitary, may be an exception because of the staggeringly favourable terms of trade which European goods commanded among the ignorant local buyers and indeed—almost by definition—because the continent was valued chiefly as a source of bullion until late in the seventeenth century. In 1665 the Royal African Company still estimated its gain from gold at twice its gain from slaves.[35]) The European conquest of the main trade-routes and of America did not change this structure fundamentally, for even the Americas exported more than they imported. It greatly diminished the cost of eastern goods by cutting out middlemen, lessening transport charges and enabling European merchants and armed bands to rob and cheat with impunity. It also greatly increased bullion supplies, presenting us with American and African Peters to be robbed to pay the Asian Pauls. Unquestionably Europe derived immense windfall gains from this. General business activity was immensely stimulated as well as capital accumulated; but our exports of manufactures were on the whole *not* greatly expanded. Colonial powers—in good medieval business tradition—followed a policy of systematic restriction of output and systematic monopoly. Hence there was no reason why exports of home manufactures should benefit.

The benefit which Europe drew from these initial conquests was thus in the nature of a single bonus rather than a regular dividend. When it was exhausted, crisis was likely to follow. Among the colonial powers costs and overheads rose faster than profits. In both east and west we may distinguish three stages: that of easy profits, that of crisis, and with luck

[34] An expansion of the total area of serf export-agriculture, e.g. in the Black Sea area, might have offset this. But this did not take place until the eighteenth century, possibly owing to Turkish strength and grain policy earlier: D. Ionescu, *Agrarverfassung Rumaeniens* (Leipzig, 1909), pp. 10–19; A. Mehlan, 'D. grossen Balkanmessen in der Tuerkenzeit', *Vierteljahrschrift f. Soz-. und Wirtschaftgesch.*, xxxi (1938), pp. 2–7.

[35] *Cal. S. P. Col., 1661–8*, p. 266.

eventually that of a stable and more modest prosperity. In the initial phase conquest or interloping brought temporarily unchallenged profits at low costs. In the east, where profits rested on the monopoly of a restricted output of spices and the like, the crisis was probably brought on by the steep rise in 'protection costs' against old and new rivals; rising all the more steeply as the colonial power tried to screw up the monopoly price. It has been estimated that the Portuguese spice trade barely paid its way for these reasons.[36] In the west, where they rested on the cheap bulk production of bullion and other raw materials, 'protection costs' probably played a smaller part, though they also rose with piracy and competition. However, there the technical limits of the primitive 'rat-hole' mining of the Spaniards were soon reached (even allowing for the uses of the mercury process), and very possibly the labour force was virtually worked to death, being treated as an expendable asset.[37] At any rate American silver exports diminished after 1610 or so. Eventually, of course, in the east colonial powers adjusted themselves to the new level of overheads and perhaps found new sources of local taxation to offset them. In the west the familiar structure of quasi-feudal large estates came into being in the seventeenth century.[38] Since the economic basis of the Spanish colonial system was broader than the Portuguese, the results of crisis would be more far-reaching. Thus the early emigration to the Americas temporarily stimulated the export of goods from the home country; but as, inevitably, many of the colonists' wants came to be supplied locally, the expanded manufactures of Spain had to pay the price. The attempt to tighten the metropolitan monopoly merely made matters worse by discouraging the development, among other things, of the potentially revolutionary plantation economy.[39] The effects of the influx of bullion into Spain are too well known to need discussion.

It is therefore understandable that the 'old colonial system' passed through a profound crisis; and that its effects on the general European economy were far-reaching. A new pattern of colonial exploitation which produced steadily rising exports of manufactures from Europe did indeed replace it. (Acting largely on their own the sugar planters of northern Brazil had shown the way to it from the end of the sixteenth century.) Yet the lure of the old monopoly profits was irresistible to all those who had a chance of capturing them. Even the Dutch remained resolutely 'old-fashioned' in their colonialism until the eighteenth century, though

[36] F. C. Lane, 'National Wealth and Protection Costs' in Clarkson and Cochran eds., *War as a Social Institution* (New York, 1941), pp. 36 ff.

[37] C. G. Motten, *Mexican Silver and the Enlightenment* (Philadelphia and London, 1950), chaps. 2–3.

[38] Thus from the end of the seventeenth century the Dutch East India Company expanded the income from colonial taxes, previously about 9 per cent of its revenue, much more rapidly than trading profits. Lannoy and Linden, op. cit., pp. 266–7. F. Chevalier, *La Formation des grands domaines en Mexique. Terres et Société au XVI–XVIIe siècles* (Paris, 1952).

[39] For the ending of sugar plantations in the early seventeenth century, E. O. v. Lippmann, op. cit.

their entrepôt position in Europe saved them from the consequences of colonial inefficiency. Old colonialism did not grow over into new colonialism; it collapsed and was replaced by it.

THE CONTRADICTIONS OF THE HOME MARKETS

There can be little doubt that the sixteenth century came nearer to creating the conditions for a really widespread adoption of the capitalist mode of production than any previous age; perhaps because of the impetus given by overseas loot, perhaps because of the encouragement of rapidly growing population and markets and rising prices. (It is not the object of this article to discuss the reasons which caused this expansion to follow the 'feudal crisis' of the fourteenth and fifteenth centuries.) A powerful combination of forces, including even large feudal interests,[40] seriously threatened the resistance of gild-dominated towns. Rural industry, of the 'putting-out' type, which had previously been largely confined to textiles, spread in various countries and to new branches of production (for example metals), especially towards the end of the period. Yet the expansion bred its own obstacles. We may briefly consider some of them.

Except perhaps in England no 'agrarian revolution' of a capitalist type accompanied industrial change, as it was to do in the eighteenth century; though there was plenty of upheaval in the countryside. Here again we find the generally feudal nature of the social framework distorting and diverting forces which might otherwise have made for a direct advance towards modern capitalism. In the east, where agrarian change took the form of revival of serfdom by exporting lords, the conditions for such development were inhibited locally, though made possible elsewhere. In other regions the price-rise, the upheavals in landownership, and the growth of demand for agrarian produce might well have led to the emergence of capitalist farming by gentlemen and the kulak-type of peasant on a greater scale than appears to have occurred.[41] Yet what happened? French lords (often 'bourgeois' who had bought themselves into feudal status) reversed the trend to peasant independence from the middle of the sixteenth century, and increasingly recovered lost ground.[42] Towns, merchants and local middlemen invested in the land, partly no doubt because of the security of farm produce in an age of inflation, partly because the surplus was easy to draw from it in a feudal manner, their exploitation being all the more effective for being combined with usury; partly perhaps in direct political rivalry with feudalists.[43] Indeed, the relationship of

463

Hobsbawm

THE CRISIS
OF THE
SEVENTEENTH
CENTURY

[40] cf. H. Aubin, 'D. Anfaenge d. Grossen schlesischen Leineweberei', *Viertel-jahrschr. f. Soz-. und Wirtschaftgesch.*, xxxv (1942), pp. 154–73.

[41] P. Raveau, *L'Agriculture . . . en Poitou au XVIᵉ s.* (Paris, 1926), p. 127; Marc Bloch, *Les Caractères Originaux de l'histoire rurale française* (new edn., Paris, 1952), pp. 148–9; but the 'gentilhomme campagnard' is not *ipso facto* a capitalist farmer.

[42] Bloch, op. cit.; Braudel, op. cit., pp. 624 ff.

[43] Bloch, op. cit., pp. 145–46; P. Raveau, op. cit., pp. 249 ff; A. Kraemer, *D. wechselnde . . . Bedeutung d. Landbesitzes d. Stadt Breslau*, op. cit., p. 48, for systematic buying of land from 1500 to the Thirty Years' War.

towns and their inhabitants as a whole to the surrounding peasantry was still, as always in a generally feudal society, that of a special kind of feudal lord. (The peasants in the town-dominated cantons of Switzerland and in inland Netherlands were not actually emancipated until the French Revolution.[44]) The mere existence of urban investment in agriculture or urban influence over the countryside, therefore, did not imply the creation of rural capitalism. Thus the spread of share-cropping in France, though theoretically marking a step towards capitalism, in fact often produced merely a bourgeoisie parasitic on a peasantry increasingly exhausted by it, and by the rising demands of the State; and consequent decline.[45] The old social structure predominated still.

Two results may have followed from this. First, it is improbable that there was much technical innovation, though the first (Italian) handbook on crop rotation appeared in the mid-sixteenth century, and certain that the increase in agrarian output did not keep pace with demand.[46] Hence towards the end of the period there are signs of diminishing returns and food-shortage, of exporting areas using up their crops for local needs, etc., preludes to the famines and epidemics of the crisis-period.[47] Second, the rural population, subject to the double pressure of landlords and townsmen (not to mention the State), and in any case much less capable of protecting itself against famine and war than they, suffered.[48] In some regions this shortsighted 'squeeze' may actually have led to a declining trend in productivity during the seventeenth century.[49] The countryside was sacrificed to lord, town and State. Its appalling rate of mortality—if the relatively prosperous Beauvaisis is any guide—was second only to that of the domestic out-workers, also increasingly rural.[50] Expansion under these conditions bred crisis.

What happened in the non-agricultural sectors depended largely on the agricultural. Costs of manufacture may have been unduly raised by the more rapid rise of agrarian than of industrial prices, thus narrowing the

[44] Baasch, Hollaend. Wirtschaftsgeschichte, p. 50; Roupnel, op. cit.

[45] Marx, Capital iii, xlvii, sect. v, on métayage; G. de Falguérolles, 'Décadence de l'économie agricole à Lempaut (Languedoc); Annales du Midi, liii (1941), pp. 142–167—an important article.

[46] Raveau, op. cit., chap. iii. For the non-innovating character of French agricultural handbooks, G. Lizerand, Le Régime rural de l'ancienne France (Paris, 1942), pp. 79–81. M. J. Elsas, Umriss einer Geschichte d. Preise u. Loehne in Deutschland (Leiden, 1949), for stable agricultural productivity.

[47] G. Coniglio, Il regno di Napoli al tempo de Carlo V (Naples, 1951), and Braudel, op. cit.; V. Barbour, Capitalism in Amsterdam (Baltimore, 1950), pp. 26–27; A. Juergens, Z. schleswig-holsteinschen Handelsgeschichte im 16. u. 17. Jh. (Berlin, 1914), pp. 10–12, for change from an exporting to an importing area at end of sixteenth century.

[48] Because they relied on local food supplies, while towns imported in any case, often from great distances. J. Meuvret, 'La Géographie du prix des céréales', Revista de Economia, iv (Lisbon, 1951), pp. 63–69. Falguérolles, op. cit., for peasants ceasing to eat wheat, which they had to sell to pay taxes.

[49] Falguérolles, op. cit., argues so.

[50] Goubert, op. cit. (above, n. 5); and below chap. 6.

profit-margin of manufacturers.[51] (However, manufacturers increasingly used the cheap labour of rural out-workers, who were again exploited to the point of debility.) The market also had its difficulties. The rural market as a whole must have proved disappointing. Many freeholding peasants benefited from the price-rise and the demand for their goods, provided they had enough land to feed themselves even in bad years, a regular surplus for sale, and a good head for business.[52] But if such yeomen bought much more than before, they bought less than townsmen of equal standing, being more self-sufficient.[53] The experience of nineteenth-century France shows that a middle and rich peasantry is about as uninviting a market for mass manufactures as may be found, and does not encourage capitalists to revolutionize production. Its wants are traditional; most of its wealth goes into more land and cattle, or into hoards, or into new building, or even into sheer waste, like those gargantuan weddings, funerals, and other feasts which disturbed continental princes at the turn of the sixteenth century.[54] The increase in the demand from the non-agricultural sector (towns, luxury market, government demand, etc.) may for a time have obscured the fact that it grew less rapidly than productive capacity, and that the persistent decline in the real income of wage-earners in the long inflation may actually, according to Nef, have stopped 'the growth of the demand for some industrial products'.[55] However, the slumps in the export markets from the late 1610s onwards brought the fact home.

Once the decline had begun, of course, an additional factor increased the difficulties of manufacture: the rise in labour costs. For there is evidence that—in the towns at least—the bargaining power of labour rose sharply during the crisis, perhaps owing to the fall or stagnation in town populations. At any rate real wages rose in England, Italy, Spain and Germany, and the mid-century saw the formation of effective journeymen's organizations in most western countries.[56] This may not have

465
Hobsbawm
THE CRISIS
OF THE
SEVENTEENTH
CENTURY

[51] Elsas, op. cit., O. Roehlk, *Hansisch-Norwegische Handelspolitik im 16. Jh.* (Neumünster, 1935), pp. 74–75 for an excellent discussion of this, though relating to the 'price-scissors' between corn and fish prices; G. D. Ramsay, 'The Report of the Royal Commission on the Clothing Industry, 1640', *Eng. Hist. Rev.,* lvii (1942), pp. 485–6.

[52] Bloch, op. cit., on this important last point.

[53] M. Campbell, *The English Yeoman* (New Haven, 1942), pp. 186–7, chap. vi *passim,* and Hoskins, *Past and Present,* no. 4 (1953).

[54] H. Widmann, *Geschichte Salzburgs* (Gotha, 1914), iii, p. 354; Feller, op. cit., ii, p. 368; H. Schnell, *Mecklenburg im Zeitalter d. Reformation* (Berlin, 1900), p. 201.

[55] 'Prices and Industiral Capitalism', *Econ. Hist. Rev.,* vii (1936–7), pp. 184–5.

[56] D. Knoop and G. P. Jones, *The Medieval Mason* (Manchester, 1949), pp. 207–12; Cipolla, 'The Decline of Italy' (cited n. 9), p. 184; Elsas, op. cit.; E. J. Hamilton, *War and Prices in Spain 1651–1800* (Harvard, 1947), p. 219. G. Unwin, *Industrial Organisation in the Sixteenth and Seventeenth Centuries* (Oxford, 1904), chap. viii; G. Des Marez, *Le Compagnonnage des Chapeliers Bruxellois* (Bruxelles, 1909), pp. 17–21; E. Martin St. Léon, *Le Compagnonnage* (Paris,

affected the labour costs of the putting-out industries, as their workers were in a weaker position to benefit from the situation, and their piece-rate wages were more easily cut. However, it is clearly not a negligible factor. Moreover, the slackening of population increase and the stabilization of prices must have depressed manufactures further.

These different aspects of the crisis may be reduced to a single formula: economic expansion took place within a social framework which it was not yet strong enough to burst, and in ways adapted to it rather than to the world of modern capitalism. Specialists in the Jacobean period must determine what actually precipitated the crisis: the decline in American silver, the collapse of the Baltic market or some of many other possible factors. Once the first crack appeared, the whole unstable structure was bound to totter. It did totter, and in the subsequent period of economic crisis and social upheaval the decisive shift from capitalist enterprise adapted to a generally feudal framework to capitalist enterprise transforming the world in its own pattern, took place. The Revolution in England was thus the most dramatic incident in the crisis, and its turning-point. 'This nation', wrote Samuel Fortrey in 1663 in his *England's Interest and Improvement,* 'can expect no less than to become the most great and flourishing of all others.' [57] It could and it did; and the effects on the world were to be portentous.

J. H. ELLIOTT

By the winter of 1640,[1] the Empire which had dominated the world scene for the best part of a century seemed at last, after many a false alarm, to be on the verge of collapse. In October of that year, after the revolt of Catalonia but before the revolt of Portugal, the English ambassador in Madrid wrote home of 'the state of Christendom, which begins already to be

1901); L. Guéneau, *L'Organisation de travail à Nevers au XVIIe et XVIIIe siècle 1660–1790* (Paris, 1919), pp. 79 ff; J. Gebauer, *Gesch. d. Stadt Hildesheim* (Hildesheim and Leipzig, 1922), pp. 221 ff; etc.

[57] Samuel Fortrey, *England's Interest and Improvement* (London, 1673 edn.), p. 8.

Source: J. H. Elliott, "The Decline of Spain," *Past and Present,* No. 20 (1961), and reprinted in Trevor Aston (ed.), *Crisis in Europe* (London, 1965), pp. 177–205. Copyright © 1965 by Routledge & Kegan Paul, Ltd., London. Reprinted by permission of the author and publishers.

[1] An earlier version of this essay (originally published in no. 20, 1961) was read as a paper to the Stubbs Society at Oxford, and I have deliberately left it as a contribution to discussion, based on a general survey of the present state of knowledge, rather than attempting to transform it into a detailed analysis. I have treated the period 1598–1648 in closer detail in a chapter on the Spanish peninsula in the forthcoming vol. iv of the *New Cambridge Modern History.* Any reader of this article will appreciate how much I, in company with other historians of Spain, owe to the ideas of M. Pierre Vilar in his 'Le Temps du Quichotte; *Europe* (Paris), xxxiv (1956), pp. 3–16.

unequally balanced'.[2] Six months later he was writing: 'Concerning the state of this kingdom, I could never have imagined to have seen it as it now is, for their people begin to fail, and those that remain, by a continuance of bad successes, and by their heavy burdens, are quite out of heart.'[3] Olivares's great bid between 1621 and 1640 to turn back the pages of history to the heroic days of Philip II had visibly failed; and, like everything about Olivares, his failure was on the grand scale. The man whom eulogists had portrayed in the days of his greatness as Atlas, supporting on his shoulders the colossal structure of the Monarchy, was now, Samson-like, bringing it crashing down with him in his fall.

The dissolution of Spanish power in the 1640s appears so irrevocable and absolute that it is hard to regard it as other than inevitable. The traditional textbook approach to European history of the sixteenth and seventeenth centuries has further helped to establish the idea of the inevitability of Spain's defeat in its war with France. Spanish power is first presented at its height under Philip II. Then comes, with the reign of Philip III, the *decline of Spain,* with the roots of decline traced back to Philip II, or Charles V, or even to Ferdinand and Isabella, depending upon the nationality, or the pertinacity, of the writer. After the lamentable scenes that have just been portrayed, the early years of Philip IV come as something of an embarrassment, since the ailing patient not only refuses to die, but even shows vigorous and unexpected signs of life. But fortunately the inexplicable recovery is soon revealed as no more than a hallucination. When a resurgent France under Richelieu at last girds itself for action, Spain's bluff is called. Both diagnosis and prognostication are triumphantly vindicated, and the patient dutifully expires.

It is not easy to reconcile this attractively simple presentation of early seventeenth-century history with our increasing knowledge of the discontent and unrest in Richelieu's France.[4] If Spain may still be regarded as a giant with feet of clay, France itself is coming to seem none too steady on the ground. This naturally tends to cast doubt on the validity of any concept of a French triumph in the first half of the century as being a foregone conclusion. Yet the lingering survival of the traditional view is easily understood. France had a population of some sixteen million, as against Spain's seven or eight, and it is commonly argued that, in the end, weight of numbers is bound to tell. It is also argued that the fact of Spain's decline is notorious and irrefutable, and that a power in decline will not win the final battle.

The argument from the size of populations is notoriously dangerous when used of a period when governments lacked the resources and the

[2] P(ublic) R(ecord) O(ffice, London) SP 94.42 f. 51, Hopton to Windebank, 22 Sept./2 Oct. 1640.

[3] PRO SP 94.42 f. 144, Hopton to Vane, 3/13 April 1641.

[4] See B. P. Porshnev, *Die Volksaufstände in Frankreich vor der Fronde* (Leipzig, 1954) and R. Mousnier, 'Recherches sur les Soulèvements Populaires en France avant la Fronde', *Revue d'Histoire Moderne et Contemporaine,* v (1958), pp. 81–113.

techniques to mobilize their subjects for war. Victory in war ultimately depended on the capacity of a state to maintain a continuing supply of men (not necessarily nationals) and of credit, and this capacity was by no means the exclusive prerogative of the large state. But the decisive argument in favour of an inevitable French victory is obviously the second: that Spain was in a state of irrevocable decline.

The phrase *decline of Spain* automatically conjures up a series of well-known images. Most of these are to be found in Professor Earl J. Hamilton's famous article,[5] which remains the classic statement of the theme: 'the progressive decline in the character of the rulers'; mortmain and vagabondage, the contempt of manual labour, monetary chaos and excessive taxation, the power of the Church and the folly of the Government. These so-called 'factors' in the decline of Spain have a long and respectable ancestry, and both their existence and their importance are irrefutable. Most of them can indeed be traced back to the writings of seventeenth-century Spaniards themselves—to the treatises of the economic writers of *arbitristas*, of whom Hamilton says that 'history records few instances of either such able diagnosis of fatal social ills by any group of moral philosophers or of such utter disregard by statesmen of sound advice'. The word *decline* itself was used of Spain at least as early as 1600 when González de Cellorigo, perhaps the most acute of all the *arbitristas*, discussed 'how our Spain . . . is subject to the process of decline (*declinación*) to which all other republics are prone'.[6] Vigorously as González de Cellorigo himself rejected the determinist thesis, the condition of Spain seemed to his contemporaries graphic evidence of the validity of the cyclical idea of history, of which the concept of decline formed an integral part.

The skillful dissection of the Spanish body politic by contemporary Spaniards, each anxious to offer the patient his own private nostrum, proved of inestimable value to writers of later generations: to Protestants of the later seventeenth century, and to rationalist historians of the eighteenth and nineteenth, who saw in the decline of Spain the classic instance of the fatal consequences of ignorance, sloth and clericalism. Apart from its important additions on Spanish wages and prices, and its rejection of the traditional thesis about the grave results of the expulsion of the Moriscos, Hamilton's article would seem to belong, in content as in approach, to the eighteenth- and nineteenth-century historiographical tradition.

It would be pleasant to be able to record that, in the twenty years since Hamilton's article was published, our knowledge and understanding of seventeenth-century Spain have been significantly enlarged. But, in most of its aspects, our picture of the reigns of Philip III and IV remains

---

[5] 'The Decline of Spain', *Econ. Hist. Rev.*, 1st ser., viii (1938), pp. 168–79.

[6] Martín González de Cellorigo, *Memorial de la Política necesaria y útil Restauración a la República de España* (Valladolid, 1600), p. 1. I am indebted to Manchester University Library for the loan of a microfilm of this important work, of which I have been able to find no copy in this country.

very much as it was drawn by Martin Hume in the old *Cambridge Modern History* over fifty years ago. The one significant exception to this story of historiographical stagnation is to be found in Hamilton's own field of monetary history. Whatever the defects either of Hamilton's methods or of his generalizations, both of them subject to growing criticism, historians now possess a vast amount of information on Spanish monetary history which was not available to Hume; and the work of a generation of historians, culminating in the monumental study of Seville and the Atlantic by M. and Mme. Chaunu,[7] has revealed much that is new and important about the character of Spain's economic relations with its American possessions.

It could, however, be argued that these advances in the fiscal and commercial history of Habsburg Spain have been achieved only at the expense of other equally important aspects of its economic life. Hamilton's pioneering example has encouraged an excessive concentration on the *external* influences on the Spanish economy, such as American silver, to the neglect of *internal* economic conditions.[8] Little more is known now than was known fifty years ago about Spanish forms of land tenure and cultivation, or about population changes, or about the varying fortunes of the different regions or social groups in the peninsula. It could also be argued that Hamilton's lead, together with the whole trend of contemporary historical writing, has produced a disproportionate concentration on *economic* conditions. Explanations of the decline in terms of Spanish religious or intellectual history have become unfashionable. This is understandable in view of the naïveté of many such explanations in the past, but it is hard to see how an adequate synthesis can be achieved until detailed research is undertaken into such topics as the working of the Spanish Church, of the Religious Orders and the educational system. At present, we possess an overwhelmingly economic interpretation of Spain's decline, which itself is highly arbitrary in that it focuses attention only on certain selected aspects of the Spanish economy.

If this leads to distortions, as it inevitably must, these become all the greater when, as so often happens, the decline of Spain is treated in isolation. The very awareness of crisis among late sixteenth- and early seventeenth-century Spaniards prompted a flood of pessimistic commentaries, which helped to make the subject exceptionally well documented. The extent of the documentation and the critical acuteness of the commentators, naturally tended to encourage the assumption that Spain's plight was in some ways unique; and this itself has led to a search for the origins of that plight in specifically Spanish circumstances and in the dubious realm of allegedly unchanging national characteristics. But considerably more is

[7] H. and P. Chaunu, *Séville et l'Atlantique (1504–1650)*, 8 vols. (Paris, 1955–9).

[8] This point is well made in the useful bibliographical survey of recent work on this period of Spanish history: J. Vicens Vives, J. Reglá and J. Nadal, 'L'Espagne aux XVIe et XVIIe Siècles', *Revue Historique*, ccxx (1958), pp. 1–42.

known now than was known twenty or thirty years ago about the nature of social and economic conditions in seventeenth-century western Europe as a whole. Much of the seventeenth century has come to be regarded as a period of European economic crisis—of commercial contraction and demographic stagnation after the spectacular advances of the sixteenth century—and certain features which once seemed peculiarly Spanish are now tending to assume a more universal character. The impoverished *hidalgos* of Spain do not now seem so very different from the discontented *hobereaux* of France or the gentry of England. Nor does the contempt for manual labour, on which historians of Spain are prone to dwell, seem any longer an attitude unique to the peninsula. A study like that by Coleman on English labour in the seventeenth century [9] suggests how 'idleness', whether voluntary or involuntary, was a general problem of European societies of the time, and can be regarded as the consequence, as much as the cause, of a backward economy: as the outcome of the inability of a predominantly agrarian society to offer its population regular employment or adequate remuneration for its labour.

Seventeenth-century Spain needs, therefore, to be set firmly back into the context of contemporary conditions, and particularly conditions in the Mediterranean world, before recourse is had to alleged national characteristics as an explanation of economic backwardness. It may be that idleness *was* in fact more widespread, and contempt for manual labour more deep-rooted, in Spain than elsewhere, but the first task must be to *compare:* to compare Spanish conditions with those of other contemporary societies, and then, if it is possible to isolate any features which appear unique to Spain, to search for their origins not only in the realm of national character, but also in the conditions of the soil and the nature of land-holding, and in the country's social and geographical structure.

Some of the difficulties in breaking free from traditional assumptions about the decline of Spain must be ascribed to the powerful connotations of the word 'decline': a word which obscures more than it explains. Behind the phrase *decline of Spain* there lurk different, although interrelated, phenomena. The decline of Spain can, in the first place, be regarded as part of that general setback to economic advance which mid-seventeenth-century Europe is said to have experienced, although the Spanish regression may well prove to have been more intense or to have lasted longer. Secondly, it describes something more easily measured: the end of the period of Spanish hegemony in Europe and the relegation of Spain to the rank of the second-rate powers. This implies a deterioration in Spain's military and naval strength, at least in relation to that of other states, and a decrease in its ability to mobilize the manpower and credit required to maintain its traditional primacy in Europe.

Any attempt to analyse the reasons for the decline of Spanish *power* in

[9] D. C. Coleman, 'Labour in the English Economy of the Seventeenth Century', *Econ. Hist. Rev.,* 2nd ser., viii (1956), pp. 280–95.

the middle decades of the seventeenth century must obviously begin with an examination of the foundations of that power in an earlier age. Olivares, between 1621 and 1643, was pursuing a foreign policy which recalls that of Philip II in the 1580s and 1590s. The general aims of that policy were the same: the destruction of heresy and the establishment of some form of Spanish hegemony over Europe. The nominal cost of the policy was also the same though the real cost was greater. Philip III's ministers maintained that Philip II was spending nearly 13 million ducats a year between 1593 and 1597; Philip IV's ministers in 1636 estimated an expenditure of just over 13 million for the coming year,[10] and estimates were always liable to prove too conservative, in view of the rising premium on silver in terms of Castilian *vellón* (copper coinage), and of the sudden emergency expenses that invariably arose in time of war.

While the policy, as well as its nominal cost, remained the same under Philip IV as under Philip II, the basis of Spanish power under the two kings was also unchanged. It was, as it had always been, the resources of the Crown of Castile. Philip IV's best troops, like Philip II's, were Castilians. Philip IV's principal revenues, like Philip II's, came from the purse of the Castilian taxpayer, and Philip IV relied, like his grandfather, on the additional income derived from the American possessions of Castile.

The primacy of the Crown of Castile within the Spanish Monarchy, stemming as it did from its unique value to its kings, was obvious and acknowledged. 'The King is Castilian and nothing else, and that is how he appears to the other kingdoms', wrote one of the most influential ministers at the Court of Philip III.[11] Olivares found himself as dependent on Castile as Philip II had been. But the assistance that Castile could render Olivares proved to be less effective than the assistance it rendered Philip II, and was extracted at an even greater expense. From this, it would seem that we are faced with a diminution of Castile's capacity to bear the cost of empire, and consequently with the problem, in the first instance, not so much of the decline of Spain as of the *decline of Castile,* which is something rather different.

Three principal foundations of Castile's sixteenth-century primacy were its population, its productivity and its overseas wealth. If the process by which these foundations were slowly eroded could be traced in detail, we should have a clearer picture of the chronology of Castile's decline. But at present our knowledge is fragmentary and inadequate, and all that is possible is to suggest something of what has been done, and the areas still to be investigated.

Spain's great imperial successes of the sixteenth century had been achieved primarily by the courage and vitality of the surplus population of an overcrowded Castile. Figures for the population of sixteenth-century

[10] A(rchivo) G(eneral de) S(imancas) Hacienda leg(ajo) 522–750 no. 231, Consulta, 23 Aug. 1636.

[11] AGS Cámara de Castilla leg. 2796 Pieza 9 Inquisición f. 329, Don Pedro Franqueza to Dr. Fadrique Cornet, 22 Jan. 1605.

Spain are scanty and unreliable, but it would probably now be generally agreed that Castile's population increased during much of the century, as it increased elsewhere in Europe, with the fastest rate of increase in the 1530s. The population of the peninsula, excluding Portugal, in the middle of the sixteenth century, is thought to have been about 7½ million, of which 6½ million were to be found in Castile.[12] But perhaps even more significant than the overwhelming numerical predominance of the Castilian population is its superior density. As late as 1594 there were 22 inhabitants to the square kilometre in Castile, as against only 13.6 in the Crown of Aragon. The great empty spaces of modern Castile seem so timeless and so inevitable, that it requires an effort of the imagination to realize that Castile in the sixteenth century was relatively more populous than the rich Levantine provinces; and here, indeed, is to be found one of the fundamental changes in the structure of Spanish history. In the early 1590s the central regions of Castile accounted for 30.9 per cent of the population of Spain, whereas they now account for only 16.2 per cent. The political preponderance of Castile within Spain therefore rested in the sixteenth century, as it now no longer rests, on a population that was not only larger but also more densely settled.

This relatively dense Castilian population, living in an arid land with a predominantly pastoral economy—a land which found increasing difficulty in feeding its rising numbers—provided the colonists for the New World and the recruits for the *tercios*. It is not known how many Castilians emigrated to America (a figure of 150,000 has been suggested for the period up to 1550), nor how many died on foreign battlefields; nor is it even known how many were required for the armies of Philip II. Although foreign troops already represented an important proportion of the Spanish Army under Philip II, the contrast between military conditions under Philip II and Philip IV is none the less striking. Native Castilians, who formed the *corps d'élite* of the army, were increasingly difficult to recruit. By the 1630s, Olivares was desperate for manpower. Provincial governors were reporting the impossibility of raising new levies, and the majority of the recruits were miserable conscripts. 'I have observed these levies', wrote the English ambassador in 1635, 'and I find the horses so weak as the most of them will never be able to go to the rendezvous, and those very hardly gotten. The infantry so unwilling to serve as they are carried like galley-slaves in chains, which serves not the turn, and so far short in number of what is purposed, as they come not to one of three.'[13]

The explanation of this increased difficulty in recruiting Castilian soldiers may be found to lie primarily in changed military conditions. Philip

[12] For this and the following information about population figures, see J. Vicens Vives, *Historia Económica de España* (Barcelona, 1959), pp. 301 ff; Ramón Carande, *Carlos V y sus Banqueros,* i (Madrid, 1943), p. 43; and J. Ruiz Almansa, 'La Población Española en el Siglo XVI', *Revista Internacional de Sociología,* iii (1943), pp. 115–36.

[13] B(ritish) M(useum) Egerton MS. 1820, f. 474, Hopton to Windebank, 31 May 1635.

IV had more men under arms than Philip II, and the demand on Castile was correspondingly greater; better chances of earning good wages or of obtaining charity at home may have diminished the attractions of military service abroad; the change from the warrior Charles V to a sedentary, bureaucratic monarch in Philip II, no doubt had its influence on the Castilian nobles, whose retreat from arms would in turn add to the difficulty of recruiting their vassals for war. All these problems deserve investigation,[14] but, in the search for the origins of Olivares's troubles over manpower, it would be natural to look also to the exhaustion of Castile's demographic resources.

Here, contemporary accounts may be misleading. There are numerous complaints of depopulation in late sixteenth-century Castile, but some of these can be explained by movements of population within the peninsula rather than by any total fall in numbers. There was a marked drift of population from the countryside to the towns, most of which grew considerably between 1530 and 1594; and there was also, during the course of the century, a continuous migration from *north* Castile—the most dynamic part of the country under Ferdinand and Isabella—into central Castile and Andalusia. This southwards migration, which may be regarded as a continuation by the populace of the *reconquista*,[15] was not completed before 1600. For all those Castilians who could not themselves cross the Atlantic, Andalusia became the El Dorado. The population of Seville, the gateway to the Atlantic, rose from 45,000 in 1530 to 90,000 in 1594, and, between those dates, the populations of all but two of the larger towns of the southern half of Spain increased, while several of the northern towns, like Medina del Campo, recorded a marked decline.

A survey of conditions in north Castile alone might therefore provide a false picture of the state of the population in the Crown of Castile as a whole, and it does not seem on present evidence that an overall decline in population can be established before the end of the 1590s. All that *can* be said is that Castile's population became concentrated in the towns, particularly those of the centre and south, and that it lost some of its most vital elements through emigration and military service. Then, in 1599 and 1600, famine and plague swept up through Andalusia and Castile, causing fearful ravages in the countryside and in the densely packed cities. Unfortunately, there are no figures for the losses of these years. One village, near Valladolid, reported that no more than eighty inhabitants survived out of 300,[16] but it is impossible to say how this figure compares with others elsewhere.

Although the traditional view of its importance has recently been questioned,[17] it is hard to avoid the conclusion that the plague of

[14] Some of them are in fact now being examined by Mr. I. A. A. Thompson of Christ's College, Cambridge, who is researching into the Spanish military system in the late sixteenth and early seventeenth centuries.

[15] Chaunu, *Séville et l'Atlantique,* viii (1), pp. 257–8 and 265.

[16] AGS Hacienda leg. 293–409 no. 222, Consulta, 27 Aug. 1601.

[17] Chaunu, op. cit., viii (2), pt. 2, pp. 1267–8.

1599–1600 marks the turning-point in the demographic history of Castile. Hamilton's figures, while too unsatisfactory as a series for the immediate years of the plague to allow any comprehensive statistical deductions, do at least point to a very sharp increase of wages over prices in the following decade, and suggest something of the gravity of the manpower crisis through which Castile was passing.

This crisis was exacerbated by the expulsion of the Moriscos ten years after the plague. The figures of the expelled Moriscos used to range to anything up to 1 million. Hamilton reduced them to 100,000. The recent meticulous study of the size and distribution of the Morisco population by M. Lapeyre,[18] shows that between 1609 and 1614 some 275,000 Moriscos were expelled from Spain. Of these 275,000 perhaps 90,000 came from Castile and Andalusia, and the rest from the Crown of Aragon—above all, Valencia, which lost a quarter of its population. If Hamilton underestimated the number of the Moriscos, he also underestimated the economic consequences of their expulsion. The consequences to the Valencian economy were very grave,[19] but it is important to remember that the Valencian and Castilian economies were distinct, and that Castile would be only marginally affected by the disruption of the economic life of Valencia. But Castile also lost 90,000 Moriscos of its own. These Moriscos, unlike those of Valencia and Aragon, were predominantly town-dwelling, and they undertook many of the more menial tasks in Castilian life. Their disappearance would naturally produce an immediate dislocation in the Castilian economy, which is reflected in the relationship between prices and wages for the crucial years of the expulsion, but it is not known how far this dislocation was remedied by Old Christians taking over the jobs previously occupied by Moriscos.

The present picture of the Castilian population, therefore, suggests a rapid increase slackening off towards the end of the sixteenth century, and then a catastrophic loss at the very end of the century, followed by the further loss of 90,000 inhabitants through the expulsion of the Moriscos. After that, almost nothing is known. Figures available for towns in 1646 show heavy losses, and there was another disastrous plague between 1647 and 1650. Where Hamilton suggests a 25 per cent decline during the course of the seventeenth century, there are others who believe that the population remained stationary rather than actually diminishing. All that can be said at present with any certainty is that Olivares was making heavy demands on the manpower of a country whose population had lost its buoyancy and resilience, and had ceased to grow.

In so far, then, as Castile's primacy rested on its reserves of manpower, there was a marked downward turn in its potentialities after the 1590s. Castile's national wealth, on which the Habsburgs relied for the bulk of their revenues, also shows signs of depletion. One of the principal diffi-

[18] Henri Lapeyre, *Géographie de l'Espagne Morisque* (Paris, 1959).

[19] See J. Reglá, 'La Expulsión de los Moriscos y sus Consecuencias', *Hispania*, xiii (1953), pp. 215–67 and 402–79.

culties involved in measuring the extent of this depletion is our ignorance of economic conditions in Castile in the first half of the sixteenth century. It is hard to chart the descent when one is still trying to locate the summit. But the researches of Carande and of Lapeyre [20] have gone far to confirm that the first half of the sixteenth century is a period of quickened economic activity in Castile and Andalusia, presumably in response to a growing demand. This was a time of population increase and of sharply rising prices. Indeed, Dr. Nadal has recently shown, on the basis of Hamilton's own figures, that there was a faster proportional rise of prices in the first half of the century than in the second, although American silver shipments were much greater in the second half than in the first.[21] The average annual rise in prices from 1501–62 was 2.8 percent, as against 1.3 per cent from 1562–1600, and the highest maximum rise in any decade occurred between 1521 and 1530, long before the discovery of Potosí. This sharp upswing in prices during Charles V's reign may be attributable to a rising scale of aristocratic expenditure, to the dramatic growth of Charles V's debts, which he financed by the distribution of *juros,* or credit bonds, and to a vastly increased demand: an increased demand for food from Castile's growing population, an increased demand in north Europe for Castilian wool, and an increased demand for wine and oil and textiles, and for almost all the necessities of life, from the new American market. This was the period which saw the development of large-scale wine and oil production in Andalusia, and of cloth production in the towns of Castile, to meet the needs of the New World; and it was also the great age of the Castilian fairs—international institutions which linked the Castilian economy to that of Italy and northern Europe in a complicated network of reciprocal obligation.

If it is accepted that the reign of Charles V represents a period of economic expansion for Castile, the first clear signs of a check to this expansion appear in 1548, when the country was experiencing one of the five-year periods of highest price increase for the entire sixteenth century. In that year the Cortes of Valladolid, moved by the general complaint of high prices, petitioned the Crown to forbid the export of Castilian manufactures, even to the New World, and to permit the import of foreign goods, which would be less expensive for the Castilian consumer than Castile's own products.[22] The assumption that the export trade was pushing up Castilian prices above the general European level appeared sufficiently convincing for the Crown to agree to the Cortes' request in 1552, except in so far as Castilian exports to the Indies were concerned. The

[20] Carande, op. cit.; Henri Lapeyre, *Une Famille de Marchands: les Ruiz* (Paris, 1955); and see Ladislas Reitzer, 'Some Observations on Castilian Commerce and Finance in the Sixteenth Century', *Journal of Modern History,* xxxii (1960), pp. 213–23 for a detailed bibliography.

[21] Jorge Nadal Oller, 'La Revolución de los Precios Españoles en el Siglo XVI', *Hispania,* xix (1959), pp. 503–29.

[22] José Larraz López, *La Epoca del Mercantilismo en Castilla (1500–1700)* (Madrid, 1943), pp. 31 ff.

consequences of the new anti-mercantilism were exactly as might have been expected, and six years later the prohibition on exports was lifted at the request of the Cortes themselves. The whole episode, brief as it was, augured badly for the future of Spanish industry.

During the reign of Philip II foreign merchants succeeded in forcing wider and wider open the door that they had suddenly found so obligingly ajar in the 1550s, and Castile's industries proved unable to resist the pressure. Professor Hamilton gave the classic explanation of this industrial failure in his famous argument that in Spain, unlike France or England, wages kept pace with prices, and that therefore Spain lacked the stimulus to industrial growth which comes from a lag between wages and prices in an age of price revolution.[23] This argument, if correct, would naturally furnish a vital clue to the *decline of Spain;* but the evidence behind it has recently been critically examined, and the whole argument has been increasingly questioned.[24] Professor Phelps Brown has shown how Hamilton's own figures would indicate that a Valencian mason's wages by no means kept pace with the rising cost of living, and indeed lagged farther behind prices than those of his English equivalent [25] (although, if comparisons of this kind are to be really satisfactory, they require a knowledge of comparative diets and household budgets such as we do not yet possess). Hamilton does not provide sufficiently connected series to allow similar calculations for other parts of the peninsula, but his hypothesis that Spanish wages kept abreast of prices would seem so far to be quite unfounded. Indeed, further investigation may well show a marked deterioration in the living standards of the mass of the Castilian population during the first half of the century. Such a deterioration, combined with the high level of Castilian prices in relation to those of other European states, would go a long way towards explaining the peculiar structure of Castile's economy by the end of the century: an economy closer in many ways to that of an east-European state like Poland, exporting basic raw materials and importing luxury products, than to the economies of west-European states. In so far as industries survived in Castile they tended to be luxury industries, catering for the needs of the wealthy few and subject to growing foreign competition.

Castile's industrial development, then, would seem to have been hampered not only by the Crown's fiscal policies and by unfavourable investment conditions, but also by the lack of a sufficiently large home market.

[23] Hamilton, 'The Decline of Spain', and 'American Treasure and the Rise of Capitalism (1500–1700)', *Economica,* ix (1929), pp. 338–57.

[24] David Felix, 'Profit Inflation and Industrial Growth', *The Quarterly Journal of Economics,* lxx (1956), pp. 441–63. See also for criticisms of Hamilton: Pierre Vilar, 'Problems of the Formation of Capitalism', *Past and Present,* no. 10 (1956), pp. 15–38; Docent Ingrid Hammarström, 'The "Price Revolution" of the Sixteenth Century', *Scandinavian Econ. Hist. Rev.,* v (1957), pp. 118–54; and Jorge Nadal, 'La Revolución de los Precios'.

[25] E. H. Phelps Brown and Sheila V. Hopkins, 'Builders' Wage-rates, Prices and Population: Some Further Evidence', *Economica,* xxvi (1959), pp. 18–38.

This lack of a market for cheap manufactures points to an economy in which food prices are too high to leave the labourer and wage-earner with anything more than the bare minimum required for their housing, fuel and clothing. One of the most important reasons for the high price of food is to be found in the agrarian policies pursued by the kings of Castile even before the advent of the Habsburgs. Their traditional practice of favouring sheep-farming at the expense of tillage—a practice vigorously continued by Ferdinand and Isabella—meant that Castile entered the sixteenth century with a dangerously unbalanced economy. While the demand for corn increased as the population grew, the sheep-owners of the *Mesta* continued to receive the benefits of royal favour. The corn-growers, on the other hand, were positively hampered, not only by the presence of the ubiquitous and highly privileged sheep, but also by the *tasa del trigo* —a fixed maximum for grain prices, which, after being sporadically applied in the first years of the century, became a permanent feature of the Crown's economic policy from 1539.[26]

The consequences of this short-sighted policy towards the agricultural interest, at a time of rapid population increase, require no comment. Professor Braudel has shown how, in the last decades of the century, Castile, in common with other south-European states, became heavily dependent on grain supplies from northern and eastern Europe.[27] Castilian agriculture was simply incapable of meeting the national demand for food. What is not clear is whether agriculture was expanding, but not expanding fast enough to keep pace with the population, or whether agricultural production for the home market was actually falling off in the later sixteenth century. There are indications that more land was being cultivated in south Spain after the middle years of the century, but this may have been more to meet the needs of the American market than to satisfy home demand. The debates of the Castilian Cortes under Philip II give an impression of mounting agrarian crisis, characterized by large-scale rural depopulation, but unfortunately, apart from the tentative pioneering survey by Viñas y Mey,[28] agrarian questions in this period remain unstudied. There are signs that the smaller landowners in Castile were being squeezed out in the later sixteenth century: it was harder for them than for the large landowners to survive the misfortunes of bad years, and they were liable to run into debt and find themselves compelled to sell out to their more powerful neighbours. This still further encouraged the concentration of land in the hands of a small number of powerful landowners, at a time when mortmain and the entail system were working powerfully in the same direction. It is customary to find historians frowning upon this proc-

[26] See Eduardo Ibarra y Rodriguez, *El Problema Cerealista en España durante el Reinado de los Reyes Católicos* (Madrid, 1944), and Carande, op. cit., i. pp. 78–79.

[27] F. Braudel, *La Méditerranée et le Monde Méditerranéen à l'époque de Philippe II* (Paris, 1949), pp. 447–70.

[28] C. Viñas y Mey, *El Problema de la Tierra en la España de los Siglos XVI–XVII* (Madrid, 1941).

ess, as if the consolidation of estates in a few hands was in itself necessarily inimical to agrarian progress. But a large landlord is not automatically debarred from being an improving landlord. It would be very useful to know how far, if at all, improving landlords *were* to be found among the great lay and ecclesiastical landowners, and also to what extent they were diverted from corn-growing by the profits of sheep-farming, or by the production of wine and oil for the American market.

The discussion in the Castilian Cortes of 1598 on agrarian conditions suggests that by this time the crisis was acute,[29] and certainly the movement of the great Castilian nobles to take up residence at Court after the accession of Philip III did nothing to lessen it. Philip III's government found itself vainly legislating against absentee landlords, in the hope that an overcrowded Court could be cleared overnight, and the lackeys and servants who thronged the streets of Madrid would be compelled to return to the land. But much more than legislation against absentee landlordism was required to save Castilian agriculture. If the real causes of rural depopulation are to be found, they must be sought, in the first instance, at the level of village life. It is here that the dearth of good local histories in Spain becomes particularly serious. Apart from what can be learnt from the discussions of the Cortes, and from one useful but necessarily general article by Professor Domínguez Ortiz,[30] little can so far be said about the exact nature of the crisis that was overwhelming Castilian rural communities in the late sixteenth and early seventeenth centuries.

It is, however, clear that the Castilian village was pitifully unprotected. There was, for instance, the little village of Sanzoles, which in 1607 addressed to the Crown a petition that has survived at Simancas.[31] It raised a loan for municipal purposes, to place itself under royal jurisdiction instead of that of Zamora cathedral, and then, as the result of a series of bad harvests, found itself unable to pay the annual interest. The creditors moved in on the village and so harassed its inhabitants that eventually, out of ninety householders, no more than forty remained. Communal indebtedness was frequent among Castilian villages, and it obviously became particularly grave when even a handful of villagers moved away, and the reduced population found itself saddled with obligations that it was now even less able to meet. But the moneylender and the powerful neighbour were only two among the many natural enemies of Castilian villages. They were exposed also to the merciless attentions of the tax-collector, the recruiting-sergeant and the quartermaster. Unfortunately we do not yet possess the information to tell us what proportion of a seventeenth-century villager's income went in taxes. A speaker in the Cortes of 1623 suggested that, in a poor man's daily expenditure of 30 maravedis, 4 went in the *alcabala* and *millones* alone;[32] and besides these and other taxes paid to the Crown—taxes which the peculiar fiscal structure of Castile made

[29] *Actas de las Cortes de Castilla,* xv (Madrid, 1889), pp. 748 ff.

[30] 'La Ruina de la Aldea Castellana', *Revista Internacional de Sociología,* no. 24 (1948), pp. 99–124.

[31] AGS Hacienda leg. 345–473, Consulta, 25 Mar. 1607.

[32] *Actas de las Cortes,* xxxix, p. 142.

particularly heavy for the peasant—there were also dues to be paid to landlords and tithes to the Church. Then, in addition to the purely fiscal exactions, there were all the vexations and the financial burdens connected with the quartering and recruiting of troops. Villages along the principal military routes, particularly the road from Madrid to Seville and Cadiz, were dangerously exposed, and billeting could be very expensive —100 ducats a night for a company of 200 men, according to a report made in the 1630s.[33]

The persistence of these many afflictions over a long period of time left the villager of Castile and Andalusia very little inducement to remain on the land. He would therefore either move with his family and become swallowed up in the blessed anonymity of the great towns, or he would join the army of vagabonds that trudged the roads of Castile. We have, then, the spectacle of a nation which, at the end of the sixteenth century, is dependent on foreigners not only for its manufactures but also for its food supply, while its own population goes idle, or is absorbed into economically unproductive occupations. Accusing fingers are commonly pointed at Church and bureaucracy as important agents of decline, in that they diverted the population from more useful employment. But is it not equally likely that the growth of Church and bureaucracy was itself a consequence of contemporary conditions: of the lack of incentive to agricultural labour at the village level, and of the inability of the Castilian economy to provide its population with adequate employment? The nature of the economic system was such that one became a student or a monk, a beggar or a bureaucrat. There was nothing else to be.

What could be done to revitalize a flagging economy, and increase national productivity? There was no shortage of ideas. The *arbitristas*— the economic writers—of the early seventeenth century, men like González de Cellorigo, Sancho de Moncada, Fernández Navarrete, all put forward sensible programmes of reform. Royal expenditure must be regulated, the sale of offices halted, the growth of the Church be checked. The tax system must be overhauled, special concessions be made to agricultural labourers, rivers be made navigable and dry lands irrigated. In this way alone could Castile's productivity be increased, its commerce be restored, and its humiliating dependence on foreigners, on the Dutch and the Genoese, be brought to an end.

The ideas were there; and so also, from the truce with the Dutch in 1609, was the opportunity. This opportunity was thrown away. The ineptitude of the Lerma régime, its readiness to dissipate the precious years of peace in a perpetual round of senseless gaiety, is one of the tragedies of Spanish history, and goes far to explain the fiasco that finally overwhelmed the country under the government of Olivares. But behind this inert government, which possessed neither the courage nor the will to look its problems squarely in the face, lay a whole social system and a psychological attitude which themselves blocked the way to radical reform.

[33] BM Add. MS. 9936, Papeles tocantes a las Cortes, f. 2.

The injection of new life into the Castilian economy in the early seventeenth century would have required a vigorous display of personal enterprise, a willingness and ability to invest in agrarian and industrial projects, and to make use of the most recent technical advances. None of these—neither enterprise, nor investment, nor technical knowledge—proved to be forthcoming. 'Those who can, will not; and those who will, cannot,' wrote González de Cellorigo.[34] Why was this?

The conventional answer, useful so far as it goes, is that the social climate in Castile was unfavourable to entrepreneurial activity. The Castilians, it is said, lacked that elusive quality known as the 'capitalist spirit'. This was a militant society, imbued with the crusading ideal, accustomed by the *reconquista* and the conquest of America to the quest for glory and booty, and dominated by a Church and an aristocracy which perpetuated those very ideals least propitious for the development of capitalism. Where, in Castile, was that 'rising middle class', which, we are told, leavened the societies of northern Europe until the whole lump was leavened? 'Our republic', wrote González de Cellorigo, 'has come to be an extreme contrast of rich and poor, and there is no means of adjusting them one to another. Our condition is one in which there are rich who loll at ease or poor who beg, and we lack people of the middle sort, whom neither wealth nor poverty prevents from pursuing the rightful kind of business enjoined by Natural Law.' [35]

These words were published in 1600, and accurately describe Castilian society at that time, but they cannot be said to describe it in 1500. For, however uncapitalistic the dominant strain in sixteenth-century Castilian life, there *were* vigorous 'people of the middle sort' in the Castile of Ferdinand and Isabella and of Charles V. The towns of north Castile at that time could boast a lively bourgeoisie—men like Simón Ruiz, willing to engage their persons and their fortunes in commercial enterprise. But the decay of commercial and financial activity in north Castile, which is patent by 1575, suggests the disappearance of such people during the course of the century. What happened to them? Doubtless they acquired privileges of nobility. The passion for *hidalguía* was strong in Castile, and a title secured not only enhanced social standing, but also exemption from taxation. Yet it is hard to believe that this is an adequate explanation for the disappearance from the Castilian scene of men like Simón Ruiz. All over Europe it was the practice of merchants to buy their way into the nobility, and yet it was not everywhere so economically stultifying as it proved to be in Castile.

It would seem desirable to press farther than this, and to turn away for a time from repeating the conventional arguments about contempt for commerce and the strength of the aristocratic ideal, to the technical and neglected subject of investment opportunities.[36] What was happening to

---

[34] *Memorial de la Política*, p. 24 v.   [35] ibid., p. 54.

[36] An indication that this question may at last be arousing attention is provided by the pioneering article of Bartolomé Bennassar, 'En Vieille-Castille: Les Ventes de Rentes Perpétuelles', *Annales E.S.C.,* xve année (1960), pp. 1115–26.

wealth in sixteenth-century Castile? Much of it was obviously going, as it was going elsewhere, into building and jewelry, and all the expensive accoutrements connected with the enjoyment of a superior social status. But it was also being invested, and unproductively invested, in *censos,* or personal loans, and in *juros,* or government bonds. Sixteenth-century Castile saw the development of a highly elaborate credit system—a system which no doubt received much of its impetus from the exigencies of the Crown's finances. Anyone with money to spare—a noble, a merchant, a wealthy peasant—or institutions, like convents, could lend it to private persons, or municipal corporations, or else to the Crown, at a guaranteed 5, 7 or 10 percent. A proper study of *censos* and *juros* in Spain could tell us much about the reasons for its economic stagnation, especially if related to similar studies for other parts of Europe. *Censos* and *juros* might almost have been deliberately devised to lure money away from risky enterprises into safer channels, of no benefit to Castile's economic development. Indeed, in 1617 the Council of Finance complained that there was no chance of a Castilian economic revival as long as *censos* and *juros* offered better rates of interest than those to be gained from investment in agriculture, industry or trade.[37]

To this unwillingness to engage one's person and one's money in risky entrepreneurial undertakings, there must also be added Castile's increasing technological backwardness, as an explanation of its failure to stage an economic recovery. This backwardness is suggested by the failure of Spanish shipbuilders between the 1590s and the 1620s to keep pace with the new techniques of the north-European dockyards.[38] It was commented upon by foreign travellers, like the Frenchman Joly, who remarked in 1603 on the backwardness of the Spaniards in the sciences and the mechanical arts,[39] and Olivares himself in the 1630s was complaining of the Spanish ignorance of modern engineering techniques: 'I am certain that no man who comes from abroad to see Spain can fail to blame us roundly for our barbarism, when he sees us having to provision all the cities of Castile by pack-animal—and rightly so, for all Europe is trying out internal navigation with great profit.'[40]

While these technical deficiencies can presumably be attributed in part to the general lack of business enterprise in Castile, they should also be related to the whole climate of Castilian intellectual life. Here we are seriously hampered by the lack of a good study of the Castilian educational system. Why was it that science and technology failed to take root in Spain, at a time when they were beginning to arouse considerable interest elsewhere in Europe? It may be that further investigations will show a greater degree of scientific interest in Spain than has hitherto been as-

[37] AGS Hacienda leg. 395–547 no. 58, Consulta, 3 Sept. 1617.
[38] See A. P. Usher, 'Spanish Ships and Shipping in the Sixteenth and Seventeenth Centuries', *Facts and Factors in Economic History for E. F. Gay* (Harvard University Press, 1932), pp. 189–213.
[39] 'Voyage de Barthélemy Joly en Espagne (1603–1604)', ed. L. Barrau-Dihigo, *Revue Hispanique,* xx (1909), p. 611.
[40] BM Add. MS. 25,689 f. 237, Consulta del Conde Duque a SM.

sumed, but at present there is no evidence of this.[41] Indeed, such evidence as does exist points in an opposite direction—to the gradual separation of Habsburg Spain from the mainstream of European intellectual development. Early sixteenth-century Spain was Erasmian Spain, enjoying close cultural contacts with the most active intellectual centres of Europe. From the 1550s there was a chilling change in the cultural climate. The *alumbrados* were persecuted, Spanish students were forbidden to attend foreign universities, and Spain was gradually sealed off by a frightened monarch from contact with the contagious atmosphere of a heretical Europe. The conscious transformation of Spain into the redoubt of the true faith may have given an added intensity to Spanish religious experience under Philip II, but it also served to cut Spain off from that powerful intellectual current which was leading elsewhere to scientific inquiry and technical experiment.[42]

The period between 1590 and 1620, then, sees a rapid erosion of two of the principal foundations of Castile's sixteenth-century primacy, and consequently of Spain's imperial power: a decline both in Castile's demographic vitality and in its productivity and wealth. Recent investigations have also confirmed that it sees the erosion of the third foundation of Castile's primacy, in the form of a drastic reduction in the value, both to the Crown and to Castile, of Castile's possessions overseas. The great convoy of volumes launched by M. and Mme. Chaunu has brought home to us the enormous significance of trade between the port of Seville and Spanish America. It is, they suggest, in the 1590s that the *Carrera de las Indias* shows its first signs of serious strain. In 1597 it became clear for the first time that the American market for European goods was overstocked, but already from about 1590 the upward trend of Seville's trade with the Indies was losing speed. Although the trade fluctuated round a high level between the 1590s and 1620, its whole character was changing to the detriment of the Castilian economy. As Mexico developed its industries and Peru its agriculture, the colonies' dependence on the traditional products of the mother country grew less. There was a decreased demand in America for the Spanish cloth, and for the wine, oil and flour which bulked so large in the transatlantic shipments of the sixteenth century. The consequences of this were very serious. The galleons at Seville were increasingly laden with foreign goods, although unfortunately we do not know the relative proportions of Spanish and non-Spanish cargoes. With less demand in America for Castilian and Andalusian products, less of the American silver carried to Seville is destined for Spanish recipients, and it

[41] A collection of essays on Spanish science, of very varying quality, was published in Madrid in 1935 under the title of *Estudios sobre la Ciencia Española del Siglo XVII*, but they have not been followed up.

[42] For the intellectual isolation of Spain as a factor in the decline, see especially Santiago Ramón y Cajal, *Los Tónicos de la Voluntad*, 5th edn. (Buenos Aires, 1946), pp. 203 ff; and Claudio Sánchez-Albornoz, *España, Un Enigma Histórico* (Buenos Aires, 1956), ii, p. 553.

is significant that Spanish silver prices, which had moved upwards for a century, begin their downward movement after 1601. Moreover, the changes and the stresses in the transatlantic system began to undermine the whole structure of credit and commerce in Seville.

The principal beneficiaries of this crisis were the foreigners—the hated Genoese ('white Moors' as an irate Catalan called them [43]), the Portuguese Jews and the heretical Dutch. Foreign bankers ran the Crown's finances; foreign merchants had secured a stranglehold over the Castilian economy, and their tentacles were wrapping themselves round Seville's lucrative American trade. Castile's sense of national humiliation was increased by the truce with the Dutch in 1609, and bitterness grew as the Dutch exploited the years of peace to prise their way into the overseas Empires of Spain and Portugal. The humiliating awareness of the sharp contrast between the dying splendour of Castile and the rising power of the foreigner is one of the most important clues to the psychological climate of Philip III's Castile. It helps to accentuate that sense of impending disaster, the growing despair about the condition of Castile which prompts the bitter outbursts of the *arbitristas;* and it turns them into fierce patriots, of whom some, like Sancho de Moncada, betray a hysterical xenophobia.

The resulting mental climate goes far to explain some of the more baffling characteristics of the age of Olivares. Insufficient attention has been paid to the many signs of a revival of aggressive Castilian nationalism between 1609 and 1621—a nationalism that would seem to have been inspired by Castile's growing sense of inferiority. Consciously or subconsciously Castilians were arguing that peace with heretics, itself deeply humiliating, was politically and economically fruitless, since it had done nothing to check the advance of the English and the Dutch. Yet, if the foreigner triumphed in the contemptible arts of commerce, Castile could at least evoke the spirit of its former greatness—its military prowess. The answer to its problems was therefore a return to war.

This appears to have been the attitude of the great Castilian Viceroys of Philip III's reign, the Osunas and the Alcalás, and it was in this climate of aggressive Castilian nationalism, with its strong messianic overtones, that Olivares came to power in 1621. In the person of Olivares one finds curiously blended the two dominant strains of thought of the reign of Philip III: the reforming idealism of the *arbitristas* and the aggressive nationalism of the great Castilian proconsuls. With his boundless confidence in his own powers, Olivares determined to combine the programmes of both. He would restore Castile to economic vigour, and simultaneously he would lead it back to the great days of Philip II when it was master of the world.

But the ambitious imperial programme of the Conde Duque depended, as the imperial programme of Philip II had depended, on the population,

[43] Acadèmia de Bones Lletres, Barcelona. Dietari de Pujades i, f. 135, 1 Dec. 1602.

the productivity and the overseas wealth of Castile, and each of these had undergone a serious crisis between 1590 and 1620. It would conventionally be argued also that Philip II's imperialism was dependent, and indeed primarily dependent, on the flow of American silver coming directly to the Crown; and in so far as that flow had diminished by the second and third decades of the seventeenth century, the attempt to revive Spain's imperial greatness was in any event doomed. Here, however, the popular conception of the role played by the King's American silver supplies can be misleading. The silver remittances to the Crown at the end of Philip II's reign averaged about 2 million ducats a year. This was little more than the annual sum raised by ecclesiastical taxation in the King's dominions, and under a third of the sum which Castile alone paid the Crown each year in its three principal taxes.[44]

The American remittances were important, in the long run, less for their proportionate contribution to the Crown's total income than for the fact that they were one of the few sources of revenue not pledged for many years in advance. Their existence assured a regular supply of silver which was necessary if the bankers were to continue to provide the King with credit. During the decade 1610–20 the remittances began to fall off. Instead of the 2 millions of the early 1600s, the President of the Council of Finance reported in December 1616 that 'in the last two years hardly a million ducats have come each year',[45] and by 1620 the figure was as low as 800,000. It recovered in the 1620s, but between 1621 and 1640 1½ million ducats represented an exceptional year, and not more than a million ducats could be expected with any degree of confidence; in fact, about half the sum that Philip II could expect.

This was serious, but it was not crippling in relation to the overall revenues of the Crown. Under Philip IV, as under Philip II, it was not America but Castile that bore the main burden of Habsburg imperialism, and Castile was still paying its 6, 7, or 8 million ducats a year in taxation. But during the 1620s it became increasingly expensive for Castile to raise these sums. Since 1617 large new quantities of *vellón* coinage had been manufactured, and by 1626 the premium on silver in terms of *vellón* had risen from 4 per cent in 1620 to some 50 per cent.[46] This meant in practice that a tax collected in *vellón* would now buy abroad only half the goods and services for which it was nominally supposed to pay.

Olivares tried to compensate for the disastrous drop in the purchasing power of Castilian money by raising the level of taxation in Castile and inventing a host of ingenious fiscal devices to extract money from the privileged and the exempt. In many ways he was extremely successful.

---

[44] This can be deduced from papers and *consultas* of the Council of Finance in AGS Hacienda for the years 1598–1607, and particularly leg. 271–280.

[45] AGS Hacienda leg. 391–542 no. 1, Don Fernando Carillo to King, 23 Dec. 1616.

[46] Hamilton, *American Treasure and the Price Revolution in Spain, 1501–1650* (Harvard University Press, 1934), Table 7, p. 96.

The Castilian aristocracy was so intensively mulcted that a title, so far from being a badge of exemption, became a positive liability, and the Venetian ambassador who arrived in 1638 reported Olivares as saying that, if the war continued, no one need think of possessing his own money any more since everything would belong to the King.[47] While this fiscal policy, when applied to the Castilian nobles, caused no more than impotent rumblings of discontent, it proved to be self-defeating when adopted towards what remained of the Castilian merchant community. The long series of arbitrary confiscations of American silver remittances to individual merchants in Seville, who were 'compensated' by the grant of relatively worthless *juros*, proved fatal to the town's commercial life.[48] Olivares's tenure of power saw the final alienation of Spain's native business community from its king, and the final defeat of native commercial enterprise in the name of royal necessity. The crumbling of the elaborate credit structure of Seville and the collapse of Seville's trading system with the New World between 1639 and 1641,[49] was the price that Olivares had to pay for his cavalier treatment of Spanish merchants.

In spite of Olivares's ruthless exploitation of Castile's remaining resources, there was never enough to meet all his needs. Castile's growing inability to meet his demands for manpower and money naturally forced him to look beyond Castile for help. To save his beloved Castile, it became imperative for him to exploit the resources of the peripheral provinces of the Iberian peninsula, which had been under-taxed in relation to Castile, and which were under no obligation to provide troops for foreign service. It was this determination to draw on the resources of the Crown of Aragon and Portugal which inspired Olivares's famous scheme for the Union of Arms: a device which would compel all the provinces of the Spanish Monarchy to contribute a specified number of paid men to the royal armies.[50]

Olivares's scheme of 1626 for the Union of Arms was in effect an implicit admission of a change in the balance of economic power within the Spanish peninsula. Behind it lay the contemporary Castilian assumption that Castile's economic plight was graver than that of the other regions of Spain. How far this assumption was correct, it is not yet possible to say. The various regions of the peninsula lived their own lives and went their own ways. A decline of Castile does not necessarily imply the simultane-

[47] *Relazioni degli Stati Europei*, ed. Barozzi and Berchet. Serie 1. Spagna, ii (Venice, 1860), p. 86.

[48] See Antonio Dominguez Ortiz, 'Los Caudales de Indias y la Política Exterior de Felipe IV', *Anuario de Estudios Americanos*, xiii (1956), pp. 311–83. The same author's *Política y Hacienda de Felipe IV* (Madrid, 1960), is an important contribution to the study of the Crown's financial policy in the reign of Philip IV, based as it is on previously unused documents from Simancas.

[49] Chaunu, op. cit., viii (2), pt. 2, pp. 1793–1851.

[50] For the Union of Arms, see my chapter in the forthcoming *New Cambridge Modern History*, vol. iv, and my *The Revolt of the Catalans. A Study in the Decline of Spain (1598–1640)* (Cambridge, 1963).

ous decline of the Crown of Aragon and Portugal, both of them living in different economic systems, and shielded by separate monetary systems from the violent oscillations of the Castilian coinage.

Yet, if we look at these peripheral kingdoms, we may well think that the prospects were a good deal less hopeful than Olivares believed them to be. Aragon: a dry, impoverished land. Valencia: its economy dislocated by the expulsion of the Moriscos. Catalonia: its population growth halted about 1625,[51] its traditional trade with the Mediterranean world contracting after the plague of 1630. Portugal: its Far Eastern Empire lost to the Dutch under Philip III, its Brazilian Empire in process of being lost to the Dutch under Philip IV.

Even if Olivares overestimated the capacity of the other territories of the peninsula to bring him the help he needed, he none the less knew as well as anyone else that he was engaged in a desperate race against time. If France could be beaten swiftly, the future would still be his. Then at last he could undertake the great reforms which only awaited the return of peace, and which would enable Castile to devote itself as effectively to the task of economic reform as it had already devoted itself to the successful prosecution of the war. In 1636, at Corbie, he very nearly achieved his aim. A little more money, a few more men, and French resistance might have crumbled. But the gamble—and Olivares knew it *was* a gamble —failed, and, with its failure, Olivares was lost. The Franco-Spanish war inevitably turned after Corbie into the kind of war which Spain was least able to stand: a war of attrition, tedious and prolonged. Such a war was bound to place heavy strains on the constitutional structure of the Spanish Monarchy, just as it placed heavy strains on the constitutional structure of the French Monarchy, since Olivares and Richelieu were compelled to demand assistance from, and billet troops in, provinces which had never been assimilated and which still possessed their own semi-autonomous institutions and their own representative bodies. The Spanish Monarchy was particularly vulnerable in this respect, since both Catalonia in the east, and Portugal in the west, were uneasily and unsatisfactorily yoked to the central government in Madrid. When the pressure became too great, as it did in 1640, they rose up in arms against that government, and Castile—for so long the predominant partner in the Monarchy that it took its superiority for granted—suddenly discovered that it no longer possessed the strength to impose its will by force.

The great crisis in the structure of the Monarchy in 1640, which led directly to the dissolution of Spanish power, must therefore be regarded as the final development of that specifically Castilian crisis of 1590–1620 which this essay has attempted to describe; as the logical dénouement of the economic crisis which destroyed the foundations of Castile's power, and of the psychological crisis which impelled it into its final bid for world supremacy.

[51] Catalan population problems are admirably treated in J. Nadal and E. Giralt, *La Population Catalane de 1553 à 1717* (Paris, 1960).

It seems improbable that any account of the *decline of Spain* can substantially alter the commonly accepted version of seventeenth-century Spanish history, for there are always the same cards, however we shuffle them: mortmain and vagabondage, governmental ineptitude, and an all-pervading contempt for the harsh facts of economic life. Instead of continuing to be indiscriminately scattered they can, however, be given some pattern and coherence. Yet even when the reshuffling is finally done and all the cards are fairly distributed, it remains doubtful whether dissent will be possible from the verdict on Spain of Robert Watson's *History of the Reign of Philip III*, published in 1783: 'her power corresponded not with her inclination'; [52] nor from the even sterner verdict of a contemporary, González de Cellorigo: 'it seems as if one had wished to reduce these kingdoms to a republic of bewitched beings, living outside the natural order of things' [53]—a republic whose most famous citizen was Don Quijote de la Mancha.

[52] p. 309.   [53] *Memorial de la Política*, p. 25 v.

32. Burgher-Oligarch and Merchant-Adventurer

C. R. BOXER

It is a matter for some surprise that the Netherlands, a country the very independent existence of which was still a matter of contention in the early part of the seventeenth century, should have produced a flourishing culture and particularly a vigorous, expanding economy. The success of the Dutch Republic is all the more amazing since it occurred in a period that many historians consider one of crisis and decline (see the preceding articles by Hobsbawm and Elliott). The reasons for the Dutch success are a matter of debate, and one school has suggested that it was a function of the general condition of European politics. This position, enunciated by the noted Dutch historian Johan Huizinga, surely underemphasizes the role of native qualities in the Dutch such as industriousness, thrift, sound business practices, and a deep commitment to seafaring. The province of Holland with its capital at Amsterdam led the way in maritime activity, and the burgher-regents of the country played an important role in this advance.

    C. R. Boxer has studied particularly the maritime aspects of the Dutch success, and he presents his conclusions in The Dutch Seaborne Empire, 1600–1800, from which the following selection is drawn. He advances the thesis that the urban patriciate, especially in Amsterdam, was changing from a class primarily interested in trade and secondarily in government, to just

Source: C. R. Boxer, *The Dutch Seaborne Empire, 1600–1800* (New York: Alfred A. Knopf, 1965), pp. 31–53. Copyright © 1965 by Charles R. Boxer. Reprinted by permission of Alfred A. Knopf Inc., the author, and Hutchinson Publishing Group Ltd.

the reverse in the course of the seventeenth century. Although the ever-increasing burdens of administrative and governmental work made it more difficult for the burghers to remain merchants, family traditions, marriage connections, and a vivid awareness of the importance of maritime activity to national prosperity ensured a continuing governmental concern with trade. Boxer's treatment of the changing fortunes of the de Witt family is a fascinating example of social analysis. Similarly his discussion of the history of the Dutch East and West India Companies illustrates the interaction of the regent and merchant classes. The skill with which this analysis has been pursued is rightly one of the most important and acclaimed features of the book.

Any detailed study of the early history of the Dutch Republic should begin with Peter Geyl's The Revolt of the Netherlands, 1559–1609 *(1958) and his* The Netherlands in the Seventeenth Century, *2 vols. (1961, 1964). C. V. Wedgwood's biography* William the Silent *(1944) is well written and informative. A stimulating series of specialized essays on the relations of England and the Netherlands has been published as* Britain and the Netherlands, *edited by J. S. Bromley and E. H. Kossman (1960).*

The urban patricians who triumphed at the Treaty of Münster were in many ways different from their fathers and grandfathers who had sustained the struggle against Spain in the days of Prince Maurice and William the Silent. From being a class primarily concerned with trade and secondarily with local government and administration, the urban patriciate in 1648 was well on the way to becoming a closed oligarchy whose priorities were exactly the reverse. In 1615 a burgomaster of Amsterdam stated that the town regents were either active merchants or those who had recently retired from business. Thirty-seven years later we find the Amsterdam traders complaining that their regents were no longer merchants nor actively engaged in overseas trade, 'but derived their income from houses, lands, and money at interest'.[1] In other words, the merchants had become *rentiers*. This particular complaint was obviously exaggerated, for one has only to think of the influential Bicker brothers, merchants and regents of Amsterdam, who inspired the defence of the town against Prince William II in 1650, and whose commercial connexions spanned the greater part of the globe. Moreover, some of the regents in the towns had always lived mainly on their incomes from real estate, and gave only part-time attention to trade and commerce. But the complaint of 1652 did reflect the fact that many members of the regent class were changing over from actively participating in trade to living on their incomes from land, investments and annuities, supplemented by their usually more modest official salaries. This tendency became increasingly obvious as the 17th century progressed, and the descendants of the merchant-oligarchs of the 1630s had become burgher-oligarchs by the 1690s. It must, however, be remembered that being a member of the municipal council of Amsterdam

[1] Aitzema, *Saken van staet en oorlogh*, Vol. III, p. 762. Cf. also G. J. Renier, *The Dutch Nation*, pp. 100–7.

was a full-time occupation for those who held office by 1650. Merchants who sat on the council could hardly have given much direct attention to their own business affairs. The separation of office-holding from direct participation in trade was more or less inevitable. However, even when the regents had become a *rentier* and official class in whole or in great part, they were still closely related through investment and marriage ties with the wealthy merchants and bankers of the towns, and thus they remained aware that the prosperity of the Seven Provinces depended mainly on overseas trade. Intermarriage between the regent families and the wealthy merchants who lived on the same footing as themselves became more common as time went on, but it was not a speedy process. A merchant family had to live in style for a good many years, perhaps a generation or two, before one of its members could marry into the urban patriciate and thus gain access first to the lower and eventually to the higher ranks of municipal office.

. . . The differences between the various provinces were in some respects so considerable that generalizations concerning the social structure of the Dutch Republic are apt to be more than usually misleading. But since Holland was by far the most important of the Seven Provinces, and since the present work is mainly concerned with the Dutch Republic as a seaborne empire, we will continue to ignore the gentleman-farmers of Friesland, the hedge-squires of Guelderland, and the tenant-farmers of Overijssel, in order to concentrate our attention on the regents, the merchants, and the mariners of Holland and Zeeland.

The transition from a merchant oligarchy to a *rentier* oligarchy, which occupied the greater part of the 17th century in the province of Holland, is exemplified by three generations of the family of Johan de Witt— 'the perfect Hollander', as Sir William Temple described him, and one of the greatest Netherlanders of all time. His family had been represented on the town council of Dordrecht since the end of the 15th century, and they came into greater prominence after 1572 when they chose the side of William I and Calvinism. Cornelis de Witt, born in 1545, inherited a flourishing timber-business from his father, which he continued to manage personally but which did not take up all of his time. He was repeatedly alderman and burgomaster of Dordrecht in the years 1575–1620, representative of the province of Holland in the Zeeland admiralty 1596–9, and the largest subscriber to the Zeeland chamber of the VOC* in 1602. His three sons, Andries, Frans and Jacob, studied law and travelled abroad in their youth, in order to fit themselves later on for official and municipal employment—a practice which was becoming the general rule for regents' sons. Although Jacob continued to carry on his father's business for some years, he was already treasurer of the Synod of Dordt in 1618, and he took his father's place on the town council after the latter's death in 1622. Thenceforward, he concentrated increasingly on his official duties, and disposed of the family business between 1632 and 1651. He served repeatedly as alderman and burgomaster; he represented Dordrecht in the

* [This is the Dutch abbreviation for the East India Company—EDITOR.]

States of Holland and in the States-General; he was a member of many government committees, an envoy to Sweden in 1644, and a prominent opponent of William II in 1650.

Jacob de Witt, though taunted by a political opponent in 1647 with being from an upstart family, certainly felt himself to be a fully fledged member of the regent class, and he is credited with the observation that 'while the burgher is small, he should be kept small'. He was also typical of the pious members of the regent class in that, while remaining a regular church attendant and an assiduous bible reader who led the family prayers for his household every day, he was resolutely opposed to any interference by the Church on the political plane. His most famous son, Johan de Witt, though not so ostentatiously devout, followed his father's precepts and practice as a life-long defender of the power and privileges of the regent class. 'Unqualified and mean persons' should have nothing to do with government and administration 'which must be reserved for qualified people alone', he stated categorically. Johan de Witt, with his brother, Cornelis, received an excellent education in the classics at Dordrecht's 'Illustrious School' and read law at the University of Leiden, though he took his degree at the Huguenot University of Angers. Nor was his physical education neglected, a fact which helped his naturally strong constitution to withstand the exhausting office hours and paperwork with which he later had to cope for years on end. He was remarkably fluent in French, and acquired some knowledge of English, German and Italian. He was also a mathematician of exceptional ability, and wrote a treatise on life-annuities (1671) which entitles him to be considered as the founder of actuarial science.

In the years 1645–7, the young De Witt brothers made what Johan called 'the grand tour' (*den grooten tour*) through most of France and part of England, after paying a brief visit to their father in Stockholm. On returning home from their travels both brothers qualified to practise as advocates; but whereas Cornelis remained in Dordrecht when he was elected alderman and decided to follow his father's career, Johan, after building up a good legal practice at The Hague, became successively Pensionary of Dordrecht (December 1650) and Grand Pensionary of the States of Holland (July 1653). His marriage to the wealthy Wandela Bicker in 1655 brought him into close and advantageous contact with the leading members of the regent families who controlled the town council of Amsterdam for many years. His further career as a statesman is too well known to need recapitulation here; but it may be mentioned that though this career was exclusively an official one and his money was mostly invested in government bonds, his friends included the Amsterdam merchant-banker, Jean Deutsz, and the Leiden industrialists, the brothers De la Court. Fairly well-to-do at the beginning of his career, he left a fortune of half a million guilders at his death, as a result of his economical way of life and the shrewd investment of his own and his wife's capital.[2]

491

Boxer

BURGHER-
OLIGARCHS AND
MERCHANT-
ADVENTURERS

[2] N. Japikse, *Johan de Witt* (Amsterdam, 1928), is my chief authority for the above.

The de Witt family of Dordrecht were typical in that they had been regents of the town for several generations, but more sudden rises to the seats of municipal power were not altogether unknown before the regents became a closed and self-perpetuating *rentier*-oligarchy. Francis Banningh Cocq, the central figure of Rembrandt's *Night Watch,* who became a burgomaster of Amsterdam in 1650, was the scion of an upstart family. The erudite Nicholas Tulp, who is likewise familiar to us from another painting by Rembrandt—*The Anatomy Lesson*—was also a man of humble origins who rose to be a burgomaster of Amsterdam. But such instances became even rarer as the 17th century progressed, and still more so in the 18th. Moreover, while it may be roughly true that the regent class grew out of the merchant class, this was probably not a universal process, particularly as regards the smaller towns. The whole problem of the origins of the regent class and its gradual development into a burgher-oligarchy is one which requires a great deal of further investigation and research, as D. J. Roorda has recently shown in a penetrating study of the ruling classes in Holland in the 17th century.

Whatever their origins, the extent to which the burgher-oligarchs had become a well-defined ruling class during the administration of Johan de Witt, the period of 'the true freedom' as its adherents and admirers termed it, is apparent from the classic *Observations upon the United Provinces of the Netherlands* by Sir William Temple, who knew the Republic well in the years immediately preceding the publication of his book (1672).[3]

Those families which live upon their patrimonial estates in all the great cities, are a people differently bred and mannered from the traders, though like them in the modesty of garb and habit, and the parsimony of living. Their youth are generally bred up at schools, and at the Universities of Leiden or Utrecht, in the common studies of humane learning, but chiefly of the civil law, which is that of their country. . . . Where these families are rich, their youths after the course of their studies at home, travel for some years, as the sons of our gentry use to do; but their journeys are chiefly into England and France, not much into Italy, seldomer into Spain, nor often into the more Northern countries, unless in company or train of their public ministers. The chief end of their breeding, is to make them fit for the service of their country in the magistracy of their towns, their provinces, and their State. And of these kind of men are the civil officers of this government generally composed, being descended of families who have many times been constantly in the magistracy of their native towns for many years, and some for several ages.

Such were most or all of the chief ministers, and the persons that composed their chief councils, in the time of my residence among

---

[3] My quotations are from pp. 161–4 of the 1676 edition.

them, and not men of mean or mechanic trades, as it is commonly received among foreigners, and makes the subject of comical jests upon their government. This does not exclude many merchants, or traders in gross, from being often seen in the offices of their cities, and sometimes deputed to their States; nor several of their States, from turning their stocks in the management of some very beneficial trade by servants and houses maintained to that purpose. But the generality of the States and magistrates are of the other sort; their estates consisting in the pensions of their public charges, in the rents of lands, or interest of money upon the *Cantores*,[4] or in actions of the East-India Company, or in shares upon the adventures of great trading merchants.

Nor do these families, habituated as it were to the magistracy of their towns and provinces, usually arrive at great or excessive riches; the salaries of public employments and interest being low, but the revenue of lands being yet very much lower, and seldom exceeding the profit of two in the hundred. They content themselves with the honour of being useful to the public, with the esteem of their cities or their country, and with the ease of their fortunes; which seldom fails by the frugality of their living, grown universal by being (I suppose) at first necessary, but since honourable among them.

The mighty growth and excess of riches is seen among the merchants and traders, whose application lies wholly that way, and who are the better content to have so little share in the government, desiring only security in what they possess; troubled with no cares but those of their fortunes, and the management of their trades, and turning the rest of their time and thought to the divertisement of their lives. Yet these, when they attain great wealth, choose to breed up their sons in the way, and marry their daughters into the families of those others most generally credited in their towns, and versed in their magistracies; and thereby introduce their families into the way of government and honour, which consists not here in titles, but in public employment.

It is worth noting that Sir William Temple rated the scions of the old landed aristocracy and titled nobility far below the regent class in importance. He added that nevertheless 'they value themselves more upon their nobility than men do in other countries where 'tis more common, and would think themselves utterly dishonoured by the marriage of one that were not of their rank, though it were to make up the fortune of a noble family, by the wealth of a plebean'. In other words, the Dutch landed nobility—where it still existed—was more of a closed aristocracy,

493

Boxer

BURGHER-
OLIGARCHS AND
MERCHANT-
ADVENTURERS

---

[4] 'And the common revenue of particular men lies much in the Cantores either of the Generality, or the several Provinces, which are the Registries of these public debts' (op. cit., p. 253). Cf. V. Barbour, *Capitalism in Amsterdam in the Seventeenth Century*, pp. 81, 83.

like that of France, Spain and Portugal, than a relatively open aristocracy like that of England, where intermarriage with recently ennobled families of men who had made their money in trade, political office, or the law, was more common. The Dutch nobility were not large landowners as a general rule, and even the largest estates in Friesland could not be compared to the broad acres held by many other European landed nobles from Poland to Portugal. Sir William Temple deprecated the tendency of the Dutch nobility to ape the manners and dress of the French aristocracy, but admitted that 'they are otherwise an honest, well-natured, friendly and gentlemanly sort of men, and acquit themselves with honour and merit, where their country employs them'. They were naturally mostly Orangist in sympathy, though down to the time of William III's stadtholdership (1672–1702), the regents could always find some nobles, like Jacob van Wassenaer van Obdam, commander-in-chief of the Netherlands Navy in 1655–65, who preferred a *bourgeois* republic to a princely Stadtholderate, either from personal conviction or else from jealousy of the House of Orange. As for the social relations of the old aristocracy and gentry with the ordinary burghers, a visiting Englishman noted in 1685: 'Those that govern themselves with prudence and moderation and make themselves familiar with their inferiors are highly respected and popular, while those that are stiff and haughty are generally hated and despised.' [5]

It was a commonplace with all foreign travellers in the United Provinces during the first seven or eight decades of the 17th century that the regent and merchant classes, and even (though to a lesser extent) the titled aristocracy and the army officers, were all more sober in 'maintaining a port' than their equivalents in other countries. Sir William Temple observed how Michiel de Ruyter and Johan de Witt, 'the one, generally esteemed by foreign nations, as great a seaman, and the other as great a statesman as any of their age', were not to be distinguished in their daily dress and deportment from, respectively, 'the commonest sea-captain' and 'the commonest burgher of the town'. Their households were on the same modest scale, and though both of them amassed great wealth, neither of them was attended by more than one man-servant, whether indoors or out. 'Nor was this manner of life affected,' adds Sir William, 'or used only by these particular men, but [it] was the general fashion or mode among all the magistrates of the State: for I speak not of the military officers, who are reckoned their servants, and live in a different garb, though generally modester than in other countries.' Doubtless the sobering influence of Calvinism was at work here, and we shall see that when

[5] James Monson's unpublished account of his journey through Western Europe in 1685–6 (quoted by kind permission of the late Lord Monson from the original MS. at Burton Hall, Lincolnshire). This particular remark seems to have been copied from Jean Parival, *Les Delices de la Hollande* (1662), p. 190, an account of the United Provinces which went through many editions and rivalled Sir William Temple's *Observations* in popularity. Cf. also, Temple, *Observations* (ed. 1676), pp. 165–6; W. Carr, *An Accurate Description of the United Provinces* (ed. London, 1691), pp. 23–8.

the plain burghers of Amsterdam and Middelburg were transplanted to the East and West Indies they could indulge in as much pomp and circumstance as did their Iberian predecessors and their English rivals.

Many contemporaries noticed that during the last quarter of the 17th century the upper middle class began to adopt a more ostentatious and luxurious way of life. For instance, Michiel de Ruyter's bachelor son, Engel, lived on a much more lavish scale than his father ever did. In addition to his well-furnished town house staffed with two menservants, two maids and a coachman, Engel de Ruyter also maintained a sizeable country-house, which he used for week-ends and summer holidays. Similarly, Lieutenant-Admiral Cornelis Tromp, son of the famous 'Tarpaulin' admiral, M. H. Tromp, had a much higher standard of living than his father, 'who contented himself with a pickled herring for his breakfast'. Cornelis married into an Amsterdam regent family and spent his last years leading the life of a grand-seigneur between his town-house on the Heerengracht at Amsterdam and his luxuriously furnished country-house 'De Trompenburgh' in 's-Graveland. William Carr, the English consul at Amsterdam, whose description of the Seven Provinces was first published there in 1688, was much struck by the noticeable increase in high living among the regents and the wealthy burghers which had occurred in the sixteen years since Temple wrote his famous work. 'The old severe and frugal way of living is now almost quite out of date in Holland; there is very little to be seen of that sober modesty in apparel, diet, and habitations as formerly. Instead of convenient dwellings, the Hollanders now build stately palaces, have their delightful gardens, and houses of pleasure, keep coaches, wagons and sleighs, have very rich furniture for their horses, with trappings adorned with silver bells . . . yea, so much is the humour of the women altered, and of their children also, that no apparel can now serve them but the best and richest that France and other countries afford; and their sons are so much addicted to play that many families in Amsterdam are quite ruined by it.' [6]

495

Boxer

BURGHER-
OLIGARCHS AND
MERCHANT-
ADVENTURERS

Carr's strictures, and those of other contemporaries who could be quoted to the same effect, apply mainly if not exclusively to the Province of Holland, and above all to the wealthy *bourgeoisie* of Amsterdam and The Hague. The impress of Calvinism on this particular section of Dutch society had never been so marked as it was elsewhere, and the rich young men who made the 'grand tour' were undoubtedly influenced by what they saw in England and (above all) in France. Another factor which may have helped to foster this display of wealth was, perhaps, the return of people who had made their fortunes in the East Indies. These Dutch equivalents and precursors of the English 18th-century 'Nabobs' had become used to a luxurious way of life in the tropics, and they can hardly have felt

---

[6] Temple, *Observations* (ed. 1676), pp. 128–9; W. Carr, *Accurate Description* (ed. 1691), pp. 71–4; N. de Roever, *Uit onzer oude Amstelstad. Schetsen en taferelen betreffende het leven en de zeden harer vroegere bewoners* (3 vols., Amsterdam, 1890–1), Vol. I, p. 77 ff.

inclined to conform to a puritanical existence after their return home. Be this as it may, Dutch art and architecture of the period clearly reflect this change, though the Dutch ruling classes always remained less extravagant than the French and English aristocracies. William Carr summed-up the situation fairly enough when he observed that although the Dutch 'were not addicted to such prodigality and wantonness as the English are . . . nevertheless, the grave and sober people of Holland are very sensible of the great alteration that now is in this country'.

One of the 'grave and sober people of Holland' had sounded the alarm even at the time when Sir William Temple was admiring the frugality and modesty of the Dutch ruling class. An anonymous pamphleteer of 1662 complained that small shopkeepers, tailors, cobblers, publicans and their respective wives, now dressed in velvet and silk clothes to an extent which made it difficult to distinguish between these base-born persons and their social superiors. Things had come to such a pass, he averred, that 'Mr. Everyman thinks he is entitled to wear what he likes so long as he can pay for it'. Similarly, some small traders and artisans furnished their houses in a manner unbefitting to their lowly station in life. 'Can you bear it', he asked indignantly, 'when you see that a tailor has a room or a parlour hung with gold leather or tapestry? Or here and there, a mercer or an artisan who decorates his house as if it was a gentleman's or a burgomaster's?' He urged that this unseemly state of affairs should be ended by the promulgation of sumptuary laws, restricting the use of silk and velvet clothes to the upper middle class, and ordering the working class to dress only 'in wool and other stuffs'. The upper middle class he defined as being composed of the regents, magistrates, sheriffs, bailiffs, receivers and other senior officials, as well as merchants and traders who possessed a capital of from forty thousand to fifty thousand guilders, 'and who are taxed accordingly'. He opined that advocates and medical doctors might be considered the social equals of magistrates, but attorneys and notaries were a grade below them and ranked with clerks and sheriff's officers. Shopkeepers, small traders, and minor officials were lumped together in the lower middle-class which, in his view, was barely a cut above the artisans. He admitted that military officers formed a class apart; but he was baffled by the social status of artists and actors. Many of these were apt to be 'of a madcap humour' (*dol van geest*), though some of the former were 'divine in artistry and intelligence'. The further proposals of this anonymous pamphleteer do not concern us here, but his work is of interest as reflecting that acute class-consciousness which permeated social life in the Golden Age of the Dutch Republic and which became intensified in the following century.[7]

The grave and sober deportment of the upper middle class—their banquets and drinking-bouts always excepted—during the first half of

---

[7] J. van B. I. C. Tus, *Een onderscheyt Boeckje ofte Tractaetje van de fouten en dwalingen der politie in ons Vaderlant* (Amsterdam, 1662); Knuttel nr. 8670. Cf. also P. Zumthor, *Daily Life in Rembrandt's Holland*, pp. 224–37.

the 17th century, and their high regard for financial solvency, did not mean that nepotism, bribery, and corruption were unknown. On the contrary, they were an integral part of the social structure, though it may fairly be claimed that they were no worse than elsewhere in Europe, despite the allegations of some foreigners to the contrary. One thing which helped to keep such malpractices in bounds was that they could be exposed with relative ease in that voluminous pamphlet-literature which was such a feature of the Seven Provinces. The authorities could seldom exert a fully effective control over determined pamphleteers, owing to the lengths to which decentralization of the government was carried and to the mutual jealousy of the sovereign provinces. Pamphlets banned in one town could often be reprinted in another.

Outspoken press criticism did not, of course, prevent such scandals as the Amsterdam regents using their official position to make outrageous profits in land sales during the extension of the town in 1615; nor the regents of Hoorn from enriching themselves in the depression year of 1619 at the expense of the poor and lowly; nor the members of the Rotterdam Admiralty from embezzling official funds in 1626. It is also very doubtful if the denunciation by the Zeeland delegates to the Grand Assembly of 1650 of bribery and corruption in official circles had more than a passing effect. The delegates were obviously thinking of Cornelis Musch, the late *Griffier,* or confidential clerk to the States-General, whose shameless greed in taking bribes was notorious, and who did not hesitate to supply the Portuguese ambassador with copies of all the secret dispatches and confidential resolutions which the latter needed. A few years later, Sir George Downing, the unscrupulous English envoy at The Hague, affirmed that 'there is scarce any who come in the States-General but get in to make themselves a fortune by it and must be bought'.

The previously quoted Portuguese envoy, Sousa Coutinho, gives us an amusing glimpse of how temptation was placed in the way of a selected individual who was married and had several children. In paying a courtesy call on such a person, and discussing the matter in hand, 'one lets fall, as if by accident, a jewel worth about a thousand *cruzados* more or less (according to that person's relative standing and position) into the hand of one of the children'. The father would not make the child return the jewel, and so 'face' was saved all round. Honourable exceptions were probably more numerous than these unfriendly critics were prepared to admit, and the French ambassador, D'Estrades, was undoubtedly exaggerating when he wrote that 'hors de M. de Witt, il n'y pas un qu'on ne fasse changer d'avis pour de l'argent'. But if the 'perfect Hollander' enjoyed an exceptional reputation for honesty where his country's interests were concerned, he found it more difficult to ignore the ties of kinship and friendship when suitable candidates for office asked him to use his influence on their behalf. Even so, the favours he did his relatives and political friends on such occasions never assumed the dimensions of a major scandal.

The same could not be said of many of his contemporaries, and nepo-

497
Boxer
BURGHER-
OLIGARCHS AND
MERCHANT-
ADVENTURERS

tism was ineradicably and unavoidably ingrained in the oligarchic system of the Dutch Republic. Both the regent supporters of 'the true freedom' and the Stadtholders of the House of Orange were equally wedded to the practice of placing their respective adherents in key positions or in lucrative posts, whenever this could be done without provoking excessive scandal—and sometimes even then. In the long run, nepotism probably did more harm to the body politic than did bribery and corruption. It certainly aroused more opposition, and it increasingly divorced the interests of the ruling oligarchy from those of the middle and lower classes. The most scandalous features of this regent nepotism were reflected in the agreements made between members of a town council to take turns in appointing their relatives and friends to office or public employment. Originally oral, and later written, these 'contracts of correspondence', which were relatively rare in the 17th century, became increasingly common in the 18th. While men of ability were not necessarily kept out of office by this patronage system, the fact remained that a candidate's primary qualification was apt to be not so much his character as his family connexions. In other words, public offices in the Dutch Republic—as elsewhere for that matter, though for different reasons—came to be regarded as private, more or less negotiable, family properties. As an Englishmen long resident in Holland wrote in 1740: 'Their government is aristocratical: so that the so much boasted liberty of the Dutch is not to be understood in the general and absolute sense, but *cum grano salis*. The Burgomasters and senate compose the sovereignty [of the Towns]; and, on a vacancy by death, the Burgomaster would be highly offended if any petulant burgher presumed to murmur at his filling it up with one of his own sons, or relations.' [8]

Although the regent oligarchy became increasingly differentiated from the ordinary burghers during the 18th century, it would be wrong to lay too much stress on the gulf that separated rulers and ruled in an earlier period. Admittedly, many—perhaps most—of the regents in the 'Golden Century' would have agreed with Jacob and Johan de Witt that the small man must be kept small, and that the regents alone were fully qualified to govern their fellow-countrymen. But despite the resentment which this aristocratic hauteur sometimes aroused, and despite the widespread admiration for the House of Orange, the fact remains that for

[8] Anon., *A Description of Holland: or, The Present State of the United Provinces* (London, 1743), p. 73. For contemporary evidence of bribery and corruption in regent circles, cf. Aitzema, *Saken van staet en oorlogh*, Vol. III, pp. 525 ff.; F. de Sousa Coutinho, *Correspondência Diplomática, 1643–1650*, Vol. II, p. 49; *Ibidem*, Vol. III, pp. 163, 165, 174–6, 227–8, 234, 248, 251; Downing's correspondence during 1661 *apud* N. Japikse, *De Verwikkelingen tusschen de Republiek en Engeland* (Leiden, 1900), especially p. 183; D'Estrades' letter of 18 November 1665 *apud* N. Japikse, *Johan de Witt* (1928), p. 106 n.; J. E. Elias, *Geschiedenis van het Amsterdamsche regentenpatriciaat* (The Hague, 1923), pp. 194–6, 202–10; D. J. Roorda, 'Een zwakke stee in de Hollandse regentaristocratie: de Hoornse vroedschap in opspraak, 1670–75', in *Bijdragen voor de geschiedenis der Nederlanden*, Vol. XVI (1961), 89–116.

much of the time most people were content to accept the regents as their natural leaders. They only turned to the House of Orange in times of acute danger, such as the French invasions of 1672 and 1748. As several Dutch historians have pointed out, many large groups in the Republic, though not nearly so vocal as the Calvinist extremists or the convinced Orangists, had good reason to prefer the regent oligarchy to its strident opponents. Roman Catholics, Remonstrants, and Protestant dissenters in general, who, in the aggregate, probably formed about two-thirds of the population (*c.* 1662), realized that the regents were their main bulwark against the intolerant *predikants* of the 'True Reformed Christian Religion'. These zealots would have placed the supremacy of the orthodox Calvinist Church above that of the relatively tolerant state if they had had their way.

Nor was it only the regent class which was distrustful of the dynastic ambitions and the monarchical leanings sometimes displayed by the House of Orange. It is significant that on the occasion of William II's attack on Amsterdam in 1650, the entire population sided unhesitatingly with the oligarchic Bicker brothers. Even in the days of Johan de Witt and 'the true freedom', the regents had to take some account of public opinion, as Sir Willaim Temple observed when he wrote that 'the way to office and authority lies through those qualities which acquire the general esteem of the people'. Though the regents later became an unrepresentative minority, most of their compatriots did not dispute their right to rule during the years when they governed the Dutch Republic at the greatest period of its history.[9]

For contempoaries and for posterity, one of the most spectacular manifestations of Dutch commercial enterprise was supplied by the rise of their East and West India Companies, even though the economic importance of these two great trading corporations was in reality less than that of the more humdrum carrying-trade of Western Europe and the North Sea Fisheries. The grain-trade with the Baltic was, as De Witt observed in 1671, the 'source and root of the most notable commerce and navigation of these lands'. At the beginning of the 17th century some 1,200 Dutch vessels were engaged in this trade, and during the first half of the same century the total of Dutch ships passing the Sound outnumbered the English by roughly thirteen to one. As late as 1666 it was estimated that three-fourths of the capital active on the Amsterdam bourse was engaged in the Baltic trade. The North Sea Fisheries for herring, haddock, cod, and ling were also termed the 'chiefest trade and principal gold-mine' of the United Provinces in 1580–1639. Some forty years later, De la Court claimed that these fisheries were estimated to employ over 1,000 busses or fishing-smacks of 48–60 tons burden. He calculated that the fishing industry with its ancillary trades then employed about 450,000 persons,

499

Boxer

BURGHER-
OLIGARCHS AND
MERCHANT-
ADVENTURERS

[9] Temple, *Observations* (ed. 1676), p. 130; P. Geyl, 'Historische appreciaties van het zeventiende-eeuwse Hollands regentenregiem', in *Studies en strijdschriften* (Groningen, 1958), pp. 180–200; C. Wilson, *Profit and Power,* p. 15.

compared with about 200,000 engaged in agriculture and about 650,000 engaged in other industries. Estimates of the value of the catch vary widely, but De la Court's figure (in 1662) of Fl. 8,000,000, or not far short of £1,000,000, is probably somewhere near the truth. The fishing industry was closely controlled by guild and government regulations which ensured the high standard of the herrings barrelled in brine for export, and of the fresh and smoked fish which were widely eaten in a country where only the rich ate meat more than once a week. Enkhuizen and Rotterdam were the two chief centres of the herring fishery for most of the 17th century, as Amsterdam was for the Arctic whaling industry. This last was organized as a monopoly of the Northern Company in 1614–42, and subsequently—and more successfully—as a free activity when the States-General declined to renew the Company's charter.[10]

The failure of the grandiose plans of the monopolistic Northern Company affords an interesting contrast with the development of the East and West India Companies during the same period, although the WIC later came to a sticky end. Like other institutions in the Dutch Republic, these two India Companies had a strongly oligarchic stamp which became more marked with the passage of time. Their organization and early development also illustrate the interaction of the merchant and the regent classes on each other, and the increasingly preponderant part played by Amsterdam capitalists and investors in overseas trade.

Each of the six regional chambers of the East India Company had a board of directors, originally identical with the local directors of the amalgamating pioneer companies, who retained their positions for life. When a director died or—more rarely—resigned, his fellow-directors submitted a list of three names to the local representatives of the provincial States, who were usually the burgomasters of the town concerned and who chose one to fill the vacancy. The *Heeren* XVII* were chosen from among the regional directors who in their turn were drawn from subscribers with a minimum holding of F. 6,000 for most of the regional chambers and of Fl. 3,000 in the smaller ones of Hoorn and Enkhuizen. These leading shareholders were termed *hoofdparticipanten*. Eight of the *Heeren* XVII represented the Amsterdam chamber, four the Middelburg, with one representative from each of the other chambers. The seventeenth director was provided by rotation among all the chambers save Amsterdam.

The self-perpetuating and oligarchic nature of the directorships soon

---

[10] Pieter de la Court, *Interest van Holland, ofte gronden van Hollands Welvaren* (Amsterdam, 1662), the English version of which, entitled *The True Interest and Political Maxims of the Republic of Holland and West-Friesland* (London, 1702), was wrongly ascribed to Johan de Witt, although he did have a hand in amending De la Court's original draft. Cf. especially pp. 26–30, 40–2 of the 1702 edition, and also V. Barbour, *Capitalism in Amsterdam*, pp. 26–7; C. Wilson, *Profit and Power*, pp. 1–24, 32–47; P. Zumthor, *Daily Life in Rembrandt's Holland* (London, 1962), pp. 306–10.

* [The Board of Directors of the VOC—EDITOR.]

aroused much adverse criticism, both among the ordinary shareholders who exercised no influence whatever on the directors' policy and among the *hoofdparticipanten* who remained outside the small circle of the directors and their friends. When the Company's charter was first renewed in 1623, the States-General made a rather half-hearted effort to meet this criticism by ruling that thenceforth the directors could only be elected for a three-year term of office, and that the list of three names for a vacant directorship should be submitted by a committee which included equal numbers of directors and *hoofdparticipanten*. In the upshot, this made little practical difference. All the retiring directors were eligible for re-election, and those leading shareholders who had a vote did not wish to prejudice their own future chances of election by antagonizing the actual directors. Hence retiring directors were almost invariably re-elected, and vacancies caused by deaths continued to be filled from the same small circle of *hoofdparticipanten*—sometimes by casting lots.

The close connexion of the directors with the regent class was cogently expressed by a pamphleteer of 1622, who echoed English and French complaints about the impossibility of obtaining redress for real or alleged wrongs done by the servants of the VOC to those nations in the East. 'For, they say, if we complain to the regents and the magistrates of the towns, there sit the directors, . . . if to the admiralties, there are the directors again. If to the States-General, we find that they and the directors are sitting there together at the same time.' This intimate connexion of the directors with the regent class was the chief reason why they were able to sidetrack or to ignore criticism of their conduct by disgruntled shareholders, and to consolidate their own position as a self-perpetuating oligarchy accountable to nobody. So sure of themselves did the *Heeren* XVII feel by 1644 that they told the States-General: 'The places and strongholds which they had captured in the East Indies should not be regarded as national conquests but as the property of private merchants, who were entitled to sell those places to whomsoever they wished, even if it was to the King of Spain, or to some other enemy of the United Provinces.' It may be added that criticism of the directors by shareholders in the Company rapidly declined after 1634, when the *Heeren* XVII began to distribute generous annual dividends in cash. These ranged between 15½ per cent and 50 per cent, reaching a climax in 1715–20 with six successive dividends of 40 per cent each.[11]

Subscribers of the original working capital of the VOC were drawn from all classes of society, though naturally the rich and the well-to-do predominated, for reasons explained by a contemporary chronicler relating the success of Van Neck's voyage: 'This profit was for a few rich and powerful people, who could afford to lay out their capital for a long time; whereas the common man cannot afford to lock up his daily earnings for so long, and such people do much better by investing their money in

501

Boxer

BURGHER-
OLIGARCHS AND
MERCHANT-
ADVENTURERS

[11] O. Van Rees, *Geschiedenis der staathuishoudkunde in Nederland tot het einde der achttiende eeuw* (2 vols., Utrecht, 1865–8), Vol. II, pp. 156–60, 195.

trade with neighbouring nations.' High officials, town councillors, wealthy traders and merchant capitalists contributed the bulk of the capital, subscribing sums ranging from Fl. 10,000 to Fl. 85,000. Prominent among the original large investors were the refugee merchant-bankers from Antwerp and the southern Netherlands, and their financial preponderance was still greater at the end of a decade. As time went on these wealthy immigrants were absorbed into the regent class, and the larger shareholders bought out most of the small investors. At the same time, Amsterdam investors who had originally subscribed more than half the Company's working capital extended their tentacles into the other chambers. By the end of the 17th century, 108 Amsterdammers were holding about three-eighths of the capital stock of the Zeeland chamber, and more than half of the entire capital of the VOC was owned in Amsterdam.[12]

Apart from its financial preponderance in the VOC, Amsterdam likewise exercised a great and growing influence on the Company's policy and administration. This influence was consolidated by Mr. Pieter van Dam, who filled the post of the Company's advocate at Amsterdam from 1652 until his death in 1706. The resident English consul in 1688 compared the sixty-eight-year-old advocate with the great Johan de Witt 'for parts, though not so in [political] principle. This great minister is a man of indefatigable industry, and labours day and night in the Company's service. He reads over twice the great journal books which come from the Indies, and out of them makes minutes to prepare matters of concern necessary to be considered by the grand council of seventeen, and by the inferior committees of the Company, and prepares the orders to be sent to their chief ministers in the Indies.' That William Carr did not exaggerate is proved by Van Dam's encyclopaedic description of the Company and its activities which he compiled for the secret and confidential use of the directors between 1693 and 1701. These bulky manuscript volumes were kept from the knowledge of outsiders and remained the *vade-mecum* of successive generations of directors until the Company's dissolution in 1795.[13]

The extent to which the regent class became in some ways separated from the merchant class was reflected in the directorships of the VOC. Whereas in 1644 the *Heeren* XVII had told the States-General that the Company was the property of private merchants, in 1743 the regents who occupied the chairs of the *Heeren* XVII passed a resolution that merchants might, after all, be allowed to become directors! Out of twenty-four regents who filled the burgomasters' chairs at Amsterdam in the years 1718–48, only two were active merchants—a striking contrast with

[12] J. G. Van Dillen, *Het oudste aandeelhoudersregister van de kamer Amsterdam der Oost-Indische Compagnie* (The Hague, 1958); W. S. Unger, 'Het inschrijvings-register van de kamer Zeeland der verenigde Oost-Indische Compagnie', in the *Economisch-Historisch Jaarboek*, Vol. 24 (The Hague, 1950); H. Terpstra, *Jacob van Neck*, pp. 74–5; V. Barbour, *Capitalism in Amsterdam*, pp. 28–9, 79.

[13] W. Carr, *Accurate Description* (ed. 1691), p. 38; P. Van Dam, *Beschrijvinge van de Oost-Indische Compagnie* (ed. F. W. Stapel, 6 vols., The Hague, 1927–54).

the composition of that town council a century previously. Admittedly the contrast becomes less striking when we recall that an Amsterdam municipal councillor's job was a full-time one after about 1650. An active merchant could hardly serve as burgomaster and give much attention to his own commercial business at the same time. But here again one must not be too categorical. The Orangist *coup d'état* of 1748, which brought another group of regents to power, resulted in a balance much more favourable to commercial interests. Out of thirty-seven Amsterdam burgomasters in the period 1752–95, thirteen were active or recently retired merchants, and the remainder had close family connexions with commercial firms. It is also worth noting that from first to last a burgomaster of Amsterdam was nearly always a director of the VOC.[14]

The West India Company likewise had a marked oligarchic stamp and close connexions with the regent class, although one of its earliest promoters, the indefatigable pamphleteer Willem Usselincx, had vainly advocated that 'no magistrate should be a director and that no director should be a magistrate at one and the same time'. In the governing board of the *Heeren* XIX,* Amsterdam provided eight directors, Zeeland four, and the other three chambers two each, the nineteenth being nominated by the States-General. As with the *Heeren* XVII, the *Heeren* XIX likewise assembled for six successive years at Amsterdam, followed by two at Middelburg. The original directors were chosen by the regents of the five towns where the provincial chambers were seated, from among the leading shareholders with a minimum investment of Fl. 6,000 for Amsterdam and Fl. 4,000 for the remainder. Vacancies were filled in a similar manner to those of the VOC, by consultation and co-optation between the town regents and the directors of the chamber concerned. The small investor was for long a more important factor in the WIC than with the sister company. This was particularly noticeable in Zeeland, where it was alleged in 1648 that over a fifth of the inhabitants of Middelburg, Flushing and Veere were shareholders in the WIC.

As had happened with the older Company, the rules concerning the periodic public audit and inspection of the accounts, and the publication of balance-sheets, were either ignored or evaded by the directors. The result in both cases was the strengthening of the directors' power *vis-à-vis* the shareholders; though in the case of the WIC the *hoofdparticipanten* sometimes held their own meetings, and may have exercised more influence on their directors. A comparison of the names of the directors of both companies before 1636 shows, as might be expected, that some prominent merchant-oligarchs, such as the Bickers of Amsterdam and the Lampsins of Flushing, were represented on the boards of both corporations. While there was markedly less enthusiasm among the merchants of Amsterdam for the WIC in 1622 than they had displayed for the VOC

503

Boxer

BURGHER-
OLIGARCHS AND
MERCHANT-
ADVENTURERS

[14] J. E. Elias, *Geschiedenis van het Amsterdamsche Regentpatriciaat*, pp. 101, 216, 232–8.
* [The Board of Directors of the WIC—EDITOR.]

twenty years earlier, yet the eighty-three leading shareholders of the Amsterdam chamber of the WIC subscribed over a million florins, which was more than a third of that city's total contribution. As with the VOC, the Amsterdammers later extended their influence by buying up shares in the other regional chambers. By 1670 more than half the total capital of the WIC was owned in Amsterdam, and this town had advanced money to the other chambers.

Colonization of suitable regions was specifically envisaged in the WIC's charter of 1621, but this Company was from the first intended as an offensive weapon for striking against the roots of Iberian power in the New World. The WIC soon became involved in efforts to conquer all or part of Brazil; and the resulting naval and military expenditure far exceeded the profits derived from the sugar and other exports of its precariously held South American territory. Piet Heyn's capture of the Mexican silver-fleet in 1628 enabled the *Heeren* XIX to declare a bumper dividend of 75 per cent in 1629–30, but the Company only distributed another one or two before its dissolution in 1674. Down to about 1650, the West African trade, particularly that in Guinea gold, yielded good profits, but these were all sunk in the Brazilian financial morass. On its reorganization in 1674, investors received only 30 per cent of their deposits, but its creditors were repaid in full and the new Company was still able to borrow money at 4 per cent in 1694. By this time it had become primarily a slave-trading concern for the export of negroes from West Africa to the West Indies, where the island of Curaçao was an excellent base for contraband trade with Spanish America.

We have seen that the organization of the WIC was delayed until after the judicial murder of Oldenbarnevelt and the triumph of the militant Calvinist or Contra-Remonstrant party in which the south Netherland emigrants were powerfully represented. For this and other reasons, the WIC formed a bulwark of this party in Holland for a few years and in Zeeland for much longer; but less fervent Protestants—the so-called Arminians and Libertines—were always represented among both directors and shareholders. During the 1630s and 1640s these latter elements gained the upper hand in Holland; although, as late as 1649, Burgomaster Bicker of Amsterdam, who had sold his WIC shares many years previously at the top of the market, is alleged to have said of the semi-bankrupt Company: 'Let the Brabanters and Walloons see now what baronies they are going to get out of it!' But the internal stresses and strains which so largely contributed to the ruin of the first West India Company were caused not so much by lack of co-operation between Calvinists and Libertines on the boards of directors as by the provincial jealousy between Holland—more especially, Amsterdam—and Zeeland. This is reflected in the pamphlet literature of the time, which is both voluminous and vituperative where the WIC is concerned, whereas printed criticism of the *Heeren* XVII virtually ceased after 1625 for over 150 years.[15]

---

[15] J. F. Jameson, *Willem Usselincx, Founder of the Dutch and Swedish West India Companies* (New York, 1887); C. Ligtenberg, *Willem Usselincx* (Utrecht,

One criticism which was frequently applied to the employees of both Companies by their stay-at-home contemporaries was that those men who served in the East and West Indies were generally of inferior character. This allegation was not confined to scurrilous pamphleteers, but forms a recurrent theme in the correspondence of the directors with their senior representatives at Batavia and Recife. The great 19th-century Islamic scholar, Snouk Hurgronje, was writing with a good knowledge of these sources when he characterized the Dutch East India Company's two centuries in the East in the following scathing terms: 'The first act of the Netherlands-Indian tragedy is called "Company", and it begins almost exactly with the 17th century. The chief actors deserve our admiration for their indomitable energy, but the objective for which they worked, and the means they employed to attain it, were of such a kind that we, even with the full application of the rule that we must judge their deeds and doings by the standard of their times, have difficulty in restraining our aversion. The "experiment" began in such wise, that the inhabitants of Asia came into contact with the dregs of the Dutch nation, who treated them with almost unbearable contempt, and whose task it was to devote all their efforts to the enrichment of a group of shareholders in the Fatherland. The servants of this chartered company, kept all too short by their employers but not less greedy for gain than they, displayed a picture of corruption which overshadows the worst of what the Oriental peoples are accused of in this respect.' [16]

I hope to show in subsequent chapters that this sweeping judgement is in some respects unfair, and that it was not only the dregs of the Dutch nation who went out to the East. But it cannot be denied that Snouk Hurgronje's denunciation contains a large element of truth. The VOC, like the Portuguese Crown before it, and like the English and French Companies competing with it, paid all but a few of its servants such small wages that they could not possibly live on their pay and allowances. They were thus compelled to resort to more or less dishonest means in order to earn a livelihood. Moreover the hardships of a six or eight months' voyage, and the dangers of life in tropical countries where little or nothing was known of the prevention and cure of such deadly diseases as malaria, cholera, leprosy and dysentery, naturally deterred the great majority of people who could get any sort of a job at home from taking their chance in the East and West Indies. The reluctance of the average upper- or middle-class Dutchman to serve a monopolisitic trading company also helps to explain why the directors could seldom afford to pick and choose their subordinates but had to make the best of those they could get. What

505

Boxer

BURGHER-
OLIGARCHS AND
MERCHANT-
ADVENTURERS

1915); C. R. Boxer, *The Dutch in Brazil, 1624–1654* (Oxford, 1957); W. J. Hoboken, 'The Dutch West-India Company: The Political Background of Its Rise and Decline', in J. S. Bromley and E. H. Kossmann (eds.), *Britain and the Netherlands. Papers Delivered to the Oxford-Netherlands Historical Conference, 1959* (London, 1960), pp. 41–61; J. G. Van Dillen, 'De West-Indische Compagnie, het Calvinisme en de politiek', in *Tijdschrift voor Geschiedenis* (1961), pp. 145–71; V. Barbour, *Capitalism in Amsterdam*.

[16] *Apud* E. du Perron, *De Muze van Jan Compagnie* (Bandung, 1948), p. 13.

David Hannay wrote of the servants of the English East India Company in the 17th century is equally applicable to their contemporaries and competitors of the VOC. 'Nothing is more common, or more grotesque, than the contrast between the profuse assurances of the Company that it has every confidence in the virtue of Mr. A. who is just appointed to this or that factory, and its furious rebuke of his scandalous dishonesty written perhaps within a year and a day.' [17]

The higher ranks of the VOC and the WIC overseas were staffed mainly by men who came from the middle and lower ranks of the burgher class, with a sprinkling from the urban patriciate. Representatives of the landed nobility were conspicuous by their absence; Hendrik Adriaan van Rheede tot Drakenstein, Lord of Mijdrecht, who was governor of Malabar in 1669–77, was one of the few exceptions. Directors often found jobs for their—mostly poorer—friends and relations who were prepared to seek their fortune in the Indies; but, generally speaking, for the reasons given above, the better class of Dutchmen preferred to seek employment nearer home and only took service with either of the two India Companies as a last resort. This helps to explain why both Companies employed such a high proportion of foreigners. But it also meant that the ladder of promotion could easily be climbed by men of ability and determination; for a career in these two Companies was, despite a good deal of inevitable nepotism, in the main a *carrière ouverte aux talents*. This is proved by the numerous instances of men who entered their service in a lowly or even, in some cases, a menial capacity and rose to the highest ranks. Antonio van Diemen, the undischarged bankrupt who enlisted as a solider and became Governor-General at Batavia in 1636–45, and François Caron, the ship's cook who became Director-General there in 1647–50, are two examples of men who rose to the top exclusively through their own merits and exertions.[18] Two of the most distinguished Governor-Generals in 18th-century Batavia, Jacob Mossel (1750–61) and Reinier de Klerk (1777–80), both started their respective careers as common seamen in the East India Company's service.

On the other hand, the scandalous career of the Zeeland regent's son, Pieter Nuyts, who avowed that he 'had not come out to Asia to eat hay', and who collected Fl. 18,000 from the Company after having been dishonourably discharged at Batavia for his misconduct in Japan and Formosa (1627–30), showed what those who had influential family connexions could get away with. There was probably no important difference between the type of man who enlisted to serve in the East or in the West Indies;

---

[17] D. Hannay, *The Great Chartered Companies* (London, 1926), pp. 190–2.

[18] W. P. Coolhaas, 'Gegevens over Antonio van Diemen' (*BTLVNI*, Vol. 103, 1943–6, pp. 469–546); Ibidem, 'Een Indisch verslag uit 1631, van de hand van Antonio van Diemen' (*BMHGU*, Vol. 65, 1943–6, pp. 1–237); C. R. Boxer (ed.), *A True Description of the Mighty Kingdoms of Japan and Siam by François Caron and Joost Schouten* (London, 1935).

though one of the many individuals who served both Companies claimed in 1655 that the senior officials of the WIC were a set of 'drunken fools' who would never have been promoted to high rank by the sister Company in the East.[19]

If the general run of the two Companies' servants left much to be desired, there were always some honourable exceptions. Although the vast majority of Dutchmen, like most of their Portuguese predecessors and of their English and French rivals, went out East (or West) 'to shake the pagoda tree', there were some who were not mainly concerned with making money. I see no reason to doubt the sincerity of Jacob van Neck's avowal that 'all his life long he had a desire to see foreign countries' and that this was the main motive which took him to the East. The same can be said of the ship's surgeon, Nicholas de Graaff, who, although happily married and comfortably installed in his home town, could never resist for long the call of the sea and of the tropics.[20] Men of this type may have been relatively rare; but there were others who, having gone out to the East solely to make money, became fascinated by the life or by the people in the tropics, and recorded their impressions for posterity. The foregoing remarks, of course, apply chiefly to the members of the *bourgeoisie*, whose motives are explained in their own writings and books. We have now to consider the more numerous but less literate members of Dutch society who had to earn their daily bread in the sweat of their brow.

[19] W. P. Coolhaas, 'Een lastig heerschap tegenover een lastig volk' (*BMHGU*, Vol. 69, 1955, pp. 17–43); D. P. de Vries, *Korte Historiael ende Journaels Aenteyckeninge van verscheyden voyagiens in de vier deelen des wereldtsronde, als Europe, Africa, Asia ende America*, Hoorn, 1655 (ed. H. T. Colenbrander, The Hague, 1911, p. 178).

[20] H. Terpstra, *Jacob van Neck*, p. 185; J. C. M. Warnsinck (ed.), *Reisen van Nicolaus de Graaff gedaan naar alle gewesten des Werelds, 1639–1687* (The Hague, 1930).

507

Boxer

BURGHER-
OLIGARCHS AND
MERCHANT-
ADVENTURERS

33. The English Revolution: An Introduction

AUSTIN WOOLRYCH

*The seventeenth century, it has been recognized for some time now, was a
time of crisis, revolution, change, and upheaval throughout much of Europe,
and England was no exception. The middle decades of the century, the 1640's
and 1650's especially, formed a period of civil war in which most of the country was divided on political and religious issues. Ultimately the Puritan forces
and the New Model Army triumphed; King Charles I was tried and publicly
executed; and the country was ruled by new political forces, at first through
the "Rump" or Long Parliament, and then through the virtual dictatorship
of Oliver Cromwell, the Protector. This revolution has held an important
place in English historiography, being pictured as a movement of national
resistance to royal absolutism, or as a vindication of the rights of Parliament
and of religious freedom. While these are undeniably important elements in
the English Revolution, there is still no uniformly held opinion regarding the
causes or the significance of the events of this fateful period.*

*The British Broadcasting Corporation produced a series of talks in 1966 on
the English Revolution, and they were subsequently published in book form.
The following selection is the introductory essay to the collection, written by
Austin Woolrych, Professor of History in the University of Lancaster. His
chapter provides an admirable survey of many of the particular areas of*

Source: Austin Woolrych, *The English Revolution: An Introduction,* in E. W.
Ives, ed., *The English Revolution, 1600–1660* (London: Edward Arnold Ltd., 1968),
pp. 1–33. Copyright © 1968 by Edward Arnold. Reprinted by permission. [Foot-
notes omitted.]

research in recent writing on the subject, as well as much material helpful in understanding the nature of the various controversies. The bulk of the chapter, devoted to a historical sketch of the events of the revolution, reflects a good grasp of recent contributions to several questions of continuing interest to scholars. The student should compare Woolrych's picture of Stuart England with Elliott's view of Spain, or Goubert's discussion of France under Louis XIV, and ask what similarities and differences existed between them. Why did England experience a revolution that succeeded in this period? Why were absolutist tendencies checked? What role could Puritanism have played in the English Revolution?

The student who wishes to pursue this subject could profitably read the other chapters in The English Revolution *to begin, and then consult more specialized works like Christopher Hill's* Puritanism and Revolution *(1958) and* The Century of Revolution *(1961); C. Wilson's* England's Apprenticeship, 1603– 1763 *(1965); and C. V. Wedgwood's* The King's Peace *(1955),* The King's War *(1958), and* A Coffin for King Charles *(1964).*

I

A generation ago it would not have seemed too difficult to write a concise introductory essay on what the English Revolution was about and what happened in it. Samuel Rawson Gardiner's great histories had mapped it out so clearly; Sir Charles Firth had completed the work and presented the authorized version to a wider public in his justly famous biography of Cromwell. Building on their foundations, the young George Macaulay Trevelyan produced, in *England under the Stuarts,* an account brimful of the happy certainties of the Whig tradition. Firth passed the mantle to Godfrey Davies, whose volume in the *Oxford History of England,* published in 1937, was still in most respects an epitome of Gardiner's eighteen volumes.

Today it all looks different, and no major event in our history is more hedged about with question-marks than the Great Rebellion. This is not because the older historians were necessarily wrong, in any simple sense. The factual accuracy of Gardiner and Firth is generally as remarkable as the heroic scale of their researches. It is rather that we are no longer fully satisfied with the kind of explanations that they offered, or with the limited area of national politics on which they mainly concentrated. We have learned to ask new questions of the past. A tardy awareness of developments in the social sciences has led us to broaden the scope of historical studies and enlarge our notions of historical causation. Whatever we personally think of the doctrines of Karl Marx and Max Weber, to name only two giants, their shadows and many others fall inevitably across our pages. Even sixth-formers seem to be expected nowadays to have their views, for example, on how to interpret the rise of the gentry and the relationship between Puritanism and capitalism.

As the dust began to settle on those particular battlefields, we were left realizing how little we still knew about the distribution of wealth and power in Stuart England, or about the relations between economic circumstances and political and religious attitudes. We are emerging, a little clearer-eyed, from a period of grand speculation and hypothesis in seventeenth-century studies. The value of the hypotheses—especially those about the rising or declining fortunes of the gentry and their effects on political allegiance—may ultimately be seen to lie less in their intrinsic validity than in the stimulus they have given to a mass of more detailed and more disciplined research. They helped to show that we can best advance knowledge now by close and quantitative investigation of particular counties, particular institutions or particular social groups. Historians have grown wary of generalizing about England as though it were a homogeneous community; they take fuller account now of the fact that when a gentleman three hundred years ago spoke of his 'country' he meant his county. They see England more realistically as the sum of her many county communities, each an important unit of government, each an arena in which the gentlefolk lived out their social lives and fought out their social rivalries, each inclined to put local interests before national, and in their sum exhibiting a great variety in social make-up and political attitudes.

If we are to comprehend the kind of society in which the political, social and intellectual conflicts of the English Revolution were generated, we should begin by picturing a population less than a tenth as large as that of today and comprising an overwhelming majority of country-dwellers. Out of perhaps four and a half million people in England and Wales, about a quarter of a million lived in London. But London differed in scale from all other towns far more greatly than now. Only a small handful of provincial towns topped the ten thousand mark, and about six Englishmen out of seven lived in communities of less than a thousand souls. There was no mass-association of people in similar jobs such as modern industry and modern urban society provide, and there was therefore no framework in which class-consciousness as we know it today could form itself. The typical community was the village; the commonest occupation small-scale husbandry; the essential social unit the family. Society was a hierarchy, ranging from great nobles down to cottagers and paupers. Before the revolution brought all in doubt, people accepted the fact of social subordination, of differences of degree, and their preachers constantly told them (as Shakespeare had done) that it was part of the divine order of things. For most men, their relations of dependence upon those just above them in the local community and of influence over those just below them mattered much more than any notion of a common class interest with others of the same kind of occupation and income-level in other communities. This is one reason why interpretations of the English Revolution based on modern concepts of class are apt to look anachronistic.

In a society dominated by status rather than class, the crucial dividing line ran between the small minority who could style themselves gentlemen (or above) and the large majority who could not. Perhaps one in twenty-five of the population belonged to families in the former category.

Below that level, men might become constables, parish clerks, churchwardens or possibly overseers of the poor, but their small authority would scarcely stir a ripple beyond the bounds of their village. Those who happened to hold freehold land worth forty shillings a year might cast a vote in a parliamentary election, but these were rare occasions and only quite exceptionally involved any judgment upon national political issues. The great majority of the people lay not only blow the level of political participation but below that of political consciousness as well. When the events of the Civil War threatened to change this state of affairs and prompted questions such as the Levellers and Agitators raised at Putney, most members of the ruling class felt that the tide of revolution was carrying them a great deal too far.

Even if we think of this ruling segment as numbering about one twenty-fifth of the whole people we may tend to exaggerate its size. Women were not expected to concern themselves with politics. Moreover it was land more than any other form of wealth that gave a man status and political weight, and the number of landowners substantial enough to affect decision-making at either national or county level was not very large. Professor Aylmer, in *The King's Servants: the Civil Service of Charles I*, attempts a rough count based on the year 1633, his figures inevitably becoming less definite as he moves down the scale. There were then 122 English peers, twenty-six bishops, and slightly over 300 in a group just below the peerage which included the eldest sons of peers, Englishmen holding Scottish or Irish titles, and the new order of baronets. Then came between 1,500 and 1,800 knights, 7,000–9,000 esquires and 10,000–14,000 mere 'gentlemen'. The last category comprised the lesser landed gentry and many whose status derived not primarily from land but from commercial wealth, professional or academic standing or office under the crown. As a body they were rather on the fringe of the ruling class. It was the ten thousand or so men ranked as esquire or above who really counted politically. It was from their ranks that most of the important county offices were filled—lord lieutenant, deputy lieutenant, sheriff, justice of the peace and so on. They furnished most of the king's servants, the men who mattered in the central administration and the royal household. They took most of the seats in the House of Commons. The higher one goes in the social scale, the larger the proportion of men in each category that one finds actively engaged in national or local politics.

It was a small enough ruling class to be quite close-knit, especially within each county community. Yet as ruling classes went in the monarchies of that time it was reasonably broad, and compared with its counterparts in (say) France or Spain it was much more politically aware and politically responsible. This was partly because English kings had never been rich enough, even if they had felt the need, to erect a bureaucratic local government of professional, salaried officials. They relied on the unpaid services of the peers and leading gentry in the counties and of the most substantial citizens in the corporate towns. The heads of the leading county families executed ordinary justice upon malefactors in their quarter sessions, supervised a wide range of local administration, enforced with varying degrees of zeal a host of statutes, collected the subsidies that parliament voted, mustered the militia—the catalogue could go on a long way. In Stuart England most government was necessarily local government, and the county provided its essential framework. The great problem was for central government to secure collaboration from the county communities; the Great Rebellion marked its crucial failure. Charles I, the Long Parliament and Cromwell learned in turn how assertive and uncooperative the counties could be, for the coming of civil war increased rather than lessened the dependence of England's new masters on the local communities.

The social structure of the English landed classes differed from that of their continental counterparts in one way which had had very important consequences for the development of parliament: only a small élite among them enjoyed the status and privileges of nobility. Elsewhere in Europe, most substantial landowners were noblemen, and newcomers to the land from the ranks of the bourgeoisie sought to acquire noble titles and privileges as soon as possible. The great social divide was between nobleman and commoner, and this was reflected in the composition of national representative assemblies, where they survived. These had most commonly comprised the three separate orders of clergy, nobles and commoners (or third estate), and in many lands they had been weakened by the built-in antagonism between noble landlords and bourgeois traders or officials. There had been various outcomes: total atrophy (as in the French Estates-General), the withdrawal of the nobles and clergy, leaving only a few impotent representatives of the towns (as in Castile), the tyranny of the landowners over the bourgeoisie (as in Brandenburg and Prussia), or in the unique case of the Dutch Republic the ascendancy of an urban patriciate. Even where the estates preserved a reasonable balance between aristocratic and bourgeois interests (as in Saxony or Aragon), they hardly shared the vitality of the English parliament.

In England the titled nobility were remarkably few. There were only fifty-five English peers in 1603, and no more than 121 in 1641. Professor Lawrence Stone has argued in *The Crisis of the Aristocracy 1558–1641* that they suffered a serious though temporary fall in power and prestige under the early Stuarts. Although they largely recovered from the financial crisis that had affected most of them in the later sixteenth century, their military power had largely gone, their holdings of land (and hence their territorial influence) were much depleted, their economic recovery was too often at their tenants' expense, their rank was cheapened because the Stuarts sold noble titles for cash, and many of them became absentee landlords, resident at and dependent on a hated royal court. The great bulk of substantial landowners were not nobles but gentry: baronets, knights, esquires and gentlemen. The relative decline of the titled aristocracy gave this squirearchy a greater political and social influence than ever. But proud as the gentry were of their status, in law they were commoners, and they lacked the essential noble privileges that their French or Spanish equivalents enjoyed. The line that divided gentlemen from the social orders below them was an important one, but it was not so exactly drawn as in the continental monarchies, nor did it mark so deep a fissure. Entry into the ranks of the gentry from below required no royal patent, and a coat of arms could be had for a price. Knights and gentlemen could engage in commercial or industrial enterprises without loss of caste, they intermarried with wealthy burgher families relatively freely, and they often apprenticed their younger sons to the better trades.

Above all, if they wished to serve in parliament they had to seek election to the House of Commons. There was thus no serious clash of social interest between the two Houses, for the richest knights of the shire in the Commons rivalled not a few of the Lords in wealth, and many a peer's son sat in the lower house—forty-eight in the Long Parliament, for example. In the Commons, landed gentlemen and rich citizens sat together, though in very unequal proportions. Legally the Long Parliament should have contained just over four hundred resident burgesses and ninety knights of the shire—more than four townsmen to every one country gentlemen. In fact there were more than four landed gentlemen to every one genuine townsman, for the squires had been taking over the borough seats ever since the fifteenth century. Yet the House of Commons was a strikingly homogeneous body and it showed little tendency to split along class lines. So many great merchants had a foot on the land, so many landowners had a finger in commercial enterprise that no clear line separated them, and there was a further blurring because groups like the lawyers, the courtiers and the royal officials commonly had an interest in both town and country. The fifty or so merchants who sat in an average parliament were a respected body, but commercial wealth carried relatively less political weight than broad acres. If it seems undervalued, however, one should remember how few Englishmen outside London were town-dwellers, and how readily merchants who bought land—as they mostly did—acquired the outlook and values of the landed gentry. The ruling class of Stuart England was in a real sense a single class.

Another factor that strengthened this class in its solidarity against any abuse of government was its veneration for the common law. The Inns of Court were not only training-grounds for professional lawyers but finishing schools for sons of the gentry who wanted no more than a taste of the town and a bit of legal know-how to help them manage their estates and hold up their heads among their fellow justices. But the Inns left their stamp on many a parliament-man—on nearly two-thirds of those originally elected to the Long Parliament, for example. However little serious law they learned, they tended to reduce political or constitutional controversies to legal terms, and it was ominous when the common law, so lately a buttress of the throne, came to be used to erode its foundations. Among the intellectual forebears of the English Revolution none stands so high as Sir Edward Coke.

If we are to sketch the sequence of developments that brought England to the brink of revolution, the first problem is where to begin in time. The conventional starting-point is 1603, the year King James travelled south to take up the Tudor inheritance. In some respects it is too late. The long rise in prices had already taken its toll of the crown's revenue and the lands of the aristocracy; the exceptional mobility of noble and gentry estates was already rising towards the peak it reached in the decade 1610–19. The squirearchy, long indispensable in local government, had already consolidated their hold on the House of Commons and explored there the techniques of opposition. By the fifteen-nineties the great age of Tudor government was clearly passing and the standards of public morality among the queen's servants were already slipping.

Yet in other ways it is misleading to push the genesis of revolution back to 1603. For at least another quarter of a century no one aimed consciously at changing the basic structure of either government or society. King's servants, county magistrates and parliament-men alike sought only to preserve their time-honoured inheritance and hold in trim the precious balance between the crown's necessary prerogatives and the subject's lawful rights. The great majority of the representatives of the local communities remained basically conservative, even when they came up all angry to the Long Parliament. Nevertheless the advent of the Stuarts soon led to fresh tensions in the body politic, and is as good a point as any at which to take up the story.

The thirty-seven years that separate the general joy at James's accession from the general indignation of 1640 fall into four stages. The first spans the remaining life-time of the last of Elizabeth's great ministers, Robert Cecil, whom James made Earl of Salisbury. Until he died in 1612, Salisbury maintained something of Tudor competence in the royal administration, but his efforts were constantly undermined by the king. James was indolent and extravagant; worse, he looked upon the main offices in his gift less as places of public trust than as rewards to distribute among his friends. As Professor Trevor-Roper has put it, 'he did not choose men for his jobs, but bestowed jobs on his men.' Thereby he not only accelerated the deterioration in the public service but alienated many of his English subjects, who could not bear to see so many coveted prizes go to Scotsmen and boon companions. The long first parliament of the reign, spanning nearly seven years, probed many issues that would lead to greater conflict later. Finance was prominent among them; resentment was growing against the king's feudal rights of wardship and purveyance, and the controversial impositions—additional import duties imposed by royal prerogative—started the commons on their mounting opposition to the crown's powers of economic regulation. James by his tactlessness provoked more than one wrangle over the Commons' traditional privileges, he claiming that they depended on the favour of his grant, they retorting that their privileges were theirs by right. There were also disputes over religion. The Commons, baulked in their own attempts to initiate further reforms in the church, challenged the canons passed by convocation in 1604 and took up the cause of the Puritan ministers who were deprived of their livings under them. But this was border-skirmishing compared with what came later, and the Tudor framework of government still held.

The next stage takes us to 1621 and marks a further sharp decline in the quality of government. It was also a period of non-parliamentary rule, for in ten whole years after the dissolution of January 1611, there was only one brief and sterile parliament in 1614. For six years after Salisbury's death a faction led by the Howard clan dominated the king's counsels, and the royal service was steadily undermined by incompetence, corruption and extravagance. These were the years when James's flashy young favourites made their notorious careers out of his weakness; first Robert Carr, who rose to the earldom of Somerset, and then after Carr's scandalous downfall in 1615, George Villiers, created Earl and finally Duke of Buckingham. These were the years also when offices came to be bought and sold as never before, and by 1618 the whole royal patronage was virtually controlled by Buckingham, to his enormous profit. There was a brisk traffic in titles too. The new rank of baronet was created in 1611 simply to be sold, and the trade in peerages began four years later. When offices of state became the sport of minions and the kingdom's highest honours were put up for cash, a growing proportion of the nobility and gentry began to nurse a sense of outrage.

The conduct of national policy deepened their resentment. The Howards did all they could to align England with Spain, and even after Buckingham supplanted them, the man who most influenced James's foreign policy was Count Gondomar, the Spanish ambassador. When James took up the idea of marrying Prince Charles to a Spanish Infanta and increasingly relaxed the penal laws against the Roman Catholics, most of his subjects felt that the nationalist and protestant ideals of their proud Elizabethan past were being betrayed. This feeling intensified after the Thirty Years' War broke out on the continent, and above all when in 1620 James's daughter Elizabeth and her husband the Elector Palatine became refugees, their principality occupied by Spanish troops.

These humiliations and the growing disreputability of the king's service were driving an ominous new division through the political nation, a division between Court and Country. The terms came into contemporary usage in just this period. The 'Court interest' included not only what we should call courtiers but all who served the king in the central government and administration, all who wrung sinecures and other lucrative grants from his bounty, and by extension the many gentry in the counties who looked to his ministers and favourites as patrons. The Country by contrast embraced all those gentry who were free of dependence on the Court and were coming to regard it as a swollen and vicious parasite. The Court-Country cleavage showed clearly in the Addled Parliament of 1614, whose stormy sittings demonstrated on the one hand that James's government had quite lost the Tudor arts of managing parliament, and on the other that the Commons had not yet thrown up leaders of their own who could temper the tactics of opposition with responsible statesmanship.

This was a time too when the claims of the royal prerogative were increasingly questioned by the common lawyers, Coke chief among them. James's dismissal of Coke from the Chief Justiceship of the King's Bench in 1616 was a sad landmark, to be followed by further threats to the independence of the judiciary. To make matters worse, the prosperity of James's earlier years had by then collapsed, and the main cause was his own ill-judged decision to transfer the trading rights of the Merchant Adventurers, who controlled cloth exports to the Low Countries, to a mushroom syndicate headed by Alderman Cockayne. The crown's prerogative powers over the affairs of merchants were brought into still further disrepute by the multiplication of monopolies, and once again Buckingham and his protégés were the chief profiteers.

After a long lapse in parliamentary activity, the period from 1621 to 1629—our third stage—was one of frequent parliaments and mounting constitutional conflict. It began against a background of deepening economic depression. After a brief recovery from the Cockayne fiasco the cloth trade began to slump again even more disastrously, and a series of wretched harvests, coinciding with widespread unemployment, brought hunger and misery to many parts of England. This time the government was not to blame, for the causes lay in England's war-wracked continental markets, but the traditional palliatives that the privy council applied never took the measure of the chronic depression in our one major industry. Recovery set in by 1625, but it was never more than partial and precarious.

The parliament of 1621 however was troubled even more by political than by economic discontents. It revived the process of impeachment, which had lain disused since the Wars of the Roses, and employed it to bring down one of the king's greatest ministers, Francis Bacon, now Viscount St. Albans and Lord Chancellor. The charge was that he took bribes, but his real offences were his association with Buckingham and his championship of the royal prerogative. More impeachments were to follow, and parliament was launched on its long struggle to render the king's ministers accountable to itself. In the same year the Commons dared to challenge the king on the hitherto sacred ground of foreign policy. Their clamour for war with Spain was foolish, yet three years later Buckingham joined the warmongers, and within two years more he had England at war with France as well as Spain. The results were a scale of expenditure that made the government desperate for supplies, and a series of military and naval disgraces that bred a bitter sense of national humiliation and a crescendo of fury against the favourite.

Charles I's accession in 1625 made little immediate difference, for the old king's grip had been slackening for some time and the new one was even more completely under Buckingham's sway. But in the parliament of that year the Commons abused their power of the purse by seeking to grant the customs duties of tonnage and poundage for one year only, and their successors of 1626 refused supplies for the war altogether until their grievances were redressed. They regarded Buckingham as 'the grievance of grievances', and only another dissolution prevented them from impeaching him. Charles then appealed directly to the nation for a free gift, and when that failed in face of the gentry's solid resistance he imposed a huge forced loan. Many gentlemen refused to pay and went to gaol, and some of them raised an important test case as to the crown's right to imprison them for reasons of state without trial. The judges found for the king, but the next parliament (1628) took up the cause of the subject's liberty most vigorously. The outcome was the Petition of Right, whereby Charles was forced to acknowledge that he could neither raise taxes, gifts nor loans without parliament's consent, nor imprison his subjects without declaring the cause and entitling them to a trial at law. Soon after this victory, the nation celebrated another deliverance: Buckingham was assassinated.

Yet early in 1629 the Commons threw off the statesmanlike restraint that had secured the Petition of Right and flew at the so-called Arminian divines who enjoyed Charles I's special patronage. These high churchmen, of whom William Laud was emerging as the leader, were obnoxious to ordinary protestant Englishmen, whether Puritans or not, on several grounds: their reintroduction of altars, vestments and liturgical practices that seemed to hark back to popery; their reaction—similarly suspect —against Calvinist theology; their high clerical pretensions, especially their claim that the office and authority of bishop were *jure divino*, ordained by the law of God; their preaching that it was sin to raise the least question of the king's authority; and their efforts to recover for the church some of the wealth of which it had been plundered since the Reformation. The last parliamentary session before 1640 ended violently, with the Speaker held down weeping in his chair while the Commons acclaimed wild resolutions that anyone who promoted popery and Arminianism, or advised the levying of tonnage and poundage without parliament's consent, 'shall be reputed a capital enemy to this kingdom and commonwealth'. This suggestion that there were treasons against the state distinct from treasons against the king momentarily opened a glimpse into a terrifying future in which king, Lords and Commons, the three pillars of England's much-vaunted 'mixed monarchy', might fall irreparably apart.

Yet a long calm descended upon the country during the last phase before the Great Rebellion. These eleven years without a parliament have sometimes been called a tyranny, but they were not that. The crown assumed no new despotic powers; the counties went on as before under the rule of their leading families and the law took its customary course. Nor were they really years of personal rule by Charles I, for he quite lacked the zest and energy for such a rôle. The true centre of national government reverted to the privy council, now no longer eclipsed by one imperious favourite but an arena once more for contending factions. Lord Treasurer Weston achieved a certain ascendancy in the early sixteen-thirties, Archbishop Laud in the later. The man of most formidable stature in the king's service, Thomas, Viscount Wentworth, was kept far from the hub of affairs, first in the Council of the North and then in Ireland, and was not admitted to Charles's full trust until 1639. Charles I's councillors were not an imposing lot, but their government was not notably inefficient or corrupt by the lowish standards of the time, and it did renounce some of the worst abuses of the Buckingham period.

Why then did this government become so hated that the political nation would finally accept its direction no longer? Some textbooks account for it too simply in terms of 'illegal' taxation and Puritan opposition to Archbishop Laud. The issues were really wider. Obviously, the financial expedients whereby the crown avoided recourse to parliament were disliked in themselves. Distraint of knighthood, the doubled revenues wrung from wardship, the new monopolies under the guise of corporations, the 'compositions' exacted for encroaching on long-forgotten royal forests or contravening obsolescent statutes against depopulation or building in the suburbs of London—all these smelt of legal chicanery and often bore harshly upon individuals. Ship money was hated more because it was a land tax in disguise and because it threatened to obviate the necessity for parliaments indefinitely.

Yet England remained one of the most lightly taxed countries in Europe, and Englishmen cared not only about what they had to pay but what they were paying for. More than half Charles's revenue went to sustain his court and courtiers, and the alienation between Court and Country was growing ever deeper. The court was no longer the splendid show-case through which Elizabeth had wooed her public, no longer the natural focus of the whole world of quality, no longer the proper centre to which honourable ambition and talent gravitated in the hope of a career of public service. To most of the gentry it seemed a côterie apart, alien to their aspirations and offensive to their prejudices. There were too many papists in high places, not only in the entourage of Queen Henrietta Maria but even in the privy council itself. Neither Charles nor Laud ever wavered in his Anglican loyalties, but the association between popery and Arminianism came naturally to the average protestant Englishman. Foreign policy seemed to bear it out, for the war with Spain was quickly wound up and through most of the thirties Charles reverted to the pro-Spanish alignment of his father's time. It went hard that England should aid the Spaniards in their renewed war against the Dutch Republic, where many an Englishman had shed his blood for the protestant cause.

The religion of Laud and the Arminians displayed itself more and more as a court religion. The king upheld the divine right of bishops; the bishops inflated the hitherto accepted divine right of kings into a doctrine of virtual absolutism. The prominent presence of the three highest prelates—the Archbishops of Canterbury and York and the Bishop of London—in the privy council went against a long tradition, and was much disliked. The courts of Star Chamber and High Commission were used more conspicuously to enforce a censorship and repress critics of the régime in church and state; the savage sentences on Prynne, Bastwick, Burton and Lilburne rebounded eventually upon those who inflicted them.

The most general grievance of all came to be that what contemporaries called the fundamental laws, and we would call the constitution, were being deliberately subverted; that parliament was suppressed so that government could pursue policies in church and state that were abhorrent to most of the nation. Resistance, especially to the payment of ship money, was already beginning when in 1638 rebellion broke out in Scotland against the imposition of a prayer book similar to England's. The king's government in Scotland rapidly collapsed, and Charles's attempt to restore it by English arms failed ignominiously. Too many of his English subjects had sympathy more with the Scots' cause than with his. After this military fiasco, in 1639 Charles at last called Wentworth home to be his chief minister and made him Earl of Strafford. On Strafford's advice he summoned the first parliament for eleven years, but this Short Parliament would do nothing for him unless he redressed a comprehensive list of grievances, and he dissolved it after only three weeks. Strafford advised him that he was now 'loose and absolved from all rules of government', and in the brief interval before the reckoning came England caught a whiff of real tyranny. But in the second 'Bishops' War' of 1640 the Scots marched first, drove the English militia back from the river Tyne in disorder, and forced Charles to conclude a humiliating truce. They were to remain in occupation of the northern counties, and England was to pay their keep.

III

Nothing could now save Charles, try as he would, from calling another parliament. The Long Parliament met on 3 November 1640, and within ten months it carried through the decisive victory of the Country over the Court. The Court element in the Commons was the smallest on record, and it was helpless against the serried ranks of opposition than John Pym marshalled so skilfully. Strafford and Laud were promptly impeached, and when Strafford's prosecutors failed to pin charges on him that the Lords would accept as treason, they hustled him to the scaffold with an arbitrary act of attainder. By that time Pym and his supporters were already tackling the abuses of the last decade with a momentous series of constitutional bills, and Charles, with two armies to be paid and no resources, was powerless to refuse them.

Yet these Country politicians were mostly conservative rather than revolutionary in spirit. They wanted to restore the equilibrium of the 'balanced polity' which they had inherited from the Tudors, and which Charles I had tilted—though not so far as they made out—in the direction of continental absolutism. All the famous statutes that they passed in 1641 claimed a basis in existing law and precedent, though neither their law nor their history was very sound. Taken together, these acts marked a considerable advance towards constitutional monarchy, yet they left the essential prerogatives of the crown intact, and a wiser king than Charles would have accepted them with a better grace. The Triennial Act provided that henceforth not more than three years should ever elapse without a session of parliament. Another act secured that the present parliament—it applied to no others—should not be dissolved without its own consent. Two more acts abolished the Court of Star Chamber, together with the prerogative jurisdiction of the councils in the North and in the Marches, and the High Commission. The Tonnage and Poundage Act made all duties levied at the ports, new impositions as well as old customs, subject to parliamentary consent. Further statutes condemned ship money and the other financial expedients of the thirties, and closed the remaining loopholes for non-parliamentary taxation. Parliament thus assured its regular summons in the future, strengthened its power of the purse and established the clear supremacy of the common law, but so far it still left England with a monarch who could rule as well as reign.

There remained the question of religion, and on this the members were less united. It was probably only because the Lords rejected a bill to exclude the bishops from the upper House that the Commons debated a more radical one that would have abolished the whole ecclesiastical hierarchy 'root and branch'. Yet this Root and Branch Bill was dropped in the end, and the signs were that the moderate majority in both Houses would settle for some modifications of episcopal authority and of the prayer book rather than permit the abolition of either.

By the late summer of 1641, when parliament treated itself to its first recess, the fierce tensions of the past year were relaxing. The Scots had signed a treaty and withdrawn, and the English forces that had faced them were being disbanded. The measures already passed were as much as most moderate men wanted, and the country looked forward to a fresh start on the now tolerably secure basis of constitutional monarchy. Yet within a year England was plunged in civil war. Why?

The event which did most to precipitate the crisis was the appalling rebellion which broke out in Ulster in October and then spread rapidly through most of Ireland. The story of massacre and atrocity was heightened a hundredfold in the telling, and it magnified the bogy of popery into a huge spectre, menacing England herself. It sharpened acutely the opposition's distrust of Charles, for the Irish rebels falsely claimed his sanction for their seizure of protestant property. Charles himself gave too much ground for distrust by his absence in Scotland, whither he had gone in August in the hope of building up a party for himself among the Scottish nobles. The Irish terror necessitated the raising of a new army in England, yet if military power were put into the king's hands—and there was neither law nor precedent for putting it in anyone else's—could he be trusted to use it only against the Irish? This question enabled Pym to press for an answer to another that the parliament had so far left still open: the question of how to ensure that the king governed through ministers who commanded parliament's confidence, without encroaching on his hitherto undoubted right to choose his own servants. Pym now launched a frontal attack on that right. On 8 November he carried the Commons in a demand that the king should 'employ only such counsellors and ministers as should be approved by his parliament'—or else parliament would take the suppression of the Irish rebellion into its own hands. A fortnight later the Commons passed the Grand Remonstrance, but by a majority of only eleven. Nominally addressed to the king, it was really a manifesto to the nation of all that evil counsellors had done amiss in the past fifteen years and all that parliament intended by way of redress. In December and January Pym went further and bid for parliamentary control over the militia. It was the gravest encroachment on the royal prerogative that the Commons had yet dared.

Outside the walls of the parliament-house the atmosphere of crisis was growing thicker. The crowds that had clamoured for Strafford's head were out again in the London streets, rabbling the bishops on their way to the house of lords. Twelve of them protested that they dared no longer attend and that parliament's proceedings were void in their absence. Pym promptly impeached them. A few days later the annual elections to the Common Council of London swung decisively his way, and he found means soon after of securing the government of the City in the hands of his allies. Then in the first week of 1642 Charles committed his crowning blunder by going to the House of Commons in person to arrest Pym and four other leaders of the opposition. The City gave them refuge and called out its militia, and for a hectic week London wore the aspect of a great capital on the verge of revolution.

The immediate storm died down, and anxious men on both sides laboured to avert the threat of civil war. But the essential issues over which the war would be fought were already defined, and from now on the political nation was steadily driven towards one camp or the other. Should parliament wrest control over the militia from the crown? Should the king's choice of ministers and officers of state be subjected to parliamentary approval? Should parliament initiate a thorough reformation of the national church, and if so were episcopacy and the liturgy to be merely reformed or struck down root and branch? The radicals' demands on these points went far beyond the limited constitutional objectives of the acts that the parliament had passed so far. Unlike those acts, they could claim no basis in the ancient fundamental laws; no cloak of antiquarian respectability could be thrown over a programme that could now fairly be called revolutionary. As the issues changed, so did the alignment of parties. Between the Grand Remonstrance of November 1641 and the outbreak of war nine months later, the nation divided between Royalists and Parliamentarians, and the line of division was very different from that between Court and Country in 1640. Many of the old Country interest that had supported the legislation of 1641 were dismayed at the demands that Pym was now pressing and at his methods of enlisting support for them. Charles rallied them to his side with a series of skilful and conciliatory declarations which were largely the work of one of their own number, Edward Hyde, the future Earl of Clarendon. The old Court interest was equally split. Although many fought for the king, many others retreated into neutrality, and a sizable minority went over to the Parliamentarians.

Most Englishmen faced the threat of civil war with extreme reluctance, and the division between the two sides was never clear-cut or complete. Recent research has shown what a considerable proportion of the political nation remained neutral, or at least as neutral as it expediently could. There were of course fully committed men on both sides: 'old cavaliers' who regarded the parliament-dogs as mere rebels, and radicals who wanted a decisive transfer of executive as well as legislative power to parliament. Without them there would have been no Civil War. But the majority, even of those who engaged themselves on either side, did not see the issues in such black-and-white terms. Many Parliamentarians had no real wish either for further constitutional changes beyond those of 1641 or for the abolition of episcopacy; they were just uneasily persuaded that Charles could not be trusted to honour what he had been forced to concede unless his hands were further tied. Many Royalists on the other hand approved the recent statutes and disliked popery and Arminianism no less than their more moderate opponents. Between these large moderate groups on either side there was no profound difference of principle; their choice mainly depended on whether they regarded the untrustworthiness of the king or the risks and stigma of rebellion as the greater evil. When allegiance was so often divided by a hair's breadth, and when it so often shifted from one side to the other or hung uneasily poised between the two, we should be very wary of entertaining any simple or single explanation of the alignment of parties on the eve of civil war.

The line of division between Royalists and Parliamentarians, though different from that between Court and Country in the recent past, still ran right through the ruling class of Stuart England. Every order of society, every kind of occupation, was represented in considerable numbers on both sides. The motives that inclined men one way or the other were varied. Loyalty to the king might stem from simple sentiment or from a professional career in the royal service, and either way it was commonly reinforced by affection for the Anglican church order and liturgy, attachment to the old fundamental laws of the land, and a dread lest all this whipping up of popular support and arming of the people against their betters should subvert the whole social order that held the ranks and degrees of men in their due places. There was a note of fear in the social contempt which the cavaliers so often professed towards their adversaries. Motivation on the parliamentary side probably ranged still more widely. Radicals like Henry Parker, the pamphleteer, believed that sovereignty derived from the people and that the people's representatives should be the final arbiters in a national crisis like that of 1642—provided that the nobles and gentry in parliament maintained the exclusive right to speak for the people. There were probably some of the fringes of the political nation who questioned even this proviso, though their voices would not be heard much just yet. More general was a negative determination to put it out of the power of 'evil counsellors' at court to do the country further harm. Puritans naturally backed parliament's demand for a thorough reformation of religion, and many (like Richard Baxter) whose religious aims were not very radical were swayed by their moral judgment upon the king's party. Others were moved more by wrongs suffered at the hands of the king's agents during the years of arbitrary rule, and others again by frustration in their business enterprises through the crown's abuse of economic regulation. In some counties and towns, moreover, the split ran much along the lines of purely local feuds and factions.

There was a rough geographical division between the two sides. East Anglia, the south-east and south were predominantly Parliamentarian, while the king's cause was strongest in the south-west, in Wales and the border-counties and in the far north. Not surprisingly, Puritanism was strong in most of the former areas and religious conservatism (whether Anglican or Roman Catholic) in the latter. The Parliamentarian regions were also richer, more populous, generally more advanced both in agriculture and industry, the Royalist ones sparser, poorer and more backward. There are many difficulties however in the way of accepting the Marxist thesis that this line of cleavage implied a kind of class antagonism between a 'bourgeois' type of landowner on the one side and a 'feudal' type on the other. Yet it does look as though impoverished gentility was temperamentally more inclined to Royalism than to its opposite, and this despite Professor Trevor-Roper's theory that the core of radical opposition lay in the declining gentry of the backwoods. The remoter Royalist regions were thick with small, struggling gentlemen who were mostly as loyal as their greater neighbours, and we know that in some divided counties such as Yorkshire a higher proportion of Royalist than of Parliamentarian gentry were in financial straits. The geographical division however was far from clear-cut, for right down the centre of England from Yorkshire and Lancashire to Somerset and Wiltshire ran a chain of divided or disputed counties, and no shire in England was without some supporters of each side.

Turning to the main social groups, many more peers fought for the king than against him, though the Parliamentarian minority was quite formidable. The landed gentry however played much the most important part in both the fighting and the politics of the Civil War years and they were much more evenly divided. It is likely that over England as a whole rather more of the leading country families just below the peerage were for the king, though not by any means in every county. About the lesser gentry historians are still busy finding out, for the regional variation was very great. As for the merchants, the biggest men in London and the ruling oligarchies in some important provincial towns were predominantly Royalist, but despite such significant exceptions the majority were for the parliament. Over large areas of England the towns stood out in opposition to a predominantly Royalist countryside, as did the rural clothing areas in the West Riding, in Lancashire and elsewhere. Several contemporaries remarked how much support the parliament got from 'the middling sort' —yeomen, substantial tenant farmers, traders and clothiers in a modest way of business, solid independent craftsmen and the like. This is broadly true, though the middling sort then did not mean the same as what we understand by the middle classes. Below this level of society it is not safe to generalize, for the degree of involvement varied so much, and so does the surviving evidence.

Perhaps historians concentrate too much on the line-up of parties at the outbreak of war. It had already changed greatly since Court and Country first faced each other in the Long Parliament, and it would change again as the revolution became more radical in the later forties. The ranks would re-align and further sub-divide, for the Civil War engendered more conflicts than it resolved.

As late as February 1642 there seemed nothing inevitable about the drift into civil war. Pym's hold on the parliament could still be precarious; the king's declarations sounded plausible and his concessions tempting. Charles actually assented to an act excluding bishops from the House of Lords. He offered high office to former opponents, even to Pym himself. He was even prepared to treat, too late, over the militia and the objectionable ceremonies in Anglican worship. The trouble was that his public declarations spoke with one voice and his actions with another. Space forbids a re-telling of the intrigues and blunders that undermined confidence in him, but they played into Pym's hands. When parliament passed the Militia Ordinance in March and claimed for it the full force of law despite the refusal of the royal assent, the hopes of a peaceful settlement dwindled fast. Charles withdrew to York, and when he summoned the loyal peers and M.P.s to his side he left the radical men firmly in command at Westminster. Their demands inevitably grew more uncompromising. Both sides raised forces during the summer, and on 22 August Charles gave the formal signal for war by raising his standard at Nottingham.

We cannot follow the course of the fighting, but the changing fortunes of battle gave rise to two developments which greatly affected the political and religious outcome. The first happened when parliament, brought near to defeat in the summer of 1643, allied with the Scots. The Solemn League and Covenant between the two nations gave Scotland a voice in the eventual settlement and pledged England to establish a Presbyterian national church. But although Scottish arms helped to win the great battle of Marston Moor in July 1644, this was not the decisive victory that it should have been. Parliament's generals, the Earls of Essex and Manchester, did not want to fight the war to a finish. They feared that the consequences would go far beyond their original war aims, vague as those were, and they were anxious for a negotiated peace. Death had removed Pym from his struggle to prevent the parliament from splitting between a war party and a peace party, and the split opened wide when Oliver Cromwell charged Manchester, his own general, before the House of Commons for his 'backwardness to all action'. It was not a personal vendetta, for as soon as the charge was substantiated Cromwell and his allies dropped it in favour of more positive measures: the resignation of all peers and M.P.s from their military commands and the forging of an instrument of total victory in the New Model Army.

The New Model, with Sir Thomas Fairfax as Lord General and Cromwell at the head of the cavalry, took the field in 1645. It won the decisive battle of Naseby in June and brought the whole war to an end a year later, but its impact on the course of the revolution had only just begun. Charles surrendered to the Scots, knowing how disquieted they were at the radical Independent temper of the New Model Army. Indeed they were inclined to help him back to his throne if he would only take the Covenant and guarantee a Presbyterian settlement of religion in England as well as Scotland. This he would not do; nor would he accept the severe terms offered to him by the English parliament. The Scots handed him over to the parliament's custody, but he was not too dismayed. He had already begun a long game of temporizing and intrigue, and he reckoned to exploit the divisions among his enemies until either they lowered their conditions or he succeeded in raising military assistance abroad.

The parliament was indeed divided, and the broad cleavage between conservative and radical factions extended to the county committees which had managed the war effort at the local level. One set of issues was political, and arose from the problems of settling the kingdom in face of the king's refusal of parliament's terms. The other great issue was religion, over which a contest developed between the Presbyterian objective of a uniform, all-embracing national church and the Independents' plea for liberty of conscience. Contemporaries labelled the two main parliamentary groupings 'Presbyterian' and 'Independent', whether the matter of debate was political or religious, and in spite of the fact that in these two quite different contexts the line of division was by no means the same: political conservatives were not necessarily Presbyterians by religious conviction, nor were all the radical men religious Independents. What broadly characterized the 'political' Presbyterians was a desire to restore the king as soon as possible, a profound distrust of the New Model's intentions, acute sensitivity to any threat against the established hierarchy of rank and degree (such as they sensed in the army and in the Puritan sects), and reluctance to consider any political changes beyond what were necessary to secure the interests of their own kind. The Independents covered a wider political spectrum, ranging from moderates, who differed from the Presbyterians more in tactics than in principles, to genuine radicals, the nucleus of a republican party. They opposed any sell-out to the king; they were readier to consider constitutional and legal reforms whose benefits would extend beyond the traditional ruling class; they looked to the army as allies, being generally outvoted in parliament; and if they were not tolerationists by conviction (as many were) they were impelled that way by their dependence on the army.

The Presbyterians wanted to disband the army as soon as possible, and in the war-weary, over-taxed, economically depressed England of 1647 they naturally had much support in this aim. But they pursued it with such a shabby disregard for the soldiers' rights, including their arrears of pay, and put such blatant slights upon the men who had won their battles, that the regiments spontaneously elected 'Agitators' from the rank and file to represent their grievances. By one provocation after another the Presbyterians drove the army into open revolt. It broke out in June when the regiments marched in defiance of parliament's orders to a general rendezvous at Newmarket. Cornet Joyce carried the king off to join them there, and thither fled Cromwell, threatened now by the Presbyterians with impeachment. Officers and soldiers covenanted together not to disband until their grievances—and not theirs only but the people's —were redressed. They were talking now of much larger matters than their arrears of pay. They demanded that parliament should expel their detractors, fix a date for its own dissolution, reform its whole constitution by a rational redistribution of seats, and provide for future elections at short and regular intervals. The army, in fact, was claiming to speak for the people of England. In order to give it a single voice and to keep the Agitators within bounds, its commanders established a General Council of the Army on which each regiment was represented by two officers and two soldiers, elected by their fellows.

The Presbyterian politicians at first showed some fight, and then, when they began to yield to the army's intimidation, a mob of Londoners invaded the House of Commons and forced it to call the king back to his capital. Fairfax marched his troops in and cowed both parliament and City. But force would not in itself settle the kingdom's problems, and the generals were already seeking another solution by negotiating with Charles themselves. The pacemaker in this as in most other political moves by the army was Cromwell's very gifted son-in-law, Commissary-General Ireton. His 'Heads of the Proposals' for a conditional reinstatement of the king were in most ways more statesmanlike than the parliament's terms—more concerned with positive political reforms, more tolerant in religion, more lenient to the beaten Royalists and less of an affront to traditional regal authority. But there were three obstacles to their acceptance. The first was Charles himself, who temporized over them as he had over parliament's offers, vainly confident that time or force would bring them both lower. Then there was the question of how to make parliament accept them, even if Charles did. Finally, a growing section of the army was rebelling against the whole negotiation. The Leveller movement had been taking shape in London since the previous year, and by the autumn of 1647 it had formulated a programme for a popular commonwealth that had no place in it for either king or lords. The Levellers were working on the army through its Agitators, and in September five regiments elected new Agitators of a still more radical colour who became the spearhead of an effort to enlist the entire soldiery, if necessary in defiance of their officers, in support of a new political deal based on the suffrages of all the free people of England. Faced with the implacable hostility of the parliament and of the ruling class it represented, the Levellers were bidding for control of the army in order to forge it into an instrument of revolutionary action. The crucial confrontation between the army commanders and the Leveller-indoctrinated Agitators took place in some famous debates in Putney church. The inconclusive outcome was that Ireton and Cromwell failed to convince their radical subordinates by argument, while the latter's attempt to raise a mutiny was a fiasco.

The whole situation was more tangled and uncertain than at any time since the first outbreak of war. Charles however chose to cut through it with a sword. In November 1647, between the Putney debates and the abortive meeting, he fled from the army's custody to Carisbrooke in the Isle of Wight. There, even if he did not win the Governor to his side as he had hoped, he managed to negotiate with certain commissioners from Scotland without the army chiefs breathing down his neck. A new party had taken over from the strict Covenanters in Scotland, a party which was headed by Charles's old councillor the Duke of Hamilton and was ready to fight for his restoration without forcing him or his subjects to take the Covenant against their wills. On 26 December Charles signed a fatal Engagement with Hamilton's commissioners, they undertaking to send an army to his aid, he to call the cavaliers to arms once more.

The secret could not be kept for long. The army closed its ranks; generals and Agitators joined in vowing to bring 'Charles Stuart, that man of blood' to account for his crimes. The parliament was more divided, but in January it voted to treat with him no further. The second Civil War began in the spring of 1648 with a series of Royalist risings, the most formidable being in the originally Parliamentarian counties of Kent and Essex. But these Royalists' gallantry was thrown to waste because the Scots failed to march soon enough to support them. They were all either defeated or contained by the time in August that Cromwell fell upon the Scots at Preston and annihilated them in a three-days' running fight. The war was then virtually over, and Charles was a ruined gambler.

Yet even now it seemed that his ruin might not be total. Moderate men had seen in this last war a choice of evils—a choice between a restoration carried by Scottish arms or the final triumph of the army and its Independent allies. The one would bring an unbridled Royalist reaction; the other starkly threatened monarchy itself. And with monarchy the whole system of gentry power and social subordination stood in danger, for even if the Levellers were checked, the displacement of the ruling county families by lesser men, already widely apparent, would be bound to go further. So the Presbyterian politicians reopened negotiations with Charles and desperately sought agreement with him all through the late autumn. It was more than the army could stand. Ireton really took charge now, for Fairfax was miserably torn and Cromwell took refuge from decision in the siege of Royalist Pontefract. The army secured the king once more, marched into London early in December and purged the parliament by forcibly excluding the Presbyterian majority. Cromwell arrived on the scene at last; his long spell of perplexed self-communing was in process of giving way to a mood of fierce resolution. The Independent remnant of the House of Commons charged the king with waging war upon the people of England and erected a High Court of Justice consisting of its own more radical members and a large stiffening of army officers. Charles refused to plead before this revolutionary tribunal, but its purpose was inexorable. His head fell on a scaffold before Whitehall Palace on 30 January, 1649.

The Rump of the Long Parliament now became the supreme authority in a commonwealth without either king or House of Lords. Thus the conflict between Presbyterians and Independents was resolved by force, but there still remained the latent conflict between the Levellers and the new wielders of power in both the parliament and the army. It did not remain latent for long. The Levellers had been deluded into hoping that the army grandees would sponsor at least a modified version of their plan for a popular commonwealth based on an Agreement of the People. The Council of Officers debated it, diluted it, presented it to the Rump and allowed it to be quietly shelved. Instead of representative government broad-based on the people's suffrages, the Levellers confronted an oligarchy of calculating politicians, many of them elected more than eight years ago and all sustained by the sharp swords of the grandees. Once more they set in motion their machinery of pamphlets, petitions and mass demonstrations, and this time they raised quite serious mutinies in the army. But their hold on the soldiery could not really challenge that of Fairfax and Cromwell, and after the crushing of the mutinies their movement lost cohesion and declined.

To do the army leaders justice, the Rump was not the kind of government they really wanted, but they knew how precariously the young Commonwealth stood and how fatal a genuine appeal to the people would have been after the fearful shock of the king's execution. They faced an immediate threat from Ireland, where Cromwell conducted a ruthless campaign. Within a year a no less serious danger from Scotland called him home, for the young Charles II swallowed his pride and put himself and his cause into the hands of the Scottish Covenanters. Cromwell now took Fairfax's place as Lord General, for Fairfax had scruples about attacking former allies with whom he had sworn the Solemn League and Covenant, and he resigned. But England had either to invade or be invaded. Cromwell never found a tougher enemy than his old comrade-in-arms David Leslie, or saved himself more spectacularly from defeat than in his superb victory at Dunbar on 3 September, 1650. But the young king still had friends and arms to call upon in Scotland, and next summer he staked them all upon a southward march into England. It ended at Worcester, a year to the day after Dunbar—for Cromwell the 'crowning mercy', for the Royalists the last appearance on an English battlefield.

After three hard seasons of campaigning, Cromwell and the army now came back into politics. Their dissatisfaction with their parliamentary masters grew steadily stronger. The Rump would not undertake to dissolve itself before November 1654; it temporized endlessly over the settlement of religion and the reform of the law; it kept old sores open by confiscating hundreds of minor Royalist estates; it offended Cromwell's ideal of a united 'protestant interest' by making war on the Dutch. The army's accusations of general corruption were much exaggerated, but its basic grievance was that these worldly-minded politicians had no real care for 'the interest of the people of God' and were sticking like leeches to their positions of power and profit. The final crisis came in April 1653 when the Rump tried to rush through a bill providing at last for a new parliament—a bill which does not survive, but was for some reason profoundly unacceptable to the army. Cromwell's answer was that famous file of musketeers which cleared the chamber and locked its doors.

What happened next can only be understood in the light of mounting religious enthusiasm in a powerful section of the army. A vociferous minority, headed by Major-General Harrison, were convinced that the millennium was at hand, when Antichrist was to be overthrown and 'the saints shall take the kingdom and possess it'. Cromwell's vision was less crude than Harrison's, but he too thought he glimpsed 'the day of the power of Christ'. He could not summon an elected parliament anyway; not only had he no legal right, but having made enemies in turn of the Royalist, the Presbyterian and now most of the Independent politicians, he could expect only hostility and confusion from such a body. So he and the Council of Officers decided on a nominated assembly as the new supreme authority, and they chose and summoned 139 'men fearing God, and of approved integrity' to represent England (by counties), Wales, Scotland and Ireland. Unfortunately the officers were not at one in what they expected of this assembly. Cromwell and his more realistic colleagues envisaged a temporary government which was to educate the nation in the blessings of a commonwealth until it could once more safely choose its own governors, and they nominated mostly men of some substance and experience. Harrison and the fanatics, by contrast, intended a rule of the saints in preparation for the imminent reign of Christ as king, and they named many obscure sectarian zealots. No wonder Barebone's Parliament, as it came to be called, tended to split between a moderate majority and a firebrand minority. The latter attempted to abrogate the whole common law in favour of a simple written code; they aimed to abolish not only tithes but lay patronage over parish livings and indeed any kind of established ministry in the church. To Cromwell they seemed to be threatening not only religion but property too, and he was thoroughly relieved when in December, after five months' sitting, the moderate majority walked out in disgust and resigned their authority back into his hands.

There was nothing for it now but to take up the burden himself, for as he said 'we were running headlong into confusion and disorder.' He accepted a written constitution, the Instrument of Government, from the hands of a small group of officers headed by Major-General Lambert, and on 16 December, 1653 he was installed as Lord Protector. Government now returned to a more traditional pattern, for Protector, council of state and parliament as defined by the Instrument, were modified versions of monarch, privy council and parliament as envisaged by the reformers of the forties. Executive and legislative powers were to be separated, and the old ideal of a 'balanced polity' was reaffirmed. The Protector had to obtain the council's consent in all significant decisions of policy, and his power of veto over bills passed by parliament, provided they did not contravene the Instrument itself, was limited to twenty days. Parliaments were to be elected at least every three years under a moderate property franchise, and their seats were completely reapportioned so that the majority went to the counties and only the larger towns got separate representation.

Cromwell and the council were given emergency powers of legislation until the first new parliament met, and they used it to tackle the thorny problem of religious settlement. They rejected the Leveller and sectarian claim that religion should be wholly removed from the civil magistrate's authority. They provided for a parochial ministry, to be approved by a mixed commission of 'Triers' and supported by tithes until a less objectionable form of contribution could be devised. But they imposed no set order of worship, no formal confession of faith and no compulsory ecclesiastical discipline, while the Instrument itself guaranteed the freedom of the peaceable sects to associate and worship in their own way.

The Protectorate was not a dictatorship, either in intent or even for the most part in practice. Yet Cromwell's sincere desire for 'a government by consent' was frustrated by two harsh facts. Firstly, the constitution had been framed by a junta of officers and depended on the army to sustain it. Secondly, the parliamentary cause had undergone such fragmentation since 1642 that any basis for unity was desperately hard to find. Faced with Royalists, Presbyterians, Rumpers, Levellers, Commonwealthsmen opposed to the rule of any single person and millenarians dedicated to a dictatorship of the saints, 'where,' cried Cromwell, 'shall we find that consent?' Yet 'healing and settling' was the constant theme of his speeches. He strove to reconcile the traditional political nation to a government that would set a bulwark against any further threat of social revolution and preserve 'the ranks and orders of men, whereby England hath been known for hundreds of years: a nobleman, a gentleman, a yeoman. That,' he said, 'is a good interest of the nation, and a great one.'

It was uphill work, and like the Stuarts before him he found the limits of his success registered in his relations both with parliament and with the county communities. Two parliaments met under his Protectorate, and in each of them only arbitrary measures prevented the republican politicians who had managed the Rump from leading the majority of moderate, uncommitted members in dangerous attacks upon his personal authority and upon the whole constitution under which he ruled. As for the gentry in the counties, it would be a distortion to picture them seething continuously with discontent, for the signs are that their old ties of neighbourhood were being steadily re-knit. Yet they shared a common dislike for a 'sword government', and most of the older ruling families remained unreconciled either to their regicide masters or to the newer and lesser men who had in so many cases supplanted them in county office. Cromwell's most drastic measure to compel their co-operation was his division of England into eleven districts, each under a major-general. This followed the abortive Royalist risings of 1655, and its prime object was to provide military security against further conspiracy. But the powers of surveillance over local government which Cromwell gave to the major-generals were a measure of his failure to gain the gentry's collaboration, and nothing did his reputation more harm than his commissioning of upstart soldiers to tell the 'natural' rulers of the county communities how to go about their business. Yet it should be remembered that when parliament pronounced against the major-generals' régime, less than eighteen months after its inception, Cromwell acquiesced in its sentence.

Cromwell certainly owed some of his difficulties to his innocence of the arts of parliamentary management and to his riding too roughly over the susceptibilities of local interests. But there was more to it than mere tactics. Certain policies which he thought it his mission to uphold were so contrary to the prejudices of most of the nobility and gentry that no amount of politicking would have won their general acceptance in his time. Not even purged parliaments or well-winnowed benches of justices would go all the way with him on liberty of conscience—still less on his ideal of a 'reformation of manners' (and here we may sympathize with them). Nor would most of them support him far in humanizing the criminal law, or promoting measures of social justice, or encouraging schemes for popular education. It is a mistake to regard the Protectorate as simply a phase of conservative reaction.

Moreover Cromwell did not wholly fail in his efforts at reconciliation. Very many of the gentry came to accept his rule as preferable to any likely alternative, so long as the Royalist cause lay in ruins. Men of conservative and even Royalist backgrounds like Lord Broghill, Charles Howard, George Monck and Sir Charles Wolseley rose high in his service. The trouble was that, as their influence rose and challenged that of the army officers and Puritan radicals, a new division began to appear. It opened wide during parliament's debates on the major-generals, and again when parliament invited Cromwell to assume the crown—a move inspired by these conservative Cromwellians, and sharply and successfully opposed by the officers. When Cromwell died in September 1658 he left his task of reunifying the nation in a sadly unfinished state. Yet paradoxically the short-lived rule of his son Richard probably enjoyed a broader basis of gentry support than any other government in the last ten years or more.

It was not a Royalist reaction that overthrew Richard's Protectorate and opened the way to the collapse of the revolution but a combination of radical groups who felt that the progressive return to more traditional ways was betraying the 'Good Old Cause' for which they had fought. The republican politicians of the Rump directed a skilful propaganda at the Commonwealthsmen in the army and the more fanatical sects. The chief officers lost their nerve and deserted Richard's sinking ship, and when they forced him to dissolve his parliament in April 1659 their unruly subordinates soon compelled them to restore the Rump to the supreme authority it had enjoyed down to 1653. But both Rump and army were politically bankrupt. They quarrelled again with each other as they had quarrelled before, and from October onwards all was in confusion. Behind the futile posturings of these last legatees of the great parliamentary cause that Pym had led in 1642, England drifted into anarchy and the Great Rebellion collapsed from within. Monarchy returned to fill a vacuum; it had rapidly become the only conceivable basis on which to re-establish the rule of law. The cool midwifery of General Monck assisted its rebirth, and a huge wave of popular acclaim for King Charles II threatened to engulf everything both good and bad that the Good Old Cause had stood for. In their haste to put the clock back, few men probably realized how deeply the experience of the past twenty years would remain etched upon the political, social and intellectual life of the nation. Fewer still would have guessed how soon—a mere twenty-eight years—another revolution would vindicate much of what Pym had striven for; or that more than six times that span would elapse before parliament began seriously to reform its own constitution or enlarge the political nation.

34. 1661:
The Young King
in Quest of Glory

PIERRE GOUBERT

European history from the mid-seventeenth century until the French Revolution is often called the "age of absolutism." Indeed, many of the principal states—England, Italy, and the Netherlands apart—were quick to modify or adopt the trappings of absolute monarchy as they were developed in France under "the Sun King," Louis XIV. In older monarchies like Spain and Austria, and in ones that were either newly formed or trying to adopt Western ideas, like Prussia and Russia, there was a tendency toward wholesale importation of French political ideas, and these centered on the figure of the king.

Seventeenth-century thought endowed the king with a mystical, religious significance and identified him with the nation he headed. He was conceived of as God's chosen representative, and an absolute obedience to his will was demanded. There are several important questions about this process which deserve to be asked. Why did European political thought on the continent tend to be dominated by absolutist theory? What role did these ideas serve in the seventeenth-century state? To what extent was absolutism the creation of powerful rulers, and especially Louis XIV; to what extent the result of other forces which had been tending in this direction?

In the following selection from Louis XIV *and* Twenty Million Frenchmen, *Pierre Goubert provides an approach to some of these questions in his por-*

Source: Pierre Goubert, *Louis XIV and Twenty Million Frenchmen,* trans. Anne Carter (New York: Random House, 1972), pp. 61–78. Copyright © 1972 by Random House, Inc. Reprinted by permission of the publisher.

trayal of the young King Louis. Goubert's treatment of the king is original and refreshing, centering as it does on the writings of Louis himself. In this survey of the king's view of his position vis-à-vis ministers, generals and other subjects at home, friends and foes abroad, and finally God, we see much of Louis's own personality and ambitions, and can gauge the thrust of his policies toward absolutism. The emphasis on his own personal glory, soon identified with France herself, is a keynote of most of Louis's subsequent actions and objectives.

Pierre Goubert is a leading figure in the so-called Annales *school, which emphasizes the social characteristics of the population, and has done much work on the demography of France during the Old Regime. His main interests are reflected not only in the title but also in the substance of this volume:* Louis XIV and Twenty Million Frenchmen. *Although he suggests in this chapter that Louis XIV was a strong-willed, forceful monarch who dominated his ministers and officials, his book amply shows where and how weaknesses or resistance in the French kingdom hindered the policies of the king. Some interesting comparisons can be made between the France of Louis XIV and the England of Charles I and Cromwell, or the Russia of Peter the Great. In all three countries "revolutions" occurred between the middle and the end of the seventeenth century, but none was quite alike. The selections on the English Civil War and on Peter the Great will provide material for discussion in this context.*

The King

To show Louis in his twenty-third year is an intimidating task. So much has been said already, both by his admirers and his detractors. The best way is to let him speak for himself. In his *Mémoires* for the years 1661, 1662, 1666, 1667 and 1668, intended for the 'education of the Dauphin', he either composed, revised or at any rate approved what was written for him by such excellent secretaries as president Périgny. And since he announced, a few hours after Mazarin's death, that it was his 'will never to take a prime minister' and 'to combine all the powers of a ruler in his own person', let us watch him in action and hear his own account of his conduct during the first year of his reign.

Four words crop up constantly in his writings. These are: 'my dignity, my glory, my greatness, my reputation'. The last is the most frequent. When, in 1670 or thereabouts, the king looked back on his early days, he saw the quest for 'reputation' as the supreme goal of all his acts, past, present and certainly future as well; reputation at home, by reducing his kingdom to obedience and doing away with the 'chaos' which reigned there; reputation among the Christian Princes of Europe (with the rest he was not concerned), at that time his peaceful neighbours, none of whom made any great impression on him. But 'they did not know him yet' and he burned to confront them 'at the head of his armies'. At twenty-two years old, 'preferring in his heart, a high reputation above all things, even life itself', the king was very conscious that he would have to 'render an account of all his actions to the whole world and to all times'. Already, he was preparing himself to do so. But what qualities had he in himself to ensure his success in achieving 'that dominant and ruling passion of kings . . . their own advancement, greatness and glory'?

To begin with, there was his magnificent health. For all the small stature, which explains his high heels, his great *perruque* and upright bearing, he evidently inherited the powerful vitality of his grandfather, Henri IV. Like him, he was an indefatigable huntsman, warrior, dancer, gormandizer and lover and yet this dashing sportsman, with no time to spare for the weak or the nervous, resigned himself to spending hours every day shut up in an office, alone or with a few colleagues. Before he was twenty he had shown his amazing courage, in battle, in sickness, and in action against the Spaniards. He continued to go his own way obstinately in the face of several generations of physicians, working sixteen to eighteen hours a day studying papers, hearing reports, giving audiences and public appearances, riding on horseback and making love.

Of a far from bookish education, the lessons which seem to have stuck in his mind were chiefly those he learned from a Spaniard and an Italian, and even more those of the tempestuous years of his minority. From his mother, from whom he inherited the many Spanish traits in his character —there was a good deal of Philip II in Louis XIV with his fondness for secrecy, his concentration on his work, his taste for splendour and formality—he seems to have acquired a regular and meticulous devotion in the exercises of his faith and that cold, exquisite courtesy which never deserted him. From his godfather, the cardinal, who had finally admitted him as a silent spectator to the Council, he had learned to know Europe, with all its intrigues, the details of its princely marriages and the consciences that were for sale.

Hustled out of Paris at the age of ten and shuttled from one town to the next in the midst of wars, rebellions, dangers and epidemics of disease, he had learned the hard way that no one, or hardly anyone, was consistently loyal, not even an archbishop or the first prince of the blood. In later years he could urge his son to forgive those who injured him, but for all that he never forgot that 'in wise and able kings, resentment and anger towards their subjects is only prudence and justice' and that 'a little harshness was the greatest kindness I could do my subjects'. None were above suspicion, the clergy, the nobility with its 'thousands of petty tyrants', the *parlements,* the supposedly sovereign courts, officers, governors, or towns, since 'there is scarcely any order of the realm, Church, nobility or Third Estate that has not at some time fallen into fearful error'. The highest tribute he could pay his dead mother was to note 'how fully she had yielded up the sovereign power' and that he had 'nothing to fear from her ambition'. Fond as he was of his brother, he denied him any post of responsibility or command in which to distinguish himself: the memory of his uncle and fear of the very name of Orléans made him state firmly that 'the sons of France should never have any other retreat than the court or any place of safety but in their brother's heart'.

This universal distrust, born of experience, was the root of his reserve, of his utter self-command in affairs of state, and of his passion for secrecy which he tried to pass on to the dauphin. Louis learned to overcome the displays of emotion and the tendency to burst into tears which had marked his early manhood, or at least to keep them for the discharge of his private feelings. We may ask ourselves how many of the tears he shed for the death of Mazarin, the Queen Mother, and later on for his own queen and Monsieur, were really genuine. His real feelings were, after all, well known. Even of Mazarin, whom he professed to love, he could write in the same breath that he meant to abolish 'the very name' of prime minister in France and stress how far 'his (Mazarin's) methods and ideas differed from mine'. Controlled tears, a studied courtesy, calculated silence, the art of evasiveness (his invariable answer to all unforeseen questions was 'I'll see'), all the consummate skill of royal stage-craft—the first stroke of which, the arrest of de Retz at the end of 1652, came as a complete shock to everyone—all this became second nature to him and was undoubtedly one of his greatest assets. Based on education, experience, suspicion and a deep determination to be, in all things, the 'master', the king's ability to act in secret was essentially a triumph of the one great virtue of the age, the will.

With it went a self-confidence that was clear from the first and which is displayed with disarming frankness in the *Mémoires:* what Lavisse has called 'the pride of a Pharaoh'. Given the political, social and judicial climate in which he lived, Louis could not help but identify himself with France and believe, as Bossuet wrote later, that 'he was the whole State, and the will of all the people was locked in his'. He prepared to instruct his grandson in the axiom that 'The body of the nation resides not in France. It dwells wholly in the person of the King'. It seemed quite natural to him that the greater part of the court, the clergy and the kingdom should proclaim him God's lieutenant upon earth, and later cry with Bossuet: 'Oh kings, you are as gods!' He was early convinced that on some occasions he was directly inspired by 'I know not what blind instincts or intuitions above reason, which seem to come straight from heaven'. The king's pride was natural, even inevitable, and could be a most useful instrument in ruling. In 1661 it was at least balanced by thought and by hard work.

At Home

In 1670, his 'tenth year of going forward . . . quite steadily along the same road', Louis XIV, at the age of thirty-two, looked back and meditated on the course of his first year of personal rule. The things he remembered, those he left out, even his way of describing and stressing events, all these offer an unequalled portrait of the intrepid gallant and imperious master, his Most Christian yet libertine Majesty, the magnificent monarch whose will it was to command the admiration of all Europe.

His first job was the complete reorganization of his system of government. He completely and utterly abolished the office of prime minister on the grounds that 'there is nothing more shameful than the sight of all the practical authority on the one side and nothing but the title of king on the other': a curious tribute to his father, mother and two cardinals. This was undoubtedly the most important act of the young ruler who has been called, somewhat grandly, 'the great revolutionary of the seventeenth century'. The King's Council was a crowded affair, overfull of clerks and persons of noble birth. Louis dismissed nearly all of them, including his mother, and retained only three men: Le Tellier, Lionne and Fouquet, the latter already watched and soon to be replaced by Colbert. These were the only ministers. Not a single prelate, great nobleman or even prince of the blood, not even the wise and illustrious Turenne, had access to what was soon known as the 'High Council' at which all important matters of state were decided.

All three men were of humble birth, wide experience and proven loyalty. All three had been Mazarin's men and all three were to owe their fortune and their advancement to the king. No one of them was dominant and none put their signature to anything at all without the king's authority. 'It was not in my interest,' Louis declared, 'to take subjects of a higher degree . . . it was not my intention to share my power with them. It was necessary that they should entertain no higher hopes for themselves than I might be pleased to gratify.' As for the rest, whether too exalted, like the Chancellor, too illustrious, like Turenne or Condé, too old, too young or too dim-witted like Brienne, la Vrillière or Guénégaud, they were fobbed off with administrative posts and given no hand in the government of the realm. Thus, after the arrest of Fouquet who was too rich, too splendid and too presumptuous but no more knave than many others, there came into being the famous 'Triad': the reign of the king, what Saint-Simon was to call the 'règne de vile bourgeoisie' had begun.

Every day, the king dutifully presided over the High Council. He attended regular meetings of the *Conseil des Dépêches,* held twice a week with the Chancellor and the four secretaries of State, ministers or not, to hear the news from the provinces and watch the young masters of requests, the up-and-coming administrators, making their reports. In September he set up the *Conseil des Finances* at which, in the presence of the Chancellor, two financial intendants and Colbert, the king acted as his own financial secretary, signing accounts, endeavouring to fix a budget and make some sense of the country's finances. He was not even above occasionally taking the chair, which was always ready for him, at what he called the *'Conseil des Parties',* although he considered this of minor importance since 'it dealt only with cases between private individuals on matters of jurisdiction'. He also found time to receive petitions and read a great many of them himself, to keep himself fully informed on all matters and in particular on the state of his troops, on income and expenditure and foreign news, to distribute places, favours, pensions and benefices and in short to perform a tireless job of patient inquiry, often going into minute detail. At the same time, his trusted ministers were beginning, under his supervision, to lay the basis of the immense task of reorganization and codification which historians have too often attributed to Colbert alone.

In addition to this everyday business, there were sudden, unexpected 'masterstrokes' aimed at reducing the remnants of the Fronde, the corps, companies, orders and privileged individuals and all those responsible for the chaos which reigned at home. The first object of this general reduction to obedience was to 'cut down the power of the principal companies which, on the pretext that there is no appeal from their judgements . . . had gradually assumed the name of sovereign courts and looked on themselves as so many separate and independent authorities'. Tough words and harsh methods produced a frightened submission: the king exiled several officers of the *Cour des Aides,* silenced the Paris *Parlement* in the matter of registering royal edicts, cut the remuneration of officers by a quarter and compelled the courts, which had previously refused to do so, to acknowledge all royal decisions taken in council and not merely those ordinances and decrees which had been ratified. In short the king had, in his own words, deliberately 'mortified' his administrators of justice. But he kept his best strokes for the *parlements* whose 'overweening arrogance . . . had put the whole realm in jeopardy during [his] minority. It was necessary to humble them, less for the harm which they had done than for that which they might do in the future.' Louis did not resort to drastic measures yet. For the moment he was content to silence them and destroy in a few words their 'false picture of themselves as champions of the so-called interests of the people as against those of their prince'. 'For subjects, peace lies only in obedience: it is always less harmful for the people to endure even the bad government of kings who are judged by God alone than to attempt to check it . . . ; the reason of State which is the first of all laws (is) . . . the most difficult and incomprehensible to all those not concerned in government.' But the complete subjection of the *parlements* of the kingdom had only just begun.

The first order of the realm had already felt the weight of the king's will. Let Louis XIV speak for himself:

'The Assembly of the Clergy [this met every five years], which had been going on for a long time in Paris, was putting off the moment of breaking up, against my expressed wish. . . .' In fact the assembly claimed to be waiting for certain edicts which it had called for to be signed, sealed and delivered first. Nothing could have annoyed the young king more than this kind of bargaining. 'I let them understand that nothing more was to be gained by these kinds of methods,' he says roundly. The assembly dispersed and only then were the edicts dispatched.

Days of reckoning were also at hand for the second order of the land but, in the meantime, this was attacked indirectly. The duc d'Épernon, who had been colonel-in-chief of the infantry, had just died. His post carried with it 'unlimited' powers, including the appointment of a great many officers of lower rank who formed a reliable court of his own 'creatures . . . by whose means he was more master of the chief forces of the State than the king himself'. This post was abolished and taken over by the king himself. In a subtler, but more far-reaching reform, the powers of military governors were gradually reduced on the grounds that they were 'subject to great abuse'. Louis relieved them of the power to levy funds 'which made them too powerful and too absolute'. Then, by a quiet rearrangement of garrisons, he took away those 'troops who were their own men' and replaced them with 'others who, on the contrary, served only myself'. Before long, in certain provinces at least, the king would be putting an end to the 'tyranny' exercised by too many of the nobility with exemplary rigour and severity. But most urgent of all was to foresee and forestall any *émotions* in the kingdom such as those which had filled the century so far.

With this object in view the Third Estate—the bourgeoisie—needed to be similarly threatened. The fortifications at Bordeaux, the most obstinate and determined of the cities of the Fronde, and at Marseilles, which had given the king such a bad reception two years earlier, were kept up 'for future safety and as an example to all the rest'. Even so, some unrest did occur, 'coming close to disobedience', in Normandy, the south-west and Provence, regions with a tradition of revolt about which the king says very little. They were 'put down and punished' by the troops which Louis had resolved to 'maintain in substantial numbers' in spite of the peace.

This severity, he states, 'was the greatest kindness I could do my people'. From the first year of his reign, the armed repression of any hint of sedition became an absolute rule. It was a rule applied on very many occasions with a ferocity which only a few sensitive souls could consider barbarous. This was the price of order, obedience, reputation, glory and greatness. More masterstrokes would follow.

The king's memoirs for the year 1661 make little mention of the people of the towns or countryside. The king merely observes that in March they were 'heavily taxed, oppressed by poverty in a number of places and by their own idleness [which we should nowadays call unemployment] in others and in need, above all else of occupation and relief. Otherwise 'no unrest or the fear or appearance of unrest' had appeared in the kingdom at that time. For the relief of 'the people', the king reduced taxation by three million in 1662, saying that the peace enabled him to do so, asserting that he found work for the 'idle', and repeated that in 1661 there was 'no unrest in the kingdom' but added that anything at all approaching disobedience, such as occurred on a few occasions at Montauban, Dieppe, in Provence and at La Rochelle was at once put down and punished' by troops. In plain terms this means that the troubles were not over but were immediately suppressed by the army. The king, who had lived through the Fronde and the rebellion of half the kingdom, asked no more. There is no mention of the cost of this tranquillity, of the 'rotten' summer, the disastrous harvest of 1661, of the unusually severe famine which followed almost at once, except for a few belated remarks (in 1662) recalling his own generosity. Glory and reputation marched on regardless of such incidents. Besides, the king was in a hurry to go on and tell the dauphin of more important matters: the great and brilliant masterstrokes abroad to which the bulk of his memoirs is devoted.

Abroad

Louis XIV's view of Europe was of a society made up of more or less powerful princes belonging to more or less ancient houses, served by more or less venal ministers. In this time of peace, relations between the States came down to the family business of marriages and inheritances, money matters such as the price of a foreign minister or ally and, above all, the affairs of precedence abounding in any aristocracy.

'The kings of France, as hereditary kings . . . may boast that there is without exception in the world today no greater house than theirs, no monarchy as ancient, no greater or more absolute power.' From this dogmatic pronouncement it is clear that, in any event, precedence and predominance rightly belonged to the monarchy of the Lilies. From 1661 onwards, any occasion would serve to demonstrate this fact to the rest of Europe.

One example is the claim made by the ambassadors of the republic of Genoa to be treated as royalty at the court of France and 'always to be given audience on the same day that this was granted to some royal ambassador so that, entering the Louvre immediately after him and to the same roll of drums, it could not be distinguished whether these honours belonged to them or not'. This undeserved fanfare reminded King Louis that for a long time Genoa had been a possession of his own ancestors and had rebelled, and that 'legitimately by several titles' it belonged to the house of France. Louis XIV therefore made it clear to the Genoese that he would not endure their 'absurd pretensions' any longer which made them 'quake with fear'. This was, admittedly, an impressive gesture involving no great risk. It was another matter to impress the emperor with the superiority of the French crown.

Louis XIV therefore took pains to explain at length 'how far the emperors of today are from the greatness of titles (of Caesar and Roman Emperors) to which they aspire' and how they had unlawfully taken on themselves the succession of Charlemagne who was, in reality, the forbear of the kings of France alone. Moreover they were only elected rulers and 'in being elected must submit to whatever conditions are imposed on them'. As a result they had little authority, small revenues and, unless they had anywhere of their own, 'only the town of Bamberg' to live in. All this was not, it should be stressed, entirely disinterested because the emperor had thought it beneath his dignity to write first inviting Louis to attend his election but had waited to receive some letter of congratulation. Louis not only refused to write the slightest note. he actually made the emperor remove the titles of comte de Ferette and landgrave of Alsace, regions ceded by the Treaty of Munster, from the powers of his ministers and, more important still, to resign the title he had assumed in a projected league against the Turks of 'head of Christendom'.

Such victories in subtle points of European precedence were particularly dear to the young king. They prepared the ground for others still more remarkable. They might also have inspired a more cautious man with some fear of future retaliation. But in 1661, young Leopold and the timid Genoese could only bow and bide their time.

Louis XIV was busy in a more practical way, getting the last ounce of advantage from application of treaties so as to cover his northern and eastern borders which he knew to be weak and too close to Paris. On the Flemish frontier, in the marches of Lorraine and Alsace, he gained moral, territorial and financial concessions, repaired his fortresses, put them in a state of defence and equipped them with everything necessary for the conduct of a war. Finally he turned his attention to those he was already thinking of as his future enemies as they had been his father's, the emperor and the crown of Spain. He used the classic means to achieve this. He got the Elector of Trèves into the League of the Rhine, that is, as he somewhat blatantly put it (the idea was originally Mazarin's), 'into a powerful and extensive union I had formed in the middle of the Empire, upon pretext of safeguarding the Treaty of Munster and the peace of Germany'. By the Florentine marriage of an Orléans princess he strengthened his ties with the Medicis in the heart of a half-Spanish Italy.

He cemented the English alliance which had made possible the victory over Spain in 1659 by the marriage of 'Monsieur'. That both these princely, and therefore diplomatic unions had been concluded by Mazarin is a fact which Louis omits to mention. Finally he congratulates himself on bringing about the marriage of Charles II of England with Catherine of Braganza, the infanta of Portugal, even though this alliance brought the English a great deal of gold, the town of Bombay, the gateway to the Indian Empire, and the beginnings of an economic and political protectorate whose dangers France was only later to appreciate. But at this period Louis XIV regarded England as a weak, pro-French country, 'barely recovered from her past troubles and concerned only to stabilize her government under a newly restored king and moreover, naturally inclined to favour France'. This judgement was permissible in 1661: it was unfortunate that Louis pronounced it in 1670. For him, the Portuguese marriage presented the considerable advantage of dealing a blow to Spain by giving Portugal, then struggling hard for independence, an effective protector. For King Louis the constant enmity between the two thrones of France and Spain was a basic fact, borne out by a hundred years of history. 'One cannot be raised except by lowering the other,' he wrote, their 'jealousy' was 'fundamental' and everlasting. (It even excused acting 'notwithstanding the Treaty of the Pyrenees; in other words of violating it, although it went somewhat against the grain for the king to do so.) However, he forgave himself by proving to his satisfaction that 'a great many "words" of the treaty were not to be taken "literally" and that in any case the Spaniards had broken the Pyrenean Treaty first "in a thousand different ways"'. If Louis meant to enhance his 'reputation' and his glory, he would have to bring down Spain and this meant going to war with her, with or without an excuse.

This obsession with Spain, like his jealous contempt for the emperor, was the result of both recent and centuries-old events and it led Louis

XIV to underestimate not only the English but also the Dutch. All their policies, he declared, were directed at two things only: maintaining their trade and humbling the House of Orange; 'the smallest war would do them great harm . . . and their chief support was in my friendship'. Merchants, republicans, and in some sense his own protégés: all three reasons for displaying his royal condescension towards them. Of course, Louis XIV could not have guessed the future in store for the infant William of Orange. But he might have noticed that the United Provinces had grown stronger during the wars, and because of them, paid rather more attention (in 1670, with Colbert at his side) to the material might of a merchant republic. He was above wasting his displays of grandeur on the Dutch. Only real kings were worthy of his attention, and it was these alone he bothered to impress with his youthful power.

God

It remained for Louis XIV to face up to the one person he had ever desired to serve, or to thank 'with real gratitude for the favours which daily he received from him'. And so he concludes his survey of the first year of his reign with an inventory of all that he has done for God.

Any young prince eager for glory and brought up a Catholic is bound at some time to feel the breath of the crusading spirit. Louis, in addition, could not bear to see the King of Spain calling himself by his traditional title of 'Catholic Majesty' and taking on himself 'the status of outstanding Catholic'. What he found still harder to endure was that the emperor, who was merely the 'head and captain-general of a German Republic', should claim to be the 'head of Christendom, as if he had truly possessed the same Empire and the same rights as Charlemagne' from whom only Louis himself could claim direct descent . . . 'when he had defended the faith against the Saxons, the Huns and the Saracens'. Consequently, on his accession he offered '100,000 écus to the Venetians for their war in Candie' and a great many promises of assistance in 'driving the infidel' from Crete. He offered the emperor 20,000 men, and gave him 6,000 in 1664. He 'empowered' his representatives in Rome to 'form a league against the Turk', to which he would contribute 'much more than any other Christian prince'. All dreams, as we shall see.

Instead of actually taking the cross himself, Louis took up the cause of Catholic minorities in Protestant countries. He interceded 'with the Dutch on behalf of the Guelder Catholics'. At Dunkirk, held by the English, he disbursed 'considerable sums in alms to the poor . . . for fear that their wretchedness might tempt them to follow the religion of the English . . .'. Defending the Roman Catholic faith abroad enhanced Louis' reputation; he boasts of it to God; in future nothing shall prevent him from making many more such interventions; it is inconceivable to him that they should make him enemies, except for heretics and infidels who do not matter.

Louis had his own heretics too. He had some significant things to say about the Jansenists. This Most Christian King frankly despised theological argument, 'long disputes on academic subjects, no knowledge of which, it was admitted, was necessary for anyone's salvation'. He was much more worried about the threat of a schism, which was to be feared from the 'warmth of feeling' involved, from the quality of the opposition, 'very meritorious if only they had themselves been less convinced of it' , and the intervention of bishops 'of high reputation and a piety truly worthy of respect'. Jansenism, 'the newborn sect' which had introduced a spirit of 'innovation' and of division which was bound to be unwelcome to the king, was made a still graver threat because of the 'human interests' it aroused and by its partial connexion with that former figure of the Fronde and escaped prisoner, Cardinal de Retz. 'Matters of State' were involved here, and it was for political reasons that Louis continued in 1661 to persecute the followers of St. Augustine. He had already ordered the burning of the *Provinciales;* next he dispersed the 'Messieurs' and their pupils, while waiting his chance to set an Archbishop of Paris who shared his views against the daughters of Port-Royal and strike at the recalcitrant bishops and religious communities.

It was a matter of policy, too, that Louis, in a long and remarkable speech, turned his attention to 'that great number of my subjects adhering to the so-called reformed religion'. More than once, in words which are hardly ever quoted, he outlines what was to be said in favour of the Protestant religion:

> The ignorance of churchmen in the last century, their luxury and debauchery, the bad examples they set and those they were obliged to suffer . . . and all the abuses which they permitted in the conduct of individuals against the rules and public sentiments of the Church. . . . The new reformers were clearly telling the truth in many things of this kind . . . [although] on the other hand [they] were guilty of falsehood in all those concerned not with facts but with belief.

As a result the people found it hard to pick out the Huguenots' well-disguised deceit from many obvious truths. Moreover when the people saw all these heretics dying for their faith they 'were still more inclined to believe that [their] religion must be good, if they would face such perils for it'. The king's first advice to his bishops is therefore to offer only good examples and 'avert scandals' which would put off the Protestants so as to 'bring back those whom birth, education and often a great but untaught zeal maintained in all good faith in these pernicious errors'. This is not the language of the 'new Constantine, the new Theodosius' hailed by Bossuet in 1685. He does not fulminate with the Church Assembly against 'the fatal liberty of conscience'. He accepts the Edict of Nantes, confirmed several times over since 1643. But he does wish to see the Huguenots brought by slow degrees back into the true faith. He puts forward his own methods for achieving this, involving no persecution, no 'harshness', but merely the strict observance of the Edict, the suppression of everything not permitted by it, the denial of any favours to the members of the reformed religion, and the offer of a reward to 'those who yielded meekly'. In dealing with heretics, Louis put his faith in the power of money to buy consciences.

After this summing up of all the services he had rendered God 'out of real gratitude for the favours' he received 'daily', not forgetting certain decrees against 'swearing' or duelling, Louis goes on to provide his son with a few important rules about the way a king should conduct himself towards God. First, it is proper to practise the devotional exercises 'regularly' and in public and in particular to enlighten the people by making 'the stations of the cross on foot, with [his] whole household on festivals'. 'The public reverence we do to this invisible power may in short be justly called the first and most important part of our political duty since, after all, our own submission to [God] is the rule and example of that which is owed to ourselves by the people.' Louis goes even further: 'Armies, councils and all human industry would be feeble instruments to maintain us on the throne, if each man . . . did not honour a higher power of which our own is a part.' This concept of the king's public piety as a model and guarantee of the loyalty of his own subjects, is a political attitude to religion not perhaps altogether unrealistic. True, Louis does add that a certain 'inner disposition' towards religion is 'nobler and more disinterested', and that 'this selfish point of view' is 'very bad when it is the only one' and 'the outside is nothing at all without the inside'. But all the same, neither his ideas nor his expression suggest a very deep or heartfelt faith. Louis' religion, in the first decade or so of his reign, was a mixture of studied policy and a well-taught conformity. The time of his inner conversion was still a long way off. In 1661, Louis was prepared to dissolve the Company of the Holy Sacrament, to support Molière against the 'tartufes' and dare to stand godfather to his first child. His life was happily compounded of myths and gallantry, and he had already become the joyous libertine who made the glorification of adultery the fashion in both Court and City. Bossuet's next Lenten sermons were to call down his first disgrace on the head of the audacious young priest. With his clergy, the devout party, and even with God himself, Louis XIV kept his distance. As yet the Most Christian King was thinking only of his glory, not of his salvation.

The thirty-year-old king who thus described the first year of his reign for the benefit of his son, was confident that he had fulfilled his 'great, noble and delicious profession of kingship' very well indeed. For twelve years, faced with no unduly tiresome obstacle or serious setback, he went his way, 'quite steadily along the same road, relaxing none of his concentration' in order to show 'to the whole world and for all time' how a great king could achieve the triumph of his ruling passion for glory.

35. The Achievement of Peter the Great

VASILI KLYUCHEVSKY

Just as European civilization spread to Asia and America in and after the sixteenth century, so also western Europeans saw their contacts with their neighbors on the plains of central and eastern Europe increase. The Slavic peoples to the east were drawn, slowly and imperceptively, more and more within the stream of European politics, culture, and trade. Although it would have been hard to predict in the seventeenth century, the Slavic state in many respects least attuned to European ideas and most backward in terms of industry and technology would one day dominate all of eastern Europe and cast a shadow over the West. Russia changed greatly at the end of the century, and much of the credit for the improvements and reforms in society must go to her great king, Peter.

What reforms did Peter carry through? Why did he bring about changes in Russian society; what were the effects of the Petrine reforms on Russian civilization? Historians agree that Peter's reign marks an epoch in Russian history, but there is a good deal of diversity of interpretation about the nature of this epoch.

Vasili Klyuchevsky was probably the premier historian of Russia in the nineteenth century, and he held a chair at the University of Moscow. Although

Source: Vasili Klyuchevsky, *Peter the Great*, trans. L. Archibald (London: Macmillan & Co., 1958), pp. 254–265, 269–272. Reprinted by permission of St. Martin's Press, Inc., The Macmillan Company of Canada, and Macmillan London and Basingstoke.

he was an immensely popular lecturer, he agreed reluctantly and only at the end of his career to prepare his lectures in book form. Consequently his History of Russia, *part of which has been translated and issued separately under the title* Peter the Great, *represents his mature and considered views on Russian history.*

Klyuchevsky argues that Peter was not a "revolutionary," but merely made Russia "competitive" with the West. In assessing Peter's reforms, Klyuchevsky stresses that most were concerned with technology and scientific, nautical, and industrial activity, so that Peter's intentions were not slavish imitation of the West and its ideas for their own sake, but rather the introduction of knowledge and techniques that would benefit and stimulate Russian society and economic development. Peter appears in his pages, therefore, as something less than the magnetic and inventive figure that some others have seen. This study has become a classic, and it is informative to see what is from a contemporary viewpoint Klyuchevsky's ironic use of the term revolutionary. But however we describe Peter the Great, he played an important role in Russian history, and this selection will help to make clearer exactly what that role was.

First of all, how did Peter become a reformer? The name of Peter makes us think of his reforms, and indeed 'Peter the Great and his reforms' has become a cliché. 'Reformer' has become his sobriquet, and the name by which he is known to history. We tend to believe that Peter I was born with the intention of reforming his country, and that he believed that this was his predestined historical mission. Nevertheless it was a long time before Peter took this view of himself. He was certainly not brought up to believe that he would reign over a state which was good for nothing, and which he would have to rebuild from top to bottom. On the contrary, he grew up knowing that he was Tsar, though a persecuted one, and that, as long as his sister and the Miloslavskys were in power, he was in danger of losing his life, and was unlikely to occupy the throne. His games of soldiers and with boats were the sports of his childhood, suggested to him by the conversations of his entourage. He realised very early that when he grew up and began to rule, he would need an army and navy, but he was, it seems, in no hurry to ask why he would need them. He only gradually realised, when he had discovered Sophia's intrigues, that he would need soldiers to control the Streltsy who supported his sister. Peter acted on the spur of the moment, and was not concerned with making plans for the future; he regarded everything he did as an immediate necessity rather than a reform, and did not notice how his actions changed both people and established systems. Even from his first foreign tour he brought back, not plans for reform, but impressions of a civilisation which he imagined he would like to introduce into Russia; and he brought back, too, a taste for the sea, that is to say, a desire to wage war against the country which had won access to the sea away from his grandfather. Indeed it was only during the last decade of his life, when the effect of his reforms was already fairly obvious, that he realised that he had done something new and spectacular. His better understanding of what he had done, however, did not help him to understand how he might act in the future. Peter thus became a reformer by accident, as it were, and even unwillingly. The war led him on and, to the end of his life, pushed him into reforming.

In the history of a country, war generally impedes reform, since foreign war and domestic reform are mutually exclusive and reform prospers best in times of peace. But in the history of Russia the correlation is different. Since a successful war has always served to secure the *status quo,* and an unsuccessful war, by provoking internal discontent, has always forced the government to review its domestic policy and introduce reforms, the government has always tried to avoid war, often to the detriment of its international position. Reforms at home were commonly achieved at the price of disaster abroad. In Peter's time the relationship between war and domestic change was different. Reforms were stimulated by the requirements of war, which indeed dictated the nature of the reforms that were undertaken. In other times the effect of war has been to force change on an unwilling government, but Peter, as he said himself, was able to learn from war what changes were needed. Unfortunately the attempt to carry on both war and reform simultaneously was unsuccessful: war slowed up reform, and reform prolonged the war because there was opposition and frequent revolt, and the forces of the nation could not be united to finish the war.

There were also interminable controversies about whether the reforms had been sufficiently elaborated, and whether they were introduced to meet the needs of the people, or had been forced on them as an unexpected act of Peter's autocratic will. In these discussions the preparations for reform were examined. It was asked whether they were deliberately calculated to bring about improvement, or were simply forced upon Peter by urgent difficulties, and were therefore only by accident measures which led to new possibilities and a new way of life. Soloviev's view was that the reforms had been prepared by Russia's past history, and even that 'they had been demanded by the people.' Some changes had been borrowed from the West and introduced in Russia as far back as Peter's grandfather, and after him by Peter's father, elder brother, and sister. Long before Peter's reign, indeed, a fairly extensive plan for reforms had been drawn up, which in many ways anticipated his own, and in some issues went further. It is true that this programme was not fully understood by medieval Russians, for it had been prepared by a few men with new ideas who had in many ways overcome the limitations of contemporary thought. Thus although changes had long been in preparation they were by no means identical with Peter's reforms. Indeed the reorganisation of Russia could have gone in one of several directions, and, given peace, could have been spread over many generations, just as, at a later period, the emancipation of the serfs was in preparation for over a century. Under Theodore and Sophia, for instance, 'politesse à la polonaise,' to use a contemporary expression, had been introduced in carriage styles and costume, and people had begun to study the Latin and Polish languages;

547
Klyuchevsky
THE
ACHIEVEMENT
OF PETER THE
GREAT

at Court the long, wide, and ungainly medieval Russian cloak had been abolished, and, had the educational programme been taken further, the kaftan might well have been replaced by the kuntush, and the Russian dance by the polka mazurka. For the matter of that, during the century and a half after Peter's time, the medieval Russian beard was made legal again.

Peter's first reforms were adapted from the Dutch and then from the Swedish systems. Moscow was replaced by St. Petersburg, a city built on the swamps, and Peter forced the nobility and merchants to build their houses in his new capital; to achieve his purpose he transported thousands of labourers from central Russia. The reform as carried out by Peter was his personal enterprise, and though it was an enterprise of unexampled ruthlessness, it was not arbitrary and was, indeed, necessary, otherwise Russia could not have developed fast enough to deal successfully with the dangers that threatened her. Even under Catherine the Great men realised that it would have been impossible to avoid violence by leaving the modernisation of Russia to the process of time. As we have already seen, Prince Shcherbatov disapproved of Peter's reforms, and thought that their effect would be to ruin the Russian people; on the other hand, the Prince was not a defender of autocracy, and considered such a system positively harmful to a nation. Yet this part-historian, part-publicist attempted a chronological calculation in the following terms: 'In how many years, in the most favourable conditions, could Russia by herself, without the autocracy of Peter the Great, have attained her present level of education and glory?' According to his calculations, Russia would not have reached even the imperfect situation it was in at the end of the eighteenth century until, say, 1892 (i.e., one hundred years later). He assumes, of course, that Russia would be at peace, that there would be no internal troubles, and that no monarch would appear to impede the country's progress by nullifying his predecessor's efforts. And who could guarantee that there would not be in all this time a Charles XII, or Frederick II, ready to annex part of Russia and interrupt its natural development? Thus Shcherbatov, although he idealised the life of medieval Russia, was not hopeful about a successful regeneration of the country if it was 'left to the natural awakening of the people.'

It is even more difficult to estimate the influence and effect of the reforms, and this, after all, is the main problem. In order to attempt a solution it will be necessary to dissect minutely its complex component parts. So many clashes of interest, influence, and motive were involved in the Petrine reforms that we must try to distinguish between indigenous and imported ideas, between that which was foreseen and that which was arrived at haphazardly. Indeed we shall not arrive at much understanding of these reforms by looking at some simple point in isolation. We should look at three parts of this problem, first, Peter's relations with the West, second, his attitude to medieval Russia, and third, his influence on the future. In fact this last point should not be surprising, since the work of a great man commonly survives him and is even carried on by others. We must therefore include in our judgement of Peter's reforms effects which only appeared after his death. The three parts of the problem we must look into are, then, how much Peter inherited from unreformed Russia, how much he borrowed from Western Europe, and what he left Russia, or more accurately, what happened to his work after his death.

Peter inherited from medieval Russia sovereign power of a peculiar sort, and an even stranger organisation of society. At the time of the accession of the new dynasty, the sovereign power was recognised as hereditary because of its proprietorial character. As soon as it lost this proprietorial character, it was left with neither definite juridical definition nor defined scope, and began to expand or contract according to the situation and character of the monarch. Peter inherited almost complete authority, and managed to extend it even further. He created the Senate, and by so doing rid himself of the pretensions which were associated with the Boyar Duma; by abolishing the Patriarchate he also eliminated both the risk of further Nikonian scandals and of the cramping effect of the exaggerated and unctuous respect which was accorded to the Patriarch of All the Russias.

At the same time, however, it is important to remember that Peter was the first monarch to give his unlimited power a moral and political definition. Before his reign the notion of the state was identified with the person of the Tsar, in the same way as in law the owner of a house is identified with the house. Peter made a distinction between the two ideas by insisting on two oaths, one to the State, and one to the Monarch. In his ukases he repeatedly insisted that the interests of the state were supreme, and, by so doing, made the Monarch subordinate to the state. Thus the Emperor became the chief representative of the law and the guardian of general prosperity. Peter considered himself a servant of state and country, and wrote as an official would about his victory over the Swedes at Doberau: 'From the time I *began to serve,* I have never seen such firing and such discipline among our soldiers.' Indeed the expressions *interest of the state, public good,* and *useful to the whole nation,* appear in Russian legislation for the first time I think, in Peter's time.

549
Klyuchevsky
THE
ACHIEVEMENT
OF PETER THE
GREAT

None the less Peter was influenced unconsciously by historical traditions in the same way that he had been unconsciously influenced by instincts. Because he thought that his reforms were in the interest of state, and for the public good, he sacrificed his son to this supreme law. The tragic death of the Tsarevitch led to the Statute of February 5th, 1722, on the law of succession. This was the first law in the history of Russian legislation to have a constitutional character. It stated: 'We issue this Statute in order to empower the ruling sovereign to specify the person to whom he wishes the heritage to pass, and to charge that person according to his judgement.' The Statute, by way of justification, recalls the example of the Grand Prince Ivan III who arbitrarily disposed of the succession, appointing first his grandson and then his son to succeed him. Before Peter there had been no law of succession, and its order had been decided by custom and circumstance alone. Under the old dynasty, which looked on the state as its patrimony (*votchina*) it was customary for the father to pass on the throne to his son 'by testament'. A new system of succession, election by the Sobor (the National Assembly) was introduced in 1598. By the seventeenth century the new dynasty did not look on the state as its patrimony, but, while the hereditary system fell into disuse, the elective system was not yet established; the new dynasty was recognised as hereditary for one generation only, and in 1613 the oath was taken to Michael Romanov and his children, but no farther. In the absence of an established system, the throne was occupied sometimes after an election by the Sobor, and sometimes by presenting the heir to the people in the Square at Moscow, as was done by Tsar Alexis with the Tsarevitch Theodore, or as happened when the rebellious Streltsy and an irregular Sobor established the Dual Monarchy of Tsars Peter and Ivan.

Peter replaced the hereditary and elective systems of succession with a system of 'personal nomination' coupled with the right to revoke; that is to say, he re-established succession by testament, legalised a situation for which no law existed, and retarded constitutional law by returning to the *votchina* system of succession. The Statute of February 5th, 1722, merely reiterated the words of Ivan III who said 'To whom I wish to him shall I give the rule.' Not only did Peter irresponsibly reproduce the past in his innovations, but he also let it influence his social legislation.

Peter did nothing to change the organisation of society which had been set up by the *Ulozhenie*, nor did he alter a division of classes which was based on obligations to the state, nor did he attack serfdom. On the contrary, the old system of class obligation was complicated by the imposition of further burdens. Peter made education compulsory for the nobility; he divided the civil service from the military; he organised the urban taxpayers into a compact group first under the administration of the *zemskie izby,* and then under the town councils; and he made the merchants of the guilds, the upper urban class, not only pay their ordinary taxes but form companies to lease and run factories and workshops belonging to the state. In Petrine Russia factories and workshops were not privately owned, but were state enterprises administered by a merchant of the guild who was compelled to do so. Nevertheless there were compensations, for the merchants, manufacturers, and workshop superintendents were granted one of the privileges of the nobility, that of buying villages with serfs to work in the factory or workshop. Peter did not alter the nature of serfdom but did modify its structure: the many types of serfdom, each with a different legal and economic position, were combined, and one class of taxable serfs was the result. Some of the 'free idlers' were registered as inferior urban citizens, so that 'idlers shall take themselves to trade in order that nobody shall be without an occupation'; others were conscripted, or forced into bondage. Thus Peter, by abolishing the intermediate classes, continued the work of simplification started by the *Ulozhenie;* and his legislation forced the members of the intermediate classes into one or other of the main classes. It was in Peter's time that Russian society was organised in the fashion planned in seventeenth-century legislation; after Peter's reforms Russian society was divided into clearly defined classes, and every class was burdened with complicated and weighty duties. Peter's attitude to the political and social régime of old Russia, which we have discussed in other connections, has now been made clear. He neither disturbed old foundations, nor built new ones, but altered existing arrangements by separating classes previously combined, or combining classes hitherto divided. Both society and the institutions of government were made more vigorous by these changes, and the state benefited from their greater activity.

What was Peter's attitude to Western Europe? He had inherited the precept 'Do everything after the example of foreign countries', that is to say Western European countries. This precept combines large doses of despondency, a lack of confidence in Russia's strength, and self-denial. How did Peter interpret this precept? What did he think of Russian relations with Western Europe? Did he see in Western Europe a model to imitate or a master who could be dismissed at the end of the lesson? Peter thought that the biggest loss suffered by Muscovy in the seventeenth century had been the Baltic littoral, by which Russia was deprived of contact with the civilised nations of the West. Yet why did he want this contact? Peter has often been accused of being a blind and inveterate Westerner who admired everything foreign, not because it was better than the Russian, but because it was unlike anything Russian; and it was believed that he wanted rather to assimilate Russia to Western Europe than to make Russia resemble Western Europe. It is difficult to believe that as sensible a man as Peter was troubled by such fantasies.

We have already seen how, in 1697, he had travelled incognito with the Great Embassy, with the intention of acquiring general technical knowledge and recruiting West European naval technicians. Indeed it was for technical reasons that the West was necessary to Peter. He was not a blind admirer of the West; on the contrary, he mistrusted it, and was not deluded into thinking that he could establish cordial relations with the West, for he knew that the West mistrusted his country, and was hostile to it. On the anniversary in 1724 of the Peace of Nystadt, Peter wrote that all countries had tried hard to exclude the Russians from knowledge in many subjects, and particularly military affairs, but somehow the countries had let information on military affairs escape them, as if their sight had been obscured, 'as if everything was veiled in front of their eyes.' Peter found this a miracle from God, and ordered the miracle to be forcefully expressed in the forthcoming celebrations 'and boldly set out, for there is a lot of meaning here', by which he meant that the subject was very suggestive of ideas. Indeed we would gladly believe the legend which has come down to us, that Peter once said, as Osterman records it: 'We need Europe for a few decades; later on we must turn our backs on it.' Thus for Peter association with Europe was only a means to an end, and not an end in itself.

What did Peter hope to gain from a rapprochement? Before answering this question, we must remember why Peter sent scores of young Russians

551

Klyuchevsky

THE
ACHIEVEMENT
OF PETER THE
GREAT

to study abroad, and ask what type of foreigner he attracted to Russia. The young Russian was sent to study mathematics, the natural sciences, naval architecture, and navigation; the foreigners who came to Russia were officers, naval architects, sailors, artisans, mining engineers, and later on jurists and specialists in administration and finance. With their help Peter introduced into Russia useful technical knowledge and skills lacked by the Russians. Russia had no regular army: he created one. It had no fleet: he built one. It had no convenient maritime commercial outlet: with his army and navy he took the eastern littoral of the Baltic. Mining was barely developed, and manufacturing hardly existed, yet by Peter's death there were more than two hundred factories and workshops in the country. The establishment of industry depended on technical knowledge, so Peter founded a naval academy, and many schools of navigation, medicine, artillery and engineering, including some where Latin and mathematics were taught, as well as nearly fifty elementary schools in provincial and sub-provincial main towns. He even provided nearly fifty garrison schools for soldiers' children. There was insufficient revenue, so Peter more than trebled it. There was no rationally organised administration capable of managing this new and complicated business, so foreign experts were called on to help to create a new central administration.

The above is, of course, an incomplete account of Peter's achievements, but it does show what he hoped to do with the help of Western Europe. Peter called on Western Europe to work and train Russians in financial and administrative affairs, and in the technical sciences. He did not want to borrow the results of Western technique, but wanted to appropriate the skill and knowledge, and build industries on the Western European model. The intelligent Russian of the seventeenth century realised that it was essential to increase Russia's productive capacity, by exploiting the country's natural and virgin riches, in order that the increased requirements of the state might be more easily met. Peter shared this point of view, and gave effect to it as did nobody before or after him, and he is therefore unique in the history of Russia. In foreign policy he concentrated on solving the Baltic problem.

It would be difficult to assess the value of the many industries he introduced. The evidence of the increased wealth was not a higher standard of living, but increased revenue. All increased earnings were, in fact, used to pay for the war. Peter's intention had been general economic reform, but the only evidence of success was the improved financial position. When Pososhkov wrote to Peter in 1724 that 'it was a great and difficult business to enrich all the people', he was not explaining a theory but sadly stating what he, and many others, had observed to be fact. In Peter's time men worked not for themselves but for the state, and after working better and harder than their fathers, probably died a great deal poorer. Peter did not leave the state in debt for one kopeck, nor did he waste a working day at the expense of future generations. On the contrary, he left his descendants rich reserves to draw on. His superiority lies in the fact that he was a creditor of the future, not a debtor. We will pursue this point later when we discuss the results of his reform. Were we to draw up a balance sheet of Peter's activities, excluding those affecting Russia's security and international position, but including those affecting the people's welfare, we would find that his great economic ambitions (which were the basis for his reforms) failed in their purpose, and, in fact, their only success was financial.

Thus Peter took from the old Russia the absolute power, the law, and the class structure; from the West he borrowed the technical knowledge required to organise the army, the navy, the economy, and the government. Where then was the revolution which renewed or transformed the Russian way of life, which introduced not only new institutions, but new principles (whether they were good or bad is, for the moment, immaterial). Peter's contemporaries, however, thought that the reforms were revolutionary, and they communicated their opinion to their descendants. But the reforms did not stop the Russians from doing things in their own way, and it was not the innovations that agitated them so much as the methods Peter used. Some of the results of the reforms were only felt in the future, and their significance was certainly not understood by everyone, and contemporaries anyhow only knew the effect the reforms had on them. Some reactions, however, were immediate, and these Peter had to account for.

The reforms were influenced not only by Peter's personality, but by wars and internecine struggles. Although the war had caused Peter to introduce reforms, it had an adverse influence on their development and success, because they were effected in an atmosphere of confusion usually consequent on war. The difficulties and demands of war forced Peter to do everything hastily.

Unfortunately Peter's methods alienated those indifferent to his reforms, and turned them into stubborn opponents. Peter used force, not example, and relied on men's instincts, and not on their moral impulses. Governing his country from the post-chaise and stagehouse, he thought always of business, never of people, and, sure of his own power, he neglected to pay sufficient attention to the passive resistance of the masses. A reforming zeal and a faith in autocracy were Peter's two hands; unfortunately one hand paralysed the energy of the other. Peter thought that he could supplement the lack of proper resources by using power to urge people on, and aimed at the impossible. As a result the officials became so intimidated and inefficient that they lost their ability to do what they were normally quite capable of doing. As Peter, for all his zeal, was unable to use people's strength, so the people, in their state of inert and passive resistance, were unable to appreciate Peter's efforts.

Thus without exaggerating or belittling the work of Peter the Great, we can summarise it as follows: the reforms were brought on by the essential requirements of state and people; the need for reform was understood by an authoritative, intelligent, energetic, and talented individual, one of those who, for no apparent reason, appear from time to time. Further, he was gifted, and, animated by a sense of duty, was resolved 'not to

553

Klyuchevsky

THE
ACHIEVEMENT
OF PETER THE
GREAT

spare his life in the service of his country'. When Peter came to the throne, Russia was not in an advantageous position compared with other European countries. Towards the end of the sixteenth century the Russians had created a great state, which was one of the largest in Europe; in the seventeenth century, however, it began to fail in moral and material strength. Peter's reforms did not aim directly at changing the political, social, or moral order, nor did they aim at forcing Russian life into an alien Western European pattern. The reforms only aimed at providing the Russian State and people with Western European intellectual and material resources, so that Russia might take its just position in Europe, and its people increase their productive capacity. But Peter had to do all this in a hurry, in the middle of a dangerous and bitter war, by using constraint at home; he had to struggle with the rapacity of his rascally officials, a gross landed nobility, and the prejudices and fears instilled by an ignorant clergy. The first reforms had been modest and limited, aimed only at reconstructing the army and developing the financial resources of the state; later, however, the reforms were the occasion for an obstinate battle which disturbed the existing pattern of living, and upset society. Started and carried through by the sovereign, the people's usual leader, the reforms were undertaken in conditions of upheaval, almost of revolution, not because of their objects but because of their methods, and by the impressions they made on the nerves and imaginations of the people. Perhaps it was more of a shock than a revolution, but the shock was the unforeseen and unintended consequence of the reforms.

Let us end by giving our opinion of Peter's reforms. The contradiction in his work, his errors, his hesitations, his obstinacy, his lack of judgement in civil affairs, his uncontrollable cruelty, and, on the other hand, his wholehearted love of his country, his stubborn devotion to his work, the broad, enlightened outlook he brought to bear on it, his daring plans conceived with creative genius and concluded with incomparable energy, and finally the success he achieved by the incredible sacrifices of his people and himself, all these different characteristics make it difficult to paint one painting. Moreover they explain the diverse impression he made on people; he sometimes provoked unqualified admiration, sometimes unqualified hostility. Generally the criticism prevailed because even his good actions were accompanied by disgusting methods.

Peter's reforms were the occasion for a struggle between the despot and the people's inertia. The Tsar hoped to arouse the energies and initiative of a society subdued by serfdom with the menace of his power, and strove, with the help of the noblemen, the oppressors of serfs, to introduce into Russia the European sciences and education which were essential to social progress. He also wanted the serf, while remaining a serf, to act responsibly and freely. The conjunction of despotism and liberty, of civilisation and serfdom, was a paradox which was not resolved in the two centuries after Peter. It is true that Russians of the eighteenth century tried to reconcile the Petrine reforms with humanitarian instincts, and Prince Shcherbatov, who was opposed to autocracy, devoted a treatise to explaining and even justifying Peter's vices and arbitrary conduct. Shcherbatov recognised that the enlightenment introduced into Russia by Peter benefited the country, and attacked Peter's critics on the grounds that they themselves had been the recipients of a culture, bestowed on them by the autocracy, which permitted them to distinguish the evils inherent in the autocratic system. Peter's faith in the miraculous power of education, and his respect for scientific knowledge, inspired the servile with little understanding of the meaning of civilisation; this understanding grew slowly, and was eventually transformed into a desire for truth and liberty.

Autocracy as a political principle is in itself odious. Yet we can reconcile ourselves to the individual who exercises this unnatural power when he adds self-sacrifice to it, and, although an autocrat, devotes himself unsparingly to the public good, risking destruction even on difficulties caused by his own work. We reconcile ourselves in the same way to the impetuous showers of spring, which strip branches from the trees, but none the less refresh the air, and by their downpour bring on the growth of the new seed.

Klyuchevsky
THE
ACHIEVEMENT
OF PETER THE
GREAT

36. The Scientific Role: The Conditions of Its Establishment in Europe

JOSEPH BEN-DAVID

37. Newton and the World of Law

A. RUPERT HALL

The age in which we live, and into which most of the students who will read these pages have been born, is called the atomic age. The name is appropriate, for the past quarter-century has witnessed incredible and staggering advances in man's knowledge and mastery of the world around him. Because of the tremendous opportunities that these advances afford man as well as the grim challenges that they set him, modern science occupies a prominent place in contemporary society. It is also a particular hallmark of Western civilization, since the crucial breakthroughs in scientific thought comprising the scientific revolution took place first in European society. There are several questions that ought to be raised about these facts. How and why did our sense of the scientific role arise? In what did the achievements of the scientific revolution consist, and how did they affect the world of the seventeenth century, and successive ages?

In the first of these selections, Joseph Ben-David investigates the growth of what he calls "the sociology of science," of how modern views and concepts of the place and function of scientific inquiry in society developed. The classical Greeks, he maintains, were capable of making many of the theoretical formulations that led to the discoveries of the sixteenth and seventeenth centuries, but they had no practical incentive to do so. Some scholars have

Source: Joseph Ben-David, "The Scientific Role: The Conditions of its Establishment in Europe," *Minerva,* Vol. IV (1965), pp. 15–17; 21–24; 26–28; 29–31; and 35–50. Reprinted by permission.

argued from a similar position that there was little technological advance in classical antiquity because ancient economies were largely slave-based without incentive to search for labor-saving devices, and that this outlook was ultimately responsible for the decline of classical civilization. Although Ben-David does not go so far in discussing the Greeks, he does lay great emphasis on two factors in the rise of modern science: the need for practical results and applications of scientific inquiry in order to produce adequate support for such studies; and the existence of people convinced of the potential value of science to society, even before its economic worth could be demonstrated. His article traces the place of science in the medieval university through the numerous academies founded in the fifteenth century, and finally to a triumphant wider public acceptance in the 1600's, especially in northern Europe. For him, the rise of Protestantism and of new elements in the middle classes, which encouraged scientific inquiry for its practical benefits, are key factors in this process. There is much information here, as well as subject for thought and debate. What is the relationship between public attitudes encouraging scientific inquiry and the "general crisis," which Hobsbawm and others see in Europe at this period? Was the contribution of Protestantism a negative or a positive one?

Professor Hall's study focuses not on the context of scientific discovery as much as on the particular discoveries of scientists in given areas. In the following selection he demonstrates quite well the fundamentally crucial importance of Isaac Newton to the success of the work of predecessors like Copernicus, Kepler, Descartes, and Galileo. In his career the strands of innovative activity in many fields—mathematics, physics, and astronomy—come together and are blended into a "harmonious and inseparable" whole. The account of how Newton worked on different parts of the puzzle, so to speak, and gradually built up a set of theories and mathematical proofs to demonstrate that the universe was subject to intelligible laws, is a fascinating if difficult one to follow. Newton's great work, The Mathematical Principles of Natural Philosophy, *is shown to be a highly original synthesis of numerous ideas and discoveries made during the preceding century.*

For those wishing to investigate the achievements of Newton's predecessors, several good books are available: H. Butterfield, The Origins of Modern Science, 1300–1800 *(1957); A. C. Crombie,* Medieval and Early Modern Science *(1959); T. S. Kuhn,* The Copernican Revolution *(1957); and A. R. Hall,* The Scientific Revolution, 1500–1800 *(1956).*

JOSEPH BEN-DAVID

Introductory Remarks

Ancient science failed to develop not because of its immanent shortcomings but because those who did scientific work did not see themselves, nor were they seen by others, as scientists, but primarily as philosophers, medical practitioners, or astrologers. Only this can explain why the appearance of Galileo had to wait for some 1,800 years after Archimedes, or the even longer gap between Aristotle's and Theophrastus' systematisations of living and growing things and those of Linnaeus and Cuvier. Had there existed among the Greeks several generations of intellectuals conceiving of themselves as scientists—with the motivations and obligations entailed in that—they could undoubtedly have applied themselves to the discovery of a less cumbersome method of mathematical notation and have made many of the scientific advances accomplished in the sixteenth and seventeenth centuries and subsequently. It is true that much of the Greek tradition was lost in the Middle Ages as a result of catastrophes but the stagnation and deterioration of the tradition had started earlier. Furthermore, had there been a group of persons, who inherited the Greek scientific tradition and who regarded themselves as scientists, anywhere in the Christian or the Moslem world or among the Jews, the Greek achievements might have been rediscovered in the Middle Ages or, at any rate, much more efficient use would have been made of them in the fifteenth century.

The question, therefore, is what made certain men in seventeenth-century Europe, and nowhere before, view themselves as scientists and see the scientific role as one with unique and special obligations and possibilities. The general conditions necessary for this occurrence were: either there had to be some striking scientific discoveries of practical value convincing people that the practice of science was an economically worthwhile occupation, or there had to be a group of persons who believed in science as an intrinsically valuable preoccupation and who had a reasonable prospect of making their belief generally accepted, even before science proved its economic worth. In what follows I will first sketch in outline the main steps of this development. Then I will present each step in detail.

Stages in the Formation of an Autonomous Scientific Role

Traditionally, natural science was subordinated to theology and philosophy. A first step towards the modern efflorescence occurred when it began to become more differentiated from theology and philosophy with respect to its subject-matter and procedures. Even when this point was reached, science continued to be a peripheral and secondary interest, but once its continuity was assured by its patent singularity and the steadiness of the concern which it attracted, it ceased to be subject to intermittent deterioration and there was even a probability of some slow but regular accumulation of scientific knowledge. The next step occurred when this peripheral subject, which had had a low status, relative to other intellectual fields, came to be regarded by groups, with class, religious and political interests opposed to the established order, as intellectually more meaningful to them than the existing theological, philosophical and literary culture. For these groups, the sciences became a central part of their culture.

Under these circumstances, men interested in science were impelled to re-define their roles as philosophers in such a way that science became increasingly central instead of peripheral to their conception of what they were doing. With the enhancement of the wealth, power and status of the classes which adopted an outlook sympathetic to science and in opposition to the inherited outlook, the status of the new type of philosopher was elevated. With the advancement of the status of scientific activity, the numbers of intellectuals of the highest quality moving into the field increased. The final steps occurred in the seventeenth century when the political success of the classes adopting the scientistic outlook, combined with the intellectual success of the new philosophers, led to a more elaborate organization of science and the establishment of scientific journals. In the course of these developments, men who did scientific work came to regard themselves and to be regarded by others as different from philosophers. They came to regard themselves as carrying on a significantly distinctive category of activity, disjunctively separated from the intellectual activity of philosophers and theologians. Increasing in numbers and having more occasion to meet and discuss with each other, they developed their own culture, their own norms and traditions in which their scientific work was embedded. The motivation and curiosity sustained by the stabilised stimulus inherent in such intensified and persistent scientific activity made for a greater continuity in scientific development. With a larger number of persons convinced of the value of science and devoting themselves actively and fully to its cultivation, science became, in a sense, a self-perpetuating domain of culture, and more independent than before of the variations in its environment.

A further contributory factor was the relative openness and decentralisation of the social system of European intellectual life. The Continent, including England, constituted a cultural whole, as a result of the unity of the church and its adoption of Roman traditions; persons and writings travelled across political borders with relative ease. Ideas evolved in one place would be readily appreciated in another. At the same time the various political units were sufficiently different from each other to permit beginnings, which were constricted in their places of origin (because they clashed with important vested interests), to be developed elsewhere, where the same vested interests were for some reason weaker.

. . . . .

The Peripherality of Science in the Medieval University

The intellectual division of labour arising from the location of different kinds of existing studies within one corporate organisation also stimulated the further internal differentiation which gave the natural sciences their place at the universities. They were not a required part of the curriculum and any academic degree could be acquired without knowledge of them. But inevitably among so many masters and scholars studying a considerable variety of subjects, there were some who were interested in scientific problems. Logicians took up mathematical and physical problems and physicians a variety of biological problems. Informal groups emerged and were given facilities to pursue these studies outside the regular curriculum or during vacations. Even though these activities were not institutionalised, the mere size and internal differentiation of the universities permitted enough interested persons to find each other. In such a large academic "market", there was enough "demand" to maintain a marginal intellectual field, whereas in a small circle the probability of finding anyone interested in it would have been less and the stimulus to curiosity and persistent interest would have been correspondingly small.

Decentralisation played its part in all these processes. The corporate autonomy of the university in any single place would not have been sufficient to withstand the onslaught of the church authorities against the philosophers. But during the thirteenth century the faculties had the choice of moving to another city. Later, when in the fourteenth century the opportunity to move diminished in consequence of increased royal power (especially in Paris), it was still possible for individuals to go to a different country, as did the English and the Germans, and even some French scholars (*e.g.,* Marsilius of Padua and John of Jandun) who left Paris for the English or the German universities. The decline of philosophy in France and England only made Italy the new centre of its study in the fifteenth and sixteenth centuries. The intellectual differentiation continued and the fifteenth-century Italian humanists or the sixteenth-century neo-Aristotelians were completely secularised and specialised philosophers.

Since geometry and dynamics were mainly cultivated by philosophers, the fate of these studies was (up to the sixteenth century) bound up with that of the philosophical studies in general. The tradition of medieval natural science was started at Oxford by masters of Merton College. From there it spread to Paris, which had the closest intellectual commerce with Oxford. When the tradition declined in both places during the fourteenth century, as did philosophy, the centre shifted to Italy, mainly to Padua, and to the new German, Dutch and other universities. Thus, when, in the fourteenth and fifteenth centuries, special university chairs were established, this tradition, influenced probably by internal developments within the medical faculty, also led to the establishment of professorships in mathematics, astronomy, and a variety of subjects, such as natural philosophy, Aristotelian physics, etc., first in Italy and later everywhere in Europe. These scientific chairs were of subordinate importance; it was an advancement for their incumbents if they could be appointed as professors of philosophy, or even better, of theology, law or medicine. It was in any case necessary to have a degree in these latter subjects in order to be appointed to a chair. Nevertheless, the natural sciences were, by this time, more or less regularly taught—on however modest a level—by professors who were paid for teaching them.

This process of differentiation, however, was stabilised some time in the sixteenth century (varying from country to country). By then, universities introduced the teaching of classics, basing their arts curriculum on the new set of specialised disciplines advocated by the humanists. There were in addition a number of professors of mathematics, astronomy and some natural history. Finally, there was a measure of specialisation in the medical faculty; anatomy was a specialised field of study and the idea of basic medical sciences was accepted. The only further differentiation of importance to science occurred in the medical faculties where chemistry became a relatively important and definitely specialised field during the eighteenth century. Otherwise, this set of subjects did not change essentially until the end of the eighteenth century. The status of mathematics and the natural science disciplines remained low. The natural sciences did not have anything approaching the status of the humanistic subjects, not to speak of the subjects of the professional faculties. This was not sufficient for the emergence of a distinctive scientific identity. As long as one could obtain a university position in mathematics only if, in addition to mathematical knowledge, one possessed a degree in medicine (*e.g.,* Cardan), theology (*e.g.,* Luca Pacioli), or law, and as long as it contributed more to one's advancement and fame to be not just a competent mathematician but a good classical scholar (editing, for instance, Greek mathematicians for publication, *e.g.,* Regiomontanus) rather than an outstanding mathematician and not a classical scholar, there was little incentive to concentrate one's energy on scientific subjects. One or another highly motivated scholar might decide to devote his best talents to science. But there was no institutional basis to ensure that his successor would do likewise.

The situation was not much different in medicine, although the status of that faculty was higher than that of the faculty of arts. Anatomy was considered an integral part of the subject and chemistry was integral to the apothecary's art, which fell within the jurisdiction of the medical faculty. Here too, however, the important thing was the practice and theory of medicine; the scientific aspect was less important. An anatomist who was not a physician—there were some artists of this kind—was not seriously regarded. Chemistry, though by the second half of the eighteenth century an undoubtedly more developed science than any branch of medicine or biology, was at the universities lower in the order of prestige and importance than those latter subjects, corresponding to the lower art of the apothecary. As a result, there was little continuity in what science there was in the medical faculties. It was largely a function of the accidental interest of individuals. The successor of a great anatomist-physiologist might well be a well-known practitioner with no scientific interests; the level of chemistry teaching varied a great deal, since the technical aspects of the subjects were not generally appreciated as being of academic importance. (This is why, even as late as the eighteenth century, the scientific excellence which occurred in the German, Dutch, Swedish, Scottish and Swiss universities was neither general in all fields nor of long endurance.)

. . . . .

Thus although mathematics and some natural science were taught with sufficient frequency to produce a supply of potential scientists, they were not taught with enough concentration to create in a small number of persons an image of themselves as scientists. Science was a marginal activity within the university and those who learned it there saw their knowledge of it as a peripheral feature in the image they had of themselves. Those who studied science at universities did not acquire enough of it for them to form a strong attachment to it. There were not enough other persons in university circles, interaction with whom could intensify their own interest in science, which was otherwise insufficiently strong to live entirely from their own individual inner motivation. Finally it was evident that science was held in fairly low esteem by the authorities of church, state and university. For the incentive to do science wholeheartedly, all three of these conditions would have to change.

Artists and "Scientists" in Italy: The Rudimentary Formation of the Scientific Role

The first signs of a change in the evaluation of science appear in the circles of artists and engineers in fifteenth-century Italy. Till then, artists were considered mere artisans but, as a result of the general conditions which made possible a modicum of autonomy for various urban groups (already noted in connection with the rise of universities), their fortunes were improving in the fifteenth century.

In addition to the new interest in art, this improvement was perhaps even more closely related to the fact that the role of artist often overlapped, in the same person, with the roles of architect, fortification engineer and ballistic expert. In fifteenth-century Italy, the artist received an all-round training. As a youth apprenticed to the workshop of a master, he tried his hand at painting, sculpture, architecture and goldsmithery before he specialised. If outstanding, such a person entered the service of a city or of a secular or an ecclesiastical prince to be responsible for public works in art, architecture and engineering. Verrocchio, Mantegna, Leonardo da Vinci and Fra Gioconda were among these versatile artist-technicians. They received a superior kind of technical training, comprehensive and eminently practical. But the artists had little formal education, usually did not know Latin and whatever book knowledge they had could have come only from the popular compendia in the vernacular which attempted to digest all available knowledge in an uncritical fashion. There had already been contacts between scholars and architects before the fifteenth century, the latter consulting the former about classical technological manuscripts. But starting from the first half of the fifteenth century with the school of Filippo Brunelleschi—which included Luca della Robbia, Donatello and Ghiberti—these contacts between scholars and architects became more continuous and conventional. The school of Brunelleschi included Leone Battista Alberti, a rich and learned scholar who became an architect, or rather, an architectural theorist and consultant to the group.

The connections between the artists and the university-trained scholars were based partly on common technical interests. The artists and architects were interested in problems of perspective, the engineers in statics and dynamics. They could both benefit from the scholars who knew the available classical literature and could formulate in articulate principles what the artists could not. At the same time the scholars benefited from their contact with the artists whose practical experience helped to make meaningful the content of the ancient texts. Greek geometry and science became more intelligible when studied in connection with design, construction, or ballistics rather than as pure book learning. The interest of painters in anatomy and botany provided a powerful tool for the anatomists and naturalists.

The artists had certain "status problems" in common with scientists. The artists and technologists had hiterto been relatively low in their position in society. The only practical way to assert the status of their calling and to prove the spiritual value of what had been traditionally considered as a lowly manual art was through giving evidence of the connection between their work and a recognised scholarly pursuit. They were, however, little interested in the acquisition of classical languages and had no sense for philosophical speculation. The only scholars with whom they had a common interest were those cultivating the sciences.

This gradually changed the self-image of the scientifically-inclined scholar. In the university community on which his status had up till then depended entirely, his interests were considered as of merely peripheral importance. If he wanted to obtain recognition, he had to prove his worth in the more central fields of scholarship. Now, however, there was an upcoming profession, that of the artists, for whom philosophy was first and foremost science. Viewing themselves through the eyes of these new clients or public, who appreciated what they had to offer, the scientist-scholars gained self-confidence. There was a basis here for viewing science and mathematics as the centre of a new philosophy still to be created.

· · · · ·

Meanwhile, in the northern countries of Europe there emerged, starting from the 1530s, a growing trend towards extolling the virtues of arts and crafts and the knowledge of nature. This began in the writings of Ludovico Vives, Erasmus, Montaigne and Rabelais and can be traced through Palissy to Bacon's new philosophy. This intellectual trend ran hand in hand with the continued growth in the social importance of new classes whose outlook was sympathetic neither with the scholastic nor the humanistic intellectual establishments. In Italy, on the other hand, artists and technologists had been—in spite of attempts in this direction—unable to break away from the domination of the guilds. The scientists as well as the small number of very eminent artists were now moving in a quite different, upper class, humanistic environment—the environment of the academies. This environment embraced those merchants—at least the most successful among them—who were being absorbed into the nobility in Italy. This was due partly to the nature of Italian city-state democracy, and partly to the fact that, unlike the position in Northern Europe, there were no Protestants with great influence in these important classes to foster among them an oppositional intellectual outlook potentially congenial to science. Thus at a time when the Northern European class structure became increasingly fluid and a mobile "middle" class was increasing in size, in awareness of itself and in self-sufficiency, the Italian class structure recrystallised into something approximating its earlier form.

The Reconquest of Science by the Non-Scientific Culture in Italy

Our description of the Italian class system as increasingly rigid and that of Northern Europe as increasingly fluid, and—parallel with this— Italian science as approaching stagnation and Northern European science as developing at a growing rate, may be regarded as somewhat ambiguous. Looking backward from the vantage point of the second half of the seventeenth century, the statement appears correct, but viewing the situation from the perspective of the sixteenth and the early seventeenth century, it seems misleading. The merging of the merchants into the Italian nobility may be considered as a sign of open-mindedness towards commercial occupations such as was not known in the majority of European countries before the nineteenth century; the participation of the guilds in the governments of cities ensured a wider extension of civic rights than anywhere else; and the interest in science, as well as in all other branches of learning and art, was more widespread in Italy than in any other country. In what sense is it then justified to view the turning of the scientists to the upper class social framework of the academies as a foreshadowing of decline? Perhaps it would be more correct to interpret it as the first appropriation of a new scientific culture by part of one of the ruling classes in Europe, to be followed at some distance by the rest?

For our purpose, the main point is that in other parts of Europe the cause of science was taken up by a class of persons who stood to gain from certain changes in the social order. In Italy by contrast, science became, by the sixteenth century, the concern of a minority within a class which had attained what it wanted and which was interested in the stability of the social order.

. . . . .

The academies provided a flexible framework for the expression of the cultural interests of different groups of intellectuals where those interests could not be fulfilled by existing institutions. The existence of such institutions in Italy as a means of coping with newly emerged interests would seem to indicate the relative openness of Italian social structure, as compared with the rest of Europe, where academies were only created in imitation of the Italian models.

As a matter of fact, however, what appears as openness is better interpreted as evidence of rigidity. A price had to be paid for the relatively easy absorption of the leading merchants into the nobility and for the relative ease with which the new cultural pursuits were accommodated within academies, and the academies within the official hierarchy of cultural institutions. The price which had to be paid was the assumption of the habits of thought, attitudes and style of the upper classes, to the point where the spirit of innovation eventually expired.

One of the results was the abandonment of the practical concerns of science. Whereas in England and in France, propaganda for the official recognition of science was based on its potential usefulness to technology and production, in Italy its claims were justified by arguments from Platonic philosophy or neo-Platonic mysticism. The cause of science in Northern Europe was supported, not only by certain, usually upper class, intellectual circles actually cultivating it but by a considerable element of merchants, artisans and seafarers. In Italy it was espoused only by an upper class intellectual clique trying to displace the official university philosophers and modernise the intellectual outlook of the Catholic church.

Copernican astronomy was the issue around which the conflict crystallised in Italy between the opposition and the official intellectual establishment. It had obvious philosophical implications which were useful for the opposition movement but in the end it embroiled the movement with the church. The oppositional as well as the conspirational and esoteric nature of the movement is attested by the names of the academies in the sixteenth century: Incogniti (Naples), 1546–48; Segreti (Naples), 1560, (Vicenza), 1570, (Siena), 1580; Animosi (Bologna), 1562, (Padua), 1573; Affidati (Bologna), 1548. The reappearance of the same names in different places shows the existence of links between different local groups. None of these names reappears in the next centuries, when the movement came out into the open and renounced its oppositional orientation.

The first group of significance was perhaps the short-lived Affidati in Padua. Founded in 1573 by the Abbot Ascanio Martinengo, it included professors of the university, high clergy, noblemen and internationally known scholars. It did not last long but some of its members went to Rome where some 20 years later they appeared as members of one of the most famous academies, the Accademia dei Lincei. The latter was founded in 1603 by the 18-year-old *Marchese* Cesi and joined in 1610 by the Naples physicist Giambattista della Porta, whose academy in Naples had been suppressed by the Roman Curia, and in 1611 by Galileo, who had previously resigned his unsatisfactory chair at Padua. This circle can be regarded as the first open and relatively comprehensive attempt to create a scientific institution claiming equal status to other institutions of learning. The Lincei attempted to organise instruction in natural sciences, philosophy and jurisprudence and published books on science (including one by Galileo).

It is very doubtful whether the dramatic events of the condemnation of Galileo were in themselves of far-reaching significance. The indignation aroused by the high-handed actions of the church hierarchy probably increased the popularity of science. There is indeed no sign of a cessation of the scientific activity following the condemnation of Galileo. It is true that the activities of the Lincei were curtailed after the first attempt of the Curia to suppress Galileo but some of its members and the disciples of

Galileo continued to be active throughout the first half of the century and participated in the foundation of the other famous Italian academy of the seventeenth century, the Cimento (1657–67). After the election of its patron, Prince Leopold de Medici, as a cardinal, its members, due to personal animosities, were unable to carry on with their work.

The picture, therefore, is not one of the movement gaining wider and wider support and then violently suppressed but rather of an episode well contained within an established intellectual fraternity which was decaying. By the end of the seventeenth century the scientific academies became unimportant replicas of the literary academies, consisting of local amateurs and notables; they were of no importance in international science. In medicine Italy remained a centre during the late seventeenth century, thanks to the excellence of some of its university faculties but in other sciences the centre shifted to England and France. The fate of the English and French universities at the turn of the fourteenth century when they lost their leadership to Italy now befell the Italian academies. Science and scientists remained dependent on the narrow circles within the upper classes which ruled the country and the church and were interested in learning. These were the circles which had to be convinced that natural science was important and worthwhile enough for them to give to it the full blessing of public recognition and freedom of communication, notwithstanding the weighty doctrinal difficulties which might arise from this. It would be unrealistic to believe that it could have been otherwise when the argument in favour of the Copernican theory was still inconclusive, when science could offer no more than a few bits and pieces of intellectually interesting astronomical and mechanical theories and the unbounded confidence of Galileo's prophetic genius, in contrast to the vast body of learning, wisdom and beauty represented by contemporary humanism and theology. As long as those who had to be convinced by the proponents of science were the main depositories of the traditional learning, the scientific movement was doomed to failure. For those who mattered, and probably for the majority of those who did not, science was an intellectually and aesthetically second rate, and morally and religiously potentially dangerous, activity. If taken up by an extraordinary genius like Galileo, who could write about it in accomplished literary form, it was given all the attention due to a great piece of literature. And if in addition the scientist was a man who could be consulted on great engineering architectural projects and show his brilliance in other serious and playful ways, he was honoured as a man of outstanding imaginative talents. The term "virtuoso" truly reflects these attitudes and shows the limit of the appreciation of science in Italian society in the seventeenth century.

This attitude to science was not unique to Italy and, had the fate of science depended everywhere in Europe on the same educated and "responsible" ruling class as in Italy, the emergence of a proud and self-confident body of scientists might have been postponed for a very long period of time, perhaps indefinitely. But for the good of science, the social structure in Northern Europe was different. As has been said, there existed to the North a mobile class whose aspirations, beliefs and interests—intellectually as well as economically and socially—were well served by affirming the utopian claims made on behalf of science. Furthermore, part of this class found science a religiously more acceptable intellectual pursuit than traditional philosophy. Thus when the now ebbing tide of science, receding from the scientific circles and academies of Italy, touched France and England, its direction was reversed. The changes which took place there and at that time set in motion a flood which has still to cease.

The Higher Evaluation of Science in Northern Europe

The most obvious aspect of the transformation which occurred in the scientific movement in Northern Europe was that there *science eventually became a central element in an emerging conception of progress.* This, however, was not at all clear from the beginning and many aspects of the movement there appeared to be no more than a reproduction of Italian patterns. The *rapprochement* between artists and practical men on the one hand and scholars of scientific bent on the other, such as existed in Italy from the fifteenth century onwards, was copied in Europe in the sixteenth century. The best known names are Vesalius, Dürer and Christopher Wren. The last, one of the most brilliant scientific talents and at the same time one of the greatest architects of the seventeenth century, can be seen as a late and improved version of his fifteenth-century Italian forerunners, Alberti and Brunelleschi. Similarly, the northern scientific academies owed their inspiration to Italy. Peiresc, the originator of the informal circles out of which there eventually arose the Académie des Sciences, was a student at Padua, a correspondent of Galileo and a disciple of della Porta, who had founded one of the early Italian scientific academies in Naples. He became the centre of the continent-wide circle of scientific and scholarly correspondents and visitors; there is a direct link between this circle and those which advocated the establishment of the Royal Society and the Académie des Sciences. But Peiresc only continued what had begun with Galileo, who was himself a centre of a network of correspondents and visitors.

Nonetheless, as early as the sixteenth century the differences between the Northern and the Italian patterns became evident in a variety of forms. The most important network of scientists and practical men was that concerned with navigation in England and Holland. In England this included the mathematicians Robert Recorde (1510–1558) and John Dee (1527–1606), both of whom served as consultants to large trading companies. Dee was also adviser to such famous seafarers as Martin Frobisher, Sir Humphrey Gilbert, John Davis and Sir Walter Raleigh. Thomas Digges, the astronomer who carried Copernicus' ideas an important step further, also spent some time at sea and interested himself in navigation. Henry Biggs (1561–1630), the first professor of mathematics at Gresham College in London, was a member of the Virginia Company. Gilbert's famous treatise on magnetism used the observations of the seafarers Robert Norman and William Borough. The seventeenth-century Cambridge anti-Aristotelian author William Watts used those of another seafarer, Thomas James. Richard Norwood, the London mathematician, surveyed the Bermudas for the Bermuda Company.

Contacts between scientists and practical men were not confined to matters connected with navigation. Apart from the already mentioned relationships with artists, engineers and artillery experts, there was increasing interest in machines, mining, lens grinding and the making of watches and other instruments. The field central to the contacts between scholars and practical people shifted, in contrast to Italy, from art and civil and military engineering, which were primarily the concerns of the ruling and aristocratic classes, to navigation and instrument making. These latter fields were closely tied to the concerns and the fortunes of a new, increasingly numerous and self-esteeming class of sea traders, merchants and artisans, some of the latter also dependent primarily on sea trade. (Italy was at that time rapidly losing its position as a sea-trading nation.) Compared to the social contacts of science in sixteenth-century Italy, these were relatively humble connections. The merchants and artisans were ascending in status and influence but they had still a very long way to rise. Their status was comparable to the status of the fifteenth-century Italian artist-engineers who had at that time cultivated the company of the scientists. The social outlook of these classes, however, was much more promising than that of the early Italian artist-engineers. The latter were dependent for their income and honours on the ruling families and the higher nobility, since these were the exclusive customers of the goods and services produced by them. But the merchants and artisans of England had a basis of income which was independent of the rulers.

There was an important affinity between the situation of the merchants and artisans and that of the new scientific scholars. Both had more to gain from certain changes in society than they had to gain from stability. In the scale of values of the classes responsible for the maintenance of the social order and the everyday business of the economy, science—potentially subversive of religious authority and technologically of limited importance—merited only low priority. In the outlook of this growing and increasingly important class, who were still not in positions of higher authority anywhere (except in Holland and there they were still very new to that position) but who had prospects of such ascendancy, adherence to inherited and existing patterns of thought and action did not rank so highly. A class of the persons who were experiencing a meteoric rise in their fortunes consequent on the discovery of new places, new routes, new goods and new markets, was sympathetic to the belief that scientific discoveries to be made in the future would transform the world into a much better place than it had ever been before.

The upper classes who were better educated provided a larger number of persons who were intellectually interested in science or even practiced science. But as a whole they had no important interest, social or cultural, in promoting it; indeed it often seemed to their advantage to slow down its diffusion. The relatively uneducated middle classes knew less about science but they saw in it a desirable symbol of change and improvement and they were vaguely prompted to prefer it to the older philosophies. They provided a broader potential basis for the support of science than had ever existed in Italy.

The Birth of a Scientific Utopia

This vaguely sympathetic stratum, was not, however, sufficient to establish science in its own right. Man lives not only by bread but also by the word of God and this was particularly true in the seventeenth century. Nearly everyone in Europe was religious, either Christian or Jewish. The church had managed to come to terms with philosophies which opposed its doctrine more directly than science. But it was easier to allow free speculation about abstract things such as the immortality of the soul than to submit specific questions like the movement of the earth to the test of the telescope. The speculations of the human mind about religious questions could never be conclusive. In questions in which speculation was regarded as the right method, it was a matter of God's power versus man's mind. God's ultimate power was beyond the power of man's mind and where there was a contradiction between the divine mind and human minds it was not difficult to "see" where the ultimate truth lay. But empirical science did not allow such evasion; it opposed nature as created by God to written records which were authoritatively accepted at that time as His own words or as directly inspired by Him. As a result, Catholic, Protestant or Jewish religious authorities all tended to take an attitude ranging from hostility to an extreme caution with respect to empirical science.

Among the major European religions, there was however one important difference: Protestantism (a) did not everywhere possess a constituted religious authority, and (b) its doctrines left the interpretation of the Bible to the individual believer and left him to seek his own religious enlightenment. Where a Catholic or a Jew had to suppress what might be his conviction that science would ultimately prove to be a new way to God because of the fixity of biblical interpretation, a Protestant who felt that God's will and the discoveries of science were in harmony could go ahead with good conscience, provided that he lived in an environment where church authority was unstable or weak. (Where the authority of the divines was well established, it was their usually anti-scientific interpretations which prevailed.)

Thus, while the idea that science and technology (the "practical arts") could become a better mode of education and an improved intellectual and moral culture in general was consistent with the interests and the outlook of the mobile middle classes, only certain branches of Protestants could make scientific knowledge, or a philosophy granting such knowledge complete autonomy, integral to their religious. beliefs. Only they could thereby overcome the resistance which religious belief might interpose. Protestantism thus provided the legitimation for the formulation of a new utopian world view where science, experiment and experience— the logical relationship between which was perhaps mistakenly construed—were to form the core of a new culture.

The beginnings of the ideas which link science, the practical arts and the continuous improvement of man's condition, can be traced back to the 1530s. Ludovico Vives, a Spanish Protestant scholar who was tutor at the English court, was among the first to extol the educational and intellectual virtue of the experience of the artisans. Starting from the middle of the sixteenth century, however, these Renaissance beginnings were taken up by Protestant philosophers and educationists and transformed into what Karl Mannheim called a "utopia". The beginners of this trend were Peter Ramus and Bernard Palissy and they were followed by Francis Bacon, Comenius, Samuel Hartlib and several others. They were interested in universal education and far-reaching projects of scientific and technological cooperation, which they hoped would lead to the conquest of nature and the emergence of a new civilisation. They believed in a worldly redemption to which science and technology and their effective support and organisation would lead.

None of these people was a significant scientist, nor—with the ambiguous exception of Bacon—even an important philosopher. They were publicists who were interested in practical results; they expressed programmatically the intellectual outlook of the circles of scientists and others who cooperated in the solution of practical problems. In Italy this cooperation had never been turned into an outlook with primarily practical aims of social reform. The only attempt with implications for wider issues was that of Galileo, which ended in failure. But even his aim was the conversion of the church to the right cosmological beliefs and the modernisation of the intellectual life of Italy; it was not social improvement. The fact that it was turned into such a broad practical outlook in Northern Europe was the combined result of the different social structure and of Protestantism.

Protestant "Science Policy"

It was not that all varieties of Protestantism adopted this new view of science or that they did so regardless of their situation. In small, self-contained Protestant communities, such as those in Geneva and in Scotland, in most places in Germany and, later in the seventeenth century, in Holland, science fared worse than in the great Catholic centres of Italy, France and Central Europe. These Protestant communities were small and tightly knit; being relatively undifferentiated, they had no appreciable class of intellectuals except their divines. Like the similarly organised Jewish communities, they would not tolerate anything approaching heresy. The Catholic church, on the other hand, with its tradition of learning and its own large class of differentiated intellectuals in the teaching orders, usually had more sympathy for specialised, non-religious intellectual interests.

In most places, however, Protestants were unable to form a closed religious community. On the one hand, they were in contention with the Catholics; on the other hand, the various Protestant sects fought among themselves. In those situations, no effective religious authority existed to enforce conformity in doctrine and practice. The governments of the territories where these conditions obtained were much freer than any others to adopt a sympathetic attitude to science and the scientistic utopia. Those who believed in the utopia were free to propagate their views and the official authorities could adopt the pragmatic attitude towards the matter. As a result official Protestant authorities adopted on several occasions policies of supporting science and eventually in Commonwealth England they came very near to the scientistic utopia as a basis for their official educational policy.

The first notable opportunity for the emergence of a distinctly Protestant science policy was provided by the persecution of Galileo. Any oppressive act by their greatest opponent in the competition of religions was immediately used as propaganda. The case of Galileo was a conspicuous one. A group of Protestant scholars in Paris, Strasbourg, Heidelberg and Tübingen decided, immediately following his condemnation, to translate Galileo's work into Latin. In this endeavour they received general support from several Protestant communities, otherwise not notable for their tolerance for Copernican ideas. Copies of the original work were obtained through doctrinally rigid Geneva; one member of the group was from Tübingen University, where only some time before Kepler had been prevented from earning a theological degree on account of his Copernican views.

The Dutch government also turned Galileo's disfavour to Protestant advantage, by inviting him, through Grotius, to advise it on the measurement of longitudes. Even though the advice of Galileo was not followed, official honours were bestowed on Galileo by the Dutch government and the contacts continued until interrupted by the Curia, which—probably not incorrectly—perceived that they were exploited for purposes of Protestant propaganda.

Protestant scholars with scientific interests saw this as an opportunity to connect the furtherance of the Protestant cause with gaining official support for science. Their concerted action was perhaps the earliest manifestation of an active "scientific lobby" in Protestant Europe. At least some of the intellectuals involved were acting on behalf of the promotion of science and not just for a general, religious-educational cause.

It is difficult to conclude just how long the Galileo case was used to link science with Protestantism: It was not, in any case, a major factor in the establishment of science. In England science became involved in Protestant politics in a new and more significant way. Both before and under the Commonwealth, it had become increasingly difficult to maintain public consensus on anything of potential religious importance because of the numerous theological dissensions with political implications. One of the often-mentioned features of the pre-history of the Royal Society is that the participants at the informal meetings of the circle from which the society emerged agreed not to discuss matters of religion and politics but to restrict themselves dispassionately to the neutral field of science. For apparently similar reasons, the Baconian philosophy and the support of science became part of the official policy of the Commonwealth. One of the educational-scientific publicists of Commonwealth England was John Durie, who had spent much of his time in Northern Europe working on the unification of all the evangelical churches. Both Hartlib, who supported Durie, and Haak, another member of the early group of scientists and politicians of science, were probably similarly motivated by their personal experiences of religious conflicts in Europe. They were influential in the educational policies of the Commonwealth and their ideas became official policy. The sudden rise of the popularity of the Baconian view in the late 1640s, and the appointment of Wilkins, Wallis, Petty and Goddard to university chairs testify to the success of the new ideas. Baconian science —in addition to its congeniality to the class interests of artisans and well-to-do merchants who formed the backbone of the regime—was something on which the more enlightened elements among the Puritans could agree. Scientific activity was welcomed by those who were interested in a more secular education and who shared the distaste of anything that reminded them of the old regime. Yet it was also acceptable to the more fanatical Puritan divines who thought that the study of the Bible should be sufficient education for all and who even wanted to abolish the universities altogether. Science thereby found hospitality in its own right. It did so not because it was positively supported by any particular doctrine of Protestant theology, but because it was relatively free from involvement in the theological and philosophical disputes which had ravaged the continent of Europe and which were disrupting English society as well.

This was the final stage in the development of the conditions for the emergence of a body of self-conscious and self-confident scientists who looked upon their activities as scientists as something inherently worthy of the efforts of distinguished intellects. Their support now became the official policy of the government of one of the wealthiest and most powerful nations of Europe. Science became, to use Durkheim's phrase, part of *"la vie sérieuse"*; its utilitarian promises were accepted like religious faith and its ethos of dispassionate inquiry, exactitude and empiricism were made into moral values and proudly identified by some with religion. Science had thereby entered definitely into the centre of a newly emerging culture.

Even though the first steps were taken by a short-lived revolutionary government, the groups which put this government into power and the reformatory zeal which inspired their victory survived. The Restoration did not reverse the growth of the new outlook or of the sections of society which espoused it. The support of science and a partial legitimation of the scientific outlook was one of the politically least difficult measures in the creation of a new consensus. Among the first acts of the new government was the establishment of the Royal Society. The attraction of science for men of outstanding ability and moral integrity at this crucial period was greatly furthered by this new policy.

Social Class, Protestantism and Science

The emergence of the new type of scientist has thus been linked to the rise of new social classes interested in a more open social structure and a more empirically oriented education on the one hand and to Protestantism on the other. It must be emphasised, however, that the only thing which this explains is the enhancement of the *status* of science and the change in the *role* of the scientist-scholar who now can openly and respectably become a scientist without having to be primarily something else. The change in status helped to increase scientific activity and the change in the definition of the role contributed similarly to the increased systematisation, clarity and boldness of scientific thought. These changes in the status of science and in the distinctiveness of the scientific role do not, however, explain the content of scientific discovery or the composition of the scientific community. Public support and religious grace can heighten motivation but they cannot create talent or determine what it discovers. Public opinion and religious belief cannot even create the basic motivation to engage in science. They can only reinforce or hinder it where it exists in individuals and in the stream of cultural tradition. The content of the new science was overwhelmingly determined by the scholarly tradition which consisted primarily of mathematics, astronomy, dynamics, statics and optics and, secondarily, of the medical fields of anatomy and physiology. Those who cultivated the new sciences had to be educated people with great talent and ample leisure, which meant that they usually came from a wealthy background. The rise of new social classes influenced scientists—whatever their class background might have been—by freeing them from social conventions. They were not inhibited or constrained by considerations of hierarchical dignity from expressing their enthusiasm about experimentation or from thinking in terms of practical utility. This same disposition to put aside everything except their scientific interests was also manifested in the relatively informal atmosphere and absence of status distinctions at the meetings of the Royal Society. Foreign visitors were struck by this situation and commented on it as notably different from the ubiquitous concern with honour, precedence and class distinctions which could be seen among comparable groups on the Continent.

The affinity between the new scientific disposition and Protestantism is disclosed somewhat more directly when we examine the actual composition of the scientific community. In Eruope, as a whole, men of Protestant origin were more numerous among scientists than were Catholics. Although the data on the religious background and scientists are not entirely reliable and it is difficult to estimate precisely the size of the religious communities in the countries from which they came, all the existing computations (including those of authors intent on disproving the hypothesis about the relationship between Protestantism and science) show that Protestants were disproportionately highly represented among scientists from the sixteenth to the end of the eighteenth century.

The explanatory factor has, nonetheless, to be sought not in the social and religious characteristics of the scientists of the time but in a constellation which includes the increased numbers, wealth, influence and status of the merchant and artisan classes, Protestantism, the emergence of a scientistic utopia of progress and rising interest in and support for science.

The Expansive Outlook of the Public of Science: Anglo-French Contrasts

In addition to the Italian case which has been discussed above, this approach is also supported by the history of the scientific movement in France, where a scientific movement was created by people who were overwhelmingly Catholic. The establishment of the Académie des Sciences in 1666 in Paris, though prompted by the English example, was no mere imitation of it. The informal circles and academies in France, which had preceded its establishment and which conducted the propaganda for it, were similar to those in England and had in fact been in close contact with the English group (as well as with the Italian ones). Marin Mersenne was, in the 1630s, a centre of correspondence encompassing all the known scientists of Europe and he assembled in conferences at his home the leading French scientists of the time: Descartes, Desargues, Gassendi, the brothers Pascal and Roberval. Both Mersenne and Theophraste Renaudot were in touch with members of the English group such as Haak and Hartlib and were in favour of the ideas of the latter and of Comenius on educational reform. Renaudot was of Protestant origin—he had been converted to Catholicism after the fall of La Rochelle in 1629—and Mersenne, though in holy orders, was suspected of reformist tendencies. However, there were no Protestants among the scientists of Mersenne's circle.

Of the other politicians of science active in scientific salons, Montmor, Auzout, Hedelin, Thevenot, Petit and Sorbière, only the last was a Protestant. But they were greatly influenced by the English example and by Baconian philosophy. The first editor of the *Journal des Savants,* Denis de Sallo, was dismissed under clerical pressure because of his pronounced Gallican and Jansenist leanings. The most important supporters of these groups in the royal court were Richelieu and, later, Colbert.

Thus, among the groups favouring a policy of active support of science and the adoption of the new scientistic philosophy in France, Protestants, Gallicans and Jansenists (both of the latter are doctrinally critical, anti-ecclesiastical positions) had played an important role. Like their opposite numbers in Protestant London, they, too, lived in a situation in which there was no single well-established church authority.

The structure of society in France differed from that in England. There was, it is true, a middle class in France which had somewhat similar sources of income as in England. It, too, was also somewhat expansive in outlook. But class differences in France were much more rigid and the power of the king much more pervasive than in England. Such an attempt at educational and social reform as that advocated by Renaudot did not, therefore, become the concern of any of the more important Paris circles of scientists and wealthy amateurs. (In Loudon, the native city of Renaudot, there was apparently such a group and it included both Protestants and Catholics.) The group immediately preceding the Académie des Sciences, the so-called Montmor Academy, was much more of an upper-class salon than the group from which the Royal Society arose. It was also more difficult in Paris than in London to overcome the resistance of vested interest groups such as the medical faculty, the Sorbonne, the Jesuits and others.

The result was that the Baconian outlook found little expression in the Académie des Sciences. Whereas the Royal Society was an independent corporation based on the mixed membership of the original group, including amateurs and politicians of science as well as scientists of outstanding accomplishments, the Académie was a sort of elevated scientific civil service composed only of a small number of scientists of very high reputation. These differences had the immediate effect that in France, parallel to the Académie, there continued to exist informal groups carrying on the reformist traditions of the scientistic outlook. These led directly to the philosophical movement of eighteenth-century France; the Académie on the other hand became a bulwark of specialised science. The scientistic outlook and specialised scientific research became separated from each other in France. This deprived the scientists of the supporting opinion which helped to define the scientific role.

Under the circumstances of the time, science was not likely to receive more than occasional support, dependent on personal predilection, from the well-established temporal or spiritual authorities, since its practical uses were few and its educational and moral importance could not compete with that of theology, the humanities and law. Only in the medium of a utopian outlook oriented towards an imagined, rationally attainable future could science replace existing philosophy and humanistic study as the most important source of truth. Such an outlook could only gain wide currency where (a) established church authority was weak and doctrine hence open to individual interpretation; (b) there was an actual class of people desiring economic and technological change rather than the maintenance of a balanced hierarchical order; and (c) where this class was expansive in power and influence but not yet in a position of authority and responsibility (in which case it would have had to be more practical and less utopian in its intellectual policies). In all these respects, seventeenth-century France lay somewhere between Italy and England. This is particularly evident if we consider that many a French intellectual of the period studied, taught or lived in Holland, where both the class and religious situation were much freer than in France.

This in-between situation of France in respect of social structure and religion is reflected in the internal constitution of French science. The atmosphere of the French circles was much more like that of the Italian academies than that of the English circles of scientists and their supporters. There was much direct contact between the Italian and the French groups. On the other hand, Baconian and related views had much wider popularity in France than in Italy—in fact some of the views and ideas were the work of Frenchmen such as Ramus, Palissy, Renaudot—and there had been during the second half of the century much conscious imitation of the English model.

This also explains why the scientific movement and outlook, which rose to importance in England under the Commonwealth, became centred in France during the eighteenth century. Its decline in England was the result of the fact that the Royal Society, its main institutional centre, became part of the conservative ruling establishment. The scientific movement continued, however, to thrive in France, where the social class and the intellectual circles, out of whose interaction the outlook arose, were kept apart from real power and, with the exception of a few selected academicians, from the highest honours.

The Consolidation of a European Scientific Community in the Seventeenth Century

With the establishment of the academies possessing sufficient means of support to ensure continuity and to maintain a constant flow of periodical publication, science became more autonomous than it had been hitherto. An uninterrupted scientific activity, more or less proportionate to the general growth of social resources (population and wealth) and relatively independent of the prevailing non-scientific culture, became possible. This contributed greatly to the development of the scientific identity and, beyond it, to the institutionalised role of the modern scientist.

The greatest scientists of the seventeenth century from Galileo, Descartes, Boyle, Newton and Leibniz, already possessed a science-centred world view. They wrote philosophy and theology too from this point of view and claimed a recognition for themselves as scientific philosophers. In the case of Galileo this self-image was not yet shared by the others, or at least not by some of the others, and he was seen by many as writer-philosopher-engineer, honoured mainly as a manifestation, somewhat like an artistic virtuoso, of human genius, rather than for his achievements in science. In the case of Boyle or Newton, the centrality of the scientific component or the specific scientific achievement are clearly distinguishable, both in the way these men wrote and in the way they were seen by others. No one ever confounded their scientific with their theological work. Descartes and Leibniz were in-between. They were still speculative philosophers. But their philosophical writings were much more clearly separate from their mathematical contributions than in the case of Galileo. All this shows the rapid growth of a distinctive scientific self-consciousness.

Nevertheless, all these men found it important to write about philosophy and theology too. They considered their scientific activity as directly relevant to these broad and important problems and therefore considered it their duty to explain their views about them to the intellectual public, of which they were a part in social status and institutional affiliation. In the eighteenth century the philosophical activity of scientists diminished. Very few of the great chemists, physicists or mathematicians of that period ever wrote about anything but science. This was not the result of any deliberate intention or programme but simply of the self-contained character of the growing scientific community. Scientists had their publications and academies and they could afford to use their own language and disregard matters with which they were not primarily concerned. In these self-contained circles only one's scientific achievements within one's specialised field were given marked attention, so that the criteria of reputation became specifically scientific. As long, therefore, as the continued existence of these circles was ensured by institutional means, the scientist did not have to justify himself before a general public of intellectuals. As long as the standing of science as an officially recognised value was not threatened, he did not have to vie for reputation with anyone who was not a scientist; it was enough to be recognised by the small circle of fellow scientists. They might, or might not, have had religious or philosophical problems but, as specialised scientists, they could safely forget about them while at work and leave the solution of such problems to other experts, or to meditations in their non-scientific capacities.

These arrangements were the basis for sustained scientific activity. Barring a revolutionary change which might destroy the social legitimation of science, interest in it was ensured. This being the case, a continuous flow of able minds into science and continuous scientific work only depended on economic opportunity and facilities. These were not abundantly available but the academies constituted a permanent framework of very high prestige and around this core other opportunities, such as teaching and support by private means, were sufficient to maintain a permanent network of meetings and communication and to offer, if not yet careers, at least very desirable prizes, to the able and the highly motivated.

This new situation of science did not make the fortunes of science independent of other social events. But it made science into a social institution with an internal life and structure of its own which could respond autonomously to other social events. The fortunes of science ceased to depend on the fortunes of the social groups and organisations of philosophers and the intellectual developments of philosophy; instead, science became a central focus of an independent group and a new set of institutions. From these there was a direct path of science as it developed in the nineteenth and twentieth centuries.

A. RUPERT HALL

*It is indeed a matter of great difficulty to discover, and effectually to dis-
tinguish, the true motions of particular bodies from the apparent; because
the parts of that immovable space, in which those motions are performed,
do by no means come under the observation of our senses. Yet the thing
is not altogether desperate; for we have some arguments to guide us, partly
from the apparent motions, which are the differences of the true motions;
partly from the forces, which are the causes and effects of the true motions.
. . . But how we are to obtain the true motions from their causes, effects,
and apparent differences, and the converse, shall be explained more at large
in the following treatise. For to this end it was that I composed it.*[1]

By distinguishing the real from the apparent motion of falling bodies
Galileo removed a principal objection against the Copernican system; by
discerning the beautiful simplicity of elliptical orbits behind the apparent
complexity of the planetary revolutions Kepler increased the likelihood of
its truth. Newton's achievement was founded on theirs, for by perfecting
Galilean mechanics he found the basis for a final distinction between reality and appearance that placed Kepler's astronomy beyond doubt. The two
great strands of seventeenth-century physical science were united in Newton's *Principia* (1687) through the fertile and fitting combination of
mathematics with the mechanical philosophy that yielded the laws of
gravity, when Kepler's planetary laws were shown to be but special cases
of the laws of motion foreshadowed by Galileo. Four modes of thought
represented by Newton's great predecessors Galileo, Kepler, Descartes and
Huygens now appeared not merely harmonious but inseparable, so that by
Newton's triumph the whole seventeenth-century revolution in science
was confirmed.

Yet when Isaac Newton was born in 1642, at the turning-point of that
revolution, the work of Galileo was still to be accepted, the discoveries of
Kepler were still ignored, and the impact of Descartes, Boyle and Huygens was still to be felt. During Newton's boyhood science moved decisively into a new age. New methods based on mathematics and experiment rose rapidly to ascendancy, while new theories buoyantly
exemplified the mechanistic, corpuscularian metaphysic. In England the
Royal Society, a galaxy of talent, offered an appropriate setting for Newton's transcendent genius; his intellectual inheritance was equally rich in
critical problems and the means for solving them.

Source: A. Rupert Hall. *From Galileo to Newton, 1630–1720* (New York:
Harper & Row, Publishers, 1963), pp. 276–306. Copyright © 1963 by A. Rupert
Hall. Reprinted by permission of Harper & Row, Publishers, Inc. and William
Collins Sons & Co., Ltd. [Some footnotes omitted.]

[1] *Principia*, Motte-Cajori, 12.

An outworn pattern characterised the education he received at school and university, and Newton rising from the lesser gentry lacked the social advantages of such grandees of science as Huygens and Boyle. Yet when he went into residence at Trinity College, Cambridge, in 1661 Newton had already acquired a practical mastery of Latin—still the international language of science—and probably of elementary geometry. In his first years there he studied Greek, logic, ethics, rhetoric (which meant the art of literary composition) and more mathematics. Somehow he also acquired a stumbling knowledge of French, though he never set foot abroad. From 1663 his unique gifts began to be conspicuous; a couple of years' work enabled the pupil of Isaac Barrow (a considerable mathematician who had returned recently to Cambridge as the first Lucasian professor) to outstrip his master. At the same time he was pursuing physical science in the writings of Galileo, Kepler, Descartes, Boyle and many others. Newton was a late developer; entering the university at eighteen he was three or four years older than many undergraduates, but in his student days he completed a thorough training in science and mathematics largely additional to his formal studies. In the next two years— 1665–6—all his future accomplishments took shape. For the most part he spent them at his home at Woolsthorpe in Lincolnshire, for the university was closed by the great plague; Newton's creative life as a scientist began on the farm. It was to continue through normal academic grooves. In the spring of 1667 he returned to his College, to be elected into a Fellowship and reside there for nearly thirty years. His small patrimony relieved him of the fear of academic poverty. Most dons were driven from their High Tables by boredom and the desire for a wife; Newton was neither bored nor married and by a special dispensation from the Crown, given five years after his succession to Barrow in the Lucasian chair (1669), he was allowed to retain his Fellowship without the usual necessity for taking Holy Orders. The way was clear for science.

Newton wrote of his active rustication many years later:

In the beginning of the year 1665 I found the Method of approximating series & the rule for reducing any dignity of any Binomial into such a series. The same year in May I found the method of Tangents of Gregory and Slusius, & in November had the direct method of fluxions, & the next year in January had the Theory of Colours & in May following I had entrance into ye inverse method of fluxions. And the same year I began to think of gravity extending to ye orb of the Moon, & (having found out how to estimate the force with which a globe revolving within a sphere presses the surface of the sphere), from Kepler's rule . . . I deduced that the forces which keep the Planets in their Orbs must [be] reciprocally as the squares of their distances from the centers about which they revolve: and thereby compared the force requisite to keep the Moon in her Orb with the force of gravity at the surface of the earth &

found them answer pretty nearly. All this was in the two plague years 1665 & 1666 for in those days I was in the prime of my age for invention and minded Mathematics and Philosophy more than at any time since.[2]

There are, moreover, among Newton's notebooks and papers many records of optical experiments and mathematical calculations that belong to this early period, when Newton had only just ceased to be a student. One of the early experiments is that of viewing through a prism a piece of paper brightly painted with red and blue (which Newton described in *Opticks* forty years later), when the edges of the two coloured sections seemed out of line: "soe y^t blew rays suffer a greater refraction y^n red ones", as Newton commented. He also composed a fairly full account of his new method of handling algebraic equations, and made notes on mechanics which show him discovering the law of centrifugal force and applying it to work out the strength of the Earth's pull on the moon. On his return to the university Newton was not short of ideas, nor matters to study further.

During the next few years, in fact, he gave most of his time to optics and mathematics. Presumably he continued his experiments with the prism and the colours of thin plates and almost certainly he was already drafting accounts of his mathematical discoveries and of his new theory of colours. Newton was always busy with the pen, either taking notes from his reading (with which he covered thousands of sheets), sketching out his ideas or making calculations. From January 1670 he lectured for about twenty years—on optics, mathematics, and in the last series mechanics. The burden was light, as it consisted of giving only eight lectures in the year, but Newton's were almost wholly written from original material and, indeed, went into his books in one form or another. At about the time that he succeeded Barrow, Newton's correspondence began to be extensive; through one friend in London, John Collins (1625–83), his mathematical ability became fairly widely known, just as his optics did after his Royal Society letters of 1672. Newton had also developed a keen interest in chemistry, and there were periods during all his residence in Cambridge after the first few years when he was in constant attendance upon the furnace he set up in the little garden below his rooms.

Yet it is odd that in the record of two-thirds of Newton's life in Cambridge there is so little trace of interest in the problem he was to make peculiarly his own—the problem of gravitation. None of his friends was aware that Newton had more than a passing interest in mechanics and astronomy, and practically no hint of his thoughts of 1666 escaped him in any letter. For fifteen years Newton pushed to the back of his mind one of the greatest of all scientific ideas because (apparently) it struck him as no more than a hypothesis and he thought he had better things to do than try to make more of it. He felt that he could not demonstrate his

---

[2] Cambridge University Library, ADD. MS. 3968, no. 2.

ideas of 1666 to his own mathematical satisfaction, and yet when he returned to them again in 1679 and 1684–5 the solution of the mathematical difficulties only took him a few months.

The questions in mathematical astronomy that Newton had considered at Woolsthorpe in 1666 he inherited from Descartes and Galileo. Ever since Tycho had abolished the rigid celestial orbs ("absurd and monstrous" Kepler had called them) the system of sun and planets had lacked cohesion. Plainly the planets did not wander erratically, but there was nothing to keep them fixed in their courses. Descartes had first perceived the need for a celestial balance of force, a sort of cosmic string that would prevent the planets escaping out of the solar vortex under the force of its rotation, and had sought to make the aether provide it. But he made no calculations—a Babylonian stargazer might have protested against the freedom of his assumptions. In Descartes' time there was something more serious to take into account: Kepler's laws of planetary motion. If Descartes ever isolated Kepler's theorems from the otherwise (to him) repellent farrago of weird notions in Kepler's books he paid no attention to them. In which he was no more unjust than virtually all his contemporaries.

There was another problem still. When Copernicus moved the Earth he knocked the bottom out of the old doctrine of lightness and heaviness; if bodies continued to fall they did so without any rational reason for their behaviour. Copernicus had put forward the rather vague notion that pieces of Earth or Venus or Jupiter had a tendency to run together like drops of water. William Gilbert, being a student of magnetism, correlated this notion of heaviness with magnetic attraction, which of course he found in the Earth. The attraction of Earth for earth and so on was quite specific, however, since otherwise (as Aristotle had argued long before) all the matter in the universe, it seemed, would congregate in one vast unhappy heap. Galileo successfully cleared up the difficulty about lightness by denying that there was any such thing, all bodies being absolutely heavy and only relatively light; but the actual cause or nature of this universal heaviness he left severely alone, apart from some remarks indicating that he found Gilbert's statements plausible.

Nor, while much concerned with the dynamical effects of heaviness, did Galileo contemplate at all the question of what it is that holds the solar system together. His concept of circular inertia relieved him from that necessity. It was Kepler who began to associate the problem of heaviness with that of the cohesion of the heavens, in his own highly eccentric fashion. He maintained that like matter would always be drawn to like, the distance each fragment moved being proportional to its "body" (mass). Thus, he wrote in 1609, the Earth would drag the moon down to itself, while rising a little way to meet it, if the two bodies were not restrained in their orbits by their own "animal or other equivalent forces". He estimated quantitatively the tendency towards a motion that never actually happens and pointed to the moon's influence over the tides as evidence for the reality of mutual attraction; like Descartes later, however,

Kepler did not further explore his idea dynamically. He was no less blind to the astronomical portent of the science of motion than Galileo was to the import of Kepler's descriptive laws. He could scarcely fail to be so, as he attributed activity in the heavens to virtues, powers and souls residing in the heavenly bodies. By a virtue that it emitted the sun swept the planets around, and Kepler allowed them no endeavour to escape its influence. Though the souls of the planets interacted with that of the sun to produce the ellipses (which he felt he must particularly explain) they required no restraint. The moon, the only satellite known in 1609, presented a rather different problem since it did not revolve about the sun, and so (as with Newton in 1666) it was the Earth-moon system that brought Kepler nearest to the idea that the moon has weight with respect to the Earth. But he never quite attained it.

Kepler's speculations attempted to account for the laws of ellipticity he had already discovered; with the equally important Third Law (1619) these formed thereafter the necessary conditions of any cosmological hypothesis. The Third Law—whose history from 1619 to 1665 is quite obscure—held the key to the problem of the stability of the solar system. For it indicated in what way the motions of the five planets were mathematically interdependent, so that they formed a harmonious system. It was Newton's genius to use this key, perceiving that interdependence was the product of the action of a single force.

That Newton in 1665 or 1666 was aware of Kepler's Third Law at all is intriguing. Amid the deep silence concerning Kepler's work from 1620 to 1665 a few English astronomers had discussed his theory of the orbit without noticing the Third Law. Possibly Barrow directed Newton to Kepler, for there were copies of all the relevant books in the Trinity Library; if so, it was crucial advice. Newton did what Descartes had failed to do; assuming the orbit to be circular, he calculated the force with which the planet would tend to escape from it. Expressing his measure of rotational force cumbersomely at first, Newton soon found his way to a simpler argument and the formula found in a paper perhaps written about the end of 1666, or even a little after that. Here Newton correctly defined the centrifugal force as that which, applied during the time taken to complete one revolution, would impel any body (such as a planet) from rest to the distance π^2 multiplied by the diameter of the circle (or orbit). From this relation Newton settled Galileo's problem, why bodies are not flung off the spinning Earth; at most the force of rotation was only about $\frac{1}{350}$ th of the force of gravity. Next Newton computed the force of the moon's rotation which, taking the diameter of the Earth to be a little over 6600 miles, proved to be less than $\frac{1}{4000}$ th of the force of gravity. And finally a very simple operation showed that from Kepler's Third Law the centrifugal forces acting upon the five planets—the measure of their endeavour to break away from their orbits—were in the inverse ratio of the squares of their distances from the sun.

These were results of tremendous importance. For Newton saw—though he did not explicitly say so—that a single force in the sun, decreasing as the square of the distance from it, would suffice to hold all the planets in their orbits (still assuming that these were circular). Furthermore, it was clear that the force required to hold the moon in its path was rather less than $\frac{1}{60^2}$ of the force of gravity (had he taken 8000 miles as the diameter of the Earth the answer would have been exactly $\frac{1}{60^2}$). From this, since the moon is distant from the Earth sixty Earth-radii, it would also follow that the inverse-square law would apply to the moon, if the force holding the moon in its orbit were the force of gravity familiar at the Earth's surface. Kepler was right, the moon would fall like a stone —if it were not supported by the force of its own revolution.

All this Newton had accomplished by about the end of 1666. He had made an onslaught upon a new branch of mechanics, the dynamics of revolving bodies, and he had at once gone on to consider the planets as bodies moving in a dynamic system and subject to the relations he had just discovered. This was Newton's great step, and was presumably his object from the first. Huygens had gone far in the same direction, but he had not seized upon the idea that sun and planets constitute a dynamic system, subject to mathematical laws (not the merely mechanical laws of Descartes). Precisely because Huygens never outgrew the Cartesian principles of explanation he could not do this; to him the celestial motions were effected by mechanical, aetherial pressures and therefore they could not be subject to simple mathematical laws like the inverse-square law. Newton's reasoning was founded upon Descartes' law of inertia and Galileo's law of acceleration, but the Cartesian aetherial mechanism adopted by Huygens was expressly designed to prevent the law of inertia's upsetting the planetary orbits, and to prevent their acceleration from the centre. Huygens could never see the problem in Newton's purely mathematical terms, even after the *Principia*. Newton, on the other hand, setting aside mechanistic explanations of gravity, attended only to the mathematical relationships. That stated in Kepler's Third Law declared how things are, and that he derived from pure mechanics showed what the forces must be. They matched to yield the inverse-square law, a law that simple algebra dictated once physical relationships were expressed in mathematical terms. And the calculation for the moon suggested that the centripetal force of the sun holding its system together was the same as the force of terrestrial gravity.

What Newton had done so far was not mathematically complex. He took his measurements from books—the figure for the size of the Earth came from Galileo, and was markedly too small. The dynamical principles he welded into his definition of centrifugal force he took from the common post-Galilean stock. The rest was simple geometry and algebra. But it required brilliance to see how it could be done, and the most powerful scientific insight to see why it should be done. Having come so far, to press on was mathematically far more difficult. For the planets move in ellipses; they, and the Earth, sun and moon are not the point-bodies of mechanical theory but solid masses. Did they nevertheless behave as if they were points? The agreement in the case of the moon's motion was poor, and the moon's motions were fearfully irregular—astronomers had not learnt to compute them accurately. If Newton committed himself to his new idea of gravitation, he would commit himself to the opinion that somehow the gravitational force must cause the perturbations of the moon's orbit. So far gravity only gave him a neat circular revolution. If Newton thought of Jupiter's satellites, there were similar problems there. And there was the problem of the tides, another roughly periodic motion which no one had reduced to good mathematical order. Worst of all, celestial dynamics did not have to consider two bodies alone—a sun and planet—but a system of a dozen or more, dominated by the sun indeed, yet, if the hypothesis of universal gravitation were correct, all pulling on each other, each disturbing the elegant orbits of the others. With all his might Newton never completely solved this problem so that he could be sure all possible disturbances of the pattern were self-nullifying; he always contemplated the possibility that a miracle might be needed from time to time to prevent cumulative disruption of the heavenly order.

How far Newton looked ahead to these problems in the early Cambridge years he did not say. The fact that he turned from planetary dynamics to pure mathematics and optics suggests that he was aware of some of the difficulties. Possibly he overestimated their complexity, when his own new methods were still imperfect (in fact he was scarcely to use them in writing the *Principia*). In any case he knew he would require far more rigorous mathematical proofs than any he had devised up to this time. In addition he needed more facts; astronomical measurements were still unreliable. Nor could Newton at this stage be sure that Cartesian mechanism was wholly false. One thing he gained from his work in optics was the strengthening of his early anti-Cartesian convictions, and of his belief that the mathematical way in science was the only one leading to truth.

While Newton kept silent others began to catch him up. G. A. Borelli, the mechanistic physiologist of the Accademia del Cimento, published in the very year 1666 the *Theory of the Medicean Planets,* which Newton was to praise later. Clearly the application to Jupiter's satellites was a subterfuge: Borelli was speaking of the whole solar system. Rather in Kepler's manner he imagined that the planets were revolved by the light-rays emanating from the rotating sun. Since this force was weakened by diffusion it grew feebler with distance so that (as Borelli erroneously supposed) the planets would revolve at speeds proportional to the force acting upon them, hence to their distance from the sun. From Descartes Borelli drew the lesson that an inward pull was required to balance the centrifugal force of rotation. He accordingly supposed that each planet had a constant tendency or desire to approach the sun, and to account for the ellipticity of the orbits (for Borelli was the first cosmologist to follow Kepler's Laws) he imagined further that the planet oscillated slowly, like a pendulum, on either side of its mean path. Apart from this last point, the main departure of Borelli's hypothesis from Descartes'—than which it was no more mathematical—was his suggestion of a centripetal force, which he did not dare to call an attraction and did not think of identifying with gravity, that was nevertheless hardly distinguishable from an attraction.

Borelli's universe, like that of Kepler and Descartes in their different ways, was a driven machine, spun round by the sun's vigour. As such it was far harder to analyse mathematically than a system in which the planets were supposed to spin freely. Only if theories of aether-vortices and solar emanations were abandoned would it be possible to return to Galileo's idea of free-spinning planets, with the proviso now known to be required that they must at the same time be subject to an inwards pull. With such a pull (and assuming always the absence of any resistance) it was now clear that the rectilinear, inertial motion of a planet would be bent round into a closed curve. Centripetal force was the factor making "rotary inertia" (as Galileo had conceived it) possible; that is, the idea of an inwards pull negated the notion of a material aether, and also made such an aether as a celestial driving-force unnecessary.

Robert Hooke saw his way through some of this argument, though not through all for he did not in fact renounce aetherial physics. His views, the product of a lively and often sound imagination in science, developed during the long years of Newton's reticence. He had little more to go on than intuition, the example of Descartes' system, and the analogy with the motion of a conical pendulum. Hooke was no more than an ordinary geometer. He did not even perceive until it was too late, and then with high resentment, that the question he was tackling was one of mathematical, not experimental, physics. He did not know how to calculate centrifugal forces till he learnt it from Huygens, and the intricate mathematics of motion in ellipses was utterly beyond him. Whereas Newton's theory grew out of mathematical relationships, Hooke's grew from qualitative consideration of the effects of gravity.

In the early 1660s Hooke made futile experiments to detect variations in gravity; in *Micrographia* (1665) he conjectured that the moon might have a gravitating principle like the Earth's; in the next year, improving upon Borelli, Hooke supposed that a "direct [inertial] motion" might be bent into a curve "by an attractive property of the body placed at the centre"; and in a tract on the comet of 1677 he wrote:

> I suppose the gravitating power of the Sun in the center of this part of the Heaven in which we are, hath an attractive power upon all the bodies of the Planets, and of the Earth that move about it, and that each of those again have a respect answerable. . . .

What follows makes it clear that in this place Hooke did not identify the attractive power with gravity, although in another tract four years earlier he had done so. There he had proposed to explain

> a System of the World differing in many particulars from any yet known, answering in all things to the common Rules of Mechanical Motions,

which was to be grounded on three suppositions. The first of these was the earliest statement of universal gravitation: that all celestial bodies have an attraction or gravitating power towards their own centres, whereby they attract their own parts and all other bodies within their sphere of activity. Hooke specifically said that sun, moon, Earth and planets have an influence on each others' motions. The second supposition was a statement of the law of inertia, with the special exception that the rectilinear path might be bent into a "Circle, Ellipsis, or some other more compounded Curve Line" by "some other effectual powers" acting on the moving body. The third supposition was that the attractive power diminishes with distance, but Hooke added that he had not experimentally (!) discovered the degrees of this decrease. (Such a remark shows that Hooke's was not the mathematical way.) Though Hooke's hypotheses are very significant in relation to the theory of Newton's *Principia,* there is no evidence that his contemporaries were deeply impressed by their display in lectures before the Royal Society and printed pamphlets, where indeed they were interspersed with many other less prescient hypotheses. He never put together the system of the world that he promised, nor was he ever able to offer any firm support, either experimental or mathematical, for the hypotheses on which it was to be founded. In this Hooke was undoubtedly unlucky, for he was the only man of his age to proceed, broadly speaking, along the track that led Newton to his goal. And it is sad that Newton's irritation at Hooke never allowed him to acknowledge the fact.

Meanwhile Newton himself, who was concerned with other matters and would have found nothing new in Hooke's ideas, took no notice of them. Early in 1673 he had offered his resignation to the Royal Society; Oldenburg had refused it, and (needlessly) had had Newton relieved of the payment of his subscription, remarking

> I could heartily wish, you would pass by the incongruities, y^t may have been committed by one or other of our Body towards you, and consider, that hardly any company will be found in the world, in wch there is not some or other y^t wants discretion. You may be satisfied, that the Body in general esteems and loves you. . . .[3]

Newton's reply was not encouraging. "I intend", his declared, "to be no further sollicitous about matters of Philosophy", and he begged to be excused from the writing of further replies to "philosophical letters". Nevertheless he did in the next two years answer renewed objections to his optical theory, and submit the further long paper on the colours of thin plates to the Royal Society. After that, which had provoked a fresh claim by Hooke that the subject had all been covered in *Micrographia* and a furious rejoinder from Newton, he had little further connection with the Society in the years after 1676. Oldenburg, Collins and Barrow were all soon dead, and though Newton's friendship with Boyle became warmer, the

[3] *Correspondence of Isaac Newton,* I, 284.

overtures from London ceased. Hooke and Nehemiah Grew became the Society's secretaries, and the *Philosophical Transactions* lapsed for a while.

After their latest conflict, Hooke had written a conciliatory letter to Newton in January 1676, laying the blame on Oldenburg's misrepresentations, professing admiration for Newton, and declaring himself "well pleased to see those notions promoted and improved which I long since began, but had not time to compleat". Without servility or surrender Hooke offered private correspondence in place of public dispute. Newton replied with equal civility and no greater sincerity, even assuring Hooke:

> you defer too much to my ability for searching into this subject [the theory of colours]. What Des-Cartes did was a good step. You have added much several ways, & especially in taking ye colours of thin plates into philosophical consideration. If I have seen further it is by standing on ye shoulders of Giants.[4]

(In the fable the keen-sighted pygmy saw further by being raised on a giant's shoulders; Newton was ingeniously praising and deprecating his achievements at the same time.) But the olive branch did not sprout. The two men were too close in their interests and too alien in their understanding of what science is for amity to be possible; both were unduly touchy, intellectually arrogant and sensitive to their rights of priority. Newton was in general honest (or cautious) in acknowledging experiments or measurements borrowed from others; he was habitually careless in appeasing the vanity of lesser men whose ideas, momentous to their progenitors, merely paralleled early stages of his own thought or furnished seeds for his own grander conceptions. And it was Hooke's misfortune that he was not satisfied with being what he was—which was very considerable—but wanted to be Newton too, which he was not.

The two men did not quarrel. A few notes on business passed between them after Hooke succeeded Oldenburg as Secretary of the Royal Society. Two years later (November 1679) Hooke again prompted Newton to warmer relations. He wrote the chatty kind of letter a secretary might write to an absent and discontented member of his society. It had only one important sentence, in which Hooke asked Newton's opinion of his own hypothesis "of compounding the celestial motions of the planets of a direct motion by the tangent and an attractive motion towards the central body". Abruptly, Newton's attention was drawn to mechanics, and to the recollection of scattered papers neglected for twelve years. Though in his reply Newton disclaimed awareness of Hooke's hypothesis, and avowed that he had for some years past turned his mind from science to other studies "in so much that I have long grutched the time spent in that study unless it be perhaps at idle hours sometimes for a diversion", he could not conceal the fact that his attention had been caught. For he went on to suggest a "fancy of my own" about the fall of a heavy body to the centre of the Earth, supposing there were space for it to fall the whole way.

[4] *Ibid.*, 416, 5 February 1676.

Now there was a spate of letters, from which the *Principia* was born. Sacrificing tact to his desire to score a point Hooke rejected Newton's spiral trajectory, terminating at the centre of the Earth, as a vulgar error. Unless resisted by air the falling body would return to its point of origin, describing " a kind of Elleptueid" (Hooke did not know that the curve would be an exact ellipse). Not content with that, he read the letters exposing Newton's mistake to the Royal Society. Newton was angered; eager to prove Hooke wrong, he computed the trajectory of descent *assuming that the force of gravity was uniform* between the surface and the centre; the result was a sort of clover-leaf curve, nothing like an "elliptoid". Once more Hooke caught him out. What Newton wrote was correct, he retorted (it was now 6 January 1680):

> But my supposition is that the attraction [to the centre] always is in a duplicate proportion to the Distance from the center reciprocall [i.e. as $\frac{1}{d^2}$], and Consequently that the Velocity will be in a subduplicate proportion to the Attraction, and consequently as Kepler supposes Reciprocall to the Distance. . . .[5]

Hooke went on to say that while the question under debate was trivial in itself, when applied to the celestial bodies this "curve truly calculated will shew the error of those many lame shifts made use of by astronomers to approach the true motions of the planets with their tables". From the dynamical conditions he had defined—peripheral motion and central attraction obeying the inverse-square law—it should be possible to calculate the true path of a planet which would prove to be, Hooke thought, like but not identical with the regular ellipses assumed by astronomers. (If he had supposed that Kepler's ellipses were true orbits, Hooke would obviously have used the word ellipse before and would have had no doubt as to the nature of the curve he sought.) Newton just ignored this letter. Eleven days later Hooke, hardly aware of the mortal offence he had given, appealed to him again, in terms that reveal serious inadequacies in his concept, to discover the curve:

> I doubt not that by your excellent method you will easily find out what this curve must be, and its proprietys. and suggest a physical reason of this proportion.[6]

But Newton was not going to be another man's computer. He kept his silence, and what Hooke had made him discover remained hidden for another four and a half years.

Hooke was never able to find the demonstration that Newton denied him. Given his concept of universal gravitation, when Huygens' theorems on centrifugal force were printed in 1673 he had the wit to combine them with Kepler's Third Law to deduce the inverse-square law of attraction, as Newton had done long before in 1666, *for circular motion*. He

[5] *Correspondence*, II, 309.   [6] *Ibid.*, 313, 17 January 1680.

guessed that in the heavens this law would cause the ellipse-like motion required by Kepler's First and Second Laws, but—regarding the matter physically and not mathematically—he assumed that the curve would be more complex than a geometrical ellipse, and so he told Newton that the curve of the body falling towards the centre of the Earth [would] be an "Elliptueid". (In this Hooke curiously paralleled the development of Kepler's own ideas, for Kepler had at first thought that the orbit would be more complex than a perfect ellipse.) Hooke was no Platonist. He challenged Newton to define this more complex curve; what Newton actually found was a geometrical demonstration of motion in an ellipse. Kepler's First and Second Laws were, dynamically, perfectly exact, not the approximations Hooke had taken them to be. And of this he left Hooke ignorant.

How the *Principia* came to be written is a well-known story. By 1684, besides Newton and Hooke, Halley and Wren were intuitively convinced of the inverse-square law of gravitation. None of the last three could derive orbits from that law mathematically. Halley, a young and energetic man, made a special journey to Cambridge to put the problem to the mathematical professor: "What would be the curve described by the planets on the supposition that gravity diminished as the square of the distance?"

> Newton immediately answered, *an Ellipse.* Struck with joy and amazement, Halley asked him how he knew it? Why, replied he, I have calculated it; and being asked for the calculation, he could not find it, but promised to send it to him [Halley].[7]

Newton had carelessly mislaid what other brilliant men with their best efforts could not find out! Re-working his calculation, Newton realised it could hardly stand by itself; it required, to be convincing and clear, axioms, definitions, subsidiary propositions, in short a demonstration of the use of mathematical reasoning in handling problems of mechanics. Within a few days or weeks he had decided to devote his lectures of the approaching Michaelmas Term, 1684, to *The Motions of Bodies.* Two or three months later, in October, he began to read a text that is substantially that of Book I of the *Principia.* Next month some of its propositions were despatched to Halley, in fulfilment of his promise, who hastened off to Cambridge a second time to persuade Newton to lay his work before the Royal Society. His wish prevailed, and Newton set to work to revise and expand his lectures, but the *Philosophiae Naturalis Principia Mathematica* ("Mathematical Principles of Natural Philosophy") assumed its ultimate form only gradually during the next two years.

In 1686, when Book I was duly presented to the Royal Society, Hooke and Newton quarrelled for the fourth and final time. It was a quarrel that led to Hooke's virtual retirement from the Society during the last years of

NEWTON AND
THE WORLD
OF LAW

---

[7] The quotations are from the account of Newton's nephew-in-law John Conduitt (Ball, 26 etc.), which is confirmed by Halley's letters.

his life; that strengthened Newton's desire to abandon the university and science; and that prevented the publication of *Opticks* until after Hooke's death. No doubt Hooke's charge of plagiarism against Newton was no more unjust than Newton's neglect of Hooke's just claims to recognition. Yet Newton could rightly assert that he had far surpassed Hooke—no comparison between their achievements is possible; his counter-charge that he had learned nothing from Hooke, who had proved nothing, was fair; but his jealous temperament swayed him into injustice when he proceeded to deny that Hooke had accomplished anything at all. In the course of his outpourings against Hooke, in letters to Halley (who had undertaken to pay for the printing of the *Principia* and see it through the press), Newton made some remarks of more than partisan importance underlining the obstacles that he had surmounted before the *Principia* could be written. The first, naturally, was the proof that the inverse-square law yielded an elliptical orbit. To the discovery of the law itself he attached little importance, since it was obvious after Huygens' book of 1673. The difficulty was to prove it for the astronomical ellipses as a mathematically exact law, not to infer it for circles.

> There is so strong an objection against the accurateness of this [inverse-square] proportion [Newton added] that without my demonstrations, to which Mr Hooke is yet a stranger, it cannot be believed by a judicious philosopher to be anywhere accurate.[8]

By this Newton meant that on the evidence any competent physicist would recognise the impossibility of the law's exactness; only a mathematician could turn the tables and demonstrate that—paradoxically—it was perfectly exact and physically sufficient. Kepler, said Newton (rather unreasonably), had guessed that the planetary ovals were geometric ellipses; his own demonstrations proved at one and the same time the mathematical precision of both the inverse-square law and the ellipses.

Secondly, Newton recollected,

> I never extended the duplicate proportion lower than to the superficies of the Earth, and before a certain demonstration I found the last year [1685], have suspected it did not reach accurately enough so low.[9]

It was a ready inference for Newton that the gravitational force must reside in the ultimate particles of matter, if it is a property of gross bodies. Now, even such astronomically adjacent bodies as the Earth and moon are so distant that the lines drawn between any two particles in these bodies could be considered parallel and of the same length, hence it was easy to see that the total force was the sum of the forces of the particles. In the case of a body only a few feet above the Earth's surface, like an apple on a tree, the situation was quite different. How could the summation of particulate forces be effected in this case, and where would the centre of force

---

[8] *Correspondence*, II, 437, Newton to Halley, 20 June 1686.   [9] *Ibid.*, 435.

in the Earth be located? In the *Principia* Newton confessed his doubt that the commonsense way of thinking would work:

> After I had found that the force of gravity towards a whole planet did arise from and was compounded of the forces of gravity towards all its parts, and towards every one part was in the inverse proportion of the squares of the distances from the part, I was yet in doubt whether that proportion as the square of the distance did accurately hold, or but nearly so, in the total force compounded of so many partial ones; for it might be that the proportion that was accurate enough at greater distances would be wide of the truth near the surface of the planet, where the distances of the particles are unequal, and their situations dissimilar.[10]

Doubt was removed by a group of theorems in which Newton integrated mathematically the individual forces arising from the infinitely numerous particles of two solid spheres. They proved that the centripetal (or gravitational) force between two spheres "increases or decreases in proportion to the distance between their centres according to the same law as applies to the particles themselves. And this is a noteworthy fact."[11] Once more mathematics demonstrated a physical improbability as truth: the sphere acted on any body outside it, however close, from its own centre; and this was true of any law of attraction. But if the inverse-square law applied outside the sphere, then inside it the attraction to the centre was directly as the distance.

Here were at least two instances where the physical or imaginative implausibility of the inverse-square law could only be corrected by mathematical reasoning. Newton was claiming, in effect—and he was right —that his great achievement lay not in imagining a physical hypothesis (to which there were grave objections that qualitative physical thinking could not surmount), but in proving mathematically that what seemed to be objections were on the contrary, when properly analysed, decisive testimonies to the accuracy of the theory. In other words, the theory of universal gravitation was only worth anything when it was a mathematical theory; and only as a mathematical theory could it be verified by observation in such a way as to sway conviction. Hooke, from the opposite pole, made a remark that provoked one of Newton's most furious outbursts:

> [Hooke] has done nothing, and yet written in such a way, as if he knew and had sufficiently hinted all but what remained to be determined by the drudgery of calculations and observations, excusing himself from that labour by reason of his other business, whereas he should rather have excused himself by reason of his inability. For 'tis plain, by his words, that he knew not how to go about it. Now is not this very fine? Mathematicians, that find out, settle, and do all

---

[10] *Principia,* Motte-Cajori, 415–6.
[11] *Ibid.* (1687), 203. I have tried to improve upon Motte-Cajori, 202–3.

the business, must content themselves with being nothing but dry calculators and drudges; and another, that does nothing but ~retend and grasp at all things, must carry away all the invention, as well as those that were to follow him, as of those that went before.[12]

Imagination, the ability to feign hypotheses, could give only the beginning of a theory in physics. To find out, to do everything, was to make a mathematical theory and confirm it by experiments or observations.

That is why Newton entitled his great work *The Mathematical Principles of Natural Philosophy* rather than, as he once thought, simply *On the Motion of Bodies*. To Newton, the laws of nature were not certainties of introspection, but those derived by mathematical reasoning. The method of explaining phenomena by reference to these laws was not by ingenious hypotheses, but again by mathematical reasoning. Galileo's proclamation of faith, tinged still with numerical or geometrical mysticism of Pythagorean or Platonic origin, became for Newton a plain, stern rule of procedure:

> the whole burden of philosophy seems to consist of this: from the phenomena of motion to investigate the forces of nature, and then from these forces to demonstrate the other phenomena.[13]

To follow any other course than the mathematical in this was quite simply to fail to comprehend the nature of physics. Yet even Newton was not quite free of the ancient delusion that mathematics is something more than logic, that it has in itself the roots of harmony and order, since he could find repeated in the colours of the spectrum the ancient divisions of the musical chord.

The *Principia* was, and is, a difficult book. Few of Newton's contemporaries were capable of working systematically through it, so that his celestial mechanics became widely known either through popularisations like Henry Pemberton's *View of Sir Isaac Newton's Philosophy* (1728) or through the "translation" of its theorems into the language of the calculus. As Newton wrote at the opening of Book III, *The System of the World*,

> . . . not that I would advise anyone to the previous study of every Proposition of [the First and Second] Books; for they abound with such as might cost too much time, even to readers of good mathematical learning. It is enough if one carefully reads the Definitions, the Laws of Motion, and the first three Sections of the First Book. He may then pass on to this Book. . . .[14]

John Locke, it is said, sought an assurance from Huygens that Newton's mathematics could be relied upon; he then read the *Principia* for its scientific ideas (which he adopted). No doubt many others approached it in the same way. Within only a few more years another difficulty came be-

---

[12] *Correspondence*, II, 438.   [13] *Principia*, Preface.
[14] *Principia*, Motte-Cajori, 397.

tween Newton and the reader. Newton had the ill-luck to write at the moment when the new mathematics was born, at the very moment of Leibniz's first paper on the calculus. Within a generation continental mathematicians had adopted Leibnizian methods of handling such problems as Newton had treated in the *Principia,* while the British were turning rather less rapidly to Newton's own fluxional analysis. But Newton's mechanics was fossilised in the geometrical proofs of an older generation of mathematicians—Huygens, Wallis, Barrow, Gregory; in a sense it was the last great piece of mathematical physics composed in the Greek tradition. Its form was soon to seem both old-fashioned and laborious.

Nor were the difficulties merely mathematical. To mathematicians comparable in stature to Newton, such as Huygens and Leibniz, it was his philosophy that proved unacceptable. Did the theory of gravitation assume that bodies are capable of acting upon each other at a distance without mechanical connection? Were space and time to be conceived of as Newton required? Was he perverting the apparently triumphant metaphysic of mechanism? Did he make God, as Leibniz alleged, an imperfect workman who needed to tinker continually with His creation? These were questions that transcended mathematical reasoning and experimental decision, yet until they were settled the status of Newton's work remained, in a measure, in suspense.

The *Principia* opens with twenty-five pages of *Definitions* and *Axioms* stating the basic concepts of mechanics and subsuming under the most general principles virtually all that had been accomplished in that science before 1687. Here Newton for the first time gives dynamics a clear, coherent foundation such as neither Galileo nor Huygens had offered. He defines mass, momentum, inertia, force and centripetal force, remarking of the last that he uses the words *attraction, impulse* and *propensity* indifferently since he considers centripetal forces not physically but mathematically. These definitions are followed by the famous scholium on space and time further discussed below. The axioms consist of three laws of motion and six corollaries. Law I is the law of inertia; Law II states that acceleration is proportional to force; Law III is the principle of the equivalence of action and reaction. The first two corollaries explain the parallelogram of forces and its application; the third and fourth assert that the total momentum and the centre of gravity of a system of bodies are unaffected by their mutual actions, while the fifth and sixth state that such actions are in turn unaffected by uniform or uniformly accelerated motion. In a second scholium Newton next gives examples of the use of the axioms in obtaining specific results discovered by his predecessors in mechanics; after having thus concisely laid the groundwork he proceeds to his own advance beyond them.

Book I of the *Principia* provides the complete mathematical theory on which celestial mechanics rests. It is wholly general, and in the earlier propositions a geometrical mass-point takes the place of a physical body; here Newton analyses the relations between orbits and central forces of different kinds. The outstanding result is the proof that the orbit is a conic, with the centre of attraction at one focus, if the force varies with the inverse square of the distance. The conditions of motion in such orbits are precisely laid down, and Newton shows how to determine the curvature of an orbit from a few observations of position. This was a practical problem for astronomers, as was the problem of the motion of the axes of the orbit, which he also treats. He gives also an approximate solution for finding the motions of three mutually attracting bodies, such as the sun, Earth and moon. Then he deals with the attractive forces of spherical and aspherical bodies arising from their component particles, from which it follows that the heavenly bodies can be reduced (externally) to point-masses as treated in the earlier theorems. Book I also contains a section on the motion of pendulums (relating to the theory of the Earth's shape) and closes with a discussion of the motion of particles when attracted by large bodies, from which Newton draws conclusions he thought applicable to optics.

The first Book was completed in the spring of 1686, and sent to the Royal Society: Newton had also worked on Books II and III but these were as yet in nothing like their final form. At first he intended to write Book III—containing the application to astronomy of the relationships established in the first Book—"in a popular method, that it might be read by many" but the quarrel with Hooke induced him to reconstruct it in the mathematical way. Meanwhile Book II, short at first, was considerably expanded by extra theorems. It is an interpolation in the main argument, dealing with the motions of fluids, and of bodies in fluids, in fact a treatise laying the foundations of fluid mechanics. Here the mathematics of the *Principia* reached its highest complexity, and indeed in the first edition Newton fell into a series of notable errors of mathematical reasoning. Book II also contains experimental proofs of many results (like the speed of sound) that Newton derived mathematically from purely theoretical considerations, basing himself throughout on the mechanical philosophy. Near the end he demonstrated conclusively that Cartesian vortices could not account for the observed planetary motions. Book III, continuing the astronomical theme, shows that from the masses, distances, and velocities of the sun, planets and satellites the theory of Book I predicts all the known phenomena, if gravity is postulated as the universal centripetal force obeying the inverse-square law. Newton took particular trouble with the involved motions of the moon (of which however he did not quite complete the theory), and with the theory of the tides. He established the orbits of comets as either parabolas or highly eccentric ellipses, and computed the shortening of the Earth's polar axis caused by its axial rotation.

No other work in the whole history of science equals the *Principia* either in originality and power of thought, or in the majesty of its achievement. No other so transformed the structure of science, for the *Principia* had no precursor in its revelation of the depth of exact comprehension that was accessible through mathematical physics. No other approached its authority in vindicating the mechanistic view of nature, which has been so far extended and emulated in all other parts of science. There could be only one moment at which experiment and observation, the mechanical philosophy, and advanced mathematical methods could be brought together to yield a system of thought at once tightly consistent in itself and verifiable by every available empirical test. Order could be brought to celestial physics only once, and it was Newton who brought order. His is the world of law. Since everything that happens in this world is the effect of motion, the primary, never-failing laws are the laws of motion defined at the beginning of Book I. Motion—except in the rare event of pure inertial motion—is the product of force; therefore in physics the next set of laws should define the forces that operate in nature. Of these Newton succeeded in defining only one, the law of gravity: the *Principia* is for the most part his treatise on this one force and the phenomena that arise from it. In it, such older descriptive laws as Kepler's and Boyle's are deduced as consequences of the basic law of force (though in the latter case the force is not that of gravity).* Thirdly, there are the laws of mathematics, belonging to the sphere of reason and logic indeed rather than to the sphere of physical reality, yet laws which physical reality obeys, and which scientific reasoning must not ignore. Nothing happens by chance, nothing is arbitrary, nothing is *sui generis* or a law unto itself. The philosophy of both *Principia* and *Opticks* insists that however varied, disconnected and specific the almost infinite range of events in nature may seem to be, it is so in appearance only: for in reality all the phenomena of things and all their properties must be traceable to a small set of fundamental laws of nature, and by mathematical reasoning each of them is deducible again from these laws, once they are known.

Yet Newton shrank from the belief that these laws are innate in nature; that in his view would lead to necessitarianism and the deification of matter. Matter and material properties could not be eternal and uncreated; rather matter is, and the laws of nature are, because God has willed them. The perfection of the laws implied for him a lawgiver, as the perfection of the achitecture of the universe implied a cosmic design:

> though [the planets and comets] may indeed continue in their orbits by the mere force of gravity yet they could by no means have at first derived the regular positions of their orbits from those laws . . . it is not to be conceived that mere mechanical causes could give birth to so many regular motions, since the comets range over all parts of the heavens in very eccentric orbits . . . and in their aphelions, where they move the slowest and are detained the longest, they recede to the greatest distances from each other, and hence suffer the least disturbance from their mutual attractions. This most beautiful system of the sun, planets, and comets could only proceed

* Newton's deduction of Boyle's Law from a repulsive force between the particles of a gas varying inversely as the distance (Book II, Proposition XXIII) must be considered a noble failure, however.

from the counsel and dominion of an intelligent and powerful Being. And if the fixed stars are centres of other like systems these, being formed by the like wise counsel, must be all subject to the dominion of One; especially since the light of the fixed stars is of the same nature as the light of the sun, and from every system light passes into all the other systems; and lest the systems of the fixed stars should, by their gravity, fall on each other he hath placed those systems at immense distances from each other.[15]

The ideas that Newton expressed in the General Scholium with which he concluded the second edition of the *Principia* (1713) had persisted throughout his life, for they occur in a document he wrote as a young man, before 1669. Like Descartes and Boyle, Newton saw the mechanistic universe as an argument against atheism, not in favour of it. But Newton's God—it will now be clear—was no Christian deity, nor the God of any sect. The attributes Newton conferred upon him are unexceptionable: he is living, intelligent, omnipotent, eternal, omniscient and most perfect, but he is a God of science, not theology. His kingdom is in the brain rather than the heart, for he is a God of law and certainty, not a God of hope and fear, of punishment and reward.

Even in a universe of law men can know only what is relative and superficial. They cannot detect the immutable, unvarying flow of duration, wrote Newton, or the unchanging extension of space. They can know time only by observing the succession of events, and space by measuring the distances between bodies without knowing if one or many among them move. Neither can men know the "inward substances" of material things. Only God is absolute and perceives the absolute. True, "He is not eternity and infinity, but eternal and infinite; he is not duration and space, but he endures and is present".[16] Nevertheless, because he "exists always and everywhere" God is for Newton the guarantor of the absoluteness of time and space, for absolute time and absolute space are the dimensions of God as their relative counterparts are man's. In a long Scholium following the Definitions of matter, motion and force with which the *Principia* begins Newton sought to clarify the distinction between absolute and relative dimensions, as he thought was necessary to avoid "prejudice". Indeed the distinction is for Newton a vital one, for the absolute are to him the only truly valid dimensions, while the relative vary with circumstance.

Hence the relative dimensions are not the same as absolute time and space, though they bear the same names, but rather refer to the direct measures of dimension (whether true or false) which we ordinarily use in place of the absolute measurements. If the meaning of words is to be taken from customary usage, then by the terms time, space, place and motion, we should understand direct measures of these quantities, and an expression will be unusual, and ex-

[15] *Principia,* Motte-Cajori, 543–4.   [16] *Ibid.,* 545.

clusively mathematical, if measurements in absolute terms are meant. For this reason, they are violating the sanctity of language who take these words time, place and so on to signify absolute dimensions. And they are equally guilty of defiling mathematical and philosophical truth who confuse absolute measures with their relative equivalents and with direct, physical measurements.[17]

The culprits are, of course, the Cartesians who define motion as displacement from neighbouring bodies. As Newton pointed out, this meant that the particles on the surface of a body moved while those in the interior of the same body were at rest. And their error had more serious consequences.

Absolute time, Newton thought, could be ascertained mathematically by correcting the celestial motions, or perhaps those of some more perfect timekeeper. Absolute space was beyond experience, since no body could be known to be absolutely at rest. Accordingly absolute motion— motion in absolute dimensions—could not be measured directly either. "Yet the thing is not altogether desperate", Newton thought, for he believed that absolute *rotation* was always manifested by its accompanying centrifugal force. The application is obvious, and was to be brought out in the rest of the *Principia;* now the worst of the Cartesian folly in confusing absolute with relative motion becomes plain. For in the solar system there is a centrifugal force in the planets—otherwise they would fall into the sun under gravity. Hence the philosopher who observes the due distinction between the species of motion will discern that the planetary motions are absolute, not relative, with respect to the sun and fixed stars. (This is not to deny that relative components of motion are involved also.) At last, by mathematical reasoning upon mechanical principles, the Copernican question was settled: the Earth and planets did revolve, not the sun and stars. This decision was the fruit of the distinction between absolute and relative dimensions, as Newton was to explain more at large in subsequent pages of the *Principia.* "For to this end I composed it."

Newton had solved the greatest scientific problem of his own and the preceding age. In a law-bound universe only one celestial geometry could work, that of Copernicus, Galileo, Kepler and Newton himself. Only God might know whether the sun and stars moved in the mystery of the absolute, but man had proved that the Earth did.

[17] *Principia* (1687), 10. I give a paraphrase since a literal translation is almost unintelligible. Cf. Motte-Cajori, 11.

Correlation of *Western Civilization: Recent Interpretations,* Volume I, with Western Civilization Texts

	Langer *et al.,* WESTERN CIVILIZATION, Vol. I	Clough *et al.,* A HISTORY OF THE WESTERN WORLD, 2nd ed., Vol. I	Brinton, Christopher, and Wolff, A HISTORY OF CIVILIZATION, 4th ed., Vol. I	King, May, and Fletcher, HISTORY OF CIVILIZATION
Text Chapters	Related selections in *Western Civilization: Recent Interpretations,* Volume I			
Intro.				1
1	1, 3	1–4	1–3	2–3
2	2	5–7	4–6	4–6
3	4	9–11	7–8	7–8
4		8, 14	9–10	9–10
5	5	12, 13, 15–18	11–13	
6	6	19	14	11–13
7	7	20–26	16, 18	18
8	7	27–29	15, 17	15–16
9	8	31–32, 36–37	14	17
10	10	30, 33–35	19, 26	19, 20–23
11			20, 22–23	24–25
12	9, 15		27–28	
13	11		21, 29, 32	29
14	12		24–25, 30–31	27–28
15	12, 13, 15		33–37	30–31, 33
16				32, 34
17	19			
18	16			35
19	18			
20				36–37
21	16, 17			
22	14			
23	20, 22			
24	23			
25	21, 26, 29			
26	29			
27	27			
28	28			
30	31			
31	32, 34			
32	33			
33	35			
	Langer *et al.* Vol. II			
1	24			
2	25			
3	30			
6	36, 37			